BARRON'S

HOW TO PREPARE FOR THE

AP*

COMPUTER SCIENCE
ADVANCED PLACEMENT EXAMINATION
JAVA VERSION

2ND EDITION

Roselyn Teukolsky
Ithaca High School

BARRON'S

* AP and Advanced Placement Program are registered trademarks of the College Entrance Examination Board, which was not involved with the production of and does not endorse this book.

All inquiries should be addressed to:
Barron's Educational Series, Inc.
250 Wireless Boulevard
Hauppauge, New York 11788
http://www.barronseduc.com

International Standard Book No.: 0-7641-2194-4

Library of Congress Catalog Card No.: 2003048036

Library of Congress Cataloging-in-Publication Data
Teukolsky, Roselyn.
  Barron's how to prepare for the AP computer science advanced
placement examination / Roselyn Teukolsky. – 2nd ed. (Java)
      p. cm.
    ISBN 0-7641-2194-4
      1. Computer science–Examinations, questions, etc. I. Title: How to prepare
for the AP computer science advanced placement examination. II. Title.

  QA76.28.T48 2003
  004'.076–dc21

                                                                                            2003048036

PRINTED IN THE UNITED STATES OF AMERICA
9 8 7 6 5 4 3 2

Contents

Preface   **x**

Introduction   **xi**

  General Information about the Exam xi

  Hints for Taking the Exam xii

    The Multiple-Choice Section xii

    The Free-Response Section xii

  How to Use This Book xiii

Chapter 1. Introductory Java Language Features   **1**

  Packages and Classes 1

  Types and Identifiers 3

    Identifiers 3

    Built-in Types 3

    Final Variables 4

  Operators 5

    Arithmetic Operators 5

    Relational Operators 5

    Logical Operators 7

    Assignment Operators 7

    Increment and Decrement Operators 8

    Operator Precedence 8

  Input/Output 9

    Input 9

    Output 9

    Escape Sequences 9

  Control Structures 10

    Decision-Making Control Structures 10

    Iteration 12

  Errors and Exceptions 15

  Multiple-Choice Questions on Introductory Java Language Concepts   17

  Answer Key 28

  Answers Explained 28

Chapter 2. Classes and Objects   **32**

  Objects 32

  Classes 32

  Public, Private, and Static 34

  Methods 34

    Headers 34

    Types of Methods 34

    Method Overloading 38

Scope **39**
    The this Keyword 39
References **40**
    Reference vs. Primitive Data Types 40
    The Null Reference 41
    Method Parameters 41
Multiple-Choice Questions on Classes and Objects **49**
Answer Key **64**
Answers Explained **64**

Chapter 3.   Inheritance and Polymorphism   **69**
Inheritance **69**
    Superclass and Subclass 69
    Inheritance Hierarchy 69
    Implementing Subclasses 70
    Declaring Subclass Objects 75
Polymorphism **76**
    Dynamic Binding (Late Binding) 76
Type Compatibility **77**
    Downcasting 77
    The ClassCastException 79
Abstract Classes **79**
    Abstract Class 79
    The abstract Keyword 79
Interfaces **81**
    Interface 81
    Defining an Interface 82
    The implements Keyword 82
    Using an Interface Type in a Client Program 82
    The Comparable Interface 83
Multiple-Choice Questions on Inheritance and Polymorphism . . . **86**
Answer Key **103**
Answers Explained **103**

Chapter 4.   Some Standard Classes   **108**
The Object Class **108**
    The Universal Superclass 108
    Methods in Object 108
The String Class **110**
    String Objects 110
    Constructing String Objects 111
    The Concatenation Operator 111
    Comparison of String Objects 112
    Other String Methods 113
Wrapper Classes **114**
    The Integer Class 114
    The Double Class 116
The Math Class **117**
The Random Class **118**

Initializing the Random Number Generator 118
Random Integers 118
Random Real Numbers 119
Multiple-Choice Questions on Standard Classes **120**
Answer Key **139**
Answers Explained **139**

Chapter 5. Program Design and Analysis   **146**
The Software Development Life Cycle **146**
The Waterfall Model 146
Program Specification 147
Program Design 147
Program Implementation 148
Testing and Debugging 148
Program Maintenance 149
Object-Oriented Program Design **149**
Identifying Classes 149
Identifying Behaviors 150
Determining Relationships Between Classes 150
Implementing Classes 150
Program Analysis **152**
Program Correctness 152
Assertions 152
Efficiency 153
Big-O Notation 154
Multiple-Choice Questions on Program Design and Analysis **156**
Answer Key **166**
Answers Explained **166**

Chapter 6. Arrays and Array Lists   **170**
One-Dimensional Arrays **170**
Initialization 170
Length of Array 171
Arrays as Parameters 171
Array Variables in a Class 175
Array of Class Objects 176
Analyzing Array Algorithms 177
Array Lists **179**
The `ArrayList` Class 179
The Methods of `ArrayList` 179
Using `ArrayList` 180
Two-Dimensional Arrays **181**
Declarations 182
Processing a Two-Dimensional Array 182
Two-Dimensional Array as Parameter 183
Multiple-Choice Questions on Arrays and Array Lists **185**
Answer Key **212**
Answers Explained **212**

Chapter 7. Recursion   219
Recursive Methods   219
General Form of Simple Recursive Methods 220
Writing Recursive Methods   222
Analysis of Recursive Methods   223
Sorting Algorithms That Use Recursion   224
Recursive Helper Methods   224
Recursion in 2-D Grids 227
Multiple-Choice Questions on Recursion 230
Answer Key 240
Answers Explained 240

Chapter 8. Linked Lists   244
Linked List   244
Linear Linked Lists   244
    Features of a Linked List 244
    The ListNode Class 245
    A Linear Linked List Class 247
Iterators 252
    List Traversal 252
    The Iterator Interface 252
    Implementing the Iterator Interface for a Linked List 252
    How to Use the LLLIterator Class 254
    The ListIterator Interface 255
    Implementing the ListIterator Class for a Linked List 256
    How to Use the LLL_ListIterator Class 257
Circular Linked Lists   259
    Implementing a Circular Linked List 259
    Circular Linked Lists and Iterators 261
Doubly Linked Lists   262
    Why Doubly Linked Lists? 262
    Header and Trailer Nodes 262
    Implementing Doubly Linked Lists 263
Linked Lists and Iterators 268
Run Time of Linked List vs. Array Algorithms 268
Multiple-Choice Questions on Linked Lists 269
Answer Key 293
Answers Explained 293

Chapter 9. Stacks and Queues   300
Stacks 300
    What Is a Stack? 300
    The Stack Interface 300
    Stack Implementation 301
    When to Use a Stack 302
Queues 303
    What Is a Queue? 303
    The Queue Interface 303
    Queue Implementation 304

When to Use a Queue 305
Priority Queues **305**
What Is a Priority Queue? 305
The `PriorityQueue` Interface 306
Implementation of a Priority Queue 306
When to Use a Priority Queue 307
Multiple-Choice Questions on Stacks and Queues **310**
Answer Key **322**
Answers Explained **322**

Chapter 10. Trees   **328**
Binary Trees **328**
Definitions 328
Implementation of Binary Trees 329
The `TreeNode` Class 329
A `BinaryTree` Class 331
Binary Search Trees **331**
A `BinarySearchTree` Class 332
Inserting an Element into a Binary Search Tree 332
Finding a Target Element in a Binary Search Tree 334
Creating a Binary Search Tree 335
Tree Traversal **335**
Three Methods of Traversal 335
Implementing the Traversal Algorithms 337
Recursive Tree Algorithms **337**
Recursion That Alters the Tree Structure 340
Binary Expression Trees **341**
Infix, Postfix, and Prefix Expressions 341
Binary Expression Tree 342
Evaluating a Binary Expression Tree 343
A Binary Expression Tree Program 345
Multiple-Choice Questions on Trees **348**
Answer Key **361**
Answers Explained **361**

Chapter 11. Collections   **368**
Collections in Java **368**
What Is a Collection? 368
The Collections API 368
The Collections Hierarchy **368**
Collections and Iterators **370**
The `List` Interface **371**
The Methods of `List` 371
The `ArrayList` Class 371
Using `ArrayList` 372
The `LinkedList` Class 374
Using `LinkedList` 375
`ArrayList` vs. `LinkedList` **376**
The `Set` Interface **377**

The Methods of `Set` 377
The `HashSet` Class 378
The `TreeSet` Class 378
Examples with `HashSet` and `TreeSet` 379
The `Map` Interface **382**
The Methods of `Map` 383
The `HashMap` Class 383
The `TreeMap` Class 384
Iterating over Maps 384
Examples with `HashMap` and `TreeMap` 385
Multiple-Choice Questions on Collections **388**
Answer Key **405**
Answers Explained **405**

Chapter 12. Sorting and Searching   **410**
$O(n^2)$ **Sorts: Selection and Insertion Sorts** **410**
Selection Sort 410
Insertion Sort 411
Recursive Sorts: Mergesort and Quicksort **411**
Mergesort 412
Quicksort 413
A Binary Tree Sort: Heapsort **414**
Sorting Algorithms in Java **417**
Sequential Search **420**
Binary Search **421**
Hash Coding **422**
Description 422
Resolving Collisions 422
Multiple-Choice Questions on Sorting and Searching **425**
Answer Key **443**
Answers Explained **443**

Chapter 13. The Marine Biology Simulation Case Study   **451**
General Description **451**
The `Simulation` Class **452**
Description 452
Methods 452
The `Fish` Class **453**
Description 453
Methods 454
The Different Fish Types **458**
The `DarterFish` Class 458
Methods of `DarterFish` 459
The `SlowFish` Class 461
Methods of `SlowFish` 461
The Interfaces **462**
The `Environment` Interface 462
The `Locatable` Interface 464
The `EnvDisplay` Interface 464

The SquareEnvironment Class 465
   The SquareEnvironment Constructors 465
The BoundedEnv and UnboundedEnv Classes 466
   How the Environment Is Implemented 466
The Utility Classes 471
   The Debug Class 472
   The Direction Class 472
   The Location Class 472
   The RandNumGenerator Class 473
The Java Library Utility Classes 473
   The java.util.ArrayList Class 473
   The java.awt.Color Class 474
   The java.util.Random Class 474
The Case Study and the AP Exam 474
Multiple-Choice Questions on the Case Study 476
Answer Key 493
Answers Explained 493

Practice Exam One   **501**
Computer Science A Section I 503
Computer Science A Section II 527
Answer Key 534
Answers Explained 534

Practice Exam Two   **545**
Computer Science A Section I 547
Computer Science A Section II 570
Answer Key 577
Answers Explained 577

Practice Exam Three   **589**
Computer Science AB Section I 591
Computer Science AB Section II 617
Answer Key 626
Answers Explained 626

Practice Exam Four   **641**
Computer Science AB Section I 643
Computer Science AB Section II 670
Answer Key 679
Answers Explained 679

Appendix A.   **Glossary of Useful Computer Terms**   **693**

Appendix B.   **Supplementary Code for Evaluating a Binary Expression Tree**   **696**

Index   **698**

Preface

This book is aimed at students reviewing for the AP Computer Science Exam. It would normally be used at the completion of an AP course. However, it contains a complete summary of all topics for both Level A and AB exams, and it can be used for self-study if accompanied by a suitable textbook.

The book provides a review of object-oriented programming, algorithm analysis, and data structures. It can therefore be used as a supplement to first-year college courses where Java is the programming language, and as a resource for teachers of high school and introductory college courses.

Each review chapter is followed by AP exam-style multiple-choice questions with detailed explanations of the answers.

There is a similarly thorough review of the Marine Biology Simulation Case Study.

There are four complete practice exams, two Level A and two Level AB. The exams follow the format of the AP exam, with multiple-choice and free-response sections. Detailed solutions with explanations are provided. There is no overlap of questions between the exams.

Acknowledgments

I owe thanks to many people who helped in the creation of this book.

A special thank-you to Mark Stehlik and Judy Hromcik for the care they took in reading the manuscript. Their detailed comments and advice were invaluable.

I am grateful to my excellent project editor, Wendy Sleppin of Barron's, for her friendly guidance and moral support throughout this project. I also thank Sara Black for her painstaking copy editing and all the members of the Barron's staff who worked on the production of the book.

I am grateful to Steven Andrianoff and David Levine of St. Bonaventure University, New York, for their outstanding Java workshop. Many ideas from that workshop found their way into this book.

The following people contributed (some without their knowledge!) with their advice, materials, textbooks, and expertise: Owen Astrachan, Alyce Brady, Cay Horstmann, Harvey and Paul Deitel, and Mark Weiss.

My husband, Saul, has been my partner in this project—typesetting the manuscript, producing the figures, and giving advice and moral support every step of the way. Without his help I could not—at the very least—have made the deadline!

Roselyn Teukolsky
Ithaca, NY
May 2003

Introduction

General Information about the Exam

The AP Computer Science Exam is a three-hour written exam. No books, calculators, or computers are allowed! The exam consists of two parts that have equal weight:

- Section I: 40 multiple-choice questions in 1 hour and 15 minutes.
- Section II: 4 free-response questions in 1 hour and 45 minutes.

Section I is scored by machine—you will blip your answers with a pencil on a mark-sense sheet. Each question correctly answered is worth 1 point, while incorrect answers get $\frac{1}{4}$ of a point deducted; a question left blank is ignored.

Section II is scored by human readers—you will write your answers in a booklet provided. Free-response questions typically involve writing methods in Java to solve a given problem. Sometimes there are questions analyzing algorithms or designing and modifying data structures. You may be asked to write or design an entire class. To ensure consistency in the grading, each grader follows the same rubric, and each of your four answers may be examined by more than one reader. Each question is worth 9 points, with partial credit awarded where applicable. Your name and school are hidden from the readers.

Your raw score for both sections is converted to an integer score from 1 to 5, where 1 represents "Not at all qualified" and 5 represents "Extremely well qualified." Be aware that the awarding of AP credit varies enormously from college to college.

The exam can be taken at two levels: Level A covers roughly a one-semester introductory college course, while Level AB covers roughly a two-semester course, including data structures. In terms of getting credit at colleges, it makes more sense to get a 4 or 5 on the Level A exam than a 2 or 3 on the Level AB exam.

The language of the AP exam is currently Java. Only a subset of the Java language will be tested on the exam. For a complete description of this subset, see the College Board web site at *http://www.collegeboard.com/ap/students/compsci*. **Every language topic in this review book is part of the AP Java subset unless explicitly stated otherwise. Note that the entire subset is covered in the book.**

At least one free-response and five multiple-choice questions will be based on the Marine Biology Simulation Case Study. The full text of the case study can be found at the College Board web site.

At the exam, you will be given

- A copy of the testable case study code.

- A quick reference to the interfaces and "black box" classes of the case study, with lists of their required methods.

- A quick reference to the standard Java interfaces and classes with lists of their required methods.

- (Level AB only) A copy of the `ListNode` and `TreeNode` classes.

Hints for Taking the Exam

The
Multiple-Choice
Section

- Since $\frac{1}{4}$ of a point is deducted for each wrong answer, don't guess unless you can eliminate at least two choices.

- You have a little less than two minutes per question, so don't waste time on any given question. You can always come back to it if you have time at the end.

- Seemingly complicated array questions can often be solved by hand tracing the code with a small array, two or three elements. The same is true for other data structures such as matrices, stacks, queues, or linked lists.

- Many questions ask you to compare two pieces of code that supposedly implement the same algorithm. Often one program segment will fail because it doesn't handle endpoint conditions properly (e.g., `num == 0` or `list == null`). *Be aware of endpoint conditions throughout the exam.*

- Since the mark-sense sheet is scanned by machine, make sure that you erase completely if you change an answer.

The
Free-Response
Section

- Each free-response question is worth 9 points. Take a minute to read through the whole exam so that you can start with a question that you feel confident about. It gives you a psychological leg up to have a solid question in the bag.

- Don't omit a question just because you can't come up with a complete solution. Remember, partial credit is awarded. Also, if you can't do part (a) of a question, don't omit part (b)—they are graded independently.

- Often part (b) of a question says, "You may want to use method `blurf`" (the method that was written in part a). Use it! Chances are it's the route to the best solution.

- If an algorithm is suggested to solve a problem, just follow it. Don't reinvent the wheel.

- Don't waste time writing comments: the graders generally ignore them. The occasional brief comment that clarifies a segment of code is OK.

- Points are not deducted for inefficient code unless efficiency is an issue in the question. So remember, brute-force code that works is preferable to elegant code that does not.

- Most of the standard Java library methods are not included in the AP subset. They are accepted on the exam if you use them correctly. However, there is always an alternative solution, and you should try to find it.

- Don't cross out an answer until you have written a replacement. Graders are instructed not to mark anything crossed out, even if it would have gotten credit.

- Have some awareness that this section is graded by humans. It is in your interest to have the graders understand your solutions. With this in mind,

  - Use a sharp pencil, write legibly, space your answers, and indent correctly.
  - Use self-documenting names for variables, methods, etc.
  - Use the identifiers that are given in a question. You will lose a usage point if you persist in using the wrong names.
  - Write clear readable code. This is your goal. Don't write one obscure convoluted statement when you can write two short clear statements. The APCS exam is not the place to demonstrate that you're a genius.

How to Use This Book

Each chapter in the book contains a comprehensive review of a topic, multiple-choice questions that focus on the topic, and detailed explanations of answers.

In both the text and questions/explanations, a special code font is used for parts of the text that are Java code.

```
//This is an example of code font
```

A different font is used for pseudo-code.

< Here is pseudo-code font. >

Sections in the text and multiple-choice questions that are directed at Level AB only are clearly marked as such. Unmarked text and questions are suitable for both Levels A and AB. Chapters 8–11 are for level AB only. This is stated on the first page of each of these chapters.

Following the review chapters are four practice exams with complete solutions, two for each level. There is no overlap in the questions, so Level AB students can use the Level A exams for additional practice. Some questions in the Level AB exams are also fair game for Level A students. These are clearly marked as such.

Each practice exam contains five multiple-choice questions and one free-response question on the Marine Biology Simulation Case Study.

An answer sheet is provided for the Section I questions of each exam. When you have completed an entire exam, and have checked your answers, you may wish to calculate your approximate AP score. Use the scoring worksheet provided on the back of the answer sheet.

There are two appendices at the end of the book. Appendix A is a glossary of computer terms that occasionally crop up on the exam. Appendix B contains supplementary material that is not required for the exam.

A final hint about the book: Try the questions before you peek at the answers. Good luck!

CHAPTER ONE

Introductory Java Language Features

Fifty loops shalt thou make ...
—Exodus 26:5

The AP Computer Science course includes algorithm analysis, data structures, and the techniques and methods of modern programming, specifically, object-oriented programming. A high-level programming language is used to explore these concepts. Java is the language currently in use on the AP exam.

Java was developed by James Gosling and a team at Sun Microsystems in California; it continues to evolve. The AP exam covers a clearly defined subset of Java language features that are presented throughout this book. The College Board web site, *http://www.collegeboard.com/ap/students/compsci*, contains a complete listing of this subset.

Java provides basic control structures such as the `if-else` statement, `for` loop, and `while` loop, as well as fundamental built-in data types. But the power of the language lies in user-defined types called objects, many of which can interact in a single program.

Packages and Classes

A typical Java program has user-defined classes whose objects interact with those from Java class libraries. In Java, related classes are grouped into *packages*, many of which are provided with the compiler. You can put your own classes into a package—this facilitates their use in other programs.

The package `java.lang`, which contains many commonly used classes, is automatically provided to all Java programs. To use any other package in a program, an `import` statement must be used. To import all of the classes in a package called `packagename`, use the form

```
import packagename.*;
```

To import a single class called `ClassName` from the package, use

```
import packagename.ClassName;
```

Java has a hierarchy of packages and subpackages. Subpackages are selected using multiple dots:

1

```
import packagename.subpackagename.ClassName;
```

The `import` statement allows the programmer to use the objects and methods defined in the designated package. By convention Java package names are lower-case.

A Java program must have at least one class, the one that contains the *main method*. In general, the name of the file containing each public class must match the name of the class, with the suffix `.java`. These files, which consist of human-readable Java statements, are called *source files*.

A *compiler* converts source code into machine-readable form called *bytecode*. All the bytecode is linked together by a *linker*, and the program is then executed. Here is a typical source file for a Java program.

```
/* Program FirstProg.java
   Start with a comment, giving the program name and a brief
   description of what the program does. */

import package1.*;
import package2.subpackage.ClassName;

public class FirstProg  //note that the file name is FirstProg.java
{
    public static type1 method1(parameter list)
    {
        < code for method 1 >
    }
    public static type2 method2(parameter list)
    {
        < code for method 2 >
    }

        ...

    public static void main(String[] args)
    {
        < your code >
    }
}
```

NOTE

1. All Java methods must be contained in a class, and all program statements must be placed inside a method.
2. Typically, the class that contains the `main` method does not contain many additional methods.
3. The words `class`, `public`, `static`, `void`, and `main` are *reserved words*, also called *keywords*.
4. The keyword `public` signals that the class or method is usable outside of the class, whereas `private` data members or methods (see Chapter 2) are not.
5. The keyword `static` is used for methods that will not access any objects of a class, such as the methods in the `FirstProg` class in the example above. This is typically true for all methods in a source file that contains no *instance variables* (see Chapter 2). Most methods in Java do operate on objects and are not static. The `main` method, however, must always be static.

6. The program shown on the previous page is a Java *application*. This is not to be confused with a Java *applet*, a program that runs inside a web browser or applet viewer. Applets are not part of the AP subset.

Types and Identifiers

Identifiers

An *identifier* is a name for a variable, parameter, constant, user-defined method, or user-defined class. In Java an identifier is any sequence of letters, digits, and the underscore character. Identifiers may not begin with a digit. Identifiers are case-sensitive, which means that age and Age are different. Wherever possible identifiers should be concise and self-documenting. A variable called area is more illuminating than one called a.

By convention identifiers for variables and methods are lowercase. Upper-case letters are used to separate these into multiple words, for example getName, findSurfaceArea, preTaxTotal, and so on. Note that a class name starts with a capital letter. Reserved words are entirely lowercase and may not be used as identifiers.

Built-in Types

Every identifier in a Java program has a type associated with it. The *primitive* or *built-in* types that are included in the AP Java subset are

int	Integer. For example, 2, -26, 3000
boolean	Boolean. Just two values, true or false
double	Double precision floating-point number. For example, 2.718, -367189.41, 1.6e4

(Note that primitive type char is not included in the AP Java subset.)

Integer values are stored exactly. Because there's a fixed amount of memory set aside for their storage, however, integers are bounded. If you try to store a value whose magnitude is too big in an int variable, you'll get an *overflow error*.

An identifier, for example a *variable*, is introduced into a Java program with a *declaration* that specifies its type. Some examples follow:

```
int x;
double y,z;
boolean found;
int count = 1;             //count initialized to 1
double p = 2.3, q = 4.1;   //p and q initialized to 2.3 and 4.1
```

One type can be cast to another compatible type if appropriate. For example,

```
int total, n;
double average;
    ...
average = (double) total/n;    //total cast to double to ensure
                               //real division is used
```

Alternatively,

```
average = total/(double) n;
```

Assigning an `int` to a `double` automatically casts the `int` to `double`. For example,

```
int num = 5;
double realNum = num;    //num is cast to double
```

Assigning a `double` to an `int` without a cast, however, causes a compile-time error. For example,

```
double x = 6.79;
int intNum = x;    //Error. Need an explicit cast to int
```

Note that casting a floating-point (real) number to an integer simply truncates the number. For example,

```
double cost = 10.95;
int numDollars = (int) cost;    //sets numDollars to 10
```

If your intent was to round `cost` to the nearest dollar, you needed to write

```
int numDollars = (int) (cost + 0.5);  //numDollars has value 11
```

To round a negative number to the nearest integer:

```
double negAmount = -4.8;
int roundNeg = (int) (negAmount - 0.5);   //roundNeg has value -5
```

The strategy of adding or subtracting 0.5 before casting correctly rounds in all cases.

Final Variables

A *final variable* or *user-defined constant*, identified by the keyword `final`, is used to name a quantity whose value will not change. Here are some examples of `final` declarations:

```
final double TAX_RATE = 0.08;
final int CLASS_SIZE = 35;
```

NOTE
1. Constant identifiers are, by convention, capitalized.
2. A `final` variable can be declared without initializing it immediately. For example,

```
final double TAX_RATE;
if (< some condition >)
    TAX_RATE = 0.08;
else
    TAX_RATE = 0.0;
// TAX_RATE can be assigned to just once: its value is final!
```

3. A common use for a constant is as an array bound. For example,

```
final int MAXSTUDENTS = 25;
int[] classList = new int[MAXSTUDENTS];
```

4. Using constants makes it easier to revise code. Just a single change in the `final` declaration need be made, rather than having to change every occurrence of a value.

Operators

Arithmetic
Operators

Operator	Meaning	Example
+	addition	3 + x
-	subtraction	p - q
*	multiplication	6*i
/	division	10/4 //returns 2, not 2.5!
%	mod (remainder)	11 % 8 //returns 3

NOTE

1. These operators can be applied to types int and double, even if both types occur in the same expression. For an operation involving a double and an int, the int is promoted to double, and the result is a double.
2. The mod operator %, as in the expression a % b, gives the remainder when a is divided by b. Thus 10 % 3 evaluates to 1, whereas 4.2 % 2.0 evaluates to 0.2.
3. Integer division a/b where both a and b are of type int returns the integer quotient only (i.e., the answer is truncated). Thus 22/6 gives 3, and 3/4 gives 0. If at least one of the operands is of type double, then the operation becomes regular floating-point division, and there is no truncation. You can control the kind of division that is carried out by explicitly casting (one or both of) the operands from int to double and vice versa. Thus

```
3.0/4          →    0.75
3/4.0          →    0.75
(int) 3.0/4    →    0
(double) 3/4   →    0.75
```

You must, however, be careful:

```
(double) (3/4)   →    0.0
```

since the integer division 3/4 is computed first, before casting to double.
4. The arithmetic operators follow the normal precedence rules (order of operations):

   (1) parentheses, from the inner ones out (highest precedence)
   (2) *, /, %
   (3) +, - (lowest precedence)

Here operators on the same line have the same precedence, and, in the absence of parentheses, are invoked from left to right. Thus the expression 19 % 5 * 3 + 14 / 5 evaluates to 4 * 3 + 2 = 14. Note that casting has precedence over all of the operators. Thus in the expression (double) 3/4, 3 will be cast to double before the division is done.

Relational
Operators

Operator	Meaning	Example
==	equal to	if (x == 100)
!=	not equal to	if (age != 21)
>	greater than	if (salary > 30000)
<	less than	if (grade < 65)
>=	greater than or equal to	if (age >= 16)
<=	less than or equal to	if (height <= 6)

NOTE

1. Relational operators are used in *boolean expressions* that evaluate to `true` or `false`.

```
boolean x = (a != b);      //initializes x to true if a!=b,
                           //false otherwise
return p == q;             //returns true if p equals q,
                           //false otherwise
```

2. If the operands are an `int` and a `double`, the `int` is promoted to a `double` as for arithmetic operators.

3. Relational operators should only be used in the comparison of primitive types (i.e., `int`, `double`, or `boolean`). User-defined types are compared using the `equals` and `compareTo` methods (see pp. 83 and 110).

4. Be careful when comparing floating-point values! Since floating-point numbers cannot always be represented exactly in the computer memory, they should not be compared directly using relational operators.

Comparing Floating-Point Numbers

Since floating-point numbers are manipulated and stored with a fixed number of significant digits, arithmetic operations generally produce results that must be rounded. This causes *round-off error*. One consequence is that you can't rely on using the `==` or `!=` operators to compare two `double` values for equality. They may differ in their last significant digit or two because of round-off error. Instead you should test that the magnitude of the difference between the numbers is less than some number about the size of the machine precision. The machine precision is usually denoted ϵ, and is typically about 10^{-16} for double precision (i.e., about 16 decimal digits). So you would like to test something like $|x-y| < \epsilon$. But this is no good if x and y are very large. For example, suppose $x = 1234567890.123456$ and $y = 1234567890.123457$. These numbers are essentially equal to machine precision, since they differ only in the 16th significant digit. But $|x - y| = 10^{-6}$, not 10^{-16}. Here you should check the *relative* difference:

$$\frac{|x - y|}{\min(|x|, |y|)} < \epsilon$$

But this test will fail for very small numbers, in particular if one of the numbers is zero. So the best general strategy is to test the relative difference unless the numbers are small ($< \epsilon$ say), in which case you test the absolute difference, $|x - y| < \epsilon$. Whew!

Logical Operators

Operator	Meaning	Example
!	NOT	if (!found)
&&	AND	if (x < 3 && y > 4)
||	OR	if (age < 2 || height < 4)

NOTE

1. Logical operators are applied to boolean expressions to form *compound boolean expressions* that evaluate to `true` or `false`.
2. Values of `true` or `false` are assigned according to the truth tables for the logical operators.

&&	T	F		||	T	F		!	
T	T	F		T	T	T		T	F
F	F	F		F	T	F		F	T

For example, F && T evaluates to F, while T \|\| F evaluates to T.

3. *Short-circuit evaluation.* The subexpressions in a compound boolean expression are evaluated from left to right, and evaluation automatically stops as soon as the value of the entire expression is known. For example, consider a boolean OR expression of the form A \|\| B, where A and B are some boolean expressions. If A is true, then the expression is `true` irrespective of the value of B. Similarly, if A is false, then A && B evaluates to `false` irrespective of the second operand. So in each case the second operand is not evaluated. For example,

```
if (numScores != 0 && scoreTotal/numScores > 90)
```

will not cause a run-time `ArithmeticException` (division-by-zero error) if the value of `numScores` is 0. This is because `numScores != 0` will evaluate to `false`, causing the entire boolean expression to evaluate to `false` without having to evaluate the second expression containing the division.

Assignment Operators

Operator	Example	Meaning
=	x = 2	simple assignment
+=	x += 4	x = x + 4
-=	y -= 6	y = y - 6
*=	p *= 5	p = p * 5
/=	n /= 10	n = n / 10
%=	n %= 10	n = n % 10

NOTE

1. All these operators, with the exception of simple assignment, are called *compound assignment operators*.
2. *Chaining* of assignment statements is allowed, with evaluation from right to left.

```
int next, prev, sum;
next = prev = sum = 0;  //initializes sum to 0, then prev to 0
                        //then next to 0
```

Increment and
Decrement
Operators

Operator	Example	Meaning
++	i++ or ++i	i is incremented by 1
--	k-- or --k	k is decremented by 1

Note that i++ (postfix) and ++i (prefix) both have the net effect of incrementing i by 1, but they are not equivalent. For example, if i currently has the value 5, then System.out.println(i++) will print 5 and then increment i to 6, whereas System.out.println(++i) will first increment i to 6 and then print 6. It's easy to remember: if the ++ is first, you first increment. A similar distinction occurs between k-- and --k.

Operator
Precedence

$$
\begin{array}{lll}
\text{highest precedence} \rightarrow & (1) & !, \ ++, \ -- \\
& (2) & *, \ /, \ \% \\
& (3) & +, \ - \\
& (4) & <, \ >, \ <=, \ >= \\
& (5) & ==, \ != \\
& (6) & \&\& \\
& (7) & || \\
\text{lowest precedence} \rightarrow & (8) & =, \ +=, \ -=, \ *=, \ /=, \ \%=
\end{array}
$$

Here operators on the same line have equal precedence. The evaluation of the operators with equal precedence is from left to right, except for rows (1) and (8) where the order is right to left. It is easy to remember: the only "backward" order is for the unary operators (row 1) and for the various assignment operators (row 8).

Example 1

What will be output by the following statement?

```
System.out.println(5 + 3 < 6 - 1);
```

Since + and - have precedence over <, 5 + 3 and 6 - 1 will be evaluated before evaluating the boolean expression. Since the value of the expression is false, the statement will output false.

Example 2

Suppose the int variables x, y, and z currently have the values 3, 4, and 5. What will the following statement do?

```
x += y -= z *= 2;
```

It will
    assign a value of 10 to z
    then assign a value of -6 to y
    then assign a value of -3 to x
(This is the kind of unreadable coding style you should avoid!)

Input/Output

Input

Since there are so many ways to provide input to a program, user input is not a part of the AP Java subset. If reading input is a necessary part of a question on the AP exam, it will be indicated something like this:

```
double x = call to a method that reads a floating-point number
```

or

```
double x = IO.readDouble();    //read user input
```

Reading in strings and converting them to numeric values is not in the subset.

Output

Testing of output will be restricted to `System.out.print` and `System.out.println`. Formatted output will not be tested.

`System.out` is an object in the `System` class that allows output to be displayed on the screen. The `println` method outputs an item and then goes to a new line. The `print` method outputs an item without going to a new line afterward. An item to be printed can be a string, or a number, or the value of a boolean expression (`true` or `false`). Here are some examples:

```
System.out.print("Hot");
System.out.println("dog");
```
 } prints Hotdog

```
System.out.println("Hot");
System.out.println("dog");
```
 } prints Hot
            dog

```
System.out.println(7 + 3);
```
 } prints 10

```
System.out.println(7 == 2 + 5);
```
 } prints true

```
int x = 27;
System.out.println(x);
```
 } prints 27
```
System.out.println("Value of x is " + x);
```
                        prints Value of x is 27

In the last example, the value of x, 27, is converted to the string `"27"`, which is then concatenated to the string `"Value of x is "`.

To print the "values" of user-defined objects, the `toString()` method is invoked (see p. 108).

Escape Sequences

An *escape sequence* is a backslash followed by a single character. It is used to print special characters. The three escape sequences that you should know for the AP exam are

Escape Sequence	Meaning
\n	newline
\"	double quote
\\	backslash

Here are some examples:

```
System.out.println("Welcome to\na new line");
```

prints

```
Welcome to
a new line
```

The statement

```
System.out.println("He is known as \"Hothead Harry\".");
```

prints

```
He is known as "Hothead Harry".
```

The statement

```
System.out.println("The file path is d:\\myFiles\\..");
```

prints

```
The file path is d:\myFiles\..
```

Control Structures

Control structures are the mechanism by which you make the statements of a program run in a nonsequential order. There are two general types: decision making and iteration.

Decision-Making Control Structures

These include the `if`, `if...else`, and `switch` statements. They are all selection control structures that introduce a decision-making ability into a program. Based on the truth value of a boolean expression, the computer will decide which path to follow. The `switch` statement is not part of the AP Java subset.

The `if` Statement

```
if (boolean expression)
{
    statements
}
```

Here the *statements* will be executed only if the *boolean expression* is `true`. If it is `false`, control passes immediately to the first statement following the `if` statement.

The `if...else` Statement

```
if (boolean expression)
{
    statements
}
else
{
    statements
}
```

Here if the *boolean expression* is `true`, only the *statements* immediately following the test will be executed. If the *boolean expression* is `false`, only the *statements* following the `else` will be executed.

Nested `if` Statement

If the statement part of an `if` statement is itself an `if` statement, the result is a *nested* `if` *statement*.

Example 1

```
if (boolean expr1)
    if (boolean expr2)
        statement;
```

This is equivalent to

```
if (boolean expr1 && boolean expr2)
    statement;
```

Example 2

Beware the dangling `else`! Suppose you want to read in an integer and print it if it's positive and even. Will the following code do the job?

```
int n = IO.readInt();         //read user input
if (n > 0)
    if (n % 2 == 0)
        System.out.println(n);
else
    System.out.println(n + " is not positive");
```

A user enters 7 and is surprised to see the output

```
7 is not positive
```

The reason is that `else` always gets matched with the *nearest* unpaired `if`, not the first `if` as the indenting would suggest.

There are two ways to fix the preceding code. The first is to use `{}` delimiters to group the statements correctly.

```
int n = IO.readInt();         //read user input
if (n > 0)
{
    if (n % 2 == 0)
        System.out.println(n);
}
else
    System.out.println(n + " is not positive");
```

The second way of fixing the code is to rearrange the statements.

```
int n = IO.readInt();         //read user input
if (n <= 0)
    System.out.println(n + " is not positive");
else
    if (n % 2 == 0)
        System.out.println(n);
```

Extended `if` Statement

For example,

```
String grade = IO.readString();         //read user input
if (grade.equals("A"))
    System.out.println("Excellent!");
else if (grade.equals("B"))
    System.out.println("Good");
else if (grade.equals("C") || grade.equals("D"))
    System.out.println("Poor");
else if (grade.equals("F"))
    System.out.println("Egregious!");
else
    System.out.println("Invalid grade");
```

If any of A, B, C, D, or F are entered, an appropriate message will be written and control will go to the statement immediately following the extended `if` statement. If any other string is entered, the final `else` is invoked, and the message `Invalid grade` will be written.

Iteration

Java has three different control structures that allow the computer to perform iterative tasks: the `for` loop, `while` loop, and `do...while` loop. The `do...while` loop is not in the AP Java subset.

The `for` loop

The general form of the `for` loop is

```
for (initialization; termination condition; update statement)
{
    statements          //body of loop
}
```

The termination condition is tested at the top of the loop; the update statement is performed at the bottom.

Example 1

```
//outputs 1 2 3 4
for (i=1; i<5; i++)
    System.out.print(i + " ");
```

Here's how it works. The *loop variable* i is initialized to 1, and the termination condition i < 5 is evaluated. If it is `true`, the body of the loop is executed and then the loop variable i is incremented according to the update statement. As soon as the termination condition is `false` (i.e., i >= 5), control passes to the first statement following the loop.

Example 2

```
//outputs 20 19 18 17 16 15
for (k=20; k>=15; k--)
    System.out.print(k + " ");
```

Example 3

```
//outputs 2 4 6 8 10
for (j=2; j<=10; j += 2)
    System.out.print(j + " ");
```

NOTE
1. The loop variable should not have its value changed inside the loop body.
2. The initializing and update statements can use any valid constants, variables, or expressions.
3. The scope (see p. 39) of the loop variable can be restricted to the loop body by combining the loop variable declaration with the initialization. For example,

```
for (int i=0; i<3; i++)
{
    ...
}
```

4. The following loop is syntactically valid:

```
for (i=1; i<=0; i++)
{
    ...
}
```

The loop body will not be executed at all, since the exiting condition is true before the first execution.

The while loop

The general form of the while loop is

```
while (boolean test)
{
    statements          //loop body
}
```

The *boolean test* is performed at the beginning of the loop. If true, the loop body is executed. Otherwise, control passes to the first statement following the loop. After execution of the loop body, the test is performed again. If true, the loop is executed again, and so on.

Example 1

```
int i = 1, mult3 = 3;
while (mult3 < 20)
{
    System.out.print(mult3 + " ");
    i++;
    mult3 *= i;
}                         //outputs 3 6 18
```

NOTE
1. It is possible for the body of a while loop never to be executed. This will happen if the test evaluates to false the first time.
2. Disaster will strike in the form of an infinite loop if the test can never be false. Don't forget to change the loop variable in the body of the loop in a way that leads to termination!

Example 2

```
int power2 = 1;
while (power2 != 20)
{
    System.out.println(power2);
    power2 *= 2;
}
```

Since `power2` will never exactly equal 20, the loop will grind merrily along eventually causing an integer overflow.

Example 3

```
/* Screen out bad data.
 * The loop won't allow execution to continue until a valid
 * integer is entered */
System.out.println("Enter a positive integer from 1 to 100");
int num = IO.readInt();          //read user input
while (num < 1 || num > 100)
{
    System.out.println("Number must be from 1 to 100.";
    System.out.println("Please reenter");
    num = IO.readInt();
}
```

Example 4

```
/* Uses a sentinel to terminate data entered at the keyboard.
 * The sentinel is a value that cannot be part of the data.
 * It signals the end of the list */
final int SENTINEL = -999;
System.out.println("Enter list of positive integers," +
    " end list with " + SENTINEL);
int value = IO.readInt();        //read user input
while (value != SENTINEL)
{
    process the value
    value = IO.readInt();        //read another value
}
```

Nested Loops

You create a *nested loop* when a loop is a statement in the body of another loop.

Example 1

```
for (int k=1; k<=3; k++)
{
    for (int i=1; i<=4; i++)
        System.out.print("*");
    System.out.println();
}
```

Think:

    for each of 3 rows
    {
            print 4 stars
            go to next line
    }

Output:

    ****
    ****
    ****

Example 2

This example has two loops nested in an outer loop.

```
for (int i=1; i<=6; i++)
{
    for (int j=1; j<=i; j++)
        System.out.print("+");
    for (int j=1; j<=6-i; j++)
        System.out.print("*");
    System.out.println();
}
```

Output:

    +*****
    ++****
    +++***
    ++++**
    +++++*
    ++++++

Errors and Exceptions

An *exception* is an error condition that occurs during the execution of a Java program. For example, if you divide an integer by zero, an `ArithmeticException` will be thrown. If you use a negative array index, an `ArrayIndexOutOfBoundsException` will be thrown.

An *unchecked exception* is one where you don't provide code to deal with the error. Such exceptions are automatically handled by Java's standard exception-handling methods, which terminate execution. You now need to fix your code!

A *checked exception* is one where you provide code (`try`/`catch`/`finally` statements) to handle the exception. These exceptions are generally not caused by an error in the code. For example, an unexpected end-of-file could be due to a broken network connection. Checked exceptions are not part of the AP Java subset.

Note that in Java, arithmetic operations with type `double` do not throw exceptions. For example, division by zero produces $\pm\infty$, not an error state!

The following exceptions are in the AP Java subset:

Exception	Discussed on page
ArithmeticException	15
NullPointerException	41
ClassCastException	79
ArrayIndexOutOfBoundsException	170
IndexOutOfBoundsException	180
NoSuchElementException	250, 252, 375
IllegalStateException	252, 255

Java allows you to write code that throws a standard unchecked exception. Here is a typical example:

```
if (numScores == 0)
    throw new ArithmeticException("Cannot divide by zero");
else
    findAverageScore();
```

NOTE
1. `throw` and `new` are both reserved words.
2. The error message is optional: the line could have read

```
throw new ArithmeticException();
```

3. Writing code to throw your own exceptions is not part of the Level A subset. Level AB students may be asked to throw a `NoSuchElementException` or an `IllegalStateException`.

Multiple-Choice Questions on Introductory Java Language Concepts

1. Which of the following pairs of declarations will cause an error message?

    I ```
       double x = 14.7;
       int y = x;
       ```

    II ```
       double x = 14.7;
       int y = (int) x;
       ```

    III ```
        int x = 14;
        double y = x;
        ```

    (A) None
    (B) I only
    (C) II only
    (D) III only
    (E) I and III only


2. What output will be produced by

    ```
    System.out.print("\\* This is not\n a comment *\\");
    ```

    (A) * This is not a comment *

    (B) * This is not a comment *\

    (C) * This is not
        a comment *

    (D) * This is not
        a comment *\\

    (E) * This is not
        a comment *\
    ```

3. Refer to the following code fragment:

```
double answer = 13/5;
System.out.println("13/5 = " + answer);
```

The output is

```
13/5 = 2.0
```

The programmer intends the output to be

```
13/5 = 2.6
```

Which of the following replacements for the first line of code will *not* fix the problem?
(A) `double answer = (double) 13/5;`
(B) `double answer = 13/(double) 5;`
(C) `double answer = 13.0/5;`
(D) `double answer = 13/5.0;`
(E) `double answer = (double) (13/5);`

4. What value is stored in `result` if

```
int result = 13 - 3 * 6 / 4 % 3;
```

(A) −5
(B) 0
(C) 13
(D) −1
(E) 12

5. Suppose that addition and subtraction had higher precedence than multiplication and division. Then the expression

```
2 + 3 * 12 / 7 - 4 + 8
```

would evaluate to which of the following?
(A) 11
(B) 12
(C) 5
(D) 9
(E) −4

6. Let x be a variable of type `double` that is positive. A program contains the boolean expression (`Math.pow(x,0.5) == Math.sqrt(x)`). Which of the following is the most likely reason why this expression can have the value `false`?
(A) $x^{1/2}$ is not mathematically equivalent to $\sqrt{x}$.
(B) x was imprecisely calculated in a previous program statement.
(C) The computer stores floating-point numbers with 32-bit words.
(D) There is round-off error in calculating the pow and sqrt functions.
(E) There is overflow error in calculating the pow function.

7. Consider the following code segment

```
if (n != 0 && x/n > 100)
    statement1;
else
    statement2;
```

If n is of type int and has a value of 0 when the segment is executed, what will happen?

(A) An ArithmeticException will be thrown.

(B) A syntax error will occur.

(C) *statement1*, but not *statement2*, will be executed.

(D) *statement2*, but not *statement1*, will be executed.

(E) Neither *statement1* nor *statement2* will be executed; control will pass to the first statement following the if statement.

8. What will the output be for the following poorly formatted program segment, if the input value for num is 22?

```
int num =  call to a method that reads an integer;
if (num > 0)
if (num % 5 == 0)
System.out.println(num);
else System.out.println(num + " is negative");
```

(A) 22

(B) 4

(C) 2 is negative

(D) 22 is negative

(E) Nothing will be output.

9. Look at the following poorly formatted program segment. If a = 7 and c = 6 before execution, which of the following represents the correct values of c, d, p, and t after execution? An undetermined value is represented with a question mark.

```
if (a == 6)
if (c == 6)
{
    c = 9;
    d = 9;
}
else
{
    t = 10;
    if (c == 6)
        c = 5;
}
else p = 9;
```

(A) c = 6, d = ?, p = 9, t = ?
(B) c = 5, d = ?, p = ?, t = 10
(C) c = 6, d = ?, p = ?, t = ?
(D) c = 5, d = 9, p = ?, t = 10
(E) c = 9, d = 9, p = ?, t = ?

10. What values are stored in x and y after execution of the following program segment?

```
int x=30, y=40;
if (x >= 0)
{
    if (x <= 100)
    {
        y = x*3;
        if (y < 50)
            x /= 10;
    }
    else
        y = x*2;
}
else
    y = -x;
```

(A) x=30 y=90
(B) x=30 y=-30
(C) x=30 y=60
(D) x=3 y=-3
(E) x=30 y=40

11. The boolean expression `!A && B || C` is equivalent to
    (A) `!A && (B || C)`
    (B) `((!A) && B) || C`
    (C) `(!A) && (B || C)`
    (D) `!(A && B) || C`
    (E) `!(A && B || C)`

12. Assume that a and b are integers. The boolean expression

    ```
    !(a <= b) && (a*b > 0)
    ```

    will always evaluate to `true` given that
    (A) `a = b`
    (B) `a > b`
    (C) `a < b`
    (D) `a > b` and `b > 0`
    (E) `a > b` and `b < 0`

13. Given that a, b, and c are integers, consider the boolean expression

    ```
    (a < b) || !((c == a*b) && (c < a))
    ```

    Which of the following will *guarantee* that the expression is `true`?
    (A) `c < a` is `false`.
    (B) `c < a` is `true`.
    (C) `a < b` is `false`.
    (D) `c == a*b` is `true`.
    (E) `c == a*b` is `true`, and `c < a` is `true`.

14. Given that n and count are both of type `int`, which statement is true about the following code segments?

    ```
    I for (count=1; count <= n; count++)
         System.out.println(count);

    II count = 1;
       while (count <= n)
       {
           System.out.println(count);
           count++;
       }
    ```

    (A) I and II are exactly equivalent for all input values n.
    (B) I and II are exactly equivalent for all input values n ≥ 1, but differ when n ≤ 0.
    (C) I and II are exactly equivalent only when n = 0.
    (D) I and II are exactly equivalent only when n is even.
    (E) I and II are not equivalent for any input values of n.

15. The following fragment intends that a user will enter a list of positive integers at the keyboard and terminate the list with a sentinel:

```java
int value;
final int SENTINEL = -999;
while (value != SENTINEL)
{
    //code to process value
    ...
    value = IO.readInt();        //read user input
}
```

The fragment is not correct. Which is a true statement?

(A) The sentinel gets processed.
(B) The last nonsentinel value entered in the list fails to get processed.
(C) A poor choice of SENTINEL value causes the loop to terminate before all values have been processed.
(D) Running the program with this code causes a compile-time error.
(E) Entering the SENTINEL value as the first value causes a run-time error.

16. Which *best* describes method Mystery?

```java
int Mystery(int x, int y)
//Precondition: x > y
{
    int i = 1, m = x;
    while (m % y != 0)
    {
        i++;
        m = i*x;
    }
    return m;
}
```

(A) It returns the smallest common factor of x and y, that is, the smallest positive integer divisor of both x and y.
(B) It returns the greatest common factor of x and y, that is, the largest integer divisor of both x and y.
(C) It returns the least common multiple of x and y, that is, the smallest integer that has both x and y as a factor.
(D) It returns y raised to the xth power, that is, y^x.
(E) It returns x raised to the yth power, that is, x^y.

17. Consider this code segment:

```
int x = 10, y = 0;
while (x > 5)
{
    y = 3;
    while (y < x)
    {
        y *= 2;
        if (y % x == 1)
            y += x;
    }
    x -= 3;
}
System.out.println(x + " " + y);
```

What will be output after execution of this code segment?
(A) 1   6
(B) 7   12
(C) -3   12
(D) 4   12
(E) -3   6

Questions 18 and 19 refer to the following method, checkNumber, which checks the validity of its four-digit integer parameter.

```
//Precondition:  n is a 4-digit integer
//Postcondition: validity of n has been returned
boolean checkNumber(int n)
{
    int d1,d2,d3,checkDigit,nRemaining,rem;
    //strip off digits
    checkDigit = n % 10;
    nRemaining = n/10;
    d3 = nRemaining % 10;
    nRemaining /= 10;
    d2 = nRemaining % 10;
    nRemaining /= 10;
    d1 = nRemaining % 10;
    //check validity
    rem = (d1 + d2 + d3) % 7;
    return rem == checkDigit;
}
```

A program invokes method checkNumber with the statement

```
boolean valid = checkNumber(num);
```

18. Which of the following values of num will result in valid having a value of true?
(A) 6143
(B) 6144
(C) 6145
(D) 6146
(E) 6147

19. What is the purpose of the local variable `nRemaining`?
    (A) It is not possible to separate n into digits without the help of a temporary variable.
    (B) `nRemaining` prevents the parameter `num` from being altered.
    (C) `nRemaining` enhances the readability of the algorithm.
    (D) On exiting the method, the value of `nRemaining` may be reused.
    (E) `nRemaining` is needed as the left-hand side operand for integer division.

20. What output will be produced by this code segment? (Ignore spacing.)

```
for (int i=5; i>=1; i--)
{
    for (int j=i; j>=1; j--)
        System.out.print(2*j-1);
    System.out.println();
}
```

(A) 9 7 5 3 1
    9 7 5 3
    9 7 5
    9 7
    9

(B) 9 7 5 3 1
    7 5 3 1
    5 3 1
    3 1
    1

(C) 9 7 5 3 1
    7 5 3 1 -1
    5 3 1 -1 -3
    3 1 -1 -3 -5
    1 -1 -3 -5 -7

(D) 1
    1 3
    1 3 5
    1 3 5 7
    1 3 5 7 9

(E) 1 3 5 7 9
    1 3 5 7
    1 3 5
    1 3
    1

21. Which of the following program fragments will produce this output? (Ignore spacing.)

```
2 - - - - -
- 4 - - - -
- - 6 - - -
- - - 8 - -
- - - - 10 -
- - - - - 12
```

```
I for (int i=1; i<=6; i++)
  {
      for (int k=1; k<=6; k++)
          if (k == i)
              System.out.print(2*k);
          else
              System.out.print("-");
      System.out.println();
  }
```

```
II for (int i=1; i<=6; i++)
   {
       for (int k=1; k<=i-1; k++)
           System.out.print("-");
       System.out.print(2*i);
       for (int k=1; k<=6-i; k++)
           System.out.print("-");
       System.out.println();
   }
```

```
III for (int i=1; i<=6; i++)
    {
        for (int k=1; k<=i-1; k++)
            System.out.print("-");
        System.out.print(2*i);
        for (int k=i+1; k<=6; k++)
            System.out.print("-");
        System.out.println();
    }
```

(A) I only
(B) II only
(C) III only
(D) I and II only
(E) I, II, and III

22. Consider this program segment:

```
int newNum = 0, temp;
int num = k;              //k is some predefined integer value ≥ 0
while (num > 10)
{
    temp = num % 10;
    num /= 10;
    newNum = newNum*10 + temp;
}
System.out.print(newNum);
```

Which is a true statement about the segment?

I If $100 \leq$ num ≤ 1000 initially, the final value of newNum must be in the range $10 \leq$ newNum ≤ 100.

II There is no initial value of num that will cause an infinite while loop.

III If num ≤ 10 initially, newNum will have a final value of 0.

(A) I only
(B) II only
(C) III only
(D) II and III only
(E) I, II, and III

23. Consider the method reverse:

```
//Precondition:  n > 0
//Postcondition: returns n with its digits reversed
//Example: If n = 234, method reverse returns 432
int reverse(int n)
{
    int rem, revNum=0;

    < code segment >

    return revNum;
}
```

Which of the following replacements for < *code segment* > would cause the method to work as intended?

```
I  for (int i=0; i<=n; i++)
   {
       rem = n % 10;
       revNum = revNum*10 + rem;
       n /= 10;
   }

II while (n != 0)
   {
       rem = n % 10;
       revNum = revNum*10 + rem;
       n /= 10;
   }

III for (int i = n; i != 0; i /= 10)
    {
        rem = i % 10;
        revNum = revNum*10 + rem;
    }
```

(A) I only
(B) II only
(C) I and II only
(D) II and III only
(E) I and III only

Answer Key

1. **B**	9. **A**	17. **D**
2. **E**	10. **A**	18. **B**
3. **E**	11. **B**	19. **C**
4. **E**	12. **D**	20. **B**
5. **C**	13. **A**	21. **E**
6. **D**	14. **A**	22. **D**
7. **D**	15. **D**	23. **D**
8. **D**	16. **C**	

Answers Explained

1. **(B)** When x is converted to an integer, as in segment I, information is lost. Java requires that an explicit cast to an int be made, as in segment II. Note that segment II will cause x to be truncated: the value stored in y is 14. By requiring the explicit cast, Java doesn't let you do this accidentally. In segment III y will contain the value 14.0. No explicit cast to a double is required since no information is lost.

2. **(E)** The string argument contains two escape sequences: '\\', which means print a backslash (\), and '\n', which means go to a new line. Choice E is the only choice that does both of these.

3. **(E)** For this choice, the integer division 13/5 will be evaluated to 2, which will then be cast to 2.0. The output will be 13/5 = 2.0. The compiler needs a way to recognize that real-valued division is required. All the other options provide a way.

4. **(E)** The operators *, /, and % have equal precedence, all higher than -, and must be performed first, from left to right.

```
      13 - 3 * 6 / 4 % 3
    = 13 - 18 / 4 % 3
    = 13 - 4 % 3
    = 13 - 1
    = 12
```

5. **(C)** The expression must be evaluated as if parenthesized like this:

```
    (2 + 3) * 12/(7 - 4 + 8)
```

This becomes 5 * 12/11 = 60/11 = 5.

6. **(D)** Anytime arithmetic operations are done with floating-point numbers, round-off error occurs. The Math class methods (see p. 117) such as pow and sqrt use various approximations to generate their answers to the required accuracy. Since they do different internal arithmetic, however, the round-off will usually not result in exactly the same answers. Note that choice A can't be correct since $\sqrt{x}$ and $x^{1/2}$ *are* mathematically equivalent. Choice B is wrong because no matter how x was previously calculated, the same x is input to pow and sqrt. Choice C is wrong since round-off error occurs no matter how many bits are used to represent numbers. Choice E is wrong because if x is representable on the machine (i.e., hasn't overflowed), then its square root, $x^{1/2}$, will not overflow.

7. **(D)** Short-circuit evaluation of the boolean expression will occur. The expression (n != 0) will evaluate to false, which makes the entire boolean expression false. Therefore the expression (x/n > 100) will not be evaluated. Hence no division by zero will occur, causing an **ArithmeticException** to be thrown. When the boolean expression has a value of false, only the else part of the statement, *statement2*, will be executed.

8. **(D)** Each else gets paired with the nearest unpaired if. Thus when the test (22 % 5 == 0) fails, the else part indicating that 22 is negative will be executed. This is clearly not the intent of the fragment, which can be fixed using delimiters:

```
int num =   call to a method that reads an integer;
if (num > 0)
{
    if (num % 5 == 0)
        System.out.println(num);
}
else
    System.out.println(num + " is negative");
```

9. **(A)** Since (a == 6) is false, the

```
if (c == 6) ...
else
{
    t = 10; ...
```

statement will not be executed. The second else matches up with the first if, which means that p = 9 gets executed. Variables d and t remain undefined.

10. **(A)** Since the first test (x >= 0) is true, the matching else part, y = -x, will not be executed. Since (x <= 100) is true, the matching else part, y = x*2, will not be executed. The variable y will be set to x*3 (i.e., 90) and will now fail the y < 50 test. Thus x will never be altered in this algorithm. Final values are x = 30 and y = 90.

11. **(B)** The order of precedence from highest to lowest is !, &&, ||. Thus, the order of evaluation is (!A), ((!A) && B), and finally ((!A) && B) || C.

12. **(D)** To evaluate to true, the expression must reduce to true && true. We therefore need !(false) && true. Choice D is the only condition that guarantees this: a > b provides !(false) for the left-hand expression, and a > b

and b > 0 implies both a and b positive, which leads to true for the right-hand expression. Choice E, for example, will provide true for the right-hand expression only if a < 0. You have no information about a and can't make assumptions about it.

13. **(A)** If (c < a) is false, ((c == a*b) && (c < a)) evaluates to false irrespective of the value of c == a*b. In this case, !(c == a*b && c < a) evaluates to true. Then (a < b) || true evaluates to true irrespective of the value of (a < b). In all the other choices, the given expression *may* be true. There is not enough information given to guarantee this, however.

14. **(A)** If n ≥ 1, both segments will print out the integers from 1 through n. If n ≤ 0, both segments will fail the test immediately and do nothing.

15. **(D)** The (value != SENTINEL) test occurs before value is initialized, causing an error at compile time. The code must be fixed by reading the first value before doing the test:

```
final int SENTINEL = -999;
int value = IO.readInt();
while (value != SENTINEL)
{
    //code to process value
    value = IO.readInt();
}
```

Choices A, B, C, and E are all incorrect because if the program doesn't compile, it won't run! A note, however, about choice C: -999 is a fine choice for the sentinel given that only positive integers are valid input data.

16. **(C)** The algorithm generates successive multiples of x, the larger of the two integers x and y, until it finds one that is also a multiple of y. This number will be the smallest common multiple of x and y.

17. **(D)** Here is a trace of the values of x and y during execution. Note that the condition (y % x == 1) is never true in this example.

x	10				7				4
y		3	6	12		3	6	12	

The while loop terminates when x is 4 since the test while (x > 5) fails.

18. **(B)** The algorithm finds the remainder when the sum of the first three digits of n is divided by 7. If this remainder is equal to the fourth digit, checkDigit, the method returns true, otherwise false. Note that (6+1+4) % 7 equals 4. Thus, only choice B is a valid number.

19. **(C)** As n gets broken down into its digits, nRemaining is the part of n that remains after each digit is stripped off. Thus nRemaining is a self-documenting name that helps describe what is happening. Choice A is false because every digit can be stripped off using some sequence of integer division and mod. Choice B is false because num is passed by value and therefore will not be altered when the method is exited (see p. 42). Eliminate choice D: when the method is exited, all local variables are destroyed. Choice E is nonsense.

20. **(B)** The outer loop produces five rows of output. Each pass through the inner loop goes from i down to 1. Thus five odd numbers starting at 9 are printed in the first row, four odd numbers starting at 7 in the second row, and so on.

21. **(E)** All three algorithms produce the given output. The outer for (int i ...) loop produces six rows, and the inner for (int k ...) loops produce the symbols in each row.

22. **(D)** Statement I is false, since if 100 ≤ num ≤ 109, the body of the while loop will be executed just once. (After this single pass through the loop, the value of num will be 10, and the test if (num > 10) will fail.) With just one pass, newNum will be a one-digit number, equal to temp (which was the original num % 10). Note that statement II is true: there cannot be an infinite loop because num /= 10 guarantees termination of the loop. Statement III is true because if num ≤ 10, the loop will be skipped, and newNum will keep its original value of 0.

23. **(D)** The algorithm works by stripping off the rightmost digit of n (stored in rem), multiplying the current value of revNum by 10, and adding that rightmost digit. When n has been stripped down to no digits (i.e., n == 0 is true), revNum is complete. Segment I is wrong because the number of passes through the loop depends on the number of digits in n, not the value of n itself.

CHAPTER TWO
Classes and Objects

Work is the curse of the drinking classes.
—Oscar Wilde

Objects

Every program that you write involves at least one thing that is being created or manipulated by the program. This thing, together with the operations that manipulate it, is called an *object*.

Consider, for example, a program that must test the validity of a four-digit code number that a person will enter to be able to use a photocopy machine. Rules for validity are provided. The object is a four-digit code number. Some of the operations to manipulate the object could be `readNumber`, `getSeparateDigits`, `testValidity`, and `writeNumber`.

Any given program can have several different types of objects. For example, a program that maintains a database of all books in a library has at least two objects:

1. A `Book` object, with operations like `getTitle`, `isOnShelf`, `isFiction`, and `goOutOfPrint`.
2. A `ListOfBooks` object, with operations like `search`, `addBook`, `removeBook`, and `sortByAuthor`.

An object is characterized by its *state* and *behavior*. For example, a book has a state described by its title, author, whether it's on the shelf, and so on. It also has behavior, like going out of print.

Notice that an object is an abstract idea, separate from the concrete details of a programming language. It corresponds to some real-world object that is being represented by the program.

All object-oriented programming languages have a way to represent an abstract object as a variable in a program. In Java, a variable that represents an abstract object is also called an object!

Classes

A *class* is a software blueprint for implementing objects of a given type. An object is a single *instance* of the class. In a program there will often be several different instances of a given class type.

The current state of a given object is maintained in its *data fields* or *instance variables*, provided by the class. The *methods* of the class provide both the behaviors exhibited by the object and the operations that manipulate the object. You can think of a class as a user-defined type that combines the state of the object and its related operations into a single unit.

While a class contains the implementation details of class objects, these details are hidden from other objects of the program, even though these objects may communicate with each other in the program. This is known as *information hiding* or *encapsulation*.

Here is the framework for a simple bank account class:

```java
public class BankAccount
{
    private String myPassword;
    private double myBalance;
    public static final double OVERDRAWN_PENALTY = 20.00;

    //constructors
    /* Default constructor.
     * Constructs bank account with default values */
    public BankAccount()
    {
        < implementation code >
    }

    /* Constructs bank account with specified password and balance */
    public BankAccount(String password, double balance)
    {
        < implementation code >
    }

    //accessor
    /* Returns balance of this account */
    public double getBalance()
    {
        < implementation code >
    }

    //mutators
    /* Deposits amount in bank account with given password */
    public void deposit(String password, double amount)
    {
        < implementation code >
    }

    /* Withdraws amount from bank account with given password.
     * Assesses penalty if myBalance is less than amount */
    public void withdraw(String password, double amount)
    {
        < implementation code >
    }
}
```

Public, Private, and Static

The keyword public preceding the class declaration signals that the class is usable by all *client programs*. If a class is not public, it can be used only by classes in its own package. In the AP Java subset, all classes are public.

Similarly, *public methods* are accessible to all client programs. Clients, however, are not privy to the class implementation, and may not access the private instance variables and private methods of the class. *Private methods and variables in a class can be accessed only by methods of that class.* While Java allows public instance variables, in the AP Java subset all instance variables are private.

Static final variables (constants) in a class are often declared public (see some examples of Math class constants on p. 117). The variable OVERDRAWN_PENALTY is an example in the BankAccount class. Since the variable is public, it can be used in any client method. The keyword static indicates that there is a single value of the variable that applies to the whole class, rather than a new instance for each object of the class. A client method would refer to the variable as BankAccount.OVERDRAWN_PENALTY. In its own class it is referred to as simply OVERDRAWN_PENALTY.

See p. 37 for static methods.

Methods

Headers

All method headers, with the exception of constructors (see below) and static methods (p. 37), look like this:

```
public      void     withdraw (String password, double amount)
```

access specifier   return type   method name   parameter list

NOTE
1. The *access specifier* tells which other methods can call this method (see *Public, Private, and Static* above).
2. A *return type* of void signals that the method does not return a value.
3. Items in the *parameter list* are separated by commas.

The implementation of the method directly follows the header, enclosed in a {} block.

Types of Methods

Constructors

A *constructor* creates an object of the class. You can recognize a constructor by its name—always the same as the class! Also, a constructor has no return type.

Having several constructors provides different ways of initializing class objects. For example, there are two constructors in the BankAccount class.

1. The *default constructor* has no arguments. It provides reasonable initial values for an object. Here is its implementation:

```
/* Default constructor.
 * Constructs a bank account with default values */
public BankAccount()
{
    myPassword = "";
    myBalance = 0.0;
}
```

In a client method, the declaration

```
BankAccount b = new BankAccount();
```

constructs a `BankAccount` object with a balance of zero and a password equal to the empty string. The `new` operator returns the address of this newly constructed object. The variable `b` is assigned the value of this address—we say "`b` is a *reference* to the object." Picture the setup like this:

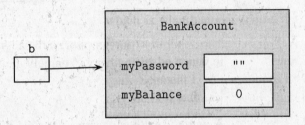

2. The constructor with parameters sets the instance variables of a `BankAccount` object to the values of those parameters.
   Here is the implementation:

```
/* Constructor. Constructs a bank account with
 * specified password and balance */
public BankAccount(String password, double balance)
{
    myPassword = password;
    myBalance = balance;
}
```

In a client program a declaration that uses this constructor needs matching parameters:

```
BankAccount c = new BankAccount("KevinC", 800.00);
```

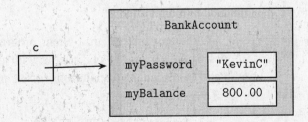

NOTE   b and c are *object variables* that store the *addresses* of their respective `BankAccount` objects. They do not store the objects themselves (see *References* on p. 40).

Accessors

An *accessor method* accesses a class object without altering the object. An accessor returns some information about the object.

The BankAccount class has a single accessor method, getBalance(). Here is its implementation:

```
/* Returns the  balance of this account */
public double getBalance()
{
    return myBalance;
}
```

A client program may use this method as follows:

```
BankAccount b1 = new BankAccount("MattW", 500.00);
BankAccount b2 = new BankAccount("DannyB", 650.50);
if (b1.getBalance() > b2.getBalance())
    ...
```

NOTE   The . *operator* (dot operator) indicates that getBalance() is a method of the class to which b1 and b2 belong, namely the BankAccount class.

Mutators

A *mutator method* changes the state of an object by modifying at least one of its instance variables.

Here are the implementations of the deposit and withdraw methods, each of which alters the value of myBalance in the BankAccount class:

```
/* Deposits amount in a bank account with the given password */
public void deposit(String password, double amount)
{
    myBalance += amount;
}
```

```
/* Withdraws amount from a bank account with the given password.
 * Assesses a penalty if myBalance is less than amount */
public void withdraw(String password, double amount)
{
    if (myBalance >= amount)
        myBalance -= amount;
    else
        myBalance -= OVERDRAWN_PENALTY;   //allows negative balance
}
```

A mutator method in a client program is invoked in the same way as an accessor: using an object variable with the dot operator. For example, assuming valid BankAccount declarations for b1 and b2:

```
b1.withdraw("MattW", 200.00);
b2.deposit("DannyB", 35.68);
```

Static Methods

Static Methods vs. Instance Methods   The methods discussed in the preceding sections—constructors, accessors, and mutators—all operate on individual objects of a class. They are called *instance methods*. A method that performs an operation for the entire class, not its individual objects, is called a *static method* (sometimes called a *class method*).

The implementation of a static method uses the keyword static in its header. There is no implied object in the code (as there is in an instance method). Thus if the code tries to call an instance method or invoke a private instance variable for this nonexistent object, a syntax error will occur.

Here's an example of a static method that might be used in the BankAccount class:

```
public static double getInterestRate()
{
    System.out.println("Enter interest rate for bank account");
    System.out.println("Enter in decimal form:");
    double rate = IO.readDouble();          // read user input
    return rate;
}
```

Since the rate that's returned by this method applies to all bank accounts in the class, not to any particular BankAccount object, it's appropriate that the method should be static.

Recall that an instance method is invoked in a client program by using an object variable followed by the dot operator followed by the method name:

```
BankAccount b = new BankAccount();
b.deposit(password, amount);       //invokes the deposit method for
                                   //BankAccount object b
```

A static method, by contrast, is invoked by using the *class name* with the dot operator:

```
double interestRate = BankAccount.getInterestRate();
```

Static Methods in a Driver Class   Often a class that contains the main() method is used as a driver program to test other classes. Usually such a class creates no objects of the class. So all the methods in the class must be static. Note that at the start of program execution, no objects exist yet. So the main() method must *always* be static.

For example, here is a program that tests a class for reading integers from the console.

```
import java.util.*;
public class GetListTest
{
    /* Read integers from the keyboard into List a */
    public static List getList()
    {
        < code to read integers into a>
        return a;
    }
```

```
                        /* Write contents of List a */
                        public static void writeList(List a)
                        {
                            System.out.println("List is : " + a);
                        }

                        public static void main(String[] args)
                        {
                            List a = getList();
                            writeList(a);
                        }
                    }
```

NOTE

1. The calls to `writeList(a)` and `getList()` do not need to be preceded by `GetListTest` plus a dot because `main` is not a client program: it is in the same class as `getList` and `writeList`.
2. If you omit the keyword `static` from the `getList` or `writeList` header, you get an error message like the following:

```
Can't make static reference to method getList()
in class GetListTest
```

The compiler has recognized that there was no object variable preceding the method call, which means that the methods were static and should have been declared as such.

Method Overloading

Overloaded methods are two or more methods in the same class that have the same name but different parameter lists. For example,

```
class DoOperations
{
    public int product(int n) {return n*n}
    public double product(double x) {return x*x}
    public double product(int x, int y) {return x*y}
        ...
```

The compiler figures out which method to call by examining the method's *signature*. The signature of a method consists of the method's name and a list of the parameter types. Thus the signatures of the overloaded `product` methods are

```
product(int)
product(double)
product(int, int)
```

Note that for overloading purposes, the return type of the method is irrelevant. You can't have two methods with identical signature but different return types. The compiler will complain that the method call is ambiguous.

Having more than one constructor in the same class is an example of overloading. Overloaded constructors provide a choice of ways to initialize objects of the class.

Scope

The *scope* of a variable or method is the region in which that variable or method is visible and can be accessed.

The instance variables, static variables, and methods of a class belong to that class's scope, which extends from the opening brace to the closing brace of the class definition. Within the class all instance variables and methods are accessible and can be referred to simply by name (no dot operator!).

A *local variable* is defined inside a method. It can even be defined inside a statement. Its scope extends from the point where it is declared to the end of the block in which its declaration occurs. A *block* is a piece of code enclosed in a {} pair. When a block is exited, the memory for a local variable is automatically recycled.

Local variables take precedence over instance variables with the same name. (Using the same name, however, creates ambiguity for the programmer, leading to errors. You should avoid the practice.)

The this Keyword

An instance method is always called for a particular object. This object is an *implicit parameter* for the method and is referred to with the keyword this.

In the implementation of instance methods, all instance variables can be written with the prefix this followed by the dot operator.

Example 1

The deposit method of the BankAccount class can refer to myBalance as follows:

```
public void deposit(String password, double amount)
{
    this.myBalance += amount;
}
```

The use of this is unnecessary in the above example.

Example 2

Consider a rational number class called Rational, which has two private instance variables:

```
private int num;        //numerator
private int denom;      //denominator
```

Now consider a constructor for the Rational class:

```
public Rational(int num, int denom)
{
    this.num = num;
    this.denom = denom;
}
```

It is definitely *not* a good idea to use the same name for the explicit parameters and the private instance variables. But if you do, you can avoid errors by referring to this.num and this.denom for the current object that is being constructed. (This particular use of this will not be tested on the exam!)

References

Reference vs.
Primitive Data
Types

All of the numerical data types, like `double` and `int`, as well as types `char` and `boolean`, are *primitive* data types. All objects are *reference* data types. The difference lies in the way they are stored.

Consider the statements

```
int num1 = 3;
int num2 = num1;
```

The variables `num1` and `num2` can be thought of as memory slots, labeled `num1` and `num2`, respectively:

If either of the above variables is now changed, the other is not affected. They each have their own memory slots.

Contrast this with the declaration of a reference data type. Recall that an object is created using `new`:

```
Date d = new Date(2, 17, 1948);
```

This declaration creates a reference variable `d` that refers to a `Date` object. The value of `d` is the address in memory of that object:

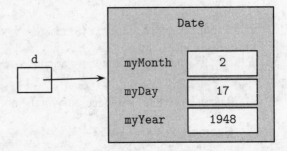

Suppose the following declaration is now made:

```
Date birthday = d;
```

This statement creates the reference variable `birthday`, which contains the same address as `d`:

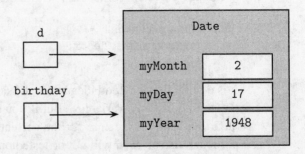

Having two references for the same object is known as *aliasing*. Aliasing can cause unintended problems for the programmer. The statement

```
d.changeDate();
```

will automatically change the object referred to by birthday as well.

What the programmer probably intended was to create a second object called birthday whose attributes exactly matched those of d. This cannot be accomplished without using new. For example,

```
Date birthday = new Date(d.getMonth(), d.getDay(), d.getYear());
```

The statement d.changeDate() will now leave the birthday object unchanged.

The Null Reference

The declaration

```
BankAccount b;
```

defines a reference b that is uninitialized. (To construct the object that b refers to requires the new operator and a BankAccount constructor.) An uninitialized object variable is called a *null reference* or *null pointer*. You can test whether a variable refers to an object or is uninitialized by using the keyword null:

```
if (b == null)
```

If a reference is not null, it can be set to null with the statement

```
b = null;
```

An attempt to invoke an instance method with a null reference may cause your program to terminate with a NullPointerException. For example,

```
public class PersonalFinances
{
    BankAccount b;                  //b is a null reference
        ...
    b.withdraw(password, amt);      //throws a NullPointerException
        ...                         //if b not constructed with new
```

NOTE

If you fail to initialize a local variable in a method before you use it, you will get a compile-time error. If you make the same mistake with an instance variable of a class, the compiler provides reasonable default values for primitive variables (0 for numbers, false for booleans), and the code may run without error. However, if you forget to initialize *reference* instance variables in a class, as in the above example, the compiler will set them to null. Any method call for an object of the class that tries to access the null reference will cause a run-time error: the program will terminate with a NullPointerException.

Method Parameters

Formal vs. Actual Parameters

The header of a method defines the *parameters* of that method. For example, consider the withdraw method of the BankAccount class:

```
public class BankAccount
{   ...
    public void withdraw(String password, double amount)
        ...
```

This method has two explicit parameters, password and amount. These are *dummy* or *formal parameters*. Think of them as place-holders for the pair of *actual parameters* or *arguments* that will be supplied by a particular method call in a client program.

For example,

```
BankAccount b = new BankAccount("TimB", 1000);
b.withdraw("TimB", 250);
```

Here "TimB" and 250 are the actual parameters that match up with password and amount for the withdraw method.

NOTE

1. The number of arguments in the method call must equal the number of parameters in the method header, and the type of each argument must be compatible with the type of each corresponding parameter.

2. In addition to its explicit parameters, the withdraw method has an implicit parameter, this, the BankAccount from which money will be withdrawn. In the method call

```
b.withdraw("TimB", 250);
```

the actual parameter that matches up with this is the object reference b.

Passing Primitive Types as Parameters

Parameters of primitive type are said to be *passed by value*. When a method is called, a new memory slot is allocated for each parameter. The value of each argument is copied into the newly created memory slot corresponding to each parameter.

During execution of the method, the parameters are local to that method. *Any changes made to the parameters will not affect the values of the arguments in the calling program.* When the method is exited, the local memory slots for the parameters are erased.

Here's an example: What will the output be?

```java
public class ParamTest
{
    public static void foo(int x, double y)
    {
        x = 3;
        y = 2.5;
    }

    public static void main(String[] args)
    {
        int a = 7;
        double b = 6.5;
        foo(a, b);
        System.out.println(a + "   " + b);
    }
}
```

The output will be

```
7   6.5
```

The arguments a and b remain unchanged, despite the method call!

This can be understood by picturing the state of the memory slots during execution of the program.

Just before the `foo(a, b)` method call:

a | b
7 | 6.5

At the time of the `foo(a, b)` method call:

a | b
7 | 6.5

x | y
7 | 6.5

Just before exiting the method: Note that the values of x and y have been changed.

a | b
7 | 6.5

x | y
3 | 2.5

After exiting the method: Note that the memory slots for x and y have been reclaimed. The values of a and b remain unchanged.

a | b
7 | 6.5

Passing Objects as Parameters

In Java both primitive types and object references are passed by value. When object references are parameters, the same mechanism of copying into local memory slots is used. The key point is that the addresses (references) are copied, not the instance variables. As with primitive types, changes made to the parameters will not change the values of the matching arguments. What this means in practice is that it is not possible for a method to replace an object with another one—you can't change the reference that was passed. It is, however, possible to change the state of the object to which the parameter refers.

Example 1

A method that changes the state of an object.

```
/* Subtracts fee from balance in b if current balance too low */
public static void chargeFee(BankAccount b, String password,
        double fee)
{
    final double MIN_BALANCE = 10.00;
    if (b.getBalance() < MIN_BALANCE)
        b.withdraw(password, fee);
}

public static void main(String[] args)
{
    final double FEE = 5.00;
```

```
            BankAccount andysAccount = new BankAccount("AndyS", 7.00);
            chargeFee(andysAccount, "AndyS", FEE);
               ...
        }
```

Here are the memory slots before the `chargeFee` method call:

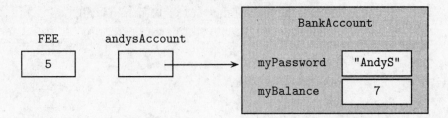

At the time of the `chargeFee` method call, copies of the matching parameters are made:

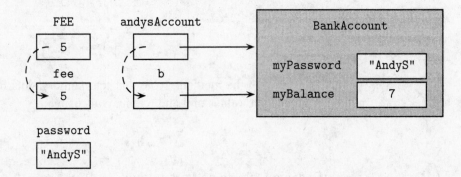

Just before exiting the method: The `myBalance` field of the `BankAccount` object has been changed.

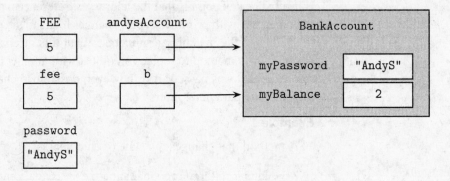

After exiting the method: All parameter memory slots have been erased, but the object remains altered.

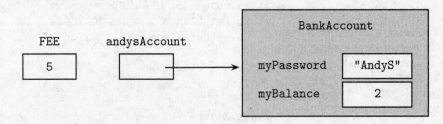

NOTE   The andysAccount reference is unchanged throughout the program segment. The object to which it refers, however, has been changed. This is significant. Contrast this with Example 2 below in which an attempt is made to replace the object itself.

Example 2

A chooseBestAccount method attempts—erroneously—to set its betterFund parameter to the BankAccount with the higher balance:

```
public static void chooseBestAccount(BankAccount better,
        BankAccount b1, BankAccount b2)
{
    if (b1.getBalance() > b2.getBalance())
        better = b1;
    else
        better = b2;
}

public static void main(String[] args)
{
    BankAccount briansFund = new BankAccount("BrianL", 10000);
    BankAccount paulsFund = new BankAccount("PaulM", 90000);
    BankAccount betterFund = null;

    chooseBestAccount(betterFund, briansFund, paulsFund);
        ...
}
```

The intent is that betterFund will be a reference to the paulsFund object after execution of the chooseBestAccount statement. A look at the memory slots illustrates why this fails.

Before the chooseBestAccount method call:

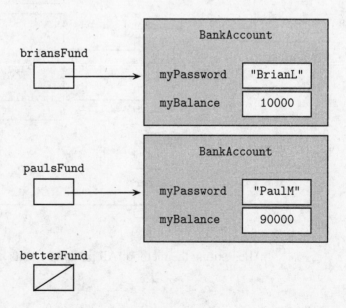

At the time of the chooseBestAccount method call: Copies of the matching references are made.

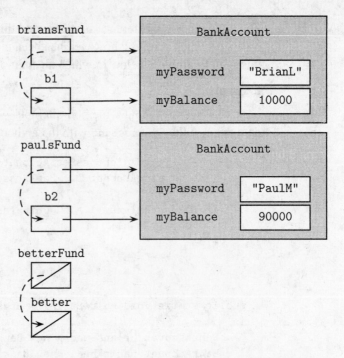

Just before exiting the method: The value of better has been changed; betterFund, however, remains unchanged.

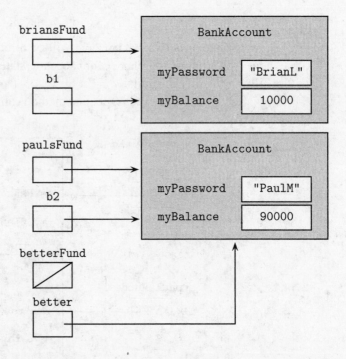

After exiting the method: All parameter slots have been erased.

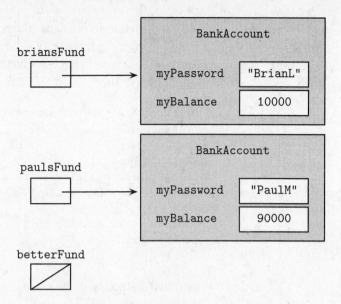

Note that the `betterFund` reference continues to be `null`, contrary to the programmer's intent.

The way to fix the problem is to modify the method so that it returns the better account. Returning an object from a method means that you are returning the address of the object.

```
public static BankAccount chooseBestAccount(BankAccount b1,
        BankAccount b2)
{
    BankAccount better;
    if (b1.getBalance() > b2.getBalance())
        better = b1;
    else
        better = b2;
    return better;
}

public static void main(String[] args)
{
    BankAccount briansFund = new BankAccount("BrianL", 10000);
    BankAccount paulsFund = new BankAccount("PaulM", 90000);
    BankAccount betterFund = chooseBestAccount(briansFund, paulsFund);
        . . .
}
```

NOTE   The effect of this is to create the `betterFund` reference, which refers to the same object as `paulsFund`:

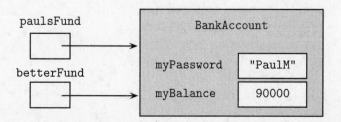

What the method does *not* do is create a new object to which betterFund refers. To do that would require the keyword new and use of a BankAccount constructor. Assuming that a getPassword() accessor has been added to the BankAccount class, the code would look like this:

```
public static BankAccount chooseBestAccount(BankAccount b1,
        BankAccount b2)
{
    BankAccount better;
    if (b1.getBalance() > b2.getBalance())
        better = new BankAccount(b1.getPassword(), b1.getBalance());
    else
        better = new BankAccount(b2.getPassword(), b2.getBalance());
    return better;
}
```

Using this modified method with the same main() method above has the following effect:

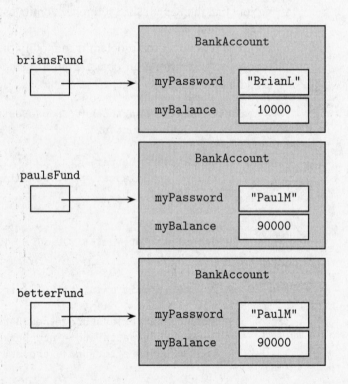

Modifying more than one object in a method can be accomplished using a *wrapper class* (see p. 114).

Multiple-Choice Questions on Classes and Objects

Questions 1–3 refer to the `Time` class declared below:

```
public class Time
{
    private int myHrs;
    private int myMins;
    private int mySecs;

    public Time()
    { implementation code }

    public Time(int h, int m, int s)
    { implementation code }

    //resets time to myHrs = h, myMins = m, mySecs = s
    public void resetTime(int h, int m, int s)
    { implementation code }

    //advances time by one second
    public void increment()
    { implementation code }

    //returns true if this time equals t, false otherwise
    public boolean equals(Time t)
    { implementation code }

    //returns true if this time is earlier than t, false otherwise
    public boolean lessThan(Time t)
    { implementation code }

    //returns time as a String in the form hrs:mins:secs
    public String toString()
    { implementation code }
}
```

1. Which of the following is a *false* statement about the methods?
    (A) `equals`, `lessThan`, and `toString` are all accessor methods.
    (B) `increment` is a mutator method.
    (C) `Time()` is the default constructor.
    (D) The `Time` class has three constructors.
    (E) There are no static methods in this class.

2. Which of the following represents correct *implementation code* for the constructor with parameters?

(A) ```
myHrs = 0;
myMins = 0;
mySecs = 0;
```

(B) ```
myHrs = h;
myMins = m;
mySecs = s;
```

(C) ```
resetTime(myHrs, myMins, mySecs);
```

(D) ```
h = myHrs;
m = myMins;
s = mySecs;
```

(E) ```
Time = new Time(h, m, s);
```

3. A client program has a `display` method that writes the time represented by its parameter:

```
public static void display (Time t)
//outputs time t in the form hrs:mins:secs
{
    < method body >
}
```

Which of the following are correct replacements for *< method body >*?

```
  I Time T = new Time(h, m, s);
    System.out.println(T);
```

```
 II System.out.println(t.myHrs + ":" + t.myMins + ":" + t.mySecs);
```

```
III System.out.println(t);
```

(A) I only
(B) II only
(C) III only
(D) II and III only
(E) I, II, and III

4. Which statement about parameters is *false*?
   (A) The scope of parameters is the method in which they are defined.
   (B) Static methods have no implicit parameter `this`.
   (C) Two overloaded methods in the same class must have parameters with different names.
   (D) All parameters in Java are passed by value.
   (E) Two different constructors in a given class can have the same number of parameters.
```

Questions 5–11 refer to the following Date class declaration:

```
public class Date
{
    private int myDay;
    private int myMonth;
    private int myYear;

    public Date()                         //default constructor
    { implementation code }

    public Date(int mo, int day, int yr)  //constructor
    { implementation code }

    public int month()                    //returns month of Date
    { implementation code }

    public int day()                      //returns day of Date
    { implementation code }

    public int year()                     //returns year of Date
    { implementation code }

    //string representation of Date as "m/d/y", e.g. 4/18/1985
    public String toString()
    { implementation code }
}
```

5. Which of the following correctly constructs a Date object?

(A) Date d = new (2, 13, 1947);

(B) Date d = new Date(2, 13, 1947);

(C) Date d;
    d = new (2, 13, 1947);

(D) Date d;
    d = Date(2, 13, 1947);

(E) Date d = Date(2, 13, 1947);

6. Which of the following will cause an error message?

  I Date d1 = new Date(8, 2, 1947);
    Date d2 = d1;

 II Date d1 = null;
    Date d2 = d1;

III Date d = null;
    int x = d.year();

(A) I only
(B) II only
(C) III only
(D) II and III only
(E) I, II, and III

7. A client program creates a Date object as follows:

```
Date d = new Date(1, 13, 2002);
```

Which of the following subsequent code segments will cause an error?
(A) String s = d.toString();
(B) int x = d.day();
(C) Date e = d;
(D) Date e = new Date(1, 13, 2002);
(E) int y = d.myYear;

8. Consider the implementation of a write() method that is added to the Date class:

```
//Write the date in the form m/d/y, for example 2/17/1948
public void write()
{
    < implementation code >
}
```

Which of the following could be used as < *implementation code* >?

I System.out.println(myMonth + "/" + myDay + "/" + myYear);

II System.out.println(month() + "/" + day() + "/" + year());

III System.out.println(this);

(A) I only
(B) II only
(C) III only
(D) II and III only
(E) I, II, and III

9. Here is a client program that uses `Date` objects:

```
public class BirthdayStuff
{
    public static Date findBirthdate()
    {
        Date bDate;
        < code to get bDate >
        return bDate;
    }

    public static void main(String[] args)
    {
        Date d = findBirthdate();
            ...
    }
}
```

Which of the following is a correct replacement for < *code to get* `bDate` >?

```
 I System.out.println("Enter birthdate: mo, day, yr: ");
   int m = IO.readInt();                    //read user input
   int d = IO.readInt();                    //read user input
   int y = IO.readInt();                    //read user input
   bDate = new Date(m, d, y);
```

```
II System.out.println("Enter birthdate: mo, day, yr: ");
   int bDate.month() = IO.readInt();        //read user input
   int bDate.day() = IO.readInt();          //read user input
   int bDate.year() = IO.readInt();         //read user input
   bDate = new Date(bDate.month(), bDate.day(), bDate.year());
```

```
III System.out.println("Enter birthdate: mo, day, yr: ");
    int bDate.myMonth = IO.readInt();       //read user input
    int bDate.myDay = IO.readInt();         //read user input
    int bDate.myYear = IO.readInt();        //read user input
    bDate = new Date(bDate.myMonth, bDate.myDay, bDate.myYear);
```

(A) I only
(B) II only
(C) III only
(D) I and II only
(E) I and III only

10. A client program for the Date class has this declaration:

    ```
    Date d1 = new Date(month, day, year);
    ```

    where month, day, and year are previously defined integer variables. The program now creates a second Date object d2 that is an exact copy of the object d1 refers to. Which of the following code segments will *not* do this correctly?

    I Date d2 = d1;

    II Date d2 = new Date(month, day, year);

    III Date d2 = new Date(d1.month(), d1.day(), d1.year());

    (A) I only
    (B) II only
    (C) III only
    (D) I, II, and III
    (E) all will do this correctly

11. The Date class is modified by adding the following mutator method:

    ```
    public void addYears(int n)     //add n years to date
    ```

    Here is part of a poorly coded client program that uses the Date class:

    ```
    public static void addCentury(Date recent, Date old)
    {
        old.addYears(100);
        recent = old;
    }

    public static void main(String[] args)
    {
        Date oldDate = new Date(1, 13, 1900);
        Date recentDate;
        addCentury(recentDate, oldDate);
            ...
    }
    ```

    Which will be true after executing this code?
    (A) A NullPointerException was thrown.
    (B) The oldDate object remains unchanged.
    (C) recentDate is a null reference.
    (D) recentDate refers to the same object as oldDate.
    (E) recentDate refers to a separate object whose contents are the same as those of oldDate.

Questions 12–15 refer to the following definition of the Rational class:

```
public class Rational
{
    private int myNum;          //numerator
    private int myDenom;        //denominator

    //constructors
    /* default constructor */
    Rational()
    { implementation code }

    /* constructor with numerator n and denominator 1 */
    Rational(int n)
    { implementation code }

    /* constructor with specified numerator and denominator */
    Rational(int numer, int denom)
    { implementation code }

    //accessors
    /* returns numerator */
    int numerator()
    { implementation code }

    /* returns denominator */
    int denominator()
    { implementation code }

    //arithmetic operations
    /* returns (this + r)
     * leaves this unchanged */
    public Rational plus(Rational r)
    { implementation code }
    //Similarly for times, minus, divide

    /* ensures myDenom > 0 */
    private void fixSigns()
    { implementation code }

    /* ensures lowest terms */
    private void reduce()
    { implementation code }
}
```

12. The method reduce() is not a public method because
    (A) Methods whose return type is void cannot be public.
    (B) Methods that change this cannot be public.
    (C) The reduce() method is not intended for use by clients of the Rational class.
    (D) The reduce() method is intended for use only by clients of the Rational class.
    (E) The reduce() method uses only the private instance variables of the Rational class.

13. The constructors in the `Rational` class allow initialization of `Rational` objects in several different ways. Which of the following will cause an error?

    (A) `Rational r1 = new Rational();`

    (B) `Rational r2 = r1;`

    (C) `Rational r3 = new Rational(2,-3);`

    (D) `Rational r4 = new Rational(3.5);`

    (E) `Rational r5 = new Rational(10);`

14. Here is the implementation code for the `plus` method:

```
/* Returns (this+r) in reduced form. Leaves this unchanged */
public Rational plus(Rational r)
{
    fixSigns();
    r.fixSigns();
    int denom = myDenom * r.myDenom;
    int num = myNum * r.myDenom + r.myNum * myDenom;
    < some more code >
}
```

    Which of the following is a correct replacement for < *some more code* >?

    (A) ```
    Rational rat(num, denom);
    rat.reduce();
    return rat;
    ```

    (B) ```
    return new Rational(num, denom);
    ```

    (C) ```
    reduce();
    Rational rat = new Rational(num, denom);
    return rat;
    ```

    (D) ```
    Rational rat = new Rational(num, denom);
    Rational.reduce();
    return rat;
    ```

    (E) ```
    Rational rat = new Rational(num, denom);
    rat.reduce();
    return rat;
    ```

15. Assume these declarations:

```
Rational a = new Rational();
Rational r = new Rational(num, denom);
int n = value;
//num, denom, and value are valid integer values
```

    Which of the following will cause a compile-time error?

    (A) `r = a.plus(r);`

    (B) `a = r.plus(new Rational(n));`

    (C) `r = r.plus(r);`

    (D) `a = n.plus(r);`

    (E) `r = r.plus(new Rational(n));`
```

16. Here are the private instance variables for a Frog object:

```
public class Frog
{
    private String mySpecies;
    private int myAge;
    private double myWeight;
    private Position myPosition;      //position (x,y) in pond
    private boolean amAlive;
        ...
```

Which of the following methods in the Frog class is the best candidate for being a static method?

(A) swim   //frog swims to new position in pond

(B) getPondTemperature   //returns temperature of pond

(C) eat   //frog eats and gains weight

(D) getWeight   //returns weight of frog

(E) die   //frog dies with some probability based
                      //on frog's age and pond temperature

17. What output will be produced by this program?

```
public class Mystery
{
    public static void strangeMethod(int x, int y)
    {
        x += y;
        y *= x;
        System.out.println(x + " " + y);
    }

    public static void main(String[] args)
    {
        int a = 6, b = 3;
        strangeMethod(a, b);
        System.out.println(a + " " + b);
    }
}
```

(A) 36
    9

(B) 3 6
    9

(C) 9 27
    9 27

(D) 6 3
    9 27

(E) 9 27
    6 3

Questions 18–20 refer to the Temperature class shown below:

```
public class Temperature
{
    private String myScale;  //valid values are "F" or "C"
    private double myDegrees;

    //constructors
    /* default constructor */
    public Temperature()
    { implementation code }

    /* constructor with specified degrees and scale */
    public Temperature(double degrees, String scale)
    { implementation code }

    //accessors
    /* Returns degrees for this temperature */
    public double getDegrees()
    { implementation code }

    /* Returns scale for this temperature */
    public String getScale()
    { implementation code }

    //mutators
    /* Precondition:   temperature is a a valid temperature
     *                 in degrees Celsius
     * Postcondition: returns this temperature, which has been
     *                 converted to degrees Fahrenheit */
    public Temperature toFahrenheit()
    { implementation code }

    /* Precondition:   temperature is a a valid temperature
     *                 in degrees Fahrenheit
     * Postcondition: returns this temperature, which has been
     *                 converted to degrees Celsius */
    public Temperature toCelsius()
    { implementation code }

    /* Raise this temperature by amt degrees and return it */
    public Temperature raise(double amt)
    { implementation code }

    /* Lower this temperature by amt degrees and return it */
    public Temperature lower(double amt)
    { implementation code }

    //other methods
    /* Returns true if the number of degrees is a valid temperature
     * in the given scale, false otherwise */
    public static boolean isValidTemp(double degrees, String scale)
    { implementation code }

        . . .

}
```

18. A client method contains this code segment:

```
Temperature t1 = new Temperature(40, "C");
Temperature t2 = t1;
Temperature t3 = t2.lower(20);
Temperature t4 = t1.toFahrenheit();
```

Which statement is *true* following execution of this segment?
(A) t1, t2, t3, and t4 all represent the identical temperature, in degrees Celsius.
(B) t1, t2, t3, and t4 all represent the identical temperature, in degrees Fahrenheit.
(C) t4 represents a Fahrenheit temperature, while t1, t2, and t3 all represent degrees Celsius.
(D) t1 and t2 refer to the same Temperature object; t3 refers to a Temperature object that is 20 degrees lower than t1 and t2, while t4 refers to an object that is t1 converted to Fahrenheit.
(E) A NullPointerException was thrown.

19. Consider the following code:

```
public class TempTest
{
    public static void main(String[] args)
    {
        System.out.println("Enter temperature scale: ");
        String scale = IO.readString();    //read user input
        System.out.println("Enter number of degrees: ");
        double degrees = IO.readDouble();   //read user input
        < code to construct a valid temperature from user input >
    }
}
```

Which is a correct replacement for < *code to construct...* >?

```
I  Temperature t = new Temperature(degrees, scale);
   if (!t.isValidTemp(degrees,scale))
       < error message and exit program >

II if (isValidTemp(degrees,scale))
       Temperature t = new Temperature(degrees, scale);
   else
       < error message and exit program >

III if (Temperature.isValidTemp(degrees,scale))
       Temperature t = new Temperature(degrees, scale);
    else
       < error message and exit program >
```

(A) I only
(B) II only
(C) III only
(D) I and II only
(E) I and III only

20. The formula to convert degrees Celsius C to Fahrenheit F is

$$F = 1.8C + 32$$

For example, $30°$ C is equivalent to $86°$ F.

An `inFahrenheit()` accessor method is added to the `Temperature` class. Here is its implementation:

```
/* Precondition:   temperature is a valid temperature in
 *                 degrees Celsius
 * Postcondition:  an equivalent temperature in degrees
 *                 Fahrenheit has been returned. Original
 *                 temperature remains unchanged */
public Temperature inFahrenheit()
{
    Temperature result;
    < more code >
    return result;
}
```

Which of the following correctly replaces < *more code* > so that the postcondition is achieved?

```
 I result = new Temperature(myDegrees*1.8 + 32, "F");
```

```
 II result = new Temperature(myDegrees*1.8, "F");
    result = result.raise(32);
```

```
III myDegrees *= 1.8;
    this = raise(32);
    result = new Temperature(myDegrees, "F");
```

(A) I only
(B) II only
(C) III only
(D) I and II only
(E) I, II, and III

MULTIPLE-CHOICE QUESTIONS ON CLASSES AND OBJECTS   61

21. Consider this program:

```
public class CountStuff
{
    public static void doSomething
    {
        int count = 0;
        ...
        //code to do something - no screen output produced
        count++;
    }

    public static void main(String[] args)
    {
        int count = 0;
        System.out.println("How many iterations?");
        int n = IO.readInt();      //read user input
        for (int i=1; i<=n; i++)
        {
            doSomething();
            System.out.println(count);
        }
    }
}
```

If the input value for n is 3, what screen output will this program subsequently produce?

(A) 0
    0
    0

(B) 1
    2
    3

(C) 3
    3
    3

(D) ?
    ?
    ?
    where ? is some undefined value.

(E) No output will be produced.

22. This question refers to the following class:

```
public class IntObject
{
    private int myInt;

    public IntObject()          //default constructor
    {myInt = 0;}
    public IntObject(int n)  //constructor
    {myInt = n;}
    public void increment()  //increment by 1
    { myInt++;}
}
```

Here is a client program that uses this class:

```
public class IntObjectTest
{
    public static IntObject someMethod(IntObject obj)
    {
        IntObject ans = obj;
        ans.increment();
        return ans;
    }

    public static void main(String[] args)
    {
        IntObject x = new IntObject(2);
        IntObject y = new IntObject(7);
        IntObject a = y;
        x = someMethod(y);
        a = someMethod(x);
    }
}
```

Just before exiting this program, what are the object values of x, y, and a, respectively?

(A) 9, 9, 9
(B) 2, 9, 9
(C) 2, 8, 9
(D) 3, 8, 9
(E) 7, 8, 9

23. Consider the following program:

```
public class Tester
{
    public void someMethod(int a, int b)
    {
        int temp = a;
        a = b;
        b = temp;
    }
}

public class TesterMain
{
    public static void main(String[] args)
    {
        int x = 6, y = 8;
        Tester tester = new Tester();
        tester.someMethod(x, y);
    }
}
```

Just before the end of execution of this program, what are the values of x, y, and temp, respectively?

(A) 6, 8, 6
(B) 8, 6, 6
(C) 6, 8, ?, where ? means undefined
(D) 8, 6, ?, where ? means undefined
(E) 8, 6, 8

Answer Key

1. **D**	9. **A**	17. **E**
2. **B**	10. **A**	18. **B**
3. **C**	11. **C**	19. **C**
4. **C**	12. **C**	20. **D**
5. **B**	13. **D**	21. **A**
6. **C**	14. **E**	22. **A**
7. **E**	15. **D**	23. **C**
8. **E**	16. **B**	

Answers Explained

1. (**D**) There are just two constructors. Constructors are recognizable by having the same name as the class, and no return type.

2. (**B**) Each of the private instance variables should be assigned the value of the matching parameter. Choice B is the only choice that does this. Choice D confuses the order of the assignment statements. Choice A gives the code for the *default* constructor, ignoring the parameters. Choice C would be correct if it were resetTime(h, m, s). As written, it doesn't assign the parameter values h, m, and s to myHrs, myMins, and mySecs. Choice E is wrong because the keyword new should be used to create a new object, not to implement the constructor!

3. (**C**) Segment III will automatically print time t in the required form since a toString method was defined for the Time class. Replacement I is wrong because it doesn't refer to the parameter, t, of the method. Replacement II is wrong because a client program may not access private data of the class.

4. (**C**) The parameter names can be the same—the *signatures* must be different. For example,

```
public void print(int x)        //prints x
public void print(double x)     //prints x
```

The signatures (method name plus parameter types) here are print(int) and print(double), respectively. The parameter name x is irrelevant. Choice A is true: all local variables and parameters go out of scope (are erased) when the method is exited. Choice B is true: static methods apply to the whole class. Only instance methods have an implicit this parameter. Choice D is true even for object parameters: their references are passed by value. Note that choice E is true because it's possible to have two different constructors with different signatures (e.g., one for an int argument and one for a double).

5. (**B**) Constructing an object requires the keyword new and a constructor of the Date class. Eliminate choices D and E since they omit new. The class name Date should appear on the right-hand side of the assignment statement, immediately following the keyword new. This eliminates choices A and C.

6. (**C**) Segment III will cause a NullPointerException to be thrown since d is a null reference. You cannot invoke a method for a null reference. Segment II has the effect of assigning null to both d1 and d2—obscure but not incorrect. Segment I creates the object reference d1 and then declares a second reference d2 that refers to the same object as d1.

7. (**E**) A client program cannot access a private instance variable.

8. (**E**) All are correct. Since write() is a Date instance method, it is OK to use the private data members in its implementation code. Segment III prints this, the current Date object. This usage is correct since write() is part of the Date class. The toString() method guarantees that the date will be printed in the required format (see p. 108).

9. (**A**) The idea here is to read in three separate variables for month, day, and year and then to construct the required date using new and the Date class constructor with three parameters. Code segment II won't work because month(), day(), and year() are accessor methods that access existing values and may not be used to read new values into bDate. Segment III is wrong because it tries to access private instance variables from a client program.

10. (**A**) Segment I will not create a second object. It will simply cause d2 to refer to the *same* object as d1, which is not what was required. The keyword new *must* be used to create a new object.

11. (**C**) When recentDate is declared in main(), its value is null. Recall that a method is not able to replace an object reference, so recentDate remains null. Note that the intent of the program is to change recentDate to refer to the updated oldDate object. The code, however, doesn't do this. Choice A is false: no methods are invoked with a null reference. Choice B is false because addYears() is a mutator method. Even though a method doesn't change the address of its object parameter, it can change the contents of the object, which is what happens here. Choices D and E are wrong because the addCentury() method cannot change the value of its recentDate argument.

12. (**C**) The reduce() method will be used only in the implementation of the instance methods of the Rational class.

13. (**D**) None of the constructors in the Rational class takes a real-valued parameter. Thus, the real-valued parameter in choice D will need to be converted to an integer. Since in general truncating a real value to an integer involves a loss of precision, it is not done automatically—you have to do it explicitly with a cast. Omitting the cast causes a compile-time error.

14. (**E**) A new Rational object must be created using the newly calculated num and denom. Then it must be reduced before being returned. Choice A is wrong because it doesn't correctly create the new object. Choice B returns a correctly constructed object, but one that has not been reduced. Choice C reduces the current object, this, instead of the new object, rat. Choice D is wrong because it invokes reduce() for the Rational class instead of the

specific rat object.

15. **(D)** The `plus` method of the `Rational` class can only be invoked by a `Rational` object. Since `n` is an `int`, the statement in choice D will cause an error.

16. **(B)** The method `getPondTemperature` is the only method that applies to more than one frog. It should therefore be static. All of the other methods relate directly to one particular Frog object. So `f.swim()`, `f.die()`, `f.getWeight()`, and `f.eat()` are all reasonable methods for a single instance `f` of a `Frog`. On the other hand, it doesn't make sense to say `f.getPondTemperature()`. It makes more sense to say `Frog.getPondTemperature()`, since the same value will apply to all frogs in the class.

17. **(E)** Here are the memory slots at the start of `strangeMethod(a, b)`:

a   b
6   3

x   y
6   3

Before exiting `strangeMethod(a, b)`:

a   b
6   3

x   y
9   27

Note that 9 27 is output before exiting. After exiting `strangeMethod(a, b)`, the memory slots are

a   b
6   3

The next step outputs 6 3.

18. **(B)** This is an example of *aliasing*. The keyword `new` is used just once, which means that just one object is constructed. Here are the memory slots after each declaration:

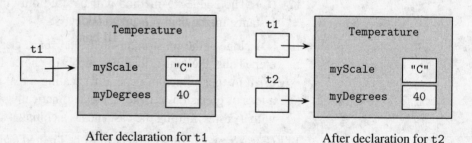

After declaration for `t1`   After declaration for `t2`

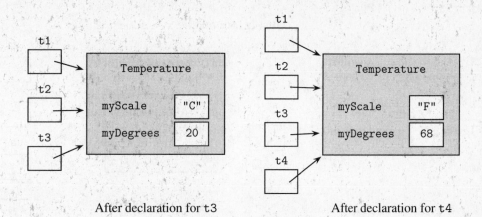

After declaration for t3   After declaration for t4

19. **(C)** Notice that `isValidTemp` is a static method for the `Temperature` class, which means that it cannot be invoked with a `Temperature` object. Thus segment I is incorrect: `t.isValidTemp` is wrong. Segment II fails because `isValidTemp` is not a method of the `TempTest` class. It therefore must be invoked with its class name, which is what happens (correctly) in segment III: `Temperature.isValidTemp`.

20. **(D)** A new `Temperature` object must be constructed to prevent the current `Temperature` from being changed. Segment I, which applies the conversion formula directly to `myDegrees`, is the best way to do this. Segment II, while not the best algorithm, does work. The statement

    ```
    result = result.raise(32);
    ```

    has the effect of raising the `result` temperature by 32 degrees, and completing the conversion. Segment III fails because

    ```
    myDegrees *= 1.8;
    ```

    alters the `myDegrees` instance variable of the current object, as does

    ```
    this = raise(32);
    ```

    To be correct, these operations must be applied to the `result` object.

21. **(A)** This is a question about the scope of variables. The scope of the `count` variable that is declared in `main()` extends up to the closing brace of `main()`. In `doSomething()` `count` is a local variable. After the method call in the `for` loop, the local variable `count` goes out of scope and the value that's being printed is the value of the `count` in `main()`, which is unchanged from 0.

22. **(A)** Here are the memory slots before the first `someMethod` call:

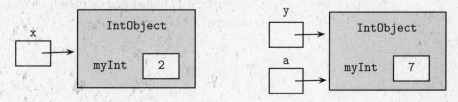

Just before exiting x = someMethod(y):

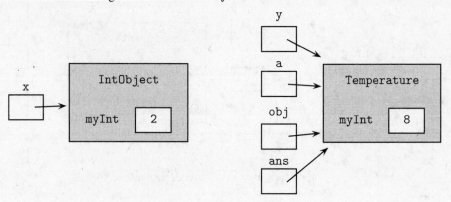

After exiting x = someMethod(y): x has been reassigned, so the object with myInt = 2 has been recycled.

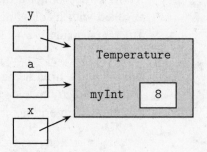

After exiting a = someMethod(x):

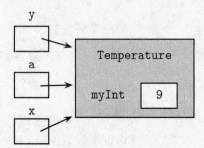

23. **(C)** Recall that when primitive types are passed as parameters, copies are made of the actual arguments. All manipulations in the method are performed on the copies, and the arguments remain unchanged. Thus x and y retain their values of 6 and 8. The local variable temp goes out of scope as soon as someMethod is exited and is therefore undefined just before the end of execution of the program.

CHAPTER THREE
Inheritance and Polymorphism

Say not you know another entirely,
till you have divided an inheritance with him.
—*Johann Kaspar Lavatar,* Aphorisms on Man

Inheritance

Superclass and Subclass

Inheritance defines a relationship between objects that share characteristics. Specifically it is the mechanism whereby a new class, called a *subclass*, is created from an existing class, called a *superclass*, by absorbing its state and behavior and augmenting these with features unique to the new class. We say that the subclass *inherits* characteristics of its superclass.

Don't get confused by the names: a subclass is bigger than a superclass—it contains more data and more methods!

Inheritance provides an effective mechanism for code reuse. Suppose the code for a superclass has been tested and debugged. Since a subclass object shares features of a superclass object, the only new code required is for the additional characteristics of the subclass.

Inheritance Hierarchy

A subclass can itself be a superclass for another subclass, leading to an *inheritance hierarchy* of classes.

For example, consider the relationship between these objects: Person, Employee, Student, GradStudent, and UnderGrad.

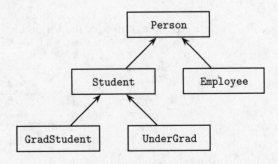

For any of these classes an arrow points to its superclass. The arrow designates the *is-a* relationship. Thus an Employee *is-a* Person; a Student *is-a* Person; a GradStudent *is-a* Student; an UnderGrad *is-a* Student. Notice that the opposite is not necessarily true: A `Person` is not necessarily a `Student`, nor is a `Student` necessarily an `UnderGrad`.

Note that the *is-a* relationship is transitive: if a `GradStudent` *is-a* `Student` and a `Student` *is-a* `Person`, then a `GradStudent` *is-a* `Person`.

Suppose the `Person` class has instance variables `name`, `socialSecurityNumber`, and `age`, and instance methods `getName`, `getSocSecNum`, `getAge`, and `printName`. Then every one of the derived classes shown inherits these variables and methods. The `Student` class may have additional instance variables `studentID` and `gpa`, plus a method `computeGrade`. All of these additional features are inherited by the subclasses `GradStudent` and `UnderGrad`. Suppose `GradStudent` and `UnderGrad` use different algorithms for computing the course grade. Then the `computeGrade` implementation can be redefined in these classes. This is called *method overriding*. If part of the original method implementation from the superclass is retained, we refer to the rewrite as *partial overriding*.

Implementing Subclasses

The `extends` Keyword

The inheritance relationship between a subclass and a superclass is specified in the declaration of the subclass, using the keyword `extends`. The general format looks like this:

```
public class Superclass
{
    //private instance variables
    //other data members
    //constructors
    //public methods
    //private methods
}

public class Subclass extends Superclass
{
    //additional private instance variables
    //additional data members
    //constructors   (Not inherited!)
    //additional public methods
    //inherited public methods whose implementation is overridden
    //additional private methods
}
```

For example, consider the following inheritance hierarchy:

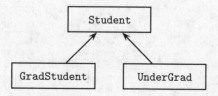

The implementation of the classes may look something like this (discussion follows the code):

```java
public class Student
{
    //data members
    public final static int NUM_TESTS = 3;
    private String myName;
    private int[] myTests;
    private String myGrade;

    //constructors
    public Student()
    {
        myName = "";
        myTests = new int[NUM_TESTS];
        myGrade = "";
    }

    public Student(String name, int[] tests, String grade)
    {
        myName = name;
        myTests = tests;
        myGrade = grade;
    }

    public String getName()
    { return myName; }

    public String getGrade()
    { return myGrade; }

    public void setGrade(String newGrade)
    { myGrade = newGrade; }

    public void computeGrade()
    {
        if (myName.equals(""))
            myGrade = "No grade";
        else if (getTestAverage() >= 65)
            myGrade = "Pass";
        else
            myGrade = "Fail";
    }

    public double getTestAverage()
    {
        double total = 0;
        for (int i=0; i<NUM_TESTS; i++)
            total += myTests[i];
        return total/NUM_TESTS;
    }
}

public class UnderGrad extends Student
{
    public UnderGrad()   //default constructor
    { super(); }
```

```
        //constructor
        public UnderGrad(String name, int[] tests, String grade)
        { super(name, tests, grade); }

        public void computeGrade()
        {
            if (getTestAverage() >= 70)
                setGrade("Pass");
            else
                setGrade("Fail");
        }
    }

public class GradStudent extends Student
{
    private int myGradID;

    //default constructor
    public GradStudent()
    {
        super();
        myGradID = 0;
    }

    //constructor
    public GradStudent(String name, int[] tests, String grade,
            int gradID)
    {
        super(name, tests, grade);
        myGradID = gradID;
    }

    public int getID()
    { return myGradID; }

    public void computeGrade()
    {
        //invokes computeGrade in Student superclass
        super.computeGrade();
        if (getTestAverage() >= 90)
            setGrade("Pass with distinction");
    }
}
```

Inheriting Instance Methods and Variables

The UnderGrad and GradStudent subclasses inherit all of the methods and variables of the Student superclass. Notice, however, that the Student instance variables myName, myTests, and myGrade are private, and are therefore not directly accessible to the methods in the UnderGrad and GradStudent subclasses. A subclass can, however, directly invoke the public accessor and mutator methods of the superclass. Thus both UnderGrad and GradStudent use getTestAverage. Additionally, both UnderGrad and GradStudent use setGrade to access indirectly—and modify—myGrade.

If, instead of private, the modifier for the instance variables in Student were protected, then the subclasses could directly access these variables. The modifier protected is used in the case study, and this is the only context in which it will be tested on the AP exam (see p. 453).

Classes on the same level in a hierarchy diagram are called *sibling classes*. Thus UnderGrad and GradStudent are siblings. Sibling classes do not inherit anything from each other. All they have in common is the identical code they inherit from their superclass.

Method Overriding and the super Keyword

A method in a superclass is overridden in a subclass by defining a method with the same return type and signature (name and parameter types). For example, the computeGrade method in the UnderGrad subclass overrides the computeGrade method in the Student superclass.

Sometimes the code for overriding a method includes a call to the superclass method. This is called partial overriding. Typically this occurs when the subclass method wants to do what the superclass does, plus something extra. This is achieved by using the keyword super in the implementation. The computeGrade method in the GradStudent subclass partially overrides the matching method in the Student class. The statement

```
super.computeGrade();
```

signals that the computeGrade method in the superclass should be invoked here. The additional test

```
if (getTestAverage() >= 90)
    ...
```

allows a GradStudent to have a grade Pass with distinction. Note that this option is open to GradStudents only.

Constructors and super

Constructors are never inherited! If no constructor is written for a subclass, the superclass default constructor with no parameters is generated. If the superclass does not have a default (zero-parameter) constructor, but only a constructor with parameters, a compiler error will occur. If there is a default constructor in the superclass, inherited data members will be initialized as for the superclass. Additional instance variables in the subclass will get a default initialization—0 for primitive types and null for reference types.

A subclass constructor can be implemented with a call to the super method, which invokes the superclass constructor. For example, the default constructor in the UnderGrad class is identical to that of the Student class. This is implemented with the statement super();

The second constructor in the UnderGrad class is called with parameters that match those in the constructor of the Student superclass.

```
public UnderGrad(String name, int[] tests, String grade)
{ super(name, tests, grade); }
```

For each constructor, the call to super has the effect of initializing the inherited instance variables myName, myTests, and myGrade exactly as they are initialized in the Student class.

Contrast this with the constructors in GradStudent. In each case, the inherited instance variables myName, myTests, and myGrade are initialized as for the Student class. Then the new instance variable, myGradID, must be explicitly initialized.

```
public GradStudent()
{
    super();
    myGradID = 0;
}

public GradStudent(String name, int[] tests, String grade,
            int gradID)
{
    super(name, tests, grade);
    myGradID = gradID;
}
```

NOTE
1. If super is used in the implementation of a subclass constructor, it can be used only in the first line of the constructor body.
2. If no constructor is provided in a subclass, the compiler provides the following default constructor:

```
public SubClass()
{
    super();       //calls default constructor of superclass
}
```

Since Student and UnderGrad have the same default constructor, it would have been safe to omit the default constructor in the UnderGrad class: The correct default would have been provided.

Rules for Subclasses

- A subclass can add new private instance variables.
- A subclass can add new public, private, or static methods.
- A subclass can override inherited methods.
- A subclass may not redefine a public method as private.
- A subclass may not override static methods of the superclass.
- A subclass must define its own constructors.
- A subclass cannot access the private members of its superclass.

Declaring Subclass Objects

When a variable of a superclass is declared in a client program, that reference can refer not only to an object of the superclass, but also to objects of any of its subclasses. Thus each of the following is legal:

```
Student s = new Student();
Student g = new GradStudent();
Student u = new UnderGrad();
```

This works because a GradStudent *is-a* Student, and an UnderGrad *is-a* Student.

Note that since a Student is not necessarily a GradStudent nor an UnderGrad, the following declarations are *not* valid:

```
GradStudent g = new Student();
Undergrad u = new Student();
```

Consider these valid declarations:

```
Student s = new Student("Brian Lorenzen", new int[] {90,94,99},
        "none");
Student u = new UnderGrad("Tim Broder", new int[] {90,90,100},
        "none");
Student g = new GradStudent("Kevin Cristella",
        new int[] {85,70,90}, "none", 1234);
```

Suppose you make the method call

```
s.setGrade("Pass");
```

The appropriate method in Student is found and the new grade assigned. The method calls

```
g.setGrade("Pass");
```

and

```
u.setGrade("Pass");
```

achieve the same effect on g and u since GradStudent and UnderGrad both inherit the setGrade method from Student. The following method calls, however, won't work:

```
int studentNum = s.getID();
int underGradNum = u.getID();
```

Neither Student s nor UnderGrad u inherit the getID method from the GradStudent class: A class does not inherit from a sibling class and a superclass does not inherit from a subclass.

Now consider the following valid method calls:

```
s.computeGrade();
g.computeGrade();
u.computeGrade();
```

Since s, g, and u have all been declared to be of type Student, will the appropriate method be executed in each case? That is the topic of the next section, *polymorphism*.

Polymorphism

A method that has been overridden in at least one subclass is said to be *polymorphic*. An example is `computeGrade`, which is redefined for both `GradStudent` and `UnderGrad`.

An object reference can also be polymorphic since it can refer to objects from different classes. For example, `Student st` could refer to an object of type `Student`, `GradStudent`, or `UnderGrad`.

Polymorphism is the mechanism of selecting the appropriate method for a particular object in a class hierarchy. The correct method is chosen because, in Java, method calls are always determined by the type of the *actual object*, not the type of the object reference. For example, even though s, g, and u are all declared to be of type `Student`, `s.computeGrade()`, `g.computeGrade()`, and `u.computeGrade()` will all perform the correct operations for their particular objects. In Java, the selection of the correct method occurs *during the run of the program*.

Dynamic Binding (Late Binding)

Making a run-time decision about which instance method to call is known as *dynamic binding* or *late binding*. Contrast it with selecting the correct method when methods are *overloaded* (see p. 38) rather than overridden. The compiler selects the correct overloaded method at compile time by comparing the methods' signatures. This is known as *static binding*, or *early binding*. In polymorphism, the actual method that will be called is not determined by the compiler.

Example 1

```
Student s = null;
Student u = new UnderGrad("Tim Broder", new int[] {90,90,100},
        "none");
Student g = new GradStudent("Kevin Cristella",
        new int[] {85,70,90}, "none", 1234);
System.out.print("Enter student status: ");
System.out.println("Grad (G), Undergrad (U), Neither (N)");
String str = IO.readString();        //read user input
if (str.equals("G"))
    s = g;
else if (str.equals("U"))
    s = u;
else
    s = new Student();
s.computeGrade();
```

When this code fragment is run, the `computeGrade` method used will depend on the type of the actual object s refers to, which in turn depends on the user input.

Example 2

```
public class StudentTest
{
    public static void computeAllGrades(Student[] studentList)
    {
        for (int i=0; i<studentList.length; i++)
            if (studentList[i] != null)
                studentList[i].computeGrade();
    }
```

```
        public static void main(String[] args)
        {
            Student[] stu = new Student[5];
            stu[0] = new Student("Brian Lorenzen",
                        new int[] {90,94,99}, "none");
            stu[1] = new UnderGrad("Tim Broder",
                        new int[] {90,90,100}, "none");
            stu[2] = new GradStudent("Kevin Cristella",
                        new int[] {85,70,90}, "none", 1234);
            computeAllGrades(stu);
        }
    }
```

Here an array of five Student references is created, all of them initially null. Three of these references, stu[0], stu[1], and stu[2], are then assigned to actual objects. The computeAllGrades method steps through the array invoking the appropriate computeGrade method for each of the objects, using dynamic binding in each case. The null test in computeAllGrades is necessary because some of the array references could be null.

NOTE   It is possible to test the actual type of an object using the keyword instanceof:

```
    for (int i=0; i<studentList.length; i++)
        if (studentList[i] instanceof GradStudent)
            System.out.println("Student " + i +
                    " is a graduate student");
        else if (studentList[i] instanceof UnderGrad)
            System.out.println("Student " + i +
                    " is an undergraduate student");
        else
            System.out.println("Student " + i +
                    " is not a grad or undergrad");
```

The instanceof keyword is not part of the AP Java subset.

Type Compatibility

Downcasting   Consider the statements

```
    Student s = new GradStudent();
    GradStudent g = new GradStudent();
    int x = s.getID();              //compile-time error
    int y = g.getID();              //legal
```

Both s and g represent GradStudent objects, so why does s.getID() cause an error? The reason is that s is of type Student and the Student class doesn't have a getID method. At compile time, only nonprivate methods of the Student class can appear to the right of the dot operator when applied to s. Don't confuse this with polymorphism: getID is not a polymorphic method. It occurs in just the GradStudent class and can therefore be called only by a GradStudent object.

The error shown above can be fixed by casting s to the correct type:

```
int x = ((GradStudent) s).getID();
```

Since s (of type Student) is actually representing a GradStudent object, such a cast can be carried out. Casting a superclass to a subclass type is called a *downcast*.

NOTE

1. The outer parentheses are necessary:

```
int x = (GradStudent) s.getID();
```

will still cause an error, despite the cast. This is because the dot operator has higher precedence than casting, so s.getID() is invoked before s is cast to GradStudent.

2. The statement

```
int y = g.getID();
```

compiles without problem because g is declared to be of type GradStudent and this is the class that contains getID. No cast is required.

Type Rules for Polymorphic Method Calls

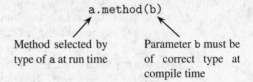

a.method(b)

Method selected by type of a at run time

Parameter b must be of correct type at compile time

- For a declaration like

  ```
  Superclass a = new Subclass();
  ```

  the type of a at compile time is Superclass; at run time it is Subclass.

- At compile time, method must be found in the class of a, that is, in Superclass. (This is true whether the method is polymorphic or not.) If method cannot be found in the class of a, you need to do an explicit cast on a to its actual type.

- For a polymorphic method, at run time the actual type of a is determined—Subclass in this example—and method is selected from Subclass. This could be an inherited method if there is no overriding method.

- The type of parameter b is checked at compile time. You may need to do an explicit cast to the subclass type to make this correct.

The
ClassCastException

The `ClassCastException` is a run-time exception thrown to signal an attempt to cast an object to a class of which it is not an instance.

```
Student u = new UnderGrad();
System.out.println((String) u);    //ClassCastException
                               //u is not an instance of String
int x = ((GradStudent) u).getID(); //ClassCastException
                       //u is not an instance of GradStudent
```

Abstract Classes

Abstract Class

An *abstract class* is a superclass that contains at least one *abstract method*. An abstract method has no implementation code, just a header. The rationale for an abstract method is that there is no good default code for the method. Every subclass will need to override this method, so why bother with a meaningless implementation in the superclass? The method appears in the abstract class as a place-holder. The implementation for the method occurs in the subclasses. Since an abstract class is always intended to be a superclass, it is sometimes called an *abstract superclass*.

The abstract
Keyword

An abstract class is declared with the keyword `abstract` in the header:

```
public abstract class AbstractClass
{
    ...
```

The keyword `extends` is used as before to declare a subclass:

```
public class SubClass extends AbstractClass
{
    ...
```

If a subclass of an abstract class does not provide implementation code for all the abstract methods of its superclass, it too becomes an abstract class and must be declared as such to avoid a compile-time error:

```
public abstract class SubClass extends AbstractClass
{
    ...
```

Here is an example of an abstract class, with two concrete (nonabstract) subclasses.

```
public abstract class Shape
{
    private String myName;

    //constructor
    public Shape(String name)
    { myName = name; }
```

```java
    public String getName()
    { return myName; }

    public abstract double area();
    public abstract double perimeter();

    public double semiPerimeter()
    { return perimeter()/2; }
}

public class Circle extends Shape
{
    private double myRadius;

    //constructor
    public Circle(double radius, String name)
    {
        super(name);
        myRadius = radius;
    }

    public double perimeter()
    { return 2 * Math.PI * myRadius; }

    public double area()
    { return Math.PI * myRadius * myRadius; }
}

public class Square extends Shape
{
    private double mySide;

    //constructor
    public Square(double side, String name)
    {
        super(name);
        mySide = side;
    }

    public double perimeter()
    { return 4 * mySide; }

    public double area()
    { return mySide * mySide; }
}
```

NOTE

1. It is meaningless to define perimeter and area methods for Shape—thus these are declared as abstract methods.
2. An abstract class can have both instance variables and concrete (nonabstract) methods. See, for example, myName, getName, and semiPerimeter in the Shape class.
3. Abstract methods are declared with the keyword abstract. There is no method body. The declaration is terminated with a semicolon.
4. No instances can be created for an abstract class:

```
Shape a;                    //legal. Null reference declared
a = new Shape("blob");   //illegal.
                         //Can't create instance of abstract class
a = new Circle(1.5, "small circle");   //legal
a = null;                              //legal
```

5. Polymorphism works with abstract classes as it does with concrete classes:

```
Shape circ = new Circle(10, "circle");
Shape sq = new Square(9.4, "square");
Shape s;
System.out.println("Which shape?");
String str = IO.readString();        //read user input
if (str.equals("circle"))
    s = circ;
else
    s = sq;
System.out.println("Area of " + s.getName() + " is "
        + s.area());
```

When to Use an Abstract Class

If a superclass has a method that is unique for each subclass, consider making the superclass—and that method—abstract.

Interfaces

Interface

An *interface* is a collection of related methods whose headers are provided without implementations. All of the methods are both public and abstract—no need to explicitly include these keywords. As such, they provide a framework of behavior for any client software.

A class that implements an interface can define any number of methods. In particular it contracts to provide implementations for *all* the methods declared in the interface. If it fails to implement any of the methods, the class must be declared abstract. A given interface can be implemented by any number of unrelated classes.

There are two important differences between an interface and an abstract class:

1. An interface cannot provide implementations for any of its methods, whereas an abstract class can.
2. An interface cannot contain instance variables, whereas an abstract class can.

NOTE

1. In addition to its method declarations, an interface can also declare constants.
2. It is not possible to construct an interface object.

Defining an Interface

An interface is declared with the `interface` keyword. For example,

```
public interface PersonalInfo
{
    String getName();           //returns name of person
    String getAddress();        //returns address of person
    int getSocialSecurityNo();  //returns social security number
}
```

NOTE

There is no access modifier for these methods—they are all public. This makes sense: the methods must be visible to the classes that will implement them.

The `implements` Keyword

Interfaces are implemented using the `implements` keyword. For example,

```
public class Student implements PersonalInfo
{
    ...
```

This declaration means that the `Student` class (defined on p. 71) has been expanded to implement the `getName`, `getAddress`, and `getSocialSecurityNo` methods. The `GradStudent` and `UnderGrad` subclasses, through inheritance, will also implement the `PersonalInfo` interface.

A class that extends a superclass can also directly implement an interface. For example, consider a small business that maintains a database of its employees, inventory, accounts, and so on. Let the class that contains all this information be called `BusinessData`, with subclasses `Employee`, `Inventory`, and so on. Then the `Employee` class could implement the `PersonalInfo` interface:

```
public class Employee extends BusinessData implements PersonalInfo
{
    ...
```

NOTE

1. The extends clause must precede the `implements` clause.
2. A class can have just one superclass, but it can implement any number of interfaces:

```
public class SubClass extends SuperClass
            implements Interface1, Interface2, ...
```

Using an Interface Type in a Client Program

Consider a program with a method `CreateLabel` that creates mailing labels for any object that implements `PersonalInfo`. Here it is demonstrated on an array of `Student`, assuming the declaration

```
public class Student implements PersonalInfo
{
    ...
```

Here is the program:

```
public class MailingLabel
{
    public static void Initialize(Student st)
    {
        < code to read in data for Student st >
    }
```

```java
        public static void FormatAndPrint(String address)
        {
            < code to format and print address >
        }


        /* Create a mailing label using p */
        public static void CreateLabel(PersonalInfo p)
        {
            System.out.println(p.getName());
            FormatAndPrint(p.getAddress());
        }

        public static void main(String[] args)
        {
            Student[] s = new Student[20];
            for (int i=0; i<s.length; i++)
            {
                Initialize(s[i]);
                CreateLabel(s[i]);
            }
        }
    }
```

NOTE

1. The `CreateLabel` method expects a `PersonalInfo` type. The actual parameter can be any object that implements `PersonalInfo`.
2. The elements of the `Student` array can be of type `Student`, `GradStudent`, or `UnderGrad`—the subclasses inherit the `getName` and `getAddress` methods.
3. Although it is not possible to construct an interface object, you can have interface references to objects of classes that implement the interface. For example,

```java
        PersonalInfo p = new PersonalInfo();      //error
        PersonalInfo p = new Student();           //OK
```

The Comparable Interface

The standard `java.lang` package contains the `Comparable` interface, which provides a useful method for comparing objects.

```java
        public interface Comparable
        {
            int compareTo(Object obj);
        }
```

Any class that implements `Comparable` must provide a `compareTo` method. This method compares the implicit object (`this`) with the parameter object (`obj`) and returns a negative integer, zero, or a positive integer depending on whether the implicit object is less than, equal to, or greater than the parameter. If the two objects being compared are not type compatible, a `ClassCastException` is thrown by the method.

Example

The abstract `Shape` class defined previously (p. 79) is modified to implement the `Comparable` interface:

```java
public abstract class Shape implements Comparable
{
    private String myName;

    //constructor
    public Shape(String name)
    { myName = name; }

    public String getName()
    { return myName; }

    public abstract double area();
    public abstract double perimeter();

    public double semiPerimeter()
    { return perimeter()/2; }

    public int compareTo(Object obj)
    {
        final double EPSILON = 1.0e-15;    //slightly bigger than
                                           //machine precision
        Shape rhs = (Shape) obj;
        double diff = area() - rhs.area();
        if (Math.abs(diff) < EPSILON * Math.abs(area()))
            return 0;
        else if (diff < 0)
            return -1;
        else
            return 1;
    }
}
```

NOTE   1. The Circle, Square, and other subclasses of Shape will all automatically implement Comparable and inherit the compareTo method.

2. It is tempting to use a simpler test for equality of areas, namely

```java
if (diff == 0)
    return 0;
```

But recall that real numbers can have round-off errors in their storage (Box p. 6). This means that the simple test may return false even though the two areas are essentially equal. A more robust test is implemented in the code given, namely to test if the relative error in diff is small enough to be considered zero.

3. The Object class is a universal superclass (see p. 108). This means that the compareTo method can take as a parameter any object reference that implements Comparable.

4. The first step of a compareTo method must cast the Object argument to the class type, in this case Shape. If this is not done, the compiler won't find the area method—remember, an Object is not necessarily a Shape.

5. The algorithm one chooses in compareTo should in general be consistent with the equals method (see p. 110): whenever object1.equals(object2) returns true, object1.compareTo(object2) returns 0.

Here is a program that finds the larger of two objects. The code is *generic*, which means that it is independent of the type of object. For the code to work, one must be able to compare two objects. This is easy to do if the objects are `Comparable`. Simply declare the objects to be of type `Comparable` and then compare them using the `compareTo` method.

```
public class FindMaxTest
{
    /* Return the larger of two objects a and b */
    public static Comparable max(Comparable a, Comparable b)
    {
        if (a.compareTo(b) > 0)
            return a;
        else
            return b;
    }

    /* Test max on two Shape objects */
    public static void main(String[] args)
    {
        Shape s1 = new Circle(3.0, "circle");
        Shape s2 = new Square(4.5, "square");
        System.out.println("Area of " + s1.getName() + " is " +
                s1.area());
        System.out.println("Area of " + s2.getName() + " is " +
                s2.area());
        Shape s3 = (Shape) max(s1, s2);
        System.out.println("The larger shape is the " +
                s3.getName());
    }
}
```

Here is the output:

```
Area of circle is 28.27
Area of square is 20.25
The larger shape is the circle
```

NOTE

1. The `max` method takes parameters of type `Comparable`. Since s1 *is-a* `Comparable` object and s2 *is-a* `Comparable` object, no casting is necessary in the method call.
2. The `max` method can be called with any two objects that implement `Comparable`, for example, two `String` objects or two `Integer` objects (see Chapter 4).
3. The objects must be type compatible (i.e., it must make sense to compare them). For example, in the program shown, if s1 *is-a* `Shape` and s2 *is-a* `String`, the `compareTo` method will throw a `ClassCastException` at the line

   ```
   Shape rhs = (Shape) obj;
   ```

4. The cast is needed in the line

   ```
   Shape s3 = (Shape) max(s1, s2);
   ```

   since `max(s1, s2)` returns a `Comparable`.
5. A primitive type is not an object and therefore cannot be passed as `Comparable`. You can, however, use a wrapper class and in this way convert a primitive type to a `Comparable` (see p. 114).

Multiple-Choice Questions on Inheritance and Polymorphism

Questions 1–10 refer to the BankAccount, SavingsAccount, and CheckingAccount classes defined below:

```java
public class BankAccount
{
    private double myBalance;

    public BankAccount()
    { myBalance = 0; }

    public BankAccount(double balance)
    { myBalance = balance; }

    public void deposit(double amount)
    { myBalance += amount; }

    public void withdraw(double amount)
    { myBalance -= amount; }

    public double getBalance()
    { return myBalance; }
}

public class SavingsAccount extends BankAccount
{
    private double myInterestRate;

    public SavingsAccount()
    { implementation code }

    public SavingsAccount(double balance, double rate)
    { implementation code }

    public void addInterest()     //Add interest to balance
    { implementation code }
}

public class CheckingAccount extends BankAccount
{
    private static final double FEE = 2.0;
    private static final double MIN_BALANCE = 50.0;

    public CheckingAccount(double balance)
    { implementation code }

    /* FEE of $2 deducted if withdrawal leaves balance less
     * than MIN_BALANCE. Allows for negative balance. */
    public void withdraw(double amount)
    { implementation code }
}
```

1. How many different nonconstructor methods can be invoked by a `SavingsAccount` object?

    (A) 1
    (B) 2
    (C) 3
    (D) 4
    (E) 5

2. Which of the following correctly implements the default constructor of the `SavingsAccount` class?

    I `myInterestRate = 0;`
       `super();`

    II `super();`
       `myInterestRate = 0;`

    III `super();`

    (A) II only
    (B) I and II only
    (C) II and III only
    (D) III only
    (E) I, II, and III

3. Which is a correct implementation of the constructor with parameters in the `SavingsAccount` class?

    (A) `myBalance = balance;`
       `myInterestRate = rate;`

    (B) `getBalance() = balance;`
       `myInterestRate = rate;`

    (C) `super();`
       `myInterestRate = rate;`

    (D) `super(balance);`
       `myInterestRate = rate;`

    (E) `super(balance, rate);`

4. Which is a correct implementation of the `CheckingAccount` constructor?

    I `super(balance);`

    II `super();`
       `deposit(balance);`

    III `deposit(balance);`

    (A) I only
    (B) II only
    (C) III only
    (D) II and III only
    (E) I, II, and III

5. Which is correct *implementation code* for the `withdraw` method in the `CheckingAccount` class?

   (A)
   ```
   super.withdraw(amount);
   if (myBalance < MIN_BALANCE)
       super.withdraw(FEE);
   ```

   (B)
   ```
   withdraw(amount);
   if (myBalance < MIN_BALANCE)
       withdraw(FEE);
   ```

   (C)
   ```
   super.withdraw(amount);
   if (getBalance() < MIN_BALANCE)
       super.withdraw(FEE);
   ```

   (D)
   ```
   withdraw(amount);
   if (getBalance() < MIN_BALANCE)
       withdraw(FEE);
   ```

   (E)
   ```
   myBalance -= amount;
   if (myBalance < MIN_BALANCE)
       myBalance -= FEE;
   ```

6. Redefining the `withdraw` method in the `CheckingAccount` class is an example of
   (A) Method overloading.
   (B) Method overriding.
   (C) Downcasting.
   (D) Dynamic binding (late binding).
   (E) Static binding (early binding).

Use the following for Questions 7–9.

A program to test the `BankAccount`, `SavingsAccount`, and `CheckingAccount` classes has these declarations:

```
BankAccount b = new BankAccount(1400);
BankAccount s = new SavingsAccount(1000, 0.04);
BankAccount c = new CheckingAccount(500);
```

7. Which method call will cause an error?
   (A) `b.deposit(200);`
   (B) `s.withdraw(500);`
   (C) `c.withdraw(500);`
   (D) `s.deposit(10000);`
   (E) `s.addInterest();`

8. In order to test polymorphism, which method must be used in the program?
   (A) Either a `SavingsAccount` constructor or a `CheckingAccount` constructor
   (B) `addInterest`
   (C) `deposit`
   (D) `withdraw`
   (E) `getBalance`

9. Which of the following will *not* cause a ClassCastException to be thrown?
    (A) ((SavingsAccount) b).addInterest();
    (B) ((CheckingAccount) b).withdraw(200);
    (C) ((CheckingAccount) c).deposit(800);
    (D) ((CheckingAccount) s).withdraw(150);
    (E) ((SavingsAccount) c).addInterest();

10. A new method is added to the BankAccount class.

```
/* Transfer amount from this BankAccount to another BankAccount.
 * Precondition: myBalance > amount */
public void transfer(BankAccount another, double amount)
{
    withdraw(amount);
    another.deposit(amount);
}
```

A program has these declarations:

```
BankAccount b = new BankAccount(650);
SavingsAccount timsSavings = new SavingsAccount(1500, 0.03);
CheckingAccount daynasChecking = new CheckingAccount(2000);
```

Which of the following will transfer money from one account to another without error?

I b.transfer(timsSavings, 50);

II timsSavings.transfer(daynasChecking, 30);

III daynasChecking.transfer(b, 55);

(A) I only
(B) II only
(C) III only
(D) I, II, and III
(E) None

11. Consider these class declarations:

```
public class Person
{
    ...
}

public class Teacher extends Person
{
    ...
}
```

Which is a true statement?

    I Teacher inherits the constructors of Person.
   II Teacher can add new methods and private instance variables.
  III Teacher can override existing private methods of Person.

(A) I only
(B) II only
(C) III only
(D) I and II only
(E) II and III only

12. Which statement about abstract classes and interfaces is *false*?
(A) An interface cannot implement any methods, whereas an abstract class can.
(B) A class can implement many interfaces but can have only one super-class.
(C) An unlimited number of unrelated classes can implement the same interface.
(D) It is not possible to construct either an abstract class object or an interface object.
(E) All of the methods in both an abstract class and an interface are public.

13. Consider the following hierarchy of classes:

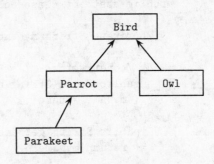

A program is written to print data about various birds:

```
public class BirdStuff
{
    public static void printName(Bird b)
    { implementation code }

    public static void printBirdCall(Parrot p)
    { implementation code }

    //several more Bird methods

    public static void main(String[] args)
    {
        Bird b1 = new Bird();
        Bird b2 = new Parrot();
        Parrot p1 = new Parrot();
        Parrot p2 = new Parakeet();
        < more code >
    }
}
```

Which of the following segments of < more code > will not cause an error?

(A) printName(p2);
     printBirdCall((Parrot) b2);

(B) printName((Parrot) b1);
     printBirdCall(b2);

(C) printName(b2);
     printBirdCall(b2);

(D) printName((Parakeet) p1);
     printBirdCall(p2);

(E) printName((Bird) p2);
     printBirdCall((Parakeet) p2);

Use the declarations below for Questions 14–16.

```java
public abstract class Solid
{
    private String myName;

    //constructor
    public Solid(String name)
    { myName = name; }

    public String getName()
    { return myName; }

    public abstract double volume();
}

public class Sphere extends Solid
{
    private double myRadius;

    //constructor
    public Sphere(String name, double radius)
    {
        super(name);
        myRadius = radius;
    }

    public double volume()
    { return (4.0/3.0) * Math.PI * myRadius * myRadius * myRadius; }
}

public class RectangularPrism extends Solid
{
    private double myLength;
    private double myWidth;
    private double myHeight;

    //constructor
    public RectangularPrism(String name, double l, double w,
            double h)
    {
        super(name);
        myLength = l;
        myWidth = w;
        myHeight = h;
    }

    public double volume()
    { return myLength * myWidth * myHeight; }
}
```

14. A program that tests these classes has the following declarations:

```
Solid s1, s2, s3, s4;
s1 = new Solid("blob");
s2 = new Sphere("sphere", 3.8);
s3 = new RectangularPrism("box", 2, 4, 6.5);
s4 = null;
```

Of these declarations, how many are incorrect?
(A) 1
(B) 2
(C) 3
(D) 4
(E) 5

15. Which is *false*?
(A) The decision about which volume method to call in a program will be resolved at run time.
(B) If the Solid class were modified to provide a default implementation for the volume method, it would no longer be an abstract class.
(C) If the Sphere and RectangularPrism classes failed to provide an implementation for the volume method, they would need to be declared as abstract classes.
(D) The fact that there is no reasonable default implementation for the volume method in the Solid class suggests that it should be an abstract method.
(E) Since Solid is abstract and its subclasses are nonabstract, polymorphism no longer applies when these classes are used in a program.

16. Here is a program that prints the volume of a solid:

```
public class SolidMain
{
    /* Output volume of Solid s */
    public static void printVolume(Solid s)
    {
        System.out.println("Volume = " + s.volume() +
            " cubic units");
    }

    public static void main(String[] args)
    {
        Solid sol;
        Solid sph = new Sphere("sphere", 4);
        Solid rec = new RectangularPrism("box", 3, 6, 9);
        Random r = new Random();
        int flipCoin = r.nextInt(2);    //returns 0 or 1
        if (flipCoin == 0)
            sol = sph;
        else
            sol = rec;
        printVolume(sol);
    }
}
```

Which is a true statement about this program?

(A) It will output the volume of the sphere or box, as intended.

(B) It will output the volume of the default Solid s, which is neither a sphere nor a box.

(C) A ClassCastException will be thrown.

(D) A compile-time error will occur because there is no implementation code for volume in the Solid class.

(E) A run-time error will occur because of parameter type mismatch in the method call printVolume(sol).

17. Consider the `Computable` interface below for performing simple calculator operations:

```
public interface Computable
{
    //return this Object + y
    Object add(Object y);

    //return this Object - y
    Object subtract(Object y);

    //return this Object * y
    Object multiply(Object y);
}
```

Which of the following is the *least* suitable class for implementing `Computable`?

(A) `LargeInteger`   `//integers with 100 digits or more`

(B) `Fraction`   `//implemented with numerator and`
                       `//denominator of type int`

(C) `IrrationalNumber` `//nonrepeating, nonterminating decimal`

(D) `Length`   `//implemented with different units, such`
                       `//as inches, centimeters, etc.`

(E) `BankAccount`   `//implemented with myBalance`

Refer to the `Player` interface shown below for Questions 18–21.

```
public interface Player
{
    /* Return integer that represents move in game */
    int getMove();

    /* Briefly describe strategy in choosing move */
    void describeStrategy();
}
```

18. A class `HumanPlayer` implements the `Player` interface. Another class, `SmartPlayer`, is a subclass of `HumanPlayer`. Which statement is *false*?
    (A) `SmartPlayer` automatically implements the `Player` interface.
    (B) `HumanPlayer` must contain implementations of both the `getMove` and `describeStrategy` methods.
    (C) It is not possible to declare a reference of type `Player`.
    (D) The `SmartPlayer` class can override the methods `getMove` and `describeStrategy` of the `HumanPlayer` class.
    (E) A method in a client program can have `Player` as a parameter type.

19. A programmer plans to write programs that simulate various games. In each case he will have several classes, each representing a different kind of competitor in the game, such as `ExpertPlayer`, `ComputerPlayer`, `RecklessPlayer`, `CheatingPlayer`, `Beginner`, `IntermediatePlayer`, and so on. It may or may not be suitable for these classes to implement the `Player` interface, depending on the particular game being simulated. In the games described below, which is the *least* suitable for having the competitor classes implement the given `Player` interface?

    (A) High-Low Guessing Game: The computer thinks of a number and the competitor who guesses it with the least number of guesses wins. After each guess the computer tells whether its number is higher or lower than the guess.

    (B) Chips: Start with a pile of chips. Each player in turn removes some number of chips. The winner is the one who removes the final chip. The first player may remove any number of chips, but not all of them. Each subsequent player must remove at least one chip and at most twice the number removed by the preceding player.

    (C) Chess: Played on a square board of 64 squares of alternating colors. There are just two players, called White and Black, the colors of their respective pieces. The players each have a set of pieces on the board that can move according to a set of rules. The players alternate moves, where a move consists of moving any one piece to another square. If that square is occupied by an opponent's piece, the piece is captured and removed from the board.

    (D) Tic-Tac-Toe: Two players alternate placing 'X' or 'O' on a 3 × 3 grid. The first player to get three in a row, where a row can be vertical, horizontal, or diagonal, wins.

    (E) Battleships: There are two players, each with a 10×10 grid hidden from his opponent. Various "ships" are placed on the grid. A move consists of calling out a grid location, trying to "hit" an opponent's ship. Players alternate moves. The first player to sink his opponent's fleet wins.

Consider these declarations for Questions 20 and 21:

```
public class HumanPlayer implements Player
{
    private String myName;

    < default constructor and constructor with parameters >

    < code to implement getMove and describeStrategy >

    public String getName()
    { implementation code }
}

public class ExpertPlayer extends HumanPlayer implements Comparable
{
    private int myRating;

    < default constructor and constructor with parameters >

    public int compareTo(Object obj)
    { implementation code }
}
```

20. Which code segment in a client program will cause an error?

```
 I  Player p1 = new HumanPlayer();
    Player p2 = new ExpertPlayer();
    int x1 = p1.getMove();
    int x2 = p2.getMove();

II  int x;
    Comparable c1 = new ExpertPlayer(< correct parameter list >);
    Comparable c2 = new ExpertPlayer(< correct parameter list >);
    if (c1.compareTo(c2) < 1)
        x = c1.getMove();
    else
        x = c2.getMove();

III int x;
    HumanPlayer h1 = new HumanPlayer(< correct parameter list >);
    HumanPlayer h2 = new HumanPlayer(< correct parameter list >);
    if (h1.compareTo(h2) < 1)
        x = ((HumanPlayer) h1).getMove();
    else
        x = ((HumanPlayer) h2).getMove();
```

(A) II only
(B) III only
(C) II and III only
(D) I, II, and III
(E) none

21. Which of the following is correct *implementation code* for the `compareTo` method in the `ExpertPlayer` class?

```
 I ExpertPlayer rhs = (ExpertPlayer) obj;
   if (myRating == rhs.myRating)
       return 0;
   else if (myRating < rhs.myRating)
       return -1;
   else
       return 1;

II ExpertPlayer rhs = (ExpertPlayer) obj;
   return myRating - rhs.myRating;

III ExpertPlayer rhs = (ExpertPlayer) obj;
    if (getName().equals(rhs.getName()))
        return 0;
    else if (getName().compareTo(rhs.getName()) < 0)
        return -1;
    else
        return 1;
```

(A) I only
(B) II only
(C) III only
(D) I and II only
(E) I, II, and III

22. Which statement about interfaces is true?

   I An interface contains only public abstract methods and public static final fields.
   II If a class implements an interface and then fails to implement any methods in that interface, then the class *must* be declared abstract.
   III While a class may implement just one interface, it may extend more than one class.

(A) I only
(B) I and II only
(C) I and III only
(D) II and III only
(E) I, II, and III

23. Which of the following classes is the least suitable candidate for implementing the `Comparable` interface?

(A) ```
    public class Point
    {
        private double x;
        private double y;

        //various methods follow
            ...
    }
    ```

(B) ```
    public class Name
    {
        private String firstName;
        private String lastName;

        //various methods follow
            ...
    }
    ```

(C) ```
    public class Car
    {
        private int modelNumber;
        private int year;
        private double price;

        //various methods follow
            ...
    }
    ```

(D) ```
    public class Student
    {
        private String name;
        private double gpa;

        //various methods follow
            ...
    }
    ```

(E) ```
    public class Employee
    {
        private String name;
        private int hireDate;
        private double salary;

        //various methods follow
            ...
    }
    ```
    ```

24. A certain interface provided by a Java package contains just a single method:

```
public interface SomeName
{
    int method1(Object o);
}
```

A programmer adds some functionality to this interface by adding another method to it, `method2`:

```
public interface SomeName
{
    int method1(Object ob1);
    void method2(Object ob2);
}
```

As a result of this addition, which of the following is true?
(A) A `ClassCastException` will occur if `ob1` and `ob2` are not compatible.
(B) All classes that implement the original `SomeName` interface will need to be rewritten because they no longer implement `SomeName`.
(C) A class that implements the original `SomeName` interface will need to modify its declaration as follows:

```
public class ClassName implements SomeName extends method2
{    ...
```

(D) `SomeName` will need to be changed to an abstract class and provide implementation code for `method2`, so that the original and upgraded versions of `SomeName` are compatible.
(E) Any new class that implements the upgraded version of `SomeName` will not compile.

25. Consider the `Temperature` class defined below:

```
public class Temperature implements Comparable
{
    private String myScale;
    private double myDegrees;

    //default constructor
    public Temperature ()
    { implementation code }

    //constructor
    public Temperature(String scale, double degrees)
    { implementation code }

    public int compareTo(Object obj)
    { implementation code }

    public String toString()
    { implementation code }
}
```

Here is a program that finds the lowest of three temperatures:

```java
public class TemperatureMain
{
    /* Find smaller of objects a and b */
    public static Comparable min(Comparable a, Comparable b)
    {
        if (a.compareTo(b) < 0)
            return a;
        else
            return b;
    }

    /* Find smallest of objects a, b, and c */
    public static Comparable minThree(Comparable a,
            Comparable b, Comparable c)
    {
        return min(min(a, b), c);
    }

    public static void main(String[] args)
    {
        < code to test minThree method >
    }
}
```

Which are correct replacements for < *code to test* minThree *method* >?

```java
I   Temperature t1 = new Temperature("C", 85);
    Temperature t2 = new Temperature("F", 45);
    Temperature t3 = new Temperature("F", 120);
    System.out.println("The lowest temperature is " +
            minThree(t1, t2, t3));

II  Comparable c1 = new Temperature("C", 85);
    Comparable c2 = new Temperature("F", 45);
    Comparable c3 = new Temperature("F", 120);
    System.out.println("The lowest temperature is " +
            minThree(c1, c2, c3));

III Comparable c1 = new Comparable("C", 85);
    Comparable c2 = new Comparable("F", 45);
    Comparable c3 = new Comparable("F", 120);
    System.out.println("The lowest temperature is " +
            minThree(c1, c2, c3));
```

(A) II only
(B) I and II only
(C) II and III only
(D) I and III only
(E) I, II, and III

26. A programmer has the task of maintaining a database of students of a large university. There are two types of students, undergraduates and graduate students. About a third of the graduate students are doctoral candidates.

All of the students have the same personal information stored, like name, address, and phone number, and also student information like courses taken and grades. Each student's GPA is computed, but differently for undergraduates and graduates. The doctoral candidates have information about their dissertations and faculty advisors.

The programmer will write a Java program to handle all the student information. Which of the following is the best design, in terms of programmer efficiency and code reusability? Note: { ... } denotes class code.

(A)
```
public interface Student { ...}
public class Undergraduate implements Student { ... }
public class Graduate implements Student { ... }
public class DocStudent extends Graduate { ... }
```

(B)
```
public abstract class Student { ...}
public class Undergraduate extends Student { ... }
public class Graduate extends Student { ... }
public class DocStudent extends Graduate { ... }
```

(C)
```
public class Student { ...}
public class Undergraduate extends Student { ... }
public class Graduate extends Student { ... }
public class DocStudent extends Graduate { ... }
```

(D)
```
public abstract class Student { ...}
public class Undergraduate extends Student { ... }
public class Graduate extends Student { ... }
public class DocStudent extends Student { ... }
```

(E)
```
public interface PersonalInformation { ... }
public class Student implements PersonalInformation { ...}
public class Undergraduate extends Student { ... }
public abstract class Graduate extends Student { ... }
public class DocStudent extends Graduate { ... }
```

Answer Key

1. **D**	10. **D**	19. **C**
2. **C**	11. **E**	20. **C**
3. **D**	12. **E**	21. **E**
4. **E**	13. **A**	22. **B**
5. **C**	14. **A**	23. **A**
6. **B**	15. **E**	24. **B**
7. **E**	16. **A**	25. **B**
8. **D**	17. **E**	26. **B**
9. **C**	18. **C**	

Answers Explained

1. (**D**) The methods are `deposit`, `withdraw`, and `getBalance`, all inherited from the `BankAccount` class, plus `addInterest`, which was defined just for the `SavingsAccount` class.

2. (**C**) Implementation I fails because `super()` *must* be the first line of the implementation whenever it is used. Implementation III may appear to be incorrect because it doesn't initialize `myInterestRate`. Since `myInterestRate`, however, is a primitive type—`double`—the compiler will provide a default initialization of 0, which was required.

3. (**D**) First, the statement `super(balance)` initializes the inherited private variable `myBalance` as for the `BankAccount` superclass. Then the statement `myInterestRate = rate` initializes `myInterestRate`, which belongs uniquely to the `SavingsAccount` class. Choice E fails because `myInterestRate` does not belong to the `BankAccount` class and therefore cannot be initialized by a super method. Choice A is wrong because the `SavingsAccount` class cannot directly access the private instance variables of its superclass. Choice B assigns a value to an accessor method, which is meaningless. Choice C is incorrect because `super()` invokes the *default* constructor of the superclass. This will cause `myBalance` of the `SavingsAccount` object to be initialized to 0, rather than `balance`, the parameter value.

4. (**E**) The constructor must initialize the inherited instance variable `myBalance` to the value of the `balance` parameter. All three segments achieve this. Implementation I does it by invoking `super(balance)`, the constructor in the superclass. Implementation II first initializes `myBalance` to 0 by invoking the *default* constructor of the superclass. Then it calls the inherited `deposit` method of the superclass to add `balance` to the account. Implementation III

works because `super()` is automatically called as the first line of the constructor code if there is no explicit call to `super`. Note that it's OK to call the `deposit` method since it's public.

5. **(C)** First the `withdraw` method of the `BankAccount` superclass is used to withdraw `amount`. A prefix of `super` must be used to invoke this method, which eliminates choices B and D. Then the balance must be tested using the accessor method `getBalance`, which is inherited. You can't test `myBalance` directly since it is private to the `BankAccount` class. This eliminates choices A and E, and provides another reason for eliminating choice B.

6. **(B)** When a superclass method is redefined in a subclass, the process is called *method overriding*. Which method to call is determined at run time. This is called *dynamic binding* (p. 76). *Method overloading* is two or more methods with different signatures in the same class (p. 38). The compiler recognizes at compile time which method to call. This is *early binding*. The process of *downcasting* is unrelated to these principles (p. 77).

7. **(E)** The `addInterest` method is defined only in the `SavingsAccount` class. It therefore cannot be invoked by a `BankAccount` object. The error can be fixed by casting s to the correct type:

   ```
   ((SavingsAccount) s).addInterest();
   ```

   The other method calls do not cause a problem because `withdraw` and `deposit` are both methods of the `BankAccount` class.

8. **(D)** The `withdraw` method is the only method that has one implementation in the superclass and a *different* implementation in a subclass. Polymorphism is the mechanism of selecting the correct method from the different possibilities in the class hierarchy. Notice that the `deposit` method, for example, is available to objects of all three bank account classes, but it's the *same* code in all three cases. So polymorphism isn't tested.

9. **(C)** You will get a `ClassCastException` whenever you try to cast an object to a class of which it is not an instance. Choice C is the only statement that doesn't attempt to do this. Look at the other choices: In choice A, b is not an instance of `SavingsAccount`. In choice B, b is not an instance of `CheckingAccount`. In choice D, s is not an instance of `CheckingAccount`. In choice E, c is not an instance of `SavingsAccount`.

10. **(D)** It is OK to use `timsSavings` and `daynasChecking` as parameters since each of these *is-a* `BankAccount` object. It is also OK for `timsSavings` and `daynasChecking` to call the `transfer` method (statements II and III), since they inherit this method from the `BankAccount` superclass.

11. **(E)** Statement I is false: a subclass must specify its own constructors. Otherwise the default constructor of the superclass will automatically be invoked. Note that statement III is true: it is OK to override private instance methods— they can even be declared public in the subclass implementation. What is *not* OK is to make the access more restrictive, for example, to override a public method and declare it private.

12. **(E)** All of the methods in an interface are by default public (the `public` keyword isn't needed). An abstract class can have both private and public

methods.

13. **(A)** There are two quick tests you can do to find the answer to this question:

    (1) Test the *is-a* relationship, namely the parameter for `printName` *is-a* `Bird`? and the parameter for `printBirdCall` *is-a* `Parrot`?

    (2) A reference cannot be cast to something it's not an instance of.

    Choice A passes both of these tests: `p2` *is-a* `Bird`, and `(Parrot) b2` *is-a* `Parrot`. Also `b2` is an instance of a `Parrot` (look at the right-hand side of the assignment), so the casting is correct. In choice B `printBirdCall(b2)` is wrong because `b2` *is-a* `Bird` and the `printBirdCall` method is expecting a `Parrot`. Therefore `b2` must be downcast to a `Parrot`. Also, the method call `printName((Parrot) b1)` fails because `b1` is an instance of a `Bird` and therefore cannot be cast to a `Parrot`. In choice C, `printName(b2)` is correct: `b2` *is-a* `Bird`. However, `printBirdCall(b2)` fails as already discussed. In choice D, `(Parakeet) p1` is an incorrect cast: `p1` is an instance of a `Parrot`. Note that `printBirdCall(p2)` is OK since `p2` *is-a* `Parrot`. In choice E, `(Bird) p2` is an incorrect cast: `p2` is an instance of `Parakeet`. Note that `printBirdCall((Parakeet) p2)` is correct: a `Parakeet` *is-a* `Parrot`, and `p2` is an instance of a `Parakeet`.

14. **(A)** The only incorrect declaration is `s1 = new Solid("blob")`: you can't declare an instance of an abstract class. Abstract class references can, however, refer to objects of concrete (nonabstract) subclasses. Thus the declarations for `s2` and `s3` are OK. Note that an abstract class reference can also be null, so the final declaration, though redundant, is correct.

15. **(E)** The point of having an abstract method is to postpone until run time the decision about which subclass version to call. This is what polymorphism is—calling the appropriate method at run time based on the type of the object.

16. **(A)** This is an example of polymorphism: the correct `volume` method is selected at run time. The parameter expected for `printVolume` is a `Solid` reference, which is what it gets in `main()`. The reference `sol` will refer either to a `Sphere` or a `RectangularPrism` object depending on the outcome of the coin flip. Since a `Sphere` is a `Solid` and a `RectangularPrism` is a `Solid`, there will be no type mismatch when these are the actual parameters in the `printVolume` method. (Note: the `Random` class is discussed in Chapter 4.)

17. **(E)** Each of choices A though D represent `Computable` objects: it makes sense to add, subtract, or multiply two large integers, two fractions, two irrational numbers, and two lengths. (One can multiply lengths to get an area, for example.) While it may make sense under certain circumstances to add or subtract two bank accounts, it does not make sense to multiply them!

18. **(C)** You can *declare a reference* of type `Player`. What you cannot do is *construct an object* of type `Player`. The following declarations are therefore legal:

    ```
    SmartPlayer s = new SmartPlayer();
    Player p1 = s;
    Player p2 = new HumanPlayer();
    ```

19. **(C)** Remember, to implement the `Player` interface a class must provide im-

plementations for getMove and describeStrategy. The describeStrategy method is suitable for all five games described. The getMove method returns a single integer, which works well for the High-Low game of choice A and the Chips game of choice B. In Tic-Tac-Toe (choice D) and Battleships (choice E) a move consists of giving a grid location. This can be provided by a single integer if the grid locations are numbered in a unique way. It's not ideal, but certainly doable. In the Chess game, however, a move cannot be described by a single integer. The player needs to specify both the grid location he is moving the piece to *and* which piece he is moving. The getMove method would need to be altered in a way that changes its return type. This makes the Player interface unsuitable.

20. **(C)** Segment II has an error in the getMove calls. References c1 and c2 are of type Comparable, which doesn't contain a getMove method. To correct these statements a cast is necessary:

    ```
    x = ((ExpertPlayer) c1).getMove();
    ```

    and similarly for the c2 call. Note that c1.compareTo(c2) is fine, since Comparable does contain the compareTo method and ExpertPlayer implements Comparable. Segment III fails because HumanPlayer does not implement Comparable and therefore does not have a compareTo method. Note that in Segment I the getMove calls are fine and require no downcasting, since p1 and p2 are of type Player and Player has the getMove method.

21. **(E)** All implementations are correct. This is *not* a question about whether it is better to compare ExpertPlayers based on their ratings or their names! One might need an alphabetized list of players, or one might need a list according to ranking. In practice, the program specification will instruct the programmer which to use. Note that segment II is correct because compareTo doesn't need to return 1 or −1. Any positive or negative integer is OK.

22. **(B)** Statement III would be correct if it read as follows: While a class may extend just one class, it may implement more than one interface.

23. **(A)** There is no good way to write a compareTo method for a Point class. Two points (x_1, y_1) and (x_2, y_2) are equal if and only if $x_1 = x_2$ and $y_1 = y_2$. But if points P_1 and P_2 are not equal, what will determine if $P_1 < P_2$ or $P_1 > P_2$? You could try using the distance from the origin. Define $P_1 > P_2$ if and only if $OP_1 > OP_2$, and $P_1 < P_2$ if and only if $OP_1 < OP_2$, where O is $(0, 0)$. This definition means that points (a, b) and (b, a) are equal, which violates the definition of equals! The problem is that there is no way to map the two-dimensional set of points to a one-dimensional distance function and still be consistent with the definition of equals. The objects in each of the other classes can be compared without a problem. In choice B, two Name objects can be ordered alphabetically. In choice C, two Car objects can be ordered by year or by price. In choice D, two Student objects can be ordered by name or GPA. In choice E, two Employee objects can be ordered by name or seniority (date of hire).

24. **(B)** Classes that implement an interface must provide implementation code for all methods in the interface. Adding method2 to the SomeName interface means that all of those classes need to be rewritten with implementation

code for method2. (This is not good—it violates the sacred principle of code reusability, and programmers relying on the interface will squeal.) Choices A, C, and D are all meaningless garbage. Choice E *may* be true if there is some other error in the new class. Otherwise, as long as the new class provides implementation code for both method1 and method2, the class will compile.

25. (**B**) Segment III is wrong because you can't construct an interface object. (Remember, Comparable is an interface!) Segments I and II both work because the minThree method is expecting three parameters, each of which is a Comparable. Since Temperature implements Comparable, each of the Temperature objects is a Comparable and can be used as a parameter in this method.

Note that the program assumes that the compareTo method is able to compare Temperature objects with different scales. This is an internal detail that would be dealt with in the compareTo method, and hidden from the client. When a class implements Comparable there is always an assumption that the compareTo method will be implemented in a reasonable way.

26. (**B**) Here is the hierarchy of classes:

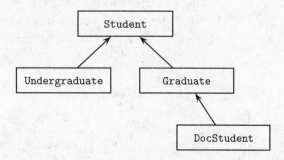

Eliminate choice D which fails to make DocStudent a subclass of Graduate. This is a poor design choice since a DocStudent *is-a* Graduate. Making Student an abstract class is desirable since the methods that are common to all students can go in there with implementations provided. The method to calculate the GPA, which differs among student types, will be declared in Student as an abstract method. Then unique implementations will be provided in both the Undergraduate and Graduate classes. Choice A is a poor design because making Student an interface means that all of its methods will need to be implemented in both the Undergraduate and Graduate classes. Many of these methods will have the same implementations. As far as possible you want to arrange for classes to inherit common methods and to avoid repeated code. Choice C is slightly inferior to choice B because you are told that all students are either graduates or undergraduates. Having the Student class abstract guarantees that you won't create an instance of a Student (who is neither a graduate nor an undergraduate). Choice E has a major design flaw: making Graduate an abstract class means that you can't create any instances of Graduate objects. Disaster! If the keyword abstract is removed from choice E, it becomes a fine design, as good as that in choice B. Once Student has implemented all the common PersonalInformation methods, these are inherited by each of the subclasses.

CHAPTER FOUR
Some Standard Classes

The Owl and the Pussycat went to sea
In a beautiful pea-green boat,
They took some honey, and plenty of money,
Wrapped up in a five-pound note.
—*Edward Lear,* The Owl and the Pussycat

The Object *Class*

The Universal Superclass

Think of Object as the superclass of the universe. Every class automatically extends Object, which means that Object is a direct or indirect superclass of every other class. In a class hierarchy tree, Object is at the top:

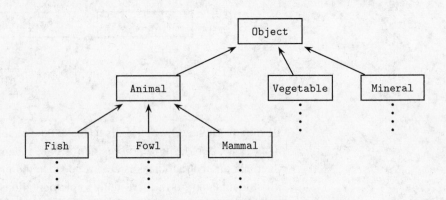

Methods in Object

There are many methods in Object, all of them inherited by every other class. Since Object is not an abstract class, all of its methods have implementations. The expectation is that these methods will be overridden in any class where the default implementation is not suitable. The required methods in the AP Java subset are toString, equals, and hashCode (which is for Level AB only).

The toString Method

```
public String toString()
```

This method returns a version of your object in String form.

When you attempt to print an object, the inherited default toString method is invoked, and what you will see is the class name followed by an @ followed by a meaningless number. For example,

```
SavingsAccount s = new SavingsAccount(500);
System.out.println(s);
```

THE OBJECT CLASS 109

produces something like

```
SavingsAccount@fea485c4
```

To have more meaningful output, you need to override the toString method for your own classes. Even if your final program doesn't need to output any objects, you should define a toString method for each class to help in debugging.

Example 1

```java
public class OrderedPair
{
    private double x;
    private double y;

    //constructors and other methods

    /* Conversion of OrderedPair to String */
    public String toString()
    {
        return "(" + x + "," + y + ")";
    }
}
```

Now the statements

```java
OrderedPair p = new OrderedPair(7,10);
System.out.println(p);
```

will invoke the overridden toString method and produce output that looks like an ordered pair:

```
(7,10)
```

Example 2

For a BankAccount class the overridden toString method may look something like this:

```java
/* Conversion of BankAccount to String */
public String toString()
{
    return "Bank Account: balance = $" + myBalance;
}
```

The statements

```java
BankAccount b = new BankAccount(600);
System.out.println(b);
```

will produce output that looks like this:

```
Bank Account: balance = $600
```

NOTE   The + sign is a concatenation operator for strings (see p. 111).

The `equals` Method

```
public boolean equals(Object other)
```

All classes inherit this method from the `Object` class. It returns `true` if this object and `other` are the same object, `false` otherwise. Being the same object means referencing the same memory slot. For example,

```
Date d1 = new Date("January", 14, 2001);
Date d2 = d1;
Date d3 = new Date("January", 14, 2001);
```

The test `if (d1.equals(d2))` returns `true`, but the test `if (d1.equals(d3))` returns `false`, since `d1` and `d3` do not refer to the same object. Often, as in this example, you may want two objects to be considered equal if their *contents* are the same. In that case, you have to override the `equals` method in your class to achieve this. Some of the standard classes described later in this chapter have overridden `equals` in this way. You will not be required to write code that overrides `equals` on the AP exam.

NOTE
1. The default implementation of `equals` is equivalent to the `==` relation for objects: in the `Date` example above, the test `if (d1 == d2)` returns `true`, the test `if (d1 == d3)` returns false.
2. The operators `<`, `>`, and so on, are not overloaded in Java. To compare objects one must use either the `equals` method or the `compareTo` method if the class implements the `Comparable` interface (see p. 83).

Level AB Only

The `hashCode` Method

Every class inherits the `hashCode` method from `Object`. The value returned by `hashCode` is an integer produced by some formula that maps your object to an address in a hash table. A given object must always produce the same hash code. Also, two objects that are equal should produce the same hash code; that is, if `obj1.equals(obj2)` is true, then `obj1` and `obj2` have the same hash code. Note that the opposite is not necessarily true. Hash codes do not have to be unique—two objects with the same hash code are not necessarily equal.

To maintain the condition that `obj1.equals(obj2)` is true implies that `obj1` and `obj2` have the same hash code, overriding `equals` means that you have to override `hashCode` at the same time. You will not be required to do this on the AP exam. You do, however, need to understand that every object is associated with an integer value called its hash code, and that objects that are equal have the same hash code.

The String *Class*

String Objects

An object of type `String` is a sequence of characters. All *string literals*, such as `"yikes!"`, are implemented as instances of this class. A string literal consists of zero or more characters, including escape sequences, surrounded by double quotes. (The quotes are not part of the `String` object.) Thus each of the following is a valid string literal:

```
""                  //empty string
"2468"
"I must\n go home"
```

String objects are *immutable*, which means that there are no methods to change them after they've been constructed. You can, however, always create a new String that is a mutated form of an existing String.

Constructing String Objects

A String object is unusual in that it can be initialized like a primitive type:

```
String s = "abc";
```

This is equivalent to

```
String s = new String("abc");
```

in the sense that in both cases s is a reference to a String object with contents "abc" (see Box on p. 113).

It is possible to reassign a String reference:

```
String s = "John";
s = "Harry";
```

This is equivalent to

```
String s = new String("John");
s = new String("Harry");
```

Notice that this is consistent with the immutable feature of String objects. "John" has not been changed, he has merely been discarded! The fickle reference s now refers to a new String, "Harry". It is also OK to reassign s as follows:

```
s = s + " Windsor";
```

s now refers to the object "Harry Windsor".

Here are other ways to initialize String objects:

```
String s1;                 //s1 is a null reference
String s2 = new String();  //s2 is an empty character sequence

String state = "Alaska";
String dessert = "baked " + state;  //dessert has value
                                     //"baked Alaska"
```

The Concatenation Operator

The dessert declaration above uses the *concatenation operator*, +, which operates on String objects. Given two String operands lhs and rhs, lhs + rhs produces a single String consisting of lhs followed by rhs. If either lhs or rhs is an object other than a String, the toString method of the object is invoked and lhs and rhs are concatenated as before. If one of the operands is a String and the other is a primitive type, then the non-String operand is converted to a String and concatenation occurs as before. If neither lhs nor rhs is a String object, an error occurs. Here are some examples:

```
int five = 5;
String state = "Hawaii-";
String tvShow = state + five + "-0";   //tvShow has value
                                       //"Hawaii-5-0"
int x = 3, y = 4;
String sum = x + y;         //error: can't assign int 7 to String
```

Suppose a Date class has a toString method that outputs dates that look like this: 2/17/1948.

```
Date d1 = new Date(8, 2, 1947);
Date d2 = new Date(2, 17, 1948);
String s = "My birthday is " + d2;  //s has value
                                    //"My birthday is 2/17/1948"
String s2 = d1 + d2;    //error: + not defined for objects
String s3 = d1.toString() + d2.toString();  //s3 has value
                                            //8/2/19472/17/1948
```

Comparison of String Objects

There are two ways to compare String objects:

1. Use the equals method that is inherited from the Object class and overridden to do the correct thing:

   ```
   if (string1.equals(string2)) ...
   ```

   This returns true if string1 and string2 are identical strings, false otherwise.

2. Use the compareTo method. The String class implements Comparable, which means that the compareTo method is provided in String. This method compares strings in dictionary order:

   • If string1.compareTo(string2) < 0, then string1 precedes string2 in the dictionary.

   • If string1.compareTo(string2) > 0, then string1 follows string2 in the dictionary.

   • If string1.compareTo(string2) == 0, then string1 and string2 are identical. (This test is an alternative to string1.equals(string2).)

Be aware that Java is case-sensitive. Thus if s1 is "cat" and s2 is "Cat", s1.equals(s2) will return false.

Characters are compared according to their position in the ASCII chart. All you need to know is that all digits precede all capital letters, which precede all lower-case letters. Thus "5" comes before "R", which comes before "a". Two strings are compared as follows: Start at the left end of each string and do a character-by-character comparison until you reach the first character in which the strings differ, the kth character, say. If the kth character of s1 comes before the kth character of s2, then s1 will come before s2, and vice versa. If the strings have identical characters, except that s1 terminates before s2, then s1 comes before s2. Here are some examples:

```
String s1 = "HOT", s2 = "HOTEL", s3 = "dog";
if (s1.compareTo(s2) < 0))      //true, s1 terminates first
   ...
if (s1.compareTo(s3) > 0))      //false, "H" comes before "d"
```

Don't Use == to Test Strings!

The expression if(string1 == string2) tests whether string1 and string2 are the same reference. It does not test the actual strings. Using == to compare strings may lead to unexpected results.

Example 1

```
String s = "oh no!";
String t = "oh no!";
if (s == t) ...
```

The test returns true even though it appears that s and t are different references. The reason is that for efficiency Java makes only one String object for equivalent string constants. This is safe in that a String cannot be altered.

Example 2

```
String s = "oh no!";
String t = new String("oh no!");
if (s == t) ...
```

The test returns false because use of new creates a new object and s and t *are* different references in this example!

The moral of the story? Use equals not == to test strings. It always does the right thing.

Other String Methods

The Java String class provides many methods, only a small number of which are in the AP Java subset. In addition to the constructors, comparison methods, and concatenation operator + discussed so far, you should know the following methods:

```
int length()
```

Returns the length of this string.

```
String substring(int startIndex)
```

Returns a new string that is a substring of this string. The substring starts with the character at startIndex and extends to the end of the string. The first character is at index zero. The method throws a StringIndexOutOfBoundsException if startIndex is negative or larger than the length of the string.

```
String substring(int startIndex, int endIndex)
```

Returns a new string that is a substring of this string. The substring starts at startIndex and extends to the character at endIndex-1. (Think of it this way: startIndex is the first character that you want; endIndex is the first character that you *don't* want.) The method throws a StringIndexOutOfBoundsException if startIndex is negative, or endIndex is larger than the length of the string, or startIndex is larger than endIndex.

---
int indexOf(String str)

Returns the index of the first occurrence of str within this string. If str is not a substring of this string, -1 is returned. The method throws a NullPointerException if str is null.

Here are some examples:

```
"unhappy".substring(2)      //returns "happy"
"cold".substring(4)         //returns "" (empty string)
"cold".substring(5)         //StringIndexOutOfBoundsException
"strawberry.substring(5,7)  //returns "be"
"crayfish".substring(4,8)   //returns "fish"
"crayfish".substring(4,9)   //StringIndexOutOfBoundsException
"crayfish".substring(5,4)   //StringIndexOutOfBoundsException

String s = "funnyfarm";
int x = s.indexOf("farm");  //x has value 5
x = s.indexOf("farmer");    //x has value -1
int y = s.length();         //y has value 9
```

Wrapper Classes

A *wrapper class* takes either an existing object or a value of primitive type, "wraps" it in an object, and provides a new set of methods for that type. The point of a wrapper class is to provide extended capabilities for the wrapped quantity:

- It can be used in generic Java methods that require objects as parameters.
- It can be used in Java container classes which require that the items be objects (see Chapter 11).

In each case, the wrapper class allows

1. Construction of an object from a single value (wrapping the primitive in a wrapper object).
2. Retrieval of the primitive value (unwrapping from the wrapper object).

Java provides a wrapper class for each of its primitive types. The two that you should know for the AP exam are the Integer and Double classes.

The Integer Class

The Integer class wraps a value of type int in an object. An object of type Integer contains just one instance variable whose type is int.

Here are the Integer methods you should know for the AP exam:

Integer(int value)

Constructs an Integer object from an int.

```
int compareTo(Object other)
```

If other is an Integer, compareTo returns 0 if this Integer is numerically equal to other, a negative integer if this Integer is less than other, and a positive integer if this Integer is greater than other.

NOTE
1. The Integer class implements Comparable.
2. The compareTo method throws a ClassCastException if the argument other is not an Integer.

```
int intValue()
```

Returns the value of this Integer as an int.

```
boolean equals(Object obj)
```

Returns true if and only if this Integer has the same int value as obj.

NOTE
1. This method overrides equals in class Object.
2. This method throws a ClassCastException if obj is not an Integer.

```
String toString()
```

Returns a String representing the value of this Integer.

Here are some examples to illustrate the Integer methods:

```
Integer intObj = new Integer(6);  //wraps 6 in Integer object
int j = intObj.intValue();        //unwraps 6 from Integer object

System.out.println("Integer value is " + intObj);
//calls toString() for intObj
```

The output is

```
Integer value is 6

Object object = new Integer(5);   //Integer is a subclass of Object

Integer intObj2 = new Integer(3);
int k = intObj2.intValue();
if (intObj.equals(intObj2))       //OK, evaluates to false
    ...
if (intObj.intValue() == intObj2.intValue())
    ...               //OK, since comparing primitive types

if (k.equals(j))     //error, k and j not objects
    ...
if ((intObj.intValue()).compareTo(intObj2.intValue()) < 0)
    ...               //error, can't use compareTo on primitive types

if (intObj.compareTo(object) < 0)  //OK
    ...
if (object.compareTo(intObj) < 0)  //error, no compareTo in Object
    ...
```

```
        if (((Integer) object).compareTo(intObj) < 0)  //OK
        ...
```

NOTE

Integer objects are immutable: there are no mutator methods in the class.

The Double Class

The `Double` class wraps a value of type `double` in an object. An object of type `Double` contains just one instance variable whose type is `double`. Like `String` and `Integer` objects, `Double` objects are also immutable.

The methods you should know for the AP exam are analogous to those for type `Integer`.

```
Double(double value)
```

Constructs a `Double` object from a `double`.

```
double doubleValue()
```

Returns the value of this `Double` as a `double`.

```
int compareTo(Object other)
```

The `Double` class implements `Comparable`. The `compareTo` method will throw a `ClassCastException` if the argument `other` is not a `Double`. If `other` is a `Double`, `compareTo` returns 0 if this `Double` is numerically equal to `other`, a negative integer if this `Double` is less than `other`, and a positive integer if this `Double` is greater than `other`.

```
boolean equals(Object obj)
```

This method overrides `equals` in class `Object`, and throws a `ClassCastException` if `obj` is not a `Double`. Otherwise it returns `true` if and only if this `Double` has the same `double` value as `obj`.

```
String toString()
```

Returns a `String` representing the value of this `Double`.

Here are some examples:

```
Double dObj = new Double(2.5);      //wraps 2.5 in Double object
double d = dObj.doubleValue();      //unwraps 2.5 from Double object

Object object = new Double(7.3);    //Double is a subclass of Object
Object intObj = new Integer(4);
if (dObj.compareTo(object) > 0)     //OK
    ...
if (dObj.compareTo(intObj) > 0)     //ClassCastException
    ...                             //can't compare Integer to Double
```

The Math *Class*

This class implements standard mathematical functions such as absolute value, square root, trigonometric functions, the log function, power function, and so on. It also contains mathematical constants such as π and e.

Here are the functions you should know for the AP exam:

```
static int abs(int x)
```

Returns the absolute value of integer x.

```
static double abs(double x)
```

Returns the absolute value of real number x.

```
static double pow(double base, double exp)
```

Returns base^{exp}. Assumes base > 0, or base $= 0$ and exp > 0, or base < 0 and exp is an integer.

```
static double sqrt(double x)
```

Returns $\sqrt{x}$, $x \geq 0$.

All of the functions and constants are implemented as static methods and variables, which means that there are no instances of Math objects. The methods are invoked using the class name, Math, followed by the dot operator.

Here are some examples of mathematical formulas and the equivalent Java statements.

1. The relationship between the radius and area of a circle:

$$r = \sqrt{A/\pi}$$

In code:

```
radius = Math.sqrt(area/Math.PI);
```

2. The amount of money A in an account after ten years, given an original deposit of P and an interest rate of 5% compounded annually, is

$$A = P(1.05)^{10}$$

In code:

```
a = p * Math.pow(1.05, 10);
```

3. The distance D between two points $P(x_P, y)$ and $Q(x_Q, y)$ on the same horizontal line is

$$D = |x_P - x_Q|$$

In code:

```
d = Math.abs(xp - xq);
```

The Random *Class*

Random numbers are generated in Java using the Math class method random, or the Random class. The AP Java subset includes just the Random class for generating random numbers.

All the classes discussed in this chapter so far are part of the java.lang package and so are automatically accessible in any program. However, to use the Random class, you need to import the appropriate package with the following statement at the top of your program:

```
import java.util.Random;
```

Initializing the Random Number Generator

A new random number generator can be created using the default constructor

```
Random r = new Random();
```

This uses the computer's clock to seed the random number generator. Each time the program is run, a different sequence of numbers will be generated (which makes life difficult if you are still debugging your program!). To create a sequence that repeats each time the program is run, initialize the random number generator with the constructor

```
Random r = new Random(seedValue);  //seedValue is of type long
                                   //Any integer can be used
```

When your program is up and running without bugs, you can remove the parameter.

Random Integers

The method call

```
r.nextInt(n)
```

generates a random integer k, where $0 \leq k < n$.

Example 1

To simulate a coin toss:

```
int toss = r.nextInt(2);        //toss has value 0 or 1
```

Example 2

To draw one number from a hat, where numbers go from 1 to 100, and each number occurs exactly once:

```
int num = r.nextInt(100) + 1;
```

r.nextInt(100) gives random integers from 0 to 99. To get an integer from 1 to 100, you must add 1.

Example 3

To get a random integer in the range 10 to 20, inclusive:

```
int num = r.nextInt(11) + 10;
```

The first term on the right-hand side produces a random integer from 0 to 10. Adding 10 produces an integer from 10 to 20.

Random Real Numbers

The method call

```
r.nextDouble()
```

produces a value x in the range $0.0 \le x < 1.0$. Values produced are approximately uniformly distributed in this range.

Example 1

To produce a random real value in the range $2.0 \le x < 3$:

```
double x = r.nextDouble() + 2;
```

Example 2

To produce a random real value in the range $4 \le x < 6$:

```
double x = 2 * r.nextDouble() + 4;
```

In general, to produce a random real value in the range `lowValue` $\le x <$ `highValue`:

```
double x = (highValue - lowValue) * r.nextDouble() + lowValue;
```

Using Random Correctly

When using Random, be sure that only one new Random object is created for each run of the program, irrespective of how many random numbers are needed. If you don't do this, the program could generate sequences of random numbers that are not very random!

There are two ways of achieving this:

1. Declare and initialize a static instance variable, for example

```
public SomeClass
{
    private static Random myRandNum = new Random();
    ...
```

Now get a random number in any method of the class by invoking

```
myRandNum.nextInt(n)     or     myRandNum.nextDouble()
```

You will not be tested on this aspect of the Random class.

2. Hide the static declaration in a class that returns a Random object. This is how the case study does it, allowing several classes to access the same Random object (see p. 473).

Multiple-Choice Questions on Standard Classes

1. Here is a program segment to find the quantity base^{exp}. Both base and exp
   are entered at the keyboard.

```
System.out.println("Enter base and exponent: ");
double base = IO.readDouble();   //read user input
double exp = IO.readDouble();    //read user input
< code to find power, which equals base^exp >
System.out.print(base + " raised to the power " + exp);
System.out.println(" equals " + power);
}
```

Which is a correct replacement for
< *code to find* power, *which equals* base^{exp} >?

```
 I double power;
   Math m = new Math();
   power = m.pow(base, exp);

II double power;
   power = Math.pow(base, exp);

III Power power;
    power = new Power(base, exp);
```

(A) I only
(B) II only
(C) III only
(D) I and II only
(E) I and III only

2. Consider the squareRoot method defined below:

```
public Double squareRoot(Double d)
//Precondition:  value of d ≥ 0
//Postcondition: returns a Double whose value is the square
//               root of the value represented by d
{
    < implementation code >
}
```

Which < *implementation code* > satisfies the postcondition?

```
 I double x = d.doubleValue();
   x = Math.sqrt(x);
   return new Double(x);

 II return new Double(Math.sqrt(d.doubleValue()));

III return ((Double) Math).sqrt(d.doubleValue());
```

(A) I only
(B) I and II only
(C) I and III only
(D) II and III only
(E) I, II, and III

3. Here are some examples of negative numbers rounded to the nearest integer.

Negative real number	Rounded to nearest integer
−3.5	−4
−8.97	−9
−5.0	−5
−2.487	−2
−0.2	0

Refer to the declaration

```
double d = -4.67;
```

Which of the following correctly rounds d to the nearest integer?

(A) `int rounded = Math.abs(d);`

(B) `Random r = new Random();`
    `int rounded = r.nextInt(d);`

(C) `int rounded = (int) (d - 0.5);`

(D) `int rounded = (int) (d + 0.5);`

(E) `int rounded = Math.abs((int) (d - 0.5));`

4. A program is to simulate plant life under harsh conditions. In the program, plants die randomly according to some probability. Here is part of a Plant class defined in the program.

```
public class Plant
{
    //create Random number generator for class
    private static Random r = new Random();

    private double myProbDeath;   //probability that plant dies,
                                  //real number between 0 and 1
    // other private instance variables

    public Plant(double probDeath, < other parameters >)
    {
        myProbDeath = probDeath;
        < initialization of other instance variables >
    }

    //plant dies
    public void die()
    {
        < statement to generate random number >
        if  (< test to determine if plant dies >)
            < code to implement plant's death >
        else
            < code to make plant continue living >
    }

    //other methods
}
```

Which of the following are correct replacements for
(1) < statement to generate random number > and
(2) < test to determine if plant dies >?

(A) (1) double x = r.nextDouble();
     (2) x == myProbDeath

(B) (1) double x = r.nextDouble();
     (2) x > myProbDeath

(C) (1) double x = r.nextDouble();
     (2) x < myProbDeath

(D) (1) int x = r.nextInt(100) + 1;
     (2) x < (int) myProbDeath

(E) (1) int x = r.nextInt(100) + 1;
     (2) x == (int) myProbDeath

5. Consider the code segment

```
Integer i = new Integer(20);
< more code >
```

Which of the following replacements for < *more code* > correctly changes i so that its integer value is 25?

  I `i = new Integer(25);`

  II `i.intValue() = 25;`

  III `Integer j = new Integer(25);`
       `i = j;`

(A) I only
(B) II only
(C) III only
(D) I and III only
(E) II and III only

6. Consider these declarations:

```
Integer intOb = new Integer(3);
Object ob = new Integer(4);
Double doubOb = new Double(3.0);
```

Which of the following will *not* cause an error?
(A) `if ((Integer) ob.compareTo(intOb) < 0) ...`
(B) `if (ob.compareTo(intOb) < 0) ...`
(C) `if (intOb.compareTo(doubOb) < 0) ...`
(D) `if (doubOb.compareTo(intOb) < 0) ...`
(E) `if (intOb.compareTo(ob) < 0) ...`

7. Refer to these declarations:

```
Integer k = new Integer(8);
Integer m = new Integer(4);
```

Which test will *not* generate an error?

  I `if (k.intValue() == m.intValue())...`

  II `if ((k.intValue()).equals(m.intValue()))...`

  III `if ((k.toString()).equals(m.toString()))...`

(A) I only
(B) II only
(C) III only
(D) I and III only
(E) I, II, and III

8. Consider the code fragment

```
Object intObj = new Integer(9);
System.out.println((String) intObj);
```

What will be output as a result of running the fragment?
(A) No output. A `ClassCastException` will be thrown.
(B) No output. An `ArithmeticException` will be thrown.
(C) 9
(D) "9"
(E) nine

9. Consider these declarations:

```
String s1 = "crab";
String s2 = new String("crab");
String s3 = s1;
```

Which expression involving these strings evaluates to `true`?

I `s1 == s2`

II `s1.equals(s2)`

III `s3.equals(s2)`

(A) I only
(B) II only
(C) II and III only
(D) I and II only
(E) I, II, and III

10. Suppose that `strA = "TOMATO"`, `strB = "tomato"`, and `strC = "tom"`. Given that `"A"` comes before `"a"` in dictionary order, which is true?
(A) `strA.compareTo(strB) < 0 && strB.compareTo(strC) < 0`
(B) `strB.compareTo(strA) < 0 || strC.compareTo(strA) < 0`
(C) `strC.compareTo(strA) < 0 && strA.compareTo(strB) < 0`
(D) `!(strA.equals(str(B)) && strC.compareTo(strB) < 0`
(E) `!(strA.equals(str(B)) && strC.compareTo(strA) < 0`

11. This question refers to the following declaration:

```
String line = "Some more silly stuff on strings!";
//the words are separated by a single space
```

What string will `str` refer to after execution of the following?

```
int x = line.indexOf("m");
String str = line.substring(10,15) + line.substring(25,25+x);
```

(A) "sillyst"
(B) "sillystr"
(C) "silly st"
(D) "silly str"
(E) "sillystrin"

12. Refer to the following method:

```
public static String weirdString(String s, String sub)
{
    String temp;
    String w = ""; //empty string
    for (int i=0; i < s.length(); i++)
    {
        temp = s.substring(i, i+1);
        if (temp.compareTo(sub) < 0)
            w = w + temp;
    }
    return w;
}
```

What will `weirdStr` contain after the following code is executed?

```
String str = "conglomeration";
String weirdStr = weirdString(str, "m");
```

(A) "cglmeai"
(B) "cgleai"
(C) "coglloeratio"
(D) "onomrton"
(E) No value. `StringIndexOutOfBoundsException`.

13. A program has a `String` variable `fullName` that stores a first name, followed by a space, followed by a last name. There are no spaces in either the first or last names. Here are some examples of `fullName` values: `"Anthony Coppola"`, `"Jimmy Carroll"`, and `"Tom DeWire"`. Consider this code segment that extracts the last name from a `fullName` variable, and stores it in `lastName` with no surrounding blanks:

```
int k = fullName.indexOf(" ");    //find index of blank
String lastName = < expression >
```

Which is a correct replacement for *expression*?

  I `fullName.substring(k);`

  II `fullName.substring(k+1);`

  III `fullName.substring(k+1, fullName.length());`

  (A) I only
  (B) II only
  (C) III only
  (D) II and III only
  (E) I and III only

14. One of the rules for converting English to Pig Latin states: If a word begins with a consonant, move the consonant to the end of the word and add "ay". Thus "dog" becomes "ogday," and "crisp" becomes "rispcay". Suppose s is a `String` containing an English word that begins with a consonant. Which of the following creates the correct corresponding word in Pig Latin? Assume the declarations

```
String ayString = "ay";
String pigString;
```

  (A) `pigString = s.substring(0, s.length()) + s.substring(0,1)`
       `+ ayString;`

  (B) `pigString = s.substring(1, s.length()) + s.substring(0,0)`
       `+ ayString;`

  (C) `pigString = s.substring(0, s.length()-1) + s.substring(0,1)`
       `+ ayString;`

  (D) `pigString = s.substring(1, s.length()-1) + s.substring(0,0)`
       `+ ayString;`

  (E) `pigString = s.substring(1, s.length()) + s.substring(0,1)`
       `+ ayString;`

15. This question refers to the getString method shown below:

```
public static String getString(String s1, String s2)
{
    int index = s1.indexOf(s2);
    return s1.substring(index, index+s2.length());
}
```

Which is true about getString? It may return a string that

  I   Is equal to s2.
 II Has no characters in common with s2.
III Is equal to s1.

(A) I and III only
(B) II and III only
(C) I and II only
(D) I, II, and III
(E) None is true.

16. Consider this method:

```
public static String doSomething(String s)
{
    final String BLANK = " ";   //BLANK contains a single space
    String str = "";            //empty string
    String temp;
    for (int i=0; i < s.length(); i++)
    {
        temp = s.substring(i, i+1);
        if (!(temp.equals(BLANK)))
            str += temp;
    }
    return str;
}
```

Which of the following is the most precise description of what doSomething does?
(A) It returns s unchanged.
(B) It returns s with all its blanks removed.
(C) It returns a String that is equivalent to s with all its blanks removed.
(D) It returns a String that is an exact copy of s.
(E) It returns a String that contains s.length() blanks.

Questions 17–19 refer to the classes Position and PositionTest below.

```java
public class Position implements Comparable
{
    private int myRow, myCol;
    /* myRow and myCol are both ≥ 0 except in
     * the default constructor where they are initialized to -1 */

    public Position()            //constructor
    {
        myRow = -1;
        myCol = -1;
    }

    public Position(int r, int c)        //constructor
    {
        myRow = r;
        myCol = c;
    }

    /* Returns row of Position */
    public int getRow()
    { return myRow; }

    /* Returns column of Position */
    public int getCol()
    { return myCol; }

    /* Returns Position north of (up from) this position */
    public Position north()
    { return new Position(myRow - 1, myCol); }

    //Similar methods south, east, and west

    /* Compares this Position to another Position object
        Returns -1 (less than), 0 (equals), or 1 (greater than) */
    public int compareTo(Object o)
    {
        Position p = (Position) o;
        if (this.getRow() < p.getRow() || this.getRow() == p.getRow()
            && this.getCol() < p.getCol())
                return -1;
        if (this.getRow() > p.getRow() || this.getRow() == p.getRow()
            && this.getCol() > p.getCol())
                return 1;
        return 0;            //row and col both equal
    }

    /* Returns string form of Position */
    public String toString()
    { return "(" + myRow + "," + myCol + ")"; }
}
```

```
public class PositionTest
{
    public static void main(String[] args)
    {
        Position p1 = new Position(2, 3);
        Position p2 = new Position(4, 1);
        Position p3 = new Position(2, 3);

        //tests to compare positions
            ...
    }
}
```

17. Which is true about the value of p1.compareTo(p2)?
    (A) It equals true.
    (B) It equals false.
    (C) It equals 0.
    (D) It equals 1.
    (E) It equals -1.

18. Which boolean expression about p1 and p3 is true?

     I p1 == p3

     II p1.equals(p3)

     III p1.compareTo(p3) == 0

    (A) I only
    (B) II only
    (C) III only
    (D) II and III only
    (E) I, II, and III

19. The Position class is modified so that the equals and hashCode methods of class Object are overridden. Here are the implementations:

```
/* Returns true if this Position equals another Position object
   false otherwise */
public boolean equals(Object o)
{
    Position p = (Position) o;
    return p.myRow == myRow && p.myCol == myCol;
}


/* Returns a hashCode for this Position */
public int hashCode()
{ return myRow * 10 + myCol; }
```

Which is *false* about the hashCode method?

  I Every Position object has a unique hashCode value.
  II For two Position objects p1 and p2, if p1.equals(p2) is true, then p1 and p2 have the same hashCode value.
  III A given hashCode value corresponds to one and only one Position object.

(A) I only
(B) II only
(C) III only
(D) I and II only
(E) I, II, and III

Questions 20 and 21 deal with the problem of swapping two integer values. Three methods are proposed to solve the problem, using primitive `int` types, `Integer` objects, and `IntPair` objects, where `IntPair` is defined as follows:

```
public class IntPair
{
    private int firstValue;
    private int secondValue;

    public IntPair(int first, int second)
    {
        firstValue = first;
        secondValue = second;
    }

    public int getFirst()
    { return firstValue; }

    public int getSecond()
    { return secondValue; }

    public void setFirst(int a)
    { firstValue = a; }

    public void setSecond(int b)
    { secondValue = b;}
}
```

20. Here are three different `Swap` methods, each intended for use in a client program.

```
I  public static void Swap(int a, int b)
   {
       int temp = a;
       a = b;
       b = temp;
   }

II public static void Swap(Integer obj_a, Integer obj_b)
   {
       Integer temp = new Integer(obj_a.intValue());
       obj_a = obj_b;
       obj_b = temp;
   }

III public static void Swap(IntPair pair)
    {
        int temp = pair.getFirst();
        pair.setFirst(pair.getSecond());
        pair.setSecond(temp);
    }
```

When correctly used in a client program with appropriate parameters, which method will swap two integers, as intended?

(A) I only

(B) II only

(C) III only

(D) II and III only

(E) I, II, and III

21. Consider the following program that uses the `IntPair` class:

```
public class TestSwap
{
    public static void Swap(IntPair pair)
    {
        int temp = pair.getFirst();
        pair.setFirst(pair.getSecond());
        pair.setSecond(temp);
    }

    public static void main(String[] args)
    {
        int x = 8, y = 6;
        < code to swap x and y >
    }
}
```

Which is a correct replacement for < *code to swap* x *and* y >?

```
 I  IntPair iPair = new IntPair(x, y);
    Swap(x, y);
    x = iPair.getFirst();
    y = iPair.getSecond();

II  IntPair iPair = new IntPair(x, y);
    Swap(iPair);
    x = iPair.getFirst();
    y = iPair.getSecond();

III IntPair iPair = new IntPair(x, y);
    Swap(iPair);
    x = iPair.setFirst();
    y = iPair.setSecond();
```

(A) I only
(B) II only
(C) III only
(D) II and III only
(E) None is correct.

Refer to the Name class below for Questions 22 and 23.

```java
public class Name implements Comparable
{
    private String firstName;
    private String lastName;

    public Name(String first, String last)  //constructor
    {
        firstName = first;
        lastName = last;
    }

    public String toString()
    { return firstName + " " + lastName; }

    public boolean equals(Object obj)
    {
        Name n = (Name) obj;
        return n.firstName.equals(firstName) &&
                n.lastName.equals(lastName);
    }

    public int hashCode()
    { implementation code }

    public int compareTo(Object obj)
    {
        Name n = (Name) obj;
        < more code >
    }
}
```

22. The `compareTo` method implements the standard name-ordering algorithm where last names take precedence over first names. Lexicographic or dictionary ordering of `Strings` is used. For example, the name Scott Dentes comes before Nick Elser, and Adam Cooper comes before Sara Cooper.

Which of the following is a correct replacement for *< more code >*?

```
I   int lastComp = lastName.compareTo(n.lastName);
    if (lastComp != 0)
        return lastComp;
    else
        return firstName.compareTo(n.firstName);

II  if (lastName.equals(n.lastName))
        return firstName.compareTo(n.firstName);
    else
        return 0;

III if (!(lastName.equals(n.lastName)))
        return firstName.compareTo(n.firstName);
    else
        return lastName.compareTo(n.lastName);
```

(A) I only
(B) II only
(C) III only
(D) I and II only
(E) I, II, and III

Level AB Only

23. Which statement about the `Name` class is *false*?
(A) `Name` objects are immutable.
(B) It is possible for the methods in `Name` to throw a `NullPointerException`.
(C) The `hashCode` method must be redefined since the `Name` class redefines the `equals` method.
(D) The `compareTo` method throws a run-time exception if the parameter is null or the parameter is incompatible with `Name` objects.
(E) Since the `Name` class implements `Comparable`, it *must* provide an implementation for an `equals` method.

24. Consider the findSum method below, which sums the integers from 1 to *k*.

```
public class SumTest
{
    public static void findSum(int k, Integer sum)
    {
        int s = 0;
        for (int i=1; i<=k; i++)
            s += i;
        sum = new Integer(s);
    }

    public static void main(String[] args)
    {
        int n = some integer value;
        Integer total = new Integer(0);
        findSum(n, total);
        System.out.println("Sum is " + total);
    }
}
```

The findSum method does not work as intended with *any* value of its int parameter. When the program is run, the output is

```
Sum is 0
```

Which of the following modifications of the program will produce correct output? The lines that are changed are highlighted in boldface.

```
I public class SumTest
  {
      public static Integer findSum(int k)
      {
          int s = 0;
          for (int i=1; i<=k; i++)
              s += i;
          return new Integer(s);
      }

      public static void main(String[] args)
      {
          int n = some integer value;
          Integer total = findSum(n);
          System.out.println("Sum is " + total);
      }
  }
```

```
II public class SumTest
   {
       public static int findSum(int k)
       {
           int s = 0;
           for (int i=1; i<=k; i++)
               s += i;
           return s;
       }
```

```
            public static void main(String[] args)
            {
                int n = some integer value;
                int total = findSum(n);
                System.out.println("Sum is " + total);
            }
        }

III public class SumTest
    {
        public static void findSum(int k, int sum)
        {
            int sum = 0;
            for (int i=1; i<=k; i++)
                sum += i;
        }

        public static void main(String[] args)
        {
            int n = some integer value;
            int total = 0;
            findSum(n, total);
            System.out.println("Sum is " + total);
        }
    }
```

(A) none
(B) I only
(C) II only
(D) III only
(E) I and II only

25. A `Temperature` class that represents temperatures in degrees Celsius or Fahrenheit is implemented with these private instance variables:

```
private double myDegrees;
private String myScale;        //can be "C" or "F"
```

A programmer wants to expand the class so that two `Temperature` objects can be compared. Which of the following plans, if implemented without error, will correctly achieve this?

  I Add an accessor method `getDegrees`:

```
public double getDegrees()
{ return myDegrees; }
```

Temperature objects in a program can then be compared as follows:

```
Temperature t1 = new Temperature(< correct parameter list >);
Temperature t2 = new Temperature(< correct parameter list >);
if (t1.getDegrees() == t2.getDegrees())
    ...
else if (t1.getDegrees() <  t2.getDegrees())
    ...
else
    ...
```

  II Have `Temperature` implement the `Comparable` interface, and add a `compareTo` method to the class.

  III Override the `equals` and `hashCode` methods for the `Temperature` class. In addition, add a `lessThan` method to the class:

```
public boolean lessThan(Object o)
//returns true if this Temperature is lower than Temperature o,
//false otherwise
```

(A) I only
(B) II only
(C) III only
(D) II and III only
(E) I, II, and III

Answer Key

1. **B**	10. **D**	19. **C**
2. **B**	11. **A**	20. **C**
3. **C**	12. **B**	21. **B**
4. **C**	13. **D**	22. **A**
5. **D**	14. **E**	23. **E**
6. **E**	15. **A**	24. **E**
7. **D**	16. **C**	25. **D**
8. **A**	17. **E**	
9. **C**	18. **C**	

Answers Explained

1. **(B)** All the Math class methods are static methods, which means there is no instance of a Math object that calls the method. The method is invoked using the class name, Math, followed by the dot operator. Thus segment II is correct, and segment I is incorrect. Segment III has no meaning in the context of this question: There is no Power class defined that calculates a power in its constructor.

2. **(B)** The Math.sqrt method must be invoked on a primitive type double, which is the reason d.doubleValue() is needed. A correct segment must create a Double object using new, which eliminates segment III. Segment III is egregiously bad: It tries to cast Math to Double. But Math is not an object! Math.sqrt is a static method.

3. **(C)** The value −4.67 must be rounded to −5. Subtracting 0.5 gives a value of −5.17. Casting to int truncates the number (chops off the decimal part) and leaves a value of −5. None of the other choices produces −5. Choice A gives the absolute value of d: 4.67. Choice B is an incorrect use of Random. The parameter for nextInt should be an integer n, $n \geq 2$. The method then returns a random int k, where $0 \leq k < n$. Choice D is the way to round a *positive* real number to the nearest integer. In the actual case it produces −4. Choice E gives the absolute value of −5, namely 5.

4. **(C)** The statement double x = r.nextDouble() generates a random double in the range $0 \leq x < 1$. Suppose myProbDeath is 0.67, or 67%. Assuming that random doubles are uniformly distributed in the interval, one can expect x to be in the range $0 \leq x < 0.67$ 67% of the time. You can therefore simulate the probability of death by testing if x is between 0 and 0.67, that is, if x < 0.67. Thus x < myProbDeath is the desired condition for plant death, eliminating

choices A and B. Choices D and E fail because `(int)` `myProbDeath` truncates `myProbDeath` to 0. The test `x < 0` will always be false, and the test `x ==` `0` will only be true if the random number generator returned exactly 0, an extremely unlikely occurrence! Neither of these choices correctly simulates the probability of death.

Note: The statement

```
private static Random r = new Random();
```

creates a single random number generator object for all plants. This use of `static` will not be tested on the AP exam.

5. **(D)** The `Integer` class has no methods that can change the contents of `i`. However, `i` can be reassigned so that it refers to another object. This happens in both segments I and III. Segment II is wrong because `intValue` is an *accessor*—it cannot be used to change the value of object `i`.

6. **(E)** Choice E works because the actual type of `ob` is `Integer`, which is what the `compareTo` method is expecting when the calling object is an `Integer`. Choices C and D will cause a `ClassCastException` since the calling and parameter objects are incompatible types. The `compareTo` method will try erroneously to cast its parameter to the type of the object calling the method. Choice A *almost* works: It fails because the dot operator has higher precedence than casting, which means that `ob.compareTo` is parsed before `ob` is cast to `Integer`, generating a message that the `compareTo` method is not in class `Object`. Choice A can be fixed with an extra pair of parentheses:

```
if (((Integer) ob).compareTo(intOb) < 0) ...
```

Choice B causes the same error message as choice A: no `compareTo` method in class `Object`.

7. **(D)** Test I is correct because it's OK to compare primitive types (in this case `int` values) using `==`. Test III works because `k.toString()` and `m.toString()` are `String`s, which should be compared with `equals`. Test II is wrong because you can't invoke a method (in this case `equals`) on an `int`.

8. **(A)** An `Integer` cannot be cast to a `String`. Don't confuse this with

```
System.out.println(intObj.toString());    //outputs 9
```

Note that if the first line of the code fragment were

```
Integer intObj = new Integer(9);
```

then the error would be detected at compile time.

9. **(C)** Here are the memory slots:

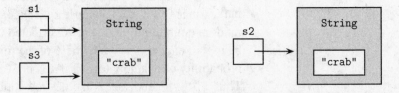

Statements II and III are true because the contents of s1 and s2 are the same, and the contents of s3 and s2 are the same. Statement I is false because s1 and s2 are not the same reference. Note that the expression s1 == s3 would be true since s1 and s3 *are* the same reference.

10. **(D)** Note that "TOMATO" precedes both "tomato" and "tom", since "T" precedes "t". Also, "tom" precedes "tomato" since the length of "tom" is less than the length of "tomato". Therefore each of the following is true:

```
strA.compareTo(strB) < 0
strA.compareTo(strC) < 0
strC.compareTo(strB) < 0
```

So

Choice A is T and F which evaluates to F
Choice B is F or F which evaluates to F
Choice C is F and T which evaluates to F
Choice D is T and T which evaluates to T
Choice E is T and F which evaluates to F

11. **(A)** x contains the index of the first occurrence of "m" in line, namely 2. (Remember that "S" is at index 0.) The method call line.substring(10,15) returns "silly", the substring starting at index 10 and extending though index 14. The method call line.substring(25,27) returns "st" (don't include the character at index 27!). The concatenation operator, +, joins these.

12. **(B)** The statement temp = s.substring(i, i+1) places in temp the string containing the character at position i. The for loop thus cycles through "conglomeration", starting at "c", and compares each single character string to "m". If that character precedes "m", a new String reference "w" is created, which consists of the current value of "w" concatenated with that character.

13. **(D)** The first character of the last name starts at the first character after the space. Thus startIndex for substring must be k+1. This eliminates expression I. Expression II takes all the characters from position k+1 to the end of the fullName string, which is correct. Expression III takes all the characters from position k+1 to position fullName.length()-1, which is also correct.

14. **(E)** Suppose s contains "cat". You want pigString = "at" + "c" + "ay". Now "at" is the substring of s starting at position 1 and ending at position s.length()-1. The correct substring call for this piece of the word is s.substring(1,s.length()), which eliminates choices A, C, and, D. (Recall that the first parameter is the starting position and the second parameter is one position past the last index of the substring.) The first letter of the word—"c" in the example—starts at position 0 and ends at position 0. The correct expression is s.substring(0,1), which eliminates choice B.

15. **(A)** Statement I is true whenever s2 occurs in s1. For example, if s1 = "catastrophe" and s2 = "cat", then getString returns "cat". Statement II will never happen. If s2 is not contained in s1, the indexOf call will return -1. Using a negative integer as the first parameter of substring will cause a StringIndexOutOfBoundsException. Statement III will be true whenever s1 equals s2.

16. **(C)** The `String temp` represents a single-character substring of `s`. The method examines each character in `s` and, if it is a nonblank, appends it to `str`, which is initially empty. Each assignment `str += temp` assigns a new reference to `str`. Thus `str` ends up as a copy of `s` but without the blanks. A reference to the final `str` object is returned. Choice A is correct in that `s` is left unchanged, but it is not the *best* characterization of what the method does. Choice B is not precise because an object parameter is never modified: changes, if any, are performed on a copy. Choices D and E are wrong because the method removes blanks.

17. **(E)** The `compareTo` method returns an `int`, so eliminate choices A and B. In the implementation of `compareTo`, the code segment that applies to the particular example is

```
if (this.getRow() < p.getRow() || ...
    return -1;
```

Since 2 < 4, the value −1 is returned.

18. **(C)** Expression III is true: the `compareTo` method is implemented to return 0 if two `Position` objects have the same row and column. Expression I is false because `object1 == object2` returns `true` only if `object1` and `object2` are the *same reference*. Expression II is tricky. One would like p1 and p3 to be equal since they have the same row and column values. This is not going to happen automatically, however. The `equals` method must explicitly be overridden for the `Position` class. If this hasn't been done, the default `equals` method, which is inherited from class `Object`, will return true only if p1 and p3 are the same reference, which is not true.

Level AB Only

19. **(C)** Here is a counterexample for statement III: a `hashCode` value of 32 corresponds to (3, 2) and (2, 12).

20. **(C)** Recall that primitive types and object references are passed by value. This means that copies are made of the actual arguments. Any changes that are made are made to the *copies*. The actual parameters remain unchanged. Thus in methods I and II the parameters will retain their original values and remain unswapped.

To illustrate, for example, why Method II fails, consider this piece of code that tests it:

```
public static void main(String[] args)
{
    int x = 8, y = 6;
    Integer xObject = new Integer(x);
    Integer yObject = new Integer(y);
    Swap(xObject, yObject);
    x = xObject.intValue();    //surprise! still has value 8
    y = yObject.intValue();    //surprise! still has value 6
    ...
}
```

Here are the memory slots before `Swap` is called:

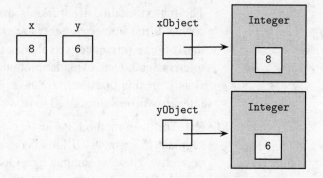

Here they are when Swap is invoked:

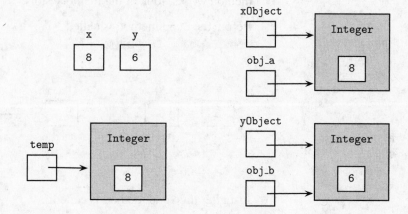

Just before exiting the Swap method:

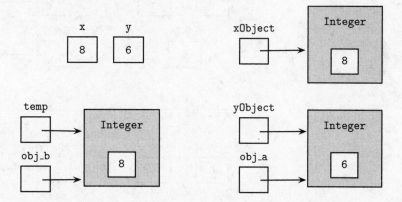

After exiting, xObject and yObject have retained their original values:

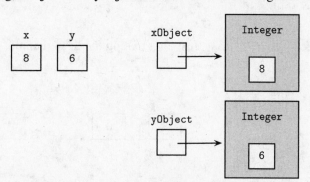

The reason method III works is that instead of the object references being changed, the object *contents* are changed. Thus, after exiting the method, the IntPair reference is as it was, but the first and second values have been interchanged. (See explanation to next question for diagrams of the memory slots.) In this question, IntPair is used as a wrapper class for a pair of integers whose values need to be swapped.

21. **(B)** The Swap method has just a single IntPair parameter, which eliminates segment I. Segment III fails because setFirst and setSecond are used incorrectly. These are mutator methods that change an IntPair object. What is desired is to return the (newly swapped) first and second values of the pair: accessor methods getFirst and getSecond do the trick. To see why this Swap method works, look at the memory slots.

Before the Swap method is called:

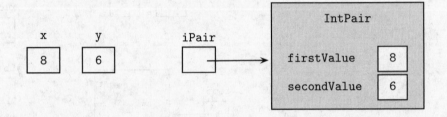

Just after the Swap method is called:

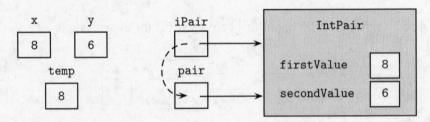

Just before exiting the Swap method:

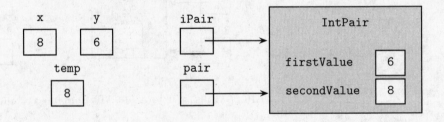

Just after exiting the Swap method:

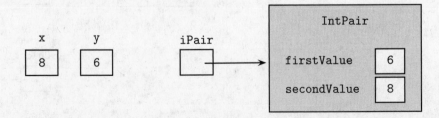

After the statements:

```
x = iPair.getFirst();
y = iPair.getSecond();
```

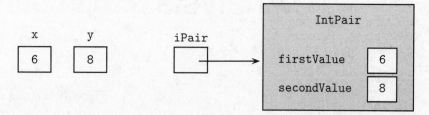

Notice that x and y have been swapped!

22. **(A)** The first statement of segment I compares last names. If these are different, the method returns the int value lastComp, which is negative if lastName precedes n.lastName, positive otherwise. If last names are the same, the method returns the int result of comparing first names. Segments II and III use incorrect algorithms for comparing names. Segment II would be correct if the else part were

```
return lastName.compareTo(n.lastName);
```

Segment III would be correct if the two return statements were interchanged.

Level AB Only

23. **(E)** The Comparable interface has just one method, compareTo. Choice E would be true if "equals" were replaced by "compareTo". Choice A is true. You know this because the Name class has no mutator methods. Thus Name objects can never be changed. Choice B is true: If a Name is initialized with null references, each of the methods will throw a NullPointerException. Choice C is true: hashCode must be redefined to satisfy the condition that two equal Name objects have the same hash code. Choice D is true: If the parameter is null, compareTo will throw a NullPointerException. If the parameter is incompatible with Name objects, its first statement will throw a ClassCastException.

24. **(E)** The point of the question is that you cannot change parameters that are passed by value. In the original program, the Integer total is passed to the findSum method with a value of 0. When the method is exited, total still refers to 0. The changes suggested in program III have the same error: If an int total is passed to the findSum method with a value of 0, when the method is exited, total will still have the value 0. One way to fix the problem is to have the findSum method return a reference to the correct sum. This is what happens in modified program I. Alternatively, have the findSum method return a simple int. Then, in main(), assign that int value to total. This is what happens in modified program II.

Level AB Only

25. **(D)** Besides the problem of comparing real numbers with ==, Method I won't work because it is meaningless to compare just degrees. For example, a temperature of 35° F is certainly not equal to 35° C. Method II is more efficient than Method III—one new method as opposed to three—but Method III, if implemented correctly, should work.

CHAPTER FIVE

Program Design and Analysis

Weeks of coding can save you hours of planning.
—Anonymous

Students of introductory computer science typically see themselves as programmers. They no sooner have a new programming project in their heads than they're at the computer, typing madly to get some code up and running. (Is this you?)

To succeed as a programmer, however, you have to combine the practical skills of a software engineer with the analytical mindset of a computer scientist. A software engineer oversees the life cycle of software development: initiation of the project, analysis of the specification, and design of the program, as well as implementation, testing, and maintenance of the final product. A computer scientist (among other things!) analyzes the implementation, correctness, and efficiency of algorithms. All these topics are tested on the APCS exam.

The Software Development Life Cycle

The Waterfall Model

The waterfall model of software development came about in the 1960s in order to bring structure and efficiency into the process of creating large programs.

Each step in the process flows into the next: The picture resembles a waterfall.

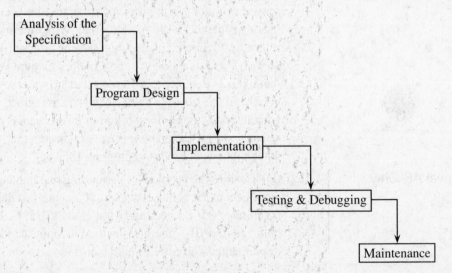

146

Even for a small-scale program these steps can save programming time and enhance the reliability of the final program.

Program Specification

The *specification* is a written description of the project. Typically it is based on a customer's requirements. The first step in writing a program is to analyze the specification, make sure you understand it, and clarify with the customer anything that is unclear.

Program Design

The design phase has two tasks.

- Identify the objects in the program, select the data structures that will implement them, and list the behaviors these objects exhibit. (This is discussed in more detail on p. 149.)

- Convert the specification into a detailed list of the tasks to be performed by the program.

Top-down Design

In a *top-down design*, the main tasks in the program are listed in order of execution. Each task is further broken down into subtasks, a process known as *stepwise refinement*. A good design provides a fairly detailed overall plan at a glance, without including the minutiae of Java code.

Example

A program must test the validity of a four-digit code number that a person will enter to be able to use a photocopy machine. Rules for validity are provided in the specification.

The major object in the program is a four-digit code number. Some of the operations needed to manipulate the object could be readNumber, testValidity, getSeparateDigits, and writeNumber. The data structure used to implement this object could be an instance variable of type int, or an instance variable of type String, or four instance variables of type int—one per digit, and so on.

The top-down design for the program that tests the validity of the number could be:

Get number
    Prompt user
    Read number   } Stepwise refinement of "Get number"

Check number
    Check for correct symbols (digits)
    Check range   } Stepwise refinement of "Check number"

Check validity
    Get separate digits
    Check if valid

Write message
    Write number
    State if valid

Algorithm

An *algorithm* is a precise step-by-step procedure that solves a problem or achieves a goal. Don't write any code for an algorithm until the steps are completely clear to you.

Program Implementation

Program implementation is the coding phase.

Top-down Implementation

In this strategy the methods in the top-down design are implemented and tested, one by one. A *driver method* is one whose sole purpose is to test another method.

Sometimes it makes more sense in the development of a program to test a calling method before testing the method it invokes. A *stub* is a dummy method that stands in for a method until the actual method has been written and tested. A stub typically has an output statement to show that it was called in the correct place, or it may return some reasonable values if necessary.

Testing and Debugging

Test Data

Not every possible input value can be tested, so a programmer should be diligent in selecting a representative set of *test data*. Typical values in each part of a domain of the program should be selected, as well as endpoint values and out-of-range values.

Example

A program must be written to insert a value into its correct position in this sorted list:

    2   5   9

Test data should include

- A value less than 2
- A value between 2 and 5
- A value between 5 and 9
- A value greater than 9
- 2, 5, and 9

Types of Errors (Bugs)

- A *compile-time error* occurs during compilation of the program. The compiler is unable to translate the program into bytecode and prints an appropriate error message. A *syntax error* is a compile-time error caused by violating the rules of the programming language. Examples include omitting semicolons or braces, using undeclared identifiers, using keywords inappropriately, having parameters that don't match in type and number, and invoking a method for an object whose class definition doesn't contain that method.

- A *run-time error* occurs during execution of the program. The Java run-time environment *throws an exception*, which means that it stops execution and prints an error message. Typical causes of run-time errors include attempting to divide by zero, using an array index that is out of bounds, attempting to open a file that cannot be found, and so on. An error that causes a program to run forever ("infinite loop") can also be regarded as a run-time error. (See also *Errors and Exceptions*, p. 15.)

- An *intent* or *logic error* is one that fails to carry out the specification of the program. The program compiles and runs but does not do the job. These are sometimes the hardest types of errors to fix.

Robustness

Always assume that any user of your program is not as smart as you are. You must therefore aim to write a *robust* program, namely one that

- Won't give inaccurate answers for some input data.
- Won't crash if the input data are invalid.
- Won't allow execution to proceed if invalid data are entered.

Examples of bad input data include out-of-range numbers, characters instead of numerical data, and a response of "maybe" when "yes" or "no" was asked for.

Note that bad input data that invalidates a computation won't be detected by Java. Your program should include code that catches the error, allows the error to be fixed, and allows program execution to resume.

Program Maintenance

Program maintenance involves upgrading the code as circumstances change. New features may be added. New programmers may come on board. To make their task easier, the original program must have clear and precise documentation for each method.

Object-Oriented Program Design

Object-oriented design uses an approach that blurs the lines of the waterfall model. Analysis of the problem, development of the design, and pieces of the implementation all overlap and influence one another.

Here are the steps in object-oriented design:

- Identify classes to be written.
- Identify behaviors (i.e., methods) for each class.
- Determine the relationships between classes.
- Write the interface (public method headers) for each class.
- Implement the methods.

Identifying Classes

Identify the objects in the program by picking out the nouns in the task description. Ignore pronouns and nouns that refer to the user. Select those nouns that are suitable as classes. Some of the other nouns may end up as attributes of the classes.

Identifying Behaviors

Find all verbs in the program description that help lead to the solution of the programming task. These will become the methods of the classes. Decide which class is responsible for each method.

Determining Relationships Between Classes

Inheritance Relationships

Look for classes with common behaviors. This will help identify superclasses. Recall the *is-a* relationship—if `object1` *is-a* `object2`, then `object2` is a candidate for a superclass.

Association Relationships

Association relationships are defined by the *has-a* relationship. For example, a `Nurse` *has-a* `Uniform`. Typically, if two classes are associated, one of them contains an instance variable whose type is the other class.

Note that a wrapper class always implements a *has-a* relationship with the object it wraps.

Implementing Classes

For each method list all of the other classes needed to implement that particular method. These classes are called *collaborators*. A class that has no collaborators is *independent*. Note that if class A is a collaborator of class B, class B is not necessarily a collaborator of class A. (This use of the word "collaborator" is a slight distortion of its ordinary English meaning!)

To implement the classes, often an incremental, *bottom-up* approach is used. This means that independent classes are fully implemented and tested before being incorporated into the overall project. These unrelated classes can be implemented by different programmers.

Next, classes that depend on just one other class are implemented and tested, and so on. This may lead to a working, bare bones version of the project. New features and enhancements will be added later.

Design flaws can be corrected at each stage of development. Remember, a design is never set in stone: it simply guides the implementation.

Here is an example of a program specification and an object-oriented approach to solving the problem.

Example

A program must create a teacher's grade book. The program should maintain a class list of students for any number of classes in the teacher's schedule. A menu should be provided that allows the teacher to

- Create a new class of students.
- Enter a set of scores for any class.
- Correct any data that's been entered.
- Display the record of any student.
- Calculate the final average and grade for all students in a class.
- Print a class list, with or without grades.
- Add a student, delete a student, or transfer a student to another class.
- Save all the data in a file.

Identifying Classes

The nouns in the task description are program, teacher, grade book, class list, student, schedule, menu, set of scores, data, record, average, grade, and file.

Eliminate each of the following:

program   (Always eliminate "program" when used in this context.)
teacher   (Eliminate, because he or she is the user.)
schedule   (This will be reflected in the name of the external file for each class, e.g., `apcs_period3.dat`.)
data, record (These are synonymous with student name, scores, grades, etc., and will be covered by these features.)
class   (This is synonymous with class list.)

The following seem to be excellent candidates for classes: `GradeBook`, `Student`, `ClassList`, and `FileHandler`. Other possibilities are `Menu` and `ScoreList`.

Relationships Between Classes

There are no inheritance relationships. There are many associations between objects, however. The `GradeBook` *has-a* `Menu`, the `ClassList` *has-a* `Student` (several, in fact!), a `Student` *has-a* `name`, `average`, `grade`, `list_of_scores`, etc. The programmer must decide whether to code these attributes as classes or primitive instance variables.

Identifying Behaviors

The verbs in the task description are: maintain <list>, provide <menu>, allow <user>, create <list>, enter <scores>, correct <data>, display <record>, calculate <average>, calculate <grade>, print <list>, add <student>, delete <student>, transfer <student>, and save <data>.

You must make some design decisions about which class is responsible for which behavior. For example, will a `ClassList` display the record of a single `Student`, or will a `Student` display his or her own record? Who will enter scores— the `GradeBook`, a `ClassList`, or a `Student`? There's no right or wrong answer. You may start it one way and reevaluate later on.

Decisions

Here are some preliminary decisions. The `GradeBook` will `provideMenu`. The menu selection will send execution to the relevant object.

The `ClassList` will maintain an updated list of each class. It will have these public methods: `addStudent`, `deleteStudent`, `transferStudent`, `createNewClass`, `printClassList`, `printScores`, and `updateList`.

Each `Student` will have complete personal and grade information. Public methods will include `setName`, `getName`, `enterScore`, `correctData`, `findAverage`, `getAverage`, `getGrade`, and `displayRecord`.

Saving and retrieving information is crucial to this program. The `FileHandler` will take care of `openFileForReading`, `openFileForWriting`, `closeFiles`, `loadClass`, and `saveClass`.

Program Analysis

Program Correctness

Testing that a program works does not prove that the program is correct. After all, you can hardly expect to test programs for every conceivable set of input data. Computer scientists have developed mathematical techniques to prove correctness in certain cases, but these are beyond the scope of the APCS course. Nevertheless, you are expected to be able to make assertions about the state of a program at various points during its execution.

Assertions

An *assertion* is a precise statement about a program at any given point. The idea is that if an assertion is proved to be true, then the program is working correctly at that point.

An informal step on the way to writing correct algorithms is to be able to make three kinds of assertions about your code.

Precondition

The *precondition* for any piece of code, whether it is a method, loop, or block, is a statement of what is true immediately before execution of that code.

Postcondition

The *postcondition* for a piece of code is a statement of what is true immediately after execution of that code.

Level AB Only

Loop invariant

A *loop invariant* applies only to a loop. It is a precise statement, in terms of the loop variables, of what is true before and after each iteration of the loop. It includes an assertion about the range of the loop variable. Informally, it describes how much of the loop's task has been completed at each stage.

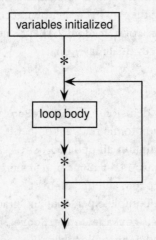

The asterisks show the points at which the loop invariant must be true:

- After initialization
- After each iteration
- After the final exit

Example

```
/* method to generate n! */
public static int factorial(int n)
//Precondition:  n ≥ 0
//Postcondition: n! has been returned
```

Level AB
(continued)

```
{
    int product = 1;
    int i = 0;
    while (i < n)
    {
        i++;
        product *= i;
    }
    return product;
}
```

After initialization	i = 0,	product = 1, i.e., 0!
After first pass	i = 1,	product = 1, i.e., 1!
After second pass	i = 2,	product = 2, i.e., 2!
...		
After kth pass	i = k,	product = k!

The loop invariant for the while loop is

```
product = i!, 0 ≤ i ≤ n
```

Here is an alternative method body for this method. (Assume the same method header, comment, and pre- and postconditions.)

```
{
    int product = 1;
    for (int i=1; i<=n; i++)
        product *= i;
    return product;
}
```

The loop invariant for the for loop is

```
product = (i-1)!, 1 ≤ i ≤ n+1
```

Here (i-1)! (rather than i!) is correct because i is incremented at the *end* of each iteration of the loop. Also, n+1 is needed in the second part of the loop invariant because i has a value of n+1 after the final exit from the loop. Remember, the invariant must also be true after the final exit.

Efficiency

An efficient algorithm is one that is economical in the use of

- CPU time. This refers to the number of machine operations required to carry out the algorithm (arithmetic operations, comparisons, data movements, etc.).
- Memory. This refers to the number and complexity of the variables used.

Some factors that affect run-time efficiency include unnecessary tests, excessive movement of data elements, and redundant computations, especially in loops.

Always aim for early detection of output conditions: your sorting algorithm should halt when the list is sorted; your search should stop if the key element has been found.

In discussing efficiency of an algorithm, we refer to the *best case*, *worst case*, and *average case*. The best case is a configuration of the data that causes the algorithm to run in the least possible amount of time. The worst case is a configuration that leads to the greatest possible run time. Typical configurations (i.e., not spe-. cially chosen data) give the average case. It is possible that best, worst, and average cases don't differ much in their run times.

For example, suppose that a list of distinct random numbers must be searched for a given key value. The algorithm used is a sequential search starting at the beginning of the list. In the best case, the key will be found in the first position examined. In the worst case, it will be in the last position or not in the list at all. On average, the key will be somewhere in the middle of the list.

Big-O Notation

Big-O notation provides a quantitative way of describing the run time or space efficiency of an algorithm. This method is independent of both the programming language and the computer used.

Level AB Only

Let n be the number of elements to be processed. For a given algorithm, express the number of comparisons, exchanges, data movements, and primitive operations as a function of n, $T(n)$. (Primitive operations involve simple built-in types and take one unit of time, for example, adding two `ints`, multiplying two `doubles`, assigning an `int`, and performing simple tests.) The type of function that you get for $T(n)$ determines the "order" of the algorithm. For example, if $T(n)$ is a linear function of n, we say the algorithm is $O(n)$ ("order n"). The idea is that for large values of n, the run time will be proportional to n. Here is a list of the most common cases.

Function Type for $T(n)$	Big-O Description
constant	$O(1)$
logarithmic	$O(\log n)$
linear	$O(n)$
quadratic	$O(n^2)$
cubic	$O(n^3)$
exponential	$O(2^n)$

Example 1

An algorithm that searches an unordered list of n elements for the largest value could need n comparisons and n reassignments to a variable `max`. Thus $T(n) \approx 2n$, which is linear, so the search algorithm is $O(n)$.

Example 2

An algorithm that prints out the last five elements of a long list stored as an array takes the same amount of time irrespective of the length of the list. Thus $T(n) = 5$, a constant, and the algorithm is $O(1)$.

Example 3

Algorithm 1 executes with $T(n) = 3n^2 - 5n + 10$ and Algorithm 2 has $T(n) = \frac{1}{2}n^2 - 50n + 100$. Both of these are quadratic, and the algorithms are therefore $O(n^2)$. Constants, low-order terms, and coefficients of the highest order term are ignored in assessing big-O run times.

NOTE

1. Big-O notation is only meaningful for n large. When n is large, there is some value n above which an $O(n^2)$ algorithm will always take longer than an $O(n)$ algorithm, or an $O(n)$ algorithm will take longer than an $O(\log n)$ algorithm, and so on.

Level AB
(continued)

2. The following table shows approximately how many computer operations could be expected given n and the big-O description of the algorithm. For example, an $O(n^2)$ algorithm performed on 100 elements would require on the order of $100^2 = 10^4$ computer operations, whereas an $O(\log_2 n)$ algorithm would require approximately seven operations.

n	$O(\log_2 n)$	$O(n)$	$O(n^2)$	$O(2^n)$
16	4	16	256	2^{16}
100	7	100	10^4	2^{100}
1000	10	1000	10^6	2^{1000}

3. Notice that one can solve only very small problems with an algorithm that has exponential behavior. At the other extreme, a logarithmic algorithm is very efficient.

Multiple-Choice Questions on Program Design and Analysis

1. A program is to be written that reads in a five-digit identification number. The specification does not state whether zero can be entered as a first digit. The programmer should
   (A) Write the code to accept zero as a first digit since zero is a valid digit.
   (B) Write the code to reject zero as a first digit since five-digit integers do not start with zero.
   (C) Eliminate zero as a possibility for any of the digits.
   (D) Treat the identification number as a four-digit number if the user enters a number starting with zero.
   (E) Check with the writer of the specification whether zero is acceptable as a first digit.

2. Refer to the following three program descriptions:

   I   Test whether there exists at least one three-digit integer whose value equals the sum of the squares of its digits.
   II Read in a three-digit code number and check if it is valid according to some given formula.
   III License plates consist of three digits and three capital letters. Read in a license plate, and check if there are any repeated characters.

   For which of the preceding program descriptions would a `ThreeDigitNumber` class be suitable?
   (A) I only
   (B) II only
   (C) III only
   (D) I and II only
   (E) I, II, and III

3. Top-down programming is illustrated by which of the following?
   (A) Writing a program from top to bottom in Java
   (B) Writing an essay describing how the program will work, without including any Java code
   (C) Using driver programs to test all methods in the order that they're called in the program
   (D) Writing and testing the lowest level methods first and then combining them to form appropriate abstract operations
   (E) Writing the program in terms of the operations to be performed and then refining these operations by adding more detail

4. Which of the following should influence your choice of a particular algorithm?

   I The run time of the algorithm
   II The memory requirements of the algorithm
   III The ease with which the logic of the algorithm can be understood

   (A) I only
   (B) III only
   (C) I and III only
   (D) I and II only
   (E) I, II, and III

5. A list of numbers is stored in a sorted array. It is required that the list be maintained in sorted order. This requirement leads to inefficient execution for which of the following processes?

   I Summing the five smallest numbers in the list
   II Finding the maximum value in the list
   III Inserting and deleting numbers

   (A) I only
   (B) III only
   (C) II and III only
   (D) I and III only
   (E) I, II, and III

6. Which of the following is *not* necessarily a feature of a robust program?
   (A) Does not allow execution to proceed with invalid data
   (B) Uses algorithms that give correct answers for extreme data values
   (C) Will run on any computer without modification
   (D) Will not allow division by zero
   (E) Will anticipate the types of errors that users of the program may make

7. A certain freight company charges its customers for shipping overseas according to this scale:

   $80 per ton for a weight of 10 tons or less
   $40 per ton for each additional ton over 10 tons but
      not exceeding 25 tons
   $30 per ton for each additional ton over 25 tons

   For example, to ship a weight of 12 tons will cost 10(80) + 2(40) = $880. To ship 26 tons will cost 10(80) + 15(40) + 1(30) = $1430.
      A method takes as parameter an integer that represents a valid shipping weight and outputs the charge for the shipment. Which of the following is the smallest set of input values for shipping weights that will adequately test this method?
   (A) 10, 25
   (B) 5, 15, 30
   (C) 5, 10, 15, 25, 30
   (D) 0, 5, 10, 15, 25, 30
   (E) 5, 10, 15, 20, 25, 30

8. A code segment calculates the mean of values stored in integers n1, n2, n3, and n4 and stores the result in average, which is of type double. What kind of error is caused with this statement?

   ```
   double average = n1 + n2 + n3 + n4 /(double) 4;
   ```

   (A) Logic
   (B) Run-time
   (C) Overflow
   (D) Syntax
   (E) Type mismatch

9. A program evaluates binary arithmetic expressions that are read from an input file. All of the operands are integers, and the only operators are +, -, *, and /. In writing the program, the programmer forgot to include a test that checks whether the right-hand operand in a division expression equals zero. If this oversight causes an error, when will the error be detected?
   (A) At compile time
   (B) While editing the program
   (C) As soon as the data from the input file is read
   (D) During evaluation of the expressions
   (E) When at least one incorrect value for the expressions is output

10. Which best describes the precondition of a method? It is an assertion that
   (A) Describes precisely the conditions that must be true at the time the method is called.
   (B) Initializes the parameters of the method.
   (C) Describes the effect of the method on its postcondition.
   (D) Explains what the method does.
   (E) States what the initial values of the local variables in the method must be.

11. Consider the following code fragment:

```
//Precondition:  a1, a2, a3 contain 3 distinct integers
//Postcondition: max contains the largest of a1,a2,a3

//first set max equal to larger of a1 and a2
if (a1 > a2)
    max = a1;
else
    max=a2;
//set max equal to larger of max and a3
if (max < a3)
    max = a3;
```

Which of the following initial setups for a1, a2, a3 will cause (1) the least number of computer operations (best case) and (2) the greatest number of computer operations (worst case) for this algorithm?

(A) (1) largest value in a1 or a2   (2) largest value in a3
(B) (1) largest value in a2 or a3   (2) largest value in a1
(C) (1) smallest value in a1   (2) largest value in a2
(D) (1) largest value in a2   (2) smallest value in a3
(E) (1) smallest value in a1 or a2   (2) largest value in a3

Refer to the following code segment for Questions 12 and 13.

```
//Compute the mean of integers 1 .. N.
//N is an integer ≥ 1 and has been initialized
int k = 1;
double mean, sum=1.0;
while (k < N)
{
    < loop body >
}
mean = sum/N;
```

12. What is the precondition for the while loop?
(A) $k \geq N$, sum = 1.0
(B) sum = 1 + 2 + 3 + ... + k
(C) $k < N$, sum = 1.0
(D) $N \geq 1$, k = 1, sum = 1.0
(E) mean = sum/N

13. What should replace < *loop body* > so that the following is the loop invariant for the `while` loop:

```
sum = 1 + 2 + ... + k, 1 ≤ k ≤ N
```

   (A) `sum += k;`
       `k++;`

   (B) `k++;`
       `sum += k;`

   (C) `sum++;`
       `k += sum;`

   (D) `k += sum;`
       `sum++;`

   (E) `sum += k;`

Questions 14 and 15 refer to the Fibonacci sequence described here. The sequence of Fibonacci numbers is 1, 1, 2, 3, 5, 8, 13, 21, ... The first two Fibonacci numbers are each 1. Each subsequent number is obtained by adding the previous two. Consider this method:

```
public static int fib(int n)
//Precondition:  n ≥ 1
//Postcondition: the nth Fibonacci number has been returned
{
    int prev=1, next=1, sum=1;
    for (int i=3; i<=n; i++)
    {
        sum = next + prev;
        prev = next;
        next = sum;
    }
    return sum;
}
```

14. Which of the following is a correct assertion about the loop variable `i`?
   (A) `1 ≤ i ≤ n`
   (B) `0 ≤ i ≤ n`
   (C) `3 ≤ i ≤ n`
   (D) `3 ≤ i ≤ n+1`
   (E) `3 < i < n+1`

15. Which of the following is a correct loop invariant for the `for` loop, assuming the correct bounds for the loop variable `i`?
   (A) `sum =` `i`th Fibonacci number
   (B) `sum =` `(i+1)`th Fibonacci number
   (C) `sum =` `(i-1)`th Fibonacci number
   (D) `sum =` `(prev-1)`th Fibonacci number
   (E) `sum =` `(next+1)`th Fibonacci number

16. An efficient algorithm that must delete the last two elements in a long list of n elements stored as an array is
    (A) $O(n)$
    (B) $O(n^2)$
    (C) $O(1)$
    (D) $O(2)$
    (E) $O(\log n)$

17. An algorithm to remove all negative values from a list of n integers sequentially examines each element in the array. When a negative value is found, each element is moved down one position in the list. The algorithm is
    (A) $O(1)$
    (B) $O(\log n)$
    (C) $O(n)$
    (D) $O(n^2)$
    (E) $O(n^3)$

18. A certain algorithm is $O(\log_2 n)$. Which of the following will be closest to the number of computer operations required if the algorithm manipulates 1000 elements?
    (A) 10
    (B) 100
    (C) 1000
    (D) 10^6
    (E) 10^9

19. A certain algorithm examines a list of n random integers and outputs the number of times the value 5 appears in the list. Using big-O notation, this algorithm is
    (A) $O(1)$
    (B) $O(5)$
    (C) $O(n)$
    (D) $O(n^2)$
    (E) $O(\log n)$

Refer to the following method for Questions 20 and 21.

```
//Precondition: a and b are initialized integers
public static int mystery(int a, int b)
{
    int total=0, count=1;
    while (count <= b)
    {
        total += a;
        count++;
    }
    return total;
}
```

20. What is the postcondition for method `mystery`?
    (A) $\text{total} = a + b$
    (B) $\text{total} = a^b$
    (C) $\text{total} = b^a$
    (D) $\text{total} = a * b$
    (E) $\text{total} = a/b$

Level AB Only

21. Which is a loop invariant for the `while` loop?
    (A) `total = (count-1)*a`, $0 \le \text{count} \le b$
    (B) `total = count*a`, $1 \le \text{count} \le b$
    (C) `total = (count-1)*a`, $1 \le \text{count} \le b$
    (D) `total = count*a`, $1 \le \text{count} \le b+1$
    (E) `total = (count-1)*a`, $1 \le \text{count} \le b+1$

22. A program is to be written that prints an invoice for a small store. A copy of the invoice will be given to the customer and will display

    - A list of items purchased.
    - The quantity, unit price, and total price for each item.
    - The amount due.

    Three candidate classes for this program are `Invoice`, `Item`, and `ItemList`, where an `Item` is a single item purchased and `ItemList` is the list of all items purchased. Which class is a reasonable choice to be responsible for the `amountDue` method, which returns the amount the customer must pay?

    I `Item`

    II `ItemList`

    III `Invoice`

    (A) I only
    (B) III only
    (C) I and II only
    (D) II and III only
    (E) I, II, and III

23. Which is a *false* statement about classes in object-oriented program design?
    (A) If a class C1 has an instance variable whose type is another class, C2, then C1 *has-a* C2.
    (B) If a class C1 is associated with another class, C2, then C1 depends on C2 for its implementation.
    (C) If classes C1 and C2 are related such that C1 *is-a* C2, then C2 *has-a* C1.
    (D) If class C1 is independent, then none of its methods will have parameters that are objects of other classes.
    (E) Classes that have common methods do not necessarily define an inheritance relationship.

24. A Java program maintains a large database of vehicles and parts for a car dealership. Some of the classes in the program are Vehicle, Car, Truck, Tire, SteeringWheel, AirBag, and Circle. The declarations below show the relationships between classes. Which is a poor choice?

    (A)
```
public class Vehicle
{   ...
    private Tire[] tires;
    private SteeringWheel sw;
    ...
}
```

    (B)
```
public class Tire extends Circle
{   ...
    //inherits methods that compute circumference
    //and center point
}
```

    (C)
```
public class Car extends Vehicle
{   ...
    //inherits private Tire[] tires from Vehicle class
    //inherits private SteeringWheel sw from Vehicle class
    ...
}
```

    (D)
```
public class Tire
{   ...
    private String rating;      //speed rating of tire
    private Circle boundary;
}
```

    (E)
```
public class SteeringWheel
{   ...
    private AirBag ab;  //AirBag is stored in SteeringWheel
    private Circle boundary;
```

25. A Java programmer has completed a preliminary design for a large program. The programmer has developed a list of classes, determined the methods for each class, established the relationships between classes, and written an interface for each class. Which class(es) should be implemented first?
    (A) Any superclasses
    (B) Any subclasses
    (C) All collaborator classes (classes that will be used to implement other classes)
    (D) The class that represents the dominant object in the program
    (E) All independent classes (classes that have no references to other classes)

Use the program description below for Questions 26–28.

A program is to be written that simulates bumper cars in a video game. The cars move on a square grid, and are located on grid points (x, y), where x and y are integers between -20 and 20. A bumper car moves in a random direction, either left, right, up, or down. If it reaches a boundary (i.e., x or y is ± 20), then it reverses direction. If it is about to collide with another bumper car, it reverses direction. Your program should be able to add bumper cars and run the simulation. One step of the simulation allows each car in the grid to move. After a bumper car has reversed direction twice, its turn is over and the next car gets to move.

26. To identify classes in the program, the nouns in the specification are listed:

    program, bumper car, grid, grid point, integer, direction, boundary, simulation

    How many nouns in the list should immediately be discarded because they are unsuitable as classes for the program?
    (A) 0
    (B) 1
    (C) 2
    (D) 3
    (E) 4

A programmer decides to include the following classes in the program. Refer to them for Questions 27 and 28.

- Simulation will run the simulation.

- Display will show the state of the game.

- BumperCar will know its identification number, position in the grid, and current direction when moving.

- GridPoint will be a position in the grid, represented by two integer fields, x_coord and y_coord.

- Grid will keep track of all bumper cars in the game, the number of cars, and their positions in the grid. It will update the grid each time a car moves. It will be implemented with a two-dimensional array of BumperCar.

27. Which operation should not be the responsibility of the GridPoint class?

    (A)   isEmpty   returns false if grid point contains a BumperCar, true otherwise

    (B)   atBoundary   returns true if x or y coordinate = ± 20, false otherwise

    (C)   left   if not at left boundary, change grid point to 1 unit left of current point

    (D)   up   if not at top of grid, change grid point to 1 unit above current point

    (E)   get_x   return x-coordinate of this point

28. Which method is not suitable for the BumperCar class?

    (A) public boolean atBoundary()
```
        //Returns true if BumperCar at boundary, false otherwise
```

    (B) public void selectRandomDirection()
```
        //Select random direction (up, down, left, or right)
        //at start of turn
```

    (C) public void reverseDirection()
```
        //Move to grid position that is in direction opposite to
        //current direction
```

    (D) public void move()
```
        //Take turn to move. Stop move after two changes
        //of direction
```

    (E) public void update()
```
        //Modify Grid to reflect new position after each stage
        //of move
```

Answer Key

1. **E**	11. **A**	21. **E**
2. **D**	12. **D**	22. **D**
3. **E**	13. **B**	23. **C**
4. **E**	14. **D**	24. **B**
5. **B**	15. **C**	25. **E**
6. **C**	16. **C**	26. **C**
7. **C**	17. **D**	27. **A**
8. **A**	18. **A**	28. **E**
9. **D**	19. **C**	
10. **A**	20. **D**	

Answers Explained

1. (**E**) A programmer should never make unilateral decisions about a program specification. When in doubt, check with the person who wrote the specification.

2. (**D**) In I and II a three-digit number is the object being manipulated. For III, however, the object is a license plate, which suggests a `LicensePlate` class.

3. (**E**) Top-down programming consists of listing the methods for the main object and then using stepwise refinement to break each method into a list of subtasks. Eliminate choices A, C, and D: Top-down programming refers to the design and planning stage and does not involve any actual writing of code. Choice B is closer to the mark, but "top-down" implies a list of operations, not an essay describing the methods.

4. (**E**) All three considerations are valid when choosing an algorithm. III is especially important if your code will be part of a larger project created by several programmers. Yet even if you are the sole writer of a piece of software, be aware that your code may one day need to be modified by others.

5. (**B**) A process that causes excessive data movement is inefficient. Inserting an element into its correct (sorted) position involves moving elements to create a slot for this element. In the worst case, the new element must be inserted into the first slot, which involves moving every element up one slot. Similarly, deleting an element involves moving elements down a slot to close the "gap." In the worst case, where the first element is deleted, all elements in the array will need to be moved. Summing the five smallest elements in the list means summing the first five elements. This requires no testing of elements and no excessive data movement, so it is efficient. Finding the maximum value in a sorted list is very fast—just select the element at the appropriate end of the list.

6. (**C**) "Robustness" implies the ability to handle all data input by the user and to give correct answers even for extreme values of data. A program that is not robust may well run on another computer without modification, and a robust program may need modification before it can run on another computer.

7. (**C**) Eliminate choice D because 0 is an invalid weight, and you may infer from the method description that invalid data have already been screened out. Eliminate choice E because it tests two values in the range 10–25. (This is not wrong, but choice C is better.) Eliminate choice A since it tests only the endpoint values. Eliminate B because it tests *no* endpoint values.

8. (**A**) The statement is syntactically correct, but as written it will not find the mean of the integers. The bug is therefore an intent or logic error. To execute as intended, the statement needs parentheses:

    ```
    double average = (n1 + n2 + n3 + n4)/(double) 4;
    ```

9. (**D**) The error that occurs is a run-time error caused by an attempt to divide by zero (`ArithmeticException`). Don't be fooled by choice C. Simply reading an expression 8/0 from the input file won't cause the error. Note that if the operands were of type `double`, the correct answer would be E. In this case, dividing by zero does not cause an exception; it gives an answer of ∞ (`Infinity`). Only on inspecting the output would it be clear that something was wrong.

10. (**A**) A precondition does not concern itself with the action of the method, the local variables, the algorithm, or the postcondition. Nor does it initialize the parameters. It simply asserts what must be true directly before execution of the method.

11. (**A**) The best case causes the fewest computer operations, and the worst case leads to the maximum number of operations. In the given algorithm, the initial test `if (a1 > a2)` and the assignment to `max` will occur irrespective of which value is the largest. The second test, `if (max < a3)`, will also always occur. The final statement, `max = a3`, will occur only if the largest value is in `a3`; thus this represents the worst case. So the best case must have the biggest value in `a1` or `a2`.

12. (**D**) The precondition is an assertion about the variables in the loop just before the loop is executed. Variables `N`, `k`, and `sum` have all been initialized to the values shown in choice D. Choice C is wrong because `k` may equal `N`. Choice A is wrong because `k` may be less than `N`. Choice E is wrong because `mean` is not defined until the loop has been exited. Choice B is wrong because it omits the assertions about `N` and `k`.

Level AB Only

13. (**B**) Note that A and B are the only reasonable choices. Choice E results in an infinite loop, and choices C and D increment `sum` by 1 instead of by `k`. For choice A, 1 is added to `sum` in the first pass through the loop, which is wrong; 2 should be added. Thus `k` should be incremented before updating `sum`. Note that for choice B after the first pass `k = 2` and `sum = 1 + 2`. After the second pass, `k = 3` and `sum = 1 + 2 + 3`. Also note that `k`'s initial value is 1 and final value on exiting the loop for the last time is `N`, as in the given loop invariant.

Level AB
(continued)

14. **(D)** Eliminate choices A, B, and E since i is initialized to 3 in the for loop. Choice C is wrong because the value of i after final exit from the loop is n+1.

15. **(C)** Eliminate choices D and E, since the loop invariant should include the loop variable in its statement. Notice that the first exit from the for loop has i = 4 and sum = 2, which is the third Fibonacci number. In general, at each exit from the loop, sum is equal to the (i-1)th Fibonacci number.

16. **(C)** Deleting a constant number of elements at the end of an array is independent of n, and therefore $O(1)$. Don't let yourself be caught by choice D: There is no such thing as $O(2)$!

17. **(D)** In the worst case, every element in the array is negative. Thus the number of data moves will be $(n-1) + (n-2) + \cdots + 2 + 1 = n(n-1)/2$. This is a quadratic function, so the algorithm is $O(n^2)$. Alternatively, you can see that each of the n elements must be examined, and in the average case it is moved about $n/2$ places. So again you get $O(n^2)$. Note that unless you are specifically asked, you should not quote the order of the best case—always assume worst case or average case behavior. Here in the best case there are no negative values in the list and so no data movements. The algorithm is $O(n)$.

18. **(A)** If $n = 1000$, $\log_2 n \approx 10$ since $2^{10} \approx 1000$.

19. **(C)** The entire list of n integers must be examined once; thus the algorithm is $O(n)$.

20. **(D)** a is being added to total b times, which means that at the end of execution total = a*b.

Level AB Only

21. **(E)** Since count is incremented at the end of the loop, total = (count-1)*a, not count*a. Thus eliminate choices B and D. Choice A is wrong because count is initialized to 1, not 0. Note that after the final exit from the loop, count has value b+1, which eliminates choice C.

22. **(D)** It makes sense for an Item to be responsible for its name, unit price, quantity, and total price. It is *not* reasonable for it to be responsible for other Items. Since an ItemList, however, will contain information for all the Items purchased, it is reasonable to have it also compute the total amountDue. It makes just as much sense to give an Invoice the responsibility for displaying information for the items purchased, as well as providing a final total, amountDue.

23. **(C)** The *is-a* relationship defines inheritance while the *has-a* relationship defines association. These types of relationship are mutually exclusive. For example, a graduate student *is-a* student. It doesn't make sense to say a student *has-a* graduate student!

24. **(B)** Even though it's convenient for a Tire object to inherit Circle methods, an inheritance relationship between a Tire and a Circle is incorrect: it is false to say that a Tire *is-a* Circle. A Tire is a car part while a Circle is a geometric shape. Notice that there is an *association* relationship between a Tire and a Circle: a Tire *has-a* Circle as its boundary.

25. **(E)** Independent classes do not have relationships with other classes and can therefore be more easily coded and tested.

26. **(C)** The word "program" is never included when it's used in this context. The word "integer" describes the type of coordinates x and y, and has no further use in the specification. While words like "direction", " boundary", and "simulation" may later be removed from consideration as classes, it is not unreasonable to keep them as candidates while you ponder the design.

27. **(A)** A `GridPoint` object knows only its x and y coordinates. It has no information about whether a `BumperCar` is at that point. Notice that operations in all of the other choices depend on the x and y coordinates of a `GridPoint` object. An `isEmpty` method should be the responsibility of the `Grid` class that keeps track of the status of each position in the grid.

28. **(E)** A `BumperCar` is responsible for itself—keeping track of its own position, selecting an initial direction, making a move, and reversing direction. It is not, however, responsible for maintaining and updating the grid. That should be done by the `Grid` class.

CHAPTER SIX
Arrays and Array Lists

Should array indices start at 0 or 1?
My compromise of 0.5 was rejected,
without, I thought, proper consideration.
—S. Kelly-Bootle

One-Dimensional Arrays

An array is a data structure used to implement a list object, where the elements in the list are of the same type; for example, a class list of 25 test scores, a membership list of 100 names, or a store inventory of 500 items.

For an array of N elements in Java, index values ("subscripts") go from 0 to $N-1$. Individual elements are accessed as follows: If arr is the name of the array, the elements are arr[0], arr[1], ..., arr[N-1]. If a negative subscript is used, or a subscript k where $k \geq N$, an ArrayIndexOutOfBoundsException is thrown.

Initialization

In Java, an array is an object; therefore, the keyword new must be used in its creation. The size of an array remains fixed once it has been created. As with String objects, however, an array reference may be reassigned to a new array of a different size.

Example

All of the following are equivalent. Each creates an array of 25 double values and assigns the reference data to this array.

1. `double[] data = new double[25];`

2. `double data[] = new double[25];`

3. `double data[];`
    `data = new double[25];`

A subsequent statement like

`data = new double[40];`

reassigns data to a new array of length 40. The memory allocated for the previous data array is recycled by Java's automatic garbage collection system.

When arrays are declared, the elements are automatically initialized to zero for the primitive numeric data types (int and double), to false for boolean variables, or to null for object references.

It is possible to declare several arrays in a single statement. For example,

```
int[] intList1, intList2;    //declares intList1 and intList2 to
                             //contain int values
int[] arr1 = new int[15], arr2 = new int[30];  //reserves 15 slots
                                               //for arr1, 30 for arr2
```

Initializer List

Small arrays whose values are known can be declared with an *initializer list*. For example, instead of writing

```
int[] coins = new int[4];
coins[0] = 1;
coins[1] = 5;
coins[2] = 10;
coins[3] = 25;
```

you can write

```
int[] coins = {1, 5, 10, 25};
```

This construction is the one case where new is not required to create an array.

Length of Array

A Java array has a final public instance variable (i.e., a constant) length, which can be accessed when you need the number of elements in the array. For example,

```
String[] names = new String[25];
< code to initialize names >

//loop to process all names in array
for (int i=0; i<names.length; i++)
    < process names >
```

NOTE
1. The array subscripts go from 0 to names.length-1; therefore, the test on i in the for loop must be strictly less than names.length.
2. length is not a method and therefore is not followed by parentheses. Contrast this with String objects, where length *is* a method and *must* be followed by parentheses. For example,

```
String s = "Confusing syntax!";
int size = s.length();    //assigns 17 to size
```

Arrays as Parameters

Since arrays are treated as objects, passing an array as a parameter means passing its object reference. No copy is made of the array. *Thus the elements of the actual array can be accessed—and modified.*

Example 1

Array elements accessed but not modified:

```
//Return index of smallest element in array arr of integers
public static int findMin(int[] arr)
{
    int min = arr[0];
    int minIndex = 0;
    for (int i=1; i<arr.length; i++)
        if (arr[i] < min)              //found a smaller element
            minIndex = i;
    return minIndex;
}
```

To call this method (in the same class that it's defined):

```
int[] array;
< code to initialize array >
int min = findMin(array);
```

NOTE
1. There are no square brackets for the argument of the method call.
2. An alternative header for the method is

```
public static int findMin(int arr[])
```

Example 2

Array elements modified:

```
//Add 3 to each element of array b
public static void changeArray(int[] b)
{
    for (int i=0; i<b.length; i++)
        b[i] += 3;
}
```

To call this method (in the same class):

```
int[] list = {1, 2, 3, 4};
changeArray(list);
System.out.print("The changed list is ");
for (int i=0; i<list.length; i++)
    System.out.print(list[i] + " ");
```

The output produced is

```
The changed list is 4 5 6 7
```

Look at the memory slots to see how this happens:

Before the method call:

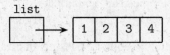

At the start of the method call:

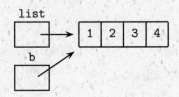

Just before exiting the method:

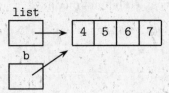

After exiting the method:

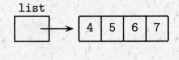

Example 3

Contrast the `changeArray` method with the following attempt to modify one array element:

```
//Add 3 to an element
public static void changeElement(int n)
{
    n += 3;
}
```

Here is some code that invokes this method:

```
int[] list = {1, 2, 3, 4};
System.out.print("Original array: ");
for (int i=0; i<list.length; i++)
    System.out.print(list[i] + " ");
changeElement(list[0]);
System.out.print("\nModified array: ");
for (int i=0; i<list.length; i++)
    System.out.print(list[i] + " ");
```

Contrary to the programmer's expectation, the output is

```
Original array: 1 2 3 4
Modified array: 1 2 3 4
```

A look at the memory slots shows why the list remains unchanged.

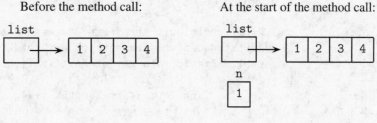

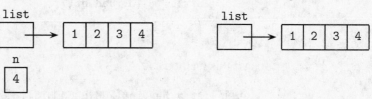

The point of this is that primitive types—including single array elements of type `int` or `double`—are passed by value. A copy is made of the actual parameter, and the copy is erased on exiting the method.

Example 4

```
//Swap arr[i] and arr[j] in array arr
public static void swap(int[] arr, int i, int j)
{
    int temp = arr[i];
    arr[i] = arr[j];
    arr[j] = temp;
}
```

To call the swap method:

```
int[] list = {1, 2, 3, 4};
swap(list, 0, 3);
System.out.print("The changed list is: ");
for (int i=0; i<list.length; i++)
    System.out.print(list[i] + " ");
```

The output shows that the program worked as intended:

```
The changed list is: 4 2 3 1
```

NOTE   Don't make the same mistake as in Example 3. The following will *not* work:

```
public static void swap(int i, int j)
{
    int temp = i;
    i = j;
    j = temp;
}
    ...
int[] list = {1, 2, 3, 4};
swap(list[0], list[3]);      //oops! list won't change
```

Example 5

Here are two different approaches for reading numbers into an array.
Approach 1

```
//Precondition:  array arr declared with NUM_ELEMENTS slots
//Postcondition: elements of arr read from the keyboard
public static void getIntegers(int[] arr)
{
    for (int i=0; i<arr.length; i++)
    {
        System.out.println("Enter integer: ");
        arr[i] = IO.readInt();          //read user input
    }
}
```

To call this method:

```
int[] list = new int[NUM_ELEMENTS];
getIntegers(list);
```

NOTE   The method getIntegers modifies the array that is passed to it.

Approach 2
Let the return type of the method be an array (actually, a reference to an array).

```
//Precondition:  array undefined
//Postcondition: returns array containing NUM_ELEMENTS integers
//               read from the keyboard
public static int[] getIntegers()
{
    int[] arr = new int[NUM_ELEMENTS];
    for (int i=0; i<arr.length; i++)
```

```
    {
        System.out.println("Enter integer: ");
        arr[i] = IO.readInt();          //read user input
    }
    return arr;
}
```

To call this method:

```
int[] list = getIntegers();
```

NOTE The following sequence of calling statements would not be wrong:

```
int[] list = new int[NUM_ELEMENTS];
list = getIntegers();
```

It is, however, unnecessary since the getIntegers method creates a new array. It's not wrong to use new twice for the same array, but it's inefficient.

Array Variables in a Class

Consider a simple Deck class in which a deck of cards is represented by the integers 0 to 51.

```
public class Deck
{
    private int[] myDeck;
    private static Random r;     //random number generator
    public final static int NUMCARDS = 52;

    //constructor
    public Deck()
    {
        myDeck = new int[NUMCARDS];

        for (int i=0; i<NUMCARDS; i++)
            myDeck[i] = i;
    }

    //write contents of Deck
    public void writeDeck()
    {
        for (int i=0; i<NUMCARDS; i++)
            System.out.print( myDeck[i] + " ");
        System.out.println();
    }

    //initialize random number generator
    public static void initializeRandom()
    { r = new Random(); }

    //swap arr[i] and arr[j] in array arr
    private void swap(int[] arr, int i, int j)
    {
        int temp = arr[i];
        arr[i] = arr[j];
        arr[j] = temp;
    }
```

```
                        //shuffle Deck
                        public void shuffle()
                        {
                            //generate a random permutation by picking a random
                            //card from those remaining and putting it in the
                            //next slot, starting from the right
                            int index;
                            for (int i=NUMCARDS-1; i>0; i--)
                            {
                                index = r.nextInt(i+1);     //int from 0 to i
                                swap(myDeck, i, index);
                            }
                        }
                    }
```

Here is a simple program that uses the Deck class:

```
    public class DeckMain
    {
        public static void main(String args[])
        {
            Deck d = new Deck();

            Deck.initializeRandom();
            d.shuffle();
            d.writeDeck();
        }
    }
```

NOTE 1. There is no evidence of the array that holds the deck of cards—myDeck is a private instance variable and is therefore invisible to clients of the Deck class.
2. The random number generator should be initialized just once in a program that shuffles decks of cards. This is why it is declared as a *static* variable. (Note: static variables will not be tested on the AP exam.)

Array of Class Objects

Suppose a large card tournament needs to keep track of many decks. The code to do this could be implemented with an array of Deck:

```
    public class ManyDecks
    {
        private Deck[] allDecks;
        private final int NUMDECKS = 500;

        //constructor
        public ManyDecks()
        {
            allDecks = new Deck[NUMDECKS];
            for (int i=0; i<NUMDECKS; i++)
                allDecks[i] = new Deck();
        }
```

```
                    //shuffle all the decks
                    public void shuffleAll()
                    {
                        //seed the random number generator for shuffling
                        Deck.initializeRandom();
                        //shuffle
                        for (int i=0; i<NUMDECKS; i++)
                            allDecks[i].shuffle();
                    }

                    //write contents of all the decks
                    public void printDecks()
                    {
                        for (int i=0; i<NUMDECKS; i++)
                            allDecks[i].writeDeck();
                    }
                }
```

NOTE   The statement

```
        allDecks = new Deck[NUMDECKS];
```

creates an array, allDecks, of 500 Deck objects. The default initialization for these Deck objects is null. In order to initialize them with actual decks, the Deck constructor must be called for each array element. This is achieved with the for loop of the ManyDecks constructor.

Analyzing Array Algorithms

Example 1

Level AB Only

(a) Discuss the efficiency of the countNegs method below. What are the best and worst case configurations of the data?

(b) What is the big-O run time?

(c) What is the loop invariant of the for loop?

```
    //Precondition:  arr[0],...,arr[arr.length-1] contain integers
    //Postcondition: number of negative values in arr has been returned
    public static int countNegs(int[] arr)
    {
        int count = 0;
        for (int i=0; i<arr.length; i++)
            if (arr[i] < 0)
                count++;
        return count;
    }
```

Solution:

(a) This algorithm sequentially examines each element in the array. In the best case, there are no negative elements, and count++ is never executed. In the worst case, all the elements are negative, and count++ is executed in each pass of the for loop.

Level AB Only

(b) The run time is $O(n)$, since each element in the list is examined.

Level AB
(continued)

(c) The loop invariant for the `for` loop is

count = number of negative values in `arr[0]`, ..., `arr[i-1]`,   and

   $0 \le i \le$ `arr.length`

Loop invariants for array algorithms can be nicely illustrated with a diagram showing a snapshot of what is happening. Each rectangle represents a portion of array `arr`. The labels on top of the rectangle are array indexes for elements at the beginning and end of each portion.

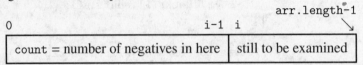

0	i-1 i	arr.length-1
count = number of negatives in here		still to be examined

Example 2

The code fragment below inserts a value, `num`, into its correct position in a sorted array of integers.

Level AB Only

(a) Discuss the efficiency of the algorithm.

(b) What is the big-O run time of the algorithm?

(c) What is the loop invariant of the `while` loop?

```
//Precondition:  arr[0],...,arr[n-1] contain integers sorted in
//               increasing order. n < arr.length
//Postcondition: num has been inserted in its correct position
{
    //find insertion point
    int i = 0;
    while (i < n && num > arr[i])
        i++;
    //if necessary, move elements arr[i]...arr[n-1] up 1 slot
    for (int j=n; j>=i+1; j--)
        arr[j] = arr[j-1];
    //insert num in i-th slot and update n
    arr[i] = num;
    n++;
}
```

Solution:

(a) In the best case, `num` is greater than all the elements in the array: Because it gets inserted at the end of the list, no elements must be moved to create a slot for it. The worst case has `num` less than all the elements in the array. In this case, `num` must be inserted in the first slot, `arr[0]`, and every element in the array must be moved up one position to create a slot.

NOTE

This algorithm illustrates a disadvantage of arrays: insertion and deletion of an element in an ordered list is inefficient, since, in the worst case, it may involve moving all the elements in the list.

Level AB Only

(b) Insertion or deletion of a single element in an ordered list is $O(n)$. Note that if n elements must be inserted (or deleted) with this algorithm, the algorithm becomes $O(n^2)$.

(c) The loop invariant for the `while` loop is

`num > arr[0]`, `num > arr[1]`, ..., `num > arr[i-1]`, where $0 \le i \le n$

Level AB
(continued)

Here is the diagram that illustrates this loop invariant:

0   i-1 i   n-1

num > all elements in here	still to be examined

Array Lists

This section contains the material that Level A students need to know. Level AB students should also see Chapter 11 for a fuller discussion of ArrayList and the other container classes.

The ArrayList
Class

The ArrayList class is part of java.util, one of Java's standard packages. An ArrayList provides an alternative way of storing a list of objects and has the following advantages over an array:

- The length of an ArrayList shrinks and grows as needed in a program, whereas an array has a fixed length that is set when the array is created.

- In an ArrayList L, the last slot is always L.size()-1, whereas in a partially filled array, you, the programmer, must keep track of the last slot currently in use.

- For an ArrayList, you can do insertion or deletion with just a single statement. Any shifting of elements is handled automatically. In an array, however, insertion or deletion requires you to write the code that shifts the elements.

Then why use an array? Well, an array has these advantages over an ArrayList:

- It is easy to store numbers (primitive types like int or double) in an array. Since an ArrayList must contain *objects*, numbers must be placed in wrapper classes (like Integer or Double) before they can be inserted in an ArrayList.

- It is easy to retrieve numbers from an array. If intList is an array of int, intList[k] automatically has type int. An element retrieved from an ArrayList is of type Object and must be cast to its actual type. If the elements are numbers (Integer or Double), the methods intValue() or doubleValue() must then be invoked before the numerical values can be used.

- It is more efficient to use an array for a list of numbers because there is no wrapping, unwrapping, or casting of the elements involved.

The Methods of
ArrayList

You should know the following methods:

```
ArrayList()
```

Constructs an empty list.

```
int size()
```

Returns the number of elements in the list.

```
boolean add(Object obj)
```

Appends obj to the end of the list. Always returns true.

```
Object get(int index)
```

Returns the element at the specified index in the list.

```
Object set(int index, Object element)
```

Replaces item at specified index in the list with specified element. Returns the element that was previously at index.

```
void add(int index, Object element)
```

Inserts element at specified index in list. If the insertion is not at the end of the list, shifts the element currently at that position and all elements following it one unit to the right (i.e., adds 1 to their indexes). Adjusts size of list.

```
Object remove(int index)
```

Removes and returns the element at the specified index in the list. Shifts all elements following that element one unit to the left (i.e., subtracts 1 from their indexes). Adjusts size of list.

NOTE   Each method above that has an index parameter—add, get, remove, and set—throws an IndexOutOfBoundsException if index is out of range. For get, remove, and set, index is out of range if

```
index < 0 || index >= size()
```

For add, however, it is OK to add an element at the end of the list. Therefore index is out of range if

```
index < 0 || index > size()
```

Using ArrayList

Example 1

```
//create an ArrayList containing 0 1 4 9
ArrayList list = new ArrayList();
for (int i=0; i<4; i++)
    list.add(new Integer(i*i));
Integer intOb = (Integer) list.get(2);  //assigns 4 to intOb
                                        //leaves a unchanged
Object x = list.set(3, new Integer(5));  //list is 0 1 4 5
                                        //x contains 9
x = list.remove(2);          //list is 0 1 5
                        //x contains 4
list.add(1, new Integer(7));   //list is 0 7 1 5
list.add(2, new Integer(8));    //list is 0 7 8 1 5
```

NOTE   If the line

```
Integer intOb = (Integer) list.get(2);
```

is replaced with

```
Integer intOb = list.get(2);
```

a compile-time error will occur. This is because the types on the left and right sides are now incompatible: The left side, `intOb`, is an `Integer`, while the right side, `list.get(2)`, is an `Object`. To avoid this problem, an explicit cast to `Integer` is required on the right side.

Example 2

```
//traversing an ArrayList
//print the elements of list, one per line
for (int i=0; i<list.size(); i++)
    System.out.println(list.get(i));
```

NOTE   The objects `list.get(i)` do not need to be cast to their actual types before printing. The above code assumes that each object in the list has a `toString` method that enables it to be printed in a meaningful way.

Example 3

```
/* Precondition:  ArrayList list contains Integer values
 *                sorted in increasing order
 * Postcondition: value inserted in its correct position in list */
public void insert(ArrayList list, Integer value)
{
    int index = 0;
    //find insertion point
    while (index < list.size() &&
            value.compareTo(list.get(index)) > 0)
        index++;
    //insert value
    list.add(index, value);
}
```

NOTE   Suppose `value` is larger than all the elements in `list`. Then the `insert` method will throw an `IndexOutOfBoundsException` if the first part of the test is omitted, namely `index<list.size()`.

Two-Dimensional Arrays

Level AB Only

A two-dimensional array (matrix) is often the data structure of choice for objects like board games, tables of values, theater seats, and mazes.

Look at the following 3×4 matrix:

```
2  6  8  7
1  5  4  0
9  3  2  8
```

Level AB
(continued)

If `mat` is the matrix variable, the row subscripts go from 0 to 2 and the column subscripts go from 0 to 3. The element `mat[1][2]` is 4, whereas `mat[0][2]` and `mat[2][3]` are both 8. As with one-dimensional arrays, if the subscripts are out of range an `ArrayIndexOutOfBoundsException` is thrown.

Declarations

Each of the following declares a two-dimensional array:

```
int[][] table;     //table can reference a 2-d array of integers
                   //table is currently a null reference
double[][] mat = new double[3][4];  //mat references a 3 × 4
                                    //array of real numbers.
                                    //Each element has value 0.0
String[][] strs = new String[2][5]; //strs references a 2 × 5
                                    //array of String objects.
                                    //Each element is null
```

An *initializer list* can be used to specify a two-dimensional array:

```
int[][] mat = { {3, 4, 5},          //row 0
                {6, 7, 8} };        //row 1
```

This defines a 2 × 3 *rectangular* array (i.e., one in which each row has the same number of elements).

The initializer list is a list of lists in which each inside list represents a row of the matrix. The quantity `mat.length` represents the number of rows. For any given row k, the quantity `mat[k].length` represents the number of elements in that row, namely the number of columns. (Java allows a variable number of elements in each row. Since these "jagged arrays" are not part of the AP Java subset, you can assume that `mat[k].length` is the same for all rows k of the matrix, i.e., that the matrix is rectangular.)

Processing a Two-Dimensional Array

Example 1

Find the sum of all elements in matrix `mat`.

```
//Precondition: mat is initialized with integer values
int sum = 0;
for (int r=0; r<mat.length; r++)
    for (int c=0; c<mat[r].length; c++)
        sum += mat[r][c];
```

NOTE

1. `mat[r][c]` represents the rth row and the cth column.
2. Rows are numbered from 0 to `mat.length-1` and columns are numbered from 0 to `mat[r].length-1`. Any index that is outside these bounds will generate an `ArrayIndexOutOfBoundsException`.

Example 2

Add 10 to each element in row 2 of matrix `mat`.

```
for (int c=0; c<mat[2].length; c++)
    mat[2][c] += 10;
```

Level AB   *NOTE*
(continued)

In the `for` loop you can use `c<mat[k].length`, where $0 \le k <$ `mat.length`, since each row has the same number of elements.

Example 3

The major and minor diagonals of a square matrix are defined as follows:

Major diagonal

Minor diagonal

You can process the diagonals as follows:

```
int[][] mat = new int[SIZE][SIZE];  //SIZE is a constant int value

for (int i=0; i<SIZE; i++)
    Process mat[i][i];              //major diagonal
        OR
    Process mat[i][SIZE-i-1];       //minor diagonal
```

Two-Dimensional
Array as Parameter

Example 1

Here is a method that counts the number of negative values in a matrix.

```
//Precondition:  mat initialized with integers
//Postcondition: returns count of negative values in mat
public static int countNegs(int[][] mat)
{
    int count = 0;
    for (int r=0; r<mat.length; r++)
        for (int c=0; c<mat[r].length; c++)
            if (mat[r][c] < 0)
                count++;
    return count;
}
```

A method in the same class can invoke this method with a statement such as

```
int negs = countNegs(mat);
```

Example 2

As with one-dimensional arrays there are two approaches for reading elements into a matrix.

Approach 1

```
//Precondition:  rows × cols matrix mat declared
//Postcondition: elements of mat read from keyboard
public static void getMatrix(int[][] mat, int rows, int cols)
{
    for (int r=0; r<rows; r++)
    {
        System.out.println("Enter row:");
        for (int c=0; c<cols; c++)
            mat[r][c] = IO.readInt();      //read user input
    }
}
```

To call this method:

```
//prompt for number of rows and columns
int rows = IO.readInt();      //read user input
int cols = IO.readInt();      //read user input
int[][] mat = new int[rows][cols];
getMatrix(mat, rows, cols);
```

Approach 2

Let the return type of the method be a two-dimensional array.

```
//Precondition:  matrix undefined. Number of rows and columns known
//Postcondition: returns matrix containing rows × cols integers
//               read from the keyboard
public static int[][] getMatrix(int rows, int cols)
{
    int[][] mat = new int[rows][cols];
    for (int r=0; r<rows; r++)
    {
        System.out.println("Enter row:");
        for (int c=0; c<cols; c++)
            mat[r][c] = IO.readInt();      //read user input
    }
    return mat;
}
```

To call this method:

```
//prompt for number of rows and columns
int rows = IO.readInt();      //read user input
int cols = IO.readInt();      //read user input
int[][] mat = getMatrix(rows, cols);
```

Multiple-Choice Questions on Arrays and Array Lists

1. Which of the following correctly initializes an array arr to contain four elements each with value 0?

   I int[] arr = {0, 0, 0, 0};

   II int[] arr = new int[4];

   III int[] arr = new int[4];
   ```
       for (int i=0; i<arr.length; i++)
           arr[i] = 0;
   ```

   (A) I only
   (B) III only
   (C) I and III only
   (D) II and III only
   (E) I, II, and III

2. The following program segment is intended to find the index of the first negative integer in arr[0] ... arr[N-1], where arr is an array of N integers.

   ```
   int i = 0;
   while (arr[i] >= 0)
   {
       i++;
   }
   location = i;
   ```

   This segment will work as intended
   (A) Always.
   (B) Never.
   (C) Whenever arr contains at least one negative integer.
   (D) Whenever arr contains at least one nonnegative integer.
   (E) Whenever arr contains no negative integers.

3. Refer to the following code segment. You may assume that arr is an array of integers.

   ```
   int sum = arr[0], i = 0;
   while (i < arr.length)
   {
       i++;
       sum += arr[i];
   }
   ```

   Which of the following will be the result of executing the segment?
   (A) Sum of arr[0], arr[1], ..., arr[arr.length-1] will be stored in sum.
   (B) Sum of arr[1], arr[2], ..., arr[arr.length-1] will be stored in sum.
   (C) Sum of arr[0], arr[1], ..., arr[arr.length] will be stored in sum.
   (D) An infinite loop will occur.
   (E) A run-time error will occur.

4. The following code fragment is intended to find the smallest value in
`arr[0] ... arr[n-1]`.

```
//Precondition:  arr[0]...arr[n-1] initialized with integers.
//               arr is an array, arr.length = n
//Postcondition: min = smallest value in arr[0]...arr[n-1]
int min = arr[0];
int i = 1;
while (i < n)
{
    i++;
    if (arr[i] < min)
        min = arr[i];
}
```

This code is incorrect. For the segment to work as intended, which of the following modifications could be made?

I Change the line

```
int i = 1;
```

to

```
int i = 0;
```

Make no other changes.

II Change the body of the `while` loop to

```
{
    if (arr[i] < min)
        min = arr[i];
    i++;
}
```

Make no other changes.

III Change the test for the `while` loop as follows:

```
while (i <= n)
```

Make no other changes.

(A) I only
(B) II only
(C) III only
(D) I and II only
(E) I, II, and III

Questions 5 and 6 refer to the following code segment. You may assume that array arr1 contains elements arr1[0], arr1[1], ..., arr1[N-1], where N = arr1.length.

```
int count = 0;
for (int i=0; i<N; i++)
    if (arr1[i] != 0)
    {
        arr1[count] = arr1[i];
        count++;
    }
int[] arr2 = new int[count];
for (int i=0; i<count; i++)
    arr2[i] = arr1[i];
```

5. If array arr1 initially contains the elements 0, 6, 0, 4, 0, 0, 2 in this order, what will arr2 contain after execution of the code segment?
    (A) 6, 4, 2
    (B) 0, 0, 0, 0, 6, 4, 2
    (C) 6, 4, 2, 4, 0, 0, 2
    (D) 0, 6, 0, 4, 0, 0, 2
    (E) 6, 4, 2, 0, 0, 0, 0

Level AB Only

6. The algorithm has run time
    (A) $O(N^2)$
    (B) $O(N)$
    (C) $O(1)$
    (D) $O(\log N)$
    (E) $O(N \log N)$

7. Consider this program segment:

```
for (int i=2; i<=k; i++)
    if (arr[i] < someValue)
        System.out.print("SMALL");
```

What is the maximum number of times that SMALL can be printed?
    (A) 0
    (B) 1
    (C) k-1
    (D) k-2
    (E) k

8. Refer to the following class:

```
public class Tester
{
    private int[] testArray = {3, 4, 5};

    //add 1 to n
    public void increment(int n)
    { n++; }

    public void testMethod()
    {
        for (int i=0; i<testArray.length; i++)
        {
            increment(testArray[i]);
            System.out.print(testArray[i] + " ");
        }
    }
}
```

What output will be produced by invoking testMethod for a Tester object?

(A) 3 4 5
(B) 4 5 6
(C) 5 6 7
(D) 0 0 0
(E) No output will be produced. An ArrayIndexOutOfBoundsException will be thrown.

9. What will be output from the following code segment, assuming it is in the same class as the doSomething method?

```
int[] arr = {1, 2, 3, 4};
doSomething(arr);
System.out.print(arr[1] + " ");
System.out.print(arr[3]);
    ...
public void doSomething(int[] list)
{
    int[] b = list;
    for (int i=0; i<b.length; i++)
        b[i] = i;
}
```

(A) 0 0
(B) 2 4
(C) 1 3
(D) 0 2
(E) 0 3

10. Consider the getData method below:

```
public void getData(int[] list)
{
    System.out.println("Enter 10 integers ");
    list = new int[10];
    for (int i=0; i< 10; i++)
        list[i] = IO.readInt();      //read user input
}
```

A method in the same class calls getData as follows:

```
int[] array = new int[10];
getData(array);
for (int i=0; i< 10; i++)
    System.out.print(array[i] + " ");
```

What will be the effect of running this code?

(A) The ten integers entered by the user will be output.

(B) Ten zeroes will be output.

(C) Ten distinct integers, different from those entered by the user, will be output.

(D) A NullPointerException will be thrown.

(E) An ArrayIndexOutOfBoundsException will be thrown.

11. The following code segment reverses the elements of arr[first] ...arr[last].

```
int k=first, j=last;
while (k < j)
{
    swap(arr, k, j);    //interchanges arr[k] and arr[j]
    k++;
    j--;
}
```

Which of the following diagrams represents the loop invariant for the while loop? (Each rectangle represents a segment of array arr. The labels above the rectangles represent the indexes of array elements at the beginning and end of each segment.)

(A)

first		k k+1		j-1 j		last
swapped		original elements		swapped		

(B)

first		k k+1		j-1 j		last
original elements		swapped		original elements		

(C)

first		k-1 k		j j+1		last
swapped		original elements		swapped		

(D)

first		k-1 k		j j+1		last
original elements		swapped		original elements		

(E)

first		k-1 k		j-1 j		last
swapped		original elements		swapped		

12. The following algorithm sets min equal to the smallest value in arr[0] ...arr[n-1]:

```
min = arr[0];
i = 1;
while (i < n)
{
    if (arr[i] < min)
        min = arr[i];
    i++;
}
```

The loop invariant for the while loop is
(A) min is smallest value in arr[0] ...arr[i], 1 ≤ i ≤ n
(B) min is smallest value in arr[0] ...arr[i-1], 1 ≤ i ≤ n-1
(C) min is smallest value in arr[0] ...arr[i], 1 ≤ i ≤ n-1
(D) min is smallest value in arr[0] ...arr[i-1], 1 < i ≤ n
(E) min is smallest value in arr[0] ...arr[i-1], 1 ≤ i ≤ n

Refer to the following class for Questions 13–15.

```
public class Address
{
    private String myName;
    private String myStreet;
    private String myCity;
    private String myState;
    private String myZip;

    //constructors
        ...

    //accessors
    public String getName()
    { return myName; }
    public String getStreet()
    { return myStreet; }
    public String getCity()
    { return myCity; }
    public String getState()
    { return myState; }
    public String getZip()
    { return myZip; }
}
```

A client method has this declaration:

```
Address[] list = new Address[100];
```

13. Here is a code segment to generate a list of *names only*.

```
for (int i=0; i<list.length; i++)
    < line of code >
```

Which is a correct < *line of code* >?
(A) `System.out.println(Address[i].getName());`
(B) `System.out.println(Address.list[i].getName());`
(C) `System.out.println(list[i].Address.getName());`
(D) `System.out.println(list[i].getName());`
(E) `System.out.println(list.getName[i]);`

14. The following code segment is to print out a list of addresses:

```
for (int i=0; i<list.length; i++)
{
    < more code >
}
```

Which is a correct replacement for < *more code* >?

I   `System.out.println(list[i].getName());`
    `System.out.println(list[i].getStreet());`
    `System.out.print(list[i].getCity() + ", ");`
    `System.out.print(list[i].getState() + " ");`
    `System.out.println(list[i].getZip());`

II `System.out.println(list[i]);`

III `System.out.println(list[i].Address);`

(A) I only
(B) II only
(C) III only
(D) I and II only
(E) I, II, and III

Refer to the following Student class for Questions 15 and 16:

```
public class Student
{
    private int idNum;
    private double gpa;
    private Address myAddress;

    //constructors
        ...

    //accessors
    public Address getAddress()
    { return myAddress; }
    public int getIdNum()
    { return idNum; }
    public double getGpa()
    { return gpa; }
}
```

15. A client method has this declaration:

```
Student[] allStudents = new Student[NUM_STUDS];   //NUM_STUDS is
                                                  //an int constant
```

Which is a correct code segment to generate a list of Student names only?

```
I Address a;
  for (int i=0; i<NUM_STUDS; i++)
  {
      a = allStudents[i].getAddress();
      System.out.println(a.getName());
  }

II for (int i=0; i<NUM_STUDS; i++)
       System.out.println(allStudents[i].getAddress().getName());

III for (int i=0; i<NUM_STUDS; i++)
        System.out.println(allStudents[i].getName());
```

(A) I only
(B) II only
(C) III only
(D) I and II only
(E) I, II, and III

16. Here is a method that locates the Student with the highest idNum:

```
//Precondition:  array s of Student is initialized
//Postcondition: Student with highest idNum has been returned
public static Student locate(Student[] s)
{
    < method body >
}
```

Which of the following could replace < *method body* > so that the method works as intended?

```
I  int max = s[0].getIdNum();
   for(int i=1; i<s.length; i++)
       if(s[i].getIdNum() > max)
       {
           max = s[i].getIdNum();
           return s[i];
       }
   return s[0];
```

```
II  int index = 0;
    int max = s[0].getIdNum();
    for(int i=1; i<s.length; i++)
        if(s[i].getIdNum() > max)
        {
            max= s[i].getIdNum();
            index = i;
        }
    return s[index];
```

```
III  int max = 0;
     for(int i=1; i<s.length; i++)
         if(s[i].getIdNum() > s[max].getIdNum())
             max = i;
     return s[max];
```

(A) I only
(B) II only
(C) III only
(D) I and III only
(E) II and III only

Questions 17–19 refer to the `Ticket` and `Transaction` classes below.

```java
public class Ticket
{
    private String myRow;
    private int mySeat;
    private double myPrice;

    //constructor
    public Ticket(String row, int seat, double price)
    {
        myRow = row;
        mySeat = seat;
        myPrice = price;
    }

    //accessors getRow(), getSeat(), and getPrice()
        ...
}

public class Transaction
{
    private int myNumTickets;
    private Ticket[] tickList;

    //constructor
    public Transaction(int numTicks)
    {
        myNumTickets = numTicks;
        tickList = new Ticket[numTicks];
        String row;
        int seat;
        double price;
        for (int i=0; i<numTicks; i++)
        {
            < read user input for row, seat, and price >
                ...

            < more code >
        }
    }

    public double totalPaid()
    //returns total amount paid for this transaction
    {
        double total = 0.0;
        < code to calculate amount >
        return total;
    }
}
```

17. Which of the following correctly replaces < *more code* > in the Transaction constructor to initialize the tickList array?

    (A) `tickList[i] = new Ticket(getRow(), getSeat(), getPrice());`

    (B) `tickList[i] = new Ticket(row, seat, price);`

    (C) `tickList[i] = new tickList(getRow(), getSeat(), getPrice());`

    (D) `tickList[i] = new tickList(row, seat, price);`

    (E) `tickList[i] = new tickList(numTicks);`

18. Which represents correct < *code to calculate amount* > in the totalPaid method?

    (A)
    ```
    for (int i=0; i<myNumTickets; i++)
        total += tickList[i].myPrice;
    ```

    (B)
    ```
    for (int i=0; i<myNumTickets; i++)
        total += tickList.getPrice[i];
    ```

    (C)
    ```
    for (int i=0; i<myNumTickets; i++)
        total += tickList[i].getPrice();
    ```

    (D)
    ```
    Transaction T;
    for (int i=0; i<T.numTicks; i++)
        total += T.tickList[i].getPrice();
    ```

    (E)
    ```
    Transaction T;
    for (int i=0; i<T.numTicks; i++)
        total += T.tickList[i].myPrice;
    ```

19. Suppose it is necessary to keep a list of all ticket transactions. A suitable declaration would be

    (A) `Transaction[] listOfSales = new Transaction[NUMSALES];`

    (B) `Transaction[] listOfSales = new Ticket[NUMSALES];`

    (C) `Ticket[] listOfSales = new Transaction[NUMSALES];`

    (D) `Ticket[] listOfSales = new Ticket[NUMSALES];`

    (E) `Transaction[] Ticket = new listOfSales[NUMSALES];`

20. A class of 30 students rated their computer science teacher on a scale of 1 to 10 (1 means awful and 10 means outstanding). The responses array is a 30-element integer array of the student responses. An 11-element array freq will count the number of occurrences of each response. For example, freq[6] will count the number of students who responded 6. The quantity freq[0] will not be used.

Here is a program that counts the students' responses and outputs the results.

```
public class StudentEvaluations
{
    public static void main(String args[])
    {
        int[] responses = {6,6,7,8,10,1,5,4,6,7,
                            5,4,3,4,4,9,8,6,7,10,
                            6,7,8,8,9,6,7,8,9,2};
        int[] freq = new int[11];
        for (int i=0; i<responses.length; i++)
            freq[responses[i]]++;
        //output results
        System.out.print("rating\tfrequency\n");
        for (int rating=1; rating<freq.length; rating++)
            System.out.print(rating + "\t" +
                freq[rating] + "\n");
    }
}
```

Suppose the last entry in the initializer list for the responses array was incorrectly typed as 12 instead of 2. What would be the result of running the program?

(A) A rating of 12 would be listed with a frequency of 1 in the output table.

(B) A rating of 1 would be listed with a frequency of 12 in the output table.

(C) An ArrayIndexOutOfBoundsException would be thrown.

(D) A StringIndexOutOfBoundsException would be thrown.

(E) A NullPointerException would be thrown.

21. Consider this class:

```
public class Book
{
    private String myTitle;
    private String myAuthor;

    //constructor
    public Book(String title, String author)
    {
        myTitle = title;
        myAuthor = author;
    }

    //display title, author
    public void display()
    { implementation code }
        . . .

}
```

A program has this declaration:

```
Book[] bookList = new Book[SOME_NUMBER];
```

Suppose bookList is initialized so that each Book in the list has a title and author. Which of the following will display the title and author of each book in bookList?

(A) ```
for (int i=0; i<bookList[i].length; i++)
    bookList[i].display();
```

(B) ```
for (int i=0; i<bookList.length; i++)
    bookList[i].display();
```

(C) ```
for (int i=0; i<bookList.length; i++)
    bookList.display();
```

(D) ```
for (int i=0; i<bookList.length; i++)
    Book.display();
```

(E) ```
for (int i=0; i<bookList.length; i++)
    Book[i].display();
```
```

22. Consider this class:

```
public class BingoCard
{
    private int[] myCard;

    /* default constructor: creates BingoCard with
     * 20 random digits in the range 1 - 90 */
    public BingoCard()
    { implementation code }

    /* display BingoCard */
    public void display()
    { implementation code }
        ...
}
```

A program that simulates a bingo game declares an array of `BingoCard` with NUMPLAYERS elements, where each element represents the card of a different player. Here is a code segment that creates all the bingo cards in the game and then displays them:

```
< declare array of BingoCard >
for (int i=0; i<NUMPLAYERS; i++)
    < construct and display each BingoCard >
```

Which of the following is a correct replacement for

(1) *< declare array of* `BingoCard` *>*,   and

(2) *< construct and display each* `BingoCard` *>*?

(A) (1) `int[] BingoCard = new BingoCard[NUMPLAYERS];`

    (2) `myCard[i] = new BingoCard();`
`myCard[i].display();`

(B) (1) `BingoCard[] players = new BingoCard[NUMPLAYERS];`

    (2) `players[i] = new BingoCard();`
`for (int k=0; k<20; k++)`
`myCard[k].display()`

(C) (1) `BingoCard[] players = new BingoCard[NUMPLAYERS];`

    (2) `BingoCard[i] = new BingoCard();`
`BingoCard[i].display();`

(D) (1) `BingoCard[] players = new BingoCard[NUMPLAYERS];`

    (2) `players[i] = new BingoCard();`
`players[i].display();`

(E) (1) `int[] players = new BingoCard[NUMPLAYERS];`

    (2) `players[i] = new BingoCard();`
`players[i].display();`

23. Let `list` be an `ArrayList` containing these `Integer` elements:

    2 5 7 6 0 1

    Which of the following statements would *not* cause an error to occur? Assume that each statement applies to the given list, independent of the other statements.
    (A) `Object ob = list.get(6);`
    (B) `Integer intOb = list.get(2);`
    (C) `list.add(6, new Integer(9));`
    (D) `Object x = list.remove(6);`
    (E) `Object y = list.set(6, new Integer(8));`

24. Refer to method `insert` below:

```
/* Precondition:   ArrayList list contains Comparable values
 *                  sorted in decreasing order
 * Postcondition: element inserted in its correct position
 *                  in list */
public void insert(ArrayList list, Comparable element)
{
    int index = 0;
    while (element.compareTo(list.get(index)) < 0)
        index++;
    list.add(index, element);
}
```

    Assuming that the type of `element` is compatible with the objects in the list, which is a *true* statement about the `insert` method?
    (A) It works as intended for all values of `element`.
    (B) It fails for all values of `element`.
    (C) It fails if `element` is greater than the first item in `list` and works in all other cases.
    (D) It fails if `element` is smaller than the last item in `list` and works in all other cases.
    (E) It fails if `element` is either greater than the first item or smaller than the last item in `list` and works in all other cases.

25. Consider the following code segment, applied to `list`, an `ArrayList` of `Integer` values.

```
int len = list.size();
for (int i=0; i<len; i++)
{
    list.add(i+1, new Integer(i));
    Object x = list.set(i, new Integer(i+2));
}
```

    If `list` is initially 6 1 8, what will it be following execution of the code segment?
    (A) 2 3 4 2 1 8
    (B) 2 3 4 6 2 2 0 1 8
    (C) 2 3 4 0 1 2
    (D) 2 3 4 6 1 8
    (E) 2 3 3 2

26. Refer to the following declarations:

```
String[] colors = {"red", "green", "black"};
ArrayList colorList = new ArrayList();
```

Which of the following correctly assigns the elements of the colors array to colorList? The final ordering of colors in colorList should be the same as in the colors array.

I for (int i=0; i<colors.length; i++)
    colorList.add(i, colors.get(i));

II for (int i=0; i<colors.length; i++)
    colorList.add(colors[i]);

III for (int i=colors.length-1; i>=0; i--)
    colorList.add(i, colors[i]);

(A) I only
(B) II only
(C) III only
(D) II and III only
(E) I, II, and III

27. Consider writing a program that reads the lines of any text file into a sequential list of lines. Which of the following is a good reason to implement the list with an ArrayList of String objects rather than an array of String objects?
(A) The get and set methods of ArrayList are more convenient than the [] notation for arrays.
(B) The size method of ArrayList provides instant access to the length of the list.
(C) An ArrayList can contain objects of any type, which leads to greater generality.
(D) If any particular text file is unexpectedly long, the ArrayList will automatically be resized. The array, by contrast, will go out of bounds.
(E) The String methods are easier to use with an ArrayList than with an array.

28. Consider writing a program that produces statistics for long lists of numerical data. Which of the following is the best reason to implement each list with an array of int (or double), rather than an ArrayList of Integer (or Double) objects?
(A) An array of primitive number types is more efficient to manipulate than an ArrayList of wrapper objects that contain numbers.
(B) Insertion of new elements into a list is easier to code for an array than for an ArrayList.
(C) Removal of elements from a list is easier to code for an array than for an ArrayList.
(D) Accessing individual elements in the middle of a list is easier for an array than for an ArrayList.
(E) Accessing all the elements is more efficient in an array than in an ArrayList.

Questions 29 and 30 are based on the Coin and Purse classes given below:

```
/* A simple coin class */
public class Coin
{
    private double myValue;
    private String myName;

    //constructor
    public Coin(double value, String name)
    {
        myValue = value;
        myName = name;
    }

    //Return the value and name of this coin

    public double getValue()
    { return myValue; }

    public String getName()
    { return myName; }

    //Define equals method for Coin objects
    public boolean equals(Object obj)
    { /* implementation not shown */ }

    //Other methods not shown
        ...
}

/* A purse holds a collection of coins */
public class Purse
{
    private ArrayList coins;

    //constructor
    //creates an empty purse
    public Purse()
    { coins = new ArrayList(); }

    //Adds aCoin to the purse
    public void add(Coin aCoin)
    { coins.add(aCoin); }

    //Returns total value of coins in purse
    public double getTotal()
    { implementation code }

}
```

29. Here is the getTotal method from the Purse class:

```
//returns total value of coins in purse
public double getTotal()
{
    double total = 0;
    < more code >
    return total;
}
```

Which of the following is a correct replacement for < *more code* >?

(A)
```
for (int i=0; i<coins.length; i++)
{
    Coin c = (Coin) coins.get(i);
    total += coins.getValue();
}
```

(B)
```
for (int i=0; i<coins.length; i++)
{
    Coin c = (Coin) coins.[i];
    total += c.getValue();
}
```

(C)
```
for (int i=0; i<coins.size(); i++)
{
    Coin c = coins.get(i);
    total += c.getValue();
}
```

(D)
```
for (int i=0; i<coins.size(); i++)
{
    Coin c = coins.get(i);
    total += coins.getValue();
}
```

(E)
```
for (int i=0; i<coins.size(); i++)
{
    Coin c = (Coin) coins.get(i);
    total += c.getValue();
}
```

30. A boolean method `find` is added to the `Purse` class:

```
/* Returns true if the purse has a coin that matches aCoin,
 * false otherwise */
public boolean find(Coin aCoin)
{
    for (int i=0; i<coins.size(); i++)
    {
        < code to find match >
    }
    return false;
}
```

Which is a correct replacement for *< code to find match >*?

```
 I  Coin c = (Coin) coins.get(i);
    if (c.equals(aCoin))
        return true;
```

```
II  Coin c = (Coin) coins.get(i);
    if ((c.getName()).equals(aCoin.getName()))
        return true;
```

```
III Coin c = (Coin) coins.get(i);
    if ((c.getValue()).equals(aCoin.getValue()))
        return true;
```

(A) I only
(B) II only
(C) III only
(D) I and II only
(E) I, II, and III

Level AB Only

31. Which of the following initializes an 8×10 matrix with integer values that are perfect squares? (0 is a perfect square.)

```
  I  int[][] mat = new int[8][10];
```

```
 II  int[][] mat = new int[8][10];
     for (int r=0; r<mat.length; r++)
         for (int c=0; c<mat[r].length; c++)
             mat[r][c] = r*r;
```

```
III  int[][] mat = new int[8][10];
     for (int c=0; c<mat[r].length; c++)
         for (int r=0; r<mat.length; r++)
             mat[r][c] = c*c;
```

(A) I only
(B) II only
(C) III only
(D) I and II only
(E) I, II, and III

Level AB
(continued)

32. Consider the following method that will alter the matrix mat:

```
public static void matStuff(int[][] mat, int row)
//Precondition: mat is initialized
{
    int numCols = mat[0].length;
    for (int col=0; col<numCols; col++)
        mat[row][col] = row;
}
```

Suppose mat is originally

$$
\begin{array}{cccc}
1 & 4 & 9 & 0 \\
2 & 7 & 8 & 6 \\
5 & 1 & 4 & 3
\end{array}
$$

After the method call matStuff(mat,2), matrix mat will be

(A)
$$
\begin{array}{cccc}
1 & 4 & 9 & 0 \\
2 & 7 & 8 & 6 \\
2 & 2 & 2 & 2
\end{array}
$$

(B)
$$
\begin{array}{cccc}
1 & 4 & 9 & 0 \\
2 & 2 & 2 & 2 \\
5 & 1 & 4 & 3
\end{array}
$$

(C)
$$
\begin{array}{cccc}
2 & 2 & 2 & 2 \\
2 & 2 & 2 & 2 \\
2 & 2 & 2 & 2
\end{array}
$$

(D)
$$
\begin{array}{cccc}
1 & 4 & 2 & 0 \\
2 & 7 & 2 & 6 \\
5 & 1 & 2 & 3
\end{array}
$$

(E)
$$
\begin{array}{cccc}
1 & 2 & 9 & 0 \\
2 & 2 & 8 & 6 \\
5 & 2 & 4 & 3
\end{array}
$$

33. Assume that a square matrix mat is defined by

```
int[][] mat = new int[SIZE][SIZE];
//SIZE is an integer constant ≥ 2
```

What does the following code segment do?

```
for (int i=0; i<SIZE-1; i++)
    for (int j=0; j<SIZE-i-1; j++)
        swap(mat, i, j, SIZE-j-1, SIZE-i-1);
```

You may assume the existence of this swap method:

```
//interchange mat[a][b] and mat[c][d]
public void swap(int[][] mat, int a, int b, int c, int d)
```

(A) Reflects mat through its major diagonal. For example,

$$
\begin{matrix} 2 & 6 \\ 4 & 3 \end{matrix} \longrightarrow \begin{matrix} 2 & 4 \\ 6 & 3 \end{matrix}
$$

(B) Reflects mat through its minor diagonal. For example,

$$
\begin{matrix} 2 & 6 \\ 4 & 3 \end{matrix} \longrightarrow \begin{matrix} 3 & 6 \\ 4 & 2 \end{matrix}
$$

(C) Reflects mat through a horizontal line of symmetry. For example,

$$
\begin{matrix} 2 & 6 \\ 4 & 3 \end{matrix} \longrightarrow \begin{matrix} 4 & 3 \\ 2 & 6 \end{matrix}
$$

(D) Reflects mat through a vertical line of symmetry. For example,

$$
\begin{matrix} 2 & 6 \\ 4 & 3 \end{matrix} \longrightarrow \begin{matrix} 6 & 2 \\ 3 & 4 \end{matrix}
$$

(E) Leaves mat unchanged.

Level AB
(*continued*)

34. A square matrix is declared as

    ```
    int[][] mat = new int[SIZE][SIZE];
    ```

    where SIZE is an appropriate integer constant. Consider the following method:

    ```
    public void mystery(int[][] mat, int value, int top, int left,
        int bottom, int right)
    {
        for (int i=left; i<=right; i++)
        {
            mat[top][i] = value;
            mat[bottom][i] = value;
        }
        for (int i=top+1; i<=bottom-1; i++)
        {
            mat[i][left] = value;
            mat[i][right] = value;
        }
    }
    ```

    Assuming that there are no out-of-range errors, which best describes what method mystery does?
    (A) Places value in corners of the rectangle with corners (top, left) and (bottom, right)
    (B) Places value in the diagonals of the square with corners (top, left) and (bottom, right)
    (C) Places value in each element of the rectangle with corners (top, left) and (bottom, right)
    (D) Places value in each element of the border of the rectangle with corners (top, left) and (bottom, right)
    (E) Places value in the topmost and bottommost rows of the rectangle with corners (top, left) and (bottom, right)

35. This question refers to the following method:

```
public static boolean isThere(String[][] mat, int row, int col,
    String symbol)
{
    boolean yes;
    int i, count=0;
    for (i=0; i<SIZE; i++)
        if (mat[i][col].equals(symbol))
            count++;
    yes = (count == SIZE);
    count = 0;
    for (i=0; i<SIZE; i++)
        if (mat[row][i].equals(symbol))
            count++;
    return (yes || count == SIZE);
}
```

Now consider this code segment:

```
public final int SIZE = 8;
String[][] mat = new String[SIZE][SIZE];
```

Which of the following conditions on a matrix mat of the type declared in the code segment will by itself guarantee that

```
isThere(mat, 2, 2, "$")
```

will have the value true when evaluated?

   I The element in row 2 and column 2 is "$"
  II All elements in both diagonals are "$"
 III All elements in column 2 are "$"

(A) I only
(B) III only
(C) I and II only
(D) I and III only
(E) II and III only

36. A two-dimensional array of `double`, `rainfall`, will be used to represent the daily rainfall for a given year. In this scheme, `rainfall[month][day]` represents the amount of rain on the given day and month. For example,

    `rainfall[1][15]`   is the amount of rain on Jan. 15
    `rainfall[12][25]`   is the amount of rain on Dec. 25

The array can be declared as follows:

```
double[][] rainfall = new double[13][32];
```

This creates 13 rows indexed from 0 to 12 and 32 columns indexed from 0 to 31, all initialized to 0.0. Row 0 and column 0 will be ignored. Column 31 in row 4 will be ignored, since April 31 is not a valid day. In years that are not leap years, columns 29, 30, and 31 in row 2 will be ignored since Feb. 29, 30, and 31 are not valid days.

Consider the method `averageRainfall` below:

```
/* Precondition:  rainfall is initialized with values
 *                representing amounts of rain on all valid
 *                days. Invalid days are initialized to 0.0.
 *                Feb 29 is not a valid day.
 * Postcondition: returns average rainfall for the year */
public double averageRainfall(double rainfall[][])
{
    double total = 0.0;
    < more code >
}
```

Which of the following is a correct replacement for < *more code* > so that the postcondition for the method is satisfied?

```
 I for (int month=1; month<rainfall.length; month++)
       for (int day=1; day<rainfall[month].length; day++)
           total += rainfall[month][day];
   return total/(13*32);

II for (int month=1; month<rainfall.length; month++)
       for (int day=1; day<rainfall[month].length; day++)
           total += rainfall[month][day];
   return total/365;

III for (int month=0; month<rainfall.length; month++)
        for (int day=0; day<rainfall[month].length; day++)
            total += rainfall[month][day];
    return total/365;
```

(A) none
(B) I only
(C) II only
(D) III only
(E) II and III only

Level AB
(continued)

37. A simple Tic-Tac-Toe board is a 3 × 3 array filled with either X's, O's, or blanks.

Here is a class for a game of Tic-Tac-Toe:

```java
public class TicTacToe
{
    private String[][] board;
    private static final int ROWS = 3;
    private static final int COLS = 3;

    //constructor. constructs empty board
    public TicTacToe()
    {
        board = new String[ROWS][COLS];
        for (int r=0; r<ROWS; r++)
            for (int c=0; c<COLS; c++)
                board[r][c] = " ";
    }

    /* Precondition:  square on Tic-Tac-Toe board is empty
     * Postcondition: symbol placed in that square */
    void makeMove(int r, int c, String symbol)
    {
        board[r][c] = symbol;
    }

    /* Creates a string representation of the board, e.g.
     *     |o |
     *     |xx |
     *     |  o|
     * Postcondition: returns the string representation */
    public String toString()
    {
        String s = "";    //empty string
        < more code >
        return s;
    }
}
```

Which segment represents a correct replacement for < *more code* > for the toString method?

```java
(A) for (int r=0; r<ROWS; r++)
    {
        for (int c=0; c<COLS; c++)
        {
            s = s + "|";
            s = s + board[r][c];
            s = s + "|\n";
        }
    }
```

Level AB
(continued)

(B)
```
for (int r=0; r<ROWS; r++)
{
    s = s + "|";
    for (int c=0; c<COLS; c++)
    {
        s = s + board[r][c];
        s = s + "|\n";
    }
}
```

(C)
```
for (int r=0; r<ROWS; r++)
{
    s = s + "|";
    for (int c=0; c<COLS; c++)
        s = s + board[r][c];
}
s = s + "|\n";
```

(D)
```
for (int r=0; r<ROWS; r++)
    s = s + "|";
for (int c=0; c<COLS; c++)
{
    s = s + board[r][c];
    s = s + "|\n";
}
```

(E)
```
for (int r=0; r<ROWS; r++)
{
    s = s + "|";
    for (int c=0; c<COLS; c++)
        s = s + board[r][c];
    s = s + "|\n";
}
```

Answer Key

1. **E**		14. **A**		27. **D**
2. **C**		15. **D**		28. **A**
3. **E**		16. **E**		29. **E**
4. **B**		17. **B**		30. **D**
5. **A**		18. **C**		31. **D**
6. **B**		19. **A**		32. **A**
7. **C**		20. **C**		33. **B**
8. **A**		21. **B**		34. **D**
9. **C**		22. **D**		35. **B**
10. **B**		23. **C**		36. **E**
11. **C**		24. **D**		37. **E**
12. **E**		25. **A**		
13. **D**		26. **B**		

Answers Explained

1. **(E)** Segment I is an initializer list which is equivalent to

```
int[] arr = new int[4];
arr[0] = 0;
arr[1] = 0;
arr[2] = 0;
arr[3] = 0;
```

Segment II creates four slots for integers, which by default are initialized to 0. The for loop in segment III is therefore unnecessary. It is not, however, incorrect.

2. **(C)** If arr contains no negative integers, the value of i will eventually exceed N-1, and arr[i] will cause an ArrayIndexOutOfBoundsException to be thrown.

3. **(E)** The intent is to sum elements arr[0], arr[1], ..., arr[arr.length-1]. Notice, however, that when i has the value arr.length-1 it is incremented to arr.length in the loop. Now the statement sum += arr[i] refers to arr[arr.length], which is out of range.

4. **(B)** There are two problems with the segment as given:
   1. arr[1] is not tested.
   2. When i has a value of n-1, incrementing i will lead to an out-of-range error for the if(arr[i] < min) test.

Modification II corrects both these errors. The change suggested in III corrects neither of these errors. The change in I corrects (1) but not (2).

5. **(A)** The code segment has the effect of removing all occurrences of 0 from array arr1. Then the nonzero elements are transferred to array arr2.

6. **(B)** The algorithm is linear. It passes once through the array, making a single assignment if a nonzero element is found.

7. **(C)** If arr[i] < someValue for all i from 2 to k, SMALL will be printed on each iteration of the for loop. Since there are k-1 iterations, the maximum number of times that SMALL can be printed is k-1.

8. **(A)** The array will not be changed by the increment method. Here are the memory slots:

Before the first call, increment(3):

Just after the first call:

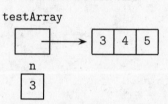

Just before exiting increment(3):

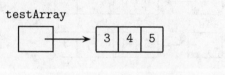

Just after exiting increment(3):

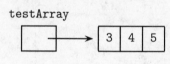
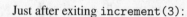

The same analysis applies to the method calls increment(4) and increment(5).

9. **(C)** Array arr is changed by doSomething. Here are the memory slots:

Just before doSomething is called:

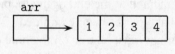

Just after doSomething is called, but before the for loop is executed:

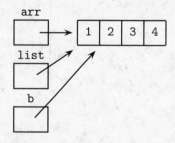

Just before exiting doSomething:

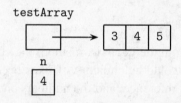
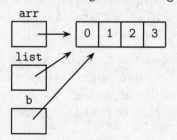

Just after exiting doSomething:

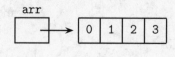

10. **(B)** The `array` object is initialized to contain 10 slots, each with a default value of 0. The `getData` method does not change the `array` reference. Here are the memory slots:

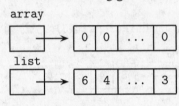

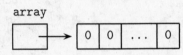

Before `getData` is invoked:

At the start of the method call:

Just before exiting `getData`:

After exiting the method:

list contains integers
entered by user

Note that if the line

```
list = new int[10];
```

is deleted from the `getData` method, the code would work as intended, and the answer would be choice A. This is because `list` and `array` would now be the same reference, and the numbers entered by the user would be stored in `array` when the method is exited.

Level AB Only

11. **(C)** Since k and j are changed at the *end* of the loop, the invariant is: `arr[first]...arr[k-1]` have been swapped with elements `arr[last]` down to `arr[j+1]`. The middle part of the array has not been processed, and these elements are still in their original positions.

12. **(E)** i is incremented at the end of the loop, which means that on exiting the loop `arr[i]` has not yet been examined. This eliminates choices A and C. The loop invariant must be true on the final exit from the loop, at which time i = n. This eliminates choice B. Choice D is wrong because i is initialized to 1. Thus 1 ≤ i ...

13. **(D)** For each i, `list[i]` is an `Address` object. To access the name of this object, use `list[i].getName()`.

14. **(A)** Since the `Address` class does not have a `toString` method, each data field must explicitly be printed. Segment II would work if there *were* a `toString` method for the class (but there isn't, so it doesn't!). Segment III doesn't make sense—the class name is not a method!

15. **(D)** Each `Student` name must be accessed through the `Address` class accessor `getName()`. The expression `allStudents[i].getAddress()` accesses the entire address of the ith student. The `myName` field is then accessed using the `getName()` accessor of the `Address` class. Segments I and II are equivalent.

Segment III would be correct if the Student class had a getName accessor method.

16. (**E**) The point of the correct solutions is that they store the *index* of the Student with the highest idNum so far. Code segment I is incorrect because it returns the first student whose idNum is greater than max, not necessarily the student with the highest idNum in the list.

17. (**B**) For each i, tickList[i] is a new Ticket object that must be constructed using the Ticket constructor. Therefore eliminate choices C, D, and E. Choice A is wrong because getRow(), getSeat(), and getPrice() are accessors for values *that already exist* for some Ticket object. Note also the absence of the dot member construct.

18. (**C**) To access the price for each Ticket in the tickList array, the getPrice() accessor in the Ticket class must be used, since myPrice is private to that class. This eliminates choices A and E. Choice B uses the array indexing brackets incorrectly. Choices D and E incorrectly declare a Transaction object. (The method applies to an existing Transaction object.)

19. (**A**) An array of type Transaction is required. This eliminates choices C and D. Choice B incorrectly uses type Ticket on the right-hand side. Choice E puts the identifier listOfSales in the wrong place.

20. (**C**) If the responses array contained an invalid value like 12, the program would attempt to add 1 to freq[12]. This is out of bounds for the freq array.

21. (**B**) It is required to display bookList[0], bookList[1],... bookList[bookList.length-1]. Thus, the correct loop body is

```
bookList[i].display();
```

This eliminates choices C, D, and E. Choice A is wrong because bookList[i].length has no meaning, since length applies to the bookList array, not to the single element bookList[i].

22. (**D**) The declaration must start with the type of value in the array, namely BingoCard. This eliminates choices A and E. Each element of the players array must be constructed with the BingoCard constructor:

```
players[i] = new BingoCard();
```

You can now eliminate choice C. Choice B has a multitude of errors. It fails in the display segment by attempting to show explicitly each element in the myCard array. But myCard is private and cannot be accessed by a client method. Also, the display method must be called by a BingoCard object, namely players[i].

23. (**C**) The effect of choice C is to adjust the size of the list to 7 and to add the Integer 9 to the last slot (i.e., the slot with index 6). Choices A, D, and E will all cause an IndexOutOfBoundsException because there is no slot with index 6: the last slot has index 5. Choice B will cause a compile-time error, since the left and right sides are incompatible types: intOb is an Integer and list.get(2) is an Object. To avoid this error, the right side of the statement in B would need to be changed to (Integer) list.get(2);.

24. **(D)** If `element` is smaller than the last item in the list, it will be compared with every item in the list. Eventually `index` will be incremented to a value that is out of bounds. To avoid this error, the test in the `while` loop should be

```
while(index < list.size() &&
        element.compareTo(list.get(index)) < 0)
```

Notice that if `element` is greater than or equal to at least one item in `list`, the test as given in the problem will eventually be false, preventing an out-of-range error.

25. **(A)** Recall that `add(index, obj)` shifts all elements, starting at `index`, one unit to the right, then inserts `obj` at position `index`. The `set(index, obj)` method replaces the element in position `index` with `obj`. So here is the state of `list` after each change:

```
i = 0    6 0 1 8
         2 0 1 8
i = 1    2 0 1 1 8
         2 3 1 1 8
i = 2    2 3 1 2 1 8
         2 3 4 2 1 8
```

26. **(B)** The declaration of the `colors` array makes the following assignments: `colors[0]="red"`, `colors[1]="green"`, and `colors[2]="black"`. The loop in segment II adds these values to `colorList` in the correct order. Segment I fails because `colors` is an array. To access the `i`th element, you need `colors[i]`. The get method is used for an `ArrayList`, not an array. Segment III, in its first pass through the loop, attempts to add `colors[2]` to index position 2 of `colorList`. This will cause an `IndexOutOfBoundsException` to be thrown, since index positions 0 and 1 do not yet exist!

27. **(D)** Arrays are of fixed length and do not shrink or grow if the size of the data set varies. An `ArrayList` automatically resizes the list. Choice A is false: the [] notation is compact and easy to use. Choice B is not a valid reason because an array L also provides instant access to its length with the quantity `L.length`. Choice C is invalid because an array can also contain objects. Also, generality is beside the point in the given program: the array must hold `String` objects. Choice E is false: whether a `String` object is `arr[i]` or `list.get(i)`, the `String` methods are equally easy to invoke.

28. **(A)** In order to add numerical elements to an `ArrayList`, you must wrap each element in a wrapper class before insertion into the list. Then, to retrieve a numerical value from an `ArrayList`, you must cast the return value of `get` to `Double` or `Integer`. Then to use the numerical values, you must call the `intValue` or `doubleValue` methods. In an array, you simply use the [] notation for assignment (as in `arr[i]=num`) or retrieval (`value=arr[i]`). Note that choices B and C are false statements: both insertion and deletion for an array involve writing code to shift elements. An `ArrayList` automatically takes care of this through its `add` and `remove` methods. Choice D is a poor reason for choosing an array. While the `get` and `set` methods of `ArrayList` might be slightly more awkward than using the [] notation, both mechanisms work pretty easily. Choice E is false: efficiency of access is roughly the same.

29. **(E)** Since `coins` is an `ArrayList`, the `size()` method must be called in the `for` loop. This eliminates choices A and B. The `get` method of `ArrayList` returns an object, which must be cast to `Coin` before it can be assigned to `c`. This eliminates choices C and D. Notice that choices A and D make the additional error of calling the `Coin` method `getValue()` with the `ArrayList` `coins` rather than with `c`, the `Coin` object.

30. **(D)** The `equals` method is defined for objects only. Since `getValue` returns a `double`, the quantities `c.getValue()` and `aCoin.getValue()` must be compared either using `==`, or as described in the box on p. 6 (better).

Level AB Only

31. **(D)** Segment II is the straightforward solution. Segment I is correct because it initializes all slots of the matrix to 0, a perfect square. (By default, all arrays of `int` or `double` are initialized to 0.) Segment III fails because `r` is undefined in the condition `c<mat[r].length`. In order to do a column-by-column traversal, you need to get the number of columns in each row. The outer `for` loop could be

    ```
    for (int c=0; c<mat[0].length; c++)
    ```

    Now segment III works. Note that since the array is rectangular, you can use any index `k` in the conditional `c<mat[k].length`, provided that `k` satisfies $0 \leq k < \texttt{mat.length}$.

32. **(A)** `matStuff` processes the row selected by the row parameter, 2 in the method call. The row value, 2, overwrites each element in row 2. Don't make the mistake of selecting choice B—the row labels are 0, 1, 2.

33. **(B)** Hand execute this for a 2×2 matrix. `i` goes from 0 to 0, `j` goes from 0 to 0, so the only interchange is swap `mat[0][0]` with `mat[1][1]`, which suggests choice B. Check with a 3×3 matrix:

    ```
    i = 0   j = 0   swap mat[0][0] with mat[2][2]
            j = 1   swap mat[0][1] with mat[1][2]
    i = 1   j = 0   swap mat[1][0] with mat[2][1]
    ```

    The elements to be interchanged are shown paired in the following figure. The result will be a reflection through the minor diagonal.

34. **(D)** The first `for` loop places `value` in the top and bottom rows of the defined rectangle. The second `for` loop fills in the remaining border elements on the sides. Note that the `top+1` and `bottom-1` initializer and terminating conditions avoid filling in the corner elements twice.

35. **(B)** For the method call `isThere(mat, 2, 2, "$")`, the code counts how many times `"$"` appears in row 2 and how many times in column 2. The method returns `true` only if `count == SIZE` for either the row or column pass (i.e., the whole of row 2 or the whole of column 2 contains the symbol `"$"`). This eliminates choices I and II.

36. **(E)** Since there are 365 valid days in a year, the divisor in calculating the average must be 365. It may appear that segments II and III are incorrect because they include rainfall for invalid days in `total`. Since these values are initialized to `0.0`, however, including them in the total won't affect the final result.

37. **(E)** There are three things that must be done in each row:

    - Add an opening boundary line:

      ```
      s = s + "|";
      ```

    - Add the symbol in each square:

      ```
      for (int c=0; c<COLS; c++)
          s = s + board[r][c];
      ```

    - Add a closing boundary line and go to the next line:

      ```
      s = s + "|\n";
      ```

    All of these statements must therefore be enclosed in the outer `for` loop, that is, `for (int r= ...`

CHAPTER SEVEN
Recursion

recursion *n. See* recursion.
—*Eric S. Raymond,* The New Hacker's Dictionary *(1991)*

Recursive Methods

A *recursive method* is a method that calls itself. For example, here is a program that calls a recursive method stackWords.

```java
public class WordPlay
{
    public static void stackWords()
    {
        String word = IO.readString();      //read user input
        if (word.equals("."))
            System.out.println();
        else
            stackWords();
        System.out.println(word);
    }

    public static void main(String args[])
    {
        System.out.println("Enter list of words, one per line.");
        System.out.println("Final word should be a period (.)");
        stackWords();
    }
}
```

Here is the output if you enter

```
hold
my
hand
.
```

You get

```
.
hand
my
hold
```

The program reads in a list of words terminated with a period, and prints the list in reverse order, starting with the period. How does this happen?

Each time the recursive call to stackWords() is made, execution goes back to the start of a new method call. The computer must remember to complete all the pending calls to the method. It does this by stacking the statements that must still be executed as follows: The first time stackWords() is called, the word "hold" is read and tested for being a period. No it's not, so stackWords() is called again. The statement to output "hold" (which has not yet been executed) goes on a stack, and execution goes to the start of the method. The word "my" is read. No, it's not a period, so the command to output "my" goes on the stack. And so on. The stack looks something like this before the recursive call in which the period is read:

System.out.println("hand");
System.out.println("my");
System.out.println("hold");

Imagine that these statements are stacked like plates. In the final stackWords() call, word has the value ".". Yes, it *is* a period, so the stackWords() line is skipped, the period is printed on the screen, and the method call terminates. The computer now completes each of the previous method calls in turn by "popping" the statements off the top of the stack. It prints "hand", then "my", then "hold", and execution of stackWords() is complete.[1]

NOTE

1. Each time stackWords() is called, a new local variable word is created.
2. The first time the method actually terminates, the program returns to complete the most recently invoked previous call. That's why the words get reversed in this example.

General Form of Simple Recursive Methods

Every recursive method has two distinct parts:

- A base case or termination condition that causes the method to end.

- A nonbase case whose actions move the algorithm toward the base case and termination.

Here is the framework for a simple recursive method that has no specific return type.

---

[1] Actually, the computer stacks the pending statements in a recursive method call more efficiently than the way described. But *conceptually* this is how it is done.

```
public void recursiveMeth( ... )
{
    if (base case)
        Perform some action
    else
    {
    Perform some other action
    recursiveMeth( ... );     //recursive method call
    }
}
```

The base case typically occurs for the simplest case of the problem, such as when an integer has a value of 0 or 1. Other examples of base cases are when some key is found, or an end-of-file is reached. A recursive algorithm can have more than one base case.

In the else or nonbase case of the framework shown, the code fragment *Perform some other action* and the method call recursiveMeth can sometimes be interchanged without altering the net effect of the algorithm. Be careful though, because what *does* change is the order of executing statements. This can sometimes be disastrous. (See the killBlob example at the end of this chapter, or the tree traversals and recursive tree algorithms in Chapter 10.)

Example 1

```
public void drawLine(int n)
{
    if (n == 0)
        System.out.println("That's all, folks!");
    else
    {
        for (int i=1; i<=n; i++)
            System.out.print("*");
        System.out.println();
        drawLine(n-1);
    }
}
```

The method call drawLine(3) produces this output:

```
***
**
*
That's all, folks!
```

NOTE

1. A method that has no pending statements following the recursive call is an example of *tail recursion*. Method drawLine is such a case, but stackWords is not.

2. The base case in the drawLine example is n==0. Notice that each subsequent call, drawLine(n-1), makes progress toward termination of the method. If your method has no base case, or if you never reach the base case, you will create *infinite recursion*. This is a catastrophic error that will cause your computer eventually to run out of memory and give you heart-stopping messages like java.lang.StackOverflowError ...

Example 2

```
//illustrates infinite recursion
public void catastrophe(int n)
{
    System.out.println(n);
    catastrophe(n);
}
```

Try running the case `catastrophe(1)` if you have lots of time to waste!

Writing Recursive Methods

To come up with a recursive algorithm, you have to be able to frame a process *recursively* (i.e., in terms of a simpler case of itself). This is different from framing it *iteratively*, which repeats a process until a final condition is met. A good strategy for writing recursive methods is to first state the algorithm recursively in words.

Example 1

Write a method that returns $n!$ (n factorial).

$n!$ defined iteratively	$n!$ defined recursively
$0! = 1$	$0! = 1$
$1! = 1$	$1! = (1)(0!)$
$2! = (2)(1)$	$2! = (2)(1!)$
$3! = (3)(2)(1)$	$3! = (3)(2!)$
$\ldots$	$\ldots$

The general recursive definition for $n!$ is

$$n! = \begin{cases} 1 & n = 0 \\ n(n-1)! & n > 0 \end{cases}$$

The definition seems to be circular until you realize that if 0! is defined, all higher factorials are defined. Code for the recursive method follows directly from the recursive definition:

```
/* Compute n! recursively.
 * Precondition:  n ≥ 0
 * Postcondition: returns n! */
public static int factorial(int n)
{
    if (n == 0)        //base case
        return 1;
    else
        return n*factorial(n-1);
}
```

Example 2

Write a recursive method `revDigs` that outputs its integer parameter with the digits reversed. For example,

$$\text{revDigs(147)} \quad \text{outputs} \quad 741$$
$$\text{revDigs(4)} \quad \text{outputs} \quad 4$$

First describe the process recursively: Output the rightmost digit. Then, if there are still digits left in the remaining number n/10, reverse its digits. Repeat this until n/10 is 0. Here is the method:

```
/* Precondition:   n ≥ 0
 * Postcondition: Outputs n with digits reversed */
public static void revDigs(int n)
{
    System.out.print(n % 10);   //rightmost digit
    if (n/10 != 0)              //base case
        revDigs(n/10);
}
```

Analysis of Recursive Methods

Recall the Fibonacci sequence 1, 1, 2, 3, 5, 8, 13, ... The nth Fibonacci number equals the sum of the previous two numbers if $n \geq 3$. Recursively,

$$\text{Fib}(n) = \begin{cases} 1, & n = 1, 2 \\ \text{Fib}(n-1) + \text{Fib}(n-2), & n \geq 3 \end{cases}$$

Here is the method:

```
/* Precondition:   n ≥ 1
 * Postcondition: Returns the nth Fibonacci number */
public static int fib(int n)
{
    if (n == 1 || n == 2)
        return 1;
    else
        return fib(n-1) + fib(n-2);
}
```

Notice that there are two recursive calls in the last line of the method. So to find Fib(5), for example, takes eight recursive calls to `fib`!

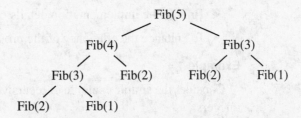

Level AB Only

In general, each call to `fib` makes two more calls, which is the tipoff for an exponential algorithm (i.e., the run time is $O(2^n)$). This is *much* slower than the $O(n)$ run time of the corresponding iterative algorithm (see Chapter 5, preamble to Question 14).

You may ask: Since every recursive algorithm can be written iteratively, when should one use recursion? Bear in mind that recursive algorithms can incur extra run time and memory. Their major plus is elegance and simplicity of code.

General Rules for Recursion

1. Avoid recursion for algorithms that involve large local arrays—too many recursive calls can cause memory overflow.
2. Use recursion when it significantly simplifies code.
3. Avoid recursion for simple iterative methods like factorial, Fibonacci, and the linear search on the next page.
4. Recursion is especially useful for

   - branching processes like traversing trees or directories.
   - divide-and-conquer algorithms like mergesort and quicksort.

Sorting Algorithms That Use Recursion

Mergesort and Quicksort are discussed in Chapter 12.

Recursive Helper Methods

A common technique in designing recursive algorithms is to have a public nonrecursive driver method that calls a private *recursive helper method* to carry out the task. The main reasons for doing this are:

- To change the value of an object reference. Recall that in Java if such an object is passed as a parameter in the method, it won't be changed. A helper must be used that returns the object reference (see *Recursion That Alters the Tree Structure* on p. 340).

- To hide the implementation details of the recursion from the user.

- To enhance the efficiency of the program.

Example 1

Consider the simple example of recursively finding the sum of the first n positive integers.

```
//returns 1 + 2 + 3 + ... + n
public static int sum(int n)
{
    if (n == 1)
        return 1;
    else
        return n + sum(n-1);
}
```

Notice that you get infinite recursion if $n \leq 0$. Suppose you want to include a test for $n > 0$ before you execute the algorithm. Placing this test in the recursive method is inefficient because if n is initially positive, it will remain positive in subsequent recursive calls. You can avoid this problem by using a driver method called getSum, which does the test on *n just once*. The recursive method sum becomes a private helper method.

```
public class FindSum
{
    /* Private recursive helper method.
     * Finds 1 + 2 + 3 + ... + n.
     * Precondition:  n > 0 */
    private static int sum(int n)
    {
        if (n == 1)
            return 1;
        else
            return n + sum(n-1);
    }

    /* Driver method */
    public static int getSum(int n)
    {
        if (n > 0)
            return sum(n);
        else
        {
            System.out.println("Error: n must be positive");
            return -1;
        }
    }
}
```

NOTE This is a trivial method used to illustrate a private recursive helper method. In practice you would never use recursion to find a simple sum!

Example 2

Consider a recursive solution to the problem of doing a sequential search for a key in an array of elements that are Comparable. If the key is found, the method returns true, otherwise it returns false.

The solution can be stated recursively as follows:

- If the key is in a[0], then the key is found.

- If not, recursively search the array starting at a[1].

- If you are past the end of the array, then the key wasn't found.

Here is a straightforward (but inefficient) implementation:

```java
public class Searcher
{
    /* Recursively search array a for key
     * Postcondition: if a[k] equals key for 0 <= k < a.length
     *                returns true, otherwise returns false  */
    public boolean search(Comparable[] a, Comparable key)
    {
        if (a.length == 0)  //base case. key not found
            return false;
        else if (a[0].compareTo(key) == 0) //base case
            return true;                    //key found
        else
        {
            Comparable[] shorter = new Comparable[a.length-1];
            for (int i=0; i<shorter.length; i++)
                shorter[i] = a[i+1];
            return search(shorter, key);
        }
    }

    public static void main(String[] args)
    {
        String[] list = {"Mary", "Joe", "Lee", "Jake"};
        Searcher s = new Searcher();
        System.out.println("Enter key: Mary, Joe, Lee or Jake.");
        String key = IO.readString();  //read user input
        boolean result = s.search(list, key);
        if (!result)
            System.out.println(key + " was not found.");
        else
            System.out.println(key + " was found.");
    }
}
```

Notice how horribly inefficient the search method is: For each recursive call a new array shorter has to be created! Much better is to use a parameter, startIndex, to keep track of where you are in the array. Replace the search method above with the following one, which calls the private helper method recurSearch:

```java
/* Driver method. Searches array a for key
 * Precondition:  a contains at least one element
 * Postcondition: if a[k] equals key for 0 <= k < a.length
 *                returns true, otherwise returns false */
public boolean search(Comparable[] a, Comparable key)
{
    return recurSearch(a, 0, key);
}

/* Recursively search array a for key, starting at startIndex
 * Precondition:  a contains at least one element and
 *                0 <= startIndex <= a.length
```

```
 *  Postcondition: if a[k] equals key for 0 <= k < a.length
 *                  returns true, otherwise returns false */
private static boolean recurSearch(Comparable[] a, int startIndex,
    Comparable key)
{
    if(startIndex == a.length)    //base case. key not found
        return false;
    else if(a[startIndex].compareTo(key) == 0) //base case
        return true;                              //key found
    else
        return recurSearch(a, startIndex+1, key);
}
```

NOTE

1. Using the parameter `startIndex` avoids having to create a new array object for each recursive call. Making `startIndex` a parameter of a helper method hides implementation details from the user.

2. Since `String` implements `Comparable`, it is OK to use an array of `String`. It would also have been OK to test with an array of `Integer` or `Double`, since they too implement `Comparable`.

3. The helper method is private, because it is called only by `search` within the `Searcher` class, and static, because it is not invoked by an object of the `Searcher` class. Contrast this with the way `search` is invoked in the main program, as `s.search...`

4. It's easy to modify the `search` method to return the index in the array where the key is found: make the return type `int` and return `startIndex` if the key is found, `-1` (say) if it isn't.

Recursion in 2-D Grids

Level AB Only

A certain type of problem crops up occasionally on the AP exam: using recursion to traverse a two-dimensional array. The problem comes in several different guises. For example,

1. A game board from which you must remove pieces.
2. A maze with walls and paths from which you must try to escape.
3. White "containers" enclosed by black "walls" into which you must "pour paint."

In each case you will be given a starting position (row, col) and instructions on what to do. The recursive solution typically involves these steps:

> *Check that the starting position is not out of range:*
> > *If (starting position satisfies some requirement)*
> > > *Perform some action to solve problem*
> > > *RecursiveCall(row+1, col)*
> > > *RecursiveCall(row−1, col)*
> > > *RecursiveCall(row, col+1)*
> > > *RecursiveCall(row, col−1)*

Level AB
(continued)

Example

On the right is an image represented as a square grid of black and white cells. Two cells in an image are part of the same "blob" if each is black and there is a sequence of moves from one cell to the other, where each move is either horizontal or vertical to an adjacent black cell. For example, the diagram represents an image that contains two blobs, one of them consisting of a single cell.

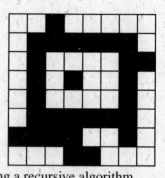

Assuming the following Image class declaration, you are to write the body of the killBlob method, using a recursive algorithm.

```
public class Image
{
    private final int BLACK = 1;
    private final int WHITE = 0;
    private int[][] image;    //square grid
    private int size;         //number of rows and columns

    public Image()    //constructor
    { implementation code }

    public void display()    //displays Image
    { implementation code }

    /* Precondition:  Image is defined with either BLACK or WHITE
                      cells
     * Postcondition: If 0 ≤ row ≤ size-1 and image[row][col]
     *                is BLACK, set all cells in the same blob
     *                to WHITE. Otherwise image is unchanged */
    public void killBlob(int row, int col)
    { implementation code }
}
```

Solution:

```
public void killBlob(int row, int col)
{
    if (row >= 0 && row < size && col >= 0 && col < size)
        if (image[row][col] == BLACK)
        {
            image[row][col] = WHITE;
            killBlob(row-1, col);
            killBlob(row+1, col);
            killBlob(row, col-1);
            killBlob(row, col+1);
        }
}
```

NOTE

1. The ordering of the four recursive calls is irrelevant.
2. The test

```
    if (image[row][col] == BLACK)
```

can be included as the last piece of the test in the first line:

Level AB
(continued)

```
    if (row >= 0 && ...
```

If `row` or `col` are out of range, the test will short-circuit, avoiding the dreaded `ArrayIndexOutOfBoundsException`.

3. If you put the statement

```
    image[row][col] = WHITE;
```

after the four recursive calls, you get an infinite recursion if your blob has more than one cell. This is because, when you visit an adjacent cell, one of its recursive calls visits the original cell. If this cell is still `BLACK`, yet more recursive calls are generated, *ad infinitum*.

A final thought: recursive algorithms can be tricky. Try to state the solution recursively *in words* before you launch into code. Oh, and don't forget the base case!

Multiple-Choice Questions on Recursion

1. Which of the following statements about recursion are true?

    I Every recursive algorithm can be written iteratively.
    II Tail recursion is always used in "divide-and-conquer" algorithms.
    III In a recursive definition, an object is defined in terms of a simpler case of itself.

    (A) I only
    (B) III only
    (C) I and II only
    (D) I and III only
    (E) II and III only

2. Which of the following, when used as the $<body>$ of method sum, will enable that method to compute $1 + 2 + \cdots + n$ correctly for any $n > 0$?

```
public static int sum(int n)
//Precondition:  n > 0
//Postcondition: 1+2+...+n has been returned
{
    < body >
}
```

    I
```
return n + sum(n-1);
```

    II
```
if (n == 1)
    return 1;
else
    return n + sum(n-1);
```

    III
```
if (n == 1)
    return 1;
else
    return sum(n) + sum(n-1);
```

    (A) I only
    (B) II only
    (C) III only
    (D) I and II only
    (E) I, II, and III

3. Refer to the method stringRecur:

```
public static void stringRecur(String s)
{
    if (s.length() < 15)
        System.out.println(s);
    stringRecur(s + "*");
}
```

When will method stringRecur terminate without error?
(A) Only when the length of the input string is less than 15
(B) Only when the length of the input string is greater than or equal to 15
(C) Only when an empty string is input
(D) For all string inputs
(E) For no string inputs

4. Refer to method strRecur:

```
public static void StrRecur(String s)
{
    if (s.length() < 15)
    {
        System.out.println(s);
        strRecur(s + "*");
    }
}
```

When will method strRecur terminate without error?
(A) Only when the length of the input string is less than 15
(B) Only when the length of the input string is greater than or equal to 15
(C) Only when an empty string is input
(D) For all string inputs
(E) For no string inputs

Questions 5 and 6 refer to method result:

```
public int result(int n)
{
    if (n == 1)
        return 2;
    else
        return 2*result(n-1);
}
```

5. What value does result(5) return?
(A) 64
(B) 32
(C) 16
(D) 8
(E) 2

6. If $n > 0$, how many times will `result` be called to evaluate `result(n)` (including the initial call)?

   (A) 2
   (B) 2^n
   (C) n
   (D) $2n$
   (E) n^2

7. Refer to method `mystery`:

   ```
   public int mystery(int n, int a, int d)
   {
       if (n == 1)
           return a;
       else
           return d + mystery(n-1, a, d);
   }
   ```

   What value is returned by the call `mystery(3, 2, 6)`?

   (A) 20
   (B) 14
   (C) 10
   (D) 8
   (E) 2

8. Refer to method `f`:

   ```
   public int f(int k, int n)
   {
       if (n == k)
           return k;
       else
           if (n > k)
               return f(k, n-k);
           else
               return f(k-n, n);
   }
   ```

   What value is returned by the call `f(6, 8)`?

   (A) 8
   (B) 4
   (C) 3
   (D) 2
   (E) 1

9. What does method `recur` do?

```
public int recur(int[] x, int n)
//x is an array of n integers
{
    int t;
    if (n == 1)
        return x[0];
    else
    {
        t = recur(x, n-1);
        if (x[n-1] > t)
            return x[n-1];
        else
            return t;
    }
}
```

(A) It finds the largest value in x and leaves x unchanged.
(B) It finds the smallest value in x and leaves x unchanged.
(C) It sorts x in ascending order and returns the largest value in x.
(D) It sorts x in descending order and returns the largest value in x.
(E) It returns x[0] or x[n-1], whichever is larger.

10. Which best describes what the `printString` method below does?

```
public void printString(String s)
{
    if (s.length() > 0)
    {
        printString(s.substring(1));
        System.out.print(s.substring(0, 1));
    }
}
```

(A) It prints string s.
(B) It prints string s in reverse order.
(C) It prints only the first character of string s.
(D) It prints only the first two characters of string s.
(E) It prints only the last character of string s.

11. Refer to the method power:

```
//Precondition:  expo is any integer, base is not zero
//Postcondition: base raised to expo power returned
public double power(double base, int expo)
{
    if (expo == 0)
        return 1;
    else if (expo > 0)
        return base*power(base, expo-1);
    else
        return < code >;
}
```

Which < code > correctly completes method power?
(Recall that $a^{-n} = 1/a^n$, $a \neq 0$; for example, $2^{-3} = 1/2^3 = 1/8$.)

(A) (1/base) * power(base, expo+1)

(B) (1/base) * power(base, expo-1)

(C) base * power(base, expo+1)

(D) base * power(base, expo-1)

(E) (1/base) * power(base, expo)

12. Consider the following method:

```
public static void doSomething(int n)
{
    if (n > 0)
    {
        doSomething(n-1);
        System.out.print(n);
        doSomething(n-1);
    }
}
```

What would be output following the call doSomething(3)?

(A) 3211211

(B) 1121213

(C) 1213121

(D) 1211213

(E) 1123211

13. A user enters several positive integers at the keyboard and terminates the list with a sentinel (-999). A writeEven method reads those integers and outputs the even integers only, in the reverse order that they are read. Thus if the user enters

```
3 5 14 6 1 8 -999
```

the output for the writeEven method will be

```
8 6 14
```

Here is the method:

```
/* Assume user enters at least one positive integer,
 * and terminates the list with -999.
 * Postcondition: All even integers in the list are
 *                 output in reverse order. */
public static void writeEven()
{
    int num = IO.readInt();     //read user input
    if (num != -999)
    {
        < code >
    }
}
```

Which < code > satisfies the postcondition of method writeEven?

```
 I if (num % 2 == 0)
        System.out.print(num + " ");
    writeEven();
```

```
II if (num % 2 == 0)
        writeEven();
    System.out.print(num + " ");
```

```
III writeEven();
    if (num % 2 == 0)
        System.out.print(num + " ");
```

(A) I only
(B) II only
(C) III only
(D) I and II only
(E) I, II, and III

Questions 14–16 refer to method t:

```
//Precondition: n ≥ 1
public static int t(int n)
{
    if (n == 1 || n == 2)
        return 2*n;
    else
        return t(n-1) - t(n-2);
}
```

14. What will be returned by t(5)?
    (A) 4
    (B) 2
    (C) 0
    (D) −2
    (E) −4

15. For the method call t(6), how many calls to t will be made, including the original call?
    (A) 6
    (B) 7
    (C) 11
    (D) 15
    (E) 25

Level AB Only

16. The run time of method t is
    (A) $O(n)$
    (B) $O(n^2)$
    (C) $O(2^n)$
    (D) $O(n^3)$
    (E) $O(\log n)$

17. This question refers to methods f1 and f2 that are in the same class:

```
public static int f1(int a, int b)
{
    if (a == b)
        return b;
    else
        return a + f2(a-1, b);
}

public static int f2(int p, int q)
{
    if (p < q)
        return p + q;
    else
        return p + f1(p-2, q);
}
```

What value will be returned by a call to f1(5, 3)?
(A) 5
(B) 6
(C) 7
(D) 12
(E) 15

18. Consider method foo:

```
public int foo(int x)
{
    if (x == 1 || x == 3)
        return x;
    else
        return x*foo(x-1);
}
```

Assuming no possibility of integer overflow, what will be the value of z after execution of the following statement?

```
int z = foo(foo(3) + foo(4));
```

(A) (15!)/(2!)
(B) 3! + 4!
(C) (7!)!
(D) (3! + 4!)!
(E) 15

Questions 19 and 20 refer to the IntFormatter class below.

```
public class IntFormatter
{
    //Write 3 digits adjacent to each other
    public static void writeThreeDigits(int n)
    {
        System.out.print(n/100);
        System.out.print((n/10) % 10);
        System.out.print(n % 10);
    }

    //Insert commas in n, every 3 digits starting at the right.
    //Precondition: n ≥ 0
    public static void writeWithCommas(int n)
    {
        if (n < 1000)
            System.out.print(n);
        else
        {
            writeThreeDigits(n % 1000);
            System.out.print(",");
            writeWithCommas(n/1000);
        }
    }
}
```

19. The method writeWithCommas is supposed to print its nonnegative int argument with commas properly inserted (every three digits, starting at the right). For example, the integer 27048621 should be printed as 27,048,621. Method writeWithCommas does not always work as intended, however. Assuming no integer overflow, which of the following integer arguments will *not* be printed correctly?
    (A) 896
    (B) 251462251
    (C) 365051
    (D) 278278
    (E) 4

20. Which change in the code of the given methods will cause method writeWithCommas to work as intended?
    (A) Interchange the lines System.out.print(n/100) and System.out.print(n % 10) in method writeThreeDigits.
    (B) Interchange the lines writeThreeDigits(n % 1000) and writeWithCommas(n/1000) in method writeWithCommas.
    (C) Change the test in writeWithCommas to if (n > 1000).
    (D) In the method writeWithCommas, change the line writeThreeDigits(n % 1000) to writeThreeDigits(n/1000).
    (E) In the method writeWithCommas, change the recursive call writeWithCommas(n/1000) to writeWithCommas(n % 1000).

21. Consider triangles that are formed by stacking squares, each with area 1.

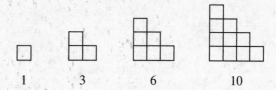

    1   3   6   10

The area of each such triangle is a *triangular number*. Note that the area of the nth such triangle equals the area of the $(n-1)$th triangle plus the new base.

Here are two different implementations of a `Triangle` class that provides a recursive method to find the area of these `Triangle` objects, given their base. (The differences between the two implementations are in bold face.)

Implementation I

```
public class Triangle
{
    private int base;

    //constructor
    public Triangle(int b)
    { base = b; }

    public int getArea()
    {
        if (base == 1)
            return 1;
        Triangle smaller =
            new Triangle(base-1);
        return base +
            smaller.getArea();
    }
}
```

Implementation II

```
public class Triangle
{
    private int base;

    //constructor
    public Triangle(int b)
    { base = b; }

    public int getArea()
    { return area(base); }

    private int area(int b)
    {
        if (b == 1)
            return 1;
        return b + area(b-1);
    }
}
```

Which of the following is a true statement?

(A) When `getArea` is invoked in a client program, neither Implementation I nor Implementation II will work correctly.

(B) Implementations I and II are equally efficient in speed and memory usage.

(C) Implementation I is more run-time efficient than Implementation II.

(D) Implementation I is more efficient in memory usage than Implementation II.

(E) Implementation II has greater run-time efficiency and memory usage efficiency than Implementation I.

Answer Key

1. **D**	8. **D**	15. **D**
2. **B**	9. **A**	16. **C**
3. **E**	10. **B**	17. **E**
4. **D**	11. **A**	18. **A**
5. **B**	12. **C**	19. **C**
6. **C**	13. **C**	20. **B**
7. **B**	14. **E**	21. **E**

Answers Explained

1. **(D)** Tail recursion is when the recursive call of a method is made as the last executable step of the method. Divide-and-conquer algorithms like those used in mergesort or quicksort have recursive calls *before* the last step. Thus, statement II is false.

2. **(B)** Code segment I is wrong because there is no base case. Code segment III is wrong because, besides anything else, sum(n) prevents the method from terminating—the base case n == 1 will not be reached.

3. **(E)** When stringRecur is invoked, it calls itself irrespective of the length of s. Since there is no action that leads to termination, the method will not terminate until the computer runs out of memory (run-time error).

4. **(D)** The base case is s.length() $\geq$ 15. Since s gets longer on each method call, the method will eventually terminate. If the original length of s is $\geq$ 15, the method will terminate without output on the first call.

5. **(B)** Letting R denote the method result, we have

$$R(5) = 2 * R(4)$$
$$= 2 * (2 * (R(3))$$
$$= \cdots$$
$$= 2 * (2 * (2 * (2 * R(1))))$$
$$= 2^5$$
$$= 32$$

6. **(C)** For result(n) there will be $(n-1)$ recursive calls before result(1), the base case, is reached. Adding the initial call gives a total of n method calls.

7. **(B)** This method returns the nth term of an arithmetic sequence with first term a and common difference d. Letting M denote method `mystery`, we have

$$M(3, 2, 6) = 6 + M(2, 2, 6)$$
$$= 6 + (6 + M(1, 2, 6)) \quad \text{(base case)}$$
$$= 6 + 6 + 2$$
$$= 14$$

8. **(D)** Here are the recursive calls that are made, in order: $f(6, 8) \to f(6, 2) \to f(4, 2) \to f(2, 2)$, base case. Thus, 2 is returned.

9. **(A)** If there is only one element in x, then `recur` returns that element. Having the recursive call at the beginning of the `else` part of the algorithm causes the `if` part for each method call to be stacked until t eventually gets assigned to x[0]. The pending `if` statements are then executed, and t is compared to each element in x. The largest value in x is returned.

10. **(B)** Since the recursive call is made directly following the base case, the `System.out.print...` statements are stacked up. These statements are then popped off the stack in reverse order, which means that the characters of the string will be printed in reverse order.

11. **(A)** The required code is for a negative `expo`. For example, `power(2, -3)` should return $2^{-3} = 1/8$. So `expo+1` for the second parameter must be correct, otherwise you will never reach `expo==0`, the base case. This eliminates choices B, D, and E. The recursive definition for b^n where $n < 0$ is

$$b^n = \begin{cases} 1, & n = 0 \\ (1/b) \cdot b^{n+1}, & n < 0 \end{cases}$$

which eliminates choice C. For example, $2^{-3} = (1/2) \cdot 2^{-2}$.

12. **(C)** The numbers to the right of the boxes show the order of execution of the statements. Let D denote `doSomething`.

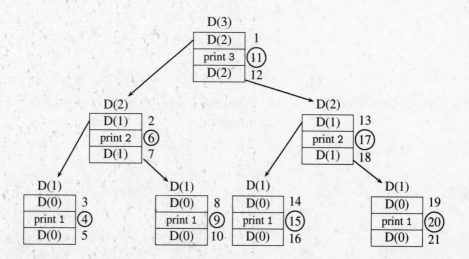

Each box represents a recursive call to `doSomething`. The numbers in the box refer to that method call only. D(0) is the base case, so the statement immediately following it is executed next. When all statements in a given box (method call) have been executed, backtrack along the arrow to find the statement that gets executed next. The circled numbers represent the statements that produce output. Following them in order, statements 4, 6, 9, 11, 15, 17, and 20 produce the output in choice C.

13. **(C)** Since even numbers are printed *before* the recursive call in segment I, they will be printed in the order in which they are read from the keyboard. Contrast this with the correct choice, segment III, in which the recursive call is made before the test for evenness. These tests will be stacked until the last number is read. Recall that the pending statements are removed from the stack in reverse order (most recent recursive call first), which leads to even numbers being printed in reverse order. Segment II is wrong because all numbers entered will be printed, irrespective of whether they are even or not. Note that segment II would work if the input list contained only even numbers.

14. **(E)** The method generates a sequence. The first two terms, $t(1)$ and $t(2)$, are 2 and 4. Each subsequent term is generated by subtracting the previous two terms. This is the sequence: 2, 4, 2, -2, -4, -2, 2, 4, ... Thus, $t(5) = -4$. Alternatively,

$$t(5) = t(4) - t(3)$$
$$= [t(3) - t(2)] - t(3)$$
$$= -t(2)$$
$$= -4$$

15. **(D)** 15. Count them! (Note that you stop at $t(2)$ since it's a base case.)

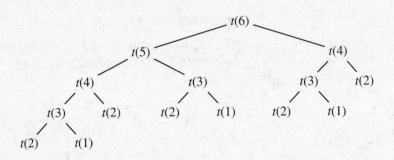

Level AB Only

16. **(C)** A simple way of seeing this is that each call makes two more calls. This is the signature of an $O(2^n)$ process.

17. **(E)** This is an example of *mutual recursion*, where two methods call each other.

$$f_1(5, 3) = 5 + f_2(4, 3)$$
$$= 5 + (4 + f_1(2, 3))$$
$$= 5 + (4 + (2 + f_2(1, 3)))$$
$$= 5 + (4 + (2 + 4))$$
$$= 15$$

Note that $f_2(1, 3)$ is a base case.

18. **(A)** foo(3) = 3 (This is a base case). Also, foo(4) = 4 ∗ foo(3) = 12. So you need to find foo(foo(3) + foo(4)) = foo(15).

$$foo(15) = 15 * foo(14)$$
$$= 15 * (14 * foo(13))$$
$$= \cdots$$
$$= 15 * 14 * \cdots * 4 * foo(3)$$
$$= 15 * 14 * \cdots * 4 * 3$$
$$= (15)!/(2!)$$

19. **(C)** Suppose that n = 365051. The method call `writeWithCommas(365051)` will write 051 and then execute the call `writeWithCommas(365)`. This is a base case, so 365 will be written out, resulting in 051,365. A number like 278278 (two sets of three identical digits) will be written out correctly, as will a "symmetrical" number like 251462251. Also, any n < 1000 is a base case and the number will be written out correctly as is.

20. **(B)** The cause of the problem is that the numbers are being written out with the sets of three digits in the wrong order. The problem is fixed by interchanging `writeThreeDigits(n % 1000)` and `writeWithCommas(n/1000)`. For example, here is the order of execution for `writeWithCommas(365051)`.

```
writeWithCommas(365) → Base case. Writes 365
System.out.print(","); → 365,
writeThreeDigits(051) → 365,051 which is correct
```

21. **(E)** Both `getArea` methods should work correctly in a client program. Implementation I, however, is less efficient since it constructs a new `Triangle` object with each recursive call. This slows down the run time and uses more memory than Implementation II, which accesses only the current `Triangle` object.

CHAPTER EIGHT
Linked Lists

But it really doesn't matter whom you put upon the list.
For they'd none of 'em be missed—they'd none of 'em be missed!
—*Gilbert and Sullivan,* The Mikado

Linked List

One way of implementing a list object in Java is as an array. An alternative implementation is as a *linked list*. Unlike an array, the elements of a linked list are not necessarily in contiguous memory slots. Instead, each element stores the address of the next item in the list. We say that it contains a *link* or *pointer* to the next item. In Java a linked list item actually stores a reference to the next object in the list. The last element of the list has a *null reference* in its pointer field to signify the end of the list.

A linked list is a *dynamic data structure*, growing and shrinking during run time. Memory slots are allocated as the need arises. Slots no longer needed are automatically recycled in Java. Contrast this with a built-in Java array, whose size is fixed at construction time.

Implementing a linked list in Java is part of the AB course and is described in this chapter. Additionally, you need to understand how to use the Java class `java.util.LinkedList` without knowing details of its implementation. This is discussed with the other "container" classes in Chapter 11.

Linear Linked Lists

Features of a
Linked List

The term "linked list" is often used to mean a *linear linked list*. Picture a linked list as a collection of memory slots called *nodes*, each of which has a data field and a pointer field.

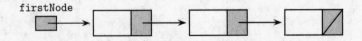

The arrows correspond to reference values in Java. The pointer field in the last item

244

is the null reference. The variable `firstNode` is a reference to the first element in the list.

A linked list can be implemented in Java using a `ListNode` class for each node and a `LinkedList` class for the whole list.

The `ListNode` Class

A `ListNode` class similar to the following will be provided on the AP exam.[1]

```
/*Linked list node */
public class ListNode
{
    private Object value;
    private ListNode next;

    public ListNode(Object initValue, ListNode initNext)
    {
        value = initValue;
        next = initNext;
    }

    public Object getValue()
    {return value;}

    public ListNode getNext()
    {return next;}

    public void setValue(Object theNewValue)
    {value = theNewValue;}

    public void setNext(ListNode theNewNext)
    {next = theNewNext;}
}
```

The Instance Variables

`private Object value`

The `value` data field is of type `Object`, which means that primitive types like `int` cannot be placed directly into a `ListNode`. They must first be wrapped in a wrapper class like `Integer` or `Double`. See Example 1 on the next page.

`private ListNode next`

The `ListNode` class is said to be *self-referential*, since it has an instance variable `next` that refers to itself. Self-referential objects can be linked together to form objects like lists, trees, stacks, and so on. Thus the variable `next` is called a *link* or *pointer*.

The Methods

`public ListNode(Object initValue, ListNode initNext)`

The `ListNode` constructor, with `initValue` and `initNext` parameters, allows a sin-

[1]Based on the College Board's *AP Computer Science AB: Implementation Classes for Linked Lists and Tree Nodes.*

gle statement to assign the value and next fields to a ListNode.

Example 1

The following statements use the constructor to create a single ListNode containing the value 8.

```
Integer intObj = new Integer(8);
ListNode p = new ListNode(intObj, null);
```

Alternatively, you can create the ListNode in a single statement:

```
ListNode p = new ListNode(new Integer(8), null);
```

> public Object getValue()

This is an accessor method that returns the value of the current ListNode. Since the type is Object, a cast to Integer, Double, or String, and so on will be needed, unless you plan to assign it to a variable of type Object.

> public ListNode getNext()

This is an accessor method that returns next, the pointer value of the the current ListNode.

> public void setValue(Object theNewValue)

This is a mutator method that allows the value of the current ListNode to be changed to theNewValue.

> public void setNext(ListNode theNewNext)

This is a mutator method that allows the next field of the current ListNode to be changed to theNewNext.

Example 2

Consider this linked list of ListNode objects, where firstNode, current, and lastNode are all of type ListNode.

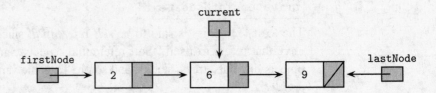

```
Integer first = (Integer) firstNode.getValue(); //first has value 2
ListNode p = current.getNext(); //p refers to ListNode containing 9
Integer last = (Integer) current.getNext().getValue();
                                              //last has value 9
```

Now consider the statements

```
current.setNext(null);
lastNode = current;
```

These two statements result in this setup:

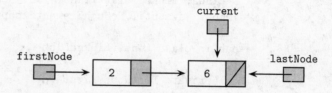

You may wonder what happened to the node containing 9. Java has automatic garbage collection that recycles any memory slot that is no longer in use (i.e., there are no references to the object in that slot).

To change the value in the first node to 5:

```
Integer num = new Integer(5);
firstNode.setValue(num);
```

Alternatively,

```
firstNode.setValue(new Integer(5));
```

Example 3

Consider a linked list of `ListNode` objects.

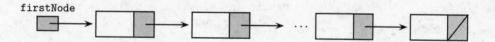

Here is a code segment that traverses the list and outputs the contents to the screen, one element per line.

```
ListNode p = firstNode;
while (p != null)
{
    System.out.println(p.getValue());
    p = p.getNext();
}
```

NOTE   The quantity `p.getValue()` does not need to be cast to the actual object type if the object in the linked list has a `toString` method. Java will polymorphically select the correct `toString` method and print the value accordingly.

A Linear Linked List Class   You are expected to know how to implement linked lists. The `LinearLinkedList` class shown below implements a singly-linked list of nodes, in which items are of type `Object`, and the references are of type `ListNode`. The instance variables are a reference to the first node, and the size of the list.

Methods provided in the class will allow

- a test for an empty list

- elements to be added or removed from either end of the list
- the size of the list to be accessed
- printing a list object by providing a toString method
- list traversal by a client, via a getFirstNode method

```
/*Linear linked list class */
import java.util.NoSuchElementException;

public class LinearLinkedList
{
    private ListNode firstNode;
    private int size;

    //Construct an empty list
    public LinearLinkedList()
    {
        size = 0;
        firstNode = null;
    }

    //Return true if list is empty, false otherwise
    public boolean isEmpty()
    {
        return size == 0;
        //or return firstNode == null;
    }

    //Return number of nodes in the list
    public int size()
    { return size; }

    //This method is needed for client traversal of list.
    //Returns reference to first node
    public ListNode getFirstNode()
    { return firstNode; }

    //Insert object o at front of list
    public void addFirst(Object o)
    {
        firstNode = new ListNode(o, firstNode);
        size++;
    }

    //Insert object o at end of list
    public void addLast(Object o)
    {
        if (isEmpty())
            firstNode = new ListNode(o, null);
        else
        {
            ListNode current = firstNode;
            while (current.getNext() != null)
                current = current.getNext();
            current.setNext(new ListNode(o, null));
```

```
    }
    size++;
}


//Remove and return first element
public Object removeFirst()
{
    if (isEmpty())
        throw new NoSuchElementException(
                "Can't remove from empty list");
    Object item = firstNode.getValue();
    firstNode = firstNode.getNext();
    size--;
    return item;
}


//Remove and return last element
public Object removeLast()
{
    if (isEmpty())
        throw new NoSuchElementException(
                "Can't remove from empty list");
    ListNode current = firstNode;
    ListNode follow = null;
    while (current.getNext() != null)   //at least 2 nodes
    {
        follow = current;
        current = current.getNext();
    }
    if (follow == null)                 //list had just 1 node
        firstNode = null;
    else
        follow.setNext(null);
    size--;
    return current.getValue();
}


//Return LinearLinkedList as String
public String toString()
{
    if (isEmpty())
        return "empty.";
    else
    {
        String s = "";
        ListNode current = firstNode;
        while (current != null)
        {
            s = s + current.getValue() + " ";
            current = current.getNext();
        }
        return s;
    }
}
}
```

NOTE   1. The `size` variable is not essential but is sometimes convenient.

2. You need to know how to throw a `NoSuchElementException`. This error occurs when there's an attempt to access a nonexistent element in a list. (See also the `next()` method of the `Iterator` interface on p. 252.) In the `LinearLinkedList` class, the exception is thrown if an attempt is made to remove an element from an empty list. To throw the exception you need to include the statement

```
import java.util.NoSuchElementException;
```

in the file with the class whose methods will throw the exception. In the relevant methods, the statement

```
if (isEmpty())
    throw new NoSuchElementException();
```

will cause the program to terminate if the list is empty. Additionally, you can provide your own error message when the exception is thrown:

```
if (isEmpty())
    throw new NoSuchElementException(
            "Can't remove from empty list");
```

For example, if the `removeFirst` and `removeLast` methods are invoked on an empty list, the message `Can't remove from empty list` is printed and the program terminates.

Here is a program that tests the `LinearLinkedList` methods:

```
/* Tests LinearLinkedList Class */

public class LinkedListTest
{
    //Read Integer objects into LinkedList a
    public static void getList(LinearLinkedList a)
    {
        final int SENTINEL = -999;

        System.out.print("Enter list of integers. ");
        System.out.println("Terminate with " + SENTINEL);
        int num = IO.readInt();    //read user input

        while (num != SENTINEL)
        {
            a.addLast(new Integer(num));
            num = IO.readInt();    //read user input
        }
    }

    //Search for key in LinkedList a.
    //Return true if found, false otherwise
    public static boolean search(LinearLinkedList a, Object key)
    {
        ListNode current = a.getFirstNode();
```

```
            while (current != null)
            {
                if(current.getValue().equals(key))
                    return true;
                current = current.getNext();
            }
            return false;
        }

        public static void main(String[] args)
        {
            LinearLinkedList a = new LinearLinkedList();

            //TESTING getList AND toString
            getList(a);
            System.out.print("List is: ");
            System.out.println(a);

            //TESTING size
            System.out.println("Length of list is " + a.size());

            //TESTING removeFirst and removeLast
            Integer first = (Integer)a.removeFirst();
            System.out.println("First element was " + first);
            Integer last = (Integer)a.removeLast();
            System.out.println("Last element was " + last);
            System.out.print("List is: ");
            System.out.println(a);

            //TESTING search
            System.out.print("Enter key value for search: ");
            Integer key = new Integer(IO.readInt());
            if (search(a, key))
                System.out.println(key + " was in the list.");
            else
                System.out.println(key + " was not in the list.");
        }
    }
```

Here is some sample output.

```
Enter list of integers. Terminate with -999
1 2 7 5 4 0 3 -999
List is: 1 2 7 5 4 0 3
Length of list is 7
First element was 1
Last element was 3
List is 2 7 5 4 0
Enter key value for search: 9
9 was not in the list
```

NOTE   The method `getFirstNode` in the `LinearLinkedList` class is a crucial method to gain access to the list for traversal outside the class.

Iterators

List Traversal

The `ListNode` and `LinearLinkedList` classes allow list traversal as follows: assign a reference to the first node using `getFirstNode` and then advance using the `getNext` method of `ListNode`. Addition and removal of items are achieved with the `setNext` and `setValue` methods of `ListNode`.

This is not ideal: A user should not have to get into the details of pointer manipulation. Ideally, the `ListNode` methods should be hidden from the user, encapsulated in the `LinearLinkedList` class.

One solution is to add a `current` instance variable to the `LinearLinkedList` class, where `current` would be a reference to a `ListNode` in the list. Methods like `add` or `remove` could then be added to the `LinearLinkedList` class. This is an improvement, but it still has disadvantages. For example,

- client traversal must still be done using `getNext`;
- more than one "current" pointer is needed if a list must be accessed in more than one place simultaneously.

A solution to both these problems is to use an *iterator* to traverse the list. An iterator is an object that maintains a current position in a collection. It provides a way to iterate through the elements, one at a time.

The `Iterator`
Interface

The package `java.util` provides an interface called `Iterator`. A class that implements `Iterator` can iterate over any collection (see Chapter 11). An iterator class provides a level of abstraction in which a list and a position in the list are two separate objects.

The Methods of `Iterator`

```
boolean hasNext()
```

Returns `true` if there's at least one more element to be examined, `false` otherwise.

```
Object next()
```

Returns the next element in the iteration. If no elements remain, the method throws a `NoSuchElementException`.

```
void remove()
```

Deletes from the collection the last element that was returned by `next`. This method can be called only once per call to `next`. It throws an `IllegalStateException` if the `next` method has not yet been called, or if the `remove` method has already been called after the last call to `next`.

Implementing the
Iterator Interface
for a Linked List

Here is a `LLLIterator` class that implements the `Iterator` interface. It will be used to traverse and manipulate a linear linked list, as implemented with the `ListNode` and `LinearLinkedList` classes.

```
/* An iterator class that steps through a linear linked list */

import java.util.Iterator;
import java.util.NoSuchElementException;

public class LLLIterator implements Iterator
{
    private ListNode current;
    private ListNode previous;         //for remove()
    private boolean OKtoRemove;        //true if OK to call remove()
    private LinearLinkedList myList;

    //constructor
    public LLLIterator(LinearLinkedList list)
    {
        myList = list;
        current = null;
        previous = null;
        OKtoRemove = false;
    }

    public boolean hasNext()
    {
        if (myList.isEmpty())
            return false;
        else if (current == null)  //at beginning of iteration
            return true;
        else
            return current.getNext() != null;
    }

    /* Advances current and returns value in current's node */
    public Object next()
    {
        if (myList.isEmpty())
            throw new NoSuchElementException
                ("List is empty");

        if (current == null)        //start of iteration
            current = myList.getFirstNode();
        else
        {
            previous = current;
            current = current.getNext();
        }
        if (current == null)       //end of list
            throw new NoSuchElementException
                ("No more elements in list");
        OKtoRemove = true;                 // OK to call remove()
        return current.getValue();
    }

    /* Precondition:  next() has been called, so current points
     *                to node that must be removed.
     *                previous points to node before current
```

```
              * Postcondition: current and previous point to node
              *                preceding node removed  */
             public void remove()
             {
                 if (! OKtoRemove)
                     throw new IllegalStateException
                         ("next() not called before remove()");
                 else
                     OKtoRemove = false;       //reset OKtoRemove
                 if (previous == null)  //first node must be removed
                     myList.removeFirst();
                 else
                     previous.setNext(current.getNext());
                 current = previous;
             }
         }
```

**How to Use the
LLLIterator Class**

Step one is to add an iterator method to the LinearLinkedList class.

```
public Iterator iterator()
{
    return new LLLIterator(this);
}
```

The method constructs a LLLIterator object for its LinearLinkedList parameter.

At the top of the file with the LinearLinkedList class (and any other file in which you use an iterator) add the statement

```
import java.util.Iterator;
```

Here are some examples showing how the LLLIterator class is used with a LinearLinkedList. Include statements like the following at the start of the client program:

```
LinearLinkedList list = new LinearLinkedList();
getList(list);              //read values into list
```

Example 1

```
//Print elements of list, 1 per line
for (Iterator itr = list.iterator(); itr.hasNext();)
    System.out.println(itr.next());
```

The iterator itr is initialized at the beginning of the linked list. Each time the method itr.next() is invoked, itr advances to the next element. This is why the for loop needs no updating statement.

Example 2

```
//Repeatedly remove first element of list and print
//the rest of the list, until no elements remain
for (Iterator itr = list.iterator(); itr.hasNext();)
{
    Object ob = itr.next();
    itr.remove();
    System.out.println(list);
}
```

If the original list is 2 4 6, the output will be

```
4 6
6
empty
```

Example 3

```
//Assume a list of Integer values
//Remove all occurrences of 6 from the list
for (Iterator itr = list.iterator(); itr.hasNext();)
{
    Integer num = (Integer) itr.next();
    if (num.intValue() == 6)
    {
        itr.remove();
        System.out.println(list);
    }
}
```

If the original list is 2 6 6 3 5 6 the output will be

```
2 6 3 5 6
2 3 5 6
2 3 5
```

Example 4

```
//Illustrate NoSuchElementException
Iterator itr = list.iterator();
while (true)
    System.out.println(itr.next());
```

The list elements will be printed, one per line. Then an attempt will be made to move past the end of the list, causing a NoSuchElementException to be thrown. The loop can be corrected by replacing true with itr.hasNext().

Example 5

```
//Illustrate IllegalStateException
Iterator itr = list.iterator();
Object ob = itr.next();
itr.remove();
itr.remove();
```

Every remove call must be preceded by a next. The second itr.remove() statement will therefore cause an IllegalStateException to be thrown.

NOTE   In a given program, the declaration

```
itr = list.iterator();
```

must be made every time you need to initialize the iterator to the beginning of the list.

The ListIterator Interface

The ListIterator interface is provided in java.util and is a subclass of Iterator. In other words,

```
public interface ListIterator extends Iterator
```

This means that `ListIterator` provides methods in addition to `next`, `hasNext`, and `remove`. There are, in fact, six new methods in `ListIterator`, of which you are expected to know just two for the AP exam: `add` and `set`.

> `void add(Object o)`

Inserts the specified element into the list. The insertion point immediately precedes the next element that would be returned by a call to `next`, if any. If the list is empty, the new element becomes the sole element in the list.

NOTE

1. A subsequent call to `next` would be unaffected by the new element—the "current" node becomes the inserted node.
2. The `add` method throws a `ClassCastException` if the type of the object added is incompatible with the elements in the list.

> `void set(Object o)`

Replaces the last element returned by `next` with the specified element. A call to `set` can only be made if neither `remove` nor `add` have been called after the last call to `next`.

NOTE

1. The method throws a `ClassCastException` if the type of the object prevents it from being added to the list. For example, if you declare a linear linked list of `Integer` and then try to add a `String`, you will generate this error.
2. The method throws an `IllegalStateException` if `next` has not been called, or if `remove` or `add` have been called after the last call to `next`.

Implementing the ListIterator Class for a Linked List

Since you are not expected to know all of the methods in the `ListIterator` interface, you will not be asked to write a class that implements `ListIterator`. You are, however, expected to know the `add` and `set` methods described above.

What follows is a framework for a `LLL_ListIterator` class. This class is a subclass of the `LLLIterator` class given in the previous section, p. 253, and it implements the `ListIterator` interface. It uses the same `LinearLinkedList` and `ListNode` classes provided in this chapter. In order to use the instance variables `current`, `previous`, `OKtoRemove`, and `myList` of the `LLLIterator` superclass, these variables were changed to `protected`. If they remained `private`, they could not be directly accessed by a derived class. Except where they are used in the Case Study, protected variables are not part of the AP Java subset—you will always use accessors and mutators to access instance variables from outside a class.

Implementation code is given for the constructor, `add`, and `set` methods.

```
/* A ListIterator class for a linear linked list */

import java.util.ListIterator;

public class LLL_ListIterator extends LLLIterator
        implements ListIterator
{
    //constructor
    public LLL_ListIterator(LinearLinkedList list)
    {
        super(list);    //same constructor as LLLIterator class
    }
```

```
        /* Precondition:  either previous and current both null
         *                 (start of iteration), or
         *.                previous and current refer to same node
         *                 (after a remove), or
         *                 previous refers to node preceding current
         * Postcondition: o has been added following current
         *                 current points to node just added
         *                 previous points to node preceding current */
        public void add(Object o)
        {
            if (current == null)  //at start of iteration
            {
                myList.addFirst(o);
                current = myList.getFirstNode();
            }
            else
            {
                //case: middle or end of list,
                //with or without preceding remove()
                current.setNext(new ListNode(o, current.getNext()));
                previous = current;
                current = current.getNext();
            }
            OKtoRemove = false;    //can't call remove or set after add
        }


        /* Precondition:  current refers to element that was last
         *                 returned by next()
         * Postcondition: element that current refers to has been
         *                 replaced by o */
        public void set(Object o)
        {
            if (! OKtoRemove)
                throw new IllegalStateException
                    ("next() not called before set()");
            current.setValue(o);
        }


        //Other methods of ListIterator interface.
        //Not required for AP exam
    }
```

How to Use the LLL_ListIterator Class

As before, a new method must be added to the LinearLinkedList class. Replace the iterator method with

```
public ListIterator listIterator()
{
    return new LLL_ListIterator(this);
}
```

Here are some examples showing how the LLL_ListIterator is used with a LinearLinkedList. First, at the top of all files that use ListIterator include the statement

```
import java.util.ListIterator;
```

Also, at the start of the client program include

```
LinearLinkedList a = new LinearLinkedList();
getList(a);        //read values into list
```

Example 1

```
//Print elements of list, 1 per line
for (ListIterator itr = a.listIterator(); itr.hasNext();)
    System.out.println(itr.next());
```

NOTE This is essentially the same code as when Iterator is used. The hasNext and next methods are inherited from the LLLIterator class.

Example 2

```
//Add element to front of list
itr = a.listIterator();
itr.add(new Integer(55));
System.out.println(a);
```

If the input for the list is 3 5 7, the output will be 55 3 5 7.

Example 3

```
//Add element to second slot in list
itr = a.listIterator();
Object obj = itr.next();
itr.add(new Double(2.7));
System.out.println(a);
```

If the input for the list is 3 5 7, the output will be 3 2.7 5 7.

Example 4

```
//Change value of the kth element in list to 100
//Precondition: list contains at least k elements
itr = a.listIterator();
for (int i=1; i<=k; i++)
    Object obj = itr.next();
itr.set(new Integer(100));
System.out.println(a);
```

If the input is 1 5 9 13 and k is 3, the output will be 1 5 100 13.

Example 5

```
//Illustrate IllegalStateException
itr = a.listIterator();
itr.set(new Integer(55));    //error: set must be preceded by next
```

Each of the following code fragments will also cause the error.

```
Object obj = itr.next();
itr.remove();
itr.set(new Integer(55));      //set must be directly
                               //preceded by next
Object obj = itr.next();
itr.add(new Integer(100));
itr.set(new Integer(15));      //set must be directly
                               //preceded by next
```

Example 6

```
//Insert element in its correct position in a linear linked list.
//Precondition: list sorted in increasing order
System.out.print("Enter integer to be inserted ");
Integer key = new Integer(IO.readInt());  //read user input
ListIterator itr = a.listIterator();
ListIterator itr2 = a.listIterator();
Object o;
while(itr.hasNext() && key.compareTo((Integer) itr.next()) > 0)
    o = itr2.next();
itr2.add(key);
System.out.println(a);
```

NOTE

1. The algorithm needs a second iterator to follow the first. This is because when you find the insertion point you've gone one node too far! The previous node must be accessed to get the pointer connections correct. The rule of thumb is this: If your algorithm needs two pointers, you should use two iterators.

2. The `itr2` iterator will be one position (node) behind `itr` when the loop is exited. This is because `itr.next()` will be executed during the *test* that terminates the loop, while `itr2.next()` will not be executed. If the loop terminates because `itr.hasNext()` is false, both iterators will be at the last slot in the list, and so the new element will be correctly inserted at the end of the list.

Circular Linked Lists

A linear linked list allows easy access to the first node but requires traversal of the whole list to reach the final node. A small change converts a linear linked list into a *circular linked list,* which allows easy access to both the first and last nodes. Let the pointer field of the last node point to the first node, instead of being `null`.

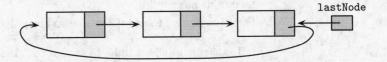

Implementing a Circular Linked List

A circular linked list can be implemented using a `ListNode` class for each node and a `CircularLinkedList` class for the whole list. The `ListNode` class is the same class used for linear linked lists. The `CircularLinkedList` class has the same methods as the `LinearLinkedList` class, but most of the implementation code is different if you use the instance variable

```
private ListNode lastNode;
```

to replace

```
private ListNode firstNode;
```

Also, instead of a getFirstNode accessor, the CircularLinkedList class would provide a getLastNode method.

Having a reference to lastNode allows easy access to both the first and last elements of the list. Insertion and deletion operations at both ends of the list can be done in $O(1)$ (constant) time. The data in the first node can be accessed with lastNode.getNext().getValue().

Note that in traversing a circular linked list, there's no longer a null reference in the last node. The lastNode reference must therefore be used as a stoplight for list traversal.

Example 1

Here is code for the addLast method of a CircularLinkedList class.

```
//insert object o at end of list
public void addLast(Object o)
{
    if (isEmpty())
    {
        lastNode = new ListNode(o, null);
        lastNode.setNext(lastNode);
    }
    else
    {
        ListNode p = new ListNode(o, lastNode.getNext());
        lastNode.setNext(p);
        lastNode = p;
    }
    size++;
}
```

NOTE
1. You may think that adding a node to an empty list can be accomplished with the single statement

   ```
   lastNode = new ListNode(o, lastNode);
   ```

   This, however, won't work. Since the current value of lastNode is null, the right-hand side, which is evaluated first, will create a node that has a null reference in its next field.
2. The else part of the addLast method can also be written as follows:

   ```
   lastNode.setNext(new ListNode(o, lastNode.getNext()));
   lastNode = lastNode.getNext();
   ```

Example 2

Here is code for the toString method of the CircularLinkedList class.

```
//return contents of circular linked list as a string
public String toString()
{
    if (isEmpty())
        return "empty";
    else
    {
        String s = "";
        ListNode current = lastNode.getNext();
        while (current != lastNode)
        {
            s = s + current.getValue() + " ";
            current = current.getNext();
        }
        s = s + current.getValue();
        return s;
    }
}
```

NOTE   The `while` loop stops when `current` refers to the last node:

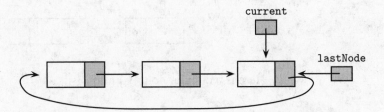

If you omit the final `s = s + current.getValue()` statement, the returned string `s` will not have the data from the last node.

Circular Linked Lists and Iterators

As with linear linked lists, iterator classes can be written for circular linked lists. Thus `CLLIterator` could implement `Iterator` and provide `next`, `hasNext`, and `remove` methods, while `CLL_ListIterator` could implement `ListIterator` and extend `Iterator`, providing the additional methods `add`, `set`, and so on.

Example

Find the sum of the integers in a circular linked list. Assume the existence of an `iterator` method for circular linked lists.

```
/* Precondition:  CircularLinkedList c contains Integers
 * Postcondition: Returns sum of Integer values in c */
public static int listSum(CircularLinkedList c)
{
    int sum = 0;
    for (Iterator itr = c.iterator(); itr.hasNext();)
        sum += ((Integer) itr.next()).intValue();
    return sum;
}
```

NOTE   You need the extra parentheses in the `sum += ...` statement because otherwise the higher precedence of the dot operator will cause `intValue()` to be invoked before the cast to `Integer`.

Doubly Linked Lists

Why Doubly Linked Lists?

Singly linked linear and circular lists have several disadvantages:

1. Traversal is in just one direction.
2. To access previous nodes, you must go to one end of the list and start again.
3. Given a reference to a node, you cannot easily delete that node. There is no direct access to the previous pointer field.

A data structure that overcomes these disadvantages is a *doubly linked list*, where each node has three fields: a data field, a reference to the next node, and a reference to the previous node. The price paid for the capability of moving in either direction of the list is the extra memory required for one more instance variable in a doubly linked list node.

Picture a doubly linked list as follows:

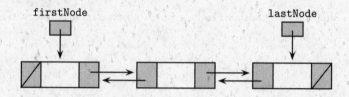

Here is a circular doubly linked list:

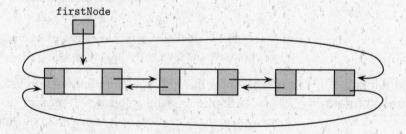

If the pointer fields are `next` and `prev`, notice that `firstNode.prev` refers to the last (rightmost) node in the list. This means that you can dispense with a `lastNode` variable: `firstNode` provides $O(1)$ access to both the first and last nodes of the list.

Header and Trailer Nodes

Header and trailer nodes are nodes at the front and back of a linked list that do not contain elements of the list. Think of them as dummy nodes with no values.

The effect of having header and trailer nodes is that you avoid some special-case testing for the first and last nodes: insertion and deletion is always done in the "middle" of the list.

Here is an empty doubly linked list with header and trailer nodes:

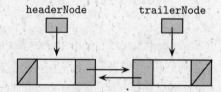

**Implementing
Doubly Linked Lists**

As with linear and circular linked lists, the implementation can be achieved with
two classes, one for the node and one for the list.

The DoublyListNode Class

The DoublyListNode class is very similar to the ListNode class. It requires an
additional pointer field, prev, and additional methods for accessing and setting
values and links for the previous node.

```
/* Doubly linked list node */

public class DoublyListNode
{
    private Object value;
    private DoublyListNode next;
    private DoublyListNode prev;

    public DoublyListNode(DoublyListNode initPrev, Object initValue,
                    DoublyListNode initNext)
    {
        prev = initPrev;
        value = initValue;
        next = initNext;
    }

    public DoublyListNode getPrev()
    { return prev; }

    public void setPrev(DoublyListNode theNewPrev)
    { prev = theNewPrev; }

    public Object getValue()
    { return value; }

    public void setValue(Object theNewValue)
    { value = theNewValue; }

    public DoublyListNode getNext()
    { return next; }

    public void setNext(DoublyListNode theNewNext)
    { next = theNewNext; }
}
```

A DoublyLinkedList Class

There are several design choices for implementing doubly linked lists—linear, circular, with or without header and/or trailer. The class below is for a linear doubly
linked list with header and trailer nodes. Having a header and trailer eliminates
many of the special end-of-list cases for insertion and deletion.

```
/* Doubly linked list class with header and trailer */

import java.util.NoSuchElementException;
```

```java
public class DoublyLinkedList
{
    private DoublyListNode headerNode;
    private DoublyListNode trailerNode;
    private int size;

    //Construct an empty list
    public DoublyLinkedList()
    {
        size = 0;
        headerNode = new DoublyListNode(null, null, null);
        trailerNode = new DoublyListNode(headerNode, null, null);
        headerNode.setNext(trailerNode);
    }

    //Return true if list is empty, false otherwise
    public boolean isEmpty()
    { return size == 0; }

    //Return number of nodes in the list
    public int size()
    { return size; }

    //Needed to traverse list
    public DoublyListNode getFirstNode()
    { return headerNode.getNext(); }

    //Needed to traverse list
    public DoublyListNode getLastNode()
    { return trailerNode.getPrev(); }

    //Insert object o at end of list
    public void addLast(Object o)
    {
        DoublyListNode p = new DoublyListNode(trailerNode.getPrev(),
                         o, trailerNode);
        trailerNode.getPrev().setNext(p);
        trailerNode.setPrev(p);
        size++;
    }

    //Insert object o at front of list
    public void addFirst(Object o)
    {implementation code similar to addLast}

    //Remove and return first element
    public Object removeFirst()
    {
        if (isEmpty())
            throw new NoSuchElementException
                ("Can't remove from empty list");

        DoublyListNode p = headerNode.getNext();
        Object item = p.getValue();
        headerNode.setNext(p.getNext());
```

```
            p.getNext().setPrev(headerNode);
            size--;
            return item;
    }

    //Remove and return last element
    public Object removeLast()
    {implementation code similar to removeFirst}

    //Add item to the left of node.
    //Precondition: node refers to an element in a nonempty list
    void addLeft(Object item, DoublyListNode node)
    {
        DoublyListNode p = new DoublyListNode(node.getPrev(),
                                item, node);
        node.setPrev(p);
        p.getPrev().setNext(p);
        size++;
    }

    //Add item to the right of node.
    //Precondition: node refers to an element in a nonempty list
    void addRight(Object item, DoublyListNode node)
    {implementation code similar to addLeft}

    //Remove element referred to by node from list.
    //Precondition: node points to element in list
    public void remove(DoublyListNode node)
    {
        node.getPrev().setNext(node.getNext());
        node.getNext().setPrev(node.getPrev());
        size--;
    }

    //Return DoublyLinkedList as String
    public String toString()
    {
        if (isEmpty())
            return "empty.";
        else
        {
            String s = "";
            DoublyListNode p = headerNode.getNext();
            while (p != trailerNode)
            {
                s = s + p.getValue() + " ";
                p = p.getNext();
            }
            return s;
        }
    }
}
```

NOTE   1. Here's an illustration of the addLeft method. Start with a nonempty doubly
         linked list, with node pointing to one of the items. Because of the header and

trailer nodes, node will not be at either end of the list:

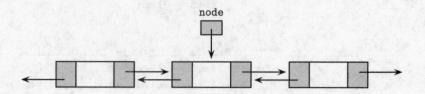

Each statement of the method is illustrated below:

```
DoublyListNode p = new DoublyListNode(node.getPrev(), item, node);
```

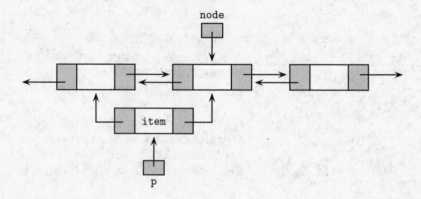

```
node.setPrev(p);
```

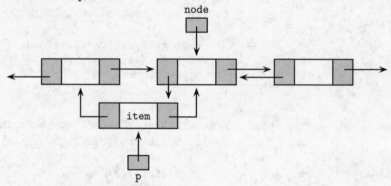

```
p.getPrev().setNext(p);
```

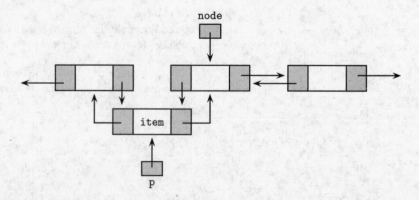

2. Here's an illustration of remove. Again, node points to some element in the "middle" of the list. This is the element that will be removed.

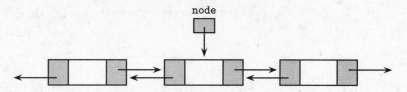

Here are pictures of what happens to the pointers:

```
node.getPrev().setNext(node.getNext());
```

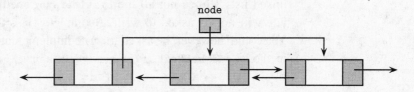

```
node.getNext().setPrev(node.getPrev());
```

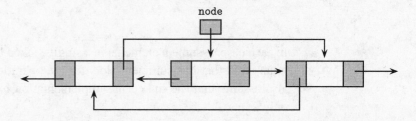

Note that as soon as the method is exited, there will be no references to the deleted element and its memory slot will be recycled.

Example

Here is a piece of code in a client method that tests addRight:

```
DoublyLinkedList a = new DoublyLinkedList();
getList(a);        //reads values into list a
DoublyListNode current = a.getFirstNode();
while (current != a.getLastNode() &&
    ((Integer) current.getValue()).intValue() != 6)
        current = current.getNext();
a.addRight(new Integer(66), current);
System.out.print("List is: ");
System.out.println(a);
```

If the list entered is 2 4 6 8, the output is

```
List is: 2 4 6 66 8
```

If the list entered is 5 10 15, the output is

```
List is: 5 10 15 66
```

NOTE   Because of the symmetry of a doubly linked list, similar results can be achieved by initializing current with a.getLastNode(), and then traveling "left" with

```
current = current.getPrev();
```

Linked Lists and Iterators

As with linear and circular linked lists, iterator classes can be written for doubly linked lists. Since not all the ListIterator methods are in the AP Java subset, you will not be asked to write a complete class that implements ListIterator. You could, however, be asked to write implementation code for one of the required methods: add, hasNext, next, remove, or set.

Run Time of Linked List vs. Array Algorithms

In each case, assume n elements in a singly-linked linear linked list (LLL) and also in an array that has sufficient slots for the operations described below. You may also assume that the linked list implementation has a reference to the first node only.

Algorithm	LLL	Array	Comment
Add or remove element at end	$O(n)$	$O(1)$	For LLL, must traverse whole list. For array, simple assignment: a[n+1] = element.
Add or remove element at front	$O(1)$	$O(n)$	For array, must move each element up one slot to create empty slot in a[0]. For LLL, simple pointer adjustment.
Linear search for key	$O(n)$	$O(n)$	In worst case, need to search entire LLL or array.
Insert element in correct position in sorted list (a) Find insertion point (b) Insert element	$O(n)$ $O(1)$	$O(n)$ $O(n)$	Insertion in LLL requires just pointer adjustments. For array, may have to move n elements to create a slot.
Delete all occurrences of value from list	$O(n)$	$O(n)$	For LLL, find value, adjust pointers, find value, adjust pointers, etc. For array, $O(n^2)$ if all elements moved each time you find value. $O(n)$ algorithm in Chapter 6, Question 5.

MULTIPLE-CHOICE QUESTIONS ON LINKED LISTS **269**

Multiple-Choice Questions on Linked Lists

Assume that all questions on linear and circular linked lists use the `ListNode` class provided on the AP exam (see p. 245).

1. The following segment is supposed to search for and remove from a linear linked list all nodes whose data fields are equal to `val`, a previously defined value. Assume that `firstNode` is accessible and references the first node in the list, and that the list is nonempty.

```
ListNode current, q;
current = firstNode;
while (current != null)
{
    if (current.getValue().equals(val))
    {
        q = current.getNext();
        current.setNext(q.getNext());
    }
    else
        current = current.getNext();
}
```

Which is true about this code segment?
(A) It works for all the nodes of the linked list.
(B) It fails for only the first node of the list.
(C) It fails for only the last node of the list.
(D) It fails for the first and last nodes of the list but works for all others.
(E) It fails for all nodes of the list.

2. A circular linked list is implemented with a `CircularLinkedList` class that has a private instance variable `lastNode`:

```
ListNode lastNode;    //refers to last node of CLL
```

The `CircularLinkedList` class has a `toString` method that converts the contents of a circular linked list to a string in the correct order. Consider a `writeList` method in the `CircularLinkedList` class:

```
/* Writes elements of CLL to screen.
 * Assumes contents of CLL have a toString method.
 * Precondition:  list is not empty.
 *                lastNode refers to last node in list
 * Postcondition: all elements printed to screen  */
public void writeList()
{ implementation code }
```

Which of the following could replace *implementation code* so that `writeList` works as intended?

```
  I System.out.println(this);

 II ListNode current = lastNode.getNext();
    while (current != lastNode)
    {
        System.out.println(current.getValue() + " ");
        current = current.getNext();
    }
    System.out.println(current.getValue());

III for (ListNode current = lastNode.getNext();
            current != lastNode; current = current.getNext())
        System.out.println(current.getValue() + " ");
```

(A) I only
(B) II only
(C) III only
(D) I and II only
(E) I, II, and III

3. Consider a `LinearLinkedList` class that has an instance variable `firstNode` of type `ListNode` and an accessor method `getFirstNode` that returns a reference to the first element in the list. Consider a client method `findKey`:

```
/* Search for key in LinearLinkedList a.
 * Return true if found, false otherwise */
public static boolean findKey(LinearLinkedList a, Object key)
{
    ListNode current = a.getFirstNode();
    while (current != null && !current.getValue().equals(key))
        current = current.getNext();
    return current != null;
}
```

Which is true about method `findKey`?
(A) `findKey` works as intended only if `key` is in the list.
(B) `findKey` works as intended only if the list is nonempty.
(C) `findKey` works as intended only if `key` is not in the last node of the list.
(D) `findKey` does not work under any circumstances.
(E) `findKey` always works as intended.

4. Consider an `insert` method in a `LinearLinkedList` class:

```
/* Precondition:  current refers to a node in a nonempty linked
 *                list sorted in increasing order
 * Postcondition: element inserted directly following node to
 *                which current points */
public void insert(ListNode current, Object element)
{
    < code >
}
```

What is the run time of < *code* >, assuming the most efficient algorithm?
(A) $O(1)$
(B) $O(n)$
(C) $O(n^2)$
(D) $O(\log n)$
(E) $O(n \log n)$

5. A circular linked list has a reference `firstNode` that points to the first element in the list, and is `null` if the list is empty. The following segment is intended to count the number of nodes in the list:

```
int count = 0;
ListNode p = firstNode.getNext();
while (p != firstNode)
{
    count++;
    p = p.getNext();
}
```

Which statement is true?
(A) The segment works as intended in all cases.
(B) The segment fails in all cases.
(C) The segment works as intended whenever the list is nonempty.
(D) The segment works as intended when the list has just one element.
(E) The segment works as intended only when the list is empty.

6. Consider the following method for removing a value from a linear linked list:

```
//Precondition:   p points to a node in a nonempty
//                linear linked list
//Postcondition: the value that p points to has been removed
//                from the list
public void remove(ListNode p)
{
    ListNode q = p.getNext();
    p.setValue(q.getValue());
    p.setNext(q.getNext());
}
```

In which of the following cases will the `remove` method fail to work as intended?

I p points to any node in the list other than the first or last node.
II p points to the last node in the list.
III p points to the first node, and there is more than one node in the list.

(A) I only
(B) II only
(C) I and II only
(D) I and III only
(E) I, II, and III

7. Suppose that the precondition of method `remove` in Question 6 is changed so that the method always works as intended. What is the run time of the algorithm?
(A) $O(n)$
(B) $O(\sqrt{n})$
(C) $O(1)$
(D) $O(n^2)$
(E) $O(\log n)$

8. Suppose that `list1` and `list2` refer to the first nodes of two linear linked lists, and that `q` points to some node in the first list. The first piece of the first list, namely all the nodes up to and including the one pointed to by `q`, is to be removed and attached to the front of `list2`, maintaining the order of the nodes. After removal, `list1` should point to the remaining nodes of its original list, and `list2` should point to the augmented list. If neither `q` nor `list1` is originally `null`, then this task is correctly performed by which of the following program segments? Assume that `p` and `q` are both correctly declared to be of type `ListNode`.

```
I  q.setNext(list2);
   list2 = list1;
   list1 = q.getNext();

II while (list1 != q.getNext())
   {
       p = list1;
       list1 = list1.getNext();
       p.setNext(list2);
       list2 = p;
   }
   list1 = p;

III p = q.getNext();
    q.setNext(list2);
    list2 = list1;
    list1 = p;
```

(A) None
(B) III only
(C) I and III only
(D) II and III only
(E) I, II, and III

Questions 9 and 10 refer to circular linked lists and a concat method described below. Circular linked lists are implemented with a CircularLinkedList class that has a private instance variable lastNode of type ListNode. The class contains, among others, the following methods:

```
public boolean isEmpty()          //returns true if list is empty
public ListNode getLastNode()     //returns lastNode
public void setLastNode(ListNode node)  //sets lastNode to node
```

Consider two CircularLinkedList objects list1 and list2. For example,

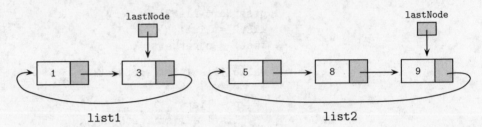

list1   list2

A method concat appends list2 to list1 and results in an augmented list1. The method call concat(list1, list2) should produce

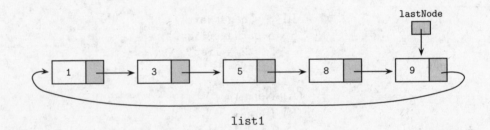

list1

If list1 is initially empty and list2 is as shown, concat(list1, list2) should produce

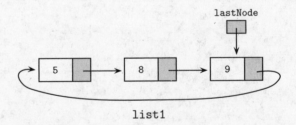

list1

If list2 is initially empty and list1 is as shown, concat(list1, list2) should produce

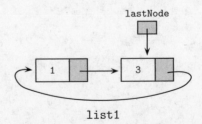

list1

Here is the concat method:

```
/* Precondition:  list1 and list2 are CircularLinkedList objects
 * Postcondition: list2 has been appended to list1  */
public static void concat(CircularLinkedList list1,
        CircularLinkedList list2)
{
    ListNode L1 = list1.getLastNode();
    ListNode L2 = list2.getLastNode();
    if (list1.isEmpty())
    {
        < code >
    }
    else
    {
        < more code >
    }
}
```

9. Which replacement for < *code* > achieves the required postcondition when
   list1 is empty?

> I list1 = list2;

> II L1 = L2;

> III list1.setLastNode(L2);

   (A) I only
   (B) II only
   (C) III only
   (D) I and III only
   (E) II and III only

10. Which could replace < *more code* > so that the postcondition of concat is satisfied? You may assume the existence of the following swap method:

```
//Interchange ListNode fields of ListNodes p1 and p2
public static void swap(ListNode p1, ListNode p2)
```

```
 I  L1.setNext(L2.getNext());
    L2.setNext(L1.getNext());
    list1.setLastNode(L2);
```

```
 II ListNode p = L1.getNext();
    L1.setNext(L2.getNext());
    L2.setNext(p);
    list1.setLastNode(L2);
```

```
III swap(list1.getLastNode(), list2.getLastNode());
    list1.setLastNode(list2.getLastNode());
```

(A) I only
(B) II only
(C) III only
(D) II and III only
(E) I and II only

11. Refer to method search:

```
/* Returns reference to first occurrence of key in list.
 * Returns null if key not in list.
 * Precondition: node points to first node in list  */
public static ListNode search(ListNode node, Object key)
{
    < code >
}
```

Which of the following replacements for < *code* > will result in method search working as intended?

```
 I if (node.getValue().equals(key))
       return node;
   else
       return search(node.getNext(), key);
```

```
 II ListNode current = node;
    while (current != null)
    {
        if(current.getValue().equals(key))
            return current;
        current = current.getNext();
    }
    return null;
```

```
III ListNode current = node;
    while (current != null && !current.getValue().equals(key))
        current = current.getNext();
    return current;
```

(A) I only
(B) II only
(C) III only
(D) II and III only
(E) I and II only

For Questions 12–16 assume that linear linked lists are implemented with a class LinearLinkedList as shown.

```
public class LinearLinkedList
{
    private ListNode firstNode;

    //constructor and other methods
        ...

    public ListNode getFirstNode()
    { return firstNode; }

    //changes firstNode
    public void setFirstNode(ListNode node)
    { firstNode = node; }

    //insert Object o at front of list
    public void addFirst(Object o)
    { implementation code }
}
```

12. This question refers to a client method `mystery`:

```
public static void mystery(LinearLinkedList list)
{
    ListNode grab, hold;
    hold = list.getFirstNode();
    list.setFirstNode(null);
    while (hold != null)
    {
        grab = hold;
        hold = hold.getNext();
        grab.setNext(list.getFirstNode());
        list.setFirstNode(grab);
    }
}
```

Assume an initial list

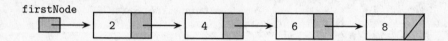

After the method call `mystery(list)`, what will the list look like?

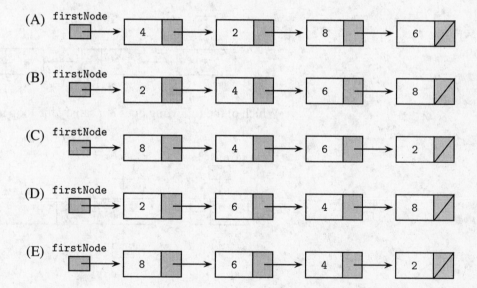

13. A client method `minimum` returns a `ListNode` that contains the smallest value in a linear linked list:

```
/* Precondition:  list is a nonempty linear linked list of
 *                Comparable objects
 * Postcondition: reference returned to ListNode with
 *                smallest value */
public static ListNode minimum(LinearLinkedList list)
{
    ListNode minSoFar = list.getFirstNode();
    ListNode p = minSoFar.getNext();
    while (p != null)
    {
        if (((Comparable) p.getValue()).compareTo
                    (minSoFar.getValue()) < 0)
            minSoFar = p;
        p = p.getNext();
    }
    return minSoFar;
}
```

Suppose `minimum(list)` is called for the following list:

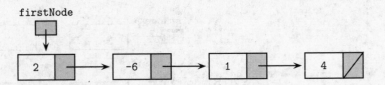

Which of the following does *not* satisfy the loop invariant for the `while` loop?

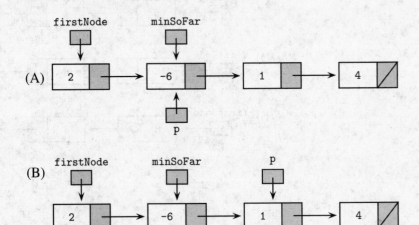

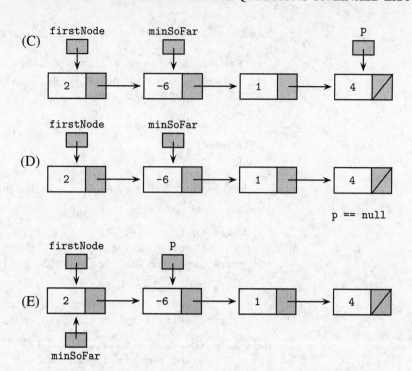

14. Suppose a method `addSecond` is added to the `LinearLinkedList` class:

```
/* Precondition:  list contains at least one element
 * Postcondition: new node containing Object o inserted at
 *                second position in list  */
public void addSecond(Object o)
{ implementation code }
```

Which of the following could replace *implementation code* so that `addSecond` works as intended?

(A) `firstNode.getNext(new ListNode(o, firstNode.getNext()));`

(B) `firstNode.setNext(o, firstNode.getNext());`

(C) `firstNode.setNext(new ListNode(o, firstNode.getNext()));`

(D) `firstNode.setNext(ListNode(o, firstNode.setNext()));`

(E) `firstNode = firstNode.getNext();`
    `firstNode.setNext(ListNode(o, firstNode));`

15. Consider an append method for the `LinearLinkedList` class:

```
/* Precondition:  list is not null
 * Postcondition: Object o added to the end of list  */
public void append(Object o)
{
    ListNode current = firstNode;
    < more code >
}
```

Which correctly replaces < *more code* > so that the postcondition of append is satisfied?

(A)
```
while (current.getNext() != null)
    current = current.getNext();
current.setNext(new ListNode(o, null));
```

(B)
```
while (current != null)
    current = current.getNext();
current.setNext(new ListNode(o, null));
```

(C)
```
while (current.getNext() != null)
    current = current.getNext();
current = new ListNode(o, null);
```

(D)
```
while (current != null)
    current = current.getNext();
current = new ListNode(o, null);
```

(E)
```
while (current.getNext() != null)
    current = current.getNext();
current.getNext(new ListNode(o, null));
```

16. Consider the following client method, print.

```
//Precondition: list is empty
public static void print(LinearLinkedList list)
{
    for (int i=1; i<=5; i++)
        list.addFirst(new Integer(i));
    ListNode p = list.getFirstNode();
    while (p != null)
    {
        System.out.print(p.getValue());
        p = p.getNext();
    }
}
```

What will be printed as a result of calling method print?
(A) 12345
(B) 54321
(C) 2345
(D) 5
(E) 1

Questions 17–19 refer to the `DoublyListNode` class on p. 263.

17. Consider a doubly linked list of `Integer` values as shown:

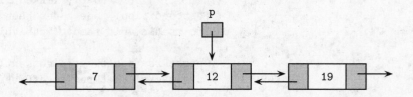

The value 9 is to be inserted between 7 and 12. Here is a code segment that achieves this:

```
Integer intObj = new Integer(9);
DoublyListNode q = new DoublyListNode(p.getPrev(), intObj, p);
< more code >
```

Which is a correct replacement for *< more code >*?

I `p.getPrev().setNext(q);`
   `p.setPrev(q);`

II `p.setPrev(q);`
   `q.getPrev().setNext(q);`

III `p.setPrev(q);`
   `p.getPrev().setNext(q);`

(A) I only
(B) II only
(C) III only
(D) I and II only
(E) I, II, and III

18. Suppose a doubly linked list does not have header or trailer nodes. Consider method `remove`:

```
/* Precondition:   p points to a node in a nonempty
 *                  doubly linked list
 * Postcondition: node p has been removed from the list */
public static void remove(DoublyListNode p)
{
    p.getPrev().setNext(p.getNext());
    p.getNext().setPrev(p.getPrev());
}
```

In which of the following cases will `remove` fail to work as intended?

I   p points to the first node in the list.
II p points to the last node in the list.
III p points to a node other than the first or last node in the list.

(A) I and II only
(B) III only
(C) I and III only
(D) I, II, and III
(E) None. Method `remove` will always work as intended.

19. Consider a doubly linked list with three nodes as shown:

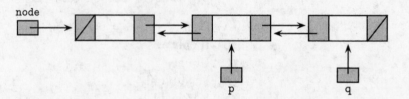

Which of the following code segments converts this list into a doubly linked circular list with three nodes? (Assume that after execution the `node` reference may point to any node.)

I   `q.setNext(node);`
    `q=q.getNext();`
    `node.setPrev(q);`

II `node.setPrev(p.getNext());`
    `p.getNext().setNext(node);`

III `p.getPrev().setPrev(q);`
    `q.setNext(p.getPrev());`

(A) I only
(B) II only
(C) III only
(D) II and III only
(E) I, II, and III

Questions 20 and 21 assume a `DoublyLinkedList` class implements doubly linked lists. Each `DoublyLinkedList` will have a header and trailer node.

```
public class DoublyLinkedList
{
    private DoublyListNode headerNode;
    private DoublyListNode trailerNode;

    //constructor
    //Creates an empty list
    public DoublyLinkedList()
    { implementation code }

    //Returns first node in list
    public DoublyListNode getFirstNode()
    { return headerNode.getNext(); }

    //other methods
        ...
}
```

20. Suppose the `DoublyLinkedList` class contains an `addRight` method.

```
/* Precondition:  node refers to an element in a nonempty list
 * Postcondition: item added to the right of node  */
public void addRight(Object item, DoublyListNode node)
{
    DoublyListNode p = new DoublyListNode(node, item,
            node.getNext());
    < more implementation code >
```

Which of the following represents *< more implementation code >* that will result in the desired postcondition?

```
 I node.setNext(p);
   node.getNext().setPrev(p);

 II node.getNext().setPrev(p);
    node.setNext(p);

III node.setNext(p);
    p.getNext().setPrev(p);
```

(A) I only
(B) II only
(C) III only
(D) I and II only
(E) II and III only

21. Here is a client method for the `DoublyLinkedList` and `DoublyListNode` classes:

```
/* Precondition:  list is a DoublyLinkedList of Integer values.
 *                list contains at least 4 nodes
 * Postcondition: An int value has been returned  */
public int DLLStuff(DoublyLinkedList list)
{
    DoublyListNode p = list.getFirstNode();
    DoublyListNode r = p.getNext();
    int val1 = ((Integer) p.getValue()).intValue();
    if (val1 %2 == 1)
    {
        p.setValue(new Integer(val1 - 1));
        p = p.getNext().getNext();
        r = p.getPrev().getPrev();
    }
    int val2 = ((Integer) r.getNext().getValue()).intValue();
    if (val2 %2 == 1)
    {
        p = r.getNext();
        int val3 = ((Integer) r.getValue()).intValue();
        val3 += 6;
        r.setValue(new Integer(val3));
        r = p.getNext().getNext();
    }
    else
        r = p.getNext();
    return ((Integer) p.getValue()).intValue() +
            ((Integer) r.getValue()).intValue();
}
```

What will be returned if `DLLStuff(list)` is called for the following doubly linked list? You may assume that `list.getFirstNode()` returns a reference to the node following the header node.

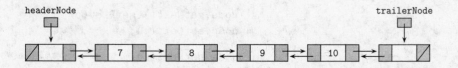

(A) 17
(B) 18
(C) 19
(D) 21
(E) An error will occur.

22. A list of items is to be maintained in random order. Operations performed on the list include

    (1) Insertion of new items at the front of the list.
    (2) Deletion of old items from the rear of the list.

    A programmer considers using a linear singly linked list (LLL), a circular singly linked list (CLL), or an array to store the items. Which of the following correctly represents the run-time efficiency of (1) insertion and (2) deletion for this list? You may assume that

    - The array has sufficient slots for insertion.
    - Linear linked lists are implemented with a reference to the first node only.
    - Circular linked lists are implemented with a reference to the last node only.
    - The most efficient algorithm possible is used in each case.

    (A) array: (1) $O(n)$ (2) $O(1)$
         LLL: (1) $O(1)$ (2) $O(n)$
         CLL: (1) $O(1)$ (2) $O(n)$

    (B) array: (1) $O(n)$ (2) $O(1)$
         LLL: (1) $O(1)$ (2) $O(n)$
         CLL: (1) $O(1)$ (2) $O(1)$

    (C) array: (1) $O(1)$ (2) $O(1)$
         LLL: (1) $O(1)$ (2) $O(1)$
         CLL: (1) $O(1)$ (2) $O(1)$

    (D) array: (1) $O(n)$ (2) $O(n)$
         LLL: (1) $O(1)$ (2) $O(n)$
         CLL: (1) $O(1)$ (2) $O(n)$

    (E) array: (1) $O(1)$ (2) $O(n)$
         LLL: (1) $O(n)$ (2) $O(1)$
         CLL: (1) $O(n)$ (2) $O(1)$

23. Consider an iterator class for a circular linked list:

```java
public class CLLIterator implements Iterator
{
    private ListNode current;
    private CircularLinkedList myList;
    //other private instance variables
        . . .

    //constructor
    public CLLIterator(CircularLinkedList list)
    {
        myList = list;
        current = null;
        //initialization of other instance variables
            . . .
    }

    //Returns true if there's at least 1 more element to be
    //examined, false otherwise
    public boolean hasNext()
    { implementation code }

    //implementation of next and remove methods
        . . .
}
```

You may assume that

- The CircularLinkedList class is implemented with a ListNode instance variable, lastNode, which refers to the last element in the circular linked list.
- An isEmpty method exists that returns true if the list is empty, false otherwise.
- The next and remove methods correctly update the value of current.

Which of the following represents correct *implementation code* for the hasNext method in the CLLIterator class?

(A)
```java
if (myList.isEmpty())
    return false;
else if (current == null)
    return true;
else
    return false;
```

(B)
```java
if (myList.isEmpty())
    return false;
else if (current == null)
    return true;
else
    return current != lastNode;
```

(C)
```java
if (myList == null || current == null)
    return true;
else
    return false;
```

```
(D) if (myList.isEmpty())
        return false;
    else if (current == null)
        return true;
    else
        return current != lastNode.getNext();

(E) if (myList == null || current == null)
        return false;
    else
        return current != lastNode;
```

In Questions 24 and 25 assume there is an `Iterator` class for `LinearLinkedList` objects.

24. Consider a `LinearLinkedList`, `list`, that has been defined with `Integer` values. Here is a code segment that removes all occurrences of 6 in `list`.

```
for (Iterator itr=list.iterator(); itr.hasNext();)
{
    < more code >
}
```

Which is a correct replacement for < *more code* >?

```
  I Integer num = (Integer) list.next();
    if (num.intValue() == 6)
        list.remove();

 II Integer itr = (Integer) itr.next();
    if (itr.intValue() == 6)
        itr.remove();

III Integer num = (Integer) itr.next();
    if (num.intValue() == 6)
        itr.remove();
```

(A) none
(B) I only
(C) II only
(D) III only
(E) I and III only

25. Consider a `LinearLinkedList`, `list`, that has at least three elements. What will the following code segment do?

```
Iterator itr = list.iterator();
Object o = itr.next();
itr.remove();
itr.remove();
```

(A) It will remove the first and second elements of the list.
(B) It will remove the second and third elements of the list.
(C) An `IllegalStateException` will be thrown.
(D) A `NoSuchElementException` will be thrown.
(E) A `ClassCastException` will be thrown.

26. This question refers to the `remove` method below:

```
public static ListNode remove(ListNode node, Object val)
{
    if (node != null)
    {
        ListNode restOfList = remove(node.getNext(), val);
        if (node.getValue().equals(val))
            return restOfList;
        else
        {
            node.setNext(restOfList);
            return node;
        }
    }
    else
        return null;
}
```

In a test of the method, a client program has this code segment:

```
LinearLinkedList list = new LinearLinkedList();
getList(list);        //read values into list
readValue(val);       //prompt for and read in val
ListNode p = remove(list.getFirstNode(), val);
list.setFirstNode(p);
```

What does `remove` do?

(A) Removes all occurrences of `val` in the list.
(B) Removes all items in the list that are not equal to `val`.
(C) Removes only the first item in the list, if and only if it equals `val`.
(D) Removes all items in the list, irrespective of value.
(E) Leaves the list unchanged.

Questions 27–29 refer to a `ListIterator` class for `LinearLinkedList` objects. You may assume that the following declaration has been made:

```
ListIterator itr = a.listIterator();   //a is a LinearLinkedList
```

27. Suppose `LinearLinkedList` a contains at least three `Integer` elements. Which of the following sequences of statements will *not* cause an `IllegalStateException` to be thrown?

    (A) ```
        Object o = itr.next();
        itr.remove();
        itr.set(new Integer(10));
        ```

    (B) ```
        itr.remove();
        Object o = itr.next();
        itr.remove();
        o = itr.next();
        ```

    (C) ```
        Object o = itr.next();
        itr.add(new Integer(5));
        itr.set(new Integer(60));
        ```

    (D) ```
        itr.add(new Integer(11));
        itr.remove();
        ```

    (E) ```
        itr.add(new Integer(55));
        itr.add(new Integer(65));
        itr.add(new Integer(75));
        ```

28. A `LinearLinkedList` of Integer objects, a, contains 2 3 7 9 11. What will the output be following this code segment? (The statements are numbered for convenience.)

    ```
    1   ListIterator itr = a.listIterator();
    2   Object obj = itr.next();
    3   itr.set(new Integer(8));
    4   obj = itr.next();
    5   itr.remove();
    6   obj = itr.next();
    7   itr.add(new Integer(5));
    8   obj = itr.next();
    9   itr.set(new Integer(6));
    10  System.out.println(a);
    ```

    (A) 8 7 5 6 11
    (B) 2 8 5 6 11
    (C) 8 7 6 9 11
    (D) 2 7 5 6 11
    (E) 2 7 6 9 11
    ```

29. A `LinearLinkedList` of `Integer` objects is sorted in increasing order. An algorithm to insert an `Integer` element `key` in its correct sorted position in the list is:

```
I  ListIterator itr = a.listIterator();
   while(itr.hasNext() &&
             key.compareTo((Integer) itr.next()) > 0)
   {}
   itr.add(key);
```

```
II  ListIterator itr = a.listIterator();
    while(itr.hasNext() &&
              key.compareTo((Integer) itr.next()) > 0)
    {
        Object o = itr.next();
    }
    itr.add(key);
```

```
III  ListIterator itr = a.listIterator();
     ListIterator itr2 = a.listIterator();
     while(itr.hasNext() &&
               key.compareTo((Integer) itr.next()) > 0)
     {
         Object o = itr2.next();
     }
     itr2.add(key);
```

(A) I only
(B) II only
(C) III only
(D) I and III only
(E) II and III only

Answer Key

1. **E**	11. **D**	21. **C**
2. **D**	12. **E**	22. **A**
3. **E**	13. **A**	23. **B**
4. **A**	14. **C**	24. **D**
5. **B**	15. **A**	25. **C**
6. **B**	16. **B**	26. **A**
7. **C**	17. **D**	27. **E**
8. **B**	18. **A**	28. **A**
9. **C**	19. **D**	29. **C**
10. **D**	20. **E**	

Answers Explained

1. **(E)** Here is what happens if `current` is pointing to a node that must be removed:

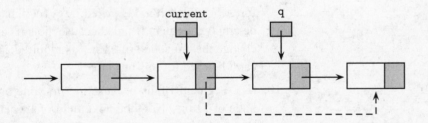

The algorithm attempts to remove the node *following* the node that should be deleted.

2. **(D)** Segment I works because the `CircularLinkedList` class has a `toString` method. The method will therefore print out the string form of the entire object. In segment II the `while` loop stops when `current` refers to the last node. To print the data in the last node you need the additional statement

   ```
   System.out.println(current.getValue());
   ```

   The `for` loop in segment III is equivalent to the `while` loop in segment II. Thus segment III would have been correct if after the loop it had the additional `System.out.println` statement.

3. **(E)** If `current` is `null`, the test will be short-circuited, and there will be no dereferencing of a null pointer in the second half of the test. Also, if `current` is `null`, `key` was not found, and the method will return `false`, which is correct.

4. **(A)** The method does not find the insertion point; it merely attaches a new node. This is a constant $O(1)$ operation.

5. **(B)** When there are no elements in the circular linked list (i.e., `firstNode` is `null`), a `NullPointerException` will be thrown: `firstNode.getNext()` tries to dereference a null pointer. If there's just one element in the list:

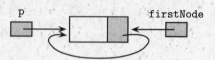

The test will fail immediately, leaving a `count` of 0. In all other cases, `count` will have a value one less than the actual number of nodes.

6. **(B)** If p points to the last node, `q = p.setNext()` will give q a value of `null`. Referring to `q.getValue()` will then cause a `NullPointerException` to be thrown.

7. **(C)** Provided p doesn't point to the last node in the list, this is a nifty algorithm that requires no list traversal. It is independent of the number of nodes in the list and is therefore $O(1)$.

8. **(B)** In segment I the statement `q.setNext(list2)` maroons the second piece of the first list: `list1` can no longer be reassigned. The first statement of segment III, `p = q.getNext()`, is crucial to avoid losing that piece of the first list. The reference assignments in segment II make no sense.

9. **(C)** Segment I is wrong because `list1` and `list2` are passed by value. Therefore when the method is exited, `list1` will have its initial value; that is, it will be empty. Segment II fails because the `setLastNode` method must be used to change the `lastNode` of `list1` as required: `getLastNode` is an accessor and can't be used for this purpose.

10. **(D)** Segment I fails because the first line breaks the connection to the first node of `list1`. Now the `next` field of L2 gets connected to the first node of `list2`, where it was to begin with! Segment II avoids this problem in its first line by using a temporary reference to hold the address of the first node in `list1`. Notice that the first three lines of segment II are exactly the code to interchange `list1.getNext()` and `list2.getNext()` correctly, so segment III is also correct.

11. **(D)** Segment I is missing a base case. It would be correct if preceded by

```
if (node == null)
    return null;
else
{ ...
```

12. **(E)** This breathless-sounding algorithm reverses pointers in the list. Here is a picture of the loop invariant for the `while` loop:

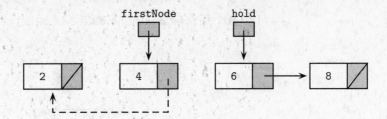

In words, `firstNode` points to the part of the list that's already been reversed, and `hold` points to the part of the original list that still needs to be taken care of.

13. **(A)** The loop invariant for the `while` loop is that `minSoFar` points to the smallest value up to and excluding the node that `p` points to. Notice that `p` is advanced right at the end of the loop (last statement), so the node that `p` points to on exiting the loop has not yet been examined.

14. **(C)** The correct code needs `firstNode.setNext(...` because the `next` field of the first node will be altered. It also needs `new ListNode...` because a new node is being created. The expression

    ```
    new ListNode(o, firstNode.getNext());
    ```

    uses the constructor of the `ListNode` class. It will be evaluated first:

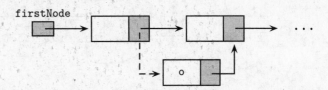

Finally `firstNode.setNext(...` sets the `next` field of `firstNode` to point to the new node (dashed arrow in the figure above).

15. **(A)** The test must be

    ```
    while (current.getNext() != null)
    ```

    so that `current` eventually points to the last node. This eliminates choices B and D. Choices C and D make the mistake of assigning `current` to the new node, which means that the node won't get attached to the list. Eliminate choice E because `setNext`, not `getNext`, must be used to modify the `next` field of the last node.

16. **(B)** Each pass through the `for` loop creates a new node at the front of the linked list, resulting in

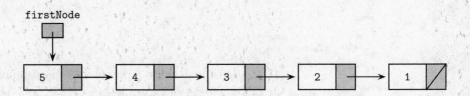

Thus, `54321` will be printed.

17. **(D)** In segment III, here's the situation after `p.setPrev(q)`:

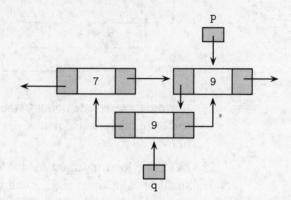

    `p.getPrev()` now refers to node q, which means that the node with 7 will not have the correct `next` pointer connection.

18. **(A)** Cases I and II both fail because a null pointer is being dereferenced. For the first node, `p.getPrev()` is `null`. For the last node, `p.getNext()` is `null`.

19. **(D)** Choice I changes the pointer connections incorrectly, as shown:

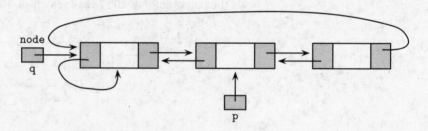

20. **(E)** Here's what goes wrong in segment I: After `node.setNext(p)`, the expression `node.getNext()` no longer refers to the node to the right of `node`. It refers to the new node! Here are the sad pointer connections following execution of segment I:

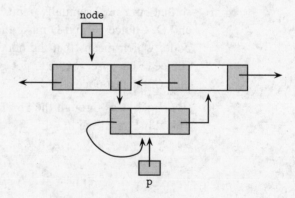

21. **(C)** After initialization p points to 7 and r points to 8. Since `val1` is 7, and 7 % 2 is 1, 7 gets changed to 6, p gets to point to 9, and r points to 6. Since `val2` is 8, and 8 % 2 != 1, the `else` part is executed: r is set to point to 10. The method then returns 9 + 10 = 19.

22. (**A**) To insert at the front of an array requires movement of all n elements to create a slot—thus, $O(n)$. Both the LLL and the CLL require just pointer adjustments to insert a node at the front: $O(1)$. To remove at the rear requires simply an adjustment on the number of elements in the array, $O(1)$. To remove from the rear of a LLL requires traversal of the list to reach the last node, $O(n)$. It would seem that a CLL would be $O(1)$ for removing an element from the rear, since the external pointer points to the last element. The problem is that to remove the last element requires accessing the pointer field of the previous node, which requires traversal along the entire list, $O(n)$.

23. (**B**) If the list is empty, there cannot be a next element, so `hasNext` is `false`. If the list isn't empty and `current` is `null`, then you're at the start of the iteration and `hasNext` is `true`. (You know you're at the start of the iteration since `current` is initialized to `null` in the constructor.) When `current == lastNode` you are at the *end* of the iteration, so `hasNext` is `false`. Until `current == lastNode`, `hasNext` is `true`. Note that choice D is almost correct, but it goes one node too far: The first node has already been examined. Don't forget that a single iterator goes through all the elements in the list just once.

24. (**D**) When you use an iterator to traverse a list, you have to use the iterator methods. Thus `itr.next()` and `itr.remove()` are the only correct expressions for these methods. This eliminates segment I. Segment II is wrong because `itr` is the iterator variable and so can't be used as the `Integer` variable.

25. (**C**) An `IllegalStateException` is thrown because there's a call to `remove` without a preceding call to `next` (see below). The intent of the code is to remove the first two items in the list. If the line

    ```
    o = itr.next();
    ```

    is inserted before the second `remove` call, the code will work as intended. Choice D is wrong: In the context of iterators, a `NoSuchElementException` is thrown if there is a call to `next` when there are no more elements in the iteration. Choice E cannot be right—the code contains no casting of objects.

26. (**A**) Here's a recursive description of the `remove` method: If the list is not empty, then if the first node contains `val`, remove that node. Now repeat this procedure for the rest of the list. The tricky part of the algorithm lies in returning the correct reference for each recursive call.

    Suppose the method is called for a linear linked list of three nodes, in which only the second node contains `val`:

    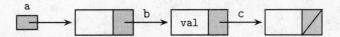

    Label the references to the three nodes a, b, and c, as shown. Here's a recursion diagram to execute `remove(a, val)`. In the diagram, r denotes `restOfList`. The circled numbers indicate the order of execution of the statements. Look at the statements in that order.

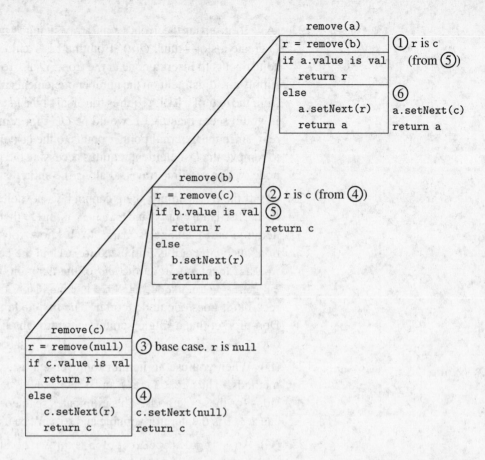

Note: A recursive method like remove that alters a linked structure (list or tree) cannot be implemented by passing a ListNode parameter that may need to be changed by the method. This is because the parameter is passed by value and will always emerge from the method with its value *unchanged*. The method must be written so that it returns a ListNode. This is how changes in the nodes get preserved. Contrast the remove method with the search method of Question 11. In the search method the list is never changed, so it's OK to have a ListNode parameter whose value emerges from the method call unchanged.

27. **(E)** An IllegalStateException will be thrown whenever

- remove is called without being preceded by next (choices B and D).
- set is called directly after add or remove (choices A and C).

Note that set must be preceded by next to avoid the error.

28. (**A**) Here is the state of the list after each given statement. The current element is highlighted.

After line 2:	2	3	7	9	11
After line 3:	8	3	7	9	11
After line 4:	8	3	7	9	11
After line 5:	8	7	9	11	
After line 6:	8	7	9	11	
After line 7:	8	7	5	9	11
After line 8:	8	7	5	9	11
After line 9:	8	7	5	6	11

29. (**C**) The problem with segments I and II is that they go too far in the list. Don't forget that every time `next` is called, the current pointer moves to the next node. Suppose the original list is 2 4 6 8, with key 3 to be inserted. In segment I the iteration stops with the current pointer at 4. Thus when the insertion point is found, there is no longer access to the previous element for a correct insertion to be made. The list ends up as 2 4 3 6 8. In segment II the loop stops with the current pointer at 6. The list ends up as 2 4 6 3 8. Note that in segment III, the correct solution, two iterators are needed: one to find the correct insertion point and one to follow behind so that insertion can be done correctly. Any algorithm that requires k pointers to keep track of different places in the list should use k iterators in the code.

CHAPTER NINE
Stacks and Queues

*A queue is an adaptor that provides a restricted subset
of Container functionality.*
—STL Programmer's Guide, *Silicon Graphics Inc.*

Stacks

What Is a Stack?

Think of a stack of plates or cafeteria trays. The last one added to the stack is the first one removed: last in first out (LIFO). And you can't remove the second tray without taking off the top one!

A *stack* is a sequence of items of the same type, in which items can be added and removed only at one end. In theory, there is no limit to the number of items on the stack.

Changes to the stack are controlled by two operations, *push* and *pop*. To push an item onto the stack is to add that item to the top of the stack. To pop the stack is to remove an item from the top of the stack. Imagine that the top of the stack floats up and down as items are pushed onto or popped off the stack. Push and pop are ideally $O(1)$ operations.

There are two other useful operations for a stack: an *isEmpty* test, which returns true or false, and *peekTop*, which inspects the top element and reports what it is. If you try to peek at or pop an empty stack, you get an *underflow* error.

The Stack Interface

There is no suitable standard stack interface in Java. An interface similar to the following will be used for questions on the AP exam:

```
public interface Stack
{
    boolean isEmpty();
    void push(Object x);
    Object pop();
    Object peekTop();
}
```

The Stack Interface Methods

```
boolean isEmpty()
```

Returns `true` if the stack is empty, `false` otherwise.

```
void push(Object x)
```

Pushes x onto the top of the stack.

```
Object pop()
```

Pops the top element off the stack. Returns this element. The method throws an exception if an attempt is made to pop an empty stack.

```
Object peekTop()
```

Returns the top element of the stack but leaves the stack unchanged. Think of it as a method that takes a peek at the top element and returns to tell what it saw. If, however, it peeks and the stack is empty, an underflow error occurs (i.e., an exception is thrown). The precondition for peekTop() is that the stack is not empty.

Stack Implementation

The AP Java subset does not provide an implementation of the Stack interface; nor will you be tested on any particular implementation. You should, however, know that a stack can be implemented with either an array or a linked list. An ArrayStack class that implements Stack is provided at *http://apcentral.collegeboard.com* for you to run programs.

On the AP exam, code such as the following will be used:

```
Stack s = new ArrayStack();        //ArrayStack implements Stack
```

Example

(Statements are numbered for reference.)

```
1   Stack s = new ArrayStack();        //creates empty stack
2   for (int i=1; i<=4; i++)
3       s.push(new Integer(2*i));      //pushes 2,4,6,8 onto stack
4   Object o = s.pop();                //removes 8 from stack
5   o = s.pop();                       //removes 6 from stack
6   Integer intOb = (Integer) s.peekTop();  //stores 4 in intOb
7                                           //s unchanged
8   if (s.isEmpty())
9       System.out.println("Bye!");
10  else
11      System.out.println("cool");   //output, since s has 2 items
12  s = new ArrayStack();             // empties s
13  if (s.isEmpty())
14      System.out.println("Bye!");   //"Bye!" output
15  else
16      System.out.println("cool");
```

Here are snapshots of the stack s.

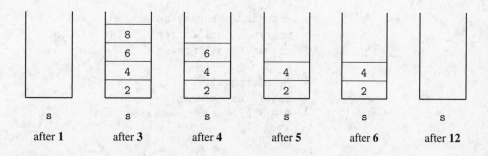

| after **1** | after **3** | after **4** | after **5** | after **6** | after **12** |

When to Use a Stack

Consider using a stack for any problem that involves backtracking (last in first out). Some examples include retracing steps in a maze and keeping track of nested structures, such as

- Expressions within other expressions.
- Methods that call other methods.
- Traversing directories and subdirectories.

In each case the stack mechanism untangles the nested structure.

Example

Write a method `validParens` to test if a Java expression has valid parentheses. An expression is valid if the number of openers (i.e., left parentheses `"("`) equals the number of enders (right parentheses `")"`). For example, `3/(a+(b*2))` is valid, but `(x-(y*(z+4)` is invalid. Note that simply checking if the number of openers equals the number of enders is insufficient: the expression `)3+4(` is not valid. To be valid, each ender must be preceded by a matching opener.

Assume that the expression is a `String` in an `Expression` class. The `validParens` method returns `true` if the parentheses in the `Expression` are valid, `false` otherwise. Here's where the stack comes in. Do a character-by-character processing. If any character substring is an opener, push it onto the stack `s`. If it's an ender and the stack is empty, the expression is invalid since there is no matching opener. If the stack is not empty, however, pop the stack. When the end of the expression is reached, the stack should be empty if the expression is valid.

Suppose that the expression to be examined is `(3+4*(5%3))`. Here is the state of the stack at various stages of the processing:

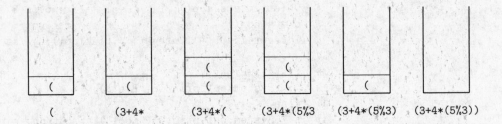

(	(3+4*	(3+4*(	(3+4*(5%3	(3+4*(5%3)	(3+4*(5%3))

Notice that the given expression is valid.

Here is part of an `Expression` class that contains the `validParens` method.

```java
/* Tests the validity of an expression */

public class Expression
{
    private String myExpression;
    private final String OPENER = "(";
    private final String ENDER = ")";

    //constructor
    public Expression()
    { code to read myExpression }
```

```
        //Returns true if parentheses valid, false otherwise
        public boolean validParens()
        {
            Stack s = new ArrayStack();
            Object obj;
            for (int i=0; i<myExpression.length(); i++)
            {
                String ch = myExpression.substring(i,i+1);
                if (ch.equals(OPENER))
                    s.push(ch);
                else if (ch.equals(ENDER))
                    if (s.isEmpty())   //no matching opener
                        return false;
                    else
                        obj = s.pop(); //pop matching opener
            }
            return s.isEmpty();        //if false, too many openers
        }

        //other methods not shown
        ...
    }
```

Queues

What Is a Queue?

Think of a line of well-behaved people waiting to board a bus. New arrivals go to the back of the line. The first one in line arrived first and is the first to board the bus: first in first out (FIFO).

A *queue* is a sequence of items of the same type in which items are removed at one end, the front, and new items are added at the other end, the back. In theory, there is no limit to the number of items in a queue.

Changes to the queue are controlled by operations *enqueue* and *dequeue.* To enqueue an item is to add that item to the *back* of the queue. To dequeue is to remove an item from the *front* of the queue. As for a stack, an *isEmpty* operation tests for an empty queue, and a *peekFront* method reports what's at the front. If you try to dequeue from or peek at an empty queue you get an underflow error.

The Queue Interface

A Queue interface similar to the following will be provided for questions on the AP exam.

```
public interface Queue
{
    boolean isEmpty();
    void enqueue(Object x);
    Object dequeue();
    Object peekFront();
}
```

The Queue Interface Methods

```
boolean isEmpty()
```

Returns true if the queue is empty, false otherwise.

```
void enqueue(Object x)
```

Inserts item at the back of the queue.

```
Object dequeue()
```

Removes an element from the front of the queue. Returns this element. The method throws an exception if an attempt is made to dequeue from an empty queue.

```
Object peekFront()
```

Returns the front element of the queue, leaving the queue unchanged. (It is analogous to peekTop() in the Stack interface.) The method throws an exception if an attempt is made to peek at an empty queue.

Queue Implementation

As with stacks, the AP Java subset does not provide an implementation of the Queue interface, nor will you be tested on any implementation. A queue can be implemented with an array or a linked list. A ListQueue class that implements Queue is provided at *http://apcentral.collegeboard.com*.

On the AP exam, code such as the following will be used:

```
Queue q = new ListQueue();      //ListQueue implements Queue
```

Example

(Statements are numbered for reference.)

```
1   Queue q = new ListQueue();                  //q is empty
2   String st = "ghijkl";
3   Object o;
4   for (int i=0; i<st.length(); i++)
5       q.enqueue(st.substring(i,i+1));    //enqueue "g", "h", "i",
6                                          //"j", "k", "l"
7   for (int i=1; i<3; i++)
8       o = q.dequeue();                   //dequeue "g", "h"
9   q.enqueue("r");
10  String str = (String) q.peekFront();   //str contains "i"
```

The state of the queue is shown below. The labels **f** and **b** underneath each figure denote the front and back of the queue.

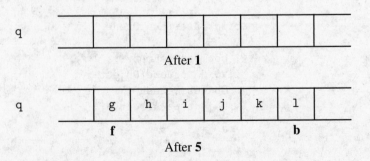

After **1**

After **5**

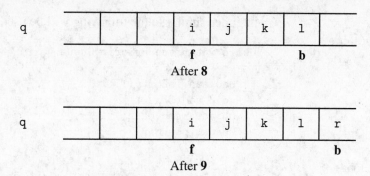

When to Use a
Queue

Think of a queue for any problem that involves processing data in the order in which it was entered. Some examples include

- Going back to the beginning and retracing steps.

- Simulations of lines—cars waiting at a car wash, people standing in line at a bank, and so on.

Example

Here is a code segment that simulates the redial feature of a telephone. Each digit that is entered is treated as a separate element and placed in a queue. When it's time to redial, the queue is emptied, and the digits are printed in the order that they were entered.

```
/* Simulate redial feature of a phone */
Queue q = new ListQueue();
System.out.println("Enter digits of phone number" +
        " separated by spaces");
System.out.println("Terminate list with negative digit.");
int digit = IO.readInt();    //read user input
while (digit >= 0)
{
    q.enqueue(new Integer(digit));
    digit = IO.readInt();
}
System.out.println();
System.out.println("The number dialed was: ");
while (!q.isEmpty())
    System.out.print((Integer) q.dequeue());
```

Priority Queues

What Is a Priority
Queue?

A *priority queue* is a collection of items of the same type, each of which contains a data field and a priority. Items are ordered by priority, in the sense that items with the highest priority are removed first.

The
PriorityQueue
Interface

An interface similar to the following will be used for questions on the AP exam:

```
public interface PriorityQueue
{
    boolean isEmpty();
    void add(Object x);
    Object removeMin();
    Object peekMin();
}
```

The PriorityQueue Interface Methods

boolean isEmpty()

Returns true if the priority queue is empty, false otherwise.

void add(Object x)

Adds x to the priority queue.

Object removeMin()

Removes the smallest item from the priority queue. This is the element with highest priority. In order for removeMin to work as intended, the items must be Comparable, with the compareTo method defined such that element e1 < e2 if and only if e1 has higher priority than e2 (see Example beginning on the next page). The removeMin method throws an unchecked exception if an attempt is made to remove an item from an empty priority queue.

Object peekMin()

Returns the smallest item in the priority queue, but leaves the priority queue unchanged. The method throws an unchecked exception if an attempt is made to peek at an empty priority queue.

Implementation of
a Priority Queue

You are not expected to know any particular implementation of the PriorityQueue interface. You should, however, understand the following general principles about implementation.

The data structure selected for a priority queue should allow for

- Rapid insertion of elements that arrive in arbitrary order.
- Rapid retrieval of the item with the highest priority.

Some possible data structures for a priority queue follow:

1. A linear linked list with elements in random order. Insertion is done at the front of the list, $O(1)$. Deletion requires a linear search for the element with highest priority, $O(n)$.
2. A linear linked list with elements sorted by priority, smallest elements in front. Deletion means removal of the first node, $O(1)$. Insertion requires a linear scan to find the insertion point, $O(n)$.
3. An array with elements in random order. Insertion is done at the end of the list, $O(1)$. Deletion requires a linear search, $O(n)$.

4. An array with elements sorted by priority, smallest elements at the end. Deletion means removing the last element in the array, $O(1)$. Insertion requires finding the insertion point and then creating a slot by moving array elements— $O(n)$ irrespective of the type of search.

5. The classic data structure for a priority queue: a *binary heap*. (See Chapter 12 for a description of a heap and an array representation of a heap.) For a priority queue, a *minimum heap* is used. The value in every node is less than or equal to the value in each of its children. For example,

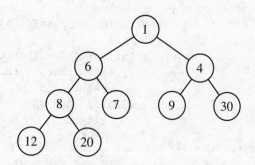

The numbers in the heap represent the *priorities* of the elements. (The lower the number, the higher the priority.) The idea is that the element with the highest priority is kept in the root of the tree, so deleting an element means removing the root element. Then restoring the heap ("reheaping") is an $O(\log n)$ operation. Insertion of an element also requires reheaping, $O(\log n)$. (It is possible to have an $O(1)$ insertion by simply adding an element to the end of the array, but then reheaping will be required to maintain the heap property.)

An `ArrayPriorityQueue` class that implements `PriorityQueue` is provided at *http://apcentral.collegeboard.com*.

On the AP exam, code such as the following will be used:

```
PriorityQueue pq = new ArrayPriorityQueue();  //ArrayPriorityQueue
                                              //implements PriorityQueue
```

When to Use a Priority Queue

Think of using a priority queue in any problem where elements enter in a random order but are removed according to their priority. For example,

- A database of patients awaiting liver transplants, where the sickest patients have the highest priority.

- Scheduling events. Events are generated in random order and each event has a time stamp denoting when the event will occur. The scheduler retrieves the events in the order they will occur.

Example

Here is a program that illustrates how a priority queue may be used. Imagine that patients awaiting an organ transplant are placed on a list. When an organ becomes available, the patient with the highest priority is contacted.

```java
public class Patient implements Comparable
{
    private String myName;
    private int myPriority;

    public Patient(String name, int priority)
    {
        myName = name;
        myPriority = priority;
    }

    public int compareTo(Object o)
    {
        Patient rhs = (Patient) o;
        if (myPriority < rhs.myPriority)
            return -1;
        else if (myPriority > rhs.myPriority)
            return 1;
        else
            return 0;
    }

    public String toString()
    {
        String s = myName + " with priority " + myPriority;
        return s;
    }
}

/* Illustrates priority queue */

public class PriQueueTest
{

    public static void main(String[] args)
    {
        PriorityQueue pq = new ArrayPriorityQueue();
        Patient p1 = new Patient("John Smith", 3);
        Patient p2 = new Patient("Mary Jones", 1);
        Patient p3 = new Patient("Kathy Gibb", 2);
        pq.add(p1);
        pq.add(p2);
        pq.add(p3);

        while (!pq.isEmpty())
        {
            System.out.println("The next patient for liver" +
                " transplant is ");
            System.out.println(pq.removeMin());
        }
    }
}
```

The output for this program is

```
    The next patient for liver transplant is
    Mary Jones with priority 1
    The next patient for liver transplant is
    Kathy Gibb with priority 2
    The next patient for liver transplant is
    John Smith with priority 3
```

NOTE With any implementation of a priority queue, the items must be of type `Comparable`. This is because the `peekMin` and `removeMin` methods have to be able to compare objects to determine which has the highest priority (the smallest element). The private instance variable `myPriority` is internal to the `Patient` class and therefore not visible to the `PriorityQueue` methods. Nor would a `getPriority` accessor in the `Patient` class help: the class implementing `PriorityQueue` has no way of knowing which accessors are available and must use a generic comparison of `Comparable` objects to determine which is the smallest.

A final thought ...

A priority queue is not a queue, it just sounds like one.
—Mark Allen Weiss

Multiple-Choice Questions on Stacks and Queues

Assume that stacks and queues are implemented with the following classes:

```
public class ArrayStack implements Stack
{ /* implementation omitted */ }

public class ListQueue implements Queue
{ /* implementation omitted */ }
```

1. A stack s of integers contains 1, 4, 5, 8, 9 in the order given, with 1 on top. What will be output by the following code segment?

```
while (((Integer) s.peekTop()).intValue() % 2 == 1)
{
    Object o = s.pop();
    System.out.print(s.peekTop());
}
```

    (A) 1
    (B) 4
    (C) 14
    (D) 159
    (E) 48

2. Methods `add(s)` and `multiply(s)` do the following to a stack s when invoked:

> The stack is popped twice.
> The two popped items are added or multiplied accordingly.
> The `Integer` result is pushed onto the stack.

What will stack s contain following execution of the following code segment?

```
int x = 3, y = 5, z = 7, w = 9;
s.push(new Integer(x));
s.push(new Integer(y));
add(s);
s.push(new Integer(w));
s.push(new Integer(z));
multiply(s);
add(s);
```

    (A) Nothing
    (B) 31
    (C) 71
    (D) 78
    (E) 128

Assume these declarations for Questions 3 and 4:

```
Queue q = new ListQueue();   //ListQueue implements Queue
int sum = 0;
Object obj;
```

3. If q is initialized, which of the following code segments will correctly sum the elements of q and leave q unchanged?

```
 I Queue temp = new ListQueue();
   while (!q.isEmpty())
   {
       obj = q.dequeue();
       sum += ((Integer) obj).intValue();
       temp.enqueue(obj);
   }
   q = temp;

 II while (!q.isEmpty())
    {
        obj = q.dequeue();
        sum += ((Integer) obj).intValue();
        q.enqueue(obj);
    }

III Queue temp = q;
    while (!temp.isEmpty())
    {
        obj = temp.dequeue();
        sum += ((Integer) obj).intValue();
    }
```

(A) I only
(B) II only
(C) III only
(D) I and III only
(E) II and III only

4. Consider the following sequence of statements:

```
Integer a = new Integer(2);
Integer b = new Integer(5);
Integer c = new Integer(4);
q.enqueue(a);
q.enqueue(b);
q.enqueue(c);
a = new Integer(a.intValue() + 1);
a = (Integer) q.dequeue();
q.enqueue(c);
q.enqueue(a);
b = a;
q.enqueue(b);
while (!q.isEmpty())
{
    a = (Integer) q.dequeue();
    System.out.print(a);
}
```

What output will be produced?
(A) 254422
(B) 54433
(C) 25433
(D) 54422
(E) 25444

5. Suppose that a queue q contains the Integer values 1, 2, 3, 4, 5, 6 in that order, with 1 at the front of q. Suppose that there are just three operations that can be performed using only one stack, s.

   (i) Dequeue x from q then print x.
   (ii) Dequeue x from q then s.push(x).
   (iii) Pop x from s then print x.

Which of the following is not a possible output list using just these operations?
(A) 123456
(B) 654321
(C) 234561
(D) 125643
(E) 345612

6. Let `intStack` be a stack of `Integer` values and `opStack` be a character stack of arithmetic operators, where each operator is a single-character `String`. A method `doOperation()` exists that

   (i) Pops two values from `intStack`.
   (ii) Pops an operator from `opStack`.
   (iii) Performs the operation.
   (iv) Pushes the result onto `intStack`.

   Assume that the `Integer` values 5, 8, 3, and 2 are pushed onto `intStack` in that order (2 pushed last), and `"*"`, `"-"`, and `"+"` are pushed onto `opStack` in that order (`"+"` pushed last). The `doOperation()` method is invoked three times. The top of `intStack` contains the result of evaluating which expression?
   (A) $((2 * 3) - 8) + 5$
   (B) $((2 + 3) - 5) * 8$
   (C) $((2 + 3) - 8) * 5$
   (D) $((5 * 8) - 3) + 2$
   (E) $((5 + 8) - 3) * 2$

7. Suppose that s and t are both stacks of `Object` and that x is a variable of type `Object`. Assume that s initially contains n elements, where n is large, and that t is initially empty. Assume further that `length(s)` gives the number of elements in s. Which is true after execution of the following code segment?

```
int len = length(s)-2;
for (int i=1; i<=len; i++)
{
    x = s.pop();
    t.push(x);
}
len = length(s)-2;
for (int i=1; i<=len; i++)
{
    x = t.pop();
    s.push(x);
}
```

   (A) s is unchanged, and x equals the third item from the bottom of s.
   (B) s is unchanged, and x equals s.peekTop().
   (C) s contains two elements, and x equals s.peekTop().
   (D) s contains two elements, and x equals the bottom element of s.
   (E) s contains two elements, and x equals t.peekTop().

8. Refer to the following program segment:

```
Queue q = new ListQueue();    //ListQueue implements Queue
Object x;
for (int i=1; i<6; i++)
    q.enqueue(new Integer(i*i));
while (!q.isEmpty())
{
    if (((Integer) q.peekFront()).intValue() % 2 == 0)
    {
        System.out.print((Integer) q.peekFront() + " ");
        x = q.dequeue();
    }
    else
    {
        x = q.dequeue();
        q.enqueue(x);
    }
}
```

Which will be true after this segment is executed?

(A) 4 16 has been printed, and the queue contains 1 9 25, with 1 at the front and 25 at the back.

(B) 16 4 has been printed, and the queue contains 1 9 25, with 1 at the front and 25 at the back.

(C) 1 4 9 16 25 has been printed, and the queue is empty.

(D) 4 16 has been printed, and the segment continues to run without termination.

(E) 4 16 4 16 4 16 ... has been printed, and the segment continues to run without termination.

9. Consider a stack s and queue q of integers. What must be true following execution of this code segment?

```
q = new ListQueue();
s = new ArrayStack();
Integer x;
for (int i=1; i<=4; i++)
    s.push(new Integer(i));
for (int i=1; i<=4; i++)
{
    x = (Integer) s.pop();
    if (x.intValue() % 2 == 0)
        q.enqueue(x);
    else
    {
        x = (Integer) q.dequeue();
        s.push(x);
    }
}
```

(A) 2 is at the back of q.
(B) s.peekTop() is 2.
(C) s is empty.
(D) q is empty.
(E) An error has occurred.

10. What output will be produced by the following code segment?

```
Stack s = new ArrayStack();    //ArrayStack implements Stack
String str = "racketeer";
String ch, x;
for (int i=0; i<str.length(); i++)
    s.push(str.substring(i, i+1));
for (int i=0; i<str.length(); i++)
{
    ch = str.substring(i, i+1);
    if (isVowel(ch))    //test if ch is a lowercase vowel,
                        //"a", "e", "i", "o", or "u"
    {
        x = (String) s.pop();
        System.out.print(x);
    }
    else
        s.push(ch);
}
```

(A) aeee
(B) eeea
(C) ctkr
(D) rktc
(E) rkct

11. Assume that linked lists are implemented with the ListNode class (p. 245). Assume also that the objects in a linked list have a toString method for printing. Refer to the following method, reverse:

```
/* Precondition:   first refers to the first node of a linear
 *                 linked list
 * Postcondition: list elements printed in reverse order  */
public void reverse(ListNode first)
{
    < code >
}
```

Which < code > will successfully achieve the postcondition of reverse?

```
I  if (first != null)
   {
       System.out.print(first.getValue() + " ");
       reverse(first.getNext());
   }
```

```
II Stack s = new ArrayStack();
   while (first != null)
   {
       s.push(first.getValue());
       first = first.getNext();
   }
   while (!s.isEmpty())
       System.out.print(s.pop() + " ");
```

```
III Queue q = new ListQueue();
    while (first != null)
    {
        q.enqueue(first.getValue());
        first = first.getNext();
    }
    while (!q.isEmpty())
        System.out.print(q.dequeue() + " ");
```

(A) I only
(B) II only
(C) III only
(D) I and II only
(E) I and III only

12. Suppose the `Stack` interface added another `pop` method, one that changes the stack but does not return the object that's being removed:

```
public void pop(Object o) //remove top item without saving it
                          //o is a dummy object
```

This is an example of
(A) polymorphism
(B) method overriding
(C) method overloading
(D) a helper method
(E) stack overflow

13. Suppose stacks are implemented with a linear linked list that has just one private instance variable, `firstNode`, which refers to the first element of the list:

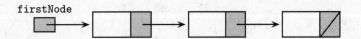

In the diagram, `firstNode` points to the top of the stack. Which of the following correctly gives the run time of (1) `push` and (2) `pop` in this implementation?

(A) (1) $O(1)$ (2) $O(1)$

(B) (1) $O(1)$ (2) $O(n)$

(C) (1) $O(n)$ (2) $O(1)$

(D) (1) $O(n)$ (2) $O(n)$

(E) (1) $O(\log n)$ (2) $O(1)$

14. Which of the following is true of a priority queue?
(A) If elements are inserted in increasing order of priority (i.e., lowest priority element inserted first), and all elements are inserted before any are removed, it works like a queue.
(B) If elements are inserted in increasing order of priority (i.e., lowest priority element inserted first), and all elements are inserted before any are removed, it works like a stack.
(C) If all elements are inserted before any are removed, it works like a queue.
(D) If elements are inserted in decreasing order of priority (i.e., highest priority element inserted first), and all elements are inserted before any are removed, it works like a stack.
(E) If elements are inserted in increasing order of priority, then it works like a queue whether or not all insertions precede any removals.

15. Refer to the following declarations:

```
//ArrayPriorityQueue implements PriorityQueue
PriorityQueue pq = new ArrayPriorityQueue();
```

The elements of the priority queue pq will be Integer values. These values will also represent the priorities of the items: smallest value = *highest* priority. Assuming that the code works as intended, what output will be produced by the following segment?

```
pq.add(new Integer(4));
pq.add(new Integer(1));
pq.add(new Integer(3));
pq.add(new Integer(2));
pq.add(new Integer(5));
while (!pq.isEmpty())
    System.out.print(pq.removeMin());
```

(A) 54321
(B) 41325
(C) 12345
(D) 52314
(E) 11111

Questions 16–18 refer to the following interface and class definition:

```
public interface Container
{
    public void insert(Object x);   //insert x into Container
    public Object remove();         //remove item from Container
}

public class C implements Container
{
    public C()         //constructor
    { implementation code }

    public void insert(Object x)   //insert x into C
    { implementation code }

    public Object remove()         //remove item from C
    { implementation code }

    //appropriate private instance variables to implement C
}
```

Here is a program segment that uses class C above:

```
Container words = new C();
String w1 = "Tom";
String w2 = "Dick";
String w3 = "Harry";
String w4 = "Moe";
words.insert(w1);
words.insert(w2);
words.insert(w3);
words.insert(w4);
String str;
str = (String) words.remove();
str = (String) words.remove();
System.out.println(str);
```

16. What will the output be if C is a stack?
    (A) Tom
    (B) Dick
    (C) Harry
    (D) Moe
    (E) There is insufficient information to determine the output.

17. What will the output be if C is a queue?
    (A) Tom
    (B) Dick
    (C) Harry
    (D) Moe
    (E) There is insufficient information to determine the output.

18. What will the output be if C is a priority queue? You may assume that priorities are assigned using the fact that items are Comparable.
    (A) Tom
    (B) Dick
    (C) Harry
    (D) Moe
    (E) There is insufficient information to determine the output.

19. What is the output from the following code segment?

```
Stack s = new ArrayStack();   //ArrayStack implements Stack
String str = "cat";
for (int i=0; i<str.length(); i++)
    s.push(str.substring(i));
while (!s.isEmpty())
{
    str = (String) s.pop();
    System.out.print(str);
}
```

    (A) catatt
    (B) tac
    (C) ttatac
    (D) tatcat
    (E) cattat

20. In the package java.util there is a Stack class that extends Java's Vector class. Thus Stack inherits all the methods of Vector. Here are three of the methods that Stack inherits:

    I void add(int i, Object x) //insert x into stack at index i

    II Object getElement(int i)   //return object at index i
                                  //leave stack unchanged

    III Object remove(int i)   //remove object at index i from stack

    Which of these methods are *not* consistent with the definition of a stack?
    (A) I only
    (B) II only
    (C) III only
    (D) II and III only
    (E) I, II, and III

21. Consider the following client method for the `ArrayStack` class:

```
/* Precondition:  stack s is defined
 * Postcondition: returns the bottom element of s
 *                s remains unchanged  */
public static Object bottom(ArrayStack s)
{
    < code >
}
```

Which replacements for < *code* > will achieve the required postcondition?

```
 I  Object o;
    while (!s.isEmpty())
        o = s.pop();
    return o;

II  Object o;
    ArrayStack t = s;
    while (!t.isEmpty())
        o = t.pop();
    return o;

III Object o;
    Stack t = new ArrayStack();
    while (!s.isEmpty())
        t.push(s.pop());
    o = t.peekTop();
    while (!t.isEmpty())
        s.push(t.pop());
    return o;
```

(A) I only
(B) II only
(C) III only
(D) I and II only
(E) I and III only

Answer Key

1. **B**		8. **D**		15. **C**	
2. **C**		9. **A**		16. **C**	
3. **A**		10. **D**		17. **B**	
4. **D**		11. **B**		18. **C**	
5. **E**		12. **C**		19. **D**	
6. **C**		13. **A**		20. **E**	
7. **E**		14. **B**		21. **C**	

Answers Explained

1. **(B)** When 1 is s.peekTop(), it passes the while test and gets popped. The current s.peekTop() is then 4, which gets printed. Now the test fails on 4, and the while loop is not executed again.

2. **(C)** After the first call to add(s), the stack will contain 8. After the call to multiply(s), it will contain 63 (on top), then 8. Therefore, after the second add(s), it will contain 71.

3. **(A)** Placing the elements in a temporary queue works because the elements will have the same order as in the original queue. Segment II seems to have a fine idea—take an element out of q, sum it, and then insert it back. Trouble is, the while loop will be infinite since q will never be empty! Segment III fails because temp is not a separate queue: It refers to the same queue as q. Any changes made to temp will therefore change q.

4. **(D)** Here is the state of the queue just before it is emptied:

	5	4	4	2	2	
	f				b	

Note that the Integer object a, which starts out with value 2, is repeatedly reassigned. The expression a = new Integer(a.intValue() + 1) results in a = 3. Then a = (Integer) q.dequeue() stores the front element of the queue in a (i.e., a = 2). The queue is a first-in-first-out structure, which means that elements are removed in the order they were inserted, from front to back as shown.

5. **(E)** For 3456 to have been printed means that 1 and 2 were dequeued and pushed onto s in that order. The order of printing would then have to be 21, not 12. Note that this means that 345621 would have been OK.

6. **(C)** The first call to doOperation() pops 2 and 3, pops +, and pushes 5, the result. The second call pops 5 and 8, pops -, and pushes -3. The third call pops -3 and 5, pops *, and pushes -15. The expression in C is the only choice that evaluates to -15.

Alternatively, work from the inside out:

pop 2, 3, and +   →   (2 + 3)
pop (2 + 3), 8, and -   →   ((2 + 3) − 8)
pop ((2 + 3) − 8), 5, and *   →   ((2 + 3) − 8) * 5

7. **(E)** The first for loop removes the top length(s)-2 elements from s, leaving two elements. Therefore length(s) equals 2. Also, x currently equals the top element of t, t.peekTop(). The second for loop is for i equals 1 to 0, so nothing is done in this loop! This leaves s with two elements, and x equal to t.peekTop().

8. **(D)** Here is q initially:

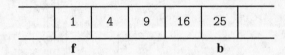

1 fails the test, is removed from the front, and is inserted at the back of the queue.
4 passes the test and is printed and removed.
9 fails and is removed and inserted at the back.
16 passes and is printed and removed.
25 fails and is removed and inserted at the back.
q now looks like this:

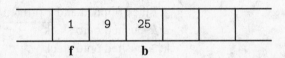

None of the elements in the queue will now pass the if test, which means that there will be an infinite sequence of removals and insertions in q. The while loop never terminates.

9. **(A)** Initially s contains 1, 2, 3, 4 with 4 on top. Here is the state of s and q after each pass through the second for loop:

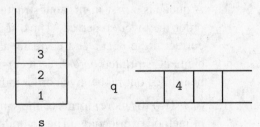

After 1st pass

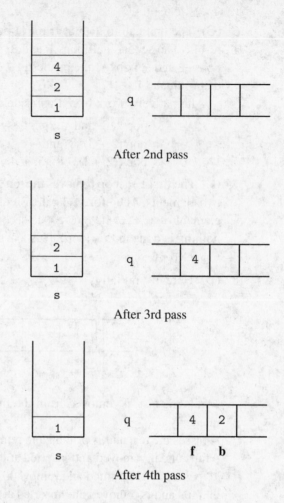

After 2nd pass

After 3rd pass

After 4th pass

10. **(D)** Here's what happens for each letter of the word:
    r: r pushed onto stack
    a: stack popped and r printed
    c: c pushed onto stack
    k: k pushed onto stack
    e: stack popped and k printed
    t: t pushed onto stack
    e: stack popped and t printed
    e: stack popped and c printed
    r: r pushed onto stack

11. **(B)** Remember that a stack is a last-in-first-out structure, which means that elements placed in it are retrieved in reverse order. So segment II is correct. A queue is a first-in-first-out structure, so the elements will be printed in the order they were received. Thus, segment III is wrong. Segment I would be correct if the print and reverse statements were interchanged. As it is, an element is printed *before* the recursive call, which means that elements will be printed out in the given order rather than being reversed.

12. **(C)** Two (or more) forms of the same method in a given class is an example of method overloading. The compiler distinguishes the methods by matching parameter types. Note that the dummy object o is necessary; otherwise, the two pop methods would have the same signature, and the compiler could not

distinguish them. The return type is not part of the signature.

13. **(A)** Simple pointer adjustments independent of the number of nodes achieve both push and pop, making them both $O(1)$:

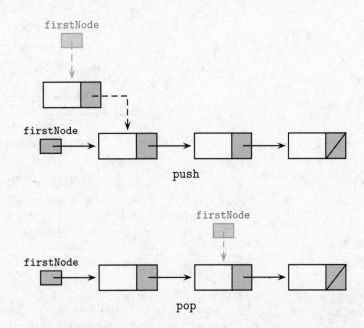

push

pop

14. **(B)** If elements are inserted in increasing order of priority, the last one in will have top priority and will be the first one out, and so on. Thus, the priority queue will work just like a stack. Choice C would be correct only if the elements were inserted in decreasing order of priority, since the first one in would then be the first one out. Choice D is wrong because the first element entered (top priority) would have to be the first one out—not a stack! Choices A and E are both wrong because higher priority elements would land at the back of the queue. Removing these would violate the first-in-first-out property of a queue.

15. **(C)** The smaller the integer, the higher the priority. Elements are deleted from a priority queue according to their priority number, highest priority (lowest value) first. This is independent of the order of the insertion.

16. **(C)** Here is the stack:

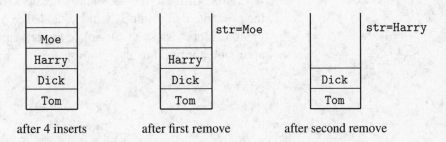

| after 4 inserts | after first remove | after second remove |

17. **(B)** Here is the queue:

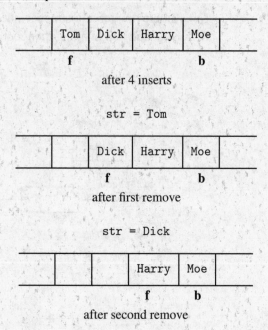

after 4 inserts

str = Tom

after first remove

str = Dick

after second remove

18. **(C)** For type `String` the ordering of priorities is alphabetical. Thus the first `remove` call removes `"Dick"`, and the second removes `"Harry"`, which is then printed.

19. **(D)** Here is the stack after the `for` loop has been executed:

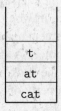

(Recall that `str.substring(i)` returns the substring of `str` starting at the ith position of `str` and extending to the end of the string.) The `while` loop pops and prints `"t"`, then `"at"`, then `"cat"`, resulting in `"tatcat"`.

20. **(E)** None of these methods are valid stack operations! Method I violates the principle that a value should be added to a stack only by pushing it onto the top. Methods II and III violate the principle that only the top element is accessible for peeking and removal.

21. **(C)** Suppose the original stack looks like this:

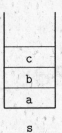

You will need a temporary stack to access the bottom element. Here are stacks s and t after the first while loop in segment III:

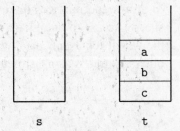

Notice that the required item, a, is now at the top of t. The second while loop restores s to its original state.

Segment I returns the correct item, but leaves s with no elements. Even though s is passed by value and the reference s remains unchanged, this doesn't protect the *contents* of s. Segment II also returns the correct element but leaves s with no elements. Assigning t to s means that any changes made to t will also be made to s.

CHAPTER TEN
Trees

> *TREE: A tall vegetable ...*
> —*Ambrose Bierce,* The Devil's Dictionary *(1911)*

In arrays and matrices there is a certain equality to the elements, with easy and speedy access to any given element. A tree, on the other hand, is a hierarchy in the way it represents data, with some elements "higher" and easier to access than others. A tree is also a structure that allows branching.

Binary Trees

Definitions

A *binary tree* is a finite set of elements that is either empty or contains a single element called the *root*, and whose remaining elements are partitioned into two disjoint subsets. Each subset is itself a binary tree, called the left or right *subtree* of the original tree.

Binary trees are often represented schematically as shown below.

Here is some vocabulary you should know:

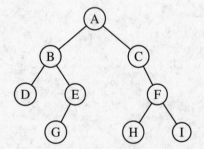

- A is the *root* of the tree. B and C are the roots of the left and right subtrees of A, and so on down the tree.

- Each element is a *node* of the tree. The tree shown has nine nodes.

- Any node whose left and right subtrees are empty is called a *leaf*. Thus D, G, H, and I are leaves.

- Note the following family relationships among nodes. A is the *parent* of B and C. B and C are the *children* of A, called the left and right child, respectively. C has no left child, just a right child, F. D and E, the children of B, are called *siblings*. Note that F is not a sibling of either D or E since it has a different parent. A leaf is a node with no children.

- Any node that occurs in a subtree of node *k* is a *descendant* of *k*. Thus every node except A is a descendant of A. Node I is a descendant of C but not of B.

- If node *k* is a descendant of node *j*, then *j* is an *ancestor* of node *k*. Thus B is an ancestor of D, E, and G, but not of F, H, and I.

- The *depth* of a node is the length of the path from the root to that node. Thus the depth of A is 0, of B is 1, and of H and I is 3.

- The *level of a node* is equal to its depth. Thus nodes D, E, and F are all at level 2. The *level of a tree* is equal to the level of its deepest leaf. Thus the level of the tree shown is 3.

- The *height* of a tree is the number of nodes on the longest path from the root to a leaf. Thus the height is one more than the level of the tree. The height is defined to be 0 for an empty tree. The height is 1 for a single node tree. The height of the tree shown on the previous page is 4.

- A *balanced tree* has approximately the same number of nodes in the left and right subtrees at each level. The tree on the previous page is balanced.

- A *full binary tree* has every leaf on the same level; and every nonleaf node has two children.

- A *complete binary tree* is either full or full through the next-to-last level, with the leaves as far left as possible in the last level.

| Implementation of Binary Trees | A binary tree can be implemented in Java using a `TreeNode` class for the nodes and a `BinaryTree` class for the tree. |

The `TreeNode` Class

A `TreeNode` class similar to the following will be provided on the AP exam.[1]

```java
/* TreeNode class for the AP exam */
public class TreeNode
{
    private Object value;
    private TreeNode left, right;

    public TreeNode(Object initValue)
    {
        value = initValue;
        left = null;
        right = null;
    }

    public TreeNode(Object initValue, TreeNode initLeft,
        TreeNode initRight)
    {
        value = initValue;
        left = initLeft;
        right = initRight;
    }
```

---

[1]Based on the College Board's *AP Computer Science AB: Implementation Classes for Linked Lists and Tree Nodes.*

```
public Object getValue()
{return value;}

public TreeNode getLeft()
{return left;}

public TreeNode getRight()
{return right;}

public void setValue(Object theNewValue)
{value = theNewValue;}

public void setLeft(TreeNode theNewLeft)
{left = theNewLeft;}

public void setRight(TreeNode theNewRight)
{right = theNewRight;}
}
```

The Instance Variables

```
private Object value
```

This is exactly like the data field of a `ListNode`. No primitive type like `int` can be placed in a `TreeNode`—it must first be wrapped in a wrapper class like `Integer` to make it an `Object`.

```
private TreeNode left, right
```

Like the `ListNode` class, the `TreeNode` class is self-referential. The variables `left` and `right` for any given `TreeNode` are pointers to the left and right subtrees of that node.

The Methods

```
public TreeNode(Object initValue)
public TreeNode(Object initValue, TreeNode initLeft,
    TreeNode initRight)
```

These constructors initialize `value` to `initValue`. The variables `left` and `right` are initialized to `null` in the first constructor and to `initLeft` and `initRight` in the second.

```
public Object getValue()
```

This is an accessor method that returns the value of the current `TreeNode`. You may need to cast this value to `Integer`, `Double`, or `String`, and so on, unless you plan to assign it to a variable of type `Object`.

```
public TreeNode getLeft()
public TreeNode getRight()
```

These are accessor methods that return `left` or `right`, the left or right pointer of the current `TreeNode`.

```
public void setValue(Object theNewValue)
```

This is a mutator method that changes the current value of TreeNode to theNewValue.

```
public void setLeft(TreeNode theNewLeft)
public void setRight(TreeNode theNewRight)
```

These are mutator methods that change the left or right field of the current TreeNode to theNewLeft or theNewRight.

A BinaryTree Class

To represent a binary tree, it makes sense to have an abstract class, since searching and insertion methods depend on the type of binary tree. Notice that these methods are declared abstract in the BinaryTree class below. A BinarySearchTree class, which is derived from BinaryTree, is shown on the next page. Implementations for insert and find are provided in that class.

Here is the abstract superclass, BinaryTree.

```
public abstract class BinaryTree
{
    private TreeNode root;

    public BinaryTree()
    { root = null; }

    public TreeNode getRoot()
    { return root; }

    public void setRoot(TreeNode theNewNode)
    { root = theNewNode; }

    public boolean isEmpty()
    { return root == null; }

    public abstract void insert(Comparable item);

    public abstract TreeNode find(Comparable key);
}
```

NOTE A binary tree class will not be provided on the AP exam, but you are expected to know how to implement binary trees.

Binary Search Trees

A *binary search tree* is a binary tree that stores elements in an ordered way that makes it efficient to find a given element and easy to access the elements in sorted order. The ordering property is conventional. The following definition of a binary search tree gives the ordering property used most often.

A binary search tree is either empty or has just one node, the root, with left and right subtrees that are binary search trees. Each node has the property that all nodes in its left subtree are less than it, and all nodes in its right subtree are greater than or equal to it. This is a binary search tree that allows duplicates. Some do not.

Here is an example:

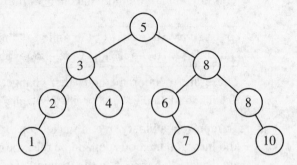

A BinarySearchTree Class

The class shown below is a subclass of the abstract `BinaryTree` class given on the previous page.

```
public class BinarySearchTree extends BinaryTree
{
    //Insert item in BinarySearchTree
    public void insert(Comparable item)
    { implementation code on the next page }

    //Returns TreeNode with key.
    //If key not in tree, returns null
    public TreeNode find(Comparable key)
    { implementation code on p. 334 }
}
```

NOTE
1. Only the abstract methods of the `BinaryTree` class, `insert` and `find`, are provided in the `BinarySearchTree` class. All the other methods of `BinaryTree`, namely `getRoot`, `setRoot`, and `isEmpty()`, are inherited.
2. No constructor is provided in `BinarySearchTree`, which means that the compiler will provide the default constructor of the `BinaryTree` superclass:

```
    public BinarySearchTree()
    { super(); }      //initializes root to null. This is fine.
```

3. The `getRoot` and `setRoot` methods in `BinarySearchTree` are used to access the private instance variable `root` of the superclass.
4. The parameters of both `insert` and `find` need to be `Comparable`, since the methods require you to compare objects.

Inserting an Element into a Binary Search Tree

Insertion Algorithm

Suppose that you wish to insert the element 9 into the preceding tree. Start by comparing with the root:

$9 > 5$, go right
$9 > 8$, go right
$9 > 8$, go right
$9 < 10$, insert to left of 10

Here is the resulting binary search tree.

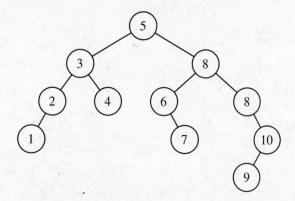

An algorithm for inserting an element uses two TreeNode pointers, p and q, say, following each other to find the insertion point. The "front" pointer q is like a kamikaze pilot plunging downward until it is null, at which point p points to the node at which the new data will be attached. A simple comparison tells whether the new node goes left or right.

The insert Method

Here is the insert method for the BinarySearchTree class:

```
//Insert item in BinarySearchTree
public void insert(Comparable item)
{
    if (getRoot() == null)
        setRoot(new TreeNode(item, null, null));
    else
    {
        TreeNode p=null, q=getRoot();
        while (q != null)
        {
            p = q;
            if (item.compareTo(p.getValue()) < 0)
                q = p.getLeft();
            else
                q = p.getRight();
        }
        if (item.compareTo(p.getValue()) < 0)
            p.setLeft(new TreeNode(item, null, null));
        else
            p.setRight(new TreeNode(item, null, null));
    }
}
```

Run-time Analysis

To insert a single element in an existing binary search tree of n elements:

1. Balanced tree: Insertion will require at most one comparison per level (i.e., no more than $\log_2 n$ comparisons). Thus the algorithm is $O(\log n)$.

2. Unbalanced tree: As many as n comparisons may be required if the tree consists of a long chain of children. Thus the algorithm is $O(n)$ in the worst case. For example,

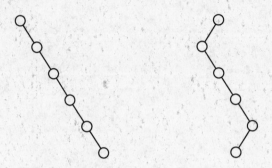

NOTE   See p. 340 for a recursive version of insert.

Finding a Target Element in a Binary Search Tree

The special ordering property of a binary search tree allows for quick and easy searching for any given element. If the target is less than the current node value, go left, otherwise go right.

The following method returns a TreeNode with the key value. It returns null if the key is not in the tree.

The find Method

Here is the find method from the BinarySearchTree class:

```
//Returns TreeNode with key.
//If key not in tree, returns null
public TreeNode find(Comparable key)
{
    TreeNode p = getRoot();
    while (p != null && key.compareTo(p.getValue())!= 0)
    {
        if (key.compareTo(p.getValue()) < 0)
            p = p.getLeft();
        else
            p = p.getRight();
    }
    return p;
}
```

Run-time Analysis

To find a single element in a binary search tree of n elements: The analysis is practically identical to that for insertion.

1. Balanced tree: A search will require at most one comparison per level (i.e., no more than $\log_2 n$ comparisons). Thus the algorithm is $O(\log n)$.
2. Unbalanced tree: As many as n comparisons may be required to search a long chain of nodes. Thus, the algorithm is $O(n)$ in the worst case.

NOTE   See Question 35 on p. 613 for a recursive version of find.

| Creating a Binary Search Tree | Creating the Tree |

Creating the Tree

The following program

- Creates a binary search tree of single-character strings.
- Tests the `find` method.

```java
/* Accesses a file of character strings, one per line,
   and inserts them into a binary search tree */
public class BinarySearchTreeTest
{
    public static void main(String[] args)
    {
        //code to open inFile
        BinaryTree tree = new BinarySearchTree();
        String ch;
        while (< there are still elements in inFile >)
        {
            ch = inFile.readLine();
            tree.insert(ch);
        }
        System.out.println("Enter character key: ");
        ch = IO.readLine();    //read user input
        TreeNode t = tree.find(ch);
        if (t == null)
            System.out.println(ch + " was not in the tree.");
        else
            System.out.println(ch + " was found in the tree!");
    }
}
```

Run-time Analysis for Creating a Binary Search Tree

1. The best case occurs if the elements are in random order, leading to a tree that is reasonably balanced, with the level of the tree approximately equal to $\log_2 n$. To create the tree, each of the n elements will require no more than $\log_2 n$ comparisons, so the run time is $O(n \log n)$.
2. An example of the worst case occurs if the elements are initially sorted or sorted in reverse order. The tree thus formed is a sequence of left or right links as shown. To create the tree, insertion of nodes requires $0 + 1 + 2 + \cdots + n - 1 = n(n-1)/2$ comparisons, which is $O(n^2)$.

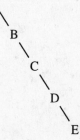

Tree Traversal

| Three Methods of Traversal | There is no natural order for accessing all the elements of a binary tree. Three different methods of traversal are used, each with its own applications. |

Inorder:	left - root - right	
Recursively:	If root is not null:	
	Traverse the left subtree inorder	
	Visit the root	
	Traverse the right subtree inorder	BAC
Preorder:	root - left - right	
Recursively:	If root is not null:	
	Visit the root	
	Traverse the left subtree preorder	
	Traverse the right subtree preorder	ABC
Postorder:	left - right - root	
Recursively:	If root is not null:	
	Traverse the left subtree postorder	
	Traverse the right subtree postorder	
	Visit the root	BCA

Example 1

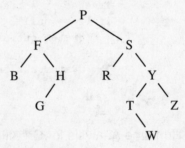

Inorder:	BFGHPRSTWYZ
Preorder:	PFBHGSRYTWZ
Postorder:	BGHFRWTZYSP

Example 2

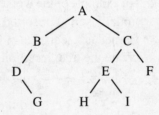

Inorder:	DGBAHEICF
Preorder:	ABDGCEHIF
Postorder:	GDBHIEFCA

Implementing the
Traversal
Algorithms

The traversals described apply to all binary trees. It therefore makes sense to add them to the `BinaryTree` superclass with their implementations. Each traversal will have a recursive helper method. Each recursive helper method follows the definition for its particular traversal and has a `TreeNode` parameter. The base case is when this parameter is `null`. The "Visit the root" step of the definition simply writes out the data in the node with `System.out.println...`

Here is the code for the `postorder` method.

```
public void postorder()
{ doPostorder(root); }

private void doPostorder(TreeNode t)
{
    if (t != null)
    {
        doPostorder(t.getLeft());
        doPostorder(t.getRight());
        System.out.print(t.getValue());
    }
}
```

NOTE

1. Similar methods can be written for inorder and preorder traversals—be sure to put the statements in the correct order!
2. Using the private helper methods (`doPostorder`, for example) allows the root parameter to remain hidden in the `BinaryTree` class. A client method can call a traversal method as follows:

```
BinaryTree tree = new BinarySearchTree();
< code to read elements into tree >
System.out.print("POSTORDER: ");
tree.postorder();     //prints the elements postorder
```

3. If the tree is a binary search tree (as in Example 1 on the previous page), an inorder traversal will print out the elements in increasing sorted order.

Recursive Tree Algorithms

Most algorithms that involve binary trees are recursive because the trees themselves are recursive structures. Many of these algorithms traverse the tree and then report some result about the tree. Some change the contents of the nodes without altering the structure of the tree (i.e., no nodes are added or removed). Other algorithms change the structure of the tree.

A typical recursive method has this scheme (in pseudo-code):

```
doTreeStuff
{
    if (root != null)          //handles base case
    {
        Handle the root           //Important! Don't forget this.
        doTreeStuff to left subtree      //recursive call
        doTreeStuff to right subtree     //recursive call
    }
}
```

This is just a general scheme. Often visiting the root postorder or inorder leads to the same correct result. Sometimes order *is* important; it depends on the actual application.

For the following examples assume that trees are implemented with the `TreeNode` class on page 329.

Example 1

```
/* Precondition:  tree is a binary tree of Integer values
 * Postcondition: returns the sum of the values in the tree,
 *                0 if the tree is empty */
public static int treeSum(TreeNode tree)
{
    if (tree == null)
        return 0;
    else
        return ((Integer) tree.getValue()).intValue()
            + treeSum(tree.getLeft()) + treeSum(tree.getRight());
}
```

Example 2

Two trees are *similar* if they have the same shape and pointer structure. Thus the following two trees are similar:

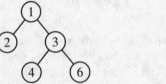

whereas these two trees are not similar:

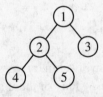 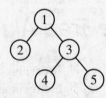

```
//Returns true if tree1 is similar to tree2, false otherwise
public static boolean similar(TreeNode tree1, TreeNode tree2)
{
    if (tree1 == null && tree2 == null)          //both null
        return true;
    else
        if (tree1 == null || tree2 == null)   //one null
            return false;
    else
        return similar(tree1.getLeft(), tree2.getLeft()) &&
            similar(tree1.getRight(), tree2.getRight());
}
```

Example 3

```
/* Precondition:  binary tree rooted at tree
 * Postcondition: creates identical tree and returns reference
 *                to its root node  */
public static TreeNode newTree(TreeNode tree)
{
    if (tree == null)       //base case
        return null;
    else
    {
        TreeNode temp = new TreeNode(null, null, null);
        temp.setValue(tree.getValue());
        temp.setLeft(newTree(tree.getLeft()));     //attach
                                                   //left subtree
        temp.setRight(newTree(tree.getRight()));   //attach
                                                   //right subtree
        return temp;
    }
}
```

NOTE   The newTree example is written with several statements to clarify the algorithm. The method can, however, be compacted as follows:

```
public static TreeNode newTree(TreeNode tree)
{
    if (tree == null)       //base case
        return null;
    else
        return new TreeNode(tree.getValue(),
            newTree(tree.getLeft()), newTree(tree.getRight()));
}
```

Example 4

Recall that the height of a binary tree is the number of nodes on the longest path from the root to a leaf. The height of an empty tree is 0. The height of any given node is the number of nodes on the longest path from that node to a leaf. To write a method that finds the height of a node, you may use the method Math.max(a, b), which returns the larger of a and b.

```
//Return the height of node t
public static int height(TreeNode t)
{
    if (t == null)
        return 0;
    else
        return 1 + Math.max(height(t.getLeft()),
            height(t.getRight()));
}
```

NOTE   The height of node t equals the height of the left or right subtree, whichever is bigger. You must add 1 because the node itself is counted in its height.

Recursion That Alters the Tree Structure

Recursive methods that change the structure of a tree by adding or removing nodes can be tricky. For example, consider using a recursive `insert` method instead of the iterative `insert` provided for the `BinarySearchTree` class (p. 333). Recall that the method inserts a new item into the tree.

A client method would call `insert` with code like the following:

```
BinaryTree tree = new BinarySearchTree();
System.out.println("Enter items to be inserted...");
while (< there are items to insert >)
{
    Object item = IO.readItem();        //read user input
    tree.insert(item);
}
```

If the `insert` method is recursive, the above method call, `tree.insert(item)`, will not work as intended because in order to make recursive calls the method must have a `TreeNode` parameter.

Suppose you modify `insert` so that it includes the required `TreeNode` parameter and change the client statement that invokes `insert` to be

```
tree.insert(tree.getRoot(), item);
```

This *still* won't work because the `TreeNode` parameter is passed by value, so the tree will remain unchanged! The way to change the tree is to *return* the changed `TreeNode`, in addition to having a `TreeNode` as a parameter for the recursive calls.

The problem is solved by making `insert` nonrecursive and having it call a private recursive helper method `recurInsert` that takes a `TreeNode` parameter and returns a `TreeNode` reference. The client method call in the code segment above remains `tree.insert(item)`.

Here is the code for both `insert` and `recurInsert`, which are added to the `BinarySearchTree` class.

```
//insert item in BinarySearchTree
public void insert(Comparable item)
{
    setRoot(recurInsert(getRoot(), item));
}


/* private helper method
 * Finds insertion point for new node and attaches it.
 * Returns reference to TreeNode along insertion path */
private TreeNode recurInsert(TreeNode t, Comparable item)
{
    if (t == null)
        return new TreeNode(item, null, null);
    else if (item.compareTo(t.getValue()) < 0)
        t.setLeft(recurInsert(t.getLeft(), item));
    else
        t.setRight(recurInsert(t.getRight(), item));
    return t;
}
```

NOTE

1. If the tree is empty, `recurInsert` simply returns the new `TreeNode` containing `item`. Otherwise, if `item` is less than the value in the current node, the algorithm recursively goes left. If `item` is greater than or equal to the value in the current node, it recursively goes right. When the insertion point is found (base case— `TreeNode` parameter is `null`), a new node is created and attached at that point.

2. The statement in the nonrecursive `insert` method

```
setRoot(recurInsert(getRoot(), item));
```

alters the root node of the tree only if the tree was originally empty or contained just one node. In fact, the recursive method `recurInsert` doesn't alter any nodes of the tree except at the insertion point. The returned node at each previous stage is simply a node along the path to the insertion point.

Recursion in Linked Structures

A recursive method that alters a linked structure (list or tree) cannot be implemented by passing a `ListNode` or `TreeNode` parameter that may need to be changed by the method. This is because the parameter is passed by value and will always emerge from the method with its value *unchanged*. The method must be written so that it returns a `ListNode` or `TreeNode`. This is how changes in the nodes get preserved. Such methods should always implement the recursion in a helper method.

In a recursive method where the list or tree is never changed, for example a recursive search algorithm that returns a boolean, it's OK to have a `ListNode` or `TreeNode` parameter whose value emerges from the method call unchanged. Such algorithms do not necessarily require helper methods, although they are often written with helpers to hide implementation details from the client.

NOTE

For an example of a recursive method that alters a linked list, see Question 26 on p. 290.

Binary Expression Trees

Infix, Postfix, and Prefix Expressions

A common application of trees is the storage and evaluation of mathematical expressions. A mathematical expression is made up of *operators* like +, −, *, /, and % and *operands*, which are numbers and variables.

There are three different representations of expressions:

infix: A + B
prefix: +AB
postfix: AB+

The "in," "pre," and "post" describe the position of the operator with respect to the operands. To convert the familiar infix form to postfix, for example, convert the pieces of the expression with highest precedence to postfix first. Then continue that way in stages.

Example 1

Convert $(A + B) * (C - D)$ to postfix.

$(A + B) * (C + D) = (AB+) * (CD-)$ //parentheses have highest precedence
$= AB + CD - *$ //treat AB+ and CD− as single operands

Example 2

Convert $(A - B)/C * D$ to prefix.

$(A - B)/C * D = ((-AB)/C) * D$ // $*$ and $/$ have equal precedence. Work
                              // from left to right
$= (/ - ABC) * D$
$= */ - ABCD$

Example 3

Convert $A - B/(C + D * E)$ to postfix.

$A - B/(C + D * E) = A - B/(C + (DE*))$
$= A - (B/CDE * +)$
$= A - BCDE * +/$
$= ABCDE * +/-$

Example 4

Convert $A - B/(C + D * E)$ to prefix.

$A - B/(C + D * E) = A - B/(C + (*DE))$
$= A - (B/(+C * DE))$
$= A - /B + C * DE$
$= -A/B + C * DE$

Binary Expression Tree

A *binary expression tree* either consists of a single root node containing an operand or stores an expression as follows. The root contains an operator that will be applied to the results of evaluating the expressions in the left and right subtrees, each of which is a binary expression tree.

A node containing an operator must have two nonempty subtrees. A node containing an operand must be a leaf. For example,

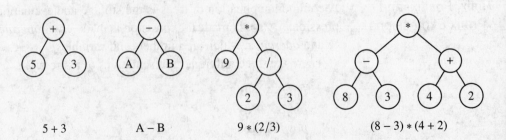

5 + 3   A − B   9 * (2/3)   (8 − 3) * (4 + 2)

NOTE   1. The level of the nodes indicates the precedence: The operation at the root will always be the *last* operation performed. Operations in the highest level nodes are performed first.

2. An expression can be generated in its infix form by an inorder traversal of the tree. (But *you* must provide the brackets!) A preorder traversal yields the prefix form, whereas a postorder traversal yields the postfix form.

Example 1

Write the infix, prefix, and postfix form of the expression represented by each binary expression tree.

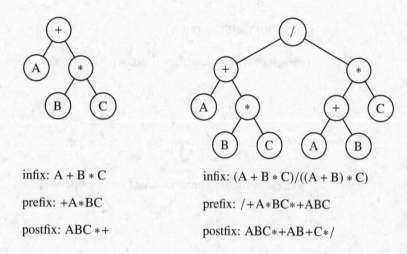

infix: A + B * C

prefix: +A*BC

postfix: ABC *+

infix: (A + B * C)/((A + B) * C)

prefix: /+A*BC*+ABC

postfix: ABC*+AB+C*/

Example 2

Evaluate the expression in the following tree.

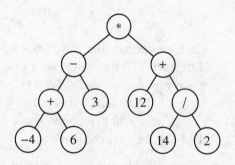

Solution: Do an inorder traversal to get the following infix form:

$$[(-4 + 6) - 3] * [12 + 14/2] = (2 - 3) * (12 + 7) = -19$$

Evaluating a Binary Expression Tree

Consider a program that places an expression in a binary expression tree and then evaluates the tree. For the purposes of this program, assume that a node contains either an operator (like "+", "−", etc.) or an integer value.

For example, a binary expression tree with the expression $(3 + 4) * 6$ would look like this:

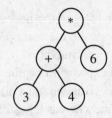

Notice that the left and right subtree of each operator node is an expression:

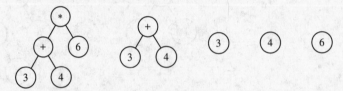

For ∗:   left subtree is   right subtree is ⑥

For +:   left subtree is ③   right subtree is ④

Each of these quantities is an expression:

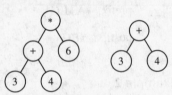

Each of these expressions is a binary operation:

Each of these expressions is a constant:

Each expression that is a binary operation is either a sum, product, quotient, or difference. This all suggests a program that has an `Expression` superclass, with `BinaryOperation` and `Constant` subclasses. Further, `BinaryOperation` should have subclasses `Sum`, `Difference`, `Product`, and `Quotient`.

Evaluating an expression consists of evaluating the left and right subtrees and applying the operator at the root. Thus

(value of tree) = (value of left subtree) • (value of right subtree)

where • is a binary operation. But

(value of left subtree) = (value of *its* left subtree) ◇ (value of *its* right subtree)

where ◇ is some other binary operation. Clearly the process is recursive. The value obtained from a given subtree depends on whether that subtree is a `Constant` or a `BinaryOperation`. If it's a `Constant`, its value is just that number (base case). If it's a `BinaryOperation`, then, depending on the operator, either a `Sum` is evaluated or a `Product` is, and so on. This procedure extends all the way down to the leaves—polymorphism is applied at each stage, determining which kind of expression to evaluate.

A Binary
Expression Tree
Program

Here are the classes used in the program[1] for evaluating a binary expression tree:

```
/* An abstract class for arithmetic expressions */
public abstract class Expression
{
    //Postcondition: Returns the value of this Expression.
    public abstract int evaluate();
}
```

NOTE   The evaluate method is abstract because evaluation depends on the type of expression being evaluated.

```
/* A class that defines expressions that are constants */
public class Constant extends Expression
{
    public Constant(int value)
    { myValue = value; }

    public int evaluate()
    { return myValue; }

    public String toString()
    { return "" + myValue; }

    private int myValue;
}
```

NOTE   The Constant class is a concrete (nonabstract) class. The evaluate method is clearly defined for a constant; simply return its value.

```
/* An abstract class that defines expressions
 * that are binary operations  */
public abstract class BinaryOperation extends Expression
{
    public BinaryOperation(String op, Expression lhs, Expression rhs)
    {
        myLeft = lhs;
        myRight = rhs;
        myOp = op;
    }

    public String toString()
    {
        return "(" + myLeft.toString() + " " + myOp
                + " " + myRight.toString() + ")";
    }

    public Expression getLeft()
    { return myLeft; }

    public Expression getRight()
    { return myRight; }
```

---

[1]This program uses the classes shown by David Levine at a workshop at St. Bonaventure and attributed to Scot Drysdale.

```
        private Expression myLeft, myRight;
        private String myOp;     // Symbolic representation of the operator
}
```

NOTE   The `BinaryOperation` class is abstract because the `evaluate` method cannot be explicitly defined here: it depends on the binary operator.

```
/* A class that defines expressions that are sums */
public class Sum extends BinaryOperation
{
    public Sum(Expression lhs, Expression rhs)
    { super("+", lhs, rhs); }

    public int evaluate()
    {return getLeft().evaluate() + getRight().evaluate();}
}
```

NOTE   1. For the `Sum` class the `evaluate` method can be defined without ambiguity:

(value of left subtree) + (value of right subtree)

2. Similar classes are defined for `Product`, `Quotient`, and `Difference`.

The `ExpressionEvaluator` program looks something like this:

```
public class ExpressionEvaluator
{
    < method to open file for reading >

    //Create binary expression tree from postfix expression in file
    public static Expression createTree()
    {implementation code}

    public static void main(String[] args)
    {
        Expression root = createTree();
        System.out.println("value of " + root.toString()
            + " is " + root.evaluate());
        System.out.println();
    }
}
```

NOTE   1. In case you're wondering how the expression got into the tree, implementation code for the `createTree` method is provided in Appendix B.
2. Notice how polymorphism is applied when `root.evaluate()` is called:

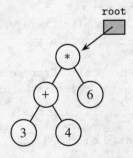

    (i) The node with * is encountered. The calling object is therefore a `Product`, which produces

`getLeft().evaluate()  *  getRight().evaluate()`

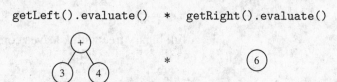

    (ii) For the left-hand side in step (i), the node with + is encountered. The calling object is therefore a `Sum`, which produces

`getLeft().evaluate()  +  getRight().evaluate()`

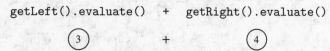

    (iii) When the nodes in step (ii) are encountered, and also the right-hand side in step (i), the controlling object in each case is a `Constant`. Thus a call to `evaluate` returns the values 3, 4, and 6, respectively.

    (iv) Thus the sum in step (ii) is 7, and the product in step (i) is 7 * 6, which is 42.

3. As you study this implementation of a binary expression tree, you may be wondering: Where did the `BinaryTree` go? The answer is that an `Expression` has replaced `TreeNode`. Each node in the tree that's created represents an `Expression`. Each `Expression` node contains a value (either a `Constant` or `BinaryOperation`) as well as a left and right pointer field that refers to another `Expression`. An `Expression`, like a `TreeNode`, is self-referential and can be linked to other `Expression` objects to form a binary expression tree.

The inheritance hierarchy in this program is an elegant way of representing the various elements that comprise the binary expression tree.

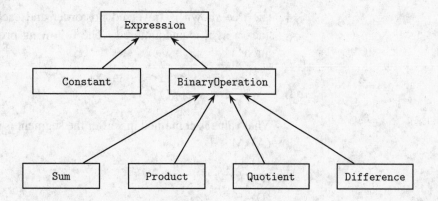

Multiple-Choice Questions on Trees

1. A full binary tree with k leaves contains how many nodes?
   - (A) k
   - (B) k^2
   - (C) 2^k
   - (D) $\log_2 k$
   - (E) $2k - 1$

2. A binary tree has level k. Which represents

   1. The maximum possible number of nodes, and
   2. The minimum possible number of nodes in the tree?

(A)	(1) 2^{k+1}	(2) $2^k + 1$
(B)	(1) 2^{k+1}	(2) k
(C)	(1) $2^{k+1} - 1$	(2) k
(D)	(1) $2^{k+1} - 1$	(2) $k + 1$
(E)	(1) $2^k + 1$	(2) 2^k

3. Which of the following represents (1) inorder, (2) preorder, and (3) postorder traversals of the tree shown?

(A)	(1) GJAPES	(2) JAGPES	(3) GAESPJ
(B)	(1) GJAEPS	(2) JGAPES	(3) GESPAJ
(C)	(1) EPSAJG	(2) PESJGA	(3) ESPGAJ
(D)	(1) GJAEPS	(2) GESPAJ	(3) JGAPES
(E)	(1) GJAPES	(2) GAESPJ	(3) JAGPES

4. The tree shown is traversed postorder and each element is pushed onto a stack s as it is encountered. The following program fragment is then executed:

   ```
   for (int i=1; i<=5; i++)
       x = s.pop();
   ```

   What value is contained in x after the segment is executed?
   - (A) M
   - (B) G
   - (C) K
   - (D) F
   - (E) P

5. Each of the following lists of numbers is inserted, in the order given, into a binary search tree. Which list produces the most balanced tree?
   - (A) 2 4 7 5 8 10
   - (B) 9 7 2 1 4 0
   - (C) 5 1 2 6 3 4
   - (D) 2 5 1 4 0 3
   - (E) 6 4 1 8 10 5

6. The element 10 is to be inserted into the binary search tree shown.

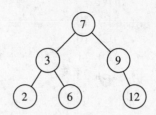

After insertion, the tree is as follows:

(A)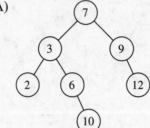

(B)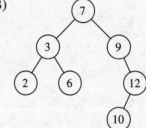

(C)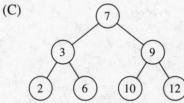

(D)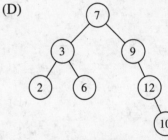

(E)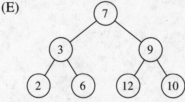

7. Array elements `a[0]`, `a[1]`, ..., `a[n-1]` are inserted into a binary search tree. The tree will then be used to search for a given element. In the *worst* case, the insertion and search, respectively, will be
   (A) $O(n^2)$, $O(n \log n)$
   (B) $O(n \log n)$, $O(n \log n)$
   (C) $O(n^2)$, $O(n)$
   (D) $O(n^2)$, $O(n^2)$
   (E) $O(n)$, $O(n)$

8. Worst-case performance of the search for a key in a *balanced* binary search tree is
   (A) $O(n^2)$
   (B) $O(n)$
   (C) $O(\log n)$
   (D) $O(2^n)$
   (E) $O(n \log n)$

9. The value of the binary expression tree shown is
   (A) 1
   (B) 4
   (C) 10
   (D) 11
   (E) 25

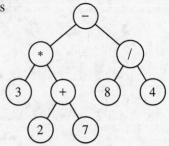

10. Which of the following correctly represents the expression A/B ∗ C % D?

(A)

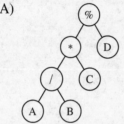

(B)

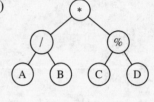

(C)

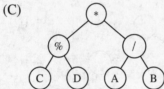

(D)

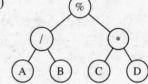

(E)

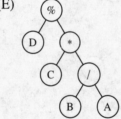

11. The (1) prefix and (2) postfix forms of the expression P + (Q − R) ∗ A/B are
    (A) (1) +P ∗ −QR/AB   (2) PQR − AB/ ∗ +
    (B) (1) PQR − AB/ ∗ +   (2) +P ∗ −QR/AB
    (C) (1) PQR − A ∗ B/+   (2) +P/ ∗ −QRAB
    (D) (1) +P/ ∗ −QRAB   (2) PQR − A ∗ B/+
    (E) (1) + ∗ P − QR/AB   (2) PQRA − ∗B/+

For Questions 12–22 assume that binary trees are implemented with the `TreeNode` class on p. 329.

12. Suppose that p refers to a node as shown. Which of the following correctly inserts the `Object` obj as the right child of the node that p points to?

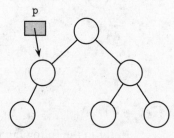

(A) `p.setRight(new TreeNode(obj, null, null));`

(B) `p = new TreeNode(obj, p.getLeft(), p.getRight());`

(C) `p.setRight(new(obj, null, null));`

(D) `p.setRight(new TreeNode(obj, p.getLeft(), p.getRight()));`

(E) `p = new TreeNode(obj, null, null);`

13. Refer to method `numNodes`:

```
//Returns the number of nodes in tree
public static int numNodes(TreeNode tree)
{
    if (tree == null)
        return 0;
    else
    {
        < code >
    }
}
```

Which replacement for *< code >* will cause the method to work as intended?

```
I  return 1 + numNodes(tree.getLeft()) +
            numNodes(tree.getRight());
```

```
II  return numNodes(tree) + numNodes(tree.getLeft()) +
            numNodes(tree.getRight());
```

```
III  return numNodes(tree.getLeft()) + numNodes(tree.getRight());
```

(A) None
(B) I only
(C) II only
(D) III only
(E) II and III only

14. Two trees are *mirror images* of each other if their roots and left and right subtrees are reflected across a vertical line as shown:

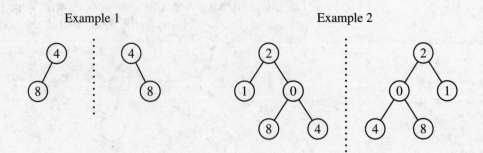

Example 1   Example 2

Refer to the following method `mirrorTree`:

```
/* Precondition:   tree refers to the root of a binary tree
 * Postcondition: a mirror image of tree is created and
 *                a reference to it is returned  */
public static TreeNode mirrorTree(TreeNode tree)
{
    if (tree == null)
        return null;
    else
    {
        < more code >
    }
}
```

Which of the following replacements for *< more code >* correctly achieves the postcondition for method `mirrorTree`?

```
I  TreeNode temp = new TreeNode(null, null, null);
   temp.setValue(tree.getValue());
   temp.setLeft(mirrorTree(tree.getRight()));
   temp.setRight(mirrorTree(tree.getLeft()));
   return temp;
```

```
II return new TreeNode(tree.getValue(),
            mirrorTree(tree.getRight()),
            mirrorTree(tree.getLeft()));
```

```
III return new TreeNode(tree.getValue(),
            mirrorTree(tree.getLeft()),
            mirrorTree(tree.getRight()));
```

(A) I only
(B) II only
(C) III only
(D) I and II only
(E) I and III only

15. Refer to method `leafSum`:

```
//Returns sum of leaves in tree, 0 for empty tree
public static int leafSum(TreeNode tree)
{
    if (tree == null)
        return 0;
    else
    {
        < code >
    }
}
```

Which replacement for < *code* > is correct?

(A)
```
    if (tree.getLeft() == null && tree.getRight() == null)
        return ((Integer) (tree.getValue())).intValue();
else
        return 1 + leafSum(tree.getLeft()) +
            leafSum(tree.getRight());
```

(B)
```
    if (tree.getLeft() == null || tree.getRight() == null)
        return ((Integer) (tree.getValue())).intValue();
else
        return 1 + leafSum(tree.getLeft()) +
            leafSum(tree.getRight());
```

(C)
```
    if (tree.getLeft() == null && tree.getRight() == null)
        return ((Integer) (tree.getValue())).intValue();
else
        return ((Integer) (tree.getValue())).intValue() +
            leafSum(tree.getLeft()) + leafSum(tree.getRight());
```

(D)
```
    if (tree.getLeft() == null || tree.getRight() == null)
        return ((Integer) (tree.getValue())).intValue();
else
        return leafSum(tree.getLeft()) +
            leafSum(tree.getRight());
```

(E)
```
    if (tree.getLeft() == null && tree.getRight() == null)
        return ((Integer) (tree.getValue())).intValue();
else
        return leafSum(tree.getLeft()) +
            leafSum(tree.getRight());
```

16. Which is true about method find?

```
//Return TreeNode with target value,
//or null if target not found
public static TreeNode find(TreeNode root, Comparable target)
{
    if (root == null)
        return null;
    else if (target.compareTo(root.getValue())== 0)
        return root;
    else if (target.compareTo(root.getValue()) < 0)
        return find(root.getLeft(), target);
    else
        return find(root.getRight(), target);
}
```

(A) Method find will never work as intended.
(B) Method find will always work as intended.
(C) Method find will only work as intended if target is not in the tree.
(D) Method find will always work as intended if the tree is a binary search tree.
(E) Method find will only work as intended if the tree is a binary search tree and target occurs no more than once in the tree.

17. Refer to method doSomething:

```
public static Object doSomething(TreeNode root)
{
    if (root != null)
        if (root.getRight() == null)
            return root.getValue();
        else
            return doSomething(root.getRight());
    return null;
}
```

Which best describes what doSomething does?
(A) It returns the largest element in a nonempty binary search tree.
(B) It returns the largest element in a nonempty tree.
(C) It returns an element at the highest level of a nonempty tree.
(D) It returns the smallest element in a nonempty binary search tree.
(E) It returns the smallest element in a nonempty tree.

18. Refer to method `traverse`, and to the binary tree of `Integer` values shown:

```
public static void traverse(TreeNode T)
{
    if (T != null)
    {
        < code >
    }
}
```

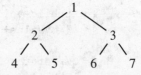

By replacing < *code* > with the three statements `traverse(T.getLeft())`, `traverse(T.getRight())`, and `System.out.print(T.getValue())` in some order, we can cause method `traverse` to execute one of six traversals. For example, by replacing < *code* > with

```
traverse(T.getLeft());
traverse(T.getRight());
System.out.print(T.getValue());
```

we would cause `traverse` to execute a postorder traversal. Which of the following replacements for < *code* > will cause the numbers 1 through 7 to be printed in ascending order when `traverse(T)` is called?

(A) ```
traverse(T.getLeft());
System.out.print(T.getValue());
traverse(T.getRight());
```

(B) ```
System.out.print(T.getValue());
traverse(T.getLeft());
traverse(T.getRight());
```

(C) ```
traverse(T.getRight());
traverse(T.getLeft());
System.out.print(T.getValue());
```

(D) ```
traverse(T.getRight());
System.out.print(T.getValue());
traverse(T.getLeft());
```

(E) It is impossible to print the numbers 1 through 7 in ascending order using this method.

19. This question uses an object from the following class:

```
/* An Integer object that can be altered */
public class IntObj
{
    private int myValue;

    public IntObj(int value)    //constructor
    { myValue = value; }

    public void increment()    //increments IntObj by 1
    { myValue++; }

    //returns Integer equivalent of IntObj
    public Integer getInteger()
    { return new Integer(myValue); }
}
```

Refer to the following method:

```
/* Precondition: tree is at root of binary tree that contains
 *               Integer values */
public static void number(TreeNode tree, IntObj nextNum)
{
    if (tree != null)
        if (tree.getLeft() == null && tree.getRight() == null)
        {
            tree.setValue(nextNum.getInteger());
            nextNum.increment();
        }
        else
        {
            number(tree.getRight(), nextNum);
            number(tree.getLeft(), nextNum);
        }
}
```

Assuming that a binary tree of Integer values is rooted at tree, which of the following trees is a possible result of executing the next two statements?

```
IntObj nextNum = new IntObj(3);
number(tree, nextNum);
```

(A)
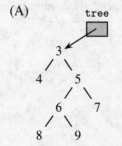

(B)
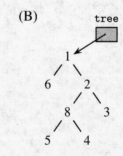

(C)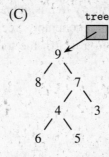

(D)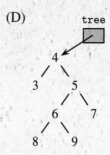

(E)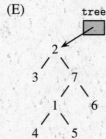

20. Refer to method whatsIt:

```java
public static int whatsIt(TreeNode tree)
{
    int x, y;
    if (tree == null)
        return -1;
    else
    {
        x = 1 + whatsIt(tree.getLeft());
        y = 1 + whatsIt(tree.getRight());
        if (x >= y)
            return x;
        else
            return y;
    }
}
```

Method whatsIt returns –1 for an empty tree. What does method whatsIt do when invoked for a nonempty tree?

(A) It returns the largest value in the tree.

(B) It returns the number of nodes in the subtree that has the greatest number of nodes.

(C) It returns the level of the tree.

(D) It returns 1 plus the level of the tree.

(E) It returns either the leftmost value or the rightmost value of a tree, whichever is larger.

21. Recall that the height of a binary tree is defined as follows: the height of an empty tree is 0; the height of a nonempty tree is the number of nodes on the longest path from the root to a leaf of the tree. Thus the height of the tree shown is 5.

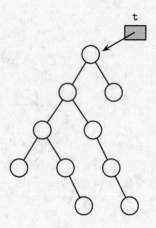

Refer to method f:

```
public static int f(TreeNode t)
{
    if (t == null)
        return 0;
    else
        return max(height(t.getLeft()) + height(t.getRight()),
            f(t.getLeft()), f(t.getRight()));
}
```

You may assume that method max(a, b, c) returns the largest of its integer arguments and that method height returns the height of its tree argument. What value is returned when f(t) is called for the tree pictured?

(A) 4

(B) 5

(C) 6

(D) 7

(E) 8

22. Consider the following binary tree of single-character `String` values:

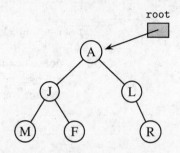

What will be output by the following code segment?

```
TreeNode current;
Queue q = new ListQueue();

if (root == null)
    System.out.println("Empty tree");
else
{
    q.enqueue(root);
    while (!q.isEmpty())
    {
        current = (TreeNode) q.dequeue();
        System.out.print(current.getValue());
        if (current.getLeft() != null)
            q.enqueue(current.getLeft());
        if (current.getRight() != null)
            q.enqueue(current.getRight());
    }
}
```

(A) MJFALR
(B) MFRJLA
(C) AJLMFR
(D) MFJRLA
(E) AJMFLR

23. A recursive method doPostorder is added to a BinaryTree class:

```
public void doPostorder(TreeNode t)
{
    if (t != null)
    {
        doPostorder(t.getLeft());
        doPostorder(t.getRight());
        System.out.print(t.getValue());
    }
}
```

Suppose this method is called for a TreeNode at the root of a tree with n elements. The run-time efficiency of doPostorder is

(A) $O(\log n)$
(B) $O(n)$
(C) $O(n \log n)$
(D) $O(n^2)$
(E) $O(2^n)$

Answer Key

1. **E**	9. **E**	17. **A**
2. **D**	10. **A**	18. **E**
3. **B**	11. **D**	19. **B**
4. **A**	12. **A**	20. **C**
5. **E**	13. **B**	21. **C**
6. **B**	14. **D**	22. **C**
7. **C**	15. **E**	23. **B**
8. **C**	16. **D**	

Answers Explained

1. (**E**) Draw some pictures and count!

# of leaves	# of nodes
1	1
2	3
4	7
8	15
16	31
32	63
...	...
k	$2k - 1$

2. (**D**) For the maximum possible number of nodes, each node must have two children. Notice the pattern:

Level	Max possible # of nodes
0	1
1	3
2	7
3	15
...	...
k	$2^{k+1} - 1$

For the minimum possible number of nodes, each node must have no more than one child. Thus, for example, a level 3 tree with the minimum number of nodes will look like this:

In each case there will be $k + 1$ nodes.

3. **(B)**
   (1) For inorder think left-root-right (i.e., G-J-right). When you now traverse the right subtree inorder, there is no left, so A comes next. Then traverse the P-E-S subtree inorder, which gives E-P-S.
   (2) For preorder think root-left-right (i.e., J-G-right). When you now traverse the right subtree, A is now the root and comes next. There is no left, so traverse the P-E-S subtree preorder, which gives P-E-S.
   (3) Similarly for postorder, thinking left-right-root produces GESPAJ.

4. **(A)** A postorder traversal yields PFMGECK, so here's the stack:

K
C
E
G
M
F
P

The fifth pop will remove element M.

5. **(E)** In each case the first number in the list will go into the root node. Subsequent numbers that are less than the first number will go into the left subtree; those greater than or equal to the first will go into the right subtree. Eliminate choices A and B, which are almost in sorted order. Each of these will form trees that are virtually long chains:

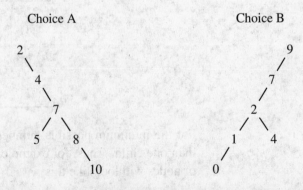

Choice C won't form a balanced tree either: all elements but one will go into the left subtree.

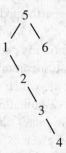

You should be able to eliminate choices A, B, and C by inspection. Comparing the trees in choices D and E shows that E yields the more balanced tree:

6. **(B)** Starting at the root, compare the new element with the current node. Go left if the element is less than the current node; otherwise go right. Insert at the first available empty slot. For the tree shown, compare 10 with 7. Since $10 > 7$, go right. Then $10 > 9$, so go right. Then $10 < 12$, a leaf, so insert left.

7. **(C)** An example of the worst case for insertion into a binary search tree occurs when the numbers are already sorted. The resulting tree will be unbalanced, a long chain of numbers:

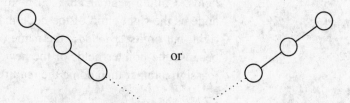

Insertion of n elements into the tree requires $0 + 1 + \cdots + n - 1 = n(n - 1)/2$ comparisons, which is $O(n^2)$. Searching this tree will require each "link" in the "chain" to be examined, much like a sequential search. This is $O(n)$.

8. **(C)** If the tree is balanced, the worst case occurs when the key is found in a leaf (i.e., at the highest level of the tree). The maximum level of a balanced tree is $\log_2 n$. Therefore, the search is $O(\log n)$.

9. **(E)** The infix form of the expression is $3 * (2 + 7) - 8/4$, which is equal to $(3 * 9) - 2 = 25$.

10. **(A)** The operators /, *, and % all have equal precedence and must therefore be performed from left to right. Thus the order of performing the operations is /, followed by *, then %. Now recall the general rule: The earlier an operation is performed, the higher its node level in the tree. In particular, the last operation performed is always the root node. So % must be in the root node, which eliminates choices B and C. Since / is performed before *, the node containing / must have a higher level than the node containing *, which eliminates choice D. Choice D fails for another reason: C * D is not part of the given expression. Choice E fails because B/A is not part of the given expression. Note that if the given expression had been $(A/B) * (C \% D)$, choice B would have been correct, since / and % would have equal first precedence and * would be the last operation performed.

11. **(D)** For both pre- and postfix, perform the operations in order of precedence, changing each subexpression to prefix or postfix as you go.
    (1) prefix:
    $$P + (Q - R) * A/B = P + [(-QR) * A]/B$$
    $$= P + (* - QRA)/B$$
    $$= P + (/ * -QRAB)$$
    $$= +P/ * -QRAB$$

    To go from the first to the second line, note that * and / have equal precedence, so use the leftmost one first.
    (2) postfix:
    $$P + (Q - R) * A/B = P + [(QR-) * A]/B$$
    $$= P + (QR - A*)/B$$
    $$= P + (QR - A * B/)$$
    $$= PQR - A * B/+$$

12. **(A)** The expression `new TreeNode(obj, null, null)` is the correct use of the `TreeNode` constructor to create a new node with `obj` that has null pointer fields. Calling `p.setRight(...` with this expression then attaches the new node as the right child of the node that `p` refers to. Choice C almost gets it right, but omits `TreeNode`, the name of the constructor. Choice D is wrong because the pointer fields of the new node must be null. Choices B and E reassign `p` rather than doing the required attachment to the node that `p` points to.

13. **(B)** Eliminate segment III; it forgot to count the root node! Segment II calls `numNodes(tree)`, which leads to infinite recursion. Segment I correctly adds 1 for the root node, and adds the number of nodes in the left and right subtrees.

14. **(D)** Segments I and II are equivalent, but segment II is more compact. The order of the pointer parameters in the constructor is left, right, so in segment II the call `mirrorTree(tree.getRight())` will attach as the left subtree of the new tree a duplicate of the right subtree of `tree`. Similarly,

`mirrorTree(tree.getLeft())` will cause a duplicate of the left subtree of `tree` to be attached as the right subtree of the new tree. Segment III is wrong because it creates an *exact* copy of the tree rather than a mirror image.

15. **(E)** This is an example where you *don't* automatically add the value in the root node. Thus eliminate choices A, B, and C, which all add something to `leafSum(tree.getLeft()) + leafSum(tree.getRight())`. The correct test for a leaf is that both the left and right pointers must be `null`. Thus eliminate choice D, which has an "or" in the test instead of an "and."

16. **(D)** The algorithm uses the binary search tree property and searches only the left subtree if `target` is less than the current root value, or only the right subtree if `target` is greater than or equal to the current root value. In a general binary tree (i.e., not a binary search tree), the given algorithm may miss the target. Note that choice E is false; the postcondition specifies that a `TreeNode` with `target` is returned, which the algorithm will do irrespective of the number of times `target` occurs in the tree.

17. **(A)** The algorithm is actually returning the rightmost element of the tree, which is not one of the choices. Note that the rightmost element of a binary search tree is the largest (check it out!), which makes A the best choice. None of the other choices *must* be true. For example, if the tree in choice C looks like the following tree, C will be false.

18. **(E)** Choice A is an inorder traversal yielding 4251637. Choice B is a preorder traversal: 1245367. Choice C is a right-to-left postorder traversal: 7635421. Choice D is a right-to-left inorder traversal: 7361524. Trying the regular postorder and the right-to-left preorder traversals (the two remaining possibilities) does not yield the required output either.

19. **(B)** This method numbers all the leaves of the tree beginning with the right subtree. The starting number given in this case is 3. The rightmost leaf becomes 3, and leaves are numbered in ascending order from right to left.

20. **(C)** In the line `x = 1 + whatsIt(tree.getLeft())`, 1 is added for each recursive call until `tree.getLeft()` is null. Similarly, 1 is added for each recursive call in the line `y = 1 + whatsIt(tree.getRight())`. Look at an example like the following tree:

Here x will end up with value 1 (two recursive calls plus −1 for the base case), whereas y will end up with the value 2 (three recursive calls plus −1 for the base case). The method in this case will return 2, the maximum of x and y, which is the level of the tree.

21. **(C)** The method call f(t) returns the maximum of the following three quantities:

    (1) Sum of heights of left and right subtrees of root node t. Here 4 + 1 = 5.
    (2) Maximum of sum of heights of left and right subtrees for *any* node in the right subtree of node t. Here this is 1.
    (3) Maximum of sum of heights of left and right subtrees for *any* node in the left subtree of node t.

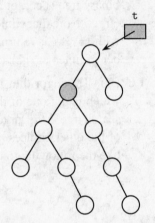

Note that the shaded node in the left subtree of node t has height of left subtree = 3, and height of right subtree = 3. No other node in the subtree returns a higher total, so the method call f(t.getLeft()) returns 6. Since max(5, 1, 6) = 6, f(t) returns 6.

22. **(C)** The algorithm yields a *level-order traversal* of the tree which visits nodes starting at the root and going from top to bottom, left to right. Suppose that the TreeNode references to the nodes are labeled with small letters as shown:

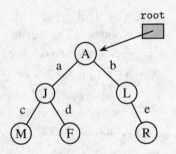

After the first pass through the while loop, A has been printed and q is

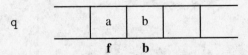

After the second pass, J has been printed and q is

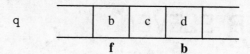

After the third pass, L has been printed and q is

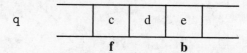

When q is empty, AJLMFR has been printed.

23. **(B)** Each aspect of a postorder traversal is linear, that is, $O(n)$. In a given traversal,

- Each node is output exactly once, thus printing is $O(n)$.
- Each `if` statement is executed once per node, thus testing for `null` is $O(n)$.
- The total number of calls to `doPostorder` is, again, once per node, thus invoking `doPostorder` is $O(n)$.

Since each operation of the method is $O(n)$, the total run time is $O(n)$.

CHAPTER ELEVEN

Collections

HASH: There is no definition for this word—
nobody knows what hash is.
—*Ambrose Bierce,* The Devil's Dictionary *(1911)*

Collections in Java

What Is a Collection?

A *collection* is any bunch of objects you can think of: members of a local bridge club, your CD collection, all book titles in the library, the moves in a chess game, the flavors at the ice cream parlor, a sack of toys. Some collections are ordered; some are not. Some allow duplicates; some do not.

The Collections API

When you write a Java program that manipulates a collection, you may use the Collections API (Application Programming Interface), which is a library provided by Java. Most of the API is in `java.util`. This library gives the programmer access to prepackaged data structures and the methods to manipulate them. The implementations of these *container classes* are invisible and should not be of concern to the programmer. The code works. And it is reusable.

All of the collections classes have the following features in common:

- They are designed to be both memory and run-time efficient.
- They provide methods for insertion and removal of items (i.e., they can grow and shrink).
- They provide for iteration over the entire collection.

The Collections Hierarchy

Inheritance is a defining feature of the Collections API. Some of the core interfaces that are used to manipulate the collections follow. They specify the operations that must be defined for any container class that implements that interface.

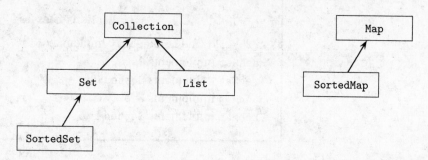

NOTE

1. The diagram shows the `Collection` interface at the root of the collections hierarchy. A `Collection` is simply a group of objects called its *elements*. `Collection` is used to manipulate collections when maximum generality is desired, much like `Object` in the hierarchy of classes.

2. `Set` and `List` are both collections. A `Set` is unordered and cannot contain duplicates. A `List` is ordered and can contain duplicates.

3. A `Map` is not considered to be a true collection and therefore has its own hierarchy tree. A `Map` is an object that maps keys to values. A `Map` cannot contain duplicate keys: each key maps to exactly one value.

4. The `SortedSet` and `SortedMap` interfaces are sorted versions of `Set` and `Map`.

You don't have to know all these interfaces for the AP exam. The only ones you are expected to know are `Set`, `List`, and `Map`. The container classes you are expected to know are `ArrayList`, `LinkedList`, `HashSet`, `TreeSet`, `HashMap`, and `TreeMap`. Using an oval to represent each class, the diagrams show which interface is directly implemented by each of these classes:

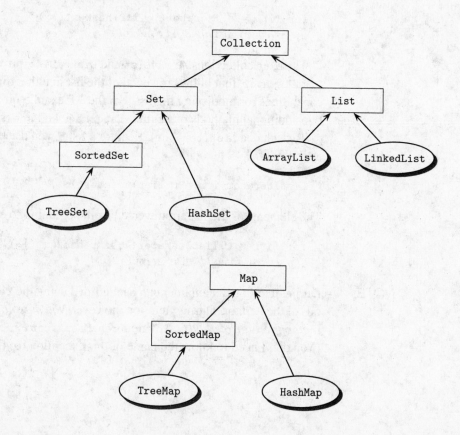

> **Collections Classes**
>
> `ArrayList` and `LinkedList` implement `List`.
> `HashSet` implements `Set`.
> `TreeSet` implements `SortedSet`.
> `HashMap` implements `Map`.
> `TreeMap` implements `SortedMap`.

Collections and Iterators

Recall that the methods of the `Iterator` interface are `next`, `hasNext`, and `remove` (see p. 252).

Each collection class defines its own implementation of the `Iterator` methods in a class that's invisible to users of the collection. An iterator object is declared for collection c using the `iterator` method as follows:

```
Iterator itr = c.iterator();
```

This statement positions the iterator at the beginning of the collection. All the elements of the collection are returned in proper sequence with the following code:

```
for (itr = c.iterator(); itr.hasNext();)
    < code with call to itr.next() >
```

The `List` collections, `ArrayList` and `LinkedList`, provide an expanded iterator, `ListIterator`, that allows traversal of the list in either direction, as well as greater capabilities for modifying the list. For the AP exam, you are expected to know just two additional methods of `ListIterator`: add and set (see p. 256).

To declare a `ListIterator` object for a list L, you use the `listIterator` method as follows:

```
ListIterator itr = L.listIterator();
```

The elements of the list are traversed from beginning to end with this code:

```
for (itr = L.listIterator(); itr.hasNext();)
    code with call to itr.next()
```

NOTE   During iteration, a container can be modified using the `remove`, `add`, and `set` methods of the iterator. During iteration, however, *you may not modify the container using noniterator methods.* A `ConcurrentModificationException` will be thrown. (You don't need to know the name of this exception for the AP exam.)

The List *Interface*

A class that implements the List interface is a sequence of elements. In other words, a list. In a list, duplicate elements are allowed. The elements of the list are indexed, with 0 being the index of the first element.

A list allows you to

- Access an element at any position in the list using its integer index.
- Insert an element anywhere in the list.
- Iterate over all elements using ListIterator or Iterator.

NOTE

1. It is generally more run-time efficient to iterate through a list than to cycle through the indexes.
2. For two list objects list1 and list2, list1.equals(list2) returns true if and only if the lists contain the same elements in the same order. This is irrespective of implementation.

The Methods of List

Here are the methods in the AP Java subset.

```
boolean add(Object obj)
```

Appends obj to the end of the list. Always returns true (contrast with add in Set, p. 377).

```
int size()
```

Returns the number of elements in the list.

```
Object get(int index)
```

Returns the element at the specified index in the list.

```
Object set(int index, Object element)
```

Replaces item at specified index in the list with specified element. Returns the element that was previously at index.

```
Iterator iterator()
```

Returns an iterator over the elements in the list, in proper sequence, starting at the first element.

```
ListIterator listIterator()
```

Returns a list iterator over the elements in the list, in proper sequence, starting at the first element.

The ArrayList Class

This is an array implementation of the List interface. The difference between an array and an ArrayList is that an ArrayList is resizable during run time, whereas an array has a fixed size at construction.

Shifting of elements, if any, caused by insertion or deletion, is handled automatically by `ArrayList`. All operations are $O(1)$, except for `add`, which is done in amortized constant time. This means that the insertion of n elements into an `ArrayList` is $O(n)$ because at some point there will be a resizing, but any single insertion can be thought of as $O(1)$.

The Methods of `ArrayList`

The following methods are in the AP Java subset (in addition to `add`, `size`, `get`, `set`, `iterator`, and `listIterator`).

```
ArrayList()
```

Constructs an empty list.

```
void add(int index, Object element)
```

Inserts `element` at specified `index` in list. If the insertion is not at the end of the list, shifts the element currently at that position and all elements following it one unit to the right (i.e., adds 1 to their indexes). Adjusts size of list.

```
Object remove(int index)
```

Removes and returns the element at the specified `index` in the list. Shifts all elements following the element one unit to the left (i.e., subtracts 1 from their indexes). Adjusts size of list.

NOTE

1. Each method above that has an `index` parameter—add, get, remove, and set— throws an `IndexOutOfBoundsException` if `index` is out of range. For get, remove, and set, index is out of range if

   ```
   index < 0 || index >= size()
   ```

   For add, however, it is OK to add an element at the end of the list. Therefore index is out of range if

   ```
   index < 0 || index > size()
   ```

2. The following constructor, which is *not* in the AP subset, is also worth knowing. It provides neat solutions to certain problems.

   ```
   ArrayList(Collection c)
   ```

   Constructs an `ArrayList` containing the elements of `c` in the same order as those in `c`.

Using `ArrayList`

Example 1

```
//Create an ArrayList of random Integers from 0 to 100
public static List getList()
{
    System.out.println("How many integers? ");
    int length = IO.readInt();    //read user input
    List list = new ArrayList();
```

```
        Random r = new Random();
        for (int i=0; i<length; i++)
            list.add(new Integer(r.nextInt(101)));  //random int
                                                     //from 0 to 100
        return list;
    }
```

NOTE

1. The variable `list` is declared to be of type `List` (the interface) but is instantiated as type `ArrayList` (the implementation). This has the advantage of making the code applicable to *any* List. For example, the single change

```
    List list = new LinkedList();
```

will produce a `getList` method that creates a linked list of random integers.

2. The `add` method in `getList` is the `List` method that appends its parameter to the end of the list.

Example 2

```
//Swap two values in list, indexed at i and j
public static void swap(List list, int i, int j)
{
    Object temp = list.get(i);
    list.set(i, list.get(j));
    list.set(j, temp);
}
```

NOTE

This is an example of *generic code* that works for any list. The `swap` method can be called with an `ArrayList` or a `LinkedList`—in fact, with any list object that implements `List`.

Example 3

```
//Remove all negatives from list a
//Precondition: a contains Integer values
public static void removeNegs(List a)
{
    Iterator i = a.iterator();
    while (i.hasNext())
    {
        if (((Integer) i.next()).intValue() < 0)
            i.remove();
    }
}
```

NOTE

1. An iterator is used because the entire list must be examined. (Compare this with the previous example where just two specific elements were accessed.)
2. Before `i.next()` can be accessed, it must be cast to its actual type, `Integer`. This is because `compareTo` is a method of `Integer`, but not of `Object`, the generic return type of `i.next()`.
3. To test for a negative value, you could compare the `Integer` `i.next()` to another `Integer` object, namely one with value 0. This has to be constructed with the expression `new Integer(0)`. The test in the `while` loop then becomes

```
    if (((Integer) i.next()).compareTo(new Integer(0)) < 0)
```

Example 4

```
//Code segment that changes every even-indexed element
//of list to 0.
//Precondition: list contains Integer values

boolean even = true;
ListIterator itr = list.listIterator();
while (itr.hasNext())
{
    itr.next();
    if (even)
        itr.set(new Integer(0));
    even = !even;
}
```

NOTE

1. A ListIterator is used because the set method is required: every second element, starting with the first, must be set to 0.
2. The loop must start with a call to next because every call to set must be preceded by next.

The LinkedList Class

This is a linked list implementation of the List interface. The implementation stores two links, one to the next element and one to the previous element. This is a doubly-linked list. The AP Java subset, however, does not include the methods of ListIterator that allow access to previous elements. This means that for the AP exam, the use of the LinkedList class will be restricted to singly-linked lists.

The methods of LinkedList provide easy access to both ends of the list. To access the middle of the list, either an iterator or the get and set methods of the List interface must be used (p. 371).

The Methods of LinkedList

The following methods are in the AP Java subset (in addition to add, size, get, set, iterator, and listIterator).

```
LinkedList()
```

Constructs an empty list.

```
void addFirst(Object obj)
```

Inserts obj at the front of the list.

```
void addLast(Object obj)
```

Appends obj to the end of the list.

```
Object getFirst()
```

Returns the first element in the list.

```
Object getLast()
```

Returns the last element in the list.

Object removeFirst()

Removes and returns the first element in the list.

Object removeLast()

Removes and returns the last element in the list.

NOTE
1. If the list is empty, the getFirst, getLast, removeFirst, and removeLast methods throw a NoSuchElementException.
2. The following constructor, which is *not* in the AP subset, is also worth knowing.

LinkedList(Collection c)

Constructs a LinkedList containing the elements of c in the same order as those in c.

Using LinkedList

The syntax for using a LinkedList is identical to that for using an ArrayList:

- To declare a LinkedList variable, use the generic List on the left side:

      List b = new LinkedList();

- To traverse the linked list, use Iterator or ListIterator with the same rules.
- When an object is returned from a list, cast it to its actual type before invoking methods with that object.
- Where possible, write code that is generic. This means that it should work for all implementations of List, not just LinkedList.

Example

```
//Return largest item in list a.
//Precondition: a is a nonempty list of Comparable objects
public static Comparable findMax(List a)
{
    Iterator itr = a.iterator();
    Comparable max = (Comparable) itr.next();  //initialize max to
                                               //first element
    while (itr.hasNext())
    {
        Comparable element = (Comparable) itr.next();
        if (max.compareTo(element) < 0)  //if max < element
            max = element;
    }
    return max;
}
```

NOTE
1. The elements of the list must be Comparable so that the compareTo method can be used.
2. In the initialization of max and the assignments to element, the object returned by itr.next() must be cast to Comparable before compareTo can be called.
3. The findMax method is generic and will work for any implementation of List. The variable max is initialized to the first element of the list and then compared with every subsequent element. It is updated if necessary.

ArrayList *vs.* LinkedList

Which implementation should you use? Since much of the code manipulating lists is generic, it appears that it makes no difference whether you use `ArrayList` or `LinkedList`.

Here are the run times for the various operations:

Operation	ArrayList	LinkedList
Insert at front	`add(0, obj)` $O(n)$. Must shift all elements to make slot.	`addFirst(obj)` $O(1)$. A constant number of pointer connections.
Insert at end	`add(obj)` $O(1)$. May, however, need to resize. $O(n)$ to add n elements.	`add(obj)` $O(1)$. A constant number of pointer connections.
Delete at front	`remove(0)` $O(n)$. Must shift all elements one unit left.	`removeFirst()` $O(1)$. A constant number of pointer connections.
Delete at end	`remove(size()-1)` $O(1)$. Adjust `size()`.	`removeLast()` $O(1)$. A constant number of pointer connections.
Insert in middle	`add(index, obj)` $O(1)$ access to insertion point. $O(n)$ insertion, since elements to right of `index` must be shifted.	`itr.add()` $O(n)$ access to insertion point, using iterator. $O(1)$ insertion.
Delete in middle	`remove(index)` $O(1)$ access to element. $O(n)$ deletion, since elements to right of `index` must be shifted.	`itr.remove()` $O(n)$ access to insertion point, using iterator. $O(1)$ deletion.
Change value in middle	`set(index, obj)` $O(1)$. Fast access.	`set(index, obj)` $O(n)$ traversal to locate element.

The choice of implementation should be driven by the run-time efficiency of your particular application. Here are some guidelines:

1. For most applications `ArrayList` is faster. This is because

   - `ArrayList` has fast access to any element in the list, while `LinkedList` requires an $O(n)$ traversal to reach an interior element.
   - `LinkedList` needs to allocate a node for each element in the list, whereas `ArrayList` does not.

2. There are two cases in which you should consider using `LinkedList`:

- If your application involves the frequent addition of elements to the front of the list. This is $O(1)$ for LinkedList but $O(n)$ for ArrayList, which requires copying and shifting elements for insertion.

- If you must iterate over the list, deleting many elements as you go. This is $O(n)$ for LinkedList, a single traversal with a constant number of pointer connections for each deletion. For ArrayList, however, the operation is $O(n^2)$: for each deleted element, the entire right side of the list must be shifted.

3. The LinkedList methods addFirst, getFirst, removeFirst, removeLast, addLast, and getLast make it convenient to use a LinkedList implementation for any program that accesses only the ends of the list. A good example is implementing a queue. What you lose is the advantage of generic code—you can no longer easily switch implementations if you decide ArrayList will be faster.

The Set Interface

A *set* is a collection that has no duplicate elements. It may contain a null element. The Set interface is based on the idea of a mathematical set.

A set allows you to

- Insert a nonduplicate element into the set.

- Remove an element from the set.

- Test if a given element is in the set.

- Iterate over the elements using Iterator.

The two Set implementations in the Collections API are

- HashSet, which stores its elements in a hash table (see p. 422).

- TreeSet, which stores its elements in a balanced binary search tree.

NOTE Two Set objects are equal if and only if they contain the same elements, irrespective of implementation.

The Methods of Set

Here are the methods in the AP Java subset:

```
boolean add(Object obj)
```

Adds obj to the set and returns true if obj was not already in the set. Leaves the set unchanged and returns false if obj was already in the set.

```
boolean contains(Object obj)
```

Returns true if the set contains obj, false otherwise.

```
boolean remove(Object obj)
```

Removes obj from the set and returns true if obj was in the set. Leaves the set unchanged and returns false if obj was not in the set.

```
int size()
```

Returns the number of elements in the set.

```
Iterator iterator()
```

Returns an iterator over the elements in the set.

The HashSet Class

The HashSet class implements the Set interface. Items are not stored in any particular order and therefore do not need to be Comparable.

The methods of HashSet in the AP Java subset are the same methods as those given for the Set interface: add, contains, remove, size, and iterator. Additionally, you should know that the iterator returns the elements in no particular order and does not guarantee that the order will stay the same over time.

You should also know the default constructor for HashSet objects:

```
HashSet()
```

Constructs an empty set.

The following constructor, which is *not* in the AP subset, is also worth knowing:

```
HashSet(Collection c)
```

Constructs a new HashSet containing the elements in Collection c. The new set contains no duplicates, even though c may contain duplicates.

The HashSet class is implemented with a hash table. As such it offers $O(1)$ run times for the operations add, remove, and contains.

The TreeSet Class

The TreeSet class implements the SortedSet interface and guarantees that the sorted set will be in ascending order, as determined by compareTo. This means that the items of a TreeSet are Comparable. They are also *mutually comparable*, which means that e1.compareTo(e2) will not throw a ClassCastException for any pair of elements e1 and e2 in the set. (Don't try to add a String object to a TreeSet of Integer items!)

As with HashSet, the TreeSet methods in the AP Java subset are those that were specified for the Set interface: add, contains, remove, size, and iterator. Note that the iterator for a TreeSet always returns the elements in ascending order.

You should also know the default constructor for TreeSet objects:

```
TreeSet()
```

Constructs an empty set.

The following constructor, which is *not* in the AP subset, is also worth knowing:

```
TreeSet(Collection c)
```

Constructs a new set, sorted in ascending order, containing the elements of c without duplicates. The elements of c must be mutually comparable.

The TreeSet class is implemented with a balanced binary search tree. It therefore provides $O(\log n)$ run time for the operations add, remove, and contains.

Examples with HashSet and TreeSet

Example 1

```
Set s = new HashSet();
s.add("Mary");
s.add("Joan");
s.add("Mary");
s.add("Dennis");
System.out.println("The size of the set is " + s.size());
Iterator itr = s.iterator();
while (itr.hasNext())
    System.out.print((String) itr.next() + " ");
System.out.println();
Set t = new TreeSet(s);
itr = t.iterator();
while (itr.hasNext())
    System.out.print((String) itr.next() + " ");
```

The output for this code fragment is

```
The size of the set is 3
Mary Joan Dennis
Dennis Joan Mary
```

NOTE

1. Again note that the collection variables s and t are declared with their interface type, Set, and constructed with their actual type (HashSet or TreeSet). This maintains flexibility to change implementations by just changing the constructor used.
2. Recall that a set does not allow duplicates. Thus only one "Mary" was added.
3. The names in the second line of output could have been printed in any order.
4. Tossing the elements of a HashSet into a TreeSet gives a quick method of getting the elements in sorted order. However, the constructor used is not in the AP Java subset. On the exam, the statement

    ```
    Set t = new TreeSet(s);
    ```

    is likely to be replaced with a statement like this:

    ```
    Set t = copySetToTreeSet(s);
    ```

    where copySetToTreeSet is described as a method that returns a TreeSet containing all the elements of Set s.

Example 2

Remove duplicates from an ArrayList.

```
/* Precondition:  ArrayList a may contain duplicate items
 * Postcondition: Returns ArrayList that is a with all
 *                duplicates removed */
public static ArrayList removeDups(ArrayList a)
{
    Set s = new HashSet(a);
    ArrayList b = new ArrayList(s);
    return b;
}
```

If ArrayList a is created from this file

```
farmer
cat
hen
apple
pear
baboon
cat
hen
cat
```

then the following list of words without duplicates is produced

```
[farmer, pear, apple, baboon, hen, cat]
```

NOTE

1. If the elements in the returned `ArrayList` need to be sorted, replace the first line of the method with

   ```
   Set s = new TreeSet(a);
   ```

   The line

   ```
   ArrayList b = new ArrayList(s);
   ```

   receives the elements in the same order that they're being stored—for `TreeSet` this is sorted in ascending order.

2. The `removeDups` method can be used in a program as follows:

   ```
   ArrayList a = new ArrayList();
   getList(a);     //read items into a
   a = removeDups(a);
   ```

3. Example 2 uses constructors for `ArrayList`, `HashSet`, and `TreeSet` that are not in the AP Java subset. To achieve the same result without those constructors, you would need to use iterators to copy one collection to another. On the AP exam, the statements

   ```
   Set s = new HashSet(a);
   ArrayList b = new ArrayList(s);
   ```

   are likely to be given as follows:

   ```
   Set s = copyListToHashSet(a);
   ArrayList b = copySetToArrayList(s);
   ```

   where `copyListToHashSet` is described as a method that returns a `HashSet` containing all the elements of `ArrayList a`, and `copySetToArrayList` returns an `ArrayList` containing all the elements of `Set s`.

Example 3

Consider a large `ArrayList` of words, `words`. You need to obtain each of the following:

> The total number of words.
> The number of *distinct* words (i.e., don't count any duplicates).
> A list of words that were duplicates (don't list any more than once!).

Finding the total number of words is trivial. Since `words` is an `ArrayList`, you can simply access its size:

```
int total = words.size();
```

To find the number of *distinct* words you can use the removeDups method of the previous example:

```
ArrayList noDups = removeDups(words);
int numDistinctWords = noDups.size();
```

To get a list of duplicate words, without listing any more than once, suggests using a set of duplicates. How can you generate this set?

Recall that the add method returns false if the set already contains the element you are trying to add. This gives a way to spot those duplicates. You can iterate through words, tossing each word into a set. When you spot a duplicate, add it to the set of duplicates.

```
List words = getWordList();
System.out.println("Words are: ");
System.out.println(words);

//create set of duplicates that were in words
Set h = new HashSet();
Set duplicates = new HashSet();
Iterator itr = words.iterator();
while (itr.hasNext())
{
    Object o = itr.next();
    if (!h.add(o))   //if add is false, found a duplicate
        duplicates.add(o);
}
if (duplicates.size() == 0)
    System.out.println("There were no duplicates!");
else
{
    System.out.println("Duplicates were: ");
    System.out.println(duplicates);
}
```

If the List of words is created from this file

```
farmer
cat
hen
apple
pear
cat
cat
farmer
hen
```

then the following output, showing the list of duplicates, is produced:

```
Duplicates were:
[farmer, cat, hen]
```

NOTE   The toString method in HashSet takes care of the output for duplicates.

Using HashSet and TreeSet

- If ordering of elements is important, use TreeSet.

- If ordering of elements is not important, use HashSet because the run time of the operations is faster.

- After creating an iterator for either Set implementation, don't modify the set with any method other than itr.remove(). You will generate an error if you do.

- The set implementations do not allow duplicates. Two objects e1 and e2 are duplicates if e1.equals(e2) is true, so for user-defined classes you need to override the default equals and hashCode methods to get the correct behavior. Remember two objects that are equal must have the same hashCode (see p. 110). If you do not do this correctly, you could have duplicate elements that are not treated as duplicates!

The Map *Interface*

A *map* is a collection of key-to-value mappings, where both key and value can be any object. A map cannot contain duplicate keys, which means that each key maps to exactly one value. Different keys, however, can map to the same value.

The Map interface allows you to

- insert a key/value pair into the map

- retrieve any value, given its key

- test if a given key is in the map

- view the elements in the map (The interface provides three different ways to view the collection: the set of keys, the set of values, and the set of key/value mappings. The AP Java subset requires that you know just one of these, the set of keys, using the keySet method.)

- iterate over the mapping elements, using Iterator. (The interface allows iteration over keys, values, or key/value pairs. You are required to know iteration over keys only. See *Iterating over Maps* on p. 384.)

The two Map implementations in the AP Java subset are HashMap and TreeMap.

The Methods of Map

Here are the methods in the AP Java subset:

```
Object put(Object key, Object value)
```

Associates `key` with `value` and inserts the pair in the map. If the map already contained a mapping for this key, the old value is replaced. The method returns either the previous value associated with `key`, or `null` if there was no previous value for this key.

```
Object get(Object key)
```

Returns the value associated with `key`. Returns `null` if the map contains no mapping for this key. Note that a return value of `null` indicates one of two situations:

1. The map contained no mapping for `key`.
2. This key was explicitly mapped to `null`.

The `containsKey` method can be used to distinguish these cases.

```
Object remove(Object key)
```

Removes the mapping for `key` from this map, if present. Returns the previous value associated with `key`, or `null` if there was no mapping for `key`. Note that a return value of `null` may also indicate that this `key` was previously mapped to a value of `null`.

```
boolean containsKey(Object key)
```

Returns `true` if the map contains a mapping for `key`, `false` otherwise.

```
int size()
```

Returns the number of key/value mappings in the map.

```
Set keySet()
```

Returns the set of keys contained in the map.

The `HashMap` Class

The `HashMap` class implements the `Map` interface with a hash table. There is no particular ordering of elements and no guarantee that any given ordering stays constant over time.

`HashMap` provides $O(1)$ run times for the `get` and `put` operations. This assumes that the keys are uniformly distributed across the hash table. There are two parameters that affect the performance of `HashMap`:

- initial capacity: the number of slots for keys in the table (called buckets);
- load factor: how full the table is allowed to get before its capacity is increased. (The default load factor of 0.75 offers a good tradeoff between time and space efficiency.)

You won't be tested on these details of the implementation, but they are helpful to understand how the class works.

The methods of `HashMap` in the AP Java subset are the same methods as those given for the `Map` interface: `put`, `get`, `remove`, `containsKey`, `size`, and `keySet`. You should also know the following default constructor for `HashMap` objects:

HashMap()

Constructs an empty map.

The following constructor, which is *not* in the AP subset, is also worth knowing:

HashMap(Map m)

Constructs a new map with the same mappings as m.

The TreeMap Class

The TreeMap class implements the SortedMap interface using a balanced binary search tree. The class guarantees ascending key order based on the ordering of the key class. TreeMap guarantees $O(\log n)$ performance for the containsKey, get, and put operations.

The operations for TreeMap that you should know are those described for the Map interface: put, get, remove, containsKey, size, and keySet. Additionally, you should know the following default constructor for TreeMap objects:

TreeMap()

Constructs an empty map.

The following constructor, which is *not* in the AP subset, is also worth knowing:

TreeMap(Map m)

Constructs a new map with the same mappings as the given map, sorted in ascending order of keys. It assumes that all possible pairs of keys are mutually comparable.

Iterating over Maps

The AP Java subset does not include an iterator method for the Map interface. This suggests that you will not be required to iterate over mappings.

You are, however, expected to be able to iterate over sets. The following idiom shows how to iterate over the set of keys for any mapping m:

```
for (Iterator i=m.keySet().iterator(); i.hasNext();)
    System.out.println(i.next());
```

This will print out the keys for map m. If m is of type HashMap, the keys will appear in some unknown order. If m is a TreeMap, the keys will be printed in ascending order.

NOTE

1. As with all the collections so far, no outside modification is allowed during an iteration.
2. If i.remove() is called during an iteration over the key set, the corresponding mapping will be removed from the map.
3. The Map interface allows iteration over the set of keys, the set of values, and the set of key/value pairs. The operations that support the latter two types of iteration are not in the AP Java subset.

Examples with
HashMap and
TreeMap

Example 1

Initialize data in a map.

```
Map employeeMap = new HashMap();
Employee emp;
for (int i=1; i<=NUM_EMPLOYEES; i++)
{
    emp = new Employee();       //declare a new Employee
    emp.setName(...);           //set the Employee's attributes
    emp.setSalary(...);         // ...
    emp.setID("E" + i);         // ...
    employeeMap.put(emp.getID(), emp);  //add employee to the
                                        //map using ID as the key
}
System.out.println(employeeMap.get("E4"));  //display the employee
                                            //whose key is E4
```

NOTE
1. Both the key and value must be objects. The employee ID is a String object.
2. It is common practice to use one of an object's attributes as a key in a map. You must be careful, however, that the key is unique. For example, using an employee's name as the key would be problematic: two different employees with the same name could not exist in the same mapping!

Example 2

```
Map h = new HashMap();
h.put("Othello", "green");
h.put("MacBeth", "red");
h.put("Hamlet", "blue");
if (!h.containsKey("Lear"))
    h.put("Lear", "black");
Map t = new TreeMap(h);
System.out.println(h.keySet());  //print the HashMap keys
System.out.println(t.keySet());  //print the TreeMap keys
```

Running this code segment produces this output:

```
[Othello, MacBeth, Hamlet, Lear]
[Hamlet, Lear, MacBeth, Othello]
```

NOTE
1. The keys are ordered for the TreeMap. They are in no particular order for the HashMap.
2. To print the set of values, you would need to use the Map method values, which is not in the AP Java subset. You can print the set of key/value pairs for a Map m with the statement

```
System.out.println(m);
```

3. The statement

```
Map t = new TreeMap(h);
```

uses a constructor that is not in the AP subset. On the AP exam, the statement is likely to be given as follows:

```
Map t = copyMapToTreeMap(h);
```

where copyMapToTreeMap is described as a method that returns a TreeMap containing all the elements of HashMap h.

Example 3

Consider a deck of cards, stored in an ArrayList, deck, of Card objects. You wish to simulate a game of cards in which each card is either in play or not in play. A HashMap can be used to mark the cards as available or not.

```
Map m = new HashMap();
for (Iterator itr = deck.iterator(); itr.hasNext();)
    m.put(itr.next(), new Integer(0));  //mark each card initially
                                        //as available
< code to proceed with game >
    ...
//select a random card from deck
Random r = new Random();
int index = r.nextInt(52);    //int from 0 to 51
Card card = deck.get(index);
Integer mark = (Integer) m.get(card);
if (mark.intValue() == 0)      //card available
{
    < code to use card  in game >
    m.put(card, new Integer(1));   //card now unavailable
}
```

Example 4

Use a HashMap to record the frequency of each word in inFile.

```
public class WordFreqs
{
    private Map m;

    /* default constructor */
    public WordFreqs()
    {
        m = new HashMap();
        loadMap(m);
    }

    /* Create HashMap of words in inFile.
     * Each key is a lowercase word.
     * Each value is the frequency of the corresponding word */
    public void loadMap(Map m)
    {
        < code to open inFile  for reading >
```

```
        while (< there are still words in inFile >)
        {
            String word = inFile.readWord();  //read one word

            //get Integer value in Map m associated with word
            Integer i = (Integer) m.get(word);
            if (i == null)     //word is a new word
                m.put(word, new Integer(1));
            else
                m.put(word, new Integer(i.intValue() + 1));
        }
        < close inFile >
    }


    /* Print word frequencies */
    public void printFrequencies()
    {
        System.out.println("Word frequencies:");
        System.out.println(m);
    }
}
```

Here is a program that tests the WordFreqs class:

```
import java.util.*;

public class GetWordFreqs
{
    public static void main(String[] args)
    {
        WordFreqs w = new WordFreqs();
        w.printFrequencies();
    }
}
```

When inFile is

```
apple pear apple orange pear grape orange apple
```

the following output is obtained:

```
Word frequencies:
(apple = 3, pear = 2, orange = 2, grape = 1)
```

Multiple-Choice Questions on Collections

For additional questions on the ArrayList class, see Questions 23–30 in Chapter 6.

1. Which is a *true* statement about the collections classes?
   (A) ArrayList and LinkedList extend List.
   (B) HashSet and TreeSet implement HashMap and TreeMap, respectively.
   (C) TreeMap and HashMap implement Map.
   (D) TreeSet implements both Set and Tree.
   (E) TreeSet extends HashSet.

2. Which of the following correctly lists all the elements in a HashSet h? You may assume that the objects in h have a toString method.

   I `for (ListIterator i = h.listIterator(); i.hasNext();)`
          `System.out.println(i.next() + " ");`

   II `for (Iterator itr = h.iterator(); itr.hasNext();)`
          `System.out.println(itr.next() + " ");`

   III `System.out.println(h);`

   (A) I only
   (B) II only
   (C) III only
   (D) I and III only
   (E) II and III only

3. Which is a correct description of the run times of the given operation for (1) TreeSet and (2) HashSet?

   (A) Inserting an element (add):   (1) $O(1)$ (2) $O(1)$

   (B) Inserting an element (add):   (1) $O(1)$ (2) $O(\log n)$

   (C) Removing an element (remove):   (1) $O(\log n)$ (2) $O(n)$

   (D) Removing an element (remove):   (1) $O(\log n)$ (2) $O(1)$

   (E) Testing if an element is in
        the set (contains):   (1) $O(n)$ (2) $O(n)$

4. A collection of Comparable objects is to be maintained in sorted ascending order. The collection can contain duplicates. Individual elements in the collection will be updated frequently. There will be no deletion of elements, and infrequent additions of new elements. The best implementation for this collection is:
   (A) An ArrayList
   (B) A LinkedList
   (C) A TreeSet
   (D) A HashSet
   (E) A TreeMap

5. Consider an `ArrayList` `list` of `Student` objects. Which of the following correctly adds a `Student` `s` at position `insertPos`. You may assume that `s` is initialized, and that `insertPos` is of type `int` and is in bounds.

   I `list.add(insertPos, s)`

   II
   ```
   for (int i=list.size(); i>=insertPos; i--)
       list[i+1] = list[i];
   list[insertPos] = s;
   list.size()++;
   ```

   III
   ```
   ListIterator itr = list.listIterator();
   int index = 0;
   while (index != insertPos)
   {
       itr.next();
       index++;
   }
   itr.add(s);
   ```

   (A) I only
   (B) II only
   (C) III only
   (D) I and III only
   (E) II and III only

6. Consider method `replace` below:

   ```
   /* Precondition:  List L is a list of objects, some of which
    *                could be null
    * Postcondition: All occurrences of val are replaced
    *                with newVal */
   public static void replace(List L, Object val, Object newVal)
   {
       for (ListIterator i=L.listIterator(); i.hasNext();)
           if (val.equals(i.next())
               i.set(newVal);
   }
   ```

   Which is true about the `replace` method?
   (A) It always works as specified.
   (B) It may cause a `NullPointerException` to be thrown.
   (C) It may cause an `IllegalStateException` to be thrown.
   (D) It may cause a `NoSuchElementException` to be thrown.
   (E) It will never work as specified; it will always cause an exception to be thrown.

7. Refer to the `filter` method shown below.

```
/* Precondition:  L is a List of objects
 * Postcondition: all elements that do not satisfy some
 *                condition, cond(obj), have been removed  */
public static void filter(List L)
{
    for (Iterator i=L.iterator(); i.hasNext();)
        if (!cond(i.next()))
            i.remove();
}
```

Which is a true statement?

(A) The code is polymorphic: It will work for any implementation of `List`.

(B) The code works without loss of generality if the last line of the method is replaced with `L.remove();`

(C) The code fails if the collection is a `List` because `ListIterator` must be used instead of `Iterator`.

(D) The code can be written without an iterator as follows:

```
for (int i=0; i<L.size(); i++)
    if (!cond(L.get(i)))
        L.remove();
```

(E) The `filter` method will throw a `NullPointerException` if any element of the collection is null.

8. Consider a map `m`, where `m` is of type `HashMap` or `TreeMap`. Suppose `s1` and `s2` are both sets, of type `HashSet` or `TreeSet`, where `s1` is the set of keys in `m`, and `s2` is the set of corresponding values in `m`. Which *must* be true?

(A) `s1.size() > s2.size()`

(B) `s1.size() >= s2.size()`

(C) `s1.size() == s2.size()`

(D) `s1.size() < s2.size()`

(E) `s1.size() <= s2.size()`

9. Refer to the method changeEven below.

```
/* Precondition:  ArrayList a contains Integer values
 * Postcondition: Every even-indexed element contains 0, i.e.,
 *                elements with index 0,2,4,... contain 0  */
public static void changeEven(ArrayList a)
{
    boolean even = true;
    ListIterator itr = a.listIterator();
    while (itr.hasNext())
    {
        if (even)
            itr.set(new Integer(0));
        itr.next();
        even = !even;
    }
}
```

Which statement is true about changeEven?

(A) It will work as intended for any ArrayList a.

(B) It will throw an IllegalStateException for every ArrayList a.

(C) It will throw an IllegalStateException only if ArrayList a has an even number of elements.

(D) It will throw an IllegalStateException only if ArrayList a has an odd number of elements.

(E) It will throw an IllegalStateException only if ArrayList a has fewer than three elements.

10. Consider the max method below, which is intended to find the largest element in a set.

```
/* Precondition:  s is a nonempty set of Comparable objects
 * Postcondition: returns largest element in s  */
public static Comparable max(Set s)
{
    Iterator itr = s.iterator();
    Comparable maxValue = (Comparable) itr.next();
    < code to find maxValue >
    return maxValue;
}
```

Which replacement for < *code to find* maxValue > achieves the desired post-condition?

```
 I  while (itr.hasNext())
    {
        if (maxValue.compareTo(itr.next()) < 0)
            maxValue = itr.next();
    }
```

```
 II while (itr.hasNext())
    {
        if (maxValue.compareTo(itr.next()) < 0)
            maxValue = (Comparable) itr.next();
    }
```

```
 III while (itr.hasNext())
    {
        Comparable current = (Comparable) itr.next();
        if (maxValue.compareTo(current) < 0)
            maxValue = current;
    }
```

(A) I only
(B) II only
(C) III only
(D) II and III only
(E) none is correct

11. Consider the following code segment:

```
List a = new ArrayList();
Set t = new TreeSet();
for (int i = 10; i>=1; i--)
    a.add(new Integer(i*i));
for (int i=0; i<a.size(); i++)
{
    Integer intObj = (Integer) a.get(i);
    int val = (intObj.intValue()) % 3;
    t.add(new Integer(val));
}
System.out.println(t);
```

What will be output as a result of executing this segment?

(A) 1, 0, 1, 1, 0, 1, 1, 0, 1, 1
(B) 1, 1, 0, 1, 1, 0, 1, 1, 0, 1
(C) 0, 0, 0, 1, 1, 1, 1, 1, 1, 1
(D) 1, 0
(E) 0, 1

12. Assume that `list` is an array of lowercase words:

```
String[] list = {salad, banana, lettuce, beef, banana,
                    < more words >}
```

What does this code segment do?

```
public static final Integer ONE = new Integer(1);
Map m = new HashMap();
for (int i=0; i<list.length; i++)
{
    Integer num = (Integer) m.get(list[i]);
    if (num == null)
        m.put(list[i], ONE);
    else
        m.put(list[i], new Integer(num.intValue() + 1));
}
```

(A) It produces in m a count of the *distinct* words in the list.
(B) It produces a table that maps each word in the list to its position in the list.
(C) It produces an alphabetized list of the words in the list and maps each word to its position in the list.
(D) It produces a frequency table that maps each word in the list to the number of times it occurs in the list.
(E) It searches list for those words that are already in m. When it finds a word in m, it updates the frequency for that word.

13. Which of the following correctly removes the first k elements from LinkedList L? You may assume that $0 \le k < $ L.size().

```
I   int count = 1;
    ListIterator itr = L.listIterator();
    while (itr.hasNext() && count <= k)
    {
        itr.remove();
        count++;
    }
```

```
II  int count = 1;
    Iterator itr = L.iterator();
    while (count <= k)
    {
        itr.next();
        itr.remove();
        count++;
    }
```

```
III for (int i=1; i<=k; i++)
        L.removeFirst();
```

(A) I only
(B) II only
(C) III only
(D) I and III only
(E) II and III only

14. Note: This question uses constructors that are not in the AP Java subset. It is included for students who have mastered the constructors that take a Collection parameter.

A certain LinkedList L may contain duplicates. Which of the following code segments removes the duplicates from L? (It is not necessary to preserve the order of the elements in the list.)

(A) `Map m = new HashMap(L);`
    `List L = new LinkedList(m);`

(B) `Set s = new HashSet(L);`
    `List L = new LinkedList(s);`

(C) `List a = new ArrayList(L);`
    `List L = new LinkedList(a);`

(D) `Map t = new TreeMap(L);`
    `List L = new LinkedList(t);`

(E) `TreeSet t = new Set(L);`
    `List L = new LinkedList(t);`

15. A new ice cream parlor in a college town is planning to introduce three new flavors: peach chocolate, mango vanilla, and lychee strawberry. The ice cream parlor will do a survey among college students and ask if they would try such a flavor. The percentage of students who would be willing to try each flavor will then be tabulated. The raw data of the survey will be stored in a large text file, and a computer program will access the file and calculate percentages. Which of the following is the most suitable data structure for tabulating the results of the survey in the computer program?

   (A) A HashMap
   (B) A HashSet
   (C) A priority queue
   (D) An $m \times n$ matrix, where m is the number of flavors and n is the number of people surveyed
   (E) m arrays, where m is the number of flavors

16. Which of the following code fragments will *not* cause an exception to be thrown?

   (A)
```
Map m = new HashMap();
Object obj = m.get("hello");
```

   (B)
```
List l = new LinkedList();
Object obj = l.getFirst();
```

   (C)
```
List a = new ArrayList();
a.add(1, "hello");
```

   (D)
```
String str = "";
Set s = new HashSet();
s.add("The");
s.add("rain");
s.add("in");
s.add("Spain");
for (Iterator i=s.iterator(); i.hasNext();)
    str = str + (Integer) i.next();
```

   (E)
```
Set t = new TreeSet();
t.add("The");
t.add("rain");
t.add("in");
t.add("Spain");
for (Iterator i=t.iterator(); i.hasNext();)
{
    i.remove();
    i.next():
}
```

Use the following description of the game of Battleships for Questions 17–20.

A programmer simulates the game of Battleships. The computer will try to sink its opponent's fleet before its own fleet is wiped out. Each player has a grid, hidden from the other player, with ships placed in straight lines, as shown.

Notice that

- No two ships occupy adjacent squares.
- The grid goes from (0, 0) in the top left-hand corner to (SIZE-1, SIZE-1) in the bottom right-hand corner.
- There are five ships of different lengths.

The players take turns shooting at each other's fleet. When a player fires a shot, he communicates the coordinates where the shot lands. His opponent responds "hit" or "miss."

The programmer is considering how the computer should keep track of its opponent's grid. He has defined a Position class and EnemyGrid class as follows:

```java
public class Position implements Comparable
{
    private int myRow, myCol;

    /* Postcondition: row() == r, col() == c */
    public Position(int r, int c)
    {
        myRow = r;
        myCol = c;
    }

    // public accessing methods

    /* Returns row of Position */
    public int row()
    { return myRow; }

    /* Returns column of Position */
    public int col()
    { return myCol; }

    /* Returns Position north of (up from) this position */
    public Position north()
    { return new Position(myRow - 1, myCol); }

    //similar methods for south, east, and west
```

```java
    /* Compares this Position to another Position object.
     * Returns either -1 (less than), 0 (equals),
     * or 1 (greater than).
     * Ascending order for Positions is row-major, namely start
     * at (0,0) and proceed row by row, left to right.  */
    public int compareTo(Object o)
    {
        Position p = (Position) o;
        if (this.row() < p.row() || this.row() == p.row() &&
                this.col() < p.col())
            return -1;
        if (this.row() > p.row() || this.row() == p.row() &&
                this.col() > p.col())
            return 1;
        return 0;        //row and col both equal
    }

    //equals and hashCode methods
        ...

    /* Returns string form of Position */
    public String toString()
    { return "(" + myRow + "," + myCol + ")"; }
}

public class EnemyGrid
{
    < private instance variables >

    //constructor
    public EnemyGrid()
    { implementation code }

    public void displayGrid()
    { implementation code }

    public Position selectNewPos()
    { implementation code }

    //Update grid with "hit" or "miss" response
    public void updateGrid(String response, Position pos)
    { implementation code }

    //other methods
        ...

}
```

17. The < *private instance variables* > of the EnemyGrid class will depend on the data structure selected to keep track of the grid. Which of the following is the *least suitable* data structure?

(A) A TreeMap in which the keys are Position objects that have already been fired at. The corresponding values are the strings "hit" or "miss".

(B) A SIZE×SIZE matrix of strings in which each grid element has the value "hit", "miss", or "untried".

(C) A LinkedList of Position objects that have been fired at and hit, sorted in increasing order.

(D) A TreeSet called hitSet, which is the set of Position objects that the computer fired at and hit, and a TreeSet called missSet, which is the set of Position objects that the computer fired at and missed.

(E) An ArrayList of all Positions in the grid, and a parallel ArrayList of strings in which the *k*th location has value "hit", "miss", or "untried", depending on the status of the *k*th Position.

18. The programmer selects a TreeMap as the data structure for the EnemyGrid. The keys are Position objects that have been fired at, and the corresponding values are the strings "hit" or "miss". You may assume that SIZE is a global constant. The EnemyGrid class thus has this < *private instance variable* >:

```
private Map posMap;
```

Here is the constructor for the class, and the updateGrid method:

```
public EnemyGrid()
{ posMap = new TreeMap();}

/* Precondition:  TreeMap contains Position/String mappings
 *                for each Position in the grid fired on
 *                so far. Position pos is in range, and is
 *                not in the map.
 * Postcondition: TreeMap contains pos and its corresponding
 *                response */
public void updateGrid(Position pos, String response)
{ implementation code }
```

Which is correct *implementation code*?

```
I  posMap.put(pos, response);

II if (!posMap.containsKey(pos))
       posMap.put(pos, response);

III Object o = posMap.get(pos);
    if (o == null)
        posMap.put(pos, response);
```

(A) I only
(B) II only
(C) III only
(D) II and III only
(E) I, II, and III

19. Which is a good reason for using `TreeMap` rather than `HashMap` in the `EnemyGrid` class?

    (A) The key set of used positions is displayed in row-major order (top to bottom, left to right), making it easy to see which positions are unused.
    (B) The value set of strings is displayed in order, making it easy to see which positions have been `"hit"` (or `"miss"`ed!).
    (C) Searching for any particular key position has faster run time in `TreeMap` than in `HashMap`.
    (D) Inserting a `Position/String` pair into the `TreeMap` has faster run time than insertion into a `HashMap`.
    (E) Retrieving a value from `TreeMap` has faster run time than retrieval from a `HashMap`.

20. Consider three different implementations for the `EnemyGrid` class:

    I A `TreeMap` in which the keys are a set of `Position` objects that have already been fired at. The corresponding values are the strings `"hit"` or `"miss"`.
    II A `SIZE×SIZE` matrix of strings in which each grid element has the value `"hit"`, `"miss"`, or `"untried"`.
    III A `TreeSet` called `hitSet` that is the set of positions fired on and hit, and a `TreeSet` called `missSet` that is the set of positions fired on and missed.

    Which statement is *false*?

    (A) Determining whether a given `Position` has been tried is more efficient with implementation II than with implementations I or III.
    (B) Updating a new position is more efficient with implementation II than with implementations I or III.
    (C) Listing all of the positions that have been used so far is more efficient with implementation II than implementation III.
    (D) Listing all of the positions, in row-major order, that have been used so far is more efficient with implementation I than implementation III.
    (E) Listing all of the positions, in row-major order, that have *not yet* been used is more efficient with implementation II than either implementations I or III.

The program description below applies to Questions 21–24.

Every year the Ithaca Bridge Club awards a versatility trophy to the player with the highest final score. A player's final score is the average of his or her top twenty scores in games each with a different partner. Thus, in order to be eligible for this trophy, a player must have played at least twenty games with at least twenty different partners during the year.

Consider writing a program that finds the winner of this trophy. Here are two classes that may be used:

```java
public class Game
{
    private String myPartner;
    private double myScore;

    public Game(String partner, double score)
    {
        myPartner = partner;
        myScore = score;
    }

    public String getPartner()
    { return myPartner; }

    public double getScore()
    { return myScore; }
}

public class Player
{
    private String myName;
    private double myFinalScore;
    private LinkedList myGames;  //a list of Games for this Player
                                 //sorted in decreasing order of score

    public Player(String name)
    {
        myName = name;
        //myGames initialized here from gameFile
    }

    public String getName()
    { return myName; }

    //Returns average of elements in a
    private double findAverage(double[] a)
    { implementation code }

    //Returns average of top 20 scores for games each with a
    //different partner, or returns -1 if player is ineligible
    //(fewer than 20 games or fewer than 20 partners)
    public double calculateFinalScore()
    { implementation code }
}
```

You may assume that every player in the club has a personalized gameFile that contains a listing of partners and corresponding scores. For example, Jimmy Carroll's gameFile may look like this:

```
Coppola Anthony        46.72
Harmon Mary            71.50
Coppola Anthony        64.27
Smith Jean             50.15
Smith Jean             48.31
Harmon Mary            75.67
    . . .
```

Notice that these scores are not in any particular order. When the data is read in by the Player constructor, however, each Game is placed in a LinkedList, sorted by score in descending order.

21. Consider the algorithm for the calculateFinalScore method for a Player. Traverse the LinkedList in order, as follows:

    - Get a Game.
    - If the partner has not been used, store the corresponding score, otherwise move on.
    - Stop when you reach the end of the list or you have twenty scores, whichever comes first.
    - If you have fewer than twenty scores, it means that this Player either played fewer than twenty games, or had fewer than twenty partners. The player is ineligible and the method should return -1.
    - If the player is eligible, return the average of the twenty scores.

    There are two collections that must be stored during execution of this algorithm:
    (1) the partners that have already been used, and
    (2) the scores that must be counted for the final average.
    Which is the most suitable implementation for
    (1) the partners, and (2) the scores?

    (A) (1) an ArrayList   (2) an ArrayList

    (B) (1) an ArrayList   (2) an array

    (C) (1) a HashSet   (2) an array

    (D) (1) a TreeSet   (2) an array

    (E) (1) a HashSet   (2) an ArrayList

22. Here is the implementation code for the `calculateFinalScore` method of the Player class:

```
/* Returns average of top 20 games, each with a different
 * partner. Returns -1 if Player is ineligible (fewer than
 * 20 games or 20 partners) */
public double calculateFinalScore()
{
    int count = 0;   //number of games counted so far
    double[] scores = new double[20];  //array of scores to be
                                       //used in finding average
    Set partnerSet = new HashSet();  //set of different
                                     //partners so far
    Iterator itr = myGames.iterator();  //iterator for
                                        //LinkedList of Games


    < code to generate scores array >

    if (count == 20)    //player eligible
        return findAverage(scores);
    else
        return -1;    //player ineligible
}
```

Which is correct < *code to generate* scores *array* >?

```
I  while (myGames.hasNext() && count < 20)
   {
       Game g = (Game) myGames.next();
       if (!partnerSet.contains(itr.getPartner()))
       {
           partnerSet.add(itr.getPartner());
           scores[count] = itr.getScore();
           count++;
       }
   }
```

```
II while (itr.hasNext() && count < 20)
   {
       Game g = (Game) itr.next();
       if (!partnerSet.contains(g.getPartner()))
       {
           partnerSet.add(g.getPartner());
           scores[count] = g.getScore();
           count++;
       }
   }
```

```
III while (itr.hasNext() && count < 20)
    {
        Object o = itr.next();
        if (!partnerSet.contains(o.getPartner()))
        {
            partnerSet.add(o.getPartner());
            scores[count] = o.getScore();
            count++;
        }
    }
```

(A) None is correct.
(B) I only
(C) II only
(D) III only
(E) II and III only

23. When the trophy race program is run, the data for all the players are inserted into an ArrayList, players, of Player objects. The list is then traversed, and all players that are eligible have their player name and final score inserted into a TreeMap. Recall that an eligible player had his or her final score returned by the method calculateFinalScore. The method returned -1 for ineligible players.

   Here is a code segment that traverses the players list:

```
for (Iterator itr = players.iterator(); itr.hasNext();)
{
    Player p = (Player) itr.next();
    if (<test>) //if this Player is eligible
    {
        <statement>;   //place (Player name, final score)
                       //pair in TreeMap t
    }
}
```

Which is (1) a correct < *test* > and (2) a correct < *statement* >?

(A) (1) p.calculateFinalScore() >= 0
     (2) t.put(p, p.calculateFinalScore())

(B) (1) p.calculateFinalScore() >= 0
     (2) t.put(p.getName(), new Double(p.calculateFinalScore()))

(C) (1) p.getScore() < 0
     (2) t.put(p.getPartner(), new Double(p.getScore()))

(D) (1) p.getScore() < 0
     (2) t.put(p, new Double(p.getScore()))

(E) (1) p >= 0
     (2) t.put(p, p.calculateFinalScore())

24. Having (player name, final score) pairs in a `TreeMap` data structure facilitates which operation?

    I Listing the final scores in descending order.
    II Listing the names of eligible players in alphabetical order.
    III Listing the eligible players and their corresponding final scores, with the names in alphabetical order.

    (A) I only
    (B) III only
    (C) II and III only
    (D) I and II only
    (E) I, II, and III

Answer Key

1. **C**		9. **B**		17. **C**	
2. **E**		10. **C**		18. **E**	
3. **D**		11. **E**		19. **A**	
4. **A**		12. **D**		20. **C**	
5. **D**		13. **E**		21. **C**	
6. **B**		14. **B**		22. **C**	
7. **A**		15. **A**		23. **B**	
8. **B**		16. **A**		24. **C**	

Answers Explained

1. **(C)** Choice A is false because `ArrayList` and `LinkedList` are not subclasses of `List`; they *implement* the `List` interface. Choice B makes no sense: `HashSet` and `TreeSet` both implement `Set`. Choice D is wrong because there is no standard collections interface called `Tree`. Choice E is wrong: `TreeSet` is not a subclass of `HashSet`; they both are implementations of `Set`.

2. **(E)** Segment I is wrong because `ListIterator` is defined only for classes that implement `List`. If h were an `ArrayList` or `LinkedList`, then segment I would be correct. Note that segment III works because all of the collections classes, including `HashSet`, have a `toString` method.

3. **(D)** The balanced binary search tree for `TreeSet` provides $O(\log n)$ run times for `add`, `remove`, and `contains` (see the run-time analysis for `insert`, p. 333, and `find`, p. 334). The hash table implementation for `HashSet` provides $O(1)$ run times for `add`, `remove`, and `contains` (see p. 422).

4. **(A)** Accessing individual elements in the list is very efficient with `ArrayList`, $O(1)$. For a `LinkedList` this operation is $O(n)$. Eliminate choices C and D—a set cannot contain duplicates. Choice E is a poor answer—the given collection is not a mapping.

5. **(D)** Segment I is the best way to do this. The `add` method of `ArrayList` allows instant access at any position in the list. Segment III is not as efficient, but it works! It uses the `ListIterator` method `add` instead of the `ArrayList` method `add`. Note that it is not necessary to include a test of `itr.hasNext()` in the `while` loop. Since it is given that `insertPos` is in bounds, the algorithm will always find the correct position before running off the end of the list. Segment II is wrong because it's treating the `ArrayList` as if it were an array: there should be no indexing brackets.

6. **(B)** Since some of the elements in L could be null, if val is null the expression val.equals(... will cause a NullPointerException to be thrown. The problem can be fixed by inserting the test if (val == null) as the first statement in the for loop, and taking the appropriate action.

7. **(A)** When the filter method is invoked for any particular List, the appropriate iterator and remove methods will be called for that implementation. This is polymorphism. Choice B is wrong because you may not alter a collection with an external method during an iteration. Strike choice C because both Iterator and ListIterator methods are defined for lists. Choice D fails because there is no remove method in ArrayList or LinkedList that has no parameters. Choice E is false since you should be able to assume an external method works as advertised.

8. **(B)** Some keys in m can map to the same value. No two values, however, can match the same key.

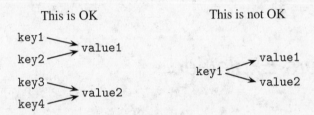

Recall that a set cannot contain duplicates. If the mapping is as shown on the left, s1 will have four elements and s2 will have two elements. If the mapping is one-to-one, then

    s1.size() == s2.size()

In general, however, the relationship will be

    s1.size() >= s2.size()

9. **(B)** The changeEven method throws an IllegalStateException since set is invoked before next on the first pass through the while loop.

10. **(C)** The object itr.next() must be cast to Comparable before it can be assigned to maxValue. This is one of the reasons segment I fails. It also fails because the itr.next() in the compareTo argument is a different object from the itr.next() assigned to maxValue in the following line! The iterator advances to the next element every time next() is called. Segment II makes the same error. Segment III is the only segment that correctly advances the iterator just once during a pass through the while loop.

11. **(E)** The add method appends new elements to the end of the list. Thus a contains 100, 81, 64, 49, 36, 25, 16, 9, 4, 1. The second for loop retrieves each element in turn, starting with 100. The remainder when the element is divided by 3 is added to the TreeSet t. The only remainders generated are 1 and 0. Therefore t contains just these two elements (no duplicates!). The output is 0, 1, since a TreeSet is ordered in ascending order.

12. **(D)** The algorithm traverses the array, starting with the first word. For each word, it checks to see if that word already exists as a key in m. If it does, it increments the corresponding value by 1. If it doesn't, it inserts the word in

m and assigns it the value 1. The set of values is thus the frequency for each word.

13. (**E**) Segment I fails because `remove` cannot be called without first calling `next`. Note that it's OK to use either `Iterator` or `ListIterator`, since both are defined for `List` collections. In segment II, notice that you don't need an `itr.hasNext()` test, since you are given that k is in range. Segment III repeatedly removes the first element using a method from `LinkedList`.

14. (**B**) The statement `Set s = new HashSet(L)` creates a set containing the elements of L, but without duplicates. (Recall that a set doesn't allow duplicates.) Then the statement `List L = new LinkedList(s)` creates a new list L with the elements of s. This has the effect of restoring L without the duplicates, but not necessarily in the original order. Choices A and D don't make sense: they place the elements of L in a map, but without a mapping! Choice C places the elements of L, duplicates and all, in `ArrayList a`. Then it restores L to its original state. Choice E tries to create an instance of a `Set`, which is wrong because `Set` is an interface. Note that E would be a correct answer if the first statement were changed to `Set t = new TreeSet(L)` (for the same reasons that choice B works).

15. (**A**) For each flavor its corresponding tally must be stored. This suggests that a mapping should be used, with flavors as keys and frequencies as the corresponding values.

16. (**A**) The `get` method of `Map` returns either the value associated with the key or `null` if the map contains no mapping for that key. In the example given, since the `HashMap` is empty, `obj` will be assigned the value `null`. Here are the errors that will be caused by each of the other choices:
    B: `NoSuchElementException`: attempting to remove an element from an empty list.
    C: `IndexOutOfBoundsException`: If the list is empty, index 1 is out of range. Index 0 would be fine for `add`.
    D: `ClassCastException`: casting a `String` to an `Integer`.
    E: `IllegalStateException`: calling `remove` before a call to `next`.

17. (**C**) There has to be some mechanism in the data structure that keeps track of whether a given position was hit *or missed*. All the data structures except the `LinkedList` in choice C have such a mechanism.

18. (**E**) Segment I associates pos with response and inserts the pair in the map. If the map already contained a mapping for this pos, the old value is replaced with response. Segment II inserts the pos/response pair in the map when it determines that this pos is new. Segment III gets the value associated with pos in the map. Since pos is not in the map, o will be `null` and, yet again, the pos/response pair will be inserted in the map. Note: it is part of the precondition that pos is not in the `TreeMap`.

19. (**A**) Choices B through E are all false statements! Choice B is wrong because only the keys are displayed in order, not the values. (Besides, what does it mean to have "hit" or "miss" in order?) All of the operations in choices C through E are $O(\log n)$ for `TreeMap` and $O(1)$ for `HashMap` if run time is the most important issue.

20. **(C)** Recall that the `TreeMap` (implementation I) contains only the positions that have been used so far. Thus listing these is a simple traversal of a tree, requiring no tests. In order to list the used positions in the matrix (implementation II), however, every element in the grid must be inspected so that the `"untried"` values are omitted. Note that choices A and B are true: accessing a given element in the matrix is $O(1)$, whereas doing so in a binary search tree is $O(\log n)$. Choice D is true because positions in the `TreeMap` are already sorted, whereas the positions in the two different `TreeSets`, while individually sorted, would have to be merged. For choice E, to list the unused positions is very easy with the matrix implementation. Simply traverse in order and list the positions that are marked `"untried"`. Finding the unused positions in implementations I and III is quite tricky, since these positions are not explicitly included in those structures. Try it!

21. **(C)** *To store the partners:* You want a collection that allows you to test in an efficient and convenient way whether the current partner is already in the collection. The `contains` method of `Set` allows an $O(1)$ test if a `HashSet` is used. A `HashSet` is better than a `TreeSet` because you have no compelling reason to keep the collection sorted. The `contains` method for `TreeSet` is $O(\log n)$, which is slower than $O(1)$. An `ArrayList` for the partners is not as good a choice as a `HashSet` because the search is $O(n)$.
   To store the scores: The length of the list is fixed at 20, and the scores are primitive `doubles`. This suggests that you use a fixed-length array. Using an array saves you from wrapping and unwrapping the `double` values during processing.

22. **(C)** Segment II does each of the following correctly:

    - Traverses the list with `itr`, the `Iterator` object.
    - Casts the `next` object in the list to `Game`.
    - Accesses the partner and score for this `Game`, using `g.getPartner()` and `g.getScore()`.
    - Accesses the `partnerSet` correctly, using `partnerSet.contains` and `partnerSet.add`.

    Segment I uses the `Iterator` and `Game` objects incorrectly. Segment III does not cast the `next` object to `Game`.

23. **(B)** If a player is ineligible, the `calculateFinalScore` method returns -1. Therefore the correct test for eligibility is

    ```
    if (p.calculateFinalScore() >= 0)
    ```

    You need `p.getName()` and `p.calculateFinalScore()` to access Player p's name and final score. You also need to create an object from the final score so that it can be placed in the `TreeMap`:

    ```
    new Double(p.calculateFinalScore())
    ```

    Be careful not to use the `getScore` method from the `Game` class!
    Note that the test should not be

    ```
    if (p.calculateFinalScore() != -1)
    ```

Never test whether a floating-point number is exactly equal to or not equal to another number (see the Box on p. 6).

24. **(C)** A `TreeMap` maintains the keys in sorted order, which in this case means that the names are in alphabetical order. Printing the `keySet` gives the names in alphabetical order (operation II). Printing the map `t` gives the (name, score) pairs as described in operation III. Note: it's certainly possible to perform a sort on the set of score values. This operation is not, however, *facilitated* by the `TreeMap` structure, which was the point of the question.

CHAPTER TWELVE
Sorting and Searching

Critics search for ages for the wrong word, which,
to give them credit, they eventually find.
—Peter Ustinov (1952)

In each of the following sorting algorithms, assume that an array of *n* elements, a[0], a[1], ..., a[n-1], is to be sorted in ascending order.

O(n²) Sorts: Selection and Insertion Sorts

Selection Sort

This is a "search-and-swap" algorithm. Here's how it works.

Find the smallest element in the array and exchange it with a[0], the first element. Now find the smallest element in the subarray a[1] ... a[n-1] and swap it with a[1], the second element in the array. Continue this process until just the last two elements remain to be sorted, a[n-2] and a[n-1]. The smaller of these two elements is placed in a[n-2]; the larger, in a[n-1]; and the sort is complete.

Trace these steps with a small array of four elements. The unshaded part is the subarray still to be searched.

<pre>
8   1   4   6

1   8   4   6   after first pass

1   4   8   6   after second pass

1   4   6   8   after third pass
</pre>

NOTE

Level AB Only

1. For an array of *n* elements, the array is sorted after *n* − 1 passes.
2. After the *k*th pass, the first *k* elements are in their final sorted position.
3. Number of comparisons in first pass: $n - 1$
   Number of comparisons in second pass: $n - 2$
   ...and so on.
   Total number of comparisons $= (n - 1) + (n - 2) + \cdots + 2 + 1 = n(n - 1)/2$, which is $O(n^2)$.
4. Irrespective of the initial order of elements, selection sort makes the same number of comparisons. Thus best, worst, and average cases are all $O(n^2)$.

410

Insertion Sort

Think of the first element in the array, a[0], as being sorted with respect to itself. The array can now be thought of as consisting of two parts, a sorted list followed by an unsorted list. The idea of insertion sort is to move elements from the unsorted list to the sorted list one at a time; as each item is moved, it is inserted into its correct position in the sorted list. In order to place the new item, some elements may need to be moved down to create a slot.

Here is the array of four elements. In each case, the boxed element is "it," the next element to be inserted into the sorted part of the list. The shaded area is the part of the list sorted so far.

8	1	4	6	
1	8	4	6	after first pass
1	4	8	6	after second pass
1	4	6	8	after third pass

NOTE

1. For an array of n elements, the array is sorted after $n - 1$ passes.
2. After the kth pass, a[0], a[1], ..., a[k] are sorted with respect to each other but not necessarily in their final sorted positions.
3. The worst case for insertion sort occurs if the array is initially sorted in reverse order, since this will lead to the maximum possible number of comparisons and moves:

Level AB Only

Number of comparisons in first pass: 1
Number of comparisons in second pass: 2

$\vdots$

Number of comparisons in $(n - 1)$th pass: $n - 1$

Total number of comparisons $= 1 + 2 + \cdots + (n - 2) + (n - 1) = n(n - 1)/2$, which is $O(n^2)$.

4. The best case for insertion sort occurs if the array is already sorted in increasing order. In this case, each pass through the array will involve just one comparison, which will indicate that "it" is in its correct position with respect to the sorted list. Therefore, no elements will need to be moved.

Level AB Only

Total number of comparisons $= n - 1$, which is $O(n)$.

5. For the average case, insertion sort must still make $n - 1$ passes (i.e., $O(n)$ passes). Each pass makes $O(n)$ comparisons, so the total number of comparisons is $O(n^2)$.

Recursive Sorts: Mergesort and Quicksort

Selection and insertion sorts are inefficient for large n, requiring approximately n passes through a list of n elements. More efficient algorithms can be devised using a "divide-and-conquer" approach, which is used in all the sorting algorithms that follow.

Mergesort

Here is a recursive description of how mergesort works:

If there is more than one element in the array
> Break the array into two halves.
> Mergesort the left half.
> Mergesort the right half.
> Merge the two subarrays into a sorted array.

Mergesort uses a `merge` method to merge two sorted pieces of an array into a single sorted array. For example, suppose array `a[0] ...a[n-1]` is such that `a[0] ...a[k]` is sorted and `a[k+1] ...a[n-1]` is sorted, both parts in increasing order. Example:

a[0]	a[1]	a[2]	a[3]	a[4]	a[5]
2	5	8	9	1	6

In this case, `a[0] ...a[3]` and `a[4] ...a[5]` are the two sorted pieces. The method call `merge(a,0,3,5)` should produce the "merged" array:

a[0]	a[1]	a[2]	a[3]	a[4]	a[5]
1	2	5	6	8	9

The middle numerical parameter in `merge` (the 3 in this case) represents the index of the last element in the first "piece" of the array. The first and third numerical parameters are the lowest and highest index, respectively, of array a.

Here's what happens in mergesort:

1. Start with an unsorted list of n elements.
2. The recursive calls break the list into n sublists, each of length 1. Note that these n arrays, each containing just one element, are sorted!
3. Recursively merge adjacent pairs of lists. There are then approximately $n/2$ lists of length 2; then, approximately $n/4$ lists of approximate length 4, and so on, until there is just one list of length n.

An example of mergesort follows:

Analysis of Mergesort:

1. The major disadvantage of mergesort is that it needs a temporary array that is as large as the original array to be sorted. This could be a problem if space is a factor.

Level AB Only

2. The merge method compares each element in the subarrays, an $O(n)$ process. It also copies the elements from a temporary array back into the original list, another $O(n)$ process. This total of $2n$ operations makes the merge part of the algorithm $O(n)$.

3. To break the array of n elements into n arrays of one element each requires $\log_2 n$ divisions, an $O(\log n)$ process. For each of the $\log_2 n$ divisions of the array, the $O(n)$ merge method is called to put it together again. Thus mergesort is $O(n \log n)$.

4. Mergesort is not affected by the initial ordering of the elements. Thus best, worst, and average cases are $O(n \log n)$.

Quicksort

For large n, quicksort is, on average, the fastest known sorting algorithm. Here is a recursive description of how quicksort works:

If there are at least two elements in the array
    Partition the array.
    Quicksort the left subarray.
    Quicksort the right subarray.

The partition method splits the array into two subarrays as follows: a *pivot* element is chosen at random from the array (often just the first element) and placed so that all items to the left of the pivot are less than or equal to the pivot, whereas those to the right are greater than or equal to it.

For example, if the array is 4, 1, 2, 7, 5, −1, 8, 0, 6, and a[0] = 4 is the pivot, the partition method produces

    −1   1   2   0 | 4 | 5   8   7   6

Here's how the partitioning works: Let a[0], 4 in this case, be the pivot. Markers up and down are initialized to index values 1 and $n - 1$, as shown. Move the up marker until a value less than the pivot is found, or down equals up. Move the down marker until a value greater than the pivot is found, or down equals up. Swap a[up] and a[down]. Continue the process until down equals up. This is the pivot position. Swap a[0] and a[pivotPosition].

```
           down →      →                          up ←
        | 4 |   1     2     7     5    −1    8     0     6
                          down →          ← ← up
        | 4 |   1     2     0     5    −1    8     7     6
                              down ← up
        | 4 |   1     2     0    −1     5    8     7     6

          −1    1     2     0    | 4 |   5    8     7     6
```

Level AB
(continued)

Notice that the pivot element, 4, is in its final sorted position.

Analysis of Quicksort

1. For the fastest run time, the array should be partitioned into two parts of roughly the same size. In this case, and on average, there are $\log_2 n$ splits. The partition algorithm is $O(n)$. Therefore the best and average case run times are $O(n \log n)$.
2. If the pivot happens to be the smallest or largest element in the array, the split is not much of a split—one of the subarrays is empty! If this happens repeatedly, quicksort degenerates into a slow, recursive version of selection sort and is $O(n^2)$ (worst case).
3. The worst case for quicksort occurs when the partitioning algorithm repeatedly divides the array into pieces of size 1 and $n - 1$. An example is when the array is initially sorted in either order and the first or last element is chosen as the pivot. Some algorithms avoid this situation by initially shuffling up the given array (!) or selecting the pivot by examining several elements of the array (such as first, middle, and last) and then taking the median.

NOTE   For both quicksort and mergesort, when a subarray gets down to some small size m, it becomes faster to sort by straight insertion. The optimal value of m is machine-dependent, but it's approximately equal to 7.

A Binary Tree Sort: Heapsort

Level AB Only

Heapsort is an elegant algorithm that uses an array implementation of a binary tree. Recall the following definitions from Chapter 10:

A *full binary tree* has every leaf on the same level and every nonleaf node has two children.

A *complete binary tree* is either full or full through the next-to-last level, with the leaves as far left as possible in the last level.

A *heap* (sometimes called a *max heap*) is a complete binary tree in which every node has a value greater than or equal to each of its children.

Example

Is each of the following a heap?

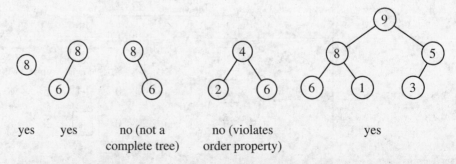

yes   yes   no (not a   no (violates   yes
                      complete tree)   order property)

Level AB   *NOTE*
(continued)

1. The largest value in a heap is in the root node.
2. A heap with *n* elements has *n*/2 subtrees that have at least one child. This counts the tree itself.

To sort array a[0], a[1], a[1], ..., a[n-1], heapsort has three main steps:

I. Slot the elements into a "mental" binary tree, level by level, from left to right as shown here. This creates a *complete* binary tree in your head, with the property that if node a[k] has children, its left child is a[2*k+1] and its right child is a[2*k + 2].

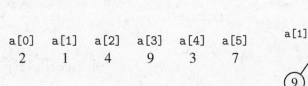

a[0]	a[1]	a[2]	a[3]	a[4]	a[5]
2	1	4	9	3	7

II. Transform the tree into a heap. Note that a[(n/2)-1] down to a[0] are roots of nonempty subtrees. (Check it out for odd and even values of n.) To form the heap, work from the "bottom" subtree up:

```
for (int rootIndex = (n/2)-1; rootIndex >= 0; rootIndex--)
    fixHeap(rootIndex, n-1);    //n-1 is the last index
```

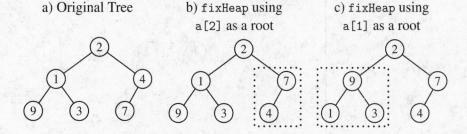

a) Original Tree   b) fixHeap using a[2] as a root   c) fixHeap using a[1] as a root

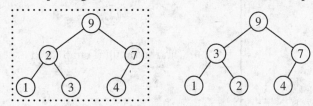

d) fixHeap using a[0] as a root   e) Tree is now a heap

This mental picture gives meaning to what is happening to the array—a sequence of swaps.

	a[0]	a[1]	a[2]	a[3]	a[4]	a[5]
Original array	2	1	4	9	3	7
fixHeap(2,5)	2	1	7	9	3	4
fixHeap(1,5)	2	9	7	1	3	4
fixHeap(0,5)	9	2	7	1	3	4
	9	3	7	1	2	4

III. Sort the array using the heap property that the biggest element is at the top of the tree: Swap a[0] and a[n-1]. Now a[n-1] is in its final sorted position in the array. Reduce the last index by one (think of it as an apple that has dropped off the tree), and restore the heap using one fewer element. Eventually there will be just one element in the tree, at which stage the array will be sorted.

```
while(n > 1)
{
    swap(0, n-1);        //swap a[0] and a[n-1]
    n--;
    fixHeap(0, n-1);     //rootIndex is 0 in each case
}
```

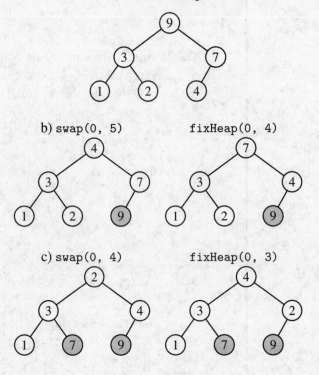

a) Tree is a heap

b) swap(0, 5)   fixHeap(0, 4)

c) swap(0, 4)   fixHeap(0, 3)

...and so on until swap(0, 1) yields

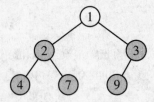

Here is the sequence of swaps in the array, starting after the tree has been formed into a heap.

Level AB
(continued)

	a[0]	a[1]	a[2]	a[3]	a[4]	a[5]
heap	9	3	7	1	2	4
swap	4	3	7	1	2	9
fix	7	3	4	1	2	9
swap	2	3	4	1	7	9
fix	4	3	2	1	7	9
swap	1	3	2	4	7	9
fix	3	1	2	4	7	9
swap	2	1	3	4	7	9
sorted!	1	2	3	4	7	9

Note that the `fixHeap` method in parts I and II of this algorithm assumes that the heap property is violated only by the root node (i.e., if you cover the root, the rest of the tree looks like a heap).

Analysis of Heapsort

1. For small n, this is not very efficient because of the initial overhead: Array elements must be rearranged to satisfy the heap property—the largest element must be moved to the "top" of the heap, and then moved again to the end of the array.
2. Heapsort is very efficient for large n.
   a) Building the original heap has $n/2$ iterations, each containing a `fixHeap` call, which, in the worst case, travels to the bottom (highest level) of the tree, $\log_2 n$ iterations. Thus building the original heap is $O(n \log n)$.
   b) The sorting loop: $(n-2)$ iterations of an $O(1)$ swap and $O(\log n)$ `fixHeap`-ing. Thus the sorting piece of the algorithm is also $O(n \log n)$.
3. Heapsort is an "in-place" sort requiring no temporary storage. Its best, average, and worst case run times are all $O(n \log n)$. The worst case is only 20 percent worse than its average run time! This means that the order of the input elements does not significantly affect the run time.

Sorting Algorithms in Java

Unlike the container classes like `ArrayList`, whose elements must be objects, arrays can hold either objects or primitive types like `int` or `double`.

Here is a method that sorts an array of `double` in descending order, using a selection sort.

```
/* Precondition:  a is an array of double
 * Postcondition: a sorted from largest to smallest using a
 *                selection sort  */

public static void selectionSort(double[] a)
{
    for (int i=0; i<a.length-1; i++)
    {
```

```
                            //find max element in a[i+1] to a[a.length-1]
                            double max = a[i];
                            int maxPos = i;    //index of largest element
                            for (int j=i+1; j<a.length; j++)
                                if (max < a[j])
                                {
                                    max = a[j];
                                    maxPos = j;
                                }
                            swap(a, i, maxPos);    //swap a[i] and a[maxPos]
                    }
                }
```

Here is the swap method:

```
    private static void swap(double[] a, int i, int j)
    {
        double temp = a[i];
        a[i] = a[j];
        a[j] = temp;
    }
```

The methods shown above work as easily for an array of int—simply change all the double declarations to int. These methods are not, however, suitable for sorting an array of objects. To sort objects, the elements must be Comparable since you need to be able to compare them.

Here is another way of organizing the code for sorting objects: a class that holds all the methods for a given type of sorting method. The class shown below uses heapsort. For an example that uses selection sort, see the introduction to Question 20 on p. 431.

Level AB Only

```
/* A class that sorts an array of objects
 * from smallest to largest using heapsort */
public class HeapSort
{
    private Comparable[] a;

    /* Constructs a HeapSort Object */
    public HeapSort(Comparable[] arr)
    {
        a = arr;
    }

    /* Swaps a[i] and a[j] in array a */
    private void swap(int i, int j)
    {
        Comparable temp = a[i];
        a[i] = a[j];
        a[j] = temp;
    }

    /* Fixes (sub)heap rooted at a[rootIndex], assuming that all
     * descendants of a[rootIndex] satisfy the heap order property
     * (i.e., order property violated only at the root node).
     * last is the last index of an element in the heap
     * i.e., last<=a.length-1  */
```

```java
private void fixHeap(int rootIndex, int last)
{
    int lChild = rootIndex*2 + 1;
    int rChild = lChild + 1;
    int maxChild;

    // Process until root value in correct place
    while (rootIndex*2 < last) //condition for node having no
                //children. If false, no more subtrees to check
    {
        if (lChild == last)   //only one child node
            maxChild = lChild;
        else
            if (a[lChild].compareTo(a[rChild]) > 0) //left child
                                    //greater than right child
                maxChild = lChild;
            else
                maxChild = rChild;

        // If heap property violated, swap values
        if (a[rootIndex].compareTo(a[maxChild]) < 0) //root less
                                            //than max child
        {
            swap(rootIndex, maxChild);
            //reassign indexes for subtree on next level
            rootIndex = maxChild;
            lChild = rootIndex*2 + 1;
            rChild = lChild + 1;
        }
        else
            break;      //heap was OK
    }
}

/* Sorts array a from smallest to largest using heapsort.
 * Precondition: a is an array of Comparable objects */
public void heapSort()
{
    int n = a.length;   //number of elements in array

    //build original heap from unsorted elements
    for (int rootIndex = (n/2)-1; rootIndex >=0; rootIndex--)
        fixHeap(rootIndex, n-1);
    //sort by swapping root value (current largest) in heap
    //with last unsorted value, then fixHeap-ing the
    //remaining part of the array
    while (n > 1)     //while more than one element in tree
    {
        swap(0, n-1);
        n--;
        fixHeap(0, n-1);
    }
}
}
```

Level AB *NOTE*
(continued)

1. The only method in this class other than the constructor that a client would call is `heapSort`. The swap and `fixHeap` methods are internal to the sorting algorithm and are therefore private.
2. The root of the binary tree is at `a[0]`. In other words, the array being sorted is `a[0], a[1], ..., a[a.length-1]`, the standard array in Java. Some implementations of `heapSort` don't use `a[0]` and insert the first element in `a[1]`.

To sort an array of objects using this class:

```java
public class SortTest
{
    < various methods >

    public static void main(String args[])
    {
        //sort an array of words
        < fill wordArray with wordList, a list of String objects >
        Comparable[] wordArray = makeArray(wordList);
        HeapSort h1 = new HeapSort(wordArray);
        h1.heapSort();
            ...

        //sort an array of Position objects
        < fill posArray with posList, a list of Position objects >
        Comparable[] posArray = makeArray(posList);
        HeapSort h2 = new HeapSort(posArray);
        h2.heapSort();
            ...
    }
}
```

NOTE   This code can be used only for objects that implement `Comparable`. The Java classes `Integer`, `Double`, and `String` all do. The `Position` class used is on p. 396. All of the `Position` coordinates are nonnegative. The `compareTo` method is defined to give `Position` objects a row-major ordering, namely top-to-bottom, left-to-right. Thus (1,4) is less than (2,0), and (1,3) is less than (1,4).

Sequential Search

Assume that you are searching for a key in a list of n elements. A sequential search starts at the first element and compares the key to each element in turn until the key is found or there are no more elements to examine in the list. If the list is sorted, in ascending order, say, stop searching as soon as the key is less than the current list element.

Level AB Only

Analysis:

1. The best case has key in the first slot, and the search is $O(1)$.
2. Worst case occurs if the key is in the last slot or not in the list. All n elements must be examined, and the algorithm is $O(n)$.
3. On average, there will be $n/2$ comparisons, which is also $O(n)$.

Binary Search

If the elements are in a *sorted* array, a divide-and-conquer approach provides a much more efficient searching algorithm. The following recursive pseudo-code algorithm shows how the *binary search* works.

Assume that a[low] ... a[high] is sorted in ascending order and that a method binSearch returns the index of key. If key is not in the array, it returns −1.

```
if (low > high)    //Base case. No elements left in array
    return -1;
else
{
    mid = (low + high)/2;
    if (key equals a[mid])    //found the key
        return mid;
    else if (key less than a[mid]) //key in left half of array
        < binSearch for key in a[low] to a[mid - 1] >
    else    //key in right half of array
        < binSearch for key in a[mid + 1] to a[high] >
}
```

NOTE When low and high cross, there are no more elements to examine, and key is not in the array.

Example: suppose 5 is the key to be found in the following array:

a[0]	a[1]	a[2]	a[3]	a[4]	a[5]	a[6]	a[7]	a[8]
1	4	5	7	9	12	15	20	21

First pass: mid = (8+0)/2 = 4.   Check a[4].
Second pass: mid = (0+3)/2 = 1.   Check a[1].
Third pass: mid = (2+3)/2 = 2.   Check a[2]. Yes! Key is found.

Level AB Only

Analysis of Binary Search:

1. In the best case, the key is found on the first try (i.e., (low + high)/2 is the index of key.) This is $O(1)$.
2. In the worst case, the key is not in the list or is at either end of a sublist. Here the n elements must be divided by 2 until there is just one element, and then that last element must be tested. This equals $1 + \log_2 n$ comparisons. Thus, in the worst case, the algorithm is $O(\log n)$. An easy way to find the number of comparisons in the worst case is to round n up to the next power of 2 and take the exponent. For example, in the array above, $n = 9$. Suppose 21 were the key. Round 9 up to 16, which equals 2^4. Thus you would need four comparisons to find it. Try it!
3. In the average case, you need about half the comparisons of the worst case, so the algorithm is still $O(\log n)$.

Hash Coding

Description

A *hash table* stores data of some type (`tableElementType`) with an associated *key field* of type `keyType`. Ideally, a hash table should provide for efficient insertion and retrieval of items.

Level AB Only

Here is a simple example of hash coding. A catalog company stores customer orders in an array as follows. The last two digits of the customer's phone number provide the index in the array for that particular customer's order. Thus two customers with phone numbers 257-3178 and 253-5169 will have their orders stored in `list[78]` and `list[69]`, respectively. In this example, the *hash table* is an array, the *key field* is a phone number, the *hash function* is (phone number mod 100), and the *hash address* is the array index.

The simplest implementation of a hash table is an array of data items. To insert or retrieve any given item, a *hash function* is performed on the key field of the item, which returns the array index or *hash address* of that item. This method cannot guarantee a unique address for each data item.

For example, suppose a small business maintains employee data in a list called `employeeList`. If the key field is `socialSecurityNo` and the hash function is (`socialSecurityNo` % 100), then 567350347 and 203479247 both hash to the same address: `employeeList[47]`.

A good hash function minimizes such *collisions* by spreading them uniformly through the key field values. A commonly used hash function in Java is

```
key.hashCode() % SIZE
```

where `key.hashCode()` is the `hashCode` value of the `key` object (see p. 110) and `SIZE` is the number of slots in the hash table.

Resolving Collisions

Hash and Search (or Open Addressing with Linear Probing)

Store the colliding element in the next available slot. An example for storing data with `keyValue` 556677003 is shown in the following table.

	employeeList
[00]	empty
[01]	453614001
[02]	empty
[03]	123467003
[04]	689286004
[05]	empty
⋮	
[99]	618272899

The hash function yields hash address 03, but `employeeList[03]` already contains data, so we try slot [04] and so on. In this example, the new data gets stored in `employeeList[05]`. If the key hashes to the last slot in the array and is filled,

Level AB
(continued)

treat it as a circular structure and go back to the beginning of the array to search for an empty slot.

In this scheme, searching for a given data item involves

1. Hash and compare.
2. If keys don't match, do a sequential search starting at that slot in the array.

Rehashing

If the first computation causes a collision, compute a new hash address using the old hash address as input. Repeat if necessary. Typically, a rehash function has form (hash address + < const >) % < number of slots > where "const" and "number of slots" are relatively prime (i.e., no common factors greater than 1). This ensures that every index will be covered.

For example, the hash function for this table is key % 10. The rehash function is (hash address + 3) % 10. (Note that 3 and 10 are relatively prime.) Here are the steps to insert 26402 into the table:

[00]	
[01]	27401
[02]	68902
[03]	
[04]	
[05]	67905
[06]	
[07]	
[08]	
[09]	27309

$26402 \% 10 = 02$ (taken)
$(2 + 3) \% 10 = 05$ (taken)
$(5 + 3) \% 10 = 08$,   which becomes the hash address of the new item.

These methods are simple to implement but are less than ideal in resolving collisions. If the table is almost full, an insertion operation becomes $O(n)$. What follows is more elegant.

Chaining

In chaining, the hash address is the index for an array of linked lists called *buckets*. Each bucket is a linear linked list of data items that share the same hash address.

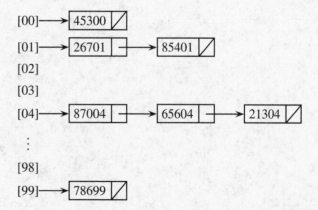

To insert an item, hash to the appropriate bucket and insert at the front of the list. Thus insertion is $O(1)$. To search for an item, apply the hash function and do a sequential search of the appropriate list. Assuming that items are uniformly distributed in the hash table, a search should occur in constant time, which is $O(1)$.

Level AB
(continued)

Features of a Good Hash Function

1. It distributes data items uniformly throughout the hash table.
2. It provides for $O(1)$ insertion and searching.

Multiple-Choice Questions on Sorting and Searching

1. The decision to choose a particular sorting algorithm should be made based on

    I   Run-time efficiency of the sort
    II Size of the array
    III Space efficiency of the algorithm

    (A) I only
    (B) II only
    (C) III only
    (D) I and II only
    (E) I, II, and III

2. The following code fragment does a sequential search to determine whether a given integer, value, is stored in an array a[0] ... a[n-1].

    ```
    int i = 0;
    while (< boolean expression >)
    {
        i++;
    }
    if (i == n)
        return -1;      //value not found
    else
        return i;       // value found at location i
    ```

    Which of the following should replace < *boolean expression* > so that the algorithm works as intended?
    (A) value != a[i]
    (B) i < n && value == a[i]
    (C) value != a[i] && i < n
    (D) i < n && value != a[i]
    (E) i < n || value != a[i]

3. A feature of data that is used for a binary search but not necessarily used for a sequential search is
    (A) Length of list.
    (B) Type of data.
    (C) Order of data.
    (D) Smallest value in the list.
    (E) Median value of the data.

4. An unsorted list of integers is stored in an array. Having the list unsorted leads to inefficient execution for which of the following operations?

    I Inserting a new element
    II Searching for a given element
    III Computing the mean of the elements

(A) I only
(B) II only
(C) III only
(D) I and II only
(E) I, II, and III

5. An algorithm for searching a large sorted array for a specific value x compares every third item in the array to x until it finds one that is greater than or equal to x. When a larger value is found, the algorithm compares x to the previous two items. If the array is sorted in increasing order, which of the following describes all cases when this algorithm uses fewer comparisons to find x than would a binary search?
(A) It will never use fewer comparisons.
(B) When x is in the middle position of the array
(C) When x is very close to the beginning of the array
(D) When x is very close to the end of the array
(E) When x is not in the array

6. Assume that a[0] ... a[N-1] is an array of N positive integers and that the following assertion is true:

$$a[0] > a[k] \text{ for all } k \text{ such that } 0 < k < N$$

Which of the following *must* be true?
(A) The array is sorted in ascending order.
(B) The array is sorted in descending order.
(C) All values in the array are identical.
(D) a[0] holds the smallest value in the array.
(E) a[0] holds the largest value in the array.

7. The following code is designed to set index to the location of the first occurrence of key in array a and to set index to −1 if key is not in a.

```
index=0;
while (a[index] != key)
    index++;
if (a[index] != key)
    index = -1;
```

In which case will this program *definitely* fail to perform the task described?
(A) When key is the first element of the array
(B) When key is the last element of the array
(C) When key is not in the array
(D) When key equals 0
(E) When key equals a[key]

8. Refer to method `search`.

```
/* Precondition:  v[0]...v[v.length-1] are initialized
 * Postcondition: Returns k such that -1 ≤ k ≤ v.length-1.
 *                If k ≥ 0 then v[k] == key. If k == -1
 *                then key != any of the elements in v  */
public static int search(int[] v, int key)
{
    int index = 0;
    while (index < v.length && v[index] < key)
        index++;
    if (index != v.length)
        return index;
    else
        return -1;
}
```

Which of the following should be added to the precondition of `search`?
(A) `v` is sorted smallest to largest.
(B) `v` is sorted largest to smallest.
(C) `v` is unsorted.
(D) There is at least one occurrence of `key` in `v`.
(E) `key` occurs no more than once in `v`.

Questions 9–14 are based on the `binSearch` method and the private instance variable a for some class:

```
private int[] a;

/* Does binary search for key in array a[0]...a[a.length-1],
 * sorted in ascending order.
 * Postcondition: Returns index such that a[index]==key.
 *                If key not in a, returns -1  */
public int binSearch(int key)
{
    int low = 0;
    int high = a.length-1;
    while (low <= high)
    {
        int mid = (low + high)/2;
        if (a[mid] == key)
            return mid;
        else if (a[mid] < key)
            low = mid + 1;
        else
            high = mid - 1;
    }
    return -1;
}
```

A binary search will be performed on the following list.

a[0]	a[1]	a[2]	a[3]	a[4]	a[5]	a[6]	a[7]
4	7	9	11	20	24	30	41

9. To find the key value 27, the search interval *after* the first pass through the while loop will be
   (A) a[0] ... a[7]
   (B) a[5] ... a[6]
   (C) a[4] ... a[7]
   (D) a[2] ... a[6]
   (E) a[6] ... a[7]

10. How many iterations will be required to determine that 27 is not in the list?
    (A) 1
    (B) 3
    (C) 8
    (D) 27
    (E) an infinite loop since 27 is not found

11. What will be stored in y after executing the following?

    ```
    int y = binSearch(4);
    ```

    (A) 20
    (B) 7
    (C) 4
    (D) 0
    (E) −1

12. If the test for the while loop is changed to

    ```
    while (low < high)
    ```

    the binSearch method does not work as intended. Which value in the given list will not be found?
    (A) 4
    (B) 7
    (C) 11
    (D) 24
    (E) 30

13. For binSearch which of the following assertions will be true following every iteration of the while loop?
    (A) key = a[mid] or key is not in a.
    (B) a[low] ≤ key ≤ a[high]
    (C) low ≤ mid ≤ high
    (D) key = a[mid], or a[low] ≤ key ≤ a[high]
    (E) key = a[mid], or a[low] ≤ key ≤ a[high], or key is not in array a.

Level AB Only

14. Suppose n = a.length. A loop invariant for the while loop is: key is not in array a, or
    (A) a[low] < key < a[high],   0 ≤ low ≤ high+1 ≤ n
    (B) a[low] ≤ key ≤ a[high],   0 ≤ low ≤ high+1 ≤ n
    (C) a[low] ≤ key ≤ a[high],   0 ≤ low ≤ high ≤ n
    (D) a[low] < key < a[high],   0 ≤ low ≤ high ≤ n
    (E) a[low] ≤ key ≤ a[high],   0 ≤ low ≤ high ≤ n−1

For Questions 15–19 refer to the `insertionSort` method and the private instance variable a, both in a Sorter class.

```
private Comparable[] a;

/* Precondition:  a[0],a[1]...a[a.length-1] is an unsorted array
 *                of Comparable objects
 * Postcondition: array a is sorted in descending order  */
public void insertionSort()
{
    for (int i=1; i<a.length; i++)
    {
        Comparable temp = a[i];
        int j = i - 1;
        while (j >= 0 && temp.compareTo(a[j]) > 0)
        {
            a[j+1] = a[j];
            j--;
        }
        a[j+1] = temp;
    }
}
```

15. An array of `Integer` is to be sorted biggest to smallest using the `insertionSort` method. If the array originally contains

     1 7 9 5 4 12

    what will it look like after the third pass of the `for` loop?
    (A) 9 7 1 5 4 12
    (B) 9 7 5 1 4 12
    (C) 12 9 7 1 5 4
    (D) 12 9 7 5 4 1
    (E) 9 7 12 5 4 1

16. When sorted biggest to smallest with `insertionSort`, which list will need the fewest changes of position for individual elements?
    (A) 5, 1, 2, 3, 4, 9
    (B) 9, 5, 1, 4, 3, 2
    (C) 9, 4, 2, 5, 1, 3
    (D) 9, 3, 5, 1, 4, 2
    (E) 3, 2, 1, 9, 5, 4

17. When sorted biggest to smallest with `insertionSort`, which list will need the greatest number of changes in position?
    (A) 5, 1, 2, 3, 4, 9
    (B) 9, 5, 1, 4, 3, 2
    (C) 9, 4, 2, 5, 1, 3
    (D) 9, 3, 5, 1, 4, 2
    (E) 3, 2, 1, 9, 5, 4

18. While typing the `insertionSort` method, a programmer by mistake enters

    ```
    while (temp.compareTo( a[j]) > 0)
    ```

    instead of

    ```
    while (j >= 0 && temp.compareTo( a[j]) > 0)
    ```

    Despite this mistake, the method works as intended the first time the programmer enters an array to be sorted in descending order. Which of the following could explain this?

    I   The first element in the array was the largest element in the array.
    II The array was already sorted in descending order.
    III The first element was less than or equal to all the other elements in the array.

    (A) I only
    (B) II only
    (C) III only
    (D) I and II only
    (E) II and III only

Level AB Only

19. A loop invariant for the outer loop (the `for` loop) is
    (A) $a[0] \geq a[1] \geq \cdots \geq a[i-1]$, $0 \leq i \leq a.length$
    (B) $a[0] > a[1] > \cdots > a[i-1]$, $1 \leq i \leq a.length$
    (C) $a[0] \geq a[1] \geq \cdots \geq a[i]$, $0 \leq i \leq a.length - 1$
    (D) $a[0] > a[1] > \cdots > a[i]$, $1 \leq i \leq a.length - 1$
    (E) $a[0] \geq a[1] \geq \cdots \geq a[i-1]$, $1 \leq i \leq a.length$

Consider the following class for Questions 20 and 21.

```java
/* A class that sorts an array of objects from
 * largest to smallest using a selection sort */
public class Sorter
{
    private Comparable[] a;

    public Sorter(Comparable[] arr)
    { a = arr;}

    /* Swap a[i] and a[j] in array a */
    private void swap(int i, int j)
    { implementation code }

    /* Sort array a from largest to smallest using selection sort.
     * Precondition: a is an array of Comparable objects */
    public void selectionSort()
    {
        for (int i=0; i<a.length-1; i++)
        {
            //find max element in a[i+1] to a[n-1]
            Comparable max = a[i];
            int maxPos = i;
            for (int j=i+1; j<a.length; j++)
                if (max.compareTo(a[j]) < 0) //max less than a[j]
                {
                    max = a[j];
                    maxPos = j;
                }
            swap(i, maxPos); //swap a[i] and a[maxPos]
        }
    }
}
```

20. If an array of `Integer` contains the following elements, what would the array look like after the third pass of `selectionSort`, sorting from high to low?

$$89 \quad 42 \quad -3 \quad 13 \quad 109 \quad 70 \quad 2$$

(A)	109	89	70	13	42	-3	2
(B)	109	89	70	42	13	2	-3
(C)	109	89	70	-3	2	13	42
(D)	89	42	13	-3	109	70	2
(E)	109	89	42	-3	13	70	2

Level AB Only

21. A loop invariant for the outer `for` loop of `selectionSort` is

(A) $a[0] \geq a[1] \geq \cdots \geq a[i-1]$, $0 \leq i \leq a.length - 1$
(B) $a[0] \geq a[1] \geq \cdots \geq a[i]$, $0 \leq i \leq a.length - 1$
(C) $a[0] \geq a[1] \geq \cdots \geq a[i-1]$, $0 \leq i \leq a.length - 2$
(D) $a[0] \geq a[1] \geq \cdots \geq a[i]$, $0 \leq i \leq a.length - 2$
(E) $a[0] \geq a[1] \geq \cdots \geq a[a.length-1]$, $0 \leq i \leq a.length - 1$

22. The elements in a long list of integers are roughly sorted in decreasing order. No more than 5 percent of the elements are out of order. Which of the following is a valid reason for using an insertion sort rather than a selection sort to sort this list into decreasing order?

    I There will be fewer comparisons of elements for insertion sort.
    II There will be fewer changes of position of elements for insertion sort.
    III There will be less space required for insertion sort.

(A) I only
(B) II only
(C) III only
(D) I and II only
(E) I, II, and III

Level AB Only

23. The code shown sorts array a[0] ... a[a.length-1] in descending order.

```
public static void sort(Comparable[] a)
{
    for (int i=0; i<a.length-1; i++)
        for (int j=0; j<a.length-i-1; j++)
            if (a[j].compareTo(a[j+1]) < 0)
                swap(a, j, j+1);  //swap a[j] and a[j+1]
}
```

This is an example of
(A) Selection sort.
(B) Insertion sort.
(C) Mergesort.
(D) Quicksort.
(E) None of the above.

24. Which of the following is a valid reason why mergesort is a better sorting algorithm than insertion sort for sorting long lists?

    I Mergesort requires less code than insertion sort.
    II Mergesort requires less storage space than insertion sort.
    III Mergesort runs faster than insertion sort.

(A) I only
(B) II only
(C) III only
(D) I and II only
(E) II and III only

25. A large array of lowercase characters is to be searched for the pattern "pqrs." The first step in a very efficient searching algorithm is to look at characters with index
(A) 0, 1, 2, ... until a "p" is encountered
(B) 0, 1, 2, ... until any letter in "p" ... "s" is encountered
(C) 3, 7, 11, ... until an "s" is encountered
(D) 3, 7, 11, ... until any letter in "p" ... "s" is encountered
(E) 3, 7, 11, ... until any letter other than "p" ... "s" is encountered

26. The array `names[0]`, `names[1]`, ..., `names[9999]` is a list of 10,000 name strings. The list is to be searched to determine the location of some name X in the list. Which of the following preconditions is necessary for a binary search?
    (A) There are no duplicate names in the list.
    (B) The number of names N in the list is large.
    (C) The list is in alphabetical order.
    (D) Name X is definitely in the list.
    (E) Name X occurs toward the end of the list.

27. Consider the following method:

```
//Precondition: a[0],a[1]...a[n-1] contain integers
public static int someMethod(int[] a, int n, int value)
{
    if (n == 0)
        return -1;
    else
    {
        if (a[n-1] == value)
            return n-1;
        else
            return someMethod(a, n-1, value);
    }
}
```

`someMethod` is an example of
    (A) Insertion sort.
    (B) Mergesort.
    (C) Selection sort.
    (D) Binary search.
    (E) Sequential search.

Level AB Only

28. The `partition` method for quicksort partitions a list as follows:

    (i) A pivot element is selected from the array.
    (ii) The elements of the list are rearranged such that all elements to the left of the pivot are less than or equal to it; all elements to the right of the pivot are greater than or equal to it.

    Partitioning the array requires which of the following?
    (A) A recursive algorithm
    (B) A temporary array
    (C) An external file for the array
    (D) A swap algorithm for interchanging array elements
    (E) A merge method for merging two sorted lists

29. Refer to method `mystery`.

```
//Precondition: a[0]...a[mid] are sorted in increasing order.
//              a[mid+1]...a[a.length-1] are sorted in
//              increasing order
public static void mystery(int[] a, int mid)
{
    int[] c = new int[a.length];
    int k, count = -1, i = 0, j = mid+1;
    while (i <= mid && j <= a.length -1)
    {
        count++;
        if (a[i] < a[j])
        {
            c[count] = a[i];
            i++;
        }
        else
        {
            c[count] = a[j];
            j++;
        }
    }
    if (i > mid)
        for (k=j; k<a.length; k++)
        {
            count++;
            c[count] = a[k];
        }
    else
        for (k=i; k<=mid; k++)
        {
            count++;
            c[count] = a[k];
        }
    for (k=0; k<=count; k++)
        a[k] = c[k];
}
```

What does method `mystery` do?

(A) Merges two parts of array a into a single sorted array.

(B) Partitions array a into two parts using a pivot element, such that all elements a[0]...a[mid] are less than the pivot, and all elements a[mid+1]...a[a.length-1] are greater than or equal to the pivot.

(C) Uses mergesort to sort array a into increasing order.

(D) Uses quicksort to sort array a into increasing order.

(E) Does a binary search of array a.

30. A binary search is to be performed on an array with 600 elements. In the *worst* case, which of the following best approximates the number of iterations of the algorithm?
    (A) 6
    (B) 10
    (C) 100
    (D) 300
    (E) 600

31. A worst case situation for insertion sort would be

    I   A list in correct sorted order.
    II A list sorted in reverse order.
    III A list in random order.

    (A) I only
    (B) II only
    (C) III only
    (D) I and II only
    (E) II and III only

Level AB Only

32. Which of the following represents a heap?

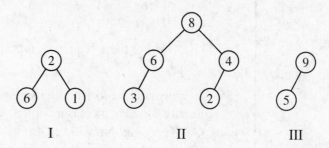

    (A) I only
    (B) II only
    (C) III only
    (D) I and III only
    (E) II and III only

33. The list

$$17 \quad 9 \quad 2 \quad 7 \quad 21 \quad 18 \quad 4 \quad 5$$

    is to be sorted into ascending order using heapsort. What is the level of the binary tree that will be formed, given that the root is at level 0?
    (A) 0
    (B) 1
    (C) 2
    (D) 3
    (E) 4

34. Assume that array a[0]...a[6] = 6 1 5 9 8 4 7 is to be sorted in increasing order using heapsort. Which of the following represents the correct sequence of swaps to be made to form the array into the original heap?

(A) 6 1 7 9 8 4 5
    6 9 7 1 8 4 5
    9 6 7 1 8 4 5
    9 8 7 1 6 4 5

(B) 6 9 5 1 8 4 7
    6 9 7 1 8 4 5
    9 6 7 1 8 4 5
    9 8 7 1 6 4 5

(C) 6 1 7 9 8 4 5
    7 1 6 9 8 4 5
    7 9 6 1 8 4 5
    9 7 6 1 8 4 5
    9 8 6 1 7 4 5

(D) 6 9 5 1 8 4 7
    9 6 5 1 8 4 7
    9 6 7 1 8 4 5
    9 8 7 1 6 4 5

(E) None of these sequences is correct.

35. An array is to be sorted into increasing order using quicksort. If the array is initially sorted in increasing order, which of the following *must* be true?
    (A) The algorithm will be $O(n)$.
    (B) The algorithm will be $O(n \log n)$.
    (C) The algorithm will be $O(n^2)$.
    (D) The efficiency of the algorithm depends on how the pivot element is selected.
    (E) The run time will be quicker if heapsort is used instead.

36. Which represents the worst case performance of the sequential search and binary search, respectively?
    (A) $O(n^2)$, $O(n \log n)$
    (B) $O(n)$, $O(n \log n)$
    (C) $O(n)$, $O(n)$
    (D) $O(n)$, $O(\log n)$
    (E) $O(n^2)$, $O(\log n)$

37. A typical algorithm to search an ordered list of numbers has an execution time of $O(\log_2 n)$. Which of the following choices is closest to the maximum number of times that such an algorithm will execute its main comparison loop when searching an ordered list of 1 million numbers?
    (A) 6
    (B) 20
    (C) 100
    (D) 120
    (E) 1000

38. A certain algorithm sequentially examines a list of n random integers and then outputs the number of times 8 occurs in the list. Using big-O notation, this algorithm is
    (A) $O(1)$
    (B) $O(\sqrt{n})$
    (C) $O(n)$
    (D) $O(n^2)$
    (E) $O(\log n)$

39. Which represents the worst case performance of mergesort, quicksort, and heapsort, respectively?
    (A) $O(n \log n)$, $O(n \log n)$, $O(n \log n)$
    (B) $O(n \log n)$, $O(n^2)$, $O(n \log n)$
    (C) $O(n^2)$, $O(n^2)$, $O(n^2)$
    (D) $O(\log n)$, $O(n^2)$, $O(\log n)$
    (E) $O(2^n)$, $O(n^2)$, $O(n \log n)$

40. Consider these three tasks:

    I A sequential search of an array of n names
    II A binary search of an array of n names in alphabetical order
    III A quicksort into alphabetical order of an array of n names that are initially in random order

    For large n, which of the following lists these tasks in order (from least to greatest) of their average case run times?

    (A)   II   I   III
    (B)   I   II   III
    (C)   II III   I
    (D) III   I   II
    (E) III   II   I

438 CHAPTER 12 SORTING AND SEARCHING

Level AB
(continued)

41. The efficiency of hash coding depends on which of the following:

    I   The number of collisions that occur
    II The size of the data items in the list
    III The method of dealing with collisions

    (A) I only
    (B) III only
    (C) I and III only
    (D) I and II only
    (E) I, II, and III

42. The following key values are to be inserted into the hash table shown in the order given:

    10   28   2   7   45   25   40   29

array index	0	1	2	3	4	5	6	7	8	9	10
key value											

The hash function is key % 11. Collisions will be resolved with the Open Addressing and Linear Probing ("hash-and-search") method. Which array slot will 29 eventually occupy?
    (A) 7
    (B) 8
    (C) 9
    (D) 10
    (E) 0

43. An array contains data that was hash coded into it. How should this array be searched for a given item?
    (A) A linear search should be used on the key data fields.
    (B) If the array is sorted on the key fields, a binary search should be used.
    (C) The Java % operation should be applied to the key of the item to obtain the correct array location.
    (D) The hashCode method of the item should be applied to the key to obtain the correct array location.
    (E) The hash function and a collision resolution algorithm should be applied to the key to find the correct location.

Level AB
(continued)

44. A certain hash function $h(x)$ on a key field places records with the following key fields into a hash table.

$$62 \quad 79 \quad 81 \quad 12 \quad 54 \quad 97 \quad 34$$

Collisions are handled with a rehashing function $r(x)$, which takes as an argument the result of applying $h(x)$. If the key values are entered in the order shown to produce the following table:

0	1	2	3	4	5	6	7	8	9	10	11	12	13	14	15	16	17	18	19
	81	62						34				12		54			97		79

then $h(x)$ and $r(x)$ are, respectively,
(A) key % 20,   (result + 13) % 20
(B) key % 20,   result % 20
(C) key % 30,   (result + 14) % 20
(D) key % 20,   (result + 7) % 20
(E) key % 30,   (result + 7) % 30

Questions 45 and 46 are based on the Sort interface and MergeSort and QuickSort classes shown below.

```
public interface Sort
{
    void sort(Comparable[] a);
}

public class MergeSort implements Sort
{
    /* Swap a[i] and a[j] in array a */
    private void swap(Comparable[] a, int i, int j)
    { implementation }

    /* Merge a[lb] to a[mi] and a[mi+1] to a[ub].
     * Precondition: a[lb] to a[mi] and a[mi+1] to a[ub] both
     *               sorted in increasing order  */
    private void merge(Comparable[] a, int lb, int mi, int ub)
    { implementation }

    /* Recursive helper method to sort a[first]...a[last]
     * from smallest to largest using mergesort
     * Precondition: a is an array of Comparable objects  */
    private void sort(Comparable[] a, int first, int last)
    {
        if (first != last)
        {
            int mid = (first+last)/2;
            sort(a, first, mid);
            sort(a, mid+1, last);
            merge(a, first, mid, last);
        }
    }

    /* Sort array a from smallest to largest using mergesort
     * Precondition: a is an array of Comparable objects  */
    public void sort(Comparable[] a)
    {
        sort(a, 0, a.length-1);
    }
}

public class QuickSort implements Sort
{
    /* Swap a[i] and a[j] in array a */
    private void swap(Comparable[] a, int i, int j)
    { implementation }

    /* Return the index pivPos such that a[first] to a[last]
     * is partitioned.
     * a[first..pivPos]<=a[pivPos] and a[pivPos..last]>=a[pivPos] */
    private int partition(Comparable[] a, int first, int last)
    { implementation }
```

Level AB
(continued)

```
/* Sort a[first] to a[last] in increasing order using
 * quicksort */
private void sort(Comparable[] a, int first, int last)
{
    if (first < last)
    {
        int pivPos = partition(a, first, last);
        sort(a, first, pivPos-1);
        sort(a, pivPos+1, last);
    }
}

/* Sort array a in increasing order */
public void sort(Comparable[] a)
{
    sort(a, 0, a.length-1);
}
}
```

45. Notice that the `MergeSort` and `QuickSort` classes both have a private helper method that implements the recursive sort routine. For this example, which of the following is *not* a valid reason for having a helper method?

    I   The helper method hides the implementation details of the sorting algorithm from the user.
    II A method with additional parameters is needed to implement the recursion.
    III Providing a helper method increases the run-time efficiency of the sorting algorithm.

    (A) I only
    (B) II only
    (C) III only
    (D) I and II only
    (E) I, II, and III

Level AB
(continued)

46. A piece of code to test the `QuickSort` and `MergeSort` classes is as follows:

```
//Create an array of Integer values
Comparable[] intArray = makeArray(intList);
< more code >
```

where `makeArray` creates an array of `Comparable` from a list `intList`. Which of the following replacements for *< more code >* is reasonable code to test `QuickSort` and `MergeSort`? You can assume `writeList` correctly writes out an array of Integer.

(A)
```
Sort q = new QuickSort();
Sort m = new MergeSort();
q.sort(intArray);
writeList(intArray);
m.sort(intArray);
writeList(intArray);
```

(B)
```
QuickSort q = new Sort();
MergeSort m = new Sort();
q.sort(intArray);
writeList(intArray);
m.sort(intArray);
writeList(intArray);
```

(C)
```
Sort q = new QuickSort();
Sort m = new MergeSort();
Comparable[] copyArray = makeArray(intList);
q.sort(intArray, 0, intArray.length-1);
writeList(intArray);
m.sort(copyArray, 0, copyArray.length-1);
writeList(copyArray);
```

(D)
```
QuickSort q = new Sort();
MergeSort m = new Sort();
Comparable[] copyArray = makeArray(intList);
q.sort(intArray);
writeList(intArray);
m.sort(copyArray);
writeList(copyArray);
```

(E)
```
Sort q = new QuickSort();
Sort m = new MergeSort();
Comparable[] copyArray = makeArray(intList);
q.sort(intArray);
writeList(intArray);
m.sort(copyArray);
writeList(copyArray);
```

Answer Key

1. **E**	17. **A**	33. **D**
2. **D**	18. **D**	34. **A**
3. **C**	19. **E**	35. **D**
4. **B**	20. **A**	36. **D**
5. **C**	21. **A**	37. **B**
6. **E**	22. **A**	38. **C**
7. **C**	23. **E**	39. **B**
8. **A**	24. **C**	40. **A**
9. **C**	25. **D**	41. **C**
10. **B**	26. **C**	42. **C**
11. **D**	27. **E**	43. **E**
12. **A**	28. **D**	44. **D**
13. **E**	29. **A**	45. **D**
14. **B**	30. **B**	46. **E**
15. **B**	31. **B**	
16. **B**	32. **C**	

Answers Explained

1. **(E)** The time and space requirements of sorting algorithms are affected by all three of the given factors, so all must be considered when choosing a particular sorting algorithm.

2. **(D)** Choice B doesn't make sense: the loop will be exited as soon as a value is found that does *not* equal a[i]. Eliminate choice A because, if value is not in the array, a[i] will eventually go out of bounds. You need the i < n part of the boolean expression to avoid this. The test i < n, however, must precede value != a[i] so that if i < n fails, the expression will be evaluated as false, the test will be short-circuited, and an out-of-range error will be avoided. Choice C does not avoid this error. Choice E is wrong because both parts of the expression must be true in order to continue the search.

3. **(C)** The binary search algorithm depends on the array being sorted. Sequential search has no ordering requirement. Both depend on choice A, the length of the list, while the other choices are irrelevant to both algorithms.

4. **(B)** Inserting a new element is quick and easy in this scheme—just add it to the end of the list. Computing the mean involves finding the sum of the elements and dividing by n, the number of elements. The execution time is the same whether the list is sorted or not. Operation II, searching, is inefficient

for an unsorted list, since a sequential search must be used. If the list were sorted, the efficient binary search algorithm, which involves fewer comparisons, could be used. In fact, if the list were sorted, even a sequential search would be more efficient than for an unsorted list: If the search item were not in list, the search could stop as soon as list elements were greater than the search item.

5. **(C)** Suppose the array has 1000 elements and x is somewhere in the first 8 slots. The algorithm described will find x using no more than five comparisons. A binary search, by contrast, will chop the array in half and do a comparison six times before examining elements in the first 15 slots of the array (array size after each chop: 500, 250, 125, 62, 31, 15).

6. **(E)** The assertion states that the first element is greater than all the other elements in the array. This eliminates choices A, C, and D. Choice B is incorrect because you have no information about the relative sizes of elements `a[1]...a[N-1]`.

7. **(C)** When `key` is not in the array, `index` will eventually be large enough that `a[index]` will cause an `ArrayIndexOutOfBoundsException`. In choices A and B, the algorithm will find `key` without error. Choice D won't fail if 0 is in the array. Choice E will work if `a[key]` is not out of range.

8. **(A)** The algorithm uses the fact that array `v` is sorted smallest to largest. The `while` loop terminates—which means that the search stops—as soon as `v[index] >= key`.

9. **(C)** The first pass uses the interval `a[0]...a[7]`. Since `mid` = $(0 + 7)/2 = 3$, `low` gets adjusted to `mid` $+1 = 4$, and the second pass uses the interval `a[4]...a[7]`.

10. **(B)** First pass: compare 27 with `a[3]`, since `low=0 high=7 mid=(0+7)/2 = 3`. Second pass: compare 27 with `a[5]`, since `low=4 high=7 mid= (4+7)/2 = 5`. Third pass: compare 27 with `a[6]`, since `low=6 high=7 mid= (6 + 7)/2 = 6`. The fourth pass doesn't happen, since `low=6`, `high=5`, and therefore the test (`low <= high`) fails. Here's the general rule for finding the number of iterations when `key` is not in the list: If n is the number of elements, round n up to the nearest power of 2, which is 8 in this case. $8 = 2^3$, which implies 3 iterations of the "divide-and-compare" loop.

11. **(D)** The method returns the index of the `key` parameter, 4. Since `a[0]` contains 4, `binSearch(4)` will return 0.

12. **(A)** Try 4. Here are the values for `low`, `high`, and `mid` when searching for 4:

> First pass: `low = 0`,   `high = 7`,   `mid = 3`
> Second pass: `low = 0`,   `high = 2`,   `mid = 1`

After this pass `high` gets adjusted to `mid` -1, which is 0. Now `low` equals `high` and the test for the `while` loop fails. The method returns -1, indicating that 4 wasn't found.

13. **(E)** When the loop is exited, either `key` = `a[mid]` (and `mid` has been returned) or `key` has not been found, in which case either `a[low]` $\leq$ `key` $\leq$ `a[high]` or `key` is not in the array. The correct assertion must account for all three possibilities.

14. **(B)** Note that low is initialized to 0 and high is initialized to n-1. It would appear that $0 \leq$ low $\leq$ high $\leq$ n-1. In the algorithm, however, if key is not in the array, low and high cross, which means low > high in that instance. The correct loop invariant inequality that takes all cases into account is, therefore, $0 \leq$ low $\leq$ high+1 $\leq$ n, which eliminates choices C, D, and E. In the algorithm, the endpoints of the new subarray to be considered are adjusted to include a[mid+1] (if it's the right half) or a[mid-1] (for the left half). This means that key can be at one of the endpoints. Thus a[low] $\leq$ key $\leq$ a[high] is the correct assertion.

15. **(B)** Start with the second element in the array.

After 1st pass:	7	1	9	5	4	12
After 2nd pass:	9	7	1	5	4	12
After 3rd pass:	9	7	5	1	4	12

16. **(B)** An insertion sort compares a[1] and a[0]. If they are not in the correct order, a[0] is moved and a[1] is inserted in its correct position. a[2] is then inserted in its correct position, and a[0] and a[1] are moved if necessary, and so on. Since B has only one element out of order, it will require the fewest changes.

17. **(A)** This list is almost sorted in reverse order. This is the worst case for insertion sort, requiring the greatest number of comparisons and moves.

18. **(D)** j >= 0 is a stopping condition that prevents an element that is larger than all those to the left of it from going off the left end of the array. If no error occurred, it means that each a[i] (i.e., temp) was less than or equal to some a[j] for j >= 0 (i.e., the insertion point was greater than index 0). Omitting the j >= 0 test will cause a run-time (out-of-range) error whenever temp is bigger than all elements to the left of it (i.e., the insertion point is 0).

19. **(E)** Note that i is initialized to 1, and after the final pass through the for loop, i equals a.length. Thus $1 \leq i \leq$ a.length, which eliminates choices A, C, and D. Eliminate choice B since there could be duplicates in the array and a[0] could equal a[1] ....

After initialization: $i = 1$ and a[0] is sorted.

After first pass: $i = 2$ and a[0] $\geq$ a[1].

After second pass: $i = 3$ and a[0] $\geq$ a[1] $\geq$ a[2].

$\vdots$

In general, after initialization and each time the for loop is completed, a[0] $\geq$ a[1] $\geq \cdots \geq$ a[i-1].

20. **(A)**

After 1st pass:	109	42	−3	13	89	70	2
After 2nd pass:	109	89	−3	13	42	70	2
After 3rd pass:	109	89	70	13	42	−3	2

21. **(A)** i is initialized to 0, and after the final pass through the for loop, i equals a.length − 1. Thus $0 \leq i \leq$ a.length − 1, which eliminates choices C and

D. Choice E is wrong because it implies that the whole array is sorted after each pass through the loop.

After initialization: $i = 0$, and no elements are sorted.

After first pass: $i = 1$, and a[0] is sorted.

After second pass: $i = 2$, and a[0] $\geq$ a[1].

$\vdots$

In general, after initialization and each time the for loop is completed, a[0] $\geq$ a[1] $\geq \cdots \geq$ a[i-1]. This rules out choice B.

22. **(A)** Look at a small array that is almost sorted:

$$10 \ 8 \ 9 \ 6 \ 2$$

For <u>insertion sort</u> you need four passes through this array.

The first pass compares 8 and 10—one comparison, no moves.

The second pass compares 9 and 8, then 9 and 10. The array becomes 10 9 8 6 2—two comparisons, two moves.

The third and fourth passes compare 6 and 8, and 2 and 6—no moves.

In summary, there are approximately one or two comparisons per pass and no more than two moves per pass.

For <u>selection sort</u>, there are four passes too.

The first pass finds the biggest element in the array and swaps it into the first position.

The array is still 10 8 9 6 2—four comparisons. There are two moves if your algorithm makes the swap in this case, otherwise no moves.

The second pass finds the biggest element from a[1] to a[4] and swaps it into the second position: 10 9 8 6 2—three comparisons, two moves.

For the third pass there are two comparisons, and one for the fourth. There are zero or two moves each time.

Summary: $4 + 3 + 2 + 1$ total comparisons and a possible two moves per pass. Notice that Reason I is valid. Selection sort makes the same number of comparisons irrespective of the state of the array. Insertion sort does far fewer comparisons if the array is almost sorted. Reason II is invalid. There are roughly the same number of data movements for insertion and selection. Insertion may even have more changes, depending on how far from their insertion points the unsorted elements are. Reason III is wrong because insertion and selection sorts have the same space requirements.

23. **(E)** In the first pass through the outer for loop, the smallest element makes its way to the end of the array. In the second pass, the next smallest element moves to the second last slot, and so on. This is different from the sorts in choices A through D; in fact, it is a bubble sort.

24. **(C)** Reject Reason I. Mergesort requires both a merge and a mergeSort method—*more* code than the relatively short and simple code for insertion sort. Reject Reason II. The merge algorithm uses a temporary array, which means *more* storage space than insertion sort. Reason III is correct. For long lists, the "divide-and-conquer" approach of mergesort gives it a faster run time than insertion sort.

25. **(D)** Since the search is for a four-letter sequence, the idea in this algorithm is that if you examine every fourth slot, you'll find a letter in the required

sequence very quickly. When you find one of these letters, you can then examine adjacent slots to check if you have the required sequence. This method will, on average, result in fewer comparisons than the strictly sequential search algorithm in choice A. Choice B is wrong. If you encounter a "q," "r," or "s" without a "p" first, you can't have found "pqrs." Choice C is wrong because you may miss the sequence completely. Choice E doesn't make sense.

26. **(C)** The main precondition for a binary search is that the list is ordered.

27. **(E)** This algorithm is just a recursive implementation of a sequential search. It starts by testing if the last element in the array, `a[n-1]`, is equal to `value`. If so, it returns the index `n-1`. Otherwise, it calls itself with `n` replaced by `n-1`. The net effect is that it examines `a[n-1]`, `a[n-2]`, ... The base case, `if (n == 0)`, occurs when there are no elements left to examine. In this case, the method returns -1, signifying that `value` was not in the array.

Level AB Only

28. **(D)** The `partition` algorithm performs a series of swaps until the pivot element is swapped into its final sorted position (see p. 413). No temporary arrays or external files are used, nor is a recursive algorithm invoked. The `merge` method is used for mergesort, not quicksort.

29. **(A)** An example of array a could be

$$2\ 6\ 8\ 1\ 3\ 4\ 5\ 10\ 12$$

In this case `mid` equals 2: `a[0]...a[2]` are sorted and `a[3]...a[8]` are sorted. The algorithm merges the two parts into

$$1\ 2\ 3\ 4\ 5\ 6\ 8\ 10\ 12$$

(Note: This merge method is needed whenever mergesort is used to sort an array.)

30. **(B)** Round 600 up to the next power of 2, which is $1024 = 2^{10}$. For the worst case, the array will be split in half $\log_2 1024 = 10$ times.

31. **(B)** If the list is sorted in reverse order, each pass through the array will involve the maximum possible number of comparisons and the maximum possible number of element movements if an insertion sort is used.

Level AB Only

32. **(C)** I violates the order property of a heap. II is not a complete binary tree.

33. **(D)** The elements will be inserted into the tree as shown, so the level of the tree is 3. (Remember that the top level of the tree is 0.)

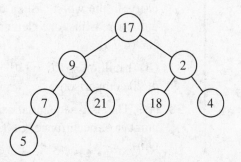

Level AB
(continued)

In fact, you don't need the tree or the actual elements!
The first element goes into level 0.
The next two elements go into level 1 (Total = 3).
The next four elements go into level 2 (Total = 7).
The next eight elements go into level 3 (Total = 15).
...and so on.
Since the given array has eight elements, you need a tree with three levels. (Note that the tree shown has not yet been formed into a heap.)

34. **(A)** The piece of code that forms the original heap is:

```
for (int rootIndex = (n/2)-1; rootIndex >= 0; rootIndex--)
    fixHeap(rootIndex,n-1);
```

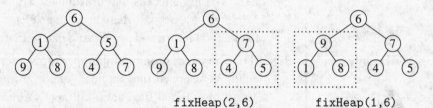

fixHeap(2,6)   fixHeap(1,6)

fixHeap(0,6)   Tree is now a heap

The sequence of swaps is:
    7 and 5
    9 and 1
    9 and 6
    8 and 6
This leads to choice A.

35. **(D)** Ideally in quicksort the pivot element should partition the array into two parts of roughly equal size. If the array is sorted and the pivot element is always the first (or last) element in the array, then one section of the array will always be empty after partitioning. This is a worst case for quicksort, $O(n^2)$. On the other hand, if the array is sorted and the pivot element is chosen near the middle of the array, quicksort will be very efficient.

36. **(D)** A sequential search, in the worst case, must examine all n elements—$O(n)$. In the worst case, a binary search will keep splitting the array in half until there is just one element left in the current subarray: $\log_2 n$ splits, which is $O(\log n)$.

37. **(B)** 1 million = $10^6 = (10^3)^2 \approx (2^{10})^2 = 2^{20}$. Thus, there will be on the order of 20 comparisons.

38. **(C)** This is a sequential search that examines each element and counts the number of occurrences of 8. Since n comparisons are made, the algorithm is $O(n)$.

Level AB
(continued)

39. **(B)** Mergesort works by breaking its array of n elements into n arrays of one element each, an $O(\log_2 n)$ process. Then it merges adjacent pairs of arrays until there is one sorted array, an $O(n)$ process. For each split of the array, the `merge` method is called. Thus, mergesort is $O(n \log n)$ irrespective of the original ordering of the elements.

Quicksort partitions the array into two parts. The algorithm is $O(n \log n)$ only if the two parts of the array are roughly equal in length. In the worst case, this is not true—the pivot is the smallest or largest element in the array. The partition method, an $O(n)$ process, will then be called n times, and the algorithm becomes $O(n^2)$.

The elements of heapsort are always placed in a balanced binary tree, which gives an $O(\log_2 n)$ process for fixing the heap. $n/2$ passes, each of which restores the heap, leads to an $O(n \log n)$ algorithm irrespective of the original ordering of the elements.

40. **(A)** A sequential search is $O(n)$, a binary search $O(\log n)$, and quicksort $O(n \log n)$. For any large positive n, $\log n < n < n \log n$.

41. **(C)** An efficient hash coding system must have as few collisions as possible (i.e., the hash addresses should be uniformly distributed throughout the table). When there are collisions, the method of allocating a new hash address should, again, distribute these addresses uniformly throughout the table. The size of the data items is irrelevant since a hash function operates just on a *key field* of the data items.

42. **(C)** Just before 29 is inserted, the table will look like this:

array index	0	1	2	3	4	5	6	7	8	9	10
key value		45	2	25			28	7	40		10

Now 29 % 11 = 7. Slots 7 and 8 are taken, so 29 goes into slot 9.

43. **(E)** Hash coded data must always be searched with a hash function applied to the key field, followed by an algorithm that resolves any collisions.

44. **(D)** In the rehash function, *result* is the current hash address. Choice A works for all numbers except 34. 34 % 20 hashes to 14, which is taken by 54. (14 + 13) % 20 rehashes to 7, which is where 34 would go if this were the correct answer. Choice B doesn't successfully resolve collisions: 34 % 20 hashes to 14, which is already taken by 54. 14 % 20 rehashes to 14, the same slot. Recall that a rehash function of the form (result + <const>) % <number of slots> must be such that <const> and <number of slots> are relatively prime (i.e., no common factors other than 1). Otherwise, the method won't generate all the hash table slots. This eliminates choice C. Choice E produces 30 slots, but the table shown has just 20 slots. Element 81, for example, has no slot under this scheme, since 81 % 30 is 21 and `list[21]` does not exist. Choice D successfully places all the numbers in the table.

45. **(D)** Reason I is valid—it's always desirable to hide implementation details from users of a method. Reason II is valid too—since `QuickSort` and `MergeSort` implement the `Sort` interface, they must have a `sort` method that takes just one parameter. But additional parameters are needed to make the

recursion work. Therefore each `sort` requires a helper method with additional parameters. Reason III is invalid in this particular example of helper methods. While there are many examples in which a helper method enhances efficiency (e.g., Example 2 on p. 225), the `sort` example is not one of them.

46. **(E)** Since `Sort` is an interface, you can't create an instance of it. This eliminates choices B and D. The `sort` methods alter the contents of their array parameter, `intArray`. Thus invoking `q.sort(intArray)` followed by `m.sort(intArray)` means that `m.sort` will always be called on a sorted array, assuming quicksort works correctly! In order to test both quicksort and mergesort on unsorted arrays, you need to make a copy of the original array, or create a different array. Eliminate choice A (and B again!), which does neither of these. Choice C is wrong because it calls the *private* `sort` methods of the classes. The `Sort` interface has just a single *public* method, `sort`, whose only argument is an array of `Comparable`. The two classes shown must provide an implementation for this `sort` method, and it is this method that must be invoked in the client program.

CHAPTER THIRTEEN
The Marine Biology Simulation Case Study

We have here other fish to fry.
—Francis Rabelais (1495–1553)

General Description

The case study is a program that simulates actions of fish in some environment, such as a lake, bay, or part of the ocean. The environment can be populated with fish from a data file that specifies the size of the environment, the number of fish, the type of fish, and the starting locations of the fish. Alternatively, a series of mouseclicks allows the initial conditions to be set up interactively.

Three types of fish populate the waters of the case study: so-called "normal" fish, as well as darter fish and slow fish.

The environment is modeled as a rectangular grid with fish moving from cell to cell in the grid. Each cell contains zero or one fish.

The simulation consists of a number of timesteps. In each timestep every fish has a chance to "act," where acting means:

- First it tries to breed, with a 1/7 probability. If it breeds, it fills all the empty adjacent cells with a baby fish. There are two cases in which it won't breed:

    1. It fails the probability test for breeding.
    2. It passes the probability test for breeding, but all the neighboring slots for babies are filled with other fish.

- If it fails to breed, it attempts to move. No fish ever moves backward. Also, if a fish is completely blocked by other fish and/or boundaries, that is, there are no available slots to move into, the fish will stay where it is. The three different fish types have different patterns of movement:

    1. A normal fish moves one space either forward or sideways. A slot is selected randomly with equal probability if there is more than one of these slots available. When the fish moves forward, it maintains its current direction. When it moves sideways, it changes direction to the direction in which it just moved.
    2. A darter fish can only move forward. If there are two empty spaces in front of it, it moves two spaces forward. If it can't move two spaces, it moves one space forward. If it can't move at all, because the cell in front of it is not empty, then it reverses its direction without moving.

3. A slow fish moves just like a normal fish. In each timestep, however, its probability of moving is just 1/5.

- Finally, the fish has a 1/5 probability of dying. When it dies, the slot that it occupies becomes vacant.

The Simulation Class

Description

The main job of the Simulation class is to provide a step method that executes just one timestep in the simulation, in which each fish is given the chance to act (breed or move, and possibly die).

In general, a class can be represented by a box diagram (shaded region) in which private instance variables and private instance methods are completely enclosed in the shaded region. Public instance methods overlap the shaded region.[1]

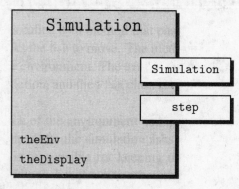

The diagram at right represents the Simulation class and shows that there is one constructor, one public method, step, and two private instance variables, theEnv and theDisplay.

Methods

```
public Simulation(Environment env, EnvDisplay display)
```

The constructor initializes theEnv and theDisplay to the env and display parameters. The Environment object is needed to provide the list of fish to the step method, and the EnvDisplay object is needed to display the state of the environment after a timestep.

```
public void step()
```

The step method carries out a single timestep of the simulation:

- It gets an array of Locatable objects (in this case, Fish) from the environment.

- It cycles through the array giving each fish a chance to act.

- It displays the environment.

- If debugging is turned on, it prints the state of the environment.

NOTE See page 462 for a review of the Environment, Locatable, and EnvDisplay interfaces.

---

[1] The class diagrams in this book are based on diagrams in *A Computer Science Tapestry* by Owen Astrachan, and diagrams by Alyce Brady in the case study narrative.

The Fish Class

Description

A Fish object has an awareness of its environment. It knows its location in the environment and its direction. Additionally it knows its identity number, color, probability of breeding, and probability of dying.

All of the methods in the Fish class are geared toward creating a Fish in its environment and having it perform an action (breeding or moving, and possibly dying).

Here is the box diagram for the Fish class.

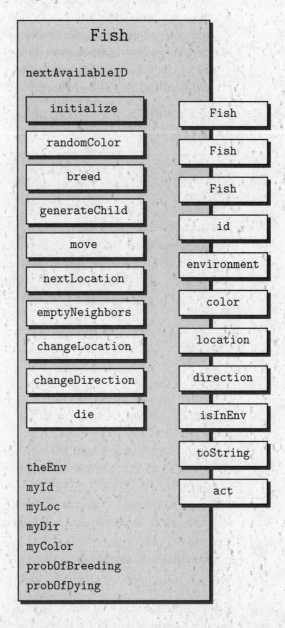

The diagram shows that there are three constructors and eight public methods. There is just one private method, initialize. This method will not be accessed by any other class. The nine other methods that are entirely enclosed inside the shaded region are *protected*. This means that while they are internal to the Fish class and will be used only to implement other Fish methods, they may be accessed by subclasses of Fish (for example, the DarterFish and SlowFish classes).

Notice nextAvailableID, a private static variable. This is a class variable, shared among all fish. It is initialized to 1 and used to give each Fish object an identification number when the fish is constructed. The constructor code increments nextAvailableID, which is then ready for the next new Fish object.

NOTE

1. Neither static variables nor protected methods will be tested on the AP exam. You must, however, understand their use within the context of the case study.
2. The original implementation of the Fish class (presented in Chapter 2 of the case study narrative) does not contain breed or die methods. In other words, the act method does little more than ask the fish to move. On the AP exam you will be expected to know the final, modified version (discussed in Chapter 3 of the case study) that includes breeding and dying.

Methods

Helper Methods for the Constructors

There are three constructors, each of which uses initialize, a private helper method.

```
private void initialize(Environment env, Location loc,
    Direction dir, Color col)
```

The initialize method initializes the theEnv, myLoc, myDir, and color instance variables from its parameters. It initializes myId from nextAvailableID, a class variable, and then increments nextAvailableID. The variables probOfBreeding and probOfDying are initialized to double values of 1.0/7.0 and 1.0/5.0, respectively. The initialize method also adds this Fish to the environment.

Another helper method used in two of the three constructors is randomColor.

```
protected Color randomColor()
```

The randomColor method generates a random color by randomly assigning the amount of red, green, and blue in a new Color object. The method uses the constructor in the Color class (see p. 474) that takes three integer parameters that denote the amount of red, green, and blue. Each int parameter must be in the range 0 to 255.

The Color class is a standard Java class found in java.awt. It is not part of the AP Java subset, but you are expected to be able to use the Color constructor and constants for questions on the case study. These will be documented in the Quick Reference provided on the AP exam (see p. 474).

The random numbers are generated using the RandNumGenerator class, a case study utility class (see p. 473). This has a single static method getInstance, which returns a Random object.

The Constructors

Each of the three constructors require that a client method constructing the fish specify the environment for the fish and its initial location in that environment.

```
public Fish(Environment env, Location loc)
```

The env and loc parameters are assigned to theEnv and myLoc by the initialize method. Additionally, `initialize` assigns a random direction to the fish using `env.randomDirection`, and a random color using `randomColor` (described on the previous page).

```
public Fish(Environment env, Location loc, Direction dir)
```

This constructor allows client code to specify a direction for the fish in addition to the environment and starting location. The `initialize` method assigns these parameters to the appropriate instance variables and additionally assigns a random color to the fish using `randomColor`.

```
public Fish(Environment env, Location loc, Direction dir,
    Color col)
```

In this constructor a client can specify both a direction and color for the fish, in addition to the environment and starting location. The `initialize` method assigns these parameters to the appropriate instance variables.

NOTE   In each of the above constructors, in addition to assigning values to `theEnv`, `myLoc`, `myDir`, and `myColor`, don't forget that the `initialize` method

- Assigns a double value of 1.0/7.0 to `probOfBreeding`.
- Assigns a double value of 1.0/5.0 to `probOfDying`.
- Assigns the current value of `nextAvailableID` to `myId`.
- Increments `nextAvailableID`.
- Adds this `Fish` object to its environment.

Accessors

```
public int id()
```

Returns the unique identification number for the fish.

```
public Environment environment()
```

Returns the fish's environment.

```
public Color color()
```

Returns the fish's color.

```
public Location location()
```

Returns the location of the fish in the environment. The `Fish` class has to provide a `location` method because it implements `Locatable` (see p. 464), an interface with the single method `location`. Note that `location` returns a `Location` object. A `Location` object has these methods: `row`, `col`, `equals`, `compareTo`, and `toString`. It also has a `hashCode` method that you won't be tested on.

```
public Direction direction()
```

Returns the direction that the fish is facing.

`public boolean isInEnv()`

Returns `true` if the fish is in the environment at the location where it thinks it is, `false` otherwise. If the program is running correctly, `isInEnv` should always return `true`. If, however, the environment is not properly updated when a fish moves or dies, the fish can get into an inconsistent state. This error will be detected by the `isInEnv` test.

`public String toString()`

Returns a string containing the fish's ID, location, and direction.

Mutator

`public void act()`

Here are the steps in the `act` method:

- Use the `isInEnv` method to check if the fish is alive and where it thinks it is. If not, return.
- Try to breed by calling the `breed` method.
- If the fish did not breed, try to move by calling the `move` method.
- Obtain a `Random` object to determine whether the fish will die in this timestep.
- If the random number obtained is within the 1 in 5 probability range for dying, call the `die` method.

Internal Helper Methods for `act`

`protected boolean breed()`

Returns `true` if the fish breeds, `false` otherwise. Here are the steps in the `breed` method:

- Obtain a `Random` object to determine whether the fish will breed in this timestep.
- If the random number obtained is within the 1 in 7 probability range for breeding, take these steps to breed:

  1. Get a list of adjacent empty neighbors.
  2. If there is at least one empty neighbor, cycle through the list and place a new fish in each location. Return `true`.
  3. If there are no available breeding locations, return `false`.

`protected void generateChild(Location loc)`

Creates a new fish that adds itself to the environment at the given location. The new fish has the color of its parent and a random direction. If debugging is turned on, information about the new fish will be printed.

`protected ArrayList emptyNeighbors()`

Returns an `ArrayList` containing the neighboring adjacent empty locations. Here is how the list is created:

- Get a list of all adjacent neighbors of the fish, empty or not. (Uses the `neighborsOf` method of the environment.)

- Cycle through this list and create a second list of empty neighbors only. (Uses the `isEmpty` test of the environment.)

- Return the list of empty neighbors.

```
protected void move()
```

Moves the fish in its environment, as follows:

- Determine the next location that the fish must move to. (Uses the method `nextLocation`.)

- If the new location is different from the current location (i.e., there was at least one valid empty neighbor)

  1. Change the fish's location to the new location.
  2. Get the direction that the fish moved. This will be the fish's new direction. (Uses `getDirection` from the environment.)
  3. Change the fish's direction to this new direction. (Uses the method `changeDirection`.) Note that the new direction will be different from the previous direction only if the the fish moved sideways.

NOTE   The steps above describe the movement of a normal fish and a slow fish (when it moves). The `move` method is overridden in the `DarterFish` class.

```
protected Location nextLocation()
```

Returns the next location for the fish. This method is called by the `move` method. A fish may move to any adjacent empty location except the one behind it. If there are no available locations, `nextLocation` returns the fish's current location. Here are the steps:

- Get an `ArrayList` of neighboring empty locations. (Uses the `emptyNeighbors` method.)

- Remove the location behind the fish as follows:

  1. Determine the direction opposite to the direction the fish is facing using the `reverse` method of the `Direction` class.
  2. Find the location behind the fish using the `getNeighbor` method of the environment. (This method takes a location and compass direction as parameters and returns the adjacent location in the specified direction.)
  3. Remove this location from the `ArrayList` of empty locations using the `remove(obj)` method of `ArrayList`.

- If debugging is turned on, print the list of possible new locations.

- If there are no valid empty neighboring locations, return the current location.

- Otherwise randomly select one of the locations in the `ArrayList` of empty neighbors and return it.

NOTE 1. The form of `remove` from an `ArrayList` used in no. 3 above is not in the AP Java subset. The form of `remove` that is in the subset takes an integer index as a parameter. The form used in the `nextLocation` method may be tested in the context of the case study.

2. The `nextLocation` method is for a normal fish only. The method is overridden in the `DarterFish` and `SlowFish` classes.

`protected void changeLocation(Location newLoc)`

Changes the fish's location to `newLoc` and records this change in the environment. This is done by assigning `newLoc` to `myLoc` and then calling the `recordMove` method of the environment.

`protected void changeDirection(Direction newDir)`

Changes the fish's direction to `newDir`.

`protected void die()`

Removes the fish from the environment. If debugging is turned on, the method prints information about the fish that's going to die. Then the fish is removed using the `remove` method of the environment.

The Different Fish Types

The case study presents three different types of fish, "normal" fish, which are encapsulated in the `Fish` superclass, plus darter fish and slow fish, which are described in the `DarterFish` and `SlowFish` subclasses:

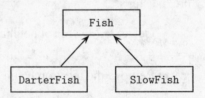

The `DarterFish` Class

A darter fish inherits all the attributes and behaviors of a normal fish. It differs from a normal fish in the way it moves. Like objects of the `Fish` superclass, a `DarterFish` object never moves in the same timestep as breeding. When it does move, however, a darter fish moves only forward, never sideways (or backward). If both the first and second cells in front of it are empty, it "darts" to the second cell. If the first cell is empty and the second cell is not, then the darter moves forward only one space. In each of these cases it maintains its current direction. If the first cell in front of a darter is not empty, then the darter fish reverses direction without changing its location.

Since the pattern of movement is different, the `move` and `nextLocation` methods of the `Fish` class are overridden in the `DarterFish` class.

Another method that must be overridden is the `generateChild` method of the `Fish` class. This is because the new babies are darter fish, not normal fish!

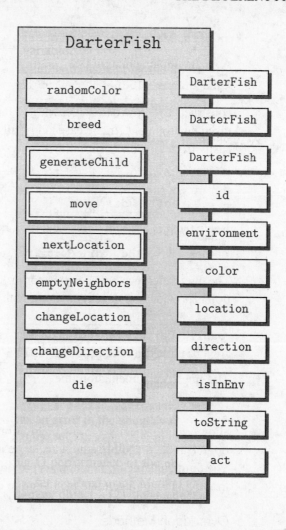

The diagram shows that a DarterFish has three constructors, and that it inherits all of the public and protected methods of the Fish class. It cannot access the private instance variables of Fish, so these are not shown in the diagram. It can, however, access them using the inherited accessor methods. The private helper method initialize of the Fish class is not accessible either. The DarterFish class, however, can indirectly make use of it by using the keyword super in its constructors.

The methods with a double frame in the diagram (generateChild, move, and nextLocation) are protected methods that are overridden in the DarterFish class.

Methods of
DarterFish

Constructors

Constructors are not inherited, and, as for the Fish class, three constructors are provided. In each case super is used with four parameters—Environment, Location, Direction, and Color—to assign values to the DarterFish attributes. Using super guarantees that the initialization code for DarterFish will be the same as for Fish, and that all attributes inherited from Fish will be similarly initialized for the darter fish.

> `public DarterFish(Environment env, Location loc)`

A single implementation line

```
super(env, loc, env.randomDirection(), Color.yellow);
```

constructs a yellow darter fish with a random direction at the given location in the given environment. In the case study, all darter fish are yellow to distinguish them easily from the other fish in the display.

> `public DarterFish(Environment env, Location loc,`
> `    Direction dir)`

Again there is a single implementation line

```
super(env, loc, dir, Color.yellow);
```

The only difference between this constructor and the previous one is that the direction is provided by the client, along with the location and environment.

> `public DarterFish(Environment env, Location loc,`
> `    Direction dir, Color col)`

The single implementation line

```
super(env, loc, dir, col);
```

allows you to specify a color in addition to the environment, location, and direction. This seems to be redundant, since all darter fish in the case study are yellow. The third constructor, however, is provided to keep the program general: someone modifying it at a later date may want to define darters with different colors.

Overridden Methods

> `protected void generateChild(Location loc)`

Creates a new darter fish at the given location. The code is identical to that in the `Fish` class, except that the child generated is of type `DarterFish`, not `Fish`.

> `protected Location nextLocation()`

Returns the location that the darter fish will move to. Here's what it does:

- If the cell in front of the darter, `oneInFront`, is empty, it examines the cell in front of that, `twoInFront`.
- If both these cells are empty, the method returns `twoInFront`, otherwise it returns `oneInFront`.
- If `oneInFront` is not empty, it returns the current location of the fish.

> `protected void move()`

Moves the darter forward as specified in `nextLocation` (see previous method). Since the distinguishing characteristics of `DarterFish` movement have been taken care of in the `nextLocation` method, the code for `move` is the same as that in `Fish`. The one difference is that, at the end, if the darter didn't move, it reverses direction. The code provides a debugging statement to reflect this.

The SlowFish
Class

A slow fish, like the darter, inherits all the attributes and behaviors of a normal fish. It differs from a normal fish in that when it doesn't breed in a given timestep, it only has a 1 in 5 chance of moving to an adjacent cell. When it *does* move, however, its pattern of movement is identical to that of a fish from the Fish class.

To implement the change, a new private instance variable, probOfMoving, is added to the SlowFish class. The test for whether a slow fish will move or not is provided in the nextLocation method, which must therefore be overridden. The move method, however, does not change and need not be redefined.

As with darter fish, the generateChild method must be overridden to reflect the fact that when a SlowFish breeds, the type of new fish created is a SlowFish.

Here is the box diagram for the SlowFish class:

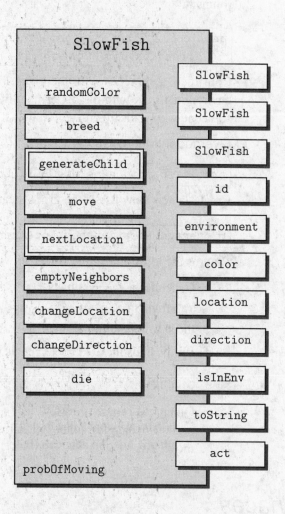

The diagram shows all the inherited public and protected methods of the Fish class and the new private instance variable probOfMoving. It also shows that there are three constructors and that generateChild and nextLocation are overridden.

Methods of
SlowFish

Constructors

As with the DarterFish class, the constructors are not inherited and must be defined in the SlowFish class. Again the keyword super must be used to initialize the instance variables inherited from Fish. In addition to these variables, the new instance variable `probOfMoving` must be initialized to `1.0/5.0`. Note that in the case study the slow fish are all red.

Here are the headers for the three constructors for `SlowFish`:

```
public SlowFish(Environment env, Location loc)
```

Constructs a red slow fish with a random direction at the given location in the given environment.

```
public SlowFish(Environment env, Location loc, Direction dir)
```

Constructs a red slow fish with the given location and direction in the given environment.

```
public SlowFish(Environment env, Location loc,
    Direction dir, Color col)
```

Constructs a slow fish with the given location, direction, and color in the given environment. As with the darter fish, this constructor is to provide flexibility for someone who wants to create a slow fish with a color other than red.

Overridden Methods

```
protected void generateChild(Location loc)
```

Creates a new slow fish at the given location.

```
protected Location nextLocation()
```

Returns the location that the slow fish will move to. Here's what it does:

- Generates a `Random` object.
- Tests whether the random number is within the probability range (1/5) for the slow fish to move.
- If it is, finds the `nextLocation` as for the `Fish` class, using the statement

  ```
  return super.nextLocation();
  ```

- Otherwise returns the slow fish's current location and, if debugging is on, prints a debugging statement to the effect that the fish was not attempting to move.

The Interfaces

The `Environment` Interface

Description

An environment object in the program models a rectangular grid of objects and keeps track of the number and location of these objects as they move or disappear. It also records the appearance of new objects in the environment.

In the marine biology simulation program, the objects are fish. They could, however, be any objects in a grid-like environment, and for this reason `Environment` is presented as an interface in the program.

NOTE

1. Level A students will not be asked to modify the environment and can treat it like a black box (i.e., an object whose internal workings are hidden). You must, however, be familiar with the public methods of `Environment` (see below).
2. Level AB students must know both the `BoundedEnv` and `UnboundedEnv` classes that implement the `Environment` interface (see p. 466). You may be asked to modify the methods in these classes or to write other classes that implement `Environment`.

Methods

```
public int numRows()
```

Returns the number of rows in this environment (`-1` if the environment is unbounded).

```
public int numCols()
```

Returns the number of columns in this environment (`-1` if the environment is unbounded).

```
public boolean isValid(Location loc)
```

Returns `true` if `loc` is valid in this environment, otherwise returns `false`. The validity of a location depends on the implementation of `Environment`. For example, in a bounded environment, an out-of-bounds location would be invalid. In all implementations, if `loc` is `null`, `isValid` should return `false`.

```
public int numCellSides()
```

Returns the number of sides around each cell. In a normal rectangular grid with rectangular cells, `numCellSides` should return 4. But imagine a grid where cells are hexagonal. Then `numCellSides` should return 6.

```
public int numAdjacentNeighbors()
```

Returns the number of adjacent neighbors around each cell. For a square cell, this method will return 4 or 8 depending on whether adjacent neighbors share just sides or sides and corners. This will be determined by an environment class constructor.

```
public Direction randomDirection()
```

Generates a random direction.

```
public Direction getDirection(Location fromLoc,
    Location toLoc)
```

Returns the direction from one location to another.

```
public Location getNeighbor(Location fromLoc,
    Direction compassDir)
```

Returns the adjacent neighbor of a location in the specified direction (whether valid or invalid).

```
public java.util.ArrayList neighborsOf(Location ofLoc)
```

Returns the adjacent neighbors of a specified location. Only neighbors that are valid locations in the environment will be included.

```
public int numObjects()
```

Returns the number of objects in this environment.

```
public Locatable[] allObjects()
```

Returns an array of all the objects in this environment.

```
public boolean isEmpty(Location loc)
```

Returns `true` if `loc` is a valid location in the context of this environment and is empty, `false` otherwise.

```
public Locatable objectAt(Location loc)
```

Returns the object at location `loc`. Returns `null` if `loc` is not in the environment or is empty.

```
public void add(Locatable obj)
```

Adds a new object `obj` to this environment at the location specified by `obj`. Precondition: `obj.location()` is a valid empty location.

```
public void remove(Locatable obj)
```

Removes the object `obj` from the environment. Precondition: `obj` is in this environment.

```
public void recordMove((Locatable obj, Location oldLoc)
```

Updates the environment to reflect the fact that an object has moved. Precondition: `obj.location()` is a valid location, and there is no other object there. Postcondition: `obj` is at the appropriate location, `obj.location()`, and either `oldLoc` is equal to `obj.location()` (there was no movement) or `oldLoc` is empty.

The Locatable Interface

The `Locatable` interface has a single method:

```
Location location()
```

Returns a `Location` object (see p. 472).

All objects in the environment must be `Locatable`, which means that their classes must have a `location` method. The `Fish`, `DarterFish`, and `SlowFish` objects are all `Locatable`: `Fish` provides the accessor method, `location`, and its derived classes inherit it.

The EnvDisplay Interface

The `EnvDisplay` interface has a single method:

```
void showEnv()
```

Shows the current state of the environment. Classes that implement `EnvDisplay` in the case study are black boxes whose implementations are hidden. What you need to know is that the Simulation class has an object of type EnvDisplay that calls the showEnv method at the end of the step method.

The SquareEnvironment *Class*

Level AB Only

Level AB students need to know how the Environment interface is implemented. You need to understand the documentation for the SquareEnvironment class which is presented as a black box class in the case study. You must, however, have a detailed knowledge of the BoundedEnv and UnboundedEnv classes.

SquareEnvironment is an abstract class that implements the Environment interface. It implements only those Environment methods needed for an environment of square cells whose neighbors are north, south, east, and west.

Here is the box diagram for the SquareEnvironment class:

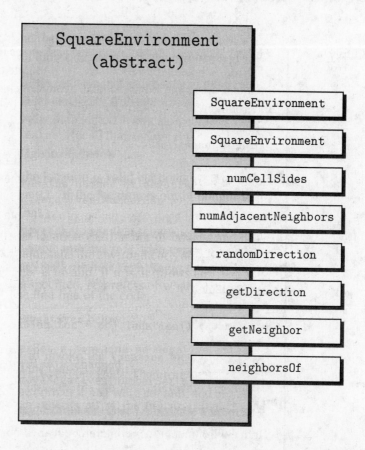

The diagram shows that the class has two constructors and six public methods. The other methods of the Environment interface are abstract and are therefore not shown in the diagram. The documentation for the methods is as described for the Environment interface on p. 463. The constructors are discussed next.

The SquareEnvironment Constructors

```
public SquareEnvironment()
```

Constructs a SquareEnvironment object in which each cell has four adjacent neighbors. (Each neighbor shares one of the cell's sides.)

Level AB
(continued)

> ```
> public SquareEnvironment(boolean includeDiagonalNeighbors)
> ```

Constructs a `SquareEnvironment` object in which cells have four or eight adjacent neighbors, depending on the value of `includeDiagonalNeighbors`. If this parameter is `true`, each cell will have eight adjacent neighbors—the adjacent neighbors on each of the four sides and the four neighbors on the diagonals (namely those neighbors that share a corner point with the cell). If `includeDiagonalNeighbors` is `false`, however, then each cell will have only four adjacent neighbors, as for a `SquareEnvironment` created with the default constructor.

NOTE   If a cell is on the boundary of a bounded environment, not all of its adjacent neighbors will be valid.

The BoundedEnv *and* UnboundedEnv *Classes*

Level AB Only

The environment classes provide a habitat for the fish in the marine biology simulation. A bounded environment is a bounded, two-dimensional grid of fish—a confined area, like a bay or lake, from which fish can't escape. An unbounded environment is a two-dimensional, grid-like expanse, like part of the ocean, containing fish that can move in and out of the environment.

Both `BoundedEnv` and `UnboundedEnv` extend `SquareEnvironment` (which implements `Environment`). This means that each class will contain the sixteen public methods of the `Environment` interface, inherited from the `SquareEnvironment` class.

The diagram on the next page represents both the `BoundedEnv` and `UnboundedEnv` classes. The diagram indicates that each class has a single constructor, the sixteen methods of `Environment`, and an overridden `toString` method. The six methods from `numCellSides` through `neighborsOf` are inherited from `SquareEnvironment`. `BoundedEnv` has two private instance variables, `theGrid` and `objectCount`, while `UnboundedEnv` has a single instance variable, `objectList`. Additionally, `indexOf` is a protected helper method in `UnboundedEnv`:

> ```
> protected int indexOf(Location loc)
> ```

Returns the index of the object at location `loc`, or –1 if there is no object at `loc`. The method is used in the `objectAt` and `remove` methods.

How the Environment Is Implemented

Both environment types contain `Locatable` objects (`Fish` are `Locatable`).

BoundedEnv	UnboundedEnv
`theGrid` is a two-dimensional array of `Locatable` objects. `objectCount` maintains a count of the number of objects in the current environment.	`objectList` is an `ArrayList` of `Locatable` objects.

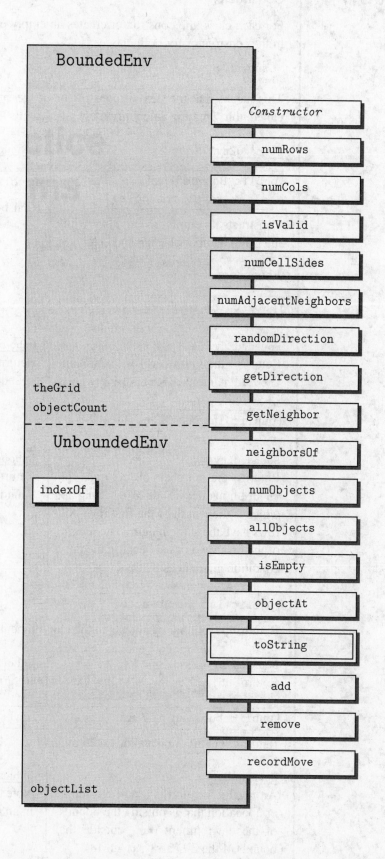

Level AB Only

Constructor

For each class, the constructor creates an empty environment. The first statement in the constructor for both classes is

```
super();
```

This means that the default constructor of the superclass `SquareEnvironment` is called, thus creating an environment whose cells have four adjacent neighbors.

BoundedEnv

```
public BoundedEnv(
    int rows, int cols)
```

Constructs an empty `BoundedEnv` with the given number of `rows` and `cols`.

UnboundedEnv

```
public UnboundedEnv()
```

Constructs an empty `UnboundedEnv`.

Accessors

```
public int numRows()
```

BoundedEnv

Returns the number of rows in `theGrid`, namely `theGrid.length`.

UnboundedEnv

Returns -1 since the environment is unbounded.

```
public int numCols()
```

BoundedEnv

Returns the number of columns in `theGrid`, namely `theGrid[0].length`, which is the length of the first row. All rows have the same length. The length of the first row is used because the precondition guarantees that `rows > 0`.

UnboundedEnv

Returns -1 since the environment is unbounded.

```
public int numObjects()
```

Returns the number of objects in the environment.

BoundedEnv

Returns `objectCount`.

UnboundedEnv

Returns `objectList.size()`.

```
public boolean isValid(Location loc)
```

Returns `true` if `loc` is valid, `false` otherwise.

BoundedEnv

An invalid location is a null reference or a location that is outside the bounds of the environment (i.e., outside the bounds of the 2-D array, `theGrid`).

UnboundedEnv

Note that all nonnull locations are valid in an unbounded environment.

Level AB
(continued)

```
public Locatable objectAt(Location loc)
```

Returns the object at the given location, `loc`.

BoundedEnv	UnboundedEnv
Returns	The method uses these steps:

BoundedEnv
Returns

```
theGrid[loc.row()][loc.col()]
```

Returns null if `loc` is empty or `loc` is out of bounds.

UnboundedEnv
The method uses these steps:

- Finds the index of `loc` using the `indexOf` helper method.
- Checks if `loc` is outside the environment by testing if index is −1.
- If `loc` is in the environment, returns the object at that index of the `ArrayList`.

Returns null if `loc` is empty or not in the environment.

```
public boolean isEmpty(Location loc)
```

Returns `true` if `loc` is both valid and empty, `false` otherwise.

BoundedEnv
Uses the statement

```
return isValid(loc) &&
    objectAt(loc) == null;
```

The validity check is needed because the `objectAt(loc) == null` part of the test will return `true` if `loc` is out of bounds, which is not the intent of this method: `isEmpty` must return `false` if `loc` is out of bounds.

UnboundedEnv
Note that all locations in an unbounded environment are valid, so all that needs to be tested is whether the object at `loc` is null—if yes, `isEmpty` is `true`; if no, `isEmpty` is `false`.

```
public Locatable[] allObjects()
```

Returns an array of all the objects in the environment.

BoundedEnv
Steps through `theGrid` row by row from top to bottom, left to right (row-major order), retrieving the object at each position and inserting it in the array if the retrieved object is not null.

UnboundedEnv
Creates the array by

- Declaring an array with `objectList.size()` slots.
- Cycling through `objectList`, retrieving each object, casting it to `Locatable`, and inserting it in the array.

```
public String toString()
```

Returns a single string that represents all the objects in the environment, in no

Level AB
(continued)

particular order. It does this by

- Initializing `String` `s` to a string with the number of objects in the environment.
- Calling `allObjects`.
- Traversing the returned array, concatenating each object to `String` `s`.

Note that the statement that does the concatenating in the last step,

```
s += theObjects[index].toString() + " ";
```

will automatically use the `toString` method of the `Fish` class, since the actual objects in the array are `Fish`. This is an example of polymorphism. Note that the code in the `BoundedEnv` class is identical to that in the `UnboundedEnv` class.

Modifiers

`public void add(Locatable obj)`

Adds a new object `obj` to the environment at the location specified by the object. A precondition for `add` is that it's a valid empty location. The method throws an `IllegalArgumentException` if the precondition is violated. Here are the steps:

BoundedEnv

- Check the precondition and throw an exception if it's not met.
- Insert `obj` into `theGrid` at the row and column indicated by `obj.location()`.
- Increment `objectCount`.

UnboundedEnv

- Get its location from the object.
- Check for empty—throw an exception if not empty.
- If it is empty, use the add method of `ArrayList` to add the object to `objectList`.

`public void remove(Locatable obj)`

Removes object `obj` from the environment. The precondition is that `obj` is in the environment. If it isn't, the method throws an `IllegalArgumentException`. Here are the steps:

BoundedEnv

- If `obj` is not in the environment at the location specified by `obj`, throw an exception.
- If `obj` is where is says it should be, `remove` puts a null reference in its place in `theGrid` and decrements `objectCount`.

UnboundedEnv

- Find the index of the object to be removed, using `indexOf(obj.location())`.
- If the index is -1, it means that `obj` is not in the environment—the method then throws the exception.
- Otherwise the object at that index is removed using the `remove(index)` method of `ArrayList`.

Level AB
(continued)

```
public void recordMove(Locatable obj, Location oldLoc)
```

Updates the environment after an object attempts to move. As a precondition, `obj.location()` is a valid location and there is no other object there. The postcondition has `obj` at `obj.location()` and either `oldLoc` is empty or `oldLoc` equals `obj.location()`, in which case there was no movement. The method throws an `IllegalArgumentException` if these conditions are violated. Here are the steps:

BoundedEnv

- Test whether `obj.location()` equals `oldLoc`. If true, there was no movement, so do nothing.

- Check the precondition: `obj.location()`, which is the object's new location, should be empty and the object at `oldLoc` should be `obj`, the parameter. If the precondition is violated, the method throws the exception.

- Move the object to its proper location in `theGrid`.

- Set the old location to null.

UnboundedEnv

The documentation and method name are somewhat misleading in the `UnboundedEnv` class. This is because the `ArrayList` does not actually keep track of its objects' locations. It simply uses the fact that all the objects in it are `Locatable` (i.e., change their locations when they move). Therefore all `recordMove` does is check that a valid move was made. Here are the steps:

- Assign `obj.location()` to `newLoc`.

- Cycle through `objectList` and count how many objects are at `newLoc` and how many at `oldLoc`.

- For the move to have been valid

    1. `objectsAtNewLoc` must equal 1, and
    2. if `oldLoc` does not equal `newLoc`, `objectsAtOldLoc` must equal 0.

- If the above conditions are violated, the exception is thrown, with a message that the precondition was violated.

The Utility Classes

There are four utility classes that are provided as black boxes. This means that you don't need to know the implementations, but you do need to know how their methods are used in the case study, and how to use the methods to modify case study code.

The Debug Class

```
static boolean isOn()
static boolean isOff()
static void turnOn()
static void turnOff()
static void restoreState()
static void print(String message)
static void println(String message)
```

The Debug.print and Debug.println methods are just like System.out.print and System.out.println, except that the string will be printed only if debugging has been turned on. You can turn debugging on and off by inserting Debug.turnOn() and Debug.turnOff() at appropriate places in the code. Any debugging messages that occur between these two statements will be printed when you run the code. Note that all of the Debug methods are static and, therefore, must be invoked with the class name followed by the dot member construct, as in Debug.print(...

The Direction Class

```
NORTH, EAST, SOUTH, WEST, NORTHEAST,
NORTHWEST, SOUTHEAST, SOUTHWEST

Direction()
Direction(int degrees)
Direction(String str)
int inDegrees()
boolean equals(Object other)
Direction toRight()
Direction toRight(int degrees)
Direction toLeft()
Direction toLeft(int degrees)
Direction reverse()
String toString()
static Direction randomDirection()
```

The following are not tested:

```
FULL_CIRCLE
int hashCode()
Direction roundedDir(int numDirections, Direction startingDir)
```

The Direction class represents a compass direction. The class provides several public constants, like Direction.EAST and Direction.NORTHWEST. Objects of type Direction are used by the fish and environment classes. A fish knows its own direction and is able to change its direction. The environment can get a random direction from a given cell to an adjacent neighbor; can get a neighboring cell that's in a given direction; and, given two cells, can return the direction from one to the other.

The Location Class

```
Location(int row, int col)
int row()
int col()
boolean equals(Object other)
int compareTo(Object other)
String toString()
```

The following is not tested:

```
int hashCode()
```

A `Location` object represents the row and column of a cell in the environment. All of the fish are `Locatable` objects, which means that they implement the `Locatable` interface. This means that they must provide a `location` method that returns a `Location` object. A fish knows its location and can change it. An environment can test if a location is valid, can generate a list of adjacent locations, can get a neighboring location in a given direction, can add and remove objects at a given location, and can record the move that a fish makes from one location to another.

The RandNumGenerator Class

```
static Random getInstance()
```

The `getInstance` method of this class returns a `Random` object that will be used to generate random numbers. The class is set up in such a way that only one `Random` object will be used in a given program, no matter how many times random numbers are generated. If this were not done, the program could generate sequences of random numbers that are not very random.

The `getInstance` method is static. Here is how it is used to get the `Random` object used in the program:

```
Random r = RandNumGenerator.getInstance();
```

Now the `nextInt` and `nextDouble` methods of `Random` can be used, depending on what is needed (see p. 118).

Random numbers are used throughout the case study:

- To generate a random color for a fish.
- To generate a random direction for a fish or for a cell in the environment.
- To test whether a fish will breed and whether a fish will die.
- To test whether a slow fish will move.
- To select the next location for a fish move, given that there's more than one available location.

The Java Library Utility Classes

The java.util.ArrayList Class

Methods for the case study:

```
boolean add(Object o)
void add(int index, Object o)
Object get(int index)
Object remove(int index)
boolean remove(Object o)
Object set(int index, Object o)
int size()
```

ArrayList is a standard Java class (see p. 371). It is used in the case study for lists of objects in which the final length of the list is not initially known:

- The neighborsOf method in the environment returns an ArrayList of valid adjacent neighbors for a given location.

- The emptyNeighbors method of the Fish class returns an ArrayList of adjacent empty locations.

Level AB Only

- The UnboundedEnv class implements the environment as an ArrayList of Locatable objects.

The java.awt.Color Class

Constants and methods for the case study:

```
black, blue, cyan, gray, green, magenta,
orange, pink, red, white, yellow

Color(int r, int g, int b)
```

This class is used to provide a fish with a color. The class has many color constants (only some of which are shown) and a constructor, whose three parameters are integers in the range 0 to 255. These provide the amount of red, green, and blue in a color. The class does not have a randomColor method—this is provided in the Fish class, whose constructors allow the creation of a fish with a random color.

The java.util.Random Class

Methods for the case study:

```
int nextInt(int n)
double nextDouble()
```

This class is described on p. 118 and is used to implement the RandNumGenerator class (see the description on the previous page).

The Case Study and the AP Exam

At least one-fourth of the AP exam will be devoted to questions on the case study. (This means at least five multiple-choice questions and one free-response question.)

Both level A and AB students will be tested on Chapters 1–4 of the case study. You must be familiar with the Fish, DarterFish, SlowFish, and Simulation classes, including their implementations. You should also be familiar with the documentation for the Environment, Locatable, and EnvDisplay interfaces; the Debug, Direction, Location, and RandNumGenerator utility classes; and the subset of methods that are used in the ArrayList, Color, and Random classes.

On the AP exam, all students will be provided with a Quick Reference that contains a list of methods for the preceding classes and interfaces. You will also receive source code for the Simulation, Fish, DarterFish, and SlowFish classes. The Fish class will contain the modifications for breeding and dying.

Only level AB students need to know Chapter 5 of the case study. This includes the documentation for the SquareEnvironment abstract class, plus documentation and implementation of the `BoundedEnv` and `UnboundedEnv` classes. The Quick Reference for level AB students will include the documentation for all the environment classes. You will also receive source code for the `BoundedEnv` and `UnboundedEnv` classes.

NOTE

- On the Quick Reference, private and protected methods will be in italics.
- The Marine Biology Simulation, including documentation, narrative, and code, can be found at this web site: *http://www.collegeboard.com/ap/students/compsci.*

Multiple-Choice Questions on the Case Study

Some of the questions in this section provide code from the case study. On the AP exam, code will not be reproduced in the questions, since you will be provided with a copy of all tested code.

1. For the SlowFish 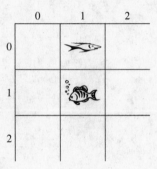 shown in location (1,1), which is a valid candidate for nextLocation()?

I (1,0)
II (1,1)
III (2,1)

(A) I only
(B) II only
(C) III only
(D) I and III only
(E) I, II, and III

2. Which class is responsible for adding a Fish object to the environment?
(A) Environment
(B) Fish
(C) BoundedEnv
(D) Simulation
(E) EnvDisplay

3. Which is a *false* statement about the use of random numbers in the Marine Biology Simulation program? Random numbers are used to
(A) Test if a fish will breed.
(B) Test if a fish will die.
(C) Test if a darter fish will move, given that it didn't breed.
(D) Test if a slow fish will move, given that it didn't breed.
(E) Give a fish a random color.

4. Which of the following best characterizes an object of the BoundedEnv class?
(A) A collection of square locations
(B) A two-dimensional grid of four-sided cells
(C) A bounded body of water containing fish
(D) A two-dimensional grid of Location objects
(E) A two-dimensional grid of Locatable objects

5. The `step` method of the `Simulation` class has a single statement in its `for` loop:

```
for (int index=0; index<theFishes.length; index++)
{
    ((Fish) theFishes[index]).act();
}
```

What would be the effect of omitting the cast of `theFishes[index]` to Fish, that is, replacing the statement with

```
theFishes[index].act();
```

(A) A compiler error will occur with a message to the effect that class `Locatable` does not contain an act method.

(B) The program will run without error, since `act` is a polymorphic method.

(C) A `ClassCastException` will be thrown.

(D) A `NullPointerException` will be thrown.

(E) An `ArrayIndexOutOfBoundsException` will be thrown.

6. Which is true about a class that implements the `Locatable` interface?

(A) It must extend the `Location` class.

(B) It must provide a `location` method.

(C) It must provide a `compareTo` method.

(D) It must provide an `equals` method.

(E) It must provide accessor methods to return its row and column.

7. Which is the *least* suitable class to implement the `Locatable` interface?

(A) A `ChessPiece` on a chess board

(B) An `Address` in a city

(C) A `Point` in three-dimensional space

(D) An `Element` in a matrix

(E) An `Animal` in a zoo

8. If `fromLoc` is the location $(3, 5)$, what is returned by this expression?

```
env.getNeighbor(fromLoc, Direction.SOUTH)
```

(A) $(2, 5)$

(B) $(3, 4)$

(C) $(4, 5)$

(D) $(3, 6)$

(E) Not enough information. You need to know the fish's direction.

9. Consider the `emptyNeighbors` method of the `Fish` class:

```
/** Finds empty locations adjacent to this fish.
 *  Returns an ArrayList containing neighboring
 *  empty locations **/
protected ArrayList emptyNeighbors()
{
    // Get all the neighbors of this fish, empty or not.
    ArrayList nbrs = environment().neighborsOf(location());

    // Figure out which neighbors are empty and add those
    // to a new list.
    ArrayList emptyNbrs = new ArrayList();
    for (int index = 0; index < nbrs.size(); index++)
    {
        Location loc = (Location) nbrs.get(index);
        if (environment().isEmpty(loc))
            emptyNbrs.add(loc);
    }

    return emptyNbrs;
}
```

Which of the following configurations of the `BoundedEnv` do not test the `if` statement of the method, if the method is called for the fish in (0,0)?

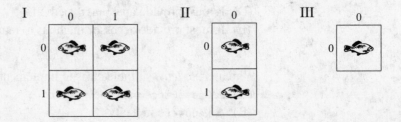

(A) I only
(B) II only
(C) III only
(D) II and III only
(E) I, II, and III

10. Consider the small bounded environment shown, containing a slow fish 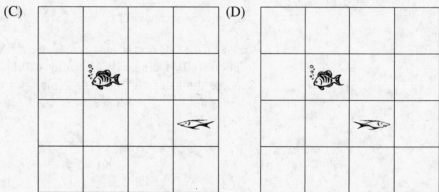 and a darter 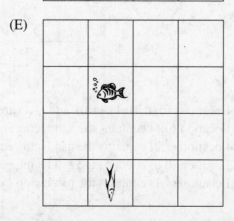.

A *valid* setup after a call to act *for the darter fish only* is

11. Consider the small 3 × 3 bounded environment, env, shown below. What locations would you expect in the ArrayList returned by the call to env.neighborsOf(loc), where loc is the location (1,2)?

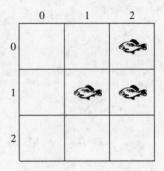

(A) (2,2)

(B) (2,1), (2,2), (0,1)

(C) (0,2), (1,1)

(D) (0,2), (1,1), (2,2)

(E) (0,2), (1,1), (2,2), (1,3)

12. Which of the following pieces of code, added to the main method, will correctly add a new fish f1 to the environment env?

(A) `Fish f1 = new Fish(env, loc); //loc is valid empty location`
    `env.add(f1);`

(B) `f1.breed();`

(C) `f1.move();`

(D) `Fish f1 = new Fish(env, loc); //loc is valid empty location`

(E) `env.recordMove(f1, newLoc);  //newLoc is new location of f1`

13. Consider a Fish object in a BoundedEnv. At its turn to act, the fish is in location (0,0), facing east. Locations (0,1), (1,0), and (1,1) are all empty. Suppose the fish fails to breed. Which is a valid situation at the end of the timestep?

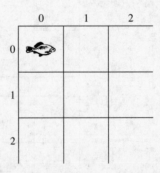

(A) Locations (0,0), (0,1), (1,0), and (1,1) are all empty.

(B) Location (0,1) contains the fish facing south.

(C) Location (1,0) contains the fish facing east.

(D) Location (0,0) contains the fish facing east.

(E) Location (1,1) contains the fish facing east.

14. Consider the `nextLocation` method of the `Fish` class. The first line of the implementation is

    ```
    ArrayList emptyNbrs = emptyNeighbors();
    ```

    What would be the effect of replacing this line with

    ```
    ArrayList emptyNbrs = environment().neighborsOf(location());
    ```

    and making no other changes to the implementation code?

    The `nextLocation` method

    I May return a location that is not empty.
    II May return the location behind this `Fish`.
    III Would *never* return the current location of this `Fish`.

    (A) I only
    (B) II only
    (C) III only
    (D) I and III only
    (E) I, II, and III

15. If a `Fish` f is in an $m \times n$ `BoundedEnv` env, $m > 1$ and $n > 1$, and the current location of f is (0,0), what will be returned by

    (1) `f.emptyNeighbors().size()`
    (2) `env.neighborsOf(f.location()).size()`

    (A)   (1) 2
          (2) 2

    (B)   (1) 4
          (2) 2

    (C)   (1) 2
          (2) 4

    (D)   (1) Insufficient information to determine
          (2) 2

    (E)   (1) Insufficient information to determine
          (2) Insufficient information to determine

16. In a 3×5 bounded environment env, which of the following locations loc is *not* guaranteed to return an `ArrayList` of size 2 for the call `env.neighborsOf(loc)`?
    (A) (0,0)
    (B) (0,1)
    (C) (0,4)
    (D) (2,0)
    (E) (2,4)

17. Consider the following incorrect implementation for the `changeLocation` method in the `Fish` class (the lines are numbered for reference):

```
1   protected void changeLocation(Location newLoc)
2   {
3       Location oldLoc = location();
4       location() = newLoc;
5       environment().recordMove(this, oldLoc);
6   }
```

Which of the following changes will fix the code?

(A) Replace line 3 with

```
Location oldLoc = myLoc;
```

and make no other changes.

(B) Replace line 4 with

```
myLoc = newLoc;
```

and make no other changes.

(C) Replace line 5 with

```
environment().recordMove(this, location());
```

and make no other changes.

(D) Replace line 5 with

```
environment().recordMove(this, newLoc);
```

and make no other changes.

(E) Omit line 5 and make no other changes.

18. Consider the 3 × 3 `BoundedEnv` shown below.

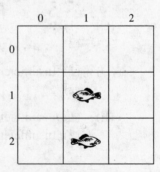

When the `Fish` in location (1,1) is about to move, which of the following contains all the valid locations that could be returned by `nextLocation`?

(A) (0,0), (0,1), (0,2), (1,0), (1,2), (2,0), (2,2)
(B) (0,1), (1,0), (1,2)
(C) (0,1), (1,0)
(D) (1,0)
(E) (0,1), (1,2)

Questions 19 and 20 refer to the idea of changing the program in a way that allows fish to age. A fish will start out with an age of 1 at its creation, and will have its age incremented by 1 each time it breeds or moves. The probability of breeding will decrease as a fish ages, and the probability of dying will increase as it ages. These probabilities will be the same for the Fish, DarterFish, and SlowFish.

19. Which groups of methods in the Fish class are likely to be modified to reflect these changes?

     I initialize
    II act, breed, move
   III generateChild

  (A) I only
  (B) II only
  (C) III only
  (D) I and II only
  (E) I, II, and III

20. In addition to the Fish class, which of the following classes should be altered to allow a fish to age?

     I DarterFish
    II SlowFish
   III BoundedEnv

  (A) none
  (B) I only
  (C) II only
  (D) III only
  (E) I and II only

21. Consider a data file that provides the initial configuration of fish in the environment. Which of the following situations should guarantee an error?

     I A file with valid dimensions but no fish
    II A file with a fish in every location in the environment
   III A file with two or more fish in the same location

  (A) I only
  (B) II only
  (C) III only
  (D) I and III only
  (E) I, II, and III

22. Which of the following is necessary to guarantee that every run of the program displays the same fish behavior?

    I The same seed value for the random number generator
    II The same input file containing configurations of fish in the environment
    III The same debugging state

    (A) I only
    (B) II only
    (C) III only
    (D) I and II only
    (E) I, II, and III

23. The original programmer of the Marine Biology Simulation program considered several different designs for the program. Which of the following most closely corresponds to the design actually chosen by the programmer?

    (A) The `Simulation` `step` method is called by a method that passes it a list of fish. The `Simulation` class asks the fish to move. The method calling `step` keeps track of the fish in the environment. The `Simulation` class is responsible for running the simulation, and the `Fish` class is responsible for knowing how to move a fish.

    (B) The `Simulation` class keeps track of the environment and asks the environment for a list of all the fish. Then the simulation asks the fish to move. The `Environment` class is responsible for keeping track of the fish in the environment and providing a list of fish to other objects when asked. The `Simulation` is responsible for running the simulation, and the `Fish` class is responsible for knowing how to move a fish.

    (C) The `Simulation` keeps track of all the fish in the environment and asks them to move. The `Simulation` class is responsible for running the simulation, and the `Fish` class is responsible for knowing how to move a fish.

    (D) The `Simulation` keeps track of both the environment and all the fish in the environment. It passes the fish to the environment and asks it to move them. Thus the `Environment` class is responsible for running the simulation and knowing how to move a fish.

    (E) The `Simulation` keeps track of the environment (or is passed it as a parameter) and asks it to move all the fish. Thus the `Environment` class is responsible for keeping track of the fish, running the simulation, and knowing how to move a fish.

24. Consider the `add` method of the `Environment` interface:

    ```
    public void add(Locatable obj)
    ```

    Which statement is *false*?
    (A) The method is used to add a new fish to the environment.
    (B) The method is used to add an existing fish that is moving to its new location.
    (C) `obj.location()` is defined for the `obj` parameter.
    (D) `obj.location()` is a valid empty location in the environment.
    (E) The object count in the environment is incremented whenever `add` is called.

25. Refer to the `Fish`, `DarterFish`, and `SlowFish` classes. Which of the following methods are polymorphic?

    I `nextLocation, move`
    II `generateChild`
    III `act, breed, die`

    (A) The methods in I only
    (B) The method in II only
    (C) The methods in III only
    (D) The methods in I and II only
    (E) The methods in I, II, and III

26. Consider running the program with just normal fish, and then again on the same computer with just darter fish, using the identical initial configuration of fish and the same random number generator seed. The expectation is that the movement of the two populations would be different, and also the breeding may differ because of the different availability of empty neighbors for the two populations. But one might expect that the dying behavior would be the same, since darter fish inherit the identical behavior for dying. This is not true, however. When the numbers for dying are recorded for the darter fish, these numbers disagree with the numbers for the normal fish. Which of the following is a likely cause of the discrepancy in the numbers?

(A) Normal fish use random numbers for movement as well as breeding and dying, whereas darter fish use them just for breeding and dying. Thus even though the sequences of random numbers are the same, the numbers are used in different places for the two programs.
(B) Since darters have a more energetic moving pattern than normal fish, their probability of dying is in fact lower than that of normal fish.
(C) Since darters move further than normal fish, there will be fewer empty locations for them to breed into, and therefore a lower percentage of darters will die.
(D) A different sequence of random numbers is produced for each run of the program because the system clock of the computer provides a different starting value in each case.
(E) Since the random numbers used in the program are of type `double`, round-off errors in the storage of these numbers could be producing two different sequences of random numbers.

27. A method is *deterministic* if, given the inputs to it, you can tell exactly what its result will be. A method is *probabilistic* if, given the inputs, there are various probabilities of different results. Which is *false* about the methods in `Fish`, `DarterFish`, and `SlowFish`?
(A) The `breed` method in `Fish` is probabilistic.
(B) The `die` method in `Fish` is deterministic.
(C) The `nextLocation` methods in `Fish`, `DarterFish`, and `SlowFish` are probabilistic.
(D) The `generateChild` methods in `Fish`, `DarterFish`, and `SlowFish` are probabilistic.
(E) The `changeDirection` method in `Fish` is deterministic.

28. Consider modifying the `SlowFish` class so that when a `SlowFish` doesn't move from its current cell, it may turn right or left (or maintain its current direction). Which of the following changes would need to be made?

    I   The `move` method of the the `Fish` class would need to be overridden in the `SlowFish` class.
    II The `changeDirection` method of the the `Fish` class would need to be overridden in the `SlowFish` class.
    III The `nextLocation` method in the `SlowFish` class would need to be modified.

    (A) I only
    (B) II only
    (C) III only
    (D) I and II only
    (E) I and III only

29. Suppose a `SlowFish` object has exactly one empty adjacent cell just before its turn to act. Which of the following *must* be true after the `act` method has been called for this fish?
    (A) If the fish neither bred nor moved, then it died.
    (B) If the fish neither bred nor died, then it moved to that empty adjacent location.
    (C) If the fish neither moved nor died, then it bred into that empty adjacent location.
    (D) If that adjacent location now contains a slow fish, the original location of the fish is now empty.
    (E) If that adjacent location now contains a slow fish, the original location of the fish may or may not contain a slow fish.

Questions 30 and 31 are based on the following:

Assume that env is a valid, empty 10×10 BoundedEnv object. Consider the following code segment:

```
Location loc1 = new Location(10, 10);
Location loc2 = new Location(2, 3);
Location loc3 = new Location(5, 1);
Location loc4 = new Location(6, 6);
Fish f1 = new Fish(env, loc2);
Fish f2 = new Fish(env, loc3);
```

30. What should be the return value of

   (1) env.isEmpty(loc1)   (2) env.isEmpty(loc2)

   (A) (1) true   (2) false
   (B) (1) true   (2) true
   (C) (1) false   (2) false
   (D) (1) false   (2) true
   (E) (1) No value. An IllegalArgumentException is thrown.   (2) false

31. What should be the return value of

   (1) env.objectAt(loc1)   (2) env.objectAt(loc4)

   (A) (1) null   (2) null
   (B) (1) false   (2) false
   (C) (1) Undefined   (2) null
   (D) (1) The object in location (10,10)   (2) The object in location (6,6)
   (E) (1) No value. An IllegalArgumentException is thrown.   (2) null

32. What is the result of running this code segment?

   ```
   BoundedEnv env = new BoundedEnv(5, 5);
   Location loc = new Location(5, 5);
   Fish f = new Fish(env, loc);
   ```

   (A) Fish f will be placed in location loc.
   (B) Both loc and f will have a value of null.
   (C) loc will retain its value of (5,5), and f will have a value of null.
   (D) An ArrayIndexOutOfBoundsException will be thrown.
   (E) An IllegalArgumentException will be thrown.

Level AB Only

33. Here is the add method of the BoundedEnv class:

```
/** Adds a new object obj to this environment at the location
 *  it specifies.
 *  (Precondition: obj.location() is a valid empty location.)
 *  throws IllegalArgumentException if the precondition is
 *  not met
**/
public void add(Locatable obj)
{
    // Check precondition.  Location should be empty.
    Location loc = obj.location();
    if (!isEmpty(loc))
        throw new IllegalArgumentException("Location " + loc +
                               " is not a valid empty location");
    // Add object to the environment.
    theGrid[loc.row()][loc.col()] = obj;
    objectCount++;
}
```

What would happen if the obj parameter passed to add were a null reference?

(A) A NoSuchElementException will be thrown.

(B) An IllegalArgumentException will be thrown.

(C) A NullPointerException will be thrown.

(D) A null reference will be added to the environment, and execution will proceed without error.

(E) Nothing will be added to the environment, and execution will proceed without error.

34. Refer to the `initialize` method of the `Fish` class (which is called by all of the `Fish` constructors) and to the `add` method of the `BoundedEnv` class. Here are the implementations of these methods:

```
/** Initializes the state of this fish.
 *  (Precondition: parameters are nonnull; loc is valid
 *  for env.)
 **/
private void initialize(Environment env, Location loc,
                Direction dir, Color col)
{
    theEnv = env;
    myId = nextAvailableID;
    nextAvailableID++;
    myLoc = loc;
    myDir = dir;
    myColor = col;
    theEnv.add(this);
    probOfBreeding = 1.0/7.0;
    probOfDying = 1.0/5.0;
}

/** Adds a new object obj to this environment at the location
 *  it specifies.
 *  (Precondition: obj.location() is a valid empty location.)
 *  throws IllegalArgumentException if the precondition is
 *  not met
 **/
public void add(Locatable obj)
{
    // Check precondition.  Location should be empty.
    Location loc = obj.location();
    if (!isEmpty(loc))
        throw new IllegalArgumentException("Location " + loc +
                            " is not a valid empty location");
    // Add object to the environment.
    theGrid[loc.row()][loc.col()] = obj;
    objectCount++;
}
```

In order to test the `add` method, the following situations are tried:

  I A run of the simulation with a fish in every valid location of the environment
 II A run of the simulation with two fish in the same location
III A run of the simulation with an out-of-bounds fish

Which of these test situations will cause an `IllegalArgumentException` to be thrown?
(A) None
(B) I only
(C) II only
(D) III only
(E) II and III only

35. In the `UnboundedEnv` class why does the constructor not initialize an `objectCount` variable?
    - (A) `objectCount` is initialized by the `SquareEnvironment` superclass constructor.
    - (B) `objectCount` is automatically initialized by the call to `super()` in the `UnboundedEnv` constructor.
    - (C) There is no need for a `numObjects` method in an unbounded environment.
    - (D) The `size` method of `ArrayList` can be used to obtain the number of objects in `UnboundedEnv`.
    - (E) Since fish can swim in and out of an unbounded environment, it is not possible to maintain an accurate object count.

36. During a test of the `UnboundedEnv` class, it was observed that any fish that moved out of the display area in the first timestep failed to move back into it in the second timestep. What is the most likely explanation for this?
    - (A) All of the fish tested were darter fish that moved forward two spaces.
    - (B) All of the fish were slow fish that failed to move in the second timestep.
    - (C) Fish don't move backward.
    - (D) Fish that move out of an unbounded environment are converted to null objects.
    - (E) There was an error in the `showEnv` method.

37. What is the big-O performance of the `objectAt` method if the environment is a
    (1) `BoundedEnv` object   (2) `UnboundedEnv` object?

    - (A)   (1) $O(1)$ (2) $O(n)$
    - (B)   (1) $O(1)$ (2) $O(1)$
    - (C)   (1) $O(n)$ (2) $O(n)$
    - (D)   (1) $O(n)$ (2) $O(1)$
    - (E)   (1) $O(n)$ (2) $O(n^2)$

38. The current implementation of `BoundedEnv` allows only for cells with four adjacent neighbors, the adjacent neighbors on all four sides. Suppose you need to modify the class so that cells have eight adjacent neighbors, those on the four sides plus the four neighbors on the diagonals. Which of the following changes to the `BoundedEnv` class are required to achieve this change?

    I Modify the constructor so that it calls `super` with a boolean parameter.
    II Modify the `isValid` method to include the diagonal neighbors.
    III Modify the `add` method so that an object can be added to a diagonal location.

    - (A) I only
    - (B) II only
    - (C) III only
    - (D) I and III only
    - (E) I, II, and III

39. Suppose the Marine Biology Simulation Case Study program is run with N fish and M steps in the simulation, where N and M are large. Assume that the environment is implemented with the UnboundedEnv class. The run-time efficiency will be

    (A) $O(N + M)$
    (B) $O(NM)$
    (C) $O(N^2 M)$
    (D) $O(M^2 N)$
    (E) $O(N^M)$

Answer Key

1. **E**	14. **D**	27. **C**
2. **B**	15. **D**	28. **A**
3. **C**	16. **B**	29. **E**
4. **E**	17. **B**	30. **C**
5. **A**	18. **C**	31. **A**
6. **B**	19. **D**	32. **E**
7. **C**	20. **A**	33. **C**
8. **C**	21. **C**	34. **E**
9. **C**	22. **D**	35. **D**
10. **A**	23. **B**	36. **C**
11. **D**	24. **B**	37. **A**
12. **D**	25. **D**	38. **A**
13. **A**	26. **A**	39. **C**

Answers Explained

1. (**E**) All are valid! The slow fish may move forward or sideways, or it may not move at all. In fact, four out of five times `nextLocation()` will return the slow fish's current location, since the probability of moving in any given timestep is approximately 1/5.

2. (**B**) A fish is added to the environment in the `initialize` method (called in the `Fish` constructors).

3. (**C**) A darter fish doesn't move at random. Whether it will move (given that it failed to breed) depends only on whether there's an empty space in front of it.

4. (**E**) The environment is a two-dimensional grid that may contain `Locatable` objects at some of its locations. (A `Locatable` object, like a `Fish`, knows its location at all times.) Thus the environment is a grid plus its objects. The choices in A, B, and D don't reflect this. Choice C does and, in fact, provides a way to think of the environment in this case study simulation. It is not, however, as precise as the description in choice E.

5. (**A**) The act method is in the `Fish` class. Therefore the calling object needs to be a `Fish`. This means that `theFishes[index]`, which is a `Locatable` object, needs to be cast to `Fish` before calling act. Choice B is wrong because act must be called by a `Fish`. A subclass of `Fish` would be OK (polymorphism), but `Locatable` is not a subclass of `Fish`. Choices C, D, and E are

wrong because the conditions for those errors are not present in this question: a `ClassCastException` is thrown when an attempt is made to cast an object to something it's not an instance of (e.g., `Locatable` to `Integer`). A `NullPointerException` occurs if a method is called by a null reference. An `ArrayIndexOutOfBoundsException` occurs when the array index is out of bounds.

6. **(B)** When a class implements an interface, it contracts to provide every method in that interface. The `Locatable` interface has just a single method, `location`. So any class that implements `Locatable` must define a `location` method.

7. **(C)** A `Locatable` object must have a `location` method in its class definition. The `location` method returns a `Location`, which has a row and a column. This implies that the object is in a two-dimensional environment. Choices A, B, D, and E suggest environments that are at least roughly two-dimensional. Choice C does not.

8. **(C)** The `getNeighbor` method returns a `Location` that is a cell adjacent to `fromLoc` in the compass direction of its second parameter. This is the cell directly below $(3, 5)$, namely $(4, 5)$.

9. **(C)** The only situation where the `if` statement won't be executed is when the body of the `for` loop is never executed. The `for` loop won't be executed if `nbrs.size()` is 0. This means that the fish has absolutely no valid neighbors, which is true only in a 1×1 environment with a fish in the lone cell.

10. **(A)** When a darter moves, it darts forward two spaces if those spaces are empty. Its direction remains the same. In each of the following choices the darter has made an invalid move: In choice B it failed to move, and it reversed direction. It only takes this action if there are no available spaces for it to move into. In choice C it darted forward two spaces and then changed direction. When a `DarterFish` changes location, it doesn't change direction. In choice D it darted forward one space even though two spaces were available. In choice E it moved liked a "normal" fish (i.e., sideways). A `DarterFish` never moves sideways.

11. **(D)** The `neighborsOf` method returns all adjacent locations that are valid. These can be empty or can contain a fish, but they cannot be out of bounds! Thus choice E fails because of the out-of-bounds location (1,3). Choice B fails because (2,1) and (0,1) are not considered adjacent in this implementation. Choice C has omitted the adjacent location (2,2), whereas choice A has omitted the adjacent locations (0,2) and (1,1).

12. **(D)** A new fish is added to the environment using `add` in its constructor. Choice A is wrong: Calling `add` outside of the `Fish` constructor is an invalid use of the method and will cause an `IllegalArgumentException` to be thrown, since there's already a fish at `f1`'s location (namely `f1`!). Choices B, C, and E are completely off the mark because `f1` already exists and is not "new."

13. **(A)** Given that the fish fails to `breed`, it *must* move into an adjacent empty cell, which eliminates choice D. Eliminate choice E—(1,1) is not adjacent to (0,0), since it doesn't share a side with (0,0). Strike choice B—when the fish moves

forward to location (0,1), it shouldn't change direction. Choice C is wrong—the fish can't keep its current direction when it moves sideways. If the fish moves sideways to (1,0), it must change direction to face south. Choice A is a valid configuration. It indicates that the fish died after it moved.

14. **(D)** The `neighborsOf` method of the `BoundedEnv` class returns all valid locations in the environment that are adjacent neighbors of its `Location` parameter. This includes locations that are not empty. Thus result I is possible. Result III is true—the location of the current `Fish` is returned only if `emptyNeighbors.size()` is zero, which is not possible with the code modification. (Every location has at least two valid neighbors.) Result II is not possible, since the subsequent code in `nextLocation` explicitly removes the location behind the `Fish` from the `ArrayList`.

15. **(D)** `f.emptyNeighbors()` returns a list of valid adjacent empty neighbors of `f`. Without information about other fish in the neighborhood, it is not possible to determine the size of this list. The `neighborsOf` method, however, returns a list of *all* valid neighboring locations, whether empty or not. Since the fish is known to be in (0,0), and the grid has at least four cells, there are two valid neighboring locations (shown shaded in the diagram).

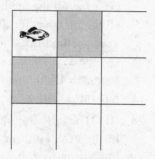

16. **(B)** (0,1) is the only location among the choices that is not a "corner" location. All of the corner locations have exactly two adjacent neighbors that are in bounds. Location (0,1) has three adjacent neighbors that are in bounds.

17. **(B)** The problem with line 4 is that a method cannot be used as the left side of an assignment statement. In particular, an accessor can't be used by a method to change values. In order to change the current location of this `Fish` to `newLoc`, the instance variable `myLoc` must be set directly to `newLoc`.

18. **(C)** The empty adjacent neighbors for the fish in (1,1) are (1,0), (0,1), and (1,2). Reject location (1,2), however, since the location directly behind the fish is removed in the `nextLocation` method.

19. **(D)** A new private instance variable, `myAge`, will need to be initialized to 1 in the `initialize` helper method. In `breed`, the test for breeding will need to be modified to take into account the fish's age. Similarly, in the `act` method, the test for dying will need to be modified. Somewhere in `act`, `breed`, or `move`, the fish's age will need to be incremented after the fish acts. Method III, `generateChild`, will not need to be altered at all, since all it does is call the `Fish` constructor, which already has the age of the fish initialized to 1.

20. **(A)** Both the `DarterFish` and `SlowFish` classes inherit the attributes and behaviors of `Fish`, including the added age features. The fish's age is ini-

tialized in the `Fish` constructor—the use of `super` will accomplish this in the `DarterFish` and `SlowFish` constructors. In its `act` and `breed` methods the `Fish` class takes care of incrementing age and adjusting probabilities for breeding and dying. Since these methods are inherited by `DarterFish` and `SlowFish`, these classes need no additional code. The environment classes are not concerned with the personal features of a fish, other than its location and direction in the environment. Thus the environment classes do not need to be modified when fishes are allowed to age.

21. **(C)** The program allows no more than one fish per location. The situations described in I and II are both valid.

22. **(D)** The same seed value for the random number generator guarantees the same sequence of random numbers for each run of the program. This in turn leads to the same results for the various actions in the program. The same input file guarantees the same configurations for each run. Situation III does not apply—fish behavior is not affected by whether debugging is on or off.

23. **(B)** Notice that the `Simulation` class has an `Environment` private instance variable, `theEnv`. Through this variable it gets `theEnv.allObjects()`, a list of all the fish. Then, in a `for` loop, it asks all the fish to act. The `Environment` class has all the methods for keeping track of the fish, and the `Fish` class has all the methods for acting—`breed`, `move`, and `die`. Eliminate choice A—the `step` method does not take a list of fish as a parameter. Eliminate choice C—the `Simulation` class has no methods that keep track of fish in the environment. Eliminate choices D and E—the `Environment` has no methods for moving a fish.

24. **(B)** The *only* use of `add` is to add a new fish to the environment. It is part of the `Fish` constructor, called by the `initialize` method. When an existing fish moves, it invokes the `changeLocation` method, which notifies the environment of the change by calling `recordMove`.

25. **(D)** The `nextLocation`, `move`, and `generateChild` methods are all overridden in the `DarterFish` and `SlowFish` classes. At run time it is determined what particular instance of `Fish` is invoking the method, and therefore which version of the method to call. This is polymorphism. The `act`, `breed`, and `die` methods are not overridden in either of the subclasses and, therefore, are not polymorphic.

26. **(A)** Choice B is false: Darters have the same probability of dying as normal fish, namely 1/5. Choice C is false: The movement and breeding of darters does not affect their probability of dying. Choice D is false: If the random numbers are produced with the same seed, the same sequence of numbers is generated. The status of the system clock is irrelevant. Choice E is wrong because round-off errors for the numbers in both sequences are the same, given that the same computer was used for both runs of the program.

27. **(C)** The `nextLocation` methods in `Fish` and `SlowFish` are probabilistic, since you can't predict with certainty where the `nextLocation` for one of these objects will be. A random number is used in determining this. Given a `DarterFish`, however, its next location is 100% predictable, based on the occupancy (or not) of two adjacent spaces directly in front of it. This means

that `nextLocation` for a `DarterFish` is deterministic. Choice A is true: Fish breed with a probability of 1/7. Note that choice B is true: Probability is used to determine if `die` will be called, but once it's called, its outcome is 100% certain—that fish is history. Choice D is true: `generateChild` gives the newborn fish a random direction and therefore it is probabilistic. Choice E is true: `changeDirection` changes the direction of the fish to be whatever direction is specified in the parameter—the outcome is 100% certain.

28. **(A)** The only change is in *how* the `SlowFish` moves. Selecting the next location doesn't change, therefore choice III is wrong. When the new direction of the `SlowFish` is determined, the inherited `changeDirection` method can be used without change, so choice II is also incorrect.

29. **(E)** There are two ways in which a slow fish got to that adjacent location: The original fish either bred or moved. If it bred (and did not subsequently die), both locations will contain a slow fish. If it bred and then died, or if it moved and stayed alive, the original location will be empty. Choices A, B, and C are false because when a slow fish acts, there's a nonzero probability that it neither breeds, moves, nor dies. Choice D is false because if the fish bred and didn't die then both the original and adjacent locations will contain slow fish.

30. **(C)** Since `loc2` contains Fish `f1`, `env.isEmpty(loc2)` should return `false`. Since `loc1` is out of bounds, it is invalid. Therefore `env.isEmpty(loc1)` returns `false`. Recall that `isEmpty(loc)` returns `true` if `loc` is both valid and empty, `false` otherwise.

31. **(A)** If the location is valid but contains no objects (true for `loc4`), `objectAt` returns `null`. If the location is out of bounds (true for `loc1`), `objectAt` also returns `null`.

32. **(E)** The location (5,5) is out of bounds and is therefore invalid. The `Fish` constructor calls the environment's `add` method, which checks if its `Location` parameter is invalid. If it is, it throws an `IllegalArgumentException`.

Level AB Only

33. **(C)** The first line of the code,

```
Location loc = obj.location();
```

will try to invoke the `location` method with a null reference, causing the `NullPointerException`. Therefore eliminate choices D and E. Choice B would be correct if `obj` were not null, and `obj.location()` were neither valid not empty. Eliminate choice A because a `NoSuchElementException` is thrown when an attempt is made to retrieve an element from an empty container (see p. 250).

34. **(E)** In situation I a fish is repeatedly added to a valid empty location without error. In situation II, when an attempt is made to add the second fish to the environment, the `!isEmpty(loc)` will be `true`, and the exception will be thrown. In situation III `isEmpty(loc)` is `false` since `loc` is invalid. Therefore again the `!isEmpty(loc)` test will be `true`, and the exception will be thrown.

35. **(D)** The expression `objectList.size()` provides the number of objects in the environment, making an `objectCount` variable unnecessary. Choice A

cannot be correct—constructors are never inherited. Choice B is wrong because there is no `objectCount` variable in `SquareEnvironment`. Choice C is contradicted by the existence of a `numObjects` method in `UnboundedEnv`. Choice E is wrong—fish that have left the environment are not included in the number of objects currently in the environment.

36. **(C)** It would take at least two timesteps for a fish to reappear, since, in order to turn around, a (normal or slow) fish must move sideways and then sideways again. Note that choice D is wrong—part of the specification for the simulation is that it keep track of all fish from the time they are born until they die, wherever they go. All of the other choices are unlikely reasons.

37. **(A)** Access to any given location in a two-dimensional array is $O(1)$. Therefore `objectAt` for `BoundedEnv` is $O(1)$. In `UnboundedEnv` the objects are stored in an `ArrayList`, which must be traversed to find the index at which the object with location `loc` is stored. This is $O(n)$. If `loc` is found, the object at that index is returned.

38. **(A)** The `SquareEnvironment` superclass has two constructors. The default constructor, which constructs an environment with cells that have just four adjacent neighbors, is invoked in the call to `super()` in the `BoundedEnv` constructor. The second constructor in `SquareEnvironment` allows for the construction of cells with eight adjacent neighbors. If the boolean parameter `includeDiagonalNeighbors` is set to `true`, all cells in the environment will have eight adjacent neighbors. This constructor can be invoked by the constructor in `BoundedEnv` if `super` is called with a boolean parameter. Changes II and III are wrong: neither `isValid` nor `add` depend on the diagonal versus nondiagonal nature of their location parameters.

39. **(C)** A single step of the simulation involves

    1. Getting an array of all N fish by calling `allObjects`. This is $O(N)$.
    2. Cycling through the array allowing each fish to act. This is $O(N^2)$, since processing each fish takes $O(N)$ operations. This is because breeding and moving cause the `objectAt` method to be called, which is $O(N)$ in an `UnboundedEnv` (see Question 38 on p. 667).

    The run time of `step` is therefore $O(N^2)$. When `step` is called M times, the run time becomes $O(N^2 M)$.

Practice
Exams

Answer Sheet: Practice Exam One

1. Ⓐ Ⓑ Ⓒ Ⓓ Ⓔ

2. Ⓐ Ⓑ Ⓒ Ⓓ Ⓔ

3. Ⓐ Ⓑ Ⓒ Ⓓ Ⓔ

4. Ⓐ Ⓑ Ⓒ Ⓓ Ⓔ

5. Ⓐ Ⓑ Ⓒ Ⓓ Ⓔ

6. Ⓐ Ⓑ Ⓒ Ⓓ Ⓔ

7. Ⓐ Ⓑ Ⓒ Ⓓ Ⓔ

8. Ⓐ Ⓑ Ⓒ Ⓓ Ⓔ

9. Ⓐ Ⓑ Ⓒ Ⓓ Ⓔ

10. Ⓐ Ⓑ Ⓒ Ⓓ Ⓔ

11. Ⓐ Ⓑ Ⓒ Ⓓ Ⓔ

12. Ⓐ Ⓑ Ⓒ Ⓓ Ⓔ

13. Ⓐ Ⓑ Ⓒ Ⓓ Ⓔ

14. Ⓐ Ⓑ Ⓒ Ⓓ Ⓔ

15. Ⓐ Ⓑ Ⓒ Ⓓ Ⓔ

16. Ⓐ Ⓑ Ⓒ Ⓓ Ⓔ

17. Ⓐ Ⓑ Ⓒ Ⓓ Ⓔ

18. Ⓐ Ⓑ Ⓒ Ⓓ Ⓔ

19. Ⓐ Ⓑ Ⓒ Ⓓ Ⓔ

20. Ⓐ Ⓑ Ⓒ Ⓓ Ⓔ

21. Ⓐ Ⓑ Ⓒ Ⓓ Ⓔ

22. Ⓐ Ⓑ Ⓒ Ⓓ Ⓔ

23. Ⓐ Ⓑ Ⓒ Ⓓ Ⓔ

24. Ⓐ Ⓑ Ⓒ Ⓓ Ⓔ

25. Ⓐ Ⓑ Ⓒ Ⓓ Ⓔ

26. Ⓐ Ⓑ Ⓒ Ⓓ Ⓔ

27. Ⓐ Ⓑ Ⓒ Ⓓ Ⓔ

28. Ⓐ Ⓑ Ⓒ Ⓓ Ⓔ

29. Ⓐ Ⓑ Ⓒ Ⓓ Ⓔ

30. Ⓐ Ⓑ Ⓒ Ⓓ Ⓔ

31. Ⓐ Ⓑ Ⓒ Ⓓ Ⓔ

32. Ⓐ Ⓑ Ⓒ Ⓓ Ⓔ

33. Ⓐ Ⓑ Ⓒ Ⓓ Ⓔ

34. Ⓐ Ⓑ Ⓒ Ⓓ Ⓔ

35. Ⓐ Ⓑ Ⓒ Ⓓ Ⓔ

36. Ⓐ Ⓑ Ⓒ Ⓓ Ⓔ

37. Ⓐ Ⓑ Ⓒ Ⓓ Ⓔ

38. Ⓐ Ⓑ Ⓒ Ⓓ Ⓔ

39. Ⓐ Ⓑ Ⓒ Ⓓ Ⓔ

40. Ⓐ Ⓑ Ⓒ Ⓓ Ⓔ

How to Calculate Your (Approximate) AP Score — AP Computer Science Level A

Multiple Choice

Number correct (out of 40) = _____

$1/4 \times$ number wrong = _____

Raw score = line 1 − line 2 = _____ ⟸ Multiple-Choice Score
(Do not round. If less than zero, enter zero.)

Free Response

Question 1 _____
(out of 9)

Question 2 _____
(out of 9)

Question 3 _____
(out of 9)

Question 4 _____
(out of 9)

Total _____ × 1.11 = _____ ⟸ Free-Response Score
(Do not round.)

Final Score

_____ + _____ = _____
Multiple-Choice Score   Free-Response Score   Final Score
(Round to nearest whole number.)

Chart to Convert to AP Grade
Computer Science A

Final Score Range	AP Grade[a]
60–80	5
45–59	4
33–44	3
25–32	2
0–24	1

[a]The score range corresponding to each grade varies from exam to exam and is approximate.

Practice Exam One

COMPUTER SCIENCE A
SECTION I

Time—1 hour and 15 minutes
Number of questions—40
Percent of total grade—50

Directions: Determine the answer to each of the following questions or incomplete statements, using separate pieces of scrap paper for any necessary scratchwork. Then decide which is the best of the choices given and fill in the corresponding oval on the answer sheet. Do not spend too much time on any one problem.

Note: Assume that the standard packages (e.g., `java.util.*`) are included in any programs that use the code segments provided in individual questions. A Quick Reference to the standard classes and interfaces with their required methods is provided.

---

1. Consider this inheritance hierarchy, in which `Novel` and `Textbook` are subclasses of `Book`.

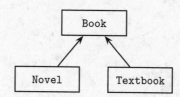

Which of the following is a *false* statement about the classes shown?
(A) The `Textbook` class can have private instance variables that are neither in `Book` nor `Novel`.
(B) Each of the classes—`Book`, `Novel`, and `Textbook`—can have a method `computeShelfLife`, whose code in `Book` and `Novel` is identical, but different from the code in `Textbook`.
(C) If the `Book` class has private instance variables `myTitle` and `myAuthor`, then `Novel` and `Textbook` inherit them but cannot directly access them.
(D) Both `Novel` and `Textbook` inherit the constructors in `Book`.
(E) If the `Book` class has a static method called `getPublisher`, this method may not be overridden in either the `Novel` or `Textbook` classes.

GO ON TO THE NEXT PAGE

2. A programmer is designing a program to catalog all books in a library. He plans to have a Book class that stores features of each book: author, title, isOnShelf, and so on, with operations like getAuthor, getTitle, getShelfInfo, and setShelfInfo. Another class, LibraryList, will store an array of Book objects. The LibraryList class will include operations such as listAllBooks, searchForBook, removeBook, and addBook. The programmer plans to implement and test the Book class first, before implementing the LibraryList class. The programmer's plan for writing this program is an example of

   (A) Top-down development.
   (B) Bottom-up development.
   (C) Stepwise refinement.
   (D) Implementing an interface.
   (E) A driver program.

Questions 3–6 refer to the Card class shown below.

```
public class Card
{
    private String mySuit;
    private int myValue;        //0 to 12

    public Card(String suit, int value)
    { implementation }

    public String getSuit()
    { return mySuit; }

    public int getValue()
    { return myValue; }

    public String toString()
    {
        String faceValue = "";
        if (myValue == 11)
            faceValue = "J";
        else if (myValue == 12)
            faceValue = "Q";
        else if (myValue == 0)
            faceValue = "K";
        else if (myValue == 1)
            faceValue = "A";
        if (myValue >= 2 && myValue <= 10)
            return myValue + " of " + mySuit;
        else
            return faceValue + " of " + mySuit;
    }
}
```

GO ON TO THE NEXT PAGE

3. Which is *true* about the methods of the Card class?
   (A) The Card class has a default constructor.
   (B) The constructor with parameters allows the suit and value for a Card to be initialized from user input.
   (C) The toString method returns a deck of Card objects as a string.
   (D) The Card class has a default method that allows comparison of Card objects.
   (E) The equals method can be used to test whether two Card objects have the same suit and value.

4. Which of the following represents correct *implementation* code for the constructor in the Card class?

   (A)
   ```
   mySuit = suit;
   myValue = value;
   ```

   (B)
   ```
   suit = mySuit;
   value = myValue;
   ```

   (C)
   ```
   Card = new Card(mySuit, myValue);
   ```

   (D)
   ```
   Card = new Card(suit, value);
   ```

   (E)
   ```
   mySuit = getSuit();
   myValue = getValue();
   ```

5. A programmer is designing a program that will play a "pick-a-card" game with a single deck of cards. Eventually the player with the highest card wins. If the programmer plans to use the Card class in the program, which of the following must be done to compare two cards for greater than or less than?

   I Modify the Card class header as follows:

   ```
   public class Card implements Comparable
   ```

   II Add a compareTo method to the Card class.

   III Add an equals method to the Card class.

   (A) I only
   (B) II only
   (C) III only
   (D) I and II only
   (E) I, II, and III

6. Which of the following correctly constructs a Card object?

   (A) `Card c = Card("spades", 10);`

   (B) `Card c = new Card("clubs", "J");`

   (C)
   ```
   Card c;
   c = Card("spades", 4);
   ```

   (D) `Card c = new Card("hearts", "8");`

   (E) `Card c = new Card("diamonds", 12);`

GO ON TO THE NEXT PAGE

To simulate a deck of cards, the following Deck class will make use of the Card class for Questions 7–9.

```
public class Deck
{
    private Card[] myDeck;
    public final static int NUMCARDS = 52;

    public Deck()
    { implementation }

    //Simulate shuffling the deck
    public void shuffle()
    { implementation }

    //other methods
        ...
}
```

Refer to this description of the Deck constructor for Questions 7 and 8.
A Deck object will be constructed as follows:
myDeck[0]...myDeck[12] will contain the spade suit
myDeck[13]...myDeck[25] will contain the heart suit
myDeck[26]...myDeck[38] will contain the diamond suit
myDeck[39]...myDeck[51] will contain the club suit
In each suit the card values range from 0 to 12. (These are converted to actual card values in the toString method of the Card class.) Here is the constructor for the Deck class:

```
public Deck()
{
    < declaration of the myDeck array >

    for (int i=0; i<NUMCARDS; i++)
    {
        < code to insert the spade cards into myDeck >
        < code to insert the heart cards into myDeck >
        < code to insert the diamond cards into myDeck >
        < code to insert the club cards into myDeck >
    }
}
```

7. Which of the following is a correct < *declaration of the* myDeck *array* >?
   (A) myDeck = new Deck[NUMCARDS];
   (B) myDeck = new Deck(suit, value);
   (C) myDeck = Deck[NUMCARDS];
   (D) myDeck = new Card(suit, value);
   (E) myDeck = new Card[NUMCARDS];

GO ON TO THE NEXT PAGE

8. Which of the following is correct < *code to insert the heart cards into* `myDeck` > so that the specification for the `myDeck` array is satisfied?

(A) `if (i/13 == 1)`
    `myDeck[i/13] = new Card("hearts", i % 13);`

(B) `if (i >= 13 && i <= 25)`
    `myDeck[i % 13] = new Card("hearts", i % 13);`

(C) `if (i/13 == 1)`
    `myDeck[i] = new Card("hearts", i % 13);`

(D) `if (i >= 13 && i <= 25)`
    `myDeck[i] = new Card("hearts", i/13);`

(E) `if (i/13 == 1)`
    `myDeck[i % 13] = new Card("hearts", i % 13);`

9. Consider the implementation of a `writeDeck` method that is added to the `Deck` class.

```
//Write the cards in myDeck, one per line
public void writeDeck()
{
    < implementation code >
}
```

Which of the following is correct < *implementation code* >?

I `System.out.println(myDeck);`

II `for (int i=0; i<NUMCARDS; i++)`
   `System.out.println(myDeck[i]);`

III `for (int i=0; i<NUMCARDS; i++)`
    `System.out.println(myDeck[i].toString());`

(A) I only
(B) II only
(C) III only
(D) I and III only
(E) II and III only

10. A method is to be written to search an array for a value that is larger than a given item and return its index. The problem specification does not indicate what should be returned if there are several such values in the array. Which of the following actions would be best?
(A) The method should be written on the assumption that there is only one value in the array that is larger than the given item.
(B) The method should be written so as to return the index of every occurrence of a larger value.
(C) The specification should be modified to indicate what should be done if there is more than one index of larger values.
(D) The method should be written to output a message if more than one larger value is found.
(E) The method should be written to delete all subsequent larger items after a suitable index is returned.

GO ON TO THE NEXT PAGE

11. When will method `whatIsIt` cause a stack overflow (i.e., cause computer memory to be exhausted)?

```
public static int whatIsIt(int x, int y)
{
    if (x > y)
        return x*y;
    else
        return whatIsIt(x-1, y);
}
```

(A) Only when $x < y$
(B) Only when $x \leq y$
(C) Only when $x > y$
(D) For all values of x and y
(E) The method will never cause a stack overflow.

12. The boolean expression `a[i] == max || !(max != a[i])` can be simplified to
(A) `a[i] == max`
(B) `a[i] != max`
(C) `a[i] < max || a[i] > max`
(D) `true`
(E) `false`

13. Suppose an `ArrayList list` is initialized with `Integer` values. Which of the following will *not* cause an `IndexOutOfBoundsException` to be thrown?

(A) `for (int i=0; i<=list.size(); i++)`
        `list.set(i, new Integer(0));`

(B) `list.add(list.size(), new Integer(0));`

(C) `Integer intOb = list.get(list.size());`

(D) `Integer intOb = list.remove(list.size());`

(E) `list.add(-1, new Integer(0));`

GO ON TO THE NEXT PAGE

Questions 14–19 refer to the Point, Quadrilateral, and Rectangle classes below:

```
public class Point
{
    private int xCoord;
    private int yCoord;

    //constructor
    public Point(int x, int y)
    {
        xCoord = x;
        yCoord = y;
    }

    //Return x coordinate of Point
    public int get_x()
    { return xCoord; }

    //Return y coordinate of Point
    public int get_y()
    { return yCoord; }

    //Change Point to new_x and new_y
    public void setPoint(int new_x, int new_y)
    {
        xCoord = new_x;
        yCoord = new_y;
    }
}

public abstract class Quadrilateral
{
    private String myLabels;    //e.g., "ABCD"

    //constructor
    public Quadrilateral(String labels)
    { myLabels = labels; }

    public String getLabels()
    { return myLabels; }

    public abstract int perimeter();
    public abstract int area();
}
```

GO ON TO THE NEXT PAGE

```
public class Rectangle extends Quadrilateral
{
    private Point myTopLeft;   //coords of top left corner
    private Point myBotRight;  //coords of bottom right corner

    //constructor
    public Rectangle(String labels, Point topLeft, Point botRight)
    { implementation }

    public int perimeter()
    { implementation }

    public int area()
    { implementation }

    /* Return true if Rectangle is valid, false otherwise.
     * Rectangle is valid if and only if "top" y-coord > "bottom" y-coord,
     * and "right" x-coord > "left" x-coord  */
    public boolean isValid()
    { implementation }

    //Return top left corner Point
    public Point getTopLeft()
    { return myTopLeft; }

    //Return bottom right corner Point
    public Point getBotRight()
    { return myBotRight; }

    //Changes the top left and bottom right corner coordinates
    //of the current Rectangle
    public void alter(Point newTopLeft, Point newBotRight)
    { implementation }
}
```

14. Which statement about the Quadrilateral class is *false*?
    (A) The perimeter and area methods are abstract because there's no suitable default code for them.
    (B) The getLabels method is not abstract because any subclasses of Quadrilateral will have the same code for this method.
    (C) If the Quadrilateral class is used in a program, it *must* be used as a superclass for at least one other class.
    (D) No instances of a Quadrilateral object can be created in a program.
    (E) Any subclasses of the Quadrilateral class *must* provide implementation code for the perimeter and area methods.

GO ON TO THE NEXT PAGE

15. Which represents correct *implementation* code for the `Rectangle` constructor?

    I `super(labels);`

    II `super(labels, topLeft, botRight);`

    III `super(labels);`
        `myTopLeft = topLeft;`
        `myBotRight = botRight;`

    (A) I only
    (B) II only
    (C) III only
    (D) I and II only
    (E) II and III only

16. Which is a *true* statement about the `Rectangle` class?

    I The `Rectangle` class implements the `Quadrilateral` interface.
    II The `Rectangle` class is a superclass of the `Point` class.
    III The `isValid` method will allow clients of the class to check the validity of any given `Rectangle` object.

    (A) I only
    (B) II only
    (C) III only
    (D) I and II only
    (E) II and III only

17. A client program of the `Rectangle` class contains the following method:

    ```
    //Precondition:  rect is a valid rectangle
    //Postcondition: returns true if rect is a square, false otherwise
    public static boolean isSquare(Rectangle rect)
    {
        return myBotRight.get_x() - myTopLeft.get_x() ==
                myTopLeft.get_y() - myBotRight.get_y();
    }
    ```

    This code is incorrect. Why?
    (A) The return statement is mathematically incorrect. It should be

    ```
    return Math.abs(myBotRight.get_x() - myTopLeft.get_x()) ==
        Math.abs(myTopLeft.get_y() - myBotRight.get_y());
    ```

    (B) The return statement is syntactically incorrect. It should be

    ```
    return myBotRight.x - myTopLeft.x ==
        myTopLeft.y - myBotRight.y;
    ```

    (C) The condition is insufficient: All four sides of the rectangle must be tested for equality.
    (D) The variables `myTopLeft` and `myBotRight` cannot be used in a client program.
    (E) The return type is incorrect. The method should return `true` or `false`.

GO ON TO THE NEXT PAGE

Consider the following classes for Questions 18 and 19:

```
public class Parallelogram extends Quadrilateral
{
    //private instance variables and constructor
        ...

    public int perimeter()
    { /* implementation not shown */ }

    public int area()
    { /* implementation not shown */ }
}

public class Square extends Rectangle
{
    //private instance variables and constructor
        ...

    public int perimeter()
    { /* implementation not shown */ }

    public int area()
    { /* implementation not shown */ }
}
```

18. A client program has this code segment:

```
Quadrilateral q1 = new Parallelogram(< parameter list >);
Quadrilateral q2 = new Square(< parameter list >);
System.out.println("Area of " + q1.getLabels() + " is " + q1.area());
System.out.println("Area of " + q2.getLabels() + " is " + q2.area());
```

Which is a *true* statement about this code?
(A) The code will cause a compile-time error because there is no getLabels method in the Parallelogram and Square classes.
(B) The code will cause a compile-time error because the area method in the Quadrilateral class is abstract.
(C) The code will run as intended: q1.area() will give the area of the appropriate parallelogram, and q2.area() will give the area of the appropriate square.
(D) The declarations are incorrect. They need to be changed as follows:

```
Parallelogram q1 = new Parallelogram(< parameter list >);
Square q2 = new Square(< parameter list >);
```

(E) The output statements are incorrect. They need to be changed as follows:

```
System.out.println("Area of " + q1.getLabels() + " is "
    + ((Parallelogram) q1).area());
System.out.println("Area of " + q2.getLabels() + " is "
    + ((Square) q2).area());
```

GO ON TO THE NEXT PAGE

19. Consider an `ArrayList`, quadList, of Quadrilateral objects: type Rectangle, Parallelogram, or Square. Refer to the following method, writeAreas:

```
/* Precondition:  quadList contains Rectangle, Parallelogram, or
 *                 Square objects in an unspecified order
 * Postcondition: area of each Quadrilateral in quadList has been printed */
public static void writeAreas(ArrayList quadList)
{
    for (int i=0; i<quadList.size(); i++)
        < code to print area of  Quadrilateral >
}
```

Which is correct *< code to print area of* Quadrilateral *>*?

(A) `System.out.println("Area of " + quadList.getLabels()`
`+ " is " + quadList.area());`

(B) `System.out.println("Area of " + quadList[i].getLabels()`
`+ " is " + quadList[i].area());`

(C) `System.out.println("Area of " + (quadList.get(i)).getLabels()`
`+ " is " + (quadList.get(i)).area());`

(D) `System.out.println("Area of " + ((Quadrilateral) quadList.get(i)).getLabels()`
`+ " is " + ((Quadrilateral) quadList.get(i)).area());`

(E) `System.out.println("Area of " + ((Quadrilateral) quadList[i]).getLabels()`
`+ " is " + ((Quadrilateral) quadList[i]).area());`

20. Refer to the `doSomething` method:

```
//< postcondition >
public static void doSomething(ArrayList a, int i, int j)
{
    Object temp = a.get(i);
    a.set(i, a.get(j));
    a.set(j, temp);
}
```

Which best describes the *< postcondition >* for doSomething?
(A) Removes from a the objects indexed at i and j.
(B) Replaces in a the object indexed at i with the object indexed at j.
(C) Replaces in a the object indexed at j with the object indexed at i.
(D) Replaces in a the objects indexed at i and j with temp.
(E) Interchanges in a the objects indexed at i and j.

GO ON TO THE NEXT PAGE

Questions 21–23 refer to the NegativeReal class below, which defines a negative real number object.

```
public class NegativeReal
{
    private Double myNegReal;

    //constructor
    //Precondition: num < 0
    public NegativeReal(double num)
    { implementation }

    //Postcondition: returns value of this NegativeReal
    public double getValue()
    { implementation }

    //Postcondition: returns this NegativeReal rounded to the nearest integer
    public int getRounded()
    { implementation }
}
```

21. Which is a correct *implementation* for the constructor of a NegativeReal object?
    (A) myNegReal = num;
    (B) myNegReal = Double(num);
    (C) myNegReal = new Double(num);
    (D) myNegReal = new Double(-num);
    (E) myNegReal = -(new Double(num));

22. Which is a correct *implementation* of the getValue method?

    I return myNegReal;

    II return myNegReal.doubleValue();

    III return doubleValue();

    (A) I only
    (B) II only
    (C) III only
    (D) II and III only
    (E) I, II, and III

GO ON TO THE NEXT PAGE

23. Here are some rounding examples:

Negative real number	Rounded to nearest integer
−3.5	−4
−8.97	−9
−5.0	−5
−2.487	−2
−0.2	0

Which implementation of `getRounded` produces the desired postcondition?

(A) `return (int) (getValue() - 0.5);`

(B) `return (int) (getValue() + 0.5);`

(C) `return (int) getValue();`

(D) `return myNegReal.intValue();`

(E) `return getValue().intValue();`

24. Consider the following method.

```
public static void whatsIt(int n)
{
    if (n > 10)
        whatsIt(n/10);
    System.out.print(n % 10);
}
```

What will be output as a result of the method call `whatsIt(347)`?

(A) 74

(B) 47

(C) 734

(D) 743

(E) 347

25. A large list of numbers is to be sorted into ascending order. Which of the following is a *true* statement?

(A) If the array is initially sorted in descending order, then insertion sort will be more efficient than selection sort.

(B) The number of comparisons for selection sort is independent of the initial arrangement of elements.

(C) The number of comparisons for insertion sort is independent of the initial arrangement of elements.

(D) The number of data movements in selection sort depends on the initial arrangement of elements.

(E) The number of data movements in insertion sort is independent of the initial arrangement of elements.

GO ON TO THE NEXT PAGE

26. Consider the code segment

```
if (n == 1)
    k++;
else if (n == 4)
    k += 4;
```

Suppose that the given segment is rewritten in the form

```
if (< condition >)
    < assignment statement >;
```

Given that n and k are integers and that the rewritten code performs the same task as the original code, which of the following could be used as

 (1) < condition > and (2) < assignment statement >?

(A) (1) n == 1 && n == 4 (2) k += n

(B) (1) n == 1 && n == 4 (2) k += 4

(C) (1) n == 1 || n == 4 (2) k += 4

(D) (1) n == 1 || n == 4 (2) k += n

(E) (1) n == 1 || n == 4 (2) k = n - k

27. Which of the following will execute *without* throwing an exception?

```
I  String s = null;
   String t = "";
   if (s.equals(t))
       System.out.println("empty strings?");

II String s = "holy";
   String t = "moly";
   if (s.equals(t))
       System.out.println("holy moly!");

III String s = "holy";
    String t = s.substring(4);
    System.out.println(s + t);
```

(A) I only
(B) II only
(C) III only
(D) I and II only
(E) II and III only

GO ON TO THE NEXT PAGE

28. Three numbers a, b, and c are said to be a *Pythagorean Triple* if and only if the sum of the squares of two of the numbers equals the square of the third. A programmer writes a method isPythTriple to test if its three parameters form a Pythagorean Triple:

```
//Returns true if a² + b² = c²; otherwise returns false
public static boolean isPythTriple(double a, double b, double c)
{
    double d = Math.sqrt(a*a + b*b);
    return d == c;
}
```

When the method was tested with known Pythagorean Triples, isPythTriple sometimes erroneously returned false. What was the most likely cause of the error?
   (A) Round-off error was caused by calculations with floating-point numbers.
   (B) Type boolean was not recognized by an obsolete version of Java.
   (C) An overflow error was caused by entering numbers that were too large.
   (D) c and d should have been cast to integers before testing for equality.
   (E) Bad test data were selected.

29. Refer to the following class, containing the mystery method.

```
public class SomeClass
{
    private int[] arr;

    //Constructor. Initializes arr to contain nonnegative
    //integers k such that 0 ≤ k ≤ 9
    public SomeClass()
    { /* implementation not shown */ }

    public int mystery()
    {
        int value = arr[0];
        for (int i=1; i < arr.length; i++)
            value = value*10 + arr[i];
        return value;
    }
}
```

Which best describes what the mystery method does?
   (A) It sums the elements of arr.
   (B) It sums the products 10*arr[0] + 10*arr[1] + ... + 10*arr[arr.length-1].
   (C) It builds an integer of the form $d_1 d_2 d_3 \ldots d_n$, where $d_1 = $ arr[0], $d_2 = $ arr[1], ..., $d_n = $ arr[arr.length-1].
   (D) It builds an integer of the form $d_1 d_2 d_3 \ldots d_n$, where $d_1 = $ arr[arr.length-1], $d_2 = $ arr[arr.length-2], ..., $d_n = $ arr[0].
   (E) It converts the elements of arr to base 10.

GO ON TO THE NEXT PAGE

Questions 30 and 31 refer to the search method in the Searcher class below.

```
public class Searcher
{
    private int[] arr;

    //Constructor. Initializes arr with integers
    public Searcher()
    { /* implementation not shown */ }

    /* Precondition:  arr[first]...arr[last] sorted in ascending order
     * Postcondition: returns index of key in arr. If key not in arr,
     *                returns -1 */
    public int search(int first, int last, int key)
    {
        int mid;
        while (first <= last)
        {
            mid = (first + last)/2;
            if (arr[mid] == key)       //found key, exit search
                return mid;
            else if (arr[mid] < key)  //key to right of arr[mid]
                first = mid + 1;
            else                       //key to left of arr[mid]
                last = mid - 1;
        }
        return -1;                     //key not in list
    }
}
```

30. Which assertion is true just before each execution of the while loop?
    (A) arr[first] < key < arr[last]
    (B) arr[first] ≤ key ≤ arr[last]
    (C) arr[first] < key < arr[last] or key is not in arr
    (D) arr[first] ≤ key ≤ arr[last] or key is not in arr
    (E) key ≤ arr[first] or key ≥ arr[last] or key is not in arr

31. Consider the array a with values as shown:

    4, 7, 19, 25, 36, 37, 50, 100, 101, 205, 220, 271, 306, 321

    where 4 is a[0] and 321 is a[13]. Suppose that the search method is called with first = 0 and last = 13 to locate the key 205. How many iterations of the while loop must be made in order to locate it?
    (A) 3
    (B) 4
    (C) 5
    (D) 10
    (E) 13

GO ON TO THE NEXT PAGE

Refer to the RandomList class for Questions 32 and 33.

```
import java.util.*;

public class RandomList
{
    private ArrayList myList;

    //constructor
    public RandomList()
    { myList = getList(); }

    /* Read random Integers from 0 to 100 inclusive into ArrayList list */
    public ArrayList getList()
    {
        System.out.println("How many integers? ");
        int listLength = IO.readInt();      //read user input
        ArrayList list = new ArrayList();
        Random r = new Random();
        for (int i=0; i<listLength; i++)
        {
            < code to add Integer to list >
        }
        return list;
    }

    /* Print all elements of this list */
    public void printList()
    {
        < code to print myList >
    }
}
```

32. Which represents correct < *code to add* Integer *to* list >?

    (A) `list[i] = new Integer(r.nextInt(101));`

    (B) `list.add(new Integer(r.nextInt(101)));`

    (C) `list[i] = new Integer(r.nextInt(100));`

    (D) `list.add(new Integer(r.nextInt(100)));`

    (E) `int num = r.nextInt(101);`
        `list.add(new num);`

GO ON TO THE NEXT PAGE

33. Which represents correct < *code to print* myList >?

```
 I for (int i=0; i<myList.size(); i++)
        System.out.print(myList.get(i) + " ");
```

```
 II for (int i=0; i<myList.size(); i++)
        System.out.print((Integer) myList.get(i) + " ");
```

```
III System.out.print(myList);
```

(A) I only
(B) II only
(C) III only
(D) II and III only
(E) I, II, and III

GO ON TO THE NEXT PAGE

Questions 34 and 35 refer to method `insert` described here. The `insert` method has two string parameters and one integer parameter. `insert` returns the string obtained by inserting the second string into the first starting at the position indicated by the integer parameter. For example, if `str1` contains `xy` and `str2` contains `cat`, then

insert(str1, str2, 0)	returns	catxy
insert(str1, str2, 1)	returns	xcaty
insert(str1, str2, 2)	returns	xycat

Here is the header for method `insert`.

```
//Precondition:  0 <= pos <= str1.length()
//Postcondition: returns < somestring >
public static String insert(String str1, String str2, int pos);
```

34. If `str1` $= a_0a_1 \ldots a_{n-1}$ and `str2` $= b_0b_1 \ldots b_{m-1}$, which of the following is a correct replacement for
    $< somestring >$?

    (A) $a_0a_1 \ldots a_{pos}b_0b_1 \ldots b_{m-1}a_{pos+1}a_{pos+2} \ldots a_{n-1}$

    (B) $a_0a_1 \ldots a_{pos+1}b_0b_1 \ldots b_{m-1}a_{pos+2}a_{pos+3} \ldots a_{n-1}$

    (C) $a_0a_1 \ldots a_{pos-1}b_0b_1 \ldots b_{m-1}a_{pos}a_{pos+1} \ldots a_{n-1}$

    (D) $a_0a_1 \ldots a_{n-1}b_0b_1 \ldots b_{m-1}$

    (E) $a_0a_1 \ldots a_{pos-1}b_0b_1 \ldots b_{pos-1}a_{pos}a_{pos+1} \ldots a_{n-1}$

35. Method `insert` follows:

    ```
    //Postcondition: returns < somestring >
    public static String insert(String str1, String str2, int pos)
    {
        String first, last;
            < more code >
        return first + str2 + last;
    }
    ```

    Which of the following is a correct replacement for $< more code >$?

    (A) ```
    first = str1.substring(0, pos);
    last = str1.substring(pos);
    ```

    (B) ```
    first = str1.substring(0, pos-1);
    last = str1.substring(pos);
    ```

    (C) ```
    first = str1.substring(0, pos+1);
    last = str1.substring(pos+1);
    ```

    (D) ```
    first = str1.substring(0, pos);
    last = str1.substring(pos+1, str1.length());
    ```

    (E) ```
    first = str1.substring(0, pos);
    last = str1.substring(pos, str1.length()+1);
    ```

GO ON TO THE NEXT PAGE
    ```

Questions 36–40 involve reasoning about the code from the Marine Biology Simulation Case Study. A Quick Reference to the case study is provided as part of this exam.

36. Consider the following statements about fish movement and breeding. Which statement must always be *true*?

    (A) If the initial configuration of fish has a fish in every location of the environment, none of the fish will be able to move in the first timestep.

    (B) If a fish has an empty neighbor behind it and no other empty neighbors, it will not be able to breed.

    (C) If a fish has no available empty neighbors for breeding, then it will move to a new location.

    (D) In each timestep of the simulation, approximately 1/7 of all fish in the environment will breed.

    (E) In each timestep of the simulation, approximately 1/5 of all fish in the environment will die.

Refer to the diagram below for Questions 37 and 38.

Consider the Fish object f   in a 3 × 3 BoundedEnv. Just before its turn to act, there are DarterFish objects   east and north of it, and SlowFish objects   west and south of it.

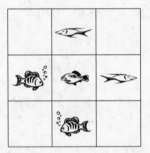

37. Suppose the BoundedEnv object is env and the Fish object is f. Just *before* the Fish object f acts, what are the values of

    (1) env.allObjects().length
    (2) env.neighborsOf(f.location()).size()

    (A) (1) 5   (2) 0
    (B) (1) 5   (2) 4
    (C) (1) 9   (2) 4
    (D) (1) 9   (2) 0
    (E) (1) 4   (2) 8

GO ON TO THE NEXT PAGE

38. Here is the configuration before the `Fish` in the center acts.

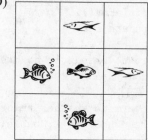

Which represents a valid setup directly after the `Fish` in the center acts?

(A)

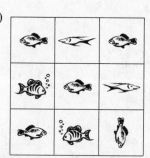

(B)

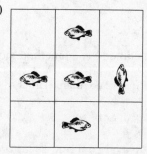

(C)

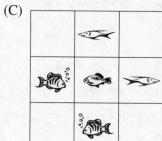

(D)

(E)

GO ON TO THE NEXT PAGE

39. Consider the act, breed, and die methods in the Fish class. Notice that the test to determine whether a fish will attempt to breed in a given timestep is done in the breed method, rather than the act method. By contrast, the test to determine whether a fish will die is done in the act method.

Suppose the breed and act methods are modified to do the tests for breeding and dying in the act method. Here is a version of breed without any tests (and without any debugging statements):

```
//Attempts to breed into neighboring locations.
//emptyNbrs is a list of valid empty neighbors
protected void breed(ArrayList emptyNbrs)
{
    //Breed to all empty locations
    for (int index=0; index<emptyNbrs.size(); index++)
    {
        Location loc = (Location) emptyNbrs.get(index);
        generateChild(loc);
    }
}
```

Using this modified breed method, here is the modified act method:

```
/** Acts for one step in the simulation.
 **/
public void act()
{
    // Make sure fish is alive and well in the environment ---
    // fish that have been removed from the environment shouldn't act.
    if (!isInEnv())
        return;

    // Try to breed. If no breeding, try to move.
    < modified code >

    // Determine whether this fish will die in this timestep.
    if (randNumGen.nextDouble() < probOfDying)
        die();
}
```

GO ON TO THE NEXT PAGE

Which replacement for < *modified code* > will allow the program to run correctly for Fish, DarterFish, and SlowFish, as it did before the changes were made?

```
 I boolean bred = false;
   Random randNumGen = RandNumGenerator.getInstance();
   if (randNumGen.nextDouble() < probOfBreeding)
   {
       ArrayList emptyNbrs = emptyNeighbors();
       if(emptyNbrs.size() > 0)
       {
           breed(emptyNbrs);
           bred = true;
       }
   }
   if (!bred)
       move();

 II boolean bred = false;
   Random randNumGen = RandNumGenerator.getInstance();
   if (randNumGen.nextDouble() < probOfBreeding)
   {
       ArrayList emptyNbrs = emptyNeighbors();
       breed(emptyNbrs);
       bred = true;
   }
   if (!bred)
       move();

III boolean bred = false;
   Random randNumGen = RandNumGenerator.getInstance();
   ArrayList emptyNbrs = emptyNeighbors();
   if (randNumGen.nextDouble() < probOfBreeding &&
           emptyNbrs.size() > 0)
   {
       breed(emptyNbrs);
       bred = true;
   }
   if (!bred)
       move();
```

(A) I only
(B) II only
(C) III only
(D) I and III only
(E) I, II, and III

GO ON TO THE NEXT PAGE

40. What conditions must be true for nextLocation to be called for a SlowFish?

    I The list of empty neighbors must have size ≥ 1.
   II The SlowFish failed to breed.
  III A random real number must be $< 1.0/5.0$.

  (A) I only
  (B) II only
  (C) III only
  (D) II and III only
  (E) I, II, and III

END OF SECTION I

IF YOU FINISH BEFORE TIME IS CALLED, YOU MAY
CHECK YOUR WORK ON THIS SECTION.

DO NOT GO ON TO SECTION II UNTIL YOU ARE TOLD TO DO SO.

COMPUTER SCIENCE A
SECTION II

Time—1 hour and 45 minutes
Number of questions—4
Percent of total grade—50

Directions: SHOW ALL YOUR WORK. REMEMBER THAT PROGRAM SEGMENTS ARE TO BE WRITTEN IN JAVA.

Note: Assume that the standard packages (e.g., `java.util.*`) are included in any programs that use the code segments provided in individual questions. A Quick Reference to the standard classes and interfaces with their required methods is provided.

---

1. Consider the problem of designing a `StockItem` class to model items in stock on the shelf of a store. Each stock item includes the following:

   - A description of the item.
   - An identity number that is a positive integer.
   - A price in dollars, rounded to the nearest cent (two decimal places).
   - The number of this particular item on the shelf.

   When a new stock item is created, it must be assigned a description, an identity number, a price, and the number on the shelf. Operations on a stock item include the following:

   - Retrieve the description of the item.
   - Retrieve the identity number of the item.
   - Retrieve the price of the item.
   - Retrieve the number of this item on the shelf.
   - Set a new price for the item.
   - Remove some quantity of this item from the shelf (if an attempt is made to remove more than the number on the shelf, all are removed).
   - Add some quantity of this item to the shelf.

   (a) Write the class declaration for the `StockItem` class. In writing this class you must

   - Choose appropriate method names.
   - Provide the functionality specified above.
   - Provide a data representation consistent with the specification above.

   DO NOT WRITE IMPLEMENTATION CODE FOR THE METHODS OR CONSTRUCTOR(S) OF THE `StockItem` CLASS. Write {implementation} under the header. For example, suppose you have a method `changeDescription`. You would indicate it like this:

   ```
   public void changeDescription{String newDescription}
   { implementation }
   ```

GO ON TO THE NEXT PAGE.

(b) Consider the class Store, which represents a list of all the StockItem objects in the store. The Store class is partially specified below:

```
public class Store
{
    private ArrayList myStockList;    //all stock items in this store

    //constructors and other methods not shown
        . . .

    //Precondition:  myStockList contains StockItem with identity number idNum
    //Postcondition: StockItem with identity number idNum has been completely
    //               removed from the shelf
    public void removeAll(int idNum)
}
```

Write the Store method removeAll, which searches for the StockItem in myStockList whose identity number matches idNum and removes all instances of that item from the shelf. You may assume that myStockList does contain the StockItem with identity number idNum.

In writing removeAll you may use any of the methods of the StockItem class that you specified in part (a).

Complete method removeAll below:

```
//Precondition:  myStockList contains StockItem with identity number idNum
//Postcondition: StockItem with identity number idNum has been completely
//               removed from the shelf
public void removeAll(int idNum)
```

2. A NumberSet, shown in the class declaration below, stores a set of Integer objects in no particular order and contains no duplicates.

```
public class NumberSet
{
    //private data members not shown
        . . .

    //Constructor initializes set to empty
    public NumberSet()
    { implementation }

    //Returns number of integers in set
    public int size()
    { implementation }

    //Adds number to set (no duplicates)
    public void insert(Integer number)
    { implementation }

    //Removes number from set if present, else does nothing
    public void remove(Integer number)
    { implementation }
```

GO ON TO THE NEXT PAGE.

```
//Returns kth Integer in sorted increasing order, where 1 ≤ k ≤ size()
public Integer findkth(int k)
{ implementation }

//Returns true if set contains number, false otherwise
public boolean contains(Integer number)
{ implementation }
}
```

The `findkth` method returns the *k*th `Integer` in sorted increasing order in the set (the *k*th smallest number), even though the implementation of `NumberSet` may not be sorted. The number *k* ranges from 1 (first in sorted order) to *N*, where *N* is the number of integers in the set. For example, if `NumberSet` s stores the numbers {5, 15, 1, −6}, here are the `int` values when `s.findkth(k)` is called.

k	int values of s.findkth(k)
1	−6
2	1
3	5
4	15

(a) Write a client method `countNegatives` that returns the number of `Integers` with negative value that occur in `NumberSet` s. In writing `countNegatives`, you may call any of the methods of the `NumberSet` class. Assume that the methods work as specified.

Complete method `countNegatives` below.

```
//Postcondition: returns the number of negative integers in s
public static int countNegatives(NumberSet s)
```

(b) Write a client method `removeNegatives` that removes all `Integer` objects with negative value from s. If there are no negative integers in s, then `removeNegatives` does nothing. In writing `removeNegatives`, you may call method `countNegatives` specified in part (a). Assume that `countNegatives` works as specified, regardless of what you wrote in part (a).

Complete method `removeNegatives` below:

```
//Postcondition: NumberSet s contains no negative integers, but is
//               otherwise unchanged
public static void removeNegatives(NumberSet s)
```

(c) Write a client method `commonElements` that returns the `NumberSet` containing just those elements occurring in both of its `NumberSet` parameters. For example, if s1 is {2, −3, 4} and s2 is {1, 3, 2, 4}, `commonElements(s1, s2)` should return the `NumberSet` {2, 4}. (If you are familiar with mathematical set theory, `commonElements` returns the intersection of s1 and s2.)

Complete method `commonElements` below.

```
//Postcondition: returns the set containing only the elements that
//               occur in both s1 and s2
public static NumberSet commonElements(NumberSet s1, NumberSet s2)
```

GO ON TO THE NEXT PAGE.

3. This question refers to the `Sentence` class below. Note: A *word* is a string of consecutive nonblank (and nonwhitespace) characters. For example, the sentence

   "Hello there!" she said.

   consists of the four words

   ```
   "Hello     there!"     she     said.
   ```

   ```java
   public class Sentence
   {
       private String mySentence;
       private int myNumWords;

       //Constructor. Creates sentence from String str
       //Precondition: words in str separated by exactly one blank
       public class Sentence(String str)
       { implementation }

       public int getNumWords()
       { return myNumWords; }

       public String getSentence()
       { return mySentence; }

       //Returns copy of String s with all blanks removed
       //Postcondition: returned string contains just one word
       private static String removeBlanks(String s)
       { implementation }

       //Returns copy of String s with all letters in lowercase
       //Postcondition: number of words in returned string equals number
       //               of words in s
       private static String lowerCase(String s)
       { implementation }

       //Returns copy of String s with all punctuation removed
       //Postcondition: number of words in returned string equals number
       //               of words in s
       private static String removePunctuation(String s)
       { implementation }
   }
   ```

   (a) Complete the `Sentence` constructor as started below. The constructor assigns `str` to `mySentence`. You should write the subsequent code that assigns a value to `myNumWords`, the number of words in `mySentence`.

   Complete the constructor below:

   ```java
   //Constructor. Creates sentence from String str
   //Precondition: words in str separated by exactly one blank
   public class Sentence(String str)
   {
       mySentence = str;
   ```

(b) Consider the problem of testing whether a string is a palindrome. A *palindrome* reads the same from left to right and right to left, ignoring spaces, punctuation, and capitalization. For example,

> A Santa lived as a devil at NASA.
> Flo, gin is a sin! I golf.
> Eva, can I stab bats in a cave?

A public method `isPalindrome` is added to the `Sentence` class. Here is the method and its implementation:

```
//Returns true if mySentence is a palindrome, false otherwise
public boolean isPalindrome()
{
    String temp = removeBlanks(mySentence);
    temp = removePunctuation(temp);
    temp = lowerCase(temp);
    return isPalindrome(temp, 0, temp.length()-1);
}
```

The overloaded `isPalindrome` method contained in the code is a private recursive helper method, also added to the `Sentence` class. You are to write the implementation of this method. It takes a "purified" string as a parameter, namely one that has been stripped of blanks and punctuation and is all lowercase letters. It also takes as parameters the first and last index of the string. It returns true if this "purified" string is a palindrome, false otherwise.

A recursive algorithm for testing if a string is a palindrome is as follows:

- If the string has length 0 or 1, it's a palindrome.
- Remove the first and last letters.
- If those two letters are the same, and the remaining string is a palindrome, then the original string is a palindrome. Otherwise it's not.

Complete the `isPalindrome` method below:

```
/* Private recursive helper method that tests whether a substring
 * of string s is a palindrome.
 * start is the index of the first character of the substring.
 * end is the index of the last character of the substring.
 * Precondition:  s contains no spaces, punctuation, or capitals
 * Postcondition: returns true if the substring is a palindrome,
 *                false otherwise */
private static boolean isPalindrome(String s, int start, int end)
```

4. This question involves reasoning about the code from the Marine Biology Simulation Case Study. A Quick Reference to the case study is provided as part of this exam.

Consider adding a new kind of fish to the simulation, a flying fish. This fish will share all the attributes already defined for the Fish class, except that its movement behavior will be different. Here's how a flying fish moves: Like a normal fish, a flying fish only moves forward or sideways, never backward. Its first choice is to jump over adjacent fish. It therefore gets a list of empty "one away" neighbors by examining cells that are adjacent to its occupied neighboring cells and in the same direction. For example, if the cell in front of the flying fish is occupied, the cell in front of that one becomes a candidate for the flying fish's next location—if it is empty. If there are any of these empty one-away neighboring locations, one is randomly chosen to become the fish's next location. As with a normal fish, if the fish moves sideways it changes direction to reflect the direction it moved. If there are no available one-away neighboring locations, the flying fish moves like a normal fish.

Here are some examples. Suppose it is the turn of the circled flying fish to move:

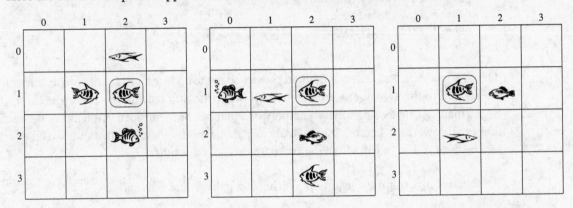

Next location: (1,0) or (3,2)   Next location must be (0,2)   Next location must be (3,1)

The following FlyingFish class will be used to implement a flying fish:

```
public class FlyingFish extends Fish
{
    //constructors
    //Three different constructors, as for the other fish, providing
    //a FlyingFish with its environment, location, direction, and color
        ...

    //redefined methods
    //Creates a new flying fish at location loc
    protected void generateChild(Location loc)
    { implementation }

    //Finds this fish's next location
    protected Location nextLocation()
    { implementation }

    //new method
    //Finds empty "one-away" locations adjacent to occupied neighbors
    //of this fish. Does not include a location behind this fish.
    //Returns an ArrayList of empty one-away locations.
    protected ArrayList targetLocations()
    { implementation }
}
```

GO ON TO THE NEXT PAGE.

(a) Write the `targetLocations` method that returns an `ArrayList` of valid, empty locations that are in a straight line adjacent to occupied neighbors of this fish. The list does not include a location behind the fish.

Write the implementation of `targetLocations` as started below (note: you should omit debugging statements):

```
//Finds empty "one-away" locations adjacent to occupied neighbors
//of this fish. Does not include a location behind this fish.
//Returns an ArrayList of empty one-away locations.
protected ArrayList targetLocations()
```

(b) Write the `nextLocation` method that finds the next location that this fish will move to. Here are the steps:

- Get a list of empty one-away neighbors.
- If there is at least one empty one-away neighbor
    return a randomly chosen one
  else
    return a location as for a normal fish in the `Fish` class.

In writing `nextLocation` you may want to call the `targetLocations` method defined in part (a). You may assume that this method works as specified irrespective of what you wrote in part (a).

Write the `nextLocation` method as started below (note: you should omit debugging statements):

```
//Finds this fish's next location
protected Location nextLocation()
```

END OF EXAMINATION

Answer Key

Section I

1. D	15. C	29. C
2. B	16. C	30. D
3. B	17. D	31. B
4. A	18. C	32. B
5. D	19. D	33. E
6. E	20. E	34. C
7. E	21. C	35. A
8. C	22. B	36. E
9. E	23. A	37. B
10. C	24. E	38. C
11. B	25. B	39. D
12. A	26. D	40. D
13. B	27. E	
14. E	28. A	

Answers Explained

Section I

1. **(D)** Constructors are never inherited. If a subclass has no constructor, the default constructor for the superclass is generated. If the superclass does not have a default constructor, a compiler error will occur.

2. **(B)** The programmer is using an object-oriented approach to writing the program, which means he will test the simplest classes first. This is bottom-up development. Choices A and C are wrong: in *top-down* development the main tasks in the program are listed in order of execution and then broken down into subtasks, which is known as *stepwise refinement*. Choice E is wrong because a driver program is one whose sole purpose is to test a given method. Implementing the simplest classes first may involve driver programs that test the various methods, but the overall plan is not an example of a driver program. Choice D is way off base—an interface is a collection of methods that will be implemented by classes that use these methods (see p. 81).

3. **(B)** A client method can read user input for aSuit and aValue, and then construct a new Card with the statement

   ```
   Card c = new Card(aSuit, aValue);
   ```

   Choice A is false because a default constructor has no parameters. The only constructor in Card has two parameters. Choice C is false because the toString method returns a single Card as a string. Choice D is false: There are no default comparison methods. In order to compare Card objects, the Card class would need to implement Comparable and provide a compareTo method. Choice E is false because the equals method, which is inherited by every class from Object, tests whether the object *references* are the same. To test whether two Card objects are equal in the sense of having the same suit and value would require that equals be overridden in the Card class.

4. **(A)** In the constructor, the private instance variables mySuit and myValue must be initialized to the appropriate parameter values. Choice A is the only choice that does this.

5. **(D)** To "pick a highest card" means that the program must be able to compare Card objects. This means that the Card class must implement Comparable, which in turn means that a compareTo method must be defined in the class (see p. 83). Option III does no harm, but equals tests for equality only, not greater than or less than, which was required for the application described.

6. **(E)** To construct a new object requires the keyword new, so eliminate choices A and C. The Card constructor takes two parameters, a String followed by an int. This eliminates choices B and D.

7. **(E)** The myDeck array is an array of Card objects. The syntax for creating the array requires the keyword new, followed by the type of elements in the array (in this case Card), followed by the number of slots (in this case NUMCARDS) in square brackets.

8. **(C)** Spades are represented by myDeck[0]...myDeck[12]. Hearts are represented by myDeck[13]...myDeck[25]. Therefore the correct test for hearts is if(i/13 == 1) and the correct assignment is myDeck[i] = ... The expression on the right-hand side must use the Card constructor. The correct Card value (second parameter) is an int from 0 to 12. This is correctly obtained with i % 13.

9. **(E)** Implementation I fails because there is no default toString method for arrays. Implementations II and III do the same thing: They invoke the toString method of the Card class.

10. **(C)** Here is one of the golden rules of programming: Don't start planning the program until every aspect of the specification is crystal clear. A programmer should never make unilateral decisions about ambiguities in a specification.

11. **(B)** When x ≤ y, a recursive call is made to whatIsIt(x-1, y). If x decreases at every recursive call, there is no way to reach a successful base case. Thus, the method never terminates and eventually exhausts all available memory.

12. **(A)** The expression !(max != a[i]) is equivalent to max == a[i], so the given expression is equivalent to a[i] == max || max == a[i], which is equivalent to a[i] == max.

13. **(B)** The index range for ArrayList is 0 ≤ index ≤ size()-1. Thus for methods get, remove, and set, the last in-bounds index is size()-1. The one exception is the add method—to add an element to the end of the list takes an index parameter list.size().

14. **(E)** Subclasses of `Quadrilateral` may also be abstract and contain `perimeter` and/or `area` as abstract methods.

15. **(C)** Segment I starts correctly, but fails to initialize the additional private variables of the `Rectangle` class. Segment II is wrong because by using `super` with `topLeft` and `botRight`, it implies that these values are used in the `Quadrilateral` superclass. This is false—there isn't even a constructor with three arguments in the superclass.

16. **(C)** Statement I is false because `Quadrilateral` is an abstract class, not an interface. (Recall that an interface provides a list of method headers without implementations.) The correct relationship between the `Quadrilateral` and `Rectangle` classes is that `Rectangle` is a subclass of `Quadrilateral` (`Rectangle extends Quadrilateral`). Statement II is false: The `Rectangle` class *uses* the `Point` class, but a `Point` is not a `Rectangle`.

17. **(D)** A client program may not access private variables of a class. This is why choice B doesn't work. Choices A and C are false: if two adjacent sides of a rectangle have the same length, the rectangle is a square. Also, since the rectangle is valid, the subtraction operations given in the method will produce positive lengths. Note that choice E is false: The method returns a boolean expression whose value is either `true` or `false`.

18. **(C)** The code segment is an example of polymorphism or dynamic binding. At run time the appropriate `area` method for each of the `Quadrilateral` objects will be invoked. Each of the other choices is false. For choice A, both `Parallelogram` and `Square` inherit `getLabels` from `Quadrilateral`. (Note that `Square` inherits `getLabels` from `Rectangle`, which inherits it from `Quadrilateral`.) For choice B, the `area` method is implemented in both the `Parallelogram` and `Square` classes, and this is the code that will be invoked for `q1.area()` and `q2.area()`. For choice D, even though q1 and q2 are declared to be of type `Quadrilateral`, `q1.area()` and `q2.area()` will select the correct operation for their particular object during run time. (This is dynamic binding—see p. 76.) For choice E, since the actual instances of q1 and q2 are `Parallelogram` and `Square`, they don't need to be cast. The correct actual types will be invoked at run time.

19. **(D)** The expression `quadList.get(i)` returns an element of type `Object`. This must be cast to `Quadrilateral` before the `getLabels` and `area` methods can be called because there is no `area` method in `Object`. The appropriate `area` method for a particular `Quadrilateral` will be determined at run time (polymorphism or dynamic binding).

20. **(E)** The algorithm has three steps:

    1. Store the object at `i` in `temp`.
    2. Place at location `i` the object at `j`.
    3. Place `temp` at location `j`.

    This has the effect of swapping the objects at `i` and `j`. Notice that choices B and C, while incomplete, are not incorrect. The question, however, asks for the *best* description of the postcondition, which is found in choice E.

21. **(C)** The expression `new Double(num)` creates a `Double` object from the `double` parameter num. This expression must be assigned to the private instance vari-

able `myNegReal`. Choices A and B do not use the keyword `new` and therefore cannot be correct. Choice D will create a `Double` with a positive value. This is incorrect since the precondition states that `num < 0`. Choice E attempts to negate a reference—no such syntax!

22. **(B)** The `Double` wrapper class contains a `doubleValue` method that returns the `double` value of any `Double` object. You need to use this method because the return type of `getValue` is `double`. Eliminate implementation I because it returns a `Double` (wrong type!). Eliminate implementation III because `doubleValue` is not a method of the `NegativeReal` class, it's a method of the `Double` class. Therefore you need to access it with a `Double` object and the dot member construct, as in implementation II.

23. **(A)** Subtracting 0.5 from a negative real number and then truncating it produces the number correctly rounded to the nearest integer. Note that casting to an `int` truncates a real number. The expression in choice B is correct for rounding a positive real number. Choice C won't round correctly. For example, −3.7 will be rounded to −3 instead of −4. Choice D will produce an error message: `intValue` is not a method in the `Double` class. Choice E attempts to use the dot member construct with a `double`, a non-object!

24. **(E)** The method call `whatsIt(347)` puts on the stack `System.out.print(7)`. The method call `whatsIt(34)` puts on the stack `System.out.print(4)`. The method call `whatsIt(3)` is a base case and writes out 3. Now the stack is popped from the top, and the 3 that was printed is followed by 4, then 7. The result is 347.

25. **(B)** Recall that insertion sort takes each element in turn and (a) finds its insertion point and (b) moves elements to insert that element in its correct place. Thus, if the array is in reverse sorted order, the insertion point will always be at the front of the array, leading to the maximum number of comparisons and data moves—very inefficient. Therefore choices A, C, and E are false.

   Selection sort finds the smallest element in the array and swaps it with `a[0]` and then finds the smallest element in the rest of the array and swaps it with `a[1]`, and so on. Thus the same number of comparisons and moves will occur, irrespective of the original arrangement of elements in the array. So choice B is true, and choice D is false.

26. **(D)** Notice that in the original code, if `n` is 1, `k` is incremented by 1, and if `n` is 4, `k` is incremented by 4. This is equivalent to saying "if `n` is 1 or 4, `k` is incremented by `n`."

27. **(E)** Segment I will throw a `NullPointerException` when `s.equals...` is invoked, because `s` is a null reference. Segment III looks suspect, but when the `startIndex` parameter of the substring method equals `s.length()`, the value returned is the empty string. If, however, `startIndex > s.length()`, a `StringIndexOutOfBoundsException` is thrown.

28. **(A)** Since results of calculations with floating-point numbers are not always represented exactly (round-off error), direct tests for equality are not reliable. Instead of the boolean expression `d == c`, a test should be done to check whether the difference of `d` and `c` is within some acceptable tolerance interval (see the Box on comparing floating point numbers, p. 6).

29. **(C)** If `arr` has elements 2, 3, 5, the values of `value` are

```
2                       //after initialization
2*10 + 3 = 23           //when i = 1
23*10 + 5 = 235         //when i = 2
```

30. **(D)** The point of the binary search algorithm is that the interval containing `key` is repeatedly narrowed down by splitting it in half. For each iteration of the `while` loop, if `key` is in the list, `arr[first]` $\leq$ `key` $\leq$ `arr[last]`. Note that (i) the endpoints of the interval must be included, and (ii) `key` is not necessarily in the list.

31. **(B)**

	first	last	mid	a[mid]
After first iteration	0	13	6	50
After second iteration	7	13	10	220
After third iteration	7	9	8	101
After fourth iteration	9	9	9	205

32. **(B)** The data structure is an `ArrayList`, not an array, so you need to use the `add` method for inserting elements into the list. This eliminates choices A and C. The method `nextInt(k)` returns a random integer from 0 to `k-1` inclusive. Thus to get integers from 0 to 100 requires a parameter of 101, which eliminates choice D. Choice E fails because it doesn't construct a new `Integer` object from `num`.

33. **(E)** All are correct! `System.out.print` takes a `String` parameter. If its parameter is an object, the `toString` method is automatically invoked. If the object's class has overridden `toString` appropriately, the correct result will be obtained (polymorphism). In segment I `myList.get(i)` returns an `Object` which is actually an `Integer`. In segment II `(Integer) myList.get(i)` is an `Integer`, and in segment III `myList` is an `ArrayList`. In each case the correct `toString` method will be invoked.

34. **(C)** Suppose, for example, `str1` is `strawberry` and `str2` is `cat`. Then `insert(str1, str2, 5)` will return the following pieces, concatenated:

$$\text{straw} + \text{cat} + \text{berry}$$
$$= a_0a_1a_2a_3a_4 + b_0b_1b_2 + a_5a_6a_7a_8a_9$$
$$= a_0a_1a_2a_3a_4b_0b_1b_2a_5a_6a_7a_8a_9$$

35. **(A)** Recall that `s.substring(k, m)` (a method of `String`) returns a substring of `s` starting at position `k` and ending at position `m-1`. Again consider the example in which `str1` is `strawberry`, `str2` is `cat`, and the method call is `insert(str1, str2, 5)`. String `str1` must be split into two parts, `first` and `last`. Then `str2` will be inserted between them. Since `str2` is inserted starting at position 5 (the "b"), `first = straw`, namely `str1.substring(0,pos)`. (Start at 0 and take all the characters up to and including location `pos-1`, namely 4.) Notice that `last`, the second substring of `str1`, must start at the index for "b", which is `pos`, the index at which `str2` was inserted. The expression `str1.substring(pos)` returns the substring of `str1` that starts at `pos` and continues to the end of the string, which was required. Note that you

don't need any "special case" tests. In the cases where str2 is inserted at the front of str1 (i.e., pos is 0) or the back of str1 (i.e., pos is str1.length()), the code for the general case works.

36. **(E)** Since the probability that a fish will die in a given timestep is 1/5, choice E is true. Note that choice D is not necessarily true—it depends on how crowded the environment is. Choice A is false because a fish may die in the first timestep, opening up a slot for another fish to move into. Choice B is false because fish can breed into *any* empty adjacent neighboring slot—it may not *move* into the slot behind it. Choice C is false because no empty neighbors to breed into means no empty neighbors to move into. The fish will stay where it is.

37. **(B)** The allObjects method returns an array of all the Locatable objects (i.e., Fish) in the environment. The picture shows five fish. The neighborsOf method returns an ArrayList containing the valid adjacent neighbors of a specified location. The location in this case is f.location(), which has four valid neighboring locations.

38. **(C)** In the initial setup the Fish has no empty neighbors—therefore it cannot breed nor move. The only other valid situation would have location (1,1) (the center location) empty, indicating that the fish died during this timestep. All other setups are invalid. In choice A, the fish bred into diagonal neighboring locations (not permissible in the BoundedEnv as currently defined). In choice B, the fish bred into adjacent locations that were not empty. In choice D the fish changed direction without moving. In choice E the fish moved diagonally—not permissible in this BoundedEnv.

39. **(D)** In order for the fish to breed, the probability for breeding must be in the correct range *and* there must be at least one neighboring adjacent cell available. If the fish doesn't breed, it moves. It appears that segment II is correct, even though it doesn't check that there's at least one empty adjacent slot available. Thus segment II sets bred to true, even though the fish tries to breed but fails for lack of available slots. If bred is true, the fish won't attempt to move. You may argue that the code still works because the fish would not have been able to move anyway because of no available slots. What ruins this argument is the darter fish—remember, when it attempts to move, if it can't find a slot, it keeps its current location, but reverses direction. (Note that randNumGen should not be declared more than once in any method. Therefore the declaration preceding the test for dying was removed from the code of the act method used in the statement of the question.)

40. **(D)** When a SlowFish fails to breed, it attempts to move. The move method calls nextLocation, but only if a random number falls within the probability range (i.e., < 1.0/5.0) for it to move. Thus conditions II and III need to be true before nextLocation is called. Condition I is incorrect: Because the list of empty neighbors is generated in the nextLocation method, it is not a condition for calling the method.

Section II

1. (a)
```
public class StockItem
{
      private String myDescription;
      private int myIdNum;
      private double myPrice;
      private int myNumOnShelf;

      public StockItem(String description, int id,
          double price, int numOnShelf)
      { implementation }

      public String getDescription()
      { implementation }

      public int getIdNum()
      { implementation }

      public double getPrice()
      { implementation }

      public int getNumOnShelf()
      { implementation }

      public void setPrice(double newPrice)
      { implementation }

      public void remove(int quantity)
      { implementation }

      public void add(int quantity)
      { implementation }
}
```

(b)
```
public void removeAll(int idNum)
{
    int i = 0;
    while (((StockItem) myStockList.get(i)).getIdNum()
              != idNum)
        i++;
    StockItem item = (StockItem) myStockList.get(i);
    item.remove(item.getNumOnShelf());
}
```
Alternatively,
```
public void removeAll(int idNum)
{
    for (int i=0; i<myStockList.size(); i++)
    {
        StockItem item = (StockItem) myStockList.get(i);
        if (item.getIdNum() == idNum)
        {
            item.remove(item.getNumOnShelf());
            break;
        }
    }
}
```

NOTE

- In part (b) the Object retrieved from the ArrayList must first be cast to StockItem before the getIdNum and remove methods can be called.
- The while loop in the first solution for part (b) will not cause an out-of-range error, since the precondition guarantees that a StockItem with the given identity number is in the list. If this is not guaranteed, you need to start the while loop test with i<myStockList.size().
- In the alternative solution shown for part (b) you want to exit the method as soon as the required StockItem has been found and processed. The break statement gets you out of the for loop and hence out of the method. The break construct will not be tested on the AP exam.

2. (a)
```
public static int countNegatives(NumberSet s)
{
    int count = 0;
    Integer zero = new Integer(0);
    while (count < s.size() &&
            s.findkth(count+1).compareTo(zero) < 0)
        count++;
    return count;
}
```

Alternatively,

```
public static int countNegatives(NumberSet s)
{
    int count = 0;
    while (count < s.size() &&
            s.findkth(count+1).intValue() < 0)
        count++;
    return count;
}
```

(b)
```
public static void removeNegatives(NumberSet s)
{
    int n = countNegatives(s);
    for (int i=1; i<=n; i++)
        s.remove(s.findkth(1));
}
```

Alternatively,

```
public static void removeNegatives(NumberSet s)
{
    while (s.findkth(1).intValue() < 0)
        s.remove(s.findkth(1));
}
```

(c)
```
public static NumberSet commonElements(NumberSet s1,
        NumberSet s2)
{
    NumberSet temp = new NumberSet();
    for (int i=1; i<=s1.size(); i++)
        if (s2.contains(s1.findkth(i)))
            temp.insert(s1.findkth(i));
    return temp;
}
```

NOTE

- To test whether an Integer is negative you must either compare it with another Integer object whose value is 0, or compare the intValue() of the Integer with the primitive int 0.
- In part (a), you must check that your solution works if s is empty. For the given algorithm, count < s.size() will fail and short circuit the test, which is desirable since s.findkth(1) will violate the precondition of findkth(k), namely that k cannot be greater than size().
- The parameter for s.findkth must be greater than 0. Hence the use of s.findkth(count+1) in part (a).
- For the first solution in part (b), you get a subtle intent error if your last step is s.remove(s.findkth(i)). Suppose that s is initially {2,−4,−6}. After s.remove(s.findkth(1)), s will be {2, −4}. After the statement s.remove(s.findkth(2)), s will be {−4}!! The point is that s is adjusted after each call to s.remove. The algorithm that works is this: If N is the number of negatives, simply remove the smallest element N times. Note that the alternative solution avoids the pitfall described by simply repeatedly removing the smallest element if it's negative.
- Part (c) could also be accomplished by going through each element in s2 and checking if it's included in s1.

3. (a)
```
public class Sentence(String str)
{
    mySentence = str;
    myNumWords = 1;
    int k = str.indexOf(" ");
    while (k != -1)    //while there are still blanks in str
    {
        myNumWords++;
        str = str.substring(k+1); //substring after blank
        k = str.indexOf(" ");     //get index of next blank
    }
}
```

(b)
```
private static boolean isPalindrome(String s, int start,
        int end)
{
    if (start >= end)  //substring has length 0 or 1
        return true;
    else
    {
        String first = s.substring(start, start+1);
        String last = s.substring(end, end+1);
        if (first.equals(last))
            return isPalindrome(s, start+1, end-1);
        else
            return false;
    }
}
```

NOTE

- In part (a), for every occurrence of a blank in mySentence, myNumWords must be incremented. (Be sure to initialize myNumWords to 1!)
- In part (a), the code locates all the blanks in mySentence by replacing str

with the substring that consists of the piece of str directly following the most recently located blank.

- Recall that indexOf returns -1 if its String parameter does not occur as a substring in its String calling object.

- In part (b) the start and end indexes move toward each other with each subsequent recursive call. This shortens the string to be tested in each call. When start and end meet, the base case has been reached.

- Notice the private static methods in the Sentence class, including the helper method you were asked to write. They are static because they are not invoked by a Sentence object (no dot member construct). The only use of these methods is to help achieve the postconditions of other methods in the class.

4. (a)
```
protected ArrayList targetLocations()
{
    Environment env = environment();
    //get all neighbors of this fish, empty or not
    ArrayList nbrs = env.neighborsOf(location());
    //remove location behind
    Direction oppDir = direction().reverse();
    Location locBehind = env.getNeighbor(location(), oppDir);
    nbrs.remove(locBehind);
    //get empty one-away neighbors
    ArrayList targetLocs = new ArrayList();
    for (int index=0; index<nbrs.size(); index++)
    {
        Location loc = (Location) nbrs.get(index);
        if (!env.isEmpty(loc))
        {
            Direction dir = env.getDirection(location(), loc);
            Location oneAway = env.getNeighbor(loc, dir);
            if (env.isEmpty(oneAway))
                targetLocs.add(oneAway);
        }
    }
    return targetLocs;
}
```

(b)
```
protected Location nextLocation()
{
    //get list of empty neighboring one-away locations
    ArrayList targetLocs = targetLocations();
    if (targetLocs.size() != 0)
    {
        //return a randomly chosen empty one-away location
        Random randNumGen = RandNumGenerator.getInstance();
        int randNum = randNumGen.nextInt(targetLocs.size());
        return (Location) targetLocs.get(randNum);
    }
    else
        return super.nextLocation();
}
```

NOTE

- In part (a) you don't need to do any validity tests for the various locations. If a neighbor is invalid (out of bounds), then the adjacent one-away neighbor will be out of bounds too, and this will be picked up when it fails the `!env.isEmpty(loc)` test.
- In part (b), if the fish has no available positions to jump into, it'll move like a normal fish. This can be achieved by calling `nextLocation` from the `Fish` superclass:

```
return super.nextLocation();
```

Answer Sheet: Practice Exam Two

1. Ⓐ Ⓑ Ⓒ Ⓓ Ⓔ
2. Ⓐ Ⓑ Ⓒ Ⓓ Ⓔ
3. Ⓐ Ⓑ Ⓒ Ⓓ Ⓔ
4. Ⓐ Ⓑ Ⓒ Ⓓ Ⓔ
5. Ⓐ Ⓑ Ⓒ Ⓓ Ⓔ
6. Ⓐ Ⓑ Ⓒ Ⓓ Ⓔ
7. Ⓐ Ⓑ Ⓒ Ⓓ Ⓔ
8. Ⓐ Ⓑ Ⓒ Ⓓ Ⓔ
9. Ⓐ Ⓑ Ⓒ Ⓓ Ⓔ
10. Ⓐ Ⓑ Ⓒ Ⓓ Ⓔ
11. Ⓐ Ⓑ Ⓒ Ⓓ Ⓔ
12. Ⓐ Ⓑ Ⓒ Ⓓ Ⓔ
13. Ⓐ Ⓑ Ⓒ Ⓓ Ⓔ
14. Ⓐ Ⓑ Ⓒ Ⓓ Ⓔ

15. Ⓐ Ⓑ Ⓒ Ⓓ Ⓔ
16. Ⓐ Ⓑ Ⓒ Ⓓ Ⓔ
17. Ⓐ Ⓑ Ⓒ Ⓓ Ⓔ
18. Ⓐ Ⓑ Ⓒ Ⓓ Ⓔ
19. Ⓐ Ⓑ Ⓒ Ⓓ Ⓔ
20. Ⓐ Ⓑ Ⓒ Ⓓ Ⓔ
21. Ⓐ Ⓑ Ⓒ Ⓓ Ⓔ
22. Ⓐ Ⓑ Ⓒ Ⓓ Ⓔ
23. Ⓐ Ⓑ Ⓒ Ⓓ Ⓔ
24. Ⓐ Ⓑ Ⓒ Ⓓ Ⓔ
25. Ⓐ Ⓑ Ⓒ Ⓓ Ⓔ
26. Ⓐ Ⓑ Ⓒ Ⓓ Ⓔ
27. Ⓐ Ⓑ Ⓒ Ⓓ Ⓔ
28. Ⓐ Ⓑ Ⓒ Ⓓ Ⓔ

29. Ⓐ Ⓑ Ⓒ Ⓓ Ⓔ
30. Ⓐ Ⓑ Ⓒ Ⓓ Ⓔ
31. Ⓐ Ⓑ Ⓒ Ⓓ Ⓔ
32. Ⓐ Ⓑ Ⓒ Ⓓ Ⓔ
33. Ⓐ Ⓑ Ⓒ Ⓓ Ⓔ
34. Ⓐ Ⓑ Ⓒ Ⓓ Ⓔ
35. Ⓐ Ⓑ Ⓒ Ⓓ Ⓔ
36. Ⓐ Ⓑ Ⓒ Ⓓ Ⓔ
37. Ⓐ Ⓑ Ⓒ Ⓓ Ⓔ
38. Ⓐ Ⓑ Ⓒ Ⓓ Ⓔ
39. Ⓐ Ⓑ Ⓒ Ⓓ Ⓔ
40. Ⓐ Ⓑ Ⓒ Ⓓ Ⓔ

How to Calculate Your (Approximate) AP Score — AP Computer Science Level A

Multiple Choice

Number correct (out of 40)   =   _____

$1/4 \times$ number wrong   =   _____

Raw score = line 1 − line 2   =   _____   ⟸   Multiple-Choice Score
                                                         (Do not round. If less
                                                         than zero, enter zero.)

Free Response

Question 1   _____
                  (out of 9)

Question 2   _____
                  (out of 9)

Question 3   _____
                  (out of 9)

Question 4   _____
                  (out of 9)

Total   _____ $\times$ 1.11   =   _____   ⟸   Free-Response Score
                                                                                (Do not round.)

Final Score

_____   +   _____   =   _____
Multiple-   Free-   Final Score
Choice   Response   (Round to nearest
Score   Score   whole number.)

Chart to Convert to AP Grade
Computer Science A

Final Score Range	AP Grade[a]
60–80	5
45–59	4
33–44	3
25–32	2
0–24	1

[a]The score range corresponding to each grade varies from exam to exam and is approximate.

Practice Exam Two

COMPUTER SCIENCE A
SECTION I

Time—1 hour and 15 minutes
Number of questions—40
Percent of total grade—50

Directions: Determine the answer to each of the following questions or incomplete statements, using separate pieces of scrap paper for any necessary scratchwork. Then decide which is the best of the choices given and fill in the corresponding oval on the answer sheet. Do not spend too much time on any one problem.

Note: Assume that the standard packages (e.g., `java.util.*`) are included in any programs that use the code segments provided in individual questions. A Quick Reference to the standard classes and interfaces with their required methods is provided.

---

1. A large Java program was thoroughly tested and found to have no bugs. What can be concluded?
   (A) All of the preconditions in the program are correct.
   (B) All of the postconditions in the program are correct.
   (C) The program may have bugs.
   (D) The program has no bugs.
   (E) Every method in the program may safely be used in other programs.

GO ON TO THE NEXT PAGE

Questions 2–5 refer to the Worker class below:

```java
public class Worker
{
    private String myName;
    private double myHourlyWage;
    private boolean isUnionMember;

    //constructors

    public Worker()
    { implementation }

    public Worker(String name, double hourlyWage, boolean union)
    { implementation }

    //accessors

    public String getName()
    { return myName; }

    public double getHourlyWage()
    { return myHourlyWage; }

    public boolean getUnionStatus()
    { return isUnionMember; }

    //modifiers

    //Permanently increase hourly wage by amt
    public void incrementWage(double amt)
    { implementation }

    //Switch value of isUnionMember from true to false and vice versa
    public void changeUnionStatus()
    { implementation }
}
```

2. Which of the following correctly implements the constructor with parameters of the Worker class?

    (A) name = myName;
        hourlyWage = myHourlyWage;
        union = isUnionMember;

    (B) myName = name;
        myHourlyWage = hourlyWage;
        isUnionMember = union;

    (C) myName = name;
        myHourlyWage = hourlyWage;
        isUnionMember = true;

    (D) Worker = new Worker(name, hourlyWage, union);

    (E) super(name, hourlyWage, union);

GO ON TO THE NEXT PAGE

3. Refer to the `incrementWage` method:

```
//Permanently increase hourly wage by amt
public void incrementWage(double amt)
{ implementation }
```

Which of the following is a correct *implementation*?
- (A) `return myHourlyWage + amt;`
- (B) `return getHourlyWage() + amt;`
- (C) `myHourlyWage += amt;`
- (D) `getHourlyWage() += amt;`
- (E) `myHourlyWage = amt;`

4. Consider the method `changeUnionStatus`:

```
//Switch value of isUnionMember from true to false and vice versa
public void changeUnionStatus()
{ implementation }
```

Which is a correct *implementation*?

```
I  if (isUnionMember)
        isUnionMember = false;
   else
        isUnionMember = true;
```

```
II isUnionMember = !isUnionMember;
```

```
III if (isUnionMember)
        isUnionMember = !isUnionMember;
```

- (A) I only
- (B) II only
- (C) III only
- (D) I and II only
- (E) I, II, and III

5. A client method `computePay` will return a worker's pay based on the number of hours worked.

```
//Precondition:  Worker w has worked the given number of hours
//Postcondition: Returns amount of pay for Worker w
public static double computePay(Worker w, double hours)
{ <code> }
```

Which replacement for < *code* > is correct?
- (A) `return myHourlyWage * hours;`
- (B) `return getHourlyWage() * hours;`
- (C) `return w.getHourlyWage() * hours;`
- (D) `return w.myHourlyWage * hours;`
- (E) `return w.getHourlyWage() * w.hours;`

GO ON TO THE NEXT PAGE

6. Consider this program segment. You may assume that wordList is an ArrayList of String objects.

```
for (int i=0; i<wordList.size(); i++)
{
    String s = (String) wordList.get(i);
    if (s.length() < 4)
        System.out.println("SHORT WORD");
}
```

What is the maximum number of times that SHORT WORD can be printed?
(A) 0
(B) 1
(C) wordList.size()
(D) wordList.size() - 1
(E) s.length()

7. The expression $20 + 21/6 * 2$ is equivalent to
(A) $20 + 3 * 2$
(B) $41/6 * 2$
(C) $20 + 21/12$
(D) $41/(6 * 2)$
(E) $20 + (3.5 * 2)$

Questions 8 and 9 refer to the following method.

```
public static int mystery(int n)
{
    if (n == 1)
        return 3;
    else
        return 3*mystery(n-1);
}
```

8. What value does mystery(4) return?
(A) 3
(B) 9
(C) 12
(D) 27
(E) 81

9. Which best describes what method mystery does?
(A) Multiplies n by 3
(B) Raises 3 to the nth power
(C) Raises n to the third power
(D) Returns $(n)(n-1)(n-2)\ldots(1)$, namely $n!$
(E) Finds the least common multiple of 3 and n

GO ON TO THE NEXT PAGE

Questions 10–13 refer to the classes Address and Customer given below.

```
public class Address
{
    private String myStreet;
    private String myCity;
    private String myState;
    private int myZipCode;

    //constructor
    public Address(String street, String city, String state, int zipCode)
    { /* implementation not shown */ }

    //accessors

    public String getStreet()
    { /* implementation not shown */ }

    public String getCity()
    { /* implementation not shown */ }

    public String getState()
    { /* implementation not shown */ }

    public int getZipCode()
    { /* implementation not shown */ }
}

public class Customer
{
    private String myName;
    private String myPhone;
    private Address myAddress;
    private int myID;

    //constructor
    public Customer(String name, String phone, Address addr, int ID)
    { implementation }

    //accessors

    //Returns address of this customer
    public Address getAddress()
    { implementation }

    public String getName()
    { /* implementation not shown */ }

    public String getPhone()
    { /* implementation not shown */ }

    public int getID()
    { /* implementation not shown */ }
}
```

GO ON TO THE NEXT PAGE

10. Which is correct *implementation* code for the getAddress method of the Customer class?

    (A) `return myAddress;`

    (B) `return addr;`

    (C) `return this.getAddress();`

    (D)
```
return myAddress.getStreet();
return myAddress.getCity();
return myAddress.getState();
return myAddress.getZipCode();
```

    (E)
```
Address a = new Address(getStreet(), getCity(), getState(), getZipCode());
return a;
```

11. Which of the following correctly creates an Address object a?

    (A) `Address a = new Address("4 Bush Lane", "Ithaca", "NY", "14850");`

    (B)
```
Address a;
a = new Address("4 Bush Lane", "Ithaca", "NY", "14850");
```

    (C) `Address a = Address("4 Bush Lane", "Ithaca", "NY", 14850);`

    (D) `Address a = new Address("4 Bush Lane", "Ithaca", "NY", 14850);`

    (E) `Address a = new Address(4 Bush Lane, Ithaca, NY, 14850);`

12. Which of the following correctly creates a Customer object c?

    I
```
Address a = new Address("125 Bismark St", "Pleasantville", "NY", 14850);
Customer c = new Customer("Jack Spratt", "747-1674", a, 7008);
```

    II
```
Customer c = new Customer("Jack Spratt", "747-1674",
    "125 Bismark St, Pleasantville, NY 14850", 7008);
```

    III
```
Customer c = new Customer("Jack Spratt", "747-1674",
    new Address("125 Bismark St", "Pleasantville", "NY", 14850), 7008);
```

    (A) I only
    (B) II only
    (C) III only
    (D) I and II only
    (E) I and III only

GO ON TO THE NEXT PAGE

13. Consider an `AllCustomers` class that has private instance variable

```
private Customer[] custList;
```

Given the ID number of a particular customer, a method of the class, `locate`, must find the correct `Customer` record and return the name of that customer. Here is the method `locate`:

```
/* Precondition:   custList contains a complete list of Customer objects.
 *                 idNum matches the ID number data member of one
 *                 of the Customer objects
 * Postcondition:  The name of the customer whose ID number
 *                 matches idNum is returned  */
public String locate(int idNum)
{
    for (int i=0; i<custList.length; i++)
        if (custList[i].getID() == idNum)
            return custList[i].getName();
    return null;      //idNum not found
}
```

A more efficient algorithm for finding the matching `Customer` object could be used if
(A) `Customer` objects were in alphabetical order by name.
(B) `Customer` objects were sorted by phone number.
(C) `Customer` objects were sorted by ID number.
(D) The `custList` array had fewer elements.
(E) The `Customer` class did not have an `Address` data member.

14. Often the most efficient computer algorithms use a divide-and-conquer approach, for example, one in which a list is repeatedly split into two pieces until a desired outcome is reached. Which of the following use a divide-and-conquer approach?

   I mergesort
   II insertion sort
   III binary search

(A) I only
(B) II only
(C) III only
(D) I and III only
(E) I, II, and III

GO ON TO THE NEXT PAGE

15. What will be output by this code segment?

```
for (int i=5; i>0; i--)
{
    for (int j=1; j<=i; j++)
        System.out.print(j*j + " ");
    System.out.println();
}
```

(A) 1
    1 4
    1 4 9
    1 4 9 16
    1 4 9 16 25

(B) 1 4 9 16 25
    1 4 9 16
    1 4 9
    1 4
    1

(C) 25 16 9 4 1
    25 16 9 4
    25 16 9
    25 16
    25

(D) 25
    25 16
    25 16 9
    25 16 9 4
    25 16 9 4 1

(E) 1 4 9 16 25
    1 4 9 16 25
    1 4 9 16 25
    1 4 9 16 25
    1 4 9 16 25

GO ON TO THE NEXT PAGE

16. Consider two methods of storing a set of nonnegative integers in which there are no duplicates.

Method One: Store the integers explicitly in an array in which the number of elements is known. For example, in this method, the set {6, 2, 1, 8, 9, 0} can be represented as follows:

0	1	2	3	4	5
6	2	1	8	9	0

6 elements

Method Two: Suppose that the range of the integers is 0 to MAX. Use a boolean array indexed from 0 to MAX. The index values represent the possible values in the set. In other words, each possible integer from 0 to MAX is represented by a different position in the array. A value of true in the array means that the corresponding integer is in the set, a value of false means that the integer is not in the set. For example, using this method the set {6, 2, 1, 8, 9, 0} would be represented as follows (T = true, F = false):

0	1	2	3	4	5	6	7	8	9	10	...	MAX
T	T	T	F	F	F	T	F	T	T	F	...	F

The following operations are to be performed on the set of integers:

   I Search for a target value in the set.
  II Print all the elements of the set.
 III Return the number of elements in the set.

Which statement is *true*?
(A) Operation I is more efficient if the set is stored using Method One.
(B) Operation II is more efficient if the set is stored using Method Two.
(C) Operation III is more efficient if the set is stored using Method One.
(D) Operation I is equally efficient for Methods One and Two.
(E) Operation III is equally efficient for Methods One and Two.

17. An algorithm for finding the average of N numbers is

$$\text{average} = \frac{\text{sum}}{N}$$

where N and sum are both integers. In a program using this algorithm, a programmer forgot to include a test that would check for N equal to zero. If N is zero, when will the error be detected?
(A) At compile time
(B) At edit time
(C) As soon as the value of N is entered
(D) During run time
(E) When an incorrect result is output

GO ON TO THE NEXT PAGE

18. What is wrong with this interface?

```
public interface Bad
{
    void someMethod(String password)
    {
        System.out.println("Psst! The password is " + password);
    }
}
```

(A) A method in an interface should be declared public.
(B) A method in an interface should be declared abstract.
(C) There should not be a method implementation.
(D) There should be a class implementation provided.
(E) There should not be any method parameters.

19. Consider the following program segment:

```
//Precondition: a[0]...a[n-1] is an initialized array of
//              integers, 0 < n ≤ a.length
    int c = 0;
    for (int i=0; i<n; i++)
        if (a[i] > 0)
        {
            a[c] = a[i];
            c++;
        }
    n = c;
```

Which is the best postcondition for the segment?
(A) a[0]...a[n-1] has been stripped of all positive integers.
(B) a[0]...a[n-1] has been stripped of all negative integers.
(C) a[0]...a[n-1] has been stripped of all occurrences of zero.
(D) The updated value of n is less than or equal to the value of n before execution of the segment.
(E) Array a contains more elements than it did before execution of the segment.

GO ON TO THE NEXT PAGE

20. If a, b, and c are integers, which of the following conditions is sufficient to *guarantee* that the expression

```
a < c || a < b && !(a == c)
```

evaluates to true?

(A) a < c
(B) a < b
(C) a > b
(D) a == b
(E) a == c

21. Airmail Express charges for shipping small packages by integer values of weight. The charges for a weight *w* in pounds are as follows:

$$0 < w \le 2 \qquad \$4.00$$
$$2 < w \le 5 \qquad \$8.00$$
$$5 < w \le 20 \quad \$15.00$$

The company does not accept packages that weigh more than 20 pounds. Which of the following represents the best set of data (weights) to test a program that calculates shipping charges?

(A) 2, 5, 20
(B) 1, 4, 16
(C) 1, 2, 3, 5, 16, 20
(D) 1, 2, 3, 5, 16, 20, 21
(E) All integers from 1 through 21

Questions 22–23 are based on the following class declaration:

```
public class AutoPart
{
    private String myDescription;
    private int myPartNum;
    private double myPrice;

    //constructor
    public AutoPart(String description, int partNum, double price)
    { implementation }

    //accessors

    public String getDescription()
    { return myDescription; }

    public int getPartNum()
    { return myPartNum; }

    public double getPrice()
    { return myPrice; }
}
```

GO ON TO THE NEXT PAGE

22. This question refers to the `findCheapest` method below, which occurs in a class that has an array of `AutoPart` as one if its private data fields:

```
private AutoPart[] allParts;
```

The `findCheapest` method examines an array of `AutoPart` and returns the part number of the `AutoPart` with the lowest price whose description matches the `part` parameter. For example, several of the `AutoPart` elements may have "headlight" as their description field. Different headlights will differ in both price and part number. If the `part` parameter is "headlight", then `findCheapest` will return the part number of the cheapest headlight.

```
/* Precondition:  allParts contains at least one element whose
 *                description matches part
 * Postcondition: Returns the part number of the cheapest AutoPart
 *                whose description matches part  */
public int findCheapest(String part)
{
    double min = LARGEVALUE;     //a value larger than the price of all auto parts
    int minIndex = -1;           //minIndex will be reassigned in for loop
    for (int i=0; i<allParts.length; i++)
        < more code >
}
```

Which of the following replacements for < *more code* > will achieve the intended postcondition of the method?

```
I  {
       if (allParts[i].getPrice() < min)
       {
           min = allParts[i].getPrice();
           minIndex = i;
       }
   }
   return allParts[minIndex].getPartNum();

II {
       if ((allParts[i].getDescription()).equals(part))
           if (allParts[i].getPrice() < min)
           {
               min = allParts[i].getPrice();
               minIndex = i;
           }
   }
   return allParts[minIndex].getPartNum();

III {
        if ((allParts[i].getDescription()).equals(part))
            if (allParts[i].getPrice() < min)
                min = allParts[i].getPrice();
    }
    return allParts[min].getPartNum();
```

(A) I only
(B) II only
(C) III only
(D) I and II only
(E) I and III only

GO ON TO THE NEXT PAGE

23. Consider the following method:

```
//Precondition: ob1 and ob2 are distinct objects
//Return smaller of ob1 and ob2
public static Object min(Object ob1, Object ob2)
{
    if (((Comparable) ob1).compareTo(ob2) < 0)
        return ob1;
    else
        return ob2;
}
```

A method in the same class has these declarations:

```
AutoPart p1 = new AutoPart(< suitable values >);
AutoPart p2 = new AutoPart(< suitable values >);
```

Which of the following statements will *not* cause an error?

(A) `System.out.println(min(p1.getDescription(), p2.getDescription()));`

(B) `System.out.println(min(p1.getPartNum(), p2.getPartNum()));`

(C) `System.out.println(min(p1.getPrice(), p2.getPrice()));`

(D) `System.out.println(min(((String) p1).getDescription(),`
`        ((String) p2).getDescription()));`

(E) `System.out.println(min(p1, p2));`

24. This question is based on the following declarations:

```
String strA = "CARROT", strB = "Carrot", strC = "car";
```

Given that all uppercase letters precede all lowercase letters when considering alphabetical order, which is true?

(A) `strA.compareTo(strB) < 0 && strB.compareTo(strC) > 0`

(B) `strC.compareTo(strB) < 0 && strB.compareTo(strA) < 0`

(C) `strB.compareTo(strC) < 0 && strB.compareTo(strA) > 0`

(D) `!(strA.compareTo(strB) == 0) && strB.compareTo(strA) < 0`

(E) `!(strA.compareTo(strB) == 0) && strC.compareTo(strB) < 0`

GO ON TO THE NEXT PAGE

25. Refer to method removeWord.

```
//Precondition:  wordList is an ArrayList of String objects
//Postcondition: All occurrences of word have been removed from wordList
public static void removeWord(ArrayList wordList, String word)
{
    for (int i=0; i<wordList.size(); i++)
        if ((wordList.get(i)).equals(word))
            wordList.remove(i);
}
```

The method does not always work as intended. Consider the method call

```
removeWord(wordList, "cat");
```

For which of the following lists will this method call fail?
(A) The cat sat on the mat
(B) The cat cat sat on the mat mat
(C) The cat sat on the cat
(D) cat
(E) The cow sat on the mat

GO ON TO THE NEXT PAGE

Questions 26–28 refer to the `ThreeDigitInteger` and `ThreeDigitCode` classes below.

```
public class ThreeDigitInteger
{
    private int myHundredsDigit;
    private int myTensDigit;
    private int myOnesDigit;
    private int myValue;

    //constructor
    //value is a 3-digit int
    public ThreeDigitInteger(int value)
    { implementation }

    //Return sum of digits for this ThreeDigitInteger
    public int digitSum()
    { implementation }

    //other methods not shown
        . . .
}


public class ThreeDigitCode extends ThreeDigitInteger
{
    private boolean myIsValid;

    //constructor
    //value is a 3-digit int
    public ThreeDigitCode(int value)
    { implementation }

    /* Returns true if ThreeDigitCode is valid, false otherwise.
     * ThreeDigitCode is valid if and only if the remainder when the sum of
     * the hundreds and tens digits is divided by 7 equals the ones digit.
     * Thus 362 is valid while 364 is not  */
    public boolean isValid()
    { implementation }
}
```

26. Which is a *true* statement about the classes shown?
    (A) The `ThreeDigitInteger` class inherits the `isValid` method from the `ThreeDigitCode` class.
    (B) The `ThreeDigitCode` class inherits all of the private instance variables and public accessor methods from the `ThreeDigitInteger` class.
    (C) The `ThreeDigitCode` class inherits the constructor from the `ThreeDigitInteger` class.
    (D) The `ThreeDigitCode` class can directly access all the private variables of the `ThreeDigitInteger` class.
    (E) The `ThreeDigitInteger` class can access the `myIsValid` instance variable of the `ThreeDigitCode` class.

GO ON TO THE NEXT PAGE

27. Which is correct *implementation* code for the `ThreeDigitCode` constructor?

```
   I  super(value);
      myIsValid = isValid();

  II  super(value, valid);

 III  myIsValid = isValid();
      super(value);
```

(A) I only
(B) II only
(C) III only
(D) I and III only
(E) I, II, and III

28. Refer to these declarations in a client program:

```
ThreeDigitInteger code = new ThreeDigitCode(127);
ThreeDigitInteger num = new ThreeDigitInteger(456);
```

Which of the following subsequent tests will *not* cause an error?

```
   I  if (code.isValid())
         ...

  II  if (num.isValid())
         ...

 III  if (((ThreeDigitCode) code).isValid())
         ...
```

(A) I only
(B) II only
(C) III only
(D) I and II only
(E) I and III only

GO ON TO THE NEXT PAGE

29. Consider the following hierarchy of classes:

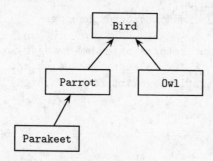

Assuming that each class has a valid default constructor, which of the following declarations in a client program are correct?

```
 I  Bird b1 = new Parrot();
    Bird b2 = new Parakeet();
    Bird b3 = new Owl();

II  Parakeet p = new Parrot();
    Owl o = new Bird();

III Parakeet p = new Bird();
```

(A) I only
(B) II only
(C) III only
(D) II and III only
(E) I, II, and III

30. Which of the following correctly appends the first five perfect squares 1, 4, 9, 16, and 25, to an existing `ArrayList list`?

(A) `for (int i=1; i<list.size(); i++)`
      `list.add(new Integer(i*i));`

(B) `for (int i=1; i<=5; i++)`
      `list.add(i*i);`

(C) `for (int i=0; i<5; i++)`
      `list.add((i+1)*(i+1));`

(D) `for (int i=1; i<6; i++)`
      `list.add(new Integer(i*i));`

(E) `for (int i=1; i<list.size(); i++)`
      `list.add(i*i);`

GO ON TO THE NEXT PAGE

31. Refer to the ExtendedRandom class below:

```java
import java.util.Random;
public class ExtendedRandom extends Random
{
    /* Postcondition: returns a random integer in the range
     *                  low to high, inclusive */
    public int nextIntInRange(int low, int high)
    {
        return < expression >
    }
}
```

Which < expression > will always return a value that satisfies the postcondition?

(A) nextInt(high - low) + low;

(B) nextInt(high - low) + low + 1;

(C) nextInt(high - low + 1) + low;

(D) nextInt(high - low + 1) + low + 1;

(E) nextInt(high) + low;

32. Consider the following mergeSort method and the private instance variable a both in the same Sorter class:

```java
private Comparable[] a;

/* Sorts a[first] to a[last] in increasing order using mergesort  */
public void mergeSort(int first, int last)
{
    if (first != last)
    {
        int mid = (first+last)/2;
        mergeSort(first, mid);
        mergeSort( mid+1, last);
        merge(first, mid, last);
    }
}
```

Method mergeSort calls method merge, which has this header:

```java
/* Merge a[lb] to a[mi] and a[mi+1] to a[ub].
 * Precondition: a[lb] to a[mi] and a[mi+1] to a[ub] both
 *                 sorted in increasing order  */
private void merge(int lb, int mi, int ub)
```

If the first call to mergeSort is mergeSort(0,3), how many *further* calls will there be to mergeSort before an array b[0]...b[3] is sorted?

(A) 2
(B) 3
(C) 4
(D) 5
(E) 6

GO ON TO THE NEXT PAGE

33. A programmer has a file of names. She is designing a program that sends junk mail letters to everyone on the list. To make the letters sound personal and friendly, she will extract each person's first name from the name string. She plans to create a parallel file of first names only. For example,

fullName	firstName
Ms. Anjali DeSouza	Anjali
Dr. John Roufaiel	John
Mrs. Mathilda Concia	Mathilda

Here is a method intended to extract the first name from a full name string.

```
/* Precondition:  fullName starts with a title followed by a period.
 *                A single space separates the title, first name, and last name.
 * Postcondition: Returns the first name only */
public static String getFirstName(String fullName)
{
    final String BLANK = " ";
    String temp, firstName;

    < code to extract first name >

    return firstName;
}
```

Which represents correct < *code to extract first name* >?

```
I   int k = fullName.indexOf(BLANK);
    temp = fullName.substring(k+1);
    k = temp.indexOf(BLANK);
    firstName = temp.substring(0, k);

II  int k = fullName.indexOf(BLANK);
    firstName = fullName.substring(k+1);
    k = firstName.indexOf(BLANK);
    firstName = firstName.substring(0, k);

III int firstBlank = fullName.indexOf(BLANK);
    int secondBlank = fullName.indexOf(BLANK);
    firstName = fullName.substring(firstBlank+1, secondBlank+1);
```

(A) I only
(B) II only
(C) III only
(D) I and II only
(E) I, II, and III

GO ON TO THE NEXT PAGE

34. Refer to the following method.

```
public static int recur(int n)
{
    if (n == 0 || n == 1)
        return 1;
    else if (n == 3)
        return 3;
    else
        return recur(n-1) + recur(n-2);
}
```

How many times is `recur(2)` called as a result of calling `recur(6)`?
(A) 2
(B) 4
(C) 8
(D) 32
(E) 64

35. A large hospital maintains a list of patients' records in no particular order. To find the record of a given patient, which represents the most efficient method that will work?
(A) Do a sequential search on the name field of the records.
(B) Do a binary search on the name field of the records.
(C) Use insertion sort to sort the records alphabetically by name; then do a sequential search on the name field of the records.
(D) Use mergesort to sort the records alphabetically by name; then do a sequential search on the name field of the records.
(E) Use mergesort to sort the records alphabetically by name; then do a binary search on the name field of the records.

GO ON TO THE NEXT PAGE

Questions 36–40 involve reasoning about the code from the Marine Biology Simulation Case Study. A Quick Reference to the case study is provided as part of this exam.

36. Refer to the state of the environment shown, with a normal fish facing west. After this fish moves to a new location, what are the possible directions that it could be facing?

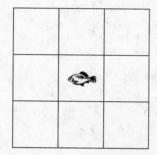

    (A) west only

    (B) east only

    (C) north or south only

    (D) north, south, or west only

    (E) north, south, east, or west

37. Let env be a 10×10 BoundedEnv object, where BoundedEnv is a class that implements the Environment interface. Consider the following code segment:

```
Location loc1 = new Location(4, 7);
Location loc2 = new Location(4, 8);
Direction dir1 = env.getDirection(loc1, loc2);
Direction dir2 = dir1.toLeft(90);
Direction dir3 = dir2.reverse();
Location loc3 = env.getNeighbor(loc2, dir3);
Location loc4 = env.getNeighbor(new Location(6, 7), dir2);
```

What locations would you expect in the ArrayList returned by env.neighborsOf(loc4) after this code segment?

    (A) (4,7), (5,6), (5,8)

    (B) (4,7), (5,6), (5,8), (6,7)

    (C) (5,7), (6,6), (7,7), (6,8)

    (D) (6,6), (7,7), (6,8)

    (E) (4,8), (5,7), (6,8), (5,9)

GO ON TO THE NEXT PAGE

38. Which of the following environments have *exactly one* possible location that `nextLocation` might return for the fish in location (1,0)?

I 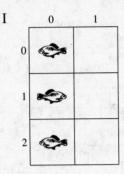   II 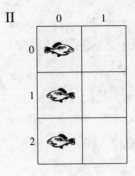   III

(A) I only
(B) II only
(C) III only
(D) I and II only
(E) I, II, and III

39. Suppose the program is modified to allow newborn fish to be any random color. Which methods of the `Fish` class must be changed?

   I The `Fish` constructor that has `color` as a parameter.
  II `generateChild`
 III `breed`

(A) I only
(B) II only
(C) III only
(D) I and II only
(E) I, II, and III

GO ON TO THE NEXT PAGE

40. Suppose the act method is modified as follows: if a fish doesn't breed, it attempts to move. If it neither bred nor moved, then it dies. In order to rewrite act as described, the move method must be modified to return a boolean. Here is the new specification for move:

```
/** Attempts to move this fish into a neighboring location.
 *  Returns true if the fish successfully moves;
 *  false otherwise.
 **/
protected boolean move()
```

Here is the modified act method:

```
/** Acts for one step in the simulation.
 **/
public void act()
{
    // Make sure fish is alive and well in the environment:
    // fish that have been removed from the environment shouldn't act.
    if (!isInEnv())
        return;
    < more code >
}
```

Which replacement for < *more code* > correctly implements the changes described above?

```
I if (!breed() && !move())
        die();

II if (!breed())
   {
        if (!move())
            die();
   }

III if (!breed())
    {
        if (!move())
        {
            Random randNumGen = RandNumGenerator.getInstance();
            if (randNumGen.nextDouble() < probOfDying)
                die();
        }
    }
```

(A) I only
(B) II only
(C) III only
(D) I and II only
(E) None is correct.

END OF SECTION I

IF YOU FINISH BEFORE TIME IS CALLED, YOU MAY
CHECK YOUR WORK ON THIS SECTION.

DO NOT GO ON TO SECTION II UNTIL YOU ARE TOLD TO DO SO.

COMPUTER SCIENCE A
SECTION II

Time—1 hour and 45 minutes
Number of questions—4
Percent of total grade—50

Directions: SHOW ALL YOUR WORK. REMEMBER THAT PROGRAM SEG-
MENTS ARE TO BE WRITTEN IN JAVA.

Note: Assume that the standard packages (e.g., `java.util.*`) are included in any programs that use the code segments provided in individual questions. A Quick Reference to
the standard classes and interfaces with their required methods is provided.

---

1. Consider a program that keeps track of transactions in a large department store. Both sales and returns
    are recorded. Three classes—`Transaction`, `Sale`, and `Return`—are used in the program, related as
    in the following inheritance hierarchy:

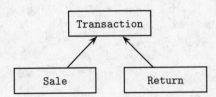

The `Transaction` class is defined below:

```
public class Transaction
{
    private String myDescription;
    private int myNumItems;
    private double myItemCost;
    public static final double TAX_RATE = 0.07;

    //constructor
    public Transaction(String description, int numItems, double itemCost)
    {
        myDescription = description;
        myNumItems = numItems;
        myItemCost = itemCost;
    }
```

GO ON TO THE NEXT PAGE.

```
        //accessors
        public String getDescription()
        { return myDescription; }

        public int getNumItems()
        { return myNumItems; }

        public double getItemCost()
        { return myItemCost; }

        public double getTotal()
        {
            double cost = myNumItems * myItemCost;
            double tax = cost * TAX_RATE;
            return cost + tax;
        }
    }
```

(a) Write the code for the Sale class. Each Sale includes

- A description of the item being sold.
- The number of this item being sold.
- The cost of this item.
- Whether the sale is cash or credit, stored as a boolean variable.
- A 10% discount for cash, with 10% stored as a final variable.

When a new Sale is created, it must be assigned an item description, the number being sold, the cost of this item, and whether the sale is cash or credit. Operations on a Sale include the following:

- Retrieve the description of the item being sold.
- Retrieve the quantity of the item being sold.
- Retrieve the cost of the item being sold.
- Retrieve whether the sale is cash or credit.
- Calculate the total for the sale. In calculating this total, a 10% discount for paying cash should be applied to the cost before the tax is calculated.

Write the code for the Sale class below.

(b) A class called DailyTransactions has the following private instance variable:

```
private Transaction[] allTransactions;   //contains all transactions in a single
                                          //day, including sales and returns
```

Write a method of the DailyTransactions class called findTransactionAverage, which computes the average of all transactions in a given day. The transactions are contained in the array allTransactions, where each object is a Sale or Return.

GO ON TO THE NEXT PAGE.

The method findTransactionAverage should

- Compute the total for all transactions.
- Divide by the number of transactions. (You may assume that there's at least one transaction.)
- Return the average.

Note that when an item is returned to the store, the amount paid is returned to the customer. For this reason the getTotal method in the Return class returns a *negative* quantity.

Complete findTransactionAverage below:

```
//Precondition:  allTransactions contains the day's transactions, each
//                of which may be a Sale or a Return
//Postcondition: average of day's transactions returned
public double findTransactionAverage()
```

2. Assume that information about candidates in a class election is stored using the Candidate and CandidateList classes below:

```
public class Candidate
{
    private String myName;
    private int myNumVotes;
    private double myVotePercent;

    //constructor
    //myVotePercent initialized to 0. Actual value set later.
    public Candidate(String name, int numVotes)
    { implementation }

    //Set myVotePercent equal to votePercent
    public void setVotePercent(double votePercent)
    { myVotePercent = votePercent; }

    //accessors

    public String getName()
    { return myName; }

    public int getNumVotes()
    { return myNumVotes; }

    public double getVotePercent()
    { return myVotePercent; }
}

public class CandidateList
{
    private Candidate[] myCList;
    private int myNumCandidates;
```

GO ON TO THE NEXT PAGE.

```
//constructor
//Reads name and number of votes for all candidates into myCList
public CandidateList()
{ implementation }


//Precondition:  myCList contains myNumCandidates elements
//               myNumCandidates equals myCList.length
//Postcondition: the vote percent for each Candidate has been
//               calculated and updated
public void computeVotePercents()
{ implementation }


//Precondition:  myCList contains complete information about all candidates,
//               including their updated vote percents
//Postcondition: returns a list of viable candidates, namely those
//               candidates who got at least 10% of the vote
public ArrayList getViableList()
{ implementation }


//Precondition:  myCList contains complete information about all candidates,
//               including their updated vote percents
//Postcondition: the names of viable candidates only have been printed,
//               one per line, followed by that candidate's vote percent
public void printViable()
{ implementation }

}
```

(a) Write the implementation of the computeVotePercents method of the CandidateList class. The computeVotePercents method should fill in the vote percent for each Candidate in myCList. A candidate's vote percent is computed by dividing the number of votes for that candidate by the total number of votes cast for all candidates and then multiplying by 100.

Complete method computeVotePercents below.

```
//Precondition:  myCList contains myNumCandidates elements
//               myNumCandidates equals myCList.length
//Postcondition: the vote percent for each Candidate has been
//               calculated and updated
public void computeVotePercents()
```

(b) Write the implementation of the getViableList method of the CandidateList class. The getViableList method should examine the elements in myCList and create an ArrayList of *viable* candidates only. A viable candidate is one who received at least 10% of the vote.

Complete method getViableList below.

```
//Precondition:  myCList contains complete information about all candidates,
//               including their updated vote percents
//Postcondition: returns a list of viable candidates, namely those
//               candidates who got at least 10% of the vote
public ArrayList getViableList()
```

GO ON TO THE NEXT PAGE.

(c) Write the implementation of the `printViable` method of the `CandidateList` class. The method `printViable` should list the names and vote percents of viable candidates only, one per line. Sample output:

```
Chris Arsenault 42.3
Anton Kriksunov 15.8
Lila Fontes 29.7
```

In writing `printViable` **you must call the** `getViableList` **method specified in part (b), and use the list returned.** Assume that `getViableList` works as specified regardless of what you wrote in part (b).

Complete method `printViable` below.

```
//Precondition:  myCList contains complete information about all candidates,
//                including their updated vote percents
//Postcondition: The names of viable candidates only have been printed,
//                one per line, followed by that candidate's vote percent
public void printViable()
```

3. Consider the problem of writing a Hi-Lo game in which a user thinks of an integer from 1 to 100 and the computer tries to guess that number with the smallest number of guesses. Each time the computer makes a guess the user makes one of three responses:

- "lower" (i.e., the number is lower than the computer's guess)
- "higher" (i.e., the number is higher than the computer's guess)
- "you got it in < however many > tries!"

The game will be programmed using the following `HiLoGame` class:

```
public class HiLoGame
{
    private int computerGuess;

    //constructor
    public HiLoGame()
    { computerGuess = 0; }

    //Explain to user how game will work
    public void giveInstructions()
    { /* implementation not shown */ }

    //Sequence of computer guesses and user responses until computer
    //guesses user's number
    public void play()
    { implementation }
}
```

(a) Write the *implementation* of the `play` method of the `HiLoGame` class. In writing `play`, the following sequence of steps should be repeated until the computer guesses the user's number:

- Output the computer's guess.
- Prompt the user for a response.
- Read the user's response. You should use the following statement to read the user's response:

```
String response = IO.readString();
```

No error checking is necessary for the response.

In writing the `play` method the computer should use a *binary search* strategy for making its guesses. This is the best strategy for the computer, one that will enable it to find the user's number with the smallest number of guesses on average.

Here's how the binary search strategy works: If the computer's guess is k and the user says "lower," the computer's guess should be midway between 1 and $k - 1$. If the user says "higher," the computer's new guess should be midway between $k + 1$ and 100. Any other response means the computer has guessed the user's number. The initial guess is midway between 1 and 100. With each subsequent guess, the interval of possible numbers is halved from what it was.

Write the `play` method below:

```
//Sequence of computer guesses and user responses until computer guesses
//user's number. Computer uses a binary search strategy for its guesses.
//Postcondition: Number of guesses made by the computer is printed
public void play()
```

(b) Using the binary search strategy, what is the maximum number of guesses the computer could make before guessing the user's number? Explain your answer.

(c) Suppose the computer used a *sequential search* strategy for guessing the user's number. What is the maximum number of guesses the computer could make before guessing the user's number? Explain your answer.

(d) Using a sequential search strategy, how many guesses *on average* would the computer need to guess the number? Explain your answer.

4. This question involves reasoning about the code from the Marine Biology Simulation Case Study. A Quick Reference to the case study is provided as part of this exam.

Consider creating a subclass of the DarterFish class called TurningDarter. A TurningDarter behaves just like a DarterFish except that instead of always moving east and west or always moving north and south, it has a small probability (0.1) of turning left or right before it tries to move forward. You may assume that when the TurningDarter does turn, it will turn left or right with equal probability.

Write the TurningDarter class. Do not include debugging statements. The class should include
- A probability of turning, equal to 0.1.
- Two constructors, one that has environment and location as parameters, and one that has environment, location, and direction as parameters. Note that all darter fish are yellow, including the turning darters.
- An overridden generateChild method, with header

```
//Creates a new turning darter fish at location loc
protected void generateChild(Location loc)
```

- An overridden nextLocation method. This method should cause the TurningDarter to turn with a probability of 0.1 and an equal probability of turning left or right. Then nextLocation should return a Location as it does for the DarterFish. Here is the header for nextLocation:

```
//Finds this fish's next location
protected Location nextLocation()
```

Write the TurningDarter class below.

END OF EXAMINATION

Answer Key

Section I

1. **C**	15. **B**	29. **A**
2. **B**	16. **C**	30. **D**
3. **C**	17. **D**	31. **C**
4. **D**	18. **C**	32. **E**
5. **C**	19. **B**	33. **D**
6. **C**	20. **A**	34. **A**
7. **A**	21. **D**	35. **A**
8. **E**	22. **B**	36. **D**
9. **B**	23. **A**	37. **B**
10. **A**	24. **C**	38. **E**
11. **D**	25. **B**	39. **B**
12. **E**	26. **B**	40. **D**
13. **C**	27. **A**	
14. **D**	28. **C**	

Answers Explained

Section I

1. **(C)** Testing a program thoroughly does not prove that a program is correct. Usually it is impossible to test every possible set of input data.

2. **(B)** Each private instance variable must be assigned the corresponding parameter value. Choice A confuses the order—the instance variables must be on the left in the assignment statements. Choice C is almost correct; but isUnionMember must be assigned the value of the parameter union, not true. Choice D tries to create a new Worker object, which assumes that the constructor already has a correct implementation! Choice E uses a statement that incorrectly implies that Worker is a subclass of some class that has an appropriate constructor. The keyword super shouldn't be used unless there's an explicit superclass defined for the given class (which will then have an extends keyword).

3. **(C)** The private instance variable myHourlyWage must be incremented by amt. Eliminate choice E, which doesn't *increment* myHourlyWage; it simply *replaces* it by amt. Choice D is wrong because you can't use a method call as the left-hand side of an assignment. Choices A and B are wrong because the incrementWage method is void and should not return a value.

4. **(D)** The value of the boolean instance variable isUnionMember must be changed to the opposite of what it currently is. Segments I and II both achieve this. Note that !true has a value of false and !false a value of true. Segment III fails to do what's required if the current value of isUnionMember is false.

5. **(C)** `computePay` is a client method and, therefore, cannot access the private variables of the class. This eliminates choices A and D. The method `getHourlyWage()` must be accessed with the dot member construct; thus choice B is wrong, and choice C is correct. Choice E is way off base—`hours` is not part of the `Worker` class, so `w.hours` is meaningless.

6. **(C)** If `s.length()` < 4 for all strings in `wordList`, then SHORT WORD will be printed on each pass through the `for` loop. Since there are `wordList.size()` passes through the loop, the maximum number of times that SHORT WORD can be printed is `wordList.size()`.

7. **(A)** The operators / and $*$ have equal precedence and both have higher precedence than +. Thus, $21/6 * 2$ must be evaluated first from left to right. $21/6$ evaluates to 3 (integer division), and so the given expression is equivalent to $20 + 3 * 2$. (The next steps in evaluating would be $20 + 6 = 26$.)

8. **(E)**

$$\text{mystery}(4) = 3 * \text{mystery}(3)$$
$$= 3 * 3 * \text{mystery}(2)$$
$$= 3 * 3 * 3 * \text{mystery}(1)$$
$$= 3 * 3 * 3 * 3$$
$$= 81$$

9. **(B)** Look at the solution to the previous question. Notice that 3 gets multiplied by itself n times (i.e., 3 gets raised to the nth power).

10. **(A)** The private instance variable `myAddress` is an `Address` object whose own instance variables have been defined for this `Customer` in the `Customer` constructor. Choice B is wrong because `addr` is a parameter name. It has neither scope nor meaning in the `getAddress` method. Choice C fails because it calls the method that you are trying to define! Choice D will exit the method at the first `return` statement. Choice E is wrong because `getStreet`, `getCity`, ... are not methods of the `Customer` class, so they cannot be accessed without an `Address` calling object. Choice E would be correct (but inefficient) if it were modified as follows:

```
Address a = new Address(myAddress.getStreet(),
    myAddress.getCity(), myAddress.getState(),
    myAddress.getZipCode());
return a;
```

11. **(D)** Constructing a new object requires the keyword `new`, which eliminates choice C. The parameters are three `String`s followed by an `int`, so eliminate choices A, B, and E.

12. **(E)** A new `Address` object must be created, to be used as the `Address` parameter in the `Customer` constructor. To do this correctly requires the keyword `new` preceding the `Address` constructor. Segment II omits `new` and does not use the `Address` constructor correctly. (In fact, it inserts a new `String` object in the `Address` slot of the `Customer` constructor.)

13. **(C)** The algorithm used in method `locate` is a sequential search, which may have to examine all the objects to find the matching one. A binary search,

which repeatedly discards a chunk of the array that does not contain the key, is more efficient. However, it can only be used if the values being examined—in this case customer ID numbers—are sorted. Note that it doesn't help to have the array sorted by name or phone number since the algorithm doesn't look at these values.

14. **(D)** Mergesort repeatedly splits an array of *n* elements in half until there are *n* arrays containing one element each. Now adjacent arrays are successively merged until there is a single merged, sorted array. A binary search repeatedly splits an array into two, narrowing the region that may contain the key. Insertion sort, however, does no array splitting. It takes elements one at a time and finds their insertion point in the sorted piece of the array. Elements are shifted to allow correct insertion of each element. Even though this algorithm maintains the array in two parts—a sorted part and yet-to-be-sorted part—this is not a divide-and-conquer approach.

15. **(B)** This code translates into

> for five rows (starting at i = 5 and decreasing i)
>> print the first i perfect squares
>> go to a new line

Thus in the first line the first five perfect squares will be printed. In the second line the first four perfect squares will be printed, and so on down to i = 1, with just one perfect square being printed.

16. **(C)** To return the number of elements in the set for Method One requires no more than returning the number of elements in the array. For Method Two, however, the number of cells that contain true must be counted, which requires a test for each of the MAX values. Note that searching for a target value in the set is more efficient for Method Two. For example, to test whether 2 is in the set, simply check if a[2] == true. In Method One, a sequential search must be done, which is less efficient. To print all the elements in Method One, simply loop over the known number of elements and print. Method Two is less efficient because the whole array must be examined: each cell must be tested for true before printing.

17. **(D)** An ArithmeticException will be thrown at run time. Note that if *N* were of type double, no exception would be thrown. The variable sum would be assigned the value Infinity, and the error would only be detected in the output.

18. **(C)** An interface should provide method declarations only. No code! Note that the methods are automatically public and abstract, so there is no need to specify this explicitly.

19. **(B)** The postcondition should be a true assertion about the major action of the segment. The segment overwrites the elements of array a with the positive elements of a. Then n is adjusted so that now the array a[0]...a[n-1] contains just positive integers. Note that even though choice D is a correct assertion about the program segment, it is not a good postcondition because it doesn't describe the main modification to array a (namely all negative integers have been removed).

20. **(A)** Note the order of precedence for the expressions involved: (1) parenthe-

ses, (2) !, (3) <, (4) ==, (5) &&, (6) ||. This means that a < c, a < b, and !(a == b) will all be evaluated before || and && are considered. The given expression then boils down to value1 || (value2 && value3), since && has higher precedence than ||. Notice that if value1 is true, the whole expression is true since true || any evaluates to true. Thus a < c will guarantee that the expression evaluates to true. None of the other conditions will guarantee an outcome of true. For example, suppose a < b (choice B). If a == c, then the whole expression will be false because you get F || F.

21. (**D**) Test data should always include a value from each range in addition to all boundary values. The given program should also handle the case in which a weight over 20 pounds is entered. Note that choice E contains redundant data and so is wasteful. There is no new information gained in testing both 3 and 4 pounds, for example.

22. (**B**) Segment II correctly keeps track of the index of the current element with the minimum price. If this is not done, the part number that must be returned will be lost. Thus segment III is incorrect. Note that min cannot be used as an index because it's a value of type double. Segment I is incorrect because it doesn't check that part matches allParts[i].getDescription(). Thus it simply finds the AutoPart with the lowest price, which is not what was required.

23. (**A**) Choices B and C are wrong because the parameters of method min must be objects, not primitive types. In choice A the parameters are String objects. Choice E fails because even though p1 and p2 are objects, they are not Comparable. (AutoPart does not implement Comparable, whereas String does.) Choice D would throw a ClassCastException: an AutoPart cannot be cast to a String.

24. (**C**) Ordering of strings involves a character-by-character comparison starting with the leftmost character of each string. Thus strA precedes strB (since "A" precedes "a") or strA.compareTo(strB) < 0. This eliminates choices B and D. Eliminate choices A and E since strB precedes strC (because "C" precedes "c") and therefore strB.compareTo(strC) < 0. Note that string1.compareTo(string2) == 0 if and only if string1 and string2 are equal strings.

25. (**B**) The remove method of ArrayList removes the indicated element, shifts the remaining elements down one slot (i.e., it does not leave gaps in the list), and adjusts the size of the list. Consider the list in choice B. The index values are shown:

```
The cat cat sat on the mat mat
 0   1   2   3   4  5   6   7
```

After the first occurrence of cat has been removed:

```
The cat sat on the mat mat
 0   1   2   3  4   5   6
```

The value of i, which was 1 when cat was removed, has now been incremented to 2 in the for loop. This means that the word to be considered next is sat. The second occurrence of cat has been missed. Thus the given code will fail whenever occurrences of the word to be removed are consecutive. You fix it by not allowing the index to increment when a removal occurs:

```
int i = 0;
while (i < wordList.size())
{
    if ((wordList.get(i)).equals(word))
        wordList.remove(i);
    else
        i++;
}
```

26. **(B)** `ThreeDigitCode` is a subclass of `ThreeDigitInteger` and therefore inherits all the instance variables and methods of `ThreeDigitInteger` except constructors. All of the statements other than B are false. For choice A, `ThreeDigitInteger` is the superclass and therefore cannot inherit from its subclass. For choice C, constructors are never inherited (see p. 73). For choice D, a subclass can access private variables of the superclass through accessor methods only (see p. 72). For choice E, a superclass cannot access any additional instance variables of its subclass.

27. **(A)** Implementation III is wrong because it violates this rule: If `super` is used in the implementation of a subclass constructor, it must be used only in the first line of the constructor body. Implementation II is wrong because the constructor has no boolean validity parameter.

28. **(C)** A compile-time error will occur for both tests I and II because at compile time the types of `code` and `num` are both `ThreeDigitInteger`, and the `ThreeDigitInteger` class does not have an `isValid` method. To avoid this error the `code` object must be cast to `ThreeDigitCode`, its actual type. Note that if you try to cast `num` to `ThreeDigitCode`, you'll get a run-time error (`ClassCastException`) because `num` is not an instance of `ThreeDigitCode`.

29. **(A)** The *is-a* relationship must work from right-to-left: a `Parrot` *is-a* `Bird`, a `Parakeet` *is-a* `Bird`, and an `Owl` *is-a* `Bird`. All are correct. This relationship fails in declarations II and III: a `Parrot` is not necessarily a `Parakeet`, a `Bird` is not necessarily an `Owl`, and a `Bird` is not necessarily a `Parakeet`.

30. **(D)** Since the current size of the `ArrayList` is unknown (and certainly can't be relied on to be 5), eliminate choices A and E. The `ArrayList` must contain *objects*, which eliminates choices B and C (and E again!). Note that the correct piece of code constructs an `Integer` object from the primitive `int` value `i*i`.

31. **(C)** Suppose you want random integers from 2 to 8, that is, `low = 2` and `high = 8`. This is 7 possible integers, so you need `nextInt(7)`, which produces 0, 1, 2, ..., or 6. Therefore the quantity `nextInt(7) + 2` produces 2, 3, 4, ..., or 8. The only expression that yields the right answer with these values is `nextInt(high - low + 1) + low`.
    Note:

    • The `ExtendedRandom` class has no constructor. The declaration

    ```
    ExtendedRandom e = new ExtendedRandom();
    ```

will invoke the compiler-supplied default constructor, which is just the default constructor of the superclass, `Random`.

- The `nextInt` method is inherited from `Random` and can, therefore, be used in the `ExtendedRandom` class without declaring a `Random` object.

32. **(E)** Here is a "box diagram" for `mergeSort(0,3)`. The boldface numbers 1–6 show the order in which the `mergeSort` calls are made.

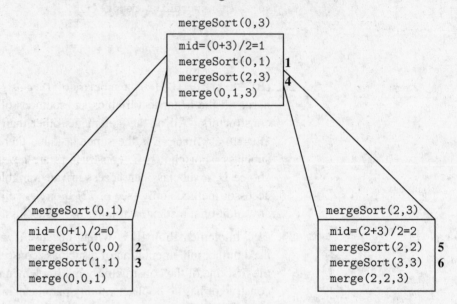

The `mergeSort` calls in which `first == last` are base case calls, which means that there will be no further method calls.

33. **(D)** Suppose `fullName` is Dr. John Roufaiel. In segment I the expression `fullName.indexOf(BLANK)` returns 3. Then `temp` gets assigned the value of `fullName.substring(4)`, which is John Roufaiel. Next k gets assigned the value `temp.indexOf(BLANK)`, namely 4, and `firstName` gets assigned `temp.substring(0, 4)`, which is all the characters from 0 to 3 inclusive, namely John. Note that segment II works the same way, except `firstName` gets assigned John Roufaiel and then reassigned John. This is not good style, since a variable name should document its contents as precisely as possible. Still, the code works. Segment III fails because `indexOf` returns the *first* occurrence of its `String` parameter. Thus `firstBlank` and `secondBlank` will both contain the same value, 3.

34. **(A)** Here are the calls that are made. Base cases are underlined.

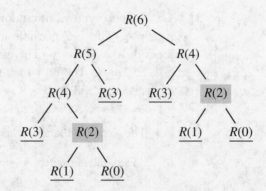

35. **(A)** Since the records are not sorted, the quickest way to find a given name is to start at the beginning of the list and sequentially search for that name. Choices C, D, and E will all work, but it's inefficient to sort and then search because all sorting algorithms take longer than simply inspecting each element. Choice B won't work: a binary search can only be used for a sorted list.

36. **(D)** After a normal fish moves, it faces the direction in which it moved. Since a fish never moves backward, the fish shown can only move north, south, or west. Therefore its final direction is north, south, or west, but not east.

37. **(B)** Here are the assigned values in the code segment: loc1 is (4,7), loc2 is (4,8), dir1 is east, dir2 is north, dir3 is south, loc3 is the cell south of (4,8), namely (5,8), and loc4 is the cell north of (6,7), namely (5,7). The question calls for the neighbors of (5,7). These are the four adjacent cells (shaded in the diagram).

38. **(E)** The only possibility in environment I is for the fish to move forward to location (1,1). The only possibility in environment II is for the fish to stay where it is in location (1,0), since it can't move backward. The only possibility in environment III is for the fish to move sideways to location (1,1), since it can't move backward.

39. **(B)** The only change needed is the choice of Fish constructor in the method generateChild. The modified statement is

```
Fish child = new Fish(environment(), loc,
    environment().randomDirection());
```

This constructor creates the new fish with a random color. Note that the breed method takes care of whether a fish will breed and which locations it will breed into. It does not concern itself with the personal attributes of the newborn fish—it calls generateChild to take care of those details.

40. **(D)** Segment III is incorrect because it violates the requirement that the fish *must* die if it neither breeds nor moves. For the code to be correct, both randNumGen and probOfDying must be removed—this results in segment II. Note that segment I is correct: if !breed() is false (i.e., breed() is true), the test will be short-circuited, and the fish won't attempt to move.

Section II

1. (a)
```
public class Sale extends Transaction
{
    private boolean myIsCash;
    private final double CASH_DISCOUNT = 0.1;

    //constructor
    public Sale(String description, int numItems,
        double itemCost, boolean isCash)
    {
        super(description, numItems, itemCost);
        myIsCash = isCash;
    }

    //return true if Sale is cash, false otherwise
    public boolean getIsCash()
    { return myIsCash; }

    public double getTotal()
    {
        double cost = getNumItems() * getItemCost();
        if (myIsCash)
        {
            double discount = cost * CASH_DISCOUNT;
            cost = cost - discount;
        }
        double tax = cost * TAX_RATE;
        return cost + tax;
    }
}
```

(b)
```
public double findTransactionAverage()
{
    double sum = 0;
    for (int i=0; i<allTransactions.length; i++)
        sum += allTransactions[i].getTotal();
    return sum/allTransactions.length;
}
```

NOTE

- In part (a) the solution shows some comments. In general, you don't need to provide comments for your code on the exam. However, short comments to clarify what you're doing are fine.
- The Sale class inherits all of the accessors from the Transaction superclass. The getDescription, getNumItems, and getItemCost methods do not need to be redefined. Their implementation doesn't change. The getTotal method, however, is different in the Sale class and therefore must be overridden.
- In part (b) the fact that getTotal is negative for a Return object means that the correct amount will automatically be added to the sum if the Transaction is a Return. The method is polymorphic and will call the appropriate getTotal method, depending on whether allTransactions[i] is a Sale or a Return.

2. (a)
```
public void computeVotePercents()
{
    int total = 0;

    //find total of all votes cast
    for (int i=0; i<myNumCandidates; i++)
        total += myCList[i].getNumVotes();

    //set vote percent for each candidate
    for (int i=0; i<myNumCandidates; i++)
    {
        double votePercent = 100 * myCList[i].getNumVotes()/
                (double) total;
        myCList[i].setVotePercent(votePercent);
    }
}
```

(b)
```
public ArrayList getViableList()
{
    ArrayList viable = new ArrayList();
    for (int i=0; i<myNumCandidates; i++)
    {
        if (myCList[i].getVotePercent() >= 10)
            viable.add(myCList[i]);
    }
    return viable;
}
```

(c)
```
public void printViable()
{
    ArrayList list = getViableList();
    for (int i=0; i<list.size(); i++)
    {
        Candidate c = (Candidate) list.get(i);
        System.out.println(c.getName() + " " +
                c.getVotePercent());
    }
}
```

NOTE
- In part (a), to get the correct, real-valued votePercent, you have to make sure that your percent calculation doesn't do integer division! You can achieve this either by casting the numerator or denominator to double, or by replacing 100 with 100.0.
- In the for loops of parts (a) and (b) you can replace i<myNumCandidates with i<myCList.length since you are given that myNumCandidates equals i<myCList.length.
- In part (c) the expression list.get(i) returns the Object in the ith slot of the ArrayList. The getName and getVotePercent methods are not in the Object class, so you need to cast list.get(i) to Candidate.

3. (a)
```
public void play()
{
    boolean done = false;
    int lo = 1, hi = 100, count = 0;
    while (!done)
    {
        computerGuess = (lo + hi)/2;
        count++;
        System.out.println("Computer guess is " +
                computerGuess);
        System.out.println("Should computer go higher
                or lower?");
        System.out.println("Or did computer guess right?");
        String response = IO.readString(); //read user input
        if (response.equals("lower"))
            hi = computerGuess - 1;
        else if (response.equals("higher"))
            lo = computerGuess + 1;
        else
        {
            System.out.println("Computer got it in " +
                count + " tries!");
            done = true;
        }
    }
}
```

(b) The computer should find the number in no more than seven tries. This is because the guessing interval is halved on each successive try:

(1) $100 \div 2 = 50$ numbers left to try

(2) $50 \div 2 = 25$ numbers left to try

(3) $25 \div 2 = 13$ numbers left to try

(4) $13 \div 2 = 7$ numbers left to try

(5) $7 \div 2 = 4$ numbers left to try

(6) $4 \div 2 = 2$ numbers left to try

(7) $2 \div 2 = 1$ number left to try

Seven iterations of the loop leaves just 1 number left to try!

(c) The maximum number of guesses is 100. A sequential search means that the computer starts at the first possible number, namely 1, and tries each successive number until it gets to 100. If the user's number is 100, the computer will take 100 guesses to reach it.

(d) On average the computer will make 50 guesses. The user is equally likely to pick any number between 1 and 100, half the time less than 50, half the time greater than 50. So on the average the distance of the number from 1 is 50.

4.
```java
public class TurningDarter extends DarterFish
{
    private double probOfTurning;

    public TurningDarter(Environment env, Location loc)
    {
        super(env, loc);
        probOfTurning = 1.0/10.0;
    }

    public TurningDarter(Environment env, Location loc,
            Direction dir)
    {
        super(env, loc, dir);
        probOfTurning = 1.0/10.0;
    }

    protected void generateChild(Location loc)
    {
        TurningDarter child = new TurningDarter(environment(),
            loc, environment().randomDirection());
    }

    protected Location nextLocation()
    {
        //turn fish with 0.1 probability.
        Random randNumGen = RandNumGenerator.getInstance();
        if (randNumGen.nextDouble() < probOfTurning)
        {
            if (randNumGen.nextInt(2) == 0)
                changeDirection(direction().toRight());
            else
                changeDirection(direction().toLeft());
        }
        return super.nextLocation();
    }
}
```

Alternative for `nextLocation` method:

```java
protected Location nextLocation()
{
    //turn fish with 0.1 probability.
    Random randNumGen = RandNumGenerator.getInstance();
    double randDouble = randNumGen.nextDouble();
    if (randDouble < 0.5*probOfTurning)
        changeDirection(direction().toRight());
    else if (randDouble < probOfTurning)
        changeDirection(direction().toLeft());
    return super.nextLocation();
}
```

NOTE
- The first constructor calls the two-parameter constructor of `DarterFish`, which gives the `TurningDarter` its environment and location values in the parameters, plus a random direction and yellow color. The second

constructor calls the three-parameter constructor of DarterFish, which gives the TurningDarter its environment, location, and direction values in the parameters, plus a yellow color.

- generateChild calls the three-parameter constructor of TurningDarter. The new child will automatically be yellow (see the previous note).

- In the nextLocation method, just one Random object, randNumGen, is declared. The first solution tests whether the fish will turn and then "flips a coin" to see if it will turn left or right. The alternative solution divides the interval from 0 to 0.1 into two: 0 to 0.05 and 0.05 to 0.1. (0.05 is included in one but not both intervals.) If the random real number randDouble lands in the first of these intervals, the fish will turn right. If it lands in the second field the fish will turn left. Otherwise the direction remains unchanged.

Answer Sheet: Practice Exam Three

1. Ⓐ Ⓑ Ⓒ Ⓓ Ⓔ
2. Ⓐ Ⓑ Ⓒ Ⓓ Ⓔ
3. Ⓐ Ⓑ Ⓒ Ⓓ Ⓔ
4. Ⓐ Ⓑ Ⓒ Ⓓ Ⓔ
5. Ⓐ Ⓑ Ⓒ Ⓓ Ⓔ
6. Ⓐ Ⓑ Ⓒ Ⓓ Ⓔ
7. Ⓐ Ⓑ Ⓒ Ⓓ Ⓔ
8. Ⓐ Ⓑ Ⓒ Ⓓ Ⓔ
9. Ⓐ Ⓑ Ⓒ Ⓓ Ⓔ
10. Ⓐ Ⓑ Ⓒ Ⓓ Ⓔ
11. Ⓐ Ⓑ Ⓒ Ⓓ Ⓔ
12. Ⓐ Ⓑ Ⓒ Ⓓ Ⓔ
13. Ⓐ Ⓑ Ⓒ Ⓓ Ⓔ
14. Ⓐ Ⓑ Ⓒ Ⓓ Ⓔ

15. Ⓐ Ⓑ Ⓒ Ⓓ Ⓔ
16. Ⓐ Ⓑ Ⓒ Ⓓ Ⓔ
17. Ⓐ Ⓑ Ⓒ Ⓓ Ⓔ
18. Ⓐ Ⓑ Ⓒ Ⓓ Ⓔ
19. Ⓐ Ⓑ Ⓒ Ⓓ Ⓔ
20. Ⓐ Ⓑ Ⓒ Ⓓ Ⓔ
21. Ⓐ Ⓑ Ⓒ Ⓓ Ⓔ
22. Ⓐ Ⓑ Ⓒ Ⓓ Ⓔ
23. Ⓐ Ⓑ Ⓒ Ⓓ Ⓔ
24. Ⓐ Ⓑ Ⓒ Ⓓ Ⓔ
25. Ⓐ Ⓑ Ⓒ Ⓓ Ⓔ
26. Ⓐ Ⓑ Ⓒ Ⓓ Ⓔ
27. Ⓐ Ⓑ Ⓒ Ⓓ Ⓔ
28. Ⓐ Ⓑ Ⓒ Ⓓ Ⓔ

29. Ⓐ Ⓑ Ⓒ Ⓓ Ⓔ
30. Ⓐ Ⓑ Ⓒ Ⓓ Ⓔ
31. Ⓐ Ⓑ Ⓒ Ⓓ Ⓔ
32. Ⓐ Ⓑ Ⓒ Ⓓ Ⓔ
33. Ⓐ Ⓑ Ⓒ Ⓓ Ⓔ
34. Ⓐ Ⓑ Ⓒ Ⓓ Ⓔ
35. Ⓐ Ⓑ Ⓒ Ⓓ Ⓔ
36. Ⓐ Ⓑ Ⓒ Ⓓ Ⓔ
37. Ⓐ Ⓑ Ⓒ Ⓓ Ⓔ
38. Ⓐ Ⓑ Ⓒ Ⓓ Ⓔ
39. Ⓐ Ⓑ Ⓒ Ⓓ Ⓔ
40. Ⓐ Ⓑ Ⓒ Ⓓ Ⓔ

How to Calculate Your (Approximate) AP Score — AP Computer Science Level AB

Multiple Choice

Number correct (out of 40) = _____

$1/4 \times$ number wrong = _____

Raw score = line 1 – line 2 = _____

Raw score $\times$ 1.25 = _____ ⟸ Multiple-Choice Score
(Do not round. If less than zero, enter zero.)

Free Response

Question 1 _____
(out of 9)

Question 2 _____
(out of 9)

Question 3 _____
(out of 9)

Question 4 _____
(out of 9)

Total _____ $\times$ 1.39 = _____ ⟸ Free-Response Score
(Do not round.)

Final Score

_____ + _____ = _____
Multiple-Choice Score Free-Response Score Final Score
(Round to nearest whole number.)

Chart to Convert to AP Grade Computer Science AB

Final Score Range	AP Grade[a]
70–100	5
60–69	4
41–59	3
31–40	2
0–30	1

[a]The score range corresponding to each grade varies from exam to exam and is approximate.

Practice Exam Three
COMPUTER SCIENCE AB
SECTION I

Time—1 hour and 15 minutes
Number of questions—40
Percent of total grade—50

Directions: Determine the answer to each of the following questions or incomplete statements, using separate pieces of scrap paper for any necessary scratchwork. Then decide which is the best of the choices given and fill in the corresponding oval on the answer sheet. Do not spend too much time on any one problem.

Note: Assume that the standard packages (e.g., `java.util.*`) are included in any programs that use the code segments provided in individual questions. A Quick Reference to the standard classes and interfaces with their required methods is provided.

---

1. The database for a large bookstore has a list of `Book` objects maintained in sorted order by title. The following operations are performed on this list:

    I Adding new books.
    II Updating information for individual books.
    III Removing books from the list.

Assuming that the most efficient algorithms are used to perform the operations, which is a *true* statement about using an `ArrayList` versus a `LinkedList` to store the database? (Assertions about run time in the choices below should be considered in terms of big-O efficiency.)

(A) Operation I has approximately the same run-time efficiency for a `LinkedList` as for an `ArrayList`.
(B) Operation II has faster run-time efficiency for a `LinkedList` than an `ArrayList`.
(C) Operation III has faster run-time efficiency for an `ArrayList` than a `LinkedList`.
(D) If a new book whose title starts with the letter "A" is to be inserted into the list, inserting into an `ArrayList` will have faster run time than inserting into a `LinkedList`.
(E) If the last book in the list must be removed, the run time will be faster for a `LinkedList` than an `ArrayList`.

GO ON TO THE NEXT PAGE

Level A Also

Questions 2–7 are based on the three classes below:

```java
public class Employee
{
    private String myName;
    private int myEmployeeNum;
    private double mySalary, myTaxWithheld;

    //constructor
    public Employee(String name, int empNum, double salary, double taxWithheld)
    { implementation }

    //Returns pre-tax salary
    public double getSalary()
    { return mySalary; }

    //accessors
    public String getName()
    { return myName; }

    public int getEmployeeNum()
    { return myEmployeeNum; }

    public double getTax()
    { return myTaxWithheld; }

    public double computePay()
    { return mySalary - myTaxWithheld; }
}
public class PartTimeEmployee extends Employee
{
    private double myPayFraction;

    //constructor
    public PartTimeEmployee(String name, int empNum, double salary,
        double taxWithheld, double payFraction)
    { implementation }

    public double getPayFraction()
    { return myPayFraction; }

    public double computePay()
    { return getSalary() * myPayFraction - getTax();}
}
public class Consultant extends Employee
{
    private static final double BONUS = 5000;
    //constructor
    public Consultant(String name, int empNum, double salary, double taxWithheld)
    { implementation }

    public double computePay()
    { implementation }
}
```

GO ON TO THE NEXT PAGE

Level A Also

2. Which of the following is correct *implementation* code for the `PartTimeEmployee` constructor?

```
 I  myPayFraction = payFraction;
    super(name, empNum, salary, taxWithheld);

II  super(name, empNum, salary, taxWithheld);
    myPayFraction = payFraction;

III myName = name;
    myEmployeeNum = empNum;
    mySalary = salary;
    myTaxWithheld = taxWithheld;
    myPayFraction = payFraction;
```

    (A) I only
    (B) II only
    (C) III only
    (D) II and III only
    (E) I, II, and III

3. The `computePay` method in the `PartTimeEmployee` and `Consultant` classes is an example of
    (A) Inheritance.
    (B) Dynamic binding (late binding).
    (C) Method overloading.
    (D) Method overriding.
    (E) Downcasting.

4. The `computePay` method in the `Consultant` class overrides the `computePay` method of the `Employee` class to add a bonus to the salary after subtracting the tax withheld. Which represents correct *implementation* of computePay for `Consultant`?

```
 I  return super.computePay() + BONUS;

II  super.computePay();
    return getSalary() + BONUS;

III return getSalary() - getTax() + BONUS;
```

    (A) I only
    (B) II only
    (C) III only
    (D) I and III only
    (E) I and II only

GO ON TO THE NEXT PAGE

Level A Also

5. Consider these valid declarations in a client program:

```
Employee e = new Employee("Noreen Rizvi", 304, 65000, 10000);
Employee p = new PartTimeEmployee("Rafael Frongillo", 287, 40000, 7000, 0.8);
Employee c = new Consultant("Dan Lepage", 694, 55000, 8500);
```

Which of the following method calls will cause an error?

(A) `double x = e.computePay();`

(B) `double y = p.computePay();`

(C) `String n = c.getName();`

(D) `int num = p.getEmployeeNum();`

(E) `double g = p.getPayFraction();`

6. Which of the following represents correct *implementation* code for the `Consultant` constructor?

   I `super();`

  II `super(name, empNum, salary, taxWithheld);`

 III
```
getName() = name;
getEmployeeNum() = empNum;
getSalary() = salary;
getTax() = taxWithheld;
```

(A) I only

(B) II only

(C) III only

(D) II and III only

(E) I, II, and III

GO ON TO THE NEXT PAGE

Level A Also

7. Consider the writePayInfo method:

```
//Writes Employee name and pay on one line
public static void writePayInfo(Employee e)
{ System.out.println(e.getName() + " " + e.computePay()); }
```

The following piece of code invokes this method:

```
Employee[] empList = new Employee[3];
empList[0] = new Employee("Lila Fontes", 1, 10000, 850);
empList[1] = new Consultant("Momo Liu", 2, 50000, 8000);
empList[2] = new PartTimeEmployee("Moses Wilks", 3, 25000, 3750, 0.6);
for (int i=0; i<empList.length; i++)
    writePayInfo(empList[i]);
```

What will happen when this code is executed?

(A) A list of employees' names and corresponding pay will be written to the screen.
(B) A NullPointerException will be thrown.
(C) A ClassCastException will be thrown.
(D) A compile-time error will occur, with the message that the getName method is not in the Consultant class.
(E) A compile-time error will occur, with the message that an instance of an Employee object cannot be created.

8. Which of the following will evaluate to true only if boolean expressions A, B, and C are all false?

(A) !A && !(B && !C)
(B) !A || !B || !C
(C) !(A || B || C)
(D) !(A && B && C)
(E) !A || !(B || !C)

9. Quicksort is performed on the following array:

$$45 \quad 40 \quad 77 \quad 20 \quad 65 \quad 52 \quad 90 \quad 15 \quad 95 \quad 79$$

The first element, 45, is used as the pivot. After one iteration of quicksort (i.e., after the first partitioning), which *must* be true?

I 45 will be the fourth element of the array.
II All elements to the left of 45 will be sorted.
III All elements to the right of 45 will be greater than or equal to 45.

(A) I only
(B) II only
(C) III only
(D) I and III only
(E) II and III only

GO ON TO THE NEXT PAGE

10. A list of numbers in unknown order is inserted into a binary search tree. Which of the following is *true*?

(A) If the tree produced is reasonably balanced, the run time to create the tree is $O(\log n)$.

(B) If the tree is balanced, the run time to search for a given element is $O(n \log n)$.

(C) The worst case run time to insert a new element into the tree is $O(n^2)$.

(D) A postorder traversal of the tree will produce the elements in ascending order.

(E) The run time to print out the elements sorted in ascending order is $O(n)$.

Level A Also

11. Consider the following class declaration:

```
public abstract class AClass
{
    private int v1;
    private double v2;

    //methods of the class
       ...
}
```

Which is *true* about AClass?

(A) Any program using this class will have an error: An abstract class cannot contain private instance variables.

(B) AClass *must* have a constructor with two parameters in order to initialize v1 and v2.

(C) All methods of AClass must be abstract.

(D) A program that uses AClass must have another class that is a subclass of AClass.

(E) In a client program, more than one instance of AClass can be created.

GO ON TO THE NEXT PAGE

12. Consider the `NumberList` class and `removeValue` method below.

```
public class NumberList
{
    private LinkedList numList;

    //constructor and other methods not shown
        ...

    //Precondition:  numList is a LinkedList of Integer objects
    //Postcondition: all occurrences of value have been removed from numList
    public void removeValue(Integer value)
    {
        Iterator itr = numList.iterator();
        while (itr.hasNext())
        {
            if (< test >)
                itr.remove();
        }
    }
}
```

Which < *test* > will produce the required postcondition?

I `itr.next().equals(value)`

II `((Integer) itr.next()).equals(value)`

III `((itr.next()).intValue()).equals(value.intValue())`

(A) I only
(B) II only
(C) III only
(D) I and II only
(E) I, II, and III

13. Refer to the following code segment:

```
int n = < some positive integer >
for (int i=n; i>=1; i/=2)
{
    process(i);
}
```

Given that `process(i)` has a run time of $O(1)$, what is the run time of the algorithm shown?
(A) $O(1)$
(B) $O(n)$
(C) $O(n^2)$
(D) $O(n/2)$
(E) $O(\log n)$

GO ON TO THE NEXT PAGE

Level A Also

Questions 14 and 15 refer to the `ElapsedTime` class below:

```
public class ElapsedTime implements Comparable
{
    private int myHours, myMins, mySecs;   //0 ≤ mySecs < 60, 0 ≤ myMins < 60

    //constructors

    public ElapsedTime()
    { myHours = 0; myMins = 0; mySecs = 0; }

    public ElapsedTime(int h, int m, int s)
    { myHours = h; myMins = m; mySecs = s; }

    public ElapsedTime(int numSecs)       //numSecs is total number of seconds
    { /* implementation not shown /* }  //of elapsed time

    //Returns number of seconds in ElapsedTime
    public int convertToSeconds()
    { /* implementation not shown /* }

    //Returns -1 if this object < obj, 0 if this object == obj,
    //and 1 if this object > obj
    public int compareTo(Object obj)
    { implementation }

    //accessors

    public int getHours()
    { return myHours; }

    public int getMins()
    { return myMins; }

    public int getSecs()
    { return mySecs; }
}
```

GO ON TO THE NEXT PAGE

Level A Also

14. Consider the `compareTo` method for the `ElapsedTime` class:

```
//Returns -1 if this object < obj, 0 if this object == obj,
//and 1 if this object > obj
public int compareTo(Object obj)
{
    ElapsedTime rhs = (ElapsedTime) obj;
    < more code >
}
```

Which is a correct replacement for *< more code >*?

```
I   if (myHours < rhs.myHours && myMins < rhs.myMins && mySecs < rhs.mySecs)
        return -1;
    else if (myHours > rhs.myHours && myMins > rhs.myMins && mySecs > rhs.mySecs)
        return 1;
    else
        return 0;
```

```
II  if (myHours < rhs.myHours)
        return -1;
    else if (myHours > rhs.myHours)
        return 1;
    else
    {
        if (myMins < rhs.myMins)
            return -1;
        else if (myMins > rhs.myMins)
            return 1;
        else
        {
            if (mySecs < rhs.mySecs)
                return -1;
            else if (mySecs > rhs.mySecs)
                return 1;
            else
                return 0;
        }
    }
```

```
III int secs = this.convertToSeconds();
    int rhsSecs = rhs.convertToSeconds();
    if (secs < rhsSecs)
        return -1;
    else if (secs == rhsSecs)
        return 0;
    else
        return 1;
```

(A) I only
(B) II only
(C) III only
(D) I and II only
(E) II and III only

GO ON TO THE NEXT PAGE

Level A Also

15. A client method `timeSum` will find the sum of two `ElapsedTime` objects.

```
//Returns sum of t1 and t2
public static ElapsedTime timeSum(ElapsedTime t1, ElapsedTime t2)
{ < implementation code > }
```

Which is correct < *implementation code* >?

```
 I int s1 = t1.convertToSeconds();
   int s2 = t2.convertToSeconds();
   return new ElapsedTime(s1 + s2);

II return new ElapsedTime(t1 + t2);

III int totSecs = t1.getSecs() + t2.getSecs();
    int seconds = totSecs % 60;
    int totMins = t1.getMins() + t2.getMins() + totSecs/60;
    int minutes = totMins % 60;
    int hours = t1.getHours() + t2.getHours() + totMins/60;
    return new ElapsedTime(hours, minutes, seconds);
```

(A) I only
(B) II only
(C) III only
(D) I and III only
(E) I, II, and III

16. A program that keeps track of the inventory items for a small store maintains the items in a `HashMap` data structure. The keys are inventory items, where each item is a string, and the corresponding values are quantities of that item that are on the shelf. Thus some entries in the map could be

Campbells Clam Chowder Soup	11
Kleenex Tissues	35
Extra-strength Bufferin	20

Inventory items are added to and removed from the `HashMap` as needed. When a listing of all inventory items is required, all items of the `HashMap` are inserted into a `TreeMap`, whose `keySet` is then printed. Using the `HashMap` and `TreeMap` data structures as described supports which of the following?

(A) Listing of all current items in alphabetical order, $O(\log n)$ insertion of new items, and $O(\log n)$ retrieval of existing items.
(B) Listing of all current items in alphabetical order, $O(1)$ insertion of new items, and $O(1)$ retrieval of existing items.
(C) Listing of all current items in no particular order, $O(1)$ insertion of new items, and $O(1)$ retrieval of existing items.
(D) Listing of all current items in no particular order, $O(\log n)$ insertion of new items, and $O(\log n)$ retrieval of existing items.
(E) Listing of all current items in no particular order, $O(1)$ insertion of new items, $O(\log n)$ retrieval of existing items.

GO ON TO THE NEXT PAGE

17. A large sorted array containing about 30,000 elements is to be searched for a value key using an iterative binary search algorithm. Assuming that key is in the array, which of the following is closest to the smallest number of iterations that will guarantee that key is found? Note: $10^3 \approx 2^{10}$.

    (A) 15
    (B) 30
    (C) 100
    (D) 300
    (E) 3000

18. Refer to the Stack interface provided. Consider the method searchAndStack:

```
//Precondition: v[0]...v[v.length-1] initialized with int values.
//              Stack s is empty. value may or may not be in v.
public static void searchAndStack(int[] v, Stack s, int value)
{
    for (int i=0; i<v.length; i++)
    {
        if (v[i] > value % 2)
            s.push(new Integer(v[i]));
        else
        {
            Object x = s.pop();
        }
    }
}
```

Suppose v initially contains 2 1 6 5 0 9, and searchAndStack(v, s, 5) is invoked. Which of the following will be true after execution of the method?

(A) The stack will be empty.
(B) The stack will contain three elements with s.peekTop() equal to 9.
(C) The stack will contain two elements with s.peekTop() equal to 9.
(D) The stack will contain two elements with s.peekTop() equal to 6.
(E) A NoSuchElementException will have been thrown.

GO ON TO THE NEXT PAGE

19. Assume that linear linked lists are implemented using the `ListNode` class provided. Refer to method `mystery` below.

```
//Precondition: firstNode refers to the first node in a linear linked list
public static ListNode mystery(ListNode firstNode)
{
    if (firstNode == null)
        return null;
    else
    {
        ListNode p = new ListNode(firstNode.getValue(),
                mystery(firstNode.getNext()));
        return p;
    }
}
```

What does method `mystery` do?

(A) It creates an exact copy of the linear linked list referred to by `firstNode` and returns a reference to this newly created list.

(B) It creates a copy in reverse order of the linear linked list referred to by `firstNode` and returns a reference to this newly created list.

(C) It reverses the pointers of the linear linked list referred to by `firstNode` and returns a reference to the original list, which is now in reverse order.

(D) It leaves the original list unchanged and returns a reference to the original list.

(E) It causes a `NullPointerException` to be thrown.

20. Suppose a queue is implemented with a circular linked list that has just one private instance variable, `lastNode`, that refers to the last element of the list:

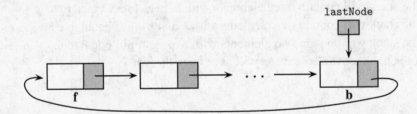

In the diagram, **f** and **b** indicate the front and back of the queue. Which of the following correctly gives the run time of (1) `enqueue` and (2) `dequeue` in this implementation?

(A)   (1) $O(n)$ (2) $O(1)$

(B)   (1) $O(1)$ (2) $O(n)$

(C)   (1) $O(n)$ (2) $O(n)$

(D)   (1) $O(1)$ (2) $O(n^2)$

(E)   (1) $O(1)$ (2) $O(1)$

GO ON TO THE NEXT PAGE

21. Let `list` be an `ArrayList` of `Integer` values sorted in increasing order. Which of the following code segments correctly lists the duplicate values of `list` in increasing order? Each duplicate value should be listed just once. You may assume that `list` contains at least one duplicate value. You may also assume the existence of the following `copyListToTreeSet` method:

```
//Postcondition: returns TreeSet that contains elements of aList
public TreeSet copyListToTreeSet(List aList)
```

I
```
Set s = copyListToTreeSet(list);
System.out.println(s);
```

II
```
Set h = new HashSet();
Set k = new TreeSet();
Iterator itr = list.iterator();
while (itr.hasNext())
{
    Object obj = itr.next();
    if (!h.add(obj))
        k.add(obj);
}
System.out.println(k);
```

III
```
Set s = copyListToTreeSet(list);
Iterator itr = s.iterator();
int index = 0;
while (itr.hasNext())
{
    int count = 0;
    Object obj = itr.next();
    while (index < list.size() && obj.equals(list.get(index)))
    {
        count++;
        index++;
    }
    if (count > 0)
        System.out.println(obj + " ");
}
```

(A) I only
(B) II only
(C) III only
(D) II and III only
(E) I, II, and III

GO ON TO THE NEXT PAGE ➡

22. A *binary expression tree* is a binary tree that stores an expression as follows. The root contains an operator that will be applied to the the results of evaluating expressions in the left and right subtrees, each of which is a binary expression tree. The *prefix* form of the expression can be generated by a preorder traversal of the binary expression tree that contains the expression. What is the prefix form of the expression in the binary expression tree shown?

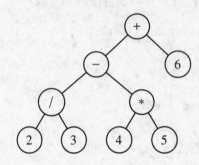

   (A) + − /2 3 ∗ 4 5 6
   (B) + ∗ −/2 3 4 5 6
   (C) + − ∗2/3 4 5 6
   (D) 2 3/4 5 ∗ −6+
   (E) 2 3/4 − 5 ∗ 6+

23. An algorithm to convert a base 10 integer n to base b, where $b < 10$, uses repeated division by b until the quotient is 0. The remainders are stored and then concatenated to form a string, starting with the most recent remainder. This string represents n in base b. For example, to convert 29 to base 3:

      3 | 29
      3 | 9   rem | 2
      3 | 3   rem | 0   29 in base 3 is 1002
      3 | 1   rem | 0
         | 0   rem | 1

To convert 53 to base 4:

      4 | 53
      4 | 13   rem | 1
      4 | 3   rem | 1   53 in base 4 is 311
         | 0   rem | 3

Which data structure is most suitable for storing the remainders during the algorithm?
   (A) A String
   (B) An array
   (C) A stack
   (D) A queue
   (E) A priority queue

GO ON TO THE NEXT PAGE

24. Assume that doubly linked lists are implemented with the `DoublyListNode` class below:

```
public class DoublyListNode
{
    private Object value;
    private DoublyListNode next, prev;

    public DoublyListNode(DoublyListNode initPrev, Object initValue,
                    DoublyListNode initNext)
    {
        prev = initPrev;
        value = initValue;
        next = initNext;
    }

    public DoublyListNode getPrev()
    { return prev; }

    public void setPrev(DoublyListNode theNewPrev)
    { prev = theNewPrev; }

    public Object getValue()
    { return value; }

    public void setValue(Object theNewValue)
    { value = theNewValue; }

    public DoublyListNode getNext()
    { return next; }

    public void setNext(DoublyListNode theNewNext)
    { next = theNewNext; }
}
```

Suppose p and q refer to two adjacent nodes in the middle of a doubly linked list as shown:

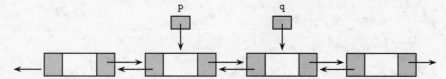

A code segment that removes both of these nodes from the list is

   I `p.getPrev().setNext(q.getNext());`
      `q.getNext().setPrev(p.getPrev());`

  II `p.setNext(q.getNext());`
      `q.setPrev(p.getPrev());`

 III `p.getNext().setPrev(q.getPrev());`
      `q.getPrev().setNext(p.getNext());`

(A) I only
(B) II only
(C) I and II only
(D) I and III only
(E) II and III only

GO ON TO THE NEXT PAGE

25. Consider a class `MatrixStuff` that has a private instance variable:

```
private int[][] mat;
```

Refer to method `alter` below that occurs in the `MatrixStuff` class. (The lines are numbered for reference.)

```
1   //Precondition:  mat is initialized with integers
2   //Postcondition: column c has been removed and the last column
3   //               is filled with zeros
4   public void alter(int[][] mat, int c)
5   {
6       for (int i=0; i<mat.length; i++)
7           for (int j=c; j<mat[0].length; j++)
8               mat[i][j] = mat[i][j+1];
9       //code to insert zeros in rightmost column
10          ...
11  }
```

The intent of the method `alter` is to remove column c. Thus if the input matrix `mat` is

$$
\begin{array}{cccc}
2 & 6 & 8 & 9 \\
1 & 5 & 4 & 3 \\
0 & 7 & 3 & 2
\end{array}
$$

the method call `mat.alter(1)` should change mat to

$$
\begin{array}{cccc}
2 & 8 & 9 & 0 \\
1 & 4 & 3 & 0 \\
0 & 3 & 2 & 0
\end{array}
$$

The method does not work as intended. Which of the following changes will correct the problem?

   I Change line 7 to

```
for (int j=c; j < mat[0].length-1; j++)
```

   and make no other changes.

   II Change lines 7 and 8 to

```
for (int j=c+1; j<mat[0].length; j++)
        mat[i][j-1] = mat[i][j];
```

   and make no other changes.

   III Change lines 7 and 8 to

```
for (int j=mat[0].length-1; j>c; j--)
        mat[i][j-1] = mat[i][j];
```

   and make no other changes.

(A) I only
(B) II only
(C) III only
(D) I and II only
(E) I, II, and III

GO ON TO THE NEXT PAGE

26. A *full binary tree* has every leaf on the same level; and every nonleaf node has two children. N integers are to be inserted into the *leaves* of a full binary tree. The final value of level in the following code segment gives the *lowest level* of tree needed to store all N elements in its leaves. Which replacement for < *boolean expression* > leads to the correct value of level? Note: Start counting levels at the root, which is level 0.

```
int level = 0;
while (< boolean expression >)
    level++;
```

(A) N < Math.pow(2, level)
(B) N >= Math.pow(2, level) && N < Math.pow(2, level+1)
(C) N > Math.pow(2, level)
(D) N > Math.pow(2, level+1)
(E) N >= Math.pow(2, level)

27. If s1 and s2 are two sets, the *union* of s1 and s2, s1 ∪ s2, is defined as the set of all elements that are either in s1 or s2 or both. For example, if s1 = {2,7,9} and s2 = {7,2,5,1}, then s1 ∪ s2 = {1,2,5,7,9}. Suppose h1 and h2 have been declared to be of type HashSet, and each has been initialized to contain objects of the same type. Which of the following code segments creates the union of h1 and h2 and stores it in union? For this question you may assume the existence of the following three methods in the same class as the segments:

```
//Postcondition: returns a HashSet that contains all the elements of Set s
public HashSet copySetToHashSet(Set s)

//Postcondition: returns an ArrayList that contains all the elements of Set s
public ArrayList copySetToArrayList(Set s)

//Postcondition: returns a HashSet that contains all the elements of List list
public HashSet copyListToHashSet(List list)
```

```
  I Set union = copySetToHashSet(h1);
    for (Iterator itr=h2.iterator(); itr.hasNext();)
        union.add(itr.next());

 II Set union = copySetToHashSet(h1);
    for (Iterator itr=h2.iterator(); itr.hasNext();)
        if(!union.contains(itr.next())
            union.add(itr.next());

III List list = copySetToArrayList(h1);
    for (Iterator itr=h2.iterator(); itr.hasNext();)
        list.add(itr.next());
    Set union = copyListToHashSet(list);
```

(A) I only
(B) II only
(C) III only
(D) II and III only
(E) I and III only

GO ON TO THE NEXT PAGE

28. A large club has a membership list of *n* names and phone numbers stored in a text file in random order, as shown:

```
RABKIN ARI 694-8176
HUBBARD JUDITH  583-2199
GOLD JONAH 394-5142
        . . .
```

The text file is edited by hand to add new members to the end of the list and to delete members who leave the club.

A programmer is to write a program that accesses the text file and prints a list of names/phone numbers in alphabetical order. Three methods are considered:

  I Read each line of the file into a string and insert it into a binary search tree. Print the list with an inorder traversal of the tree.
  II Read the lines of the file into an array of strings. Sort the array with a selection sort. Print the list.
  III Read each line of the file into a string and insert it into its correct sorted position in a linear linked list of strings. Thus, the list remains sorted after each insertion. Print the list.

Which is a *false* statement?
(A) Each of methods I, II, and III, if implemented correctly, will work.
(B) Method III, on average, has $O(n)$ run time.
(C) If the names in the text file are approximately in alphabetical order, methods I, II, and III will have the same big-O run times.
(D) If the names in the text file are randomly ordered, method I has the fastest run time.
(E) The part of the algorithm that prints the list of names is $O(n)$ in each of the three methods.

For Questions 29 and 30 refer to the `CustomerOrder` objects defined as follows:

Customer orders for a catalog company are stored in a `TreeMap` t in which the key is an invoice number (`Integer` object) and the value is the corresponding customer's order (`CustomerOrder` object). The `CustomerOrder` object contains the customer's name, address, phone number, a list of items purchased, and the total cost.

29. What will the following code segment do?

```
for (Iterator itr=t.keySet().iterator(); itr.hasNext();)
    System.out.println(itr.next());
```

(A) List the invoice numbers in no particular order.
(B) List the invoice numbers in increasing order.
(C) List the customer names in alphabetical order.
(D) List the customer names in no particular order.
(E) List the `CustomerOrder` objects in increasing order by invoice number.

GO ON TO THE NEXT PAGE

30. Instead of an invoice number, the programmer considers using the customer's name as the key and the `CustomerOrder` as the corresponding value, as before. Why is this a bad idea?

    I It is not possible to store two or more customers with the same name in map `t`.

    II It is not possible for two or more customers to order the same item.

    III It is not possible for a given customer to have more than one order.

(A) I only
(B) II only
(C) III only
(D) I and III only
(E) I, II, and III

Level A Also

31. Refer to method `match` below:

```
//Precondition:  v[0]..v[N-1] and w[0]..w[M-1] initialized with integers.
//               v[0] < v[1] < .. < v[N-1] and w[0] < w[1] < .. < w[M-1]
//Postcondition: returns true if there is an integer k that occurs in both
//               arrays, otherwise returns false
public static boolean match(int[] v, int[] w, int N, int M)
{
    int vIndex = 0, wIndex = 0;
    while (vIndex < N && wIndex < M)
    {
        if (v[vIndex] == w[wIndex])
            return true;
        else if (v[vIndex] < w[wIndex])
            vIndex++;
        else
            wIndex++;
    }
    return false;
}
```

Assuming that the method has not been exited, which assertion is true at the end of every execution of the `while` loop?

(A) `v[0]..v[vIndex-1]` and `w[0]..w[wIndex-1]` contain no common value,
    `vIndex` $\leq$ `N` and `wIndex` $\leq$ `M`.

(B) `v[0]..v[vIndex]` and `w[0]..w[wIndex]` contain no common value,
    `vIndex` $\leq$ `N` and `wIndex` $\leq$ `M`.

(C) `v[0]..v[vIndex-1]` and `w[0]..w[wIndex-1]` contain no common value,
    `vIndex` $\leq$ `N-1` and `wIndex` $\leq$ `M-1`.

(D) `v[0]..v[vIndex]` and `w[0]..w[wIndex]` contain no common value,
    `vIndex` $\leq$ `N-1` and `wIndex` $\leq$ `M-1`.

(E) `v[0]..v[N-1]` and `w[0]..w[M-1]` contain no common value,
    `vIndex` $\leq$ `N` and `wIndex` $\leq$ `M`.

GO ON TO THE NEXT PAGE

Level A Also

32. Consider the following method:

```
public static void sketch(int x1, int y1, int x2, int y2, int n)
{
    if (n <= 0)
        drawLine(x1, y1, x2, y2);
    else
    {
        int xm = (x1+x2+y1-y2)/2;
        int ym = (y1+y2+x2-x1)/2;
        sketch(x1, y1, xm, ym, n-1);
        sketch(xm, ym, x2, y2, n-1);
    }
}
```

Assume that the screen looks like a Cartesian coordinate system with the origin at the center, and that drawLine connects (x1,y1) to (x2,y2). Assume also that x1, y1, x2, and y2 are never too large or too small to cause errors. Which picture best represents the sketch drawn by the method call

```
sketch(a, 0, -a, 0, 2)
```

where a is a positive integer?

(A)

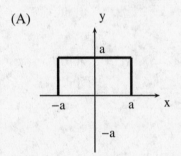

(D)

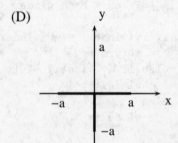

(B)

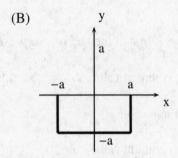

(E)

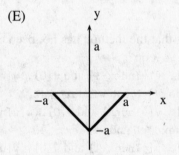

(C)

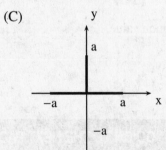

GO ON TO THE NEXT PAGE

For Questions 33–35, assume that binary trees are implemented with the TreeNode class provided.

33. Consider method printStuff:

```java
//Precondition: tree refers to the root of a binary tree
public static void printStuff(TreeNode tree)
{
    if (tree != null)
    {
        if (tree.getLeft() != null)
            System.out.println(tree.getLeft().getValue());
        printStuff(tree.getLeft());
        printStuff(tree.getRight());
    }
}
```

Which best describes what method printStuff does?
(A) Prints every element in tree except the element in the root node
(B) Prints every element in tree
(C) Prints the element in the left child of every node in tree
(D) Prints every element in the left subtree of tree
(E) Prints the element in the root node as well as every element in the left subtree of tree

GO ON TO THE NEXT PAGE

For Questions 34 and 35 consider the BinaryTree and BinarySearchTree classes below:

```
public abstract class BinaryTree
{
    private TreeNode root;

    public BinaryTree()
    { root = null; }

    public TreeNode getRoot()
    { return root; }

    public void setRoot(TreeNode theNewNode)
    { root = theNewNode; }

    public boolean isEmpty()
    { return root == null; }

    public abstract void insert(Comparable item);

    public abstract TreeNode find(TreeNode p, Comparable key);
}

public class BinarySearchTree extends BinaryTree
{
    //Insert item in BinarySearchTree
    public void insert(Comparable item)
    { implementation code }

    //Precondition: binary search tree rooted at p.
    //Returns TreeNode that contains key.
    //If key not in tree, returns null
    public TreeNode find(TreeNode p, Comparable key)
    { implementation code }
}
```

34. Which is a *false* statement about these classes?
    (A) The compiler will provide the following default constructor for the BinarySearchTree class:

    ```
    public BinarySearchTree()
    { super(); }
    ```

    (B) The insert and find methods in the BinaryTree class are abstract because their implementation depends on the type of binary tree.
    (C) The item and key parameters of insert and find need to be Comparable since the methods require you to compare objects.
    (D) The private instance variable root of the superclass cannot be altered by the BinarySearchTree class.
    (E) The following statement in a client program will cause an error:

    ```
    BinaryTree tree = new BinarySearchTree(new Integer(4));
    ```

GO ON TO THE NEXT PAGE

35. Which is correct implementation code for the `find` method?

```
I   if (p == null)
        return null;
    else if (key.compareTo(p.getValue()) == 0)
        return p;
    else if (key.compareTo(p.getValue()) < 0)
        return find(getRoot().getLeft(), key);
    else
        return find(getRoot().getRight(), key);
```

```
II  if (p == null)
        return null;
    else if (key.compareTo(p.getValue()) == 0)
        return p;
    else if (key.compareTo(p.getValue()) < 0)
        return find(p.getLeft(), key);
    else
        return find(p.getRight(), key);
```

```
III while (p != null && key.compareTo(p.getValue())!= 0)
    {
        if (key.compareTo(p.getValue()) < 0)
            p = p.getLeft();
        else
            p = p.getRight();
    }
    return p;
```

(A) I only
(B) II only
(C) III only
(D) II and III only
(E) I, II, and III

Questions 36–40 involve reasoning about the code from the Marine Biology Simulation Case Study. A Quick Reference to the case study is provided as part of this exam.

Level A Also

36. Consider using the `Environment` interface in a program that navigates a maze. The objects in the maze will be either walls or paths. Which of the following is a requirement for the classes representing `Wall` objects and `Path` objects in order to place objects of these classes into the maze?

  I Both `Wall` and `Path` objects must be `Locatable`.
  II Both `Wall` and `Path` objects must be `Comparable`.
  III Both `Wall` and `Path` objects must implement the `EnvDisplay` interface.

(A) I only
(B) II only
(C) III only
(D) I and II only
(E) I, II, and III

GO ON TO THE NEXT PAGE

Level A Also

37. Consider the small bounded environment shown, containing a slow fish and a darter.

Which of the following is an *invalid* setup after a call to act *for the slow fish only*?

(A)

(B)

(C)

(D)

(E)

GO ON TO THE NEXT PAGE

38. Refer to the `isEmpty` method in the `BoundedEnv` class:

```
/** Determines whether a specific location in this environment is
 *  empty.
 *  Returns true if loc is a valid location in the context
 *  of this environment and is empty; false otherwise
 **/
public boolean isEmpty(Location loc)
{
    return isValid(loc) && objectAt(loc) == null;
}
```

What error can occur if the `isValid(loc)` part of the test is omitted?

   I A fish may attempt to move to a location that is out of bounds.
   II A fish may attempt to move backward.
   III A fish may attempt to breed into a location that is out of bounds.

  (A) I only
  (B) II only
  (C) III only
  (D) I and III only
  (E) I, II, and III

Questions 39–40 refer to the implementation described below.

Consider implementing the unbounded environment with a `HashMap` rather than the `ArrayList` that is used in the `UnboundedEnv` class. This would be the declaration:

```
private HashMap objectMap;
```

The keys of `objectMap` would be only those locations in the environment that contain an object. The corresponding values would be the `Locatable` objects placed at those locations (i.e., the fish). No empty locations would be stored in the map.

39. What would be the big-O performance of the `objectAt` method using the `HashMap` implementation?
  (A) $O(1)$
  (B) $O(n)$
  (C) $O(\log n)$
  (D) $O(n^2)$
  (E) $O(2^n)$

GO ON TO THE NEXT PAGE

40. The allObjects method will need to be modified with the HashMap implementation. Here is the modified code:

```
/** Returns an array of all the objects in this environment.
 **/
public Locatable[] allObjects()
{
    Locatable[] objectArray = new Locatable[objectMap.size()];
    // Put all the environment objects in the array.
    < more code >
    return objectArray;
}
```

Which is a correct replacement for < *more code* >?

```
I  for (int index=0; index<objectMap.size(); index++)
   {
       objectArray[index] = (Locatable) objectMap.get(index);
   }
```

```
II for (int index=0; index<objectMap.size(); index++)
   {
       objectArray[index] = (Locatable) objectMap.get(obj.location());
   }
```

```
III int index = 0;
    for (Iterator i=objectMap.keySet().iterator(); i.hasNext();)
    {
        objectArray[index] = (Locatable) objectMap.get(i.next());
        index++;
    }
```

(A) I only
(B) II only
(C) III only
(D) II and III only
(E) I, II, and III

END OF SECTION I

IF YOU FINISH BEFORE TIME IS CALLED, YOU MAY
CHECK YOUR WORK ON THIS SECTION.

DO NOT GO ON TO SECTION II UNTIL YOU ARE TOLD TO DO SO.

COMPUTER SCIENCE AB
SECTION II

Time—1 hour and 45 minutes
Number of questions—4
Percent of total grade—50

Directions: SHOW ALL YOUR WORK. REMEMBER THAT PROGRAM SEGMENTS ARE TO BE WRITTEN IN JAVA.

Note: Assume that the standard packages (e.g., java.util.*) are included in any programs that use the code segments provided in individual questions. A Quick Reference to the standard classes and interfaces with their required methods is provided.

---

1. Consider a hash table that stores table entries of some type (DataType) with an associated key. Assume that classes TableEntry and DataType have been declared as follows:

```java
/* Hash table entry. Consists of data and associated key */
public class TableEntry
{
    private Object key;
    private DataType data;

    public TableEntry(Object theKey, DataType theData)
    {
        key = theKey;
        data = theData;
    }

    public Object getKey()
    { return key; }

    public String toString()
    { return "" + key + "   " + data; }
}

public class DataType
{
    //private instance variables
        ...
    //constructor
        ...
    //toString method for DataType object
        ...
}
```

GO ON TO THE NEXT PAGE.

Assume that the hash table will be implemented using an array of linked lists, called buckets. Each linked list or bucket will contain table entries with the same hash address.

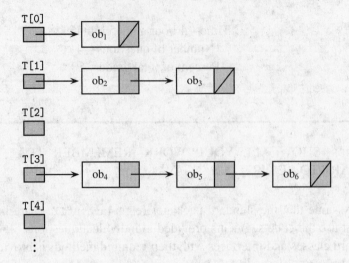

The diagram shows, for example, that ob_2 and ob_3 have hash address 1, while ob_4, ob_5, and ob_6 have hash address 3. It also shows that buckets labeled T[2] and T[4] are empty, since no entries have been inserted into them.

Here is the declaration for the HashTable class:

```
public class HashTable
{
    private int size;      //number of array elements (buckets)
    private int count;     //number of table entries
    private LinkedList[] T; //array of buckets
                           //Each bucket is a LinkedList of TableEntry objects
    //constructor
    public HashTable(int tableSize)
    { implementation }

    //Hash function returns hash address
    public int hash(Object key)
    { return key.hashCode() % size; }

    //Delete TableEntry with given key.
    //Do nothing if key not in table.
    //Precondition: key does not occur more than once in table
    public void delete(Object key)
    { implementation }

    //Insert TableEntry with data and associated key into HashTable.
    //If key already in table, replace existing data with new data.
    //Postcondition: key occurs exactly once in table
    public void insert(Object key, DataType data)
    { implementation }

    //Print contents of HashTable
    public void printTable()
    { implementation }
}
```

GO ON TO THE NEXT PAGE.

(a) Complete the constructor for the `HashTable` class. Note that the `tableSize` parameter is the number of array elements (buckets). Each bucket in the array is initially empty since the number of table entries is zero.

```
//constructor
public HashTable(int tableSize)
```

(b) Write the `delete` method for the `HashTable` class. Method `delete` removes the `TableEntry` with the given `key`. If `key` is not in the table, the method does nothing.

Complete method `delete` as started below:

```
//Delete TableEntry with given key.
//Do nothing if key not in table.
//Precondition: key does not occur more than once in table
public void delete(Object key)
```

(c) Write the `insert` method for the `HashTable` class. Method `insert` first removes any `TableEntry` with the given `key`. Then it inserts `data` with the given `key` into the table.

In writing `insert` you may call any other methods of the `HashTable` class. Assume that all these methods work as specified.

Complete method `insert` as started below:

```
//Insert TableEntry with data and associated key into HashTable.
//If key already in table, replace existing data with new data.
//Postcondition: key occurs exactly once in table
public void insert(Object key, DataType data)
```

2. A small zoo has both mammals and birds:
   - Goats that bleat and eat grass.
   - Pigs that squeal and eat swill.
   - Turkeys that gobble and eat grain.
   - Elf owls that hoot and eat insects.
   - Snowy owls that hoot and eat either hares, lemmings, or small birds, whichever are available.
   Suppose you are to write a program that simulates the zoo.

   (a) Draw a diagram that represents an `Animal` class hierarchy. Your diagram should show the relationship between all the objects in the program, with `Animal` as the superclass for all the other objects. Each class in your design should be represented by a labeled rectangle, and arrows should show the inheritance relationships between classes.
   (b) Write the code for the `Animal` class. Each `Animal` has a name, a type of covering (fur, feathers, scales, etc.), and its own particular noise that it makes. When a new animal is constructed, it must be assigned a name, noise, and covering. Each of these can be represented with a `String`. Operations on an `Animal` include the following:

      - Retrieve the name of the animal.
      - Retrieve the noise of the animal.
      - Retrieve the covering of the animal.
      - Retrieve the food of the animal. This should be an abstract method: The appropriate food for each animal will be described in its particular class.

GO ON TO THE NEXT PAGE.

(c) Given the code for a `Bird` class below, write the code for an `Owl` class.

```
public abstract class Bird extends Animal
{
    //constructor
    public Bird(String name, String noise)
    {
        super(name, noise, "feathers");
    }
}
```

An `Owl` is a `Bird` that hoots (its noise!). The food it eats depends on the type of `Owl`. Assuming that the `Animal` and `Bird` classes have been correctly defined, write the `Owl` class below.

(d) Write the code for a `SnowyOwl` class. A `SnowyOwl` is an `Owl` that will randomly eat a hare, a lemming, or a small bird (depending on what's available!). The `SnowyOwl` class should have a `Random` object to help determine which food the `SnowyOwl` will eat. You may assume the existence of the `RandNumGenerator` class used in the case study and its `getInstance()` method:

```
/*Returns a Random object used to generate random numbers */
public static Random getInstance()
{ /* Implementation not shown */ }
```

Assuming that the `Animal`, `Bird`, and `Owl` classes have been correctly defined, write the `SnowyOwl` class below.

3. An $n \times n$ *magic square* is a square array of n^2 distinct integers arranged such that the n numbers along any row, column, major diagonal, or minor diagonal have the same sum. We will consider only those magic squares that contain the first n^2 positive integers.

For example, here is a 3×3 magic square. It contains only the integers 1 through 9, each of which occurs exactly once. Each row, column, and diagonal sums to 15.

8	1	6
3	5	7
4	9	2

To check whether a two-dimensional array of integers is a magic square, you must check that
  (i) All the rows have the same sum.
 (ii) All the columns have that same sum.
(iii) Both diagonals have that same sum.

GO ON TO THE NEXT PAGE.

(a) Write method `checkDiagonalSums` as started below. Method `checkDiagonalSums` returns true if the sum of integers on both diagonals of its matrix parameter equals the second integer parameter; otherwise, it returns false. The first integer parameter represents the size of the matrix. For example,

```
checkDiagonalSums(m, 3, 15)
```

would return true for the matrix shown earlier since the sum along each diagonal is 15.

major diagonal   minor diagonal

Complete method `checkDiagonalSums` below.

```
//Precondition:  m is a size × size matrix initialized with
//               distinct positive integers from 1 to size*size
//Postcondition: returns true if sum of each diagonal equals
//               total, returns false otherwise
public static boolean checkDiagonalSums(int[][] m, int size, int total)
```

(b) This part of the question refers to the `MagicSquare` class below:

```
public class MagicSquare
{
    private int[][] myMatrix;
    private int mySize;

    //Precondition: size ≥ 3, size odd
    public MagicSquare(int size)
    {
        mySize = size;
        < code to create size × size magic square >
    }

    //Returns size × size matrix m resized to newSize × newSize.
    //If newSize > size, no elements of m are lost.
    //If newSize < size, elements in rows and columns from
    //newSize through size-1 are lost.
    private static int[][] resize(int[][] m, int newSize)
    { implementation not shown }
}
```

Complete the constructor for the `MagicSquare` class. You should provide the

< code to create size × size magic square >

Your code should create a size × size two-dimensional array of integers that represents a magic square. The following algorithm achieves this provided size is odd. Here is how it works when size is 5.

GO ON TO THE NEXT PAGE.

- Expand the 5 by 5 square to a 6 by 6 square by adding a border of cells along the top and the right edge.

		1			

- Place 1 in the middle top cell of the original square. This cell is now occupied. All other cells of the matrix are considered empty except for the top right-hand corner, which is considered occupied. (Hint: Initialize all cells to 0 except for m[1][size/2] and m[0][size].)
- Now place the remaining integers, 2 through 25, successively in the square as follows: Starting at the cell that contains 1, the general rule is to proceed diagonally upward to the right with successive integers. There are two exceptions to this general rule:

(i) When a number lands in a border cell, place it inside the original square by shifting clear across the square, either from top to bottom or from right to left. Then continue with the general rule.

(ii) If a number will land in a cell already occupied, place that number in the cell immediately beneath the last cell filled. Then continue with the general rule.

Thus, in the 5 by 5 example, 2 would go in the fourth cell along the top. Since this is a border cell, it must be placed in the fourth cell of the bottom row of the original square.

			2	9	
		1	8		
	5	7			
4	6				4
10				3	10
			2	9	

Place 3 according to the general rule. When you come to 4, it falls in the third cell up along the right border. It must therefore be placed all the way across to the left in the third cell up. Now place 5 according to the general rule. The general rule would place 6 in the square occupied by 1. Therefore, 6 must go in the cell directly below 5. The numbers 7 and 8 can be placed according to the general rule. Then 9 lands in the border and must be moved to the bottom, and so on.

Here is the completed 5 × 5 magic square:

GO ON TO THE NEXT PAGE.

17	24	1	8	15
23	5	7	14	16
4	6	13	20	22
10	12	19	21	3
11	18	25	2	9

Notice that the matrix has been resized and no longer contains the borders used to construct it.

In writing your code, you may assume that the `resize` method works as specified. You may also assume that the statement

```
int[][] m = new int[size][size];
```

creates a `size` × `size` matrix m in which each element is initialized to 0.

Complete the constructor for `MagicSquare` as started below:

```
//Precondition: size ≥ 3, size odd
public MagicSquare(int size)
{
    mySize = size;
```

4. This question involves reasoning about the code from the Marine Biology Simulation Case Study. A Quick Reference to the case study is provided as part of this exam.

The `UnboundedEnv` class is currently implemented with an `ArrayList` of `Locatable` objects. An alternative way of storing objects and their locations is in a binary search tree. The tree will contain all of the fish in the environment and will be ordered by their locations. Locations in the case study are `Comparable` and are compared as follows: If L_1 and L_2 are `Location` objects, where L_1 represents (x_1, y_1) and L_2 represents (x_2, y_2), then $L_1 < L_2$ if either $x_1 < x_2$ or $x_1 = x_2$ and $y_1 < y_2$. For example, $(2, 6) < (4, 1)$ and $(3, 4) < (3, 5)$.

Suppose the fish in the environment have positions $(2, 0)$, $(1, 2)$, $(2, 3)$, $(3, 4)$, $(0, 3)$, and $(1, 5)$. Then the corresponding binary search tree can be pictured as

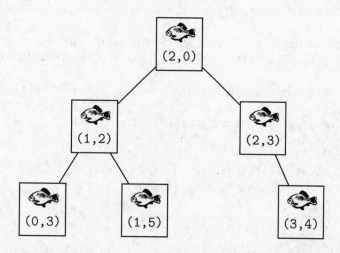

GO ON TO THE NEXT PAGE.

To implement the environment as a binary search tree, the `ArrayList objectList` will be replaced by the following private instance variables:

```
private TreeNode objectTree;
private int objectCount;     //number of objects in environment
```

(a) Since several of the methods of `UnboundedEnv` involve searching for a particular location, a private helper method `find` will be added to the class. You should write the implementation. The `find` method searches the binary search tree for the object whose location parameter is `loc` and returns the node that contains this object. The method returns `null` if it can't find an object with location `loc`.

Complete the method as started below.

```
/** Returns the node that contains the object at location loc.
 * Returns null if object with location loc is not in the tree.
 * Precondition: the tree contains all the Locatable objects in the
 *               environment. TreeNode p refers to the root of the tree
 **/
private TreeNode find(TreeNode p, Location loc)
```

(b) Write the `objectAt` method for the binary search tree implementation of the unbounded environment. The method `objectAt` returns the object at a given location in the environment and returns `null` if there is no object at that location. In writing `objectAt` you may wish to use the `find` method of part (a). You may assume that `find` works as specified irrespective of what you wrote in part (a).

Complete `objectAt` below:

```
/** Returns the object at location loc; null if loc is empty
 **/
public Locatable objectAt(Location loc)
```

(c) The binary search tree implementation of the unbounded environment requires that the `add` method be modified. The method adds a new object to the environment at a specified location, maintaining the binary search tree ordering property with respect to location. The modified method, shown below, uses an overloaded private helper method, also called `add`.

```
/** Adds a new object obj to the environment at the location the object
 * specifies.
 * Precondition: obj.location() is a valid empty location.
 * Throws an IllegalArgumentException if the precondition is not met
 **/
public void add(Locatable obj)
{
    //Check precondition. Location should be empty.
    Location loc = obj.location();
    if (!isEmpty(loc))
        throw new IllegalArgumentException("Location " + loc +
                " is not a valid empty location");

    //Add object to the environment.
    objectCount++;
    objectTree = add(objectTree, obj);  //helper method
}
```

GO ON TO THE NEXT PAGE.

Write the private helper method add. The method finds the insertion point for its Locatable parameter, attaches the new node, and returns a reference to a TreeNode.

Complete the add method below.

```
/** Private helper method
 * Find insertion point for obj in tree t and attach the new node.
 * Return reference to TreeNode
 **/
private TreeNode add(TreeNode t, Locatable obj)
```

END OF EXAMINATION

Answer Key

1. **A**	15. **D**	29. **B**
2. **B**	16. **B**	30. **D**
3. **D**	17. **A**	31. **A**
4. **D**	18. **C**	32. **B**
5. **E**	19. **A**	33. **C**
6. **B**	20. **E**	34. **D**
7. **A**	21. **B**	35. **D**
8. **C**	22. **A**	36. **A**
9. **D**	23. **C**	37. **E**
10. **E**	24. **A**	38. **D**
11. **D**	25. **D**	39. **A**
12. **D**	26. **C**	40. **C**
13. **E**	27. **E**	
14. **E**	28. **B**	

Answers Explained

1. **(A)** For adding a book to an `ArrayList`: finding the insertion point is $O(\log n)$ (binary search). Insertion is $O(n)$ (requires movement of elements). Overall: $O(n)$. For a `LinkedList`: finding the insertion point is $O(n)$. Insertion is $O(1)$. Overall: $O(n)$. Choice B is false: Accessing a single element in an `ArrayList` is $O(1)$, but $O(n)$ for a `LinkedList`. Choice C is false: To remove a book requires finding the book and then removing it. For an `ArrayList` the search is $O(\log n)$ (binary search) and removal is $O(n)$. On balance, $O(n)$. For a `LinkedList` the search is $O(n)$ and removal is $O(1)$. On balance, $O(n)$. Choice D is false: For an `ArrayList`, finding the insertion point is $O(\log n)$ (binary search). Insertion, however, requires movement of just about all the elements, $O(n)$. In the `LinkedList`, the sequential search to find the insertion point will be $O(n)$; insertion itself, $O(1)$. So both list implementations will be $O(n)$. Note that knowing that the title begins with "A" doesn't change the run-time efficiency estimate: you don't know where in the A's the title appears, and there are $O(n)$ titles beginning with "A" since you can't assume anything special about the distribution of titles among letters of the alphabet. Choice E is false: To remove the last book from both an `ArrayList` and a `LinkedList` is $O(1)$.

2. **(B)** Implementation I is wrong because it violates this rule: If super is used in the implementation of a subclass constructor, it must be used only in the first line of the constructor body. Implementation III fails because the `PartTimeEmployee` class does not have direct access to the private instance variables of the `Employee` class.

3. **(D)** *Inheritance* defines a relationship between objects that share characteristics (the *is-a* relationship). This is related to method overriding. The
`computePay` method in itself, however, is not a direct example of inheritance.
Method overriding is the process of redefining a superclass method in a subclass. Which method to call is determined at run time. This is called *dynamic
binding* (p. 76). *Method overloading* is two or more methods with the same
name but different signatures in the same class (p. 38). The process of *downcasting* is unrelated to these concepts (p. 77).

4. **(D)** Implementation I calls `super.computePay()`, which is equivalent to the
`computePay` method in the `Employee` superclass. The method returns the
quantity `mySalary-myTaxWithheld`. The `BONUS` is then correctly added to
this expression, as required. Implementation III correctly uses the public
accessor methods `getSalary` and `getTax` that the `Consultant` class has inherited. Note that the `Consultant` class does not have access to the private
instance variables `mySalary` and `myTaxWithheld` even though it inherits them
from the `Employee` class. Implementation II incorrectly returns the salary
plus `BONUS`—there is no tax withheld. The expression `super.computePay()`
returns a value equal to salary minus tax. But this is neither stored not included in the `return` statement.

5. **(E)** Note that `p` is declared to be of type `Employee`, and the `Employee` class
does not have a `getPayFraction` method. To avoid the error, `p` must be cast
to `PartTimeEmployee` as follows:

```
double g = ((PartTimeEmployee) p).getPayFraction();
```

6. **(B)** Since the `Consultant` class has no additional private instance variables,
its constructor is the same as the constructor in the `Employee` superclass. Implementation I is wrong because it calls the *default* constructor of the superclass (i.e., one without parameters). This does not exist in `Employee`, and
even if it did, it would not assign the parameter values to the private instance
variables. Implementation III is wrong because it tries to assign values to
accessor methods. These methods cannot appear on the left side of an assignment statement.

7. **(A)** The code does exactly what it looks like it should. The `writePayInfo`
parameter is of type `Employee` and each element of the `empList` array *is-a*
`Employee` and therefore does not need to be downcast to its actual instance
type. There is no `ClassCastException` (choice C) since nowhere is there an
attempt made to cast an object to a class of which it is not an instance. None
of the array elements is null; therefore, there is no `NullPointerException`
(choice B). Choice D won't happen because the `getName` method is inherited
by both the `Consultant` and `PartTimeEmployee` classes. Choice E would
occur if the `Employee` superclass were abstract, but it's not.

8. **(C)** In order for `!(A || B || C)` to be true, `(A || B || C)` must evaluate
to false. This will happen only if `A`, `B`, and `C` are *all* false. Choice A evaluates
to true when `A` and `B` are false and `C` is true. In choice B, if any *one* of `A`, `B`,
or `C` is false, the boolean expression evaluates to true. In choice D, if any one
of `A`, `B`, or `C` is false, the boolean expression evaluates to true since we have
`!(false)`. All that's required for choice E to evaluate to true is for `A` to be

false. Since `true || (any)` evaluates to true, both B and C can be either true or false.

9. **(D)** During partitioning the array looks like this:

| 45 | 40 | 77 | 20 | 65 | 52 | 90 | 15 | 95 | 79 |

| 45 | 40 | 15 | 20 | 65 | 52 | 90 | 77 | 95 | 79 |

| 20 | 40 | 15 | 45 | 65 | 52 | 90 | 77 | 95 | 79 |

Note that 45, the pivot, is in its final sorted position, the fourth element in the array. All elements to the left of 45 are less than 45 but are not sorted with respect to each other. Similarly, all elements to the right of the pivot are greater than or equal to it but are unsorted.

10. **(E)** An inorder traversal of the tree will produce the elements in ascending order. Whether the tree is balanced or not, each of the n nodes will be visited once during the traversal, which is $O(n)$. Choice A is incorrect: *Each* of the n elements may require a $\log_2 n$ search to find its slot, so creating the tree is $O(n \log n)$. Choice B is incorrect: To find a single element in a balanced tree requires no more than one comparison on each of $\log_2 n$ levels. This is $O(\log n)$. Choice C is incorrect: Even if the tree is completely unbalanced and consists of one long linked list (worst case), there will be no more than n comparisons to insert one element. This is $O(n)$. Choice D is incorrect. A postorder traversal for the binary search tree shown below produces 1, 7, 6, which is not in ascending order. In a binary search tree, the order property causes the leftmost elements to be the smallest and the rightmost the largest. Thus an *inorder* traversal will produce the elements sorted in ascending order.

11. **(D)** A program that uses an abstract class must have at least one subclass that is *not* abstract, since instances of abstract classes cannot be created. Thus choice E is false. Choice A is false: An abstract class can contain any number of private instance variables, each of which is inherited by a subclass of AClass. Note that choice C would be true if it were changed to "At least one method of AClass must be abstract." Choice B is wrong—for example v1 and v2 could be initialized in a default constructor (constructor with no parameters).

12. **(D)** The expression `itr.next()` returns an Object. When equals is invoked at run time, the object will be recognized as an Integer, and the correct equals method will be called. This is polymorphism. Thus the cast to Integer in test II is redundant. It does no harm, however, and the test works

as intended. Test III fails since `itr.next()` is an `Object`, which doesn't have an `intValue()` method. You need `((Integer) itr.next()).intValue()`. Even if you fix this, however, test III will fail because `equals` cannot be used for primitive types! Both operands in the test are type `int`.

13. **(E)** The `for` loop is executed $\log_2 n$ times (i.e., the number of times that `i`, which is initialized to n, is divided by 2 until it reaches 1).

14. **(E)** Implementation I uses faulty logic. For example, it treats an `ElapsedTime` of 5 hours 12 minutes 30 seconds as equal to 12 hours 6 minutes 20 seconds.

15. **(D)** Segment II is wrong because you can't use simple addition to add two objects: The code must be explicitly written. Segment I works because you're adding two `int` values and then invoking the constructor whose argument is the total number of seconds. Segment III works by a brute force computation of hours, minutes, and seconds.

16. **(B)** A `HashMap` stores its elements in a hash table and, therefore, provides $O(1)$ run times for its `get` and `put` operations. The key set is not stored in any particular order. Constructing a `TreeMap` with the inventory elements places them in a binary search tree and allows printing of the key set in ascending order (which is alphabetic order for `String` objects).

17. **(A)** $30,000 = 1000 \times 30 \approx 2^{10} \times 2^5 = 2^{15}$. Since a successful binary search in the worst case requires $\log_2 n$ iterations, 15 iterations will guarantee that `key` is found. (Note that $30,000 < 2^{10} \times 2^5 = 32,768$.)

18. **(C)** Since `value` 5 is odd, `value % 2` is 1. Array `v` is examined sequentially. Each time an element greater than 1 is encountered, it is pushed onto the stack. Each time an element less than or equal to 1 is encountered, the stack is popped. Thus the following sequence of actions will occur: push 2, pop, push 6, push 5, pop, push 9. Four pushes and two pops leave the stack with 2 elements, and 9 on top. Note that a `NoSuchElementException` is thrown if an attempt is made to pop an empty stack.

19. **(A)** If `mystery(firstNode)` is invoked for the following linear linked list:

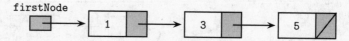

the method will create three new `ListNodes` whose pointer connections are pending:

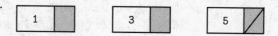

In the method call that creates the last node (containing 5), the expression `firstNode.getNext()` involves a base case, resulting in

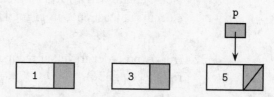

Now each of the previous method calls can be completed, resulting in the following sequence of pointer connections:

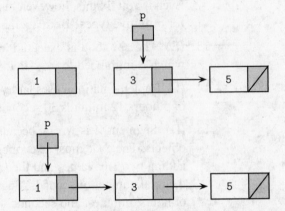

After the execution of the first recursive call has been completed, the final `ListNode` reference returned refers to the first node of a linear linked list that is identical to the original list.

20. **(E)** Just two pointer adjustments and a reassignment of `lastNode` achieve enqueue: $O(1)$.

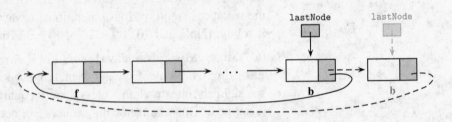

Just one pointer adjustment achieves `dequeue`: $O(1)$.

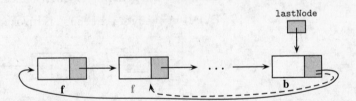

21. **(B)** Segment II places the distinct elements of `list` in `HashSet h` and the duplicates in `HashSet k`. The output correctly lists the duplicates, in increasing order, since elements of a `TreeSet` are ordered. Segment I prints all the distinct elements of `list`, excluding duplicates, which was not what was required. Segment III places all elements of `list` in a `TreeSet` and then iterates over each element of the `TreeSet` checking for duplicates in `list`. The trouble is, `count` will *always* be greater than zero, since each element of `TreeSet s` occurs at least once in `list`! The segment can be fixed by initializing `count` to -1.

22. **(A)** A preorder traversal recursively traverses a tree as follows: root - left - right (see p. 336).

23. **(C)** Notice that the remainders are generated in the opposite order that they must be output. A stack, therefore, is the perfect data structure for storage: the last remainder in will be the first out, as required.

24. **(A)** The dashed arrows show the pointer connections that must be made to remove nodes p and q from the list:

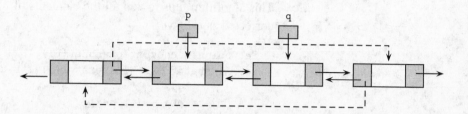

The only way to access the node to the left of p is with p.getPrev(). Similarly, the node to the right of q is q.getNext(). Thus, segment II is wrong. Segment III is completely garbled.

25. **(D)** The method as given will throw an `ArrayIndexOutOfBoundsException`. For the matrix in the example, `mat[0].length` is 4. The call `mat.alter(1)` gives c a value of 1. Thus, in the inner `for` loop, j goes from 1 to 3. When j is 3, the line `mat[i][j] = mat[i][j+1]` becomes `mat[i][3] = mat[i][4]`. Since columns go from 0 to 3, `mat[i][4]` is out of range. The changes in segments I and II both fix this problem. In each case the correct replacements are made for each row i: `mat[i][1] = mat[i][2]` and `mat[i][2] = mat[i][3]`. Segment III makes the following incorrect replacements as j goes from 3 to 2: `mat[i][2] = mat[i][3]` and `mat[i][1] = mat[i][2]`. This will cause both columns 1 and 2 to be overwritten. Before inserting zeros in the last column, `mat` will be

$$\begin{matrix} 2 & 9 & 9 & 9 \\ 1 & 3 & 3 & 3 \\ 0 & 2 & 2 & 2 \end{matrix}$$

This does not achieve the intended postcondition of the method.

26. **(C)** If $N = 1$, the required level is 0
If $N = 2$, the required level is 1
If $N = 3$ or 4, the required level is 2
If $N = 5$–8, the required level is 3
...

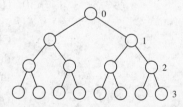

Test each of choices A–E with $N = 4$, where the desired answer is 2. Choice C works. Choices A and B fail the test on the first try and return `level = 0`. Choice D fails on the second try, leaving `level = 1`. Choice E executes the `while` loop one time too many, giving `level` a value of 3 when 2 will suffice. The conditions of the problem specify that the lowest possible level should be found.

27. **(E)** Segment I places the elements of h1 in union. Then it iterates over h2, placing in union all the elements of h2 that are not already in union. (Recall that the Set method add leaves the set unchanged if its Object parameter is already contained in the set.) Segment III takes a more circuitous route

but ends where it should. It places the elements of h1 in an `ArrayList` and then appends all the elements of h2 to the list. Note that this list may contain duplicates—the elements that are in both h1 and h2. When union is constructed from the `ArrayList`, the duplicates are eliminated, since a set contains no duplicates. Segment II fails because the `itr.next()` in the if test is not the same element as the `itr.next()` in the `union.add` statement! This algorithm fails to add all the elements of h2 to union. The code can be corrected as follows:

```
Set union = copySetToHashSet(h1);
for (Iterator itr=h2.iterator(); itr.hasNext();)
{
    Object obj = itr.next();
    if (!union.contains(obj))
        union.add(obj);
}
```

28. **(B)** Method III is $O(n^2)$: For each element in the text file, its insertion point in the linear linked list must be found. For one element, this would be $O(n)$. For n elements, it is $O(n^2)$. Choice A is true: An inorder traversal of a binary search tree accesses the values in ascending order, which is alphabetical order if the elements are strings. Choice C is true: Approximately ordered elements lead to an unbalanced binary search tree (worst case). Number of comparisons to form the tree is $1 + 2 + \cdots + (n - 2) + (n - 1) = n(n - 1)/2$, which is $O(n^2)$. Selection sort is $O(n^2)$ irrespective of the order of the elements. Choice D is true: Random order of the elements generally leads to a balanced binary search tree. Creation of the tree is then $O(n \log n)$, which is faster than the $O(n^2)$ run times of methods II and III. Choice E is true: Traversal of a linear linked list and printing elements of an array are both $O(n)$. An inorder traversal of a binary search tree visits each node once, which is $O(n)$.

29. **(B)** The statement prints the set of keys, namely the invoice numbers, so eliminate choices C, D, and E. Choice A is wrong because a `TreeMap` stores the elements in a binary search tree and prints the keys in increasing order.

30. **(D)** Recall that the keys in a map must be unique. If a name is entered that already exists in the map, the new information will replace the existing entry. Choice II will be OK with this data structure, provided the customers have different names! Different `CustomerOrder` objects *can* contain the same item that was purchased.

31. **(A)** Notice that either `vIndex` or `wIndex` is incremented at the end of the loop. This means that, when the loop is exited, the current values of `v[vIndex]` and `w[wIndex]` have not been compared. Therefore, you can only make an assertion for values `v[0]..v[vIndex-1]` and `w[0]..w[wIndex-1]`. Also, notice that if there is no common value in the arrays, the exiting condition for the `while` loop will be that the end of one of the arrays has been reached, namely `vIndex` equals N or `wIndex` equals M.

32. **(B)** Here is the "box diagram" for the recursive method calls, showing the order of execution of statements. Notice that the circled statements are the base case calls, the only statements that actually draw a line.

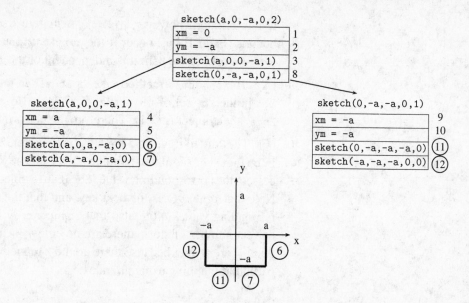

33. **(C)** The `System.out.println(tree.getLeft().getValue())` statement indicates that the data in the root node is not printed. This eliminates choices B and E. Notice that there's no `null` test on `tree.getRight()`, nor is there any `System.out.println(tree.getRight().getValue())` statement. This means that no right children are ever printed, which certainly eliminates choice A. It also eliminates choice D, since nodes in the left subtree of `tree` do contain right children.

34. **(D)** The `setRoot` method, which is inherited from the `BinaryTree` class, can be used to change the `root` reference. Note that choice A is true: The `BinarySearchTree` class doesn't inherit any constructors. The compiler does, however, provide the default constructor shown. There is no error since the superclass `BinaryTree` has a default constructor. Choice E is true because the `BinarySearchTree` class does not have a constructor with a parameter.

35. **(D)** Segment II is a correct recursive algorithm, and segment III is a correct iterative algorithm. Segment I fails because making the recursive calls with `getRoot().getLeft()` and `getRoot().getRight()` means that parameter `p` will not recurse down the tree. The only nodes inspected will be in level 0 and level 1 of the tree!

36. **(A)** Since several of the `Environment` methods deal with locations in the environment, the objects in the environment must have a location (i.e., they must be `Locatable`). None of the `Environment` methods require that the objects in it be compared or displayed, so choices II and III are not *requirements* for the objects.

37. **(E)** In choice E, the fish moved backward, which is an invalid move. All other choices are possible setups: In choice A the fish bred. In choice B it bred, then died. In choice C it neither bred, moved, nor died. In choice D it neither bred nor moved. Then it died.

38. **(D)** Both the `breed` and `nextLocation` methods call for a list of valid empty neighbors. The `isEmpty(loc)` method used to generate this list must return `true` if `loc` is both unoccupied and in bounds (i.e., valid). If the `isValid(loc)`

test is omitted, however, `isEmpty` will return `true` even if `loc` is out of bounds. Error II will occur if the `nextLocation` method fails to remove the location behind the fish; it is independent of the `isEmpty` test.

39. **(A)** The `objectAt` method takes a `Location` parameter `loc`. Searching for `loc` in the key set of `objectMap` is $O(1)$. Also, returning the corresponding `Locatable` object is $O(1)$. Therefore the performance of the method is $O(1)$.

40. **(C)** The way to traverse a `HashMap` is to use an iterator. To access the values in `objectMap`, segment III iterates over all the keys, and as each key is accessed, the corresponding value (`Locatable` object) is placed in `objectArray`. Note that `i.next()` is the next key, and that the `get` method returns the corresponding value. Note also that `objectArray` is declared with exactly the correct number of slots: there are no empty locations in the map. Segments I and II are wrong because there are no `Map` methods that allow access to any particular mapping using an index.

Section II

1. (a)
```
public HashTable(int tableSize)
{
    size = tableSize;
    count = 0;
    T = new LinkedList[size];
    for (int i=0; i<size; i++)
    {
        T[i] = new LinkedList();
    }
}
```

(b)
```
public void delete(Object key)
{
    int pos = hash(key);    //get hash address
    boolean found = false;
    ListIterator i = T[pos].listIterator();
    while (i.hasNext() && !found)
    {
        if(((TableEntry) i.next()).getKey().equals(key))
        {
            i.remove();
            found = true;
        }
    }
}
```

(c)
```
public void insert(Object key, DataType data)
{
    int pos = hash(key);
    TableEntry t = new TableEntry(key, data);
    delete(key);      //does nothing if key not in table
    T[pos].addFirst(t);
}
```

NOTE
- The `for` loop in part (a) initializes each `T[i]` to be an empty `LinkedList`.
- In parts (b) and (c) the `hash` method determines which `LinkedList` must be searched.
- The `i.next()` object in part (b) must be cast to a `TableEntry` before the `getKey` method can be called.
- The `boolean` variable `found` in part (b) is used to exit the loop if `key` is found. It is inefficient to continue the traversal after `key` is found, since `key` does not occur more than once in the table.
- In part (c) `delete(key)` must be done before adding new data, otherwise the postcondition will be violated.
- In part (c) it is also correct to use `addLast(t)` instead of `addFirst(t)` for insertion into the `LinkedList T[pos]`.

2. (a)

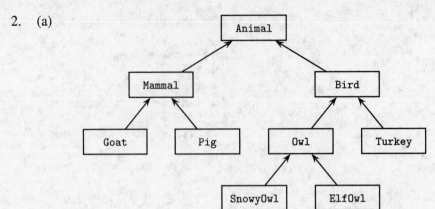

(b)
```
public abstract class Animal
{
    private String myName;
    private String myNoise;
    private String myCovering;

    //constructor
    public Animal(String name, String noise, String covering)
    {
        myName = name;
        myNoise = noise;
        myCovering = covering;
    }

    public String getName()
    { return myName; }

    public String getNoise()
    { return myNoise; }

    public String getCovering()
    { return myCovering; }

    public abstract String getFood();
}
```

(c)
```
public abstract class Owl extends Bird
{
    //constructor
    public Owl(String name)
    {
        super(name, "hoot");
    }
}
```

(d)
```
public class SnowyOwl extends Owl
{
    //constructor
    public SnowyOwl()
    {
        super("Snowy Owl");
    }
}
```

```
                    //returns type of food for this SnowyOwl
                    public String getFood()
                    {
                        Random r = RandNumGenerator.getInstance();
                        int num = r.nextInt(3);
                        if (num == 0)
                            return "hare";
                        else if (num == 1)
                            return "lemming";
                        else
                            return "small bird";
                    }
                }
```

NOTE

- Since the food type for each Animal can't be simply provided in a parameter, the getFood method must be abstract in the Animal class. This means that the Animal class must be abstract.
- Both the Bird and Owl classes inherit the abstract getFood method. Since the food type for a Bird, and also for an Owl, depends on the type of Bird or Owl, these classes don't provide implementation code for getFood. Therefore both Bird and Owl must be abstract classes.
- In parts (c) and (d) super must be used in the constructors because there's no direct access to the private variables of the Animal class.
- Note that the Bird constructor has two parameters, name and noise. The noise for an Owl, however, will always be "hoot". Therefore noise does not need to be provided as a parameter in the Owl constructor. The statement super(name,"hoot") will use the superclass (Bird) constructor to automatically assign "hoot" as an Owl's noise. Similarly, the SnowyOwl does not need any parameters in its constructor. Using the superclass (Owl) constructor will automatically provide it with its name through the statement super("SnowyOwl").
- The SnowyOwl inherits the "hoot" noise from Owl and the "feathers" covering from Bird.
- The RandNumGenerator class is set up in such a way that only one new Random object will be created in a program, no matter how many random numbers are needed (see p. 473). The given solution is therefore preferable to the line

  ```
  Random r = new Random();
  ```

  in the getFood method of SnowyOwl.

3. (a) public static boolean checkDiagonalSums(int[][] m, int size,
        int total)
    {
        int majorSum = 0, minorSum = 0;
        for (int i=0; i<size; i++)
        {
            majorSum += m[i][i];
            minorSum += m[i][size-i-1];
        }
        return majorSum == total && minorSum == total;
    }

```
(b) public MagicSquare(int size)
    {
        mySize = size;
        myMatrix = new int[size+1][size+1];
        int numSquares = size*size;
        myMatrix[0][size] = -999;   //top right corner not used
        int row = 1, col = size/2;  //starting position
        myMatrix[row][col] = 1;     //first number inserted
        for (int val=2; val <=numSquares; val++)
        {
            if (myMatrix[row-1][col+1] != 0)  //cell occupied
                row++;
            else                         //cell not occupied
            {
                row--;
                col++;
                if (row == 0)           //outside square (on top)
                    row = size;
                else if (col == size)  //outside (right side)
                    col = 0;
            }
            myMatrix[row][col] = val;
        }
        //overwrite top border by shifting each row one up
        for (int i=1; i<=size; i++)
            for (int j=0; j<size; j++)
                myMatrix[i-1][j] = myMatrix[i][j];
        //remove bottom row and right side border
        myMatrix = resize(myMatrix, size);
    }
```

NOTE
- In part (a), the line

  ```
  minorSum += m[i][size-i-1];
  ```

  can be replaced by

  ```
  minorSum += m[size-i-1][i];
  ```

- In part (a), the `return` statement can be replaced by

  ```
  if (majorSum != total || minorSum != total)
      return false;
  else
      return true;
  ```

- In part (b), a `for` loop can be used for placing each number since each of the `size*size` integers will be placed in the square exactly once, and in increasing order.
- After filling the magic square, the borders must be eliminated. This is done by shifting each row up one row and then resizing the matrix back to `size` × `size`. Resizing automatically cuts off the border on the right-hand side and eliminates the (now redundant) bottom row.

4.   (a)
```
private TreeNode find(TreeNode p, Location loc)
{
    while (p != null &&
        loc.compareTo(((Locatable) p.getValue()).
            location()) != 0)
    {
        if (loc.compareTo(((Locatable) p.getValue()).
                location()) < 0)
            p = p.getLeft();
        else
            p = p.getRight();
    }
    return p;
}
```

Here is an alternative solution that is recursive:

```
private TreeNode find(TreeNode p, Location loc)
{
    if (p == null)
        return null;
    else if (loc.compareTo(((Locatable) p.getValue()).
            location()) == 0)
        return p;
    else if (loc.compareTo(((Locatable) p.getValue()).
            location()) < 0)
        return find(p.getLeft(), loc);
    else
        return find(p.getRight(), loc);
}
```

(b)
```
public Locatable objectAt(Location loc)
{
    TreeNode t = find(objectTree, loc);
    if ( t == null )
        return null;
    return (Locatable) t.getValue();
}
```

(c)
```
private TreeNode add(TreeNode t, Locatable obj)
{
    Location loc = obj.location();
    if (t == null)
        return new TreeNode(obj, null, null);
    else if (loc.compareTo(((Locatable) t.getValue()).
            location()) < 0)
        t.setLeft(add(t.getLeft(), obj));
    else
        t.setRight(add(t.getRight(), obj));
    return t;
}
```

Here is an alternative solution that is iterative:

```
private TreeNode add(TreeNode t, Locatable obj)
{
    Location loc = obj.location();
    if (t == null)
        return new TreeNode(obj, null, null);
    else
    {
        TreeNode p = null, q = t;
        while (q != null)
        {
            p = q;
            if (loc.compareTo(((Locatable) p.getValue()).
                    location()) < 0)
                q = p.getLeft();
            else
                q = p.getRight();
        }
        if (loc.compareTo(((Locatable) p.getValue()).
                location()) < 0)
            p.setLeft(new TreeNode(obj, null, null));
        else
            p.setRight(new TreeNode(obj, null, null));
        return t;
    }
}
```

NOTE

- In part (a) p.getValue() returns an Object, which must be cast to a Locatable before its location() can be accessed.

- Location objects contain a compareTo method and thus are Comparable. If this were not true, none of these methods would work.

- In part (c) the TreeNode parameter is needed for the recursive solution, which must be able to recurse down the tree. The return value for this solution is a TreeNode reference along the insertion path. Eventually the reference at the root of the tree is returned. The iterative solution simply finds the insertion point, attaches the new node, and then returns the reference at the root of the tree. This solution does not require a TreeNode parameter—you could just use the private instance variable objectTree. The parameter was provided to give you the option of either solution.

- If you wanted to rewrite the entire UnboundedEnv class using the binary search tree implementation, you would need to restore the binary search tree after each fish acts. A fish that moves to a new location must be removed from the tree and reinserted to maintain the ordering property. (When fish breed, the new fish will automatically be inserted correctly through the add method.)

Answer Sheet: Practice Exam Four

1. Ⓐ Ⓑ Ⓒ Ⓓ Ⓔ   15. Ⓐ Ⓑ Ⓒ Ⓓ Ⓔ   29. Ⓐ Ⓑ Ⓒ Ⓓ Ⓔ

2. Ⓐ Ⓑ Ⓒ Ⓓ Ⓔ   16. Ⓐ Ⓑ Ⓒ Ⓓ Ⓔ   30. Ⓐ Ⓑ Ⓒ Ⓓ Ⓔ

3. Ⓐ Ⓑ Ⓒ Ⓓ Ⓔ   17. Ⓐ Ⓑ Ⓒ Ⓓ Ⓔ   31. Ⓐ Ⓑ Ⓒ Ⓓ Ⓔ

4. Ⓐ Ⓑ Ⓒ Ⓓ Ⓔ   18. Ⓐ Ⓑ Ⓒ Ⓓ Ⓔ   32. Ⓐ Ⓑ Ⓒ Ⓓ Ⓔ

5. Ⓐ Ⓑ Ⓒ Ⓓ Ⓔ   19. Ⓐ Ⓑ Ⓒ Ⓓ Ⓔ   33. Ⓐ Ⓑ Ⓒ Ⓓ Ⓔ

6. Ⓐ Ⓑ Ⓒ Ⓓ Ⓔ   20. Ⓐ Ⓑ Ⓒ Ⓓ Ⓔ   34. Ⓐ Ⓑ Ⓒ Ⓓ Ⓔ

7. Ⓐ Ⓑ Ⓒ Ⓓ Ⓔ   21. Ⓐ Ⓑ Ⓒ Ⓓ Ⓔ   35. Ⓐ Ⓑ Ⓒ Ⓓ Ⓔ

8. Ⓐ Ⓑ Ⓒ Ⓓ Ⓔ   22. Ⓐ Ⓑ Ⓒ Ⓓ Ⓔ   36. Ⓐ Ⓑ Ⓒ Ⓓ Ⓔ

9. Ⓐ Ⓑ Ⓒ Ⓓ Ⓔ   23. Ⓐ Ⓑ Ⓒ Ⓓ Ⓔ   37. Ⓐ Ⓑ Ⓒ Ⓓ Ⓔ

10. Ⓐ Ⓑ Ⓒ Ⓓ Ⓔ   24. Ⓐ Ⓑ Ⓒ Ⓓ Ⓔ   38. Ⓐ Ⓑ Ⓒ Ⓓ Ⓔ

11. Ⓐ Ⓑ Ⓒ Ⓓ Ⓔ   25. Ⓐ Ⓑ Ⓒ Ⓓ Ⓔ   39. Ⓐ Ⓑ Ⓒ Ⓓ Ⓔ

12. Ⓐ Ⓑ Ⓒ Ⓓ Ⓔ   26. Ⓐ Ⓑ Ⓒ Ⓓ Ⓔ   40. Ⓐ Ⓑ Ⓒ Ⓓ Ⓔ

13. Ⓐ Ⓑ Ⓒ Ⓓ Ⓔ   27. Ⓐ Ⓑ Ⓒ Ⓓ Ⓔ

14. Ⓐ Ⓑ Ⓒ Ⓓ Ⓔ   28. Ⓐ Ⓑ Ⓒ Ⓓ Ⓔ

How to Calculate Your (Approximate) AP Score — AP Computer Science Level AB

Multiple Choice

Number correct (out of 40)   =   _____

$1/4 \times$ number wrong   =   _____

Raw score = line 1 − line 2   =   _____

Raw score $\times$ 1.25   =   _____   ⟸   **Multiple-Choice Score**
(Do not round. If less
than zero, enter zero.)

Free Response

Question 1   _____
(out of 9)

Question 2   _____
(out of 9)

Question 3   _____
(out of 9)

Question 4   _____
(out of 9)

Total   _____ $\times$ 1.39   =   _____   ⟸   **Free-Response Score**
(Do not round.)

Final Score

_____   +   _____   =   _____
Multiple-   Free-   Final Score
Choice   Response   (Round to nearest
Score   Score   whole number.)

**Chart to Convert to AP Grade
Computer Science AB**

Final Score Range	AP Grade[a]
70–100	5
60–69	4
41–59	3
31–40	2
0–30	1

[a]The score range corresponding to
each grade varies from exam to exam
and is approximate.

Practice Exam Four
COMPUTER SCIENCE AB
SECTION I

Time—1 hour and 15 minutes
Number of questions—40
Percent of total grade—50

Directions: Determine the answer to each of the following questions or incomplete statements, using separate pieces of scrap paper for any necessary scratchwork. Then decide which is the best of the choices given and fill in the corresponding oval on the answer sheet. Do not spend too much time on any one problem.

Note: Assume that the standard packages (e.g., `java.util.*`) are included in any programs that use the code segments provided in individual questions. A Quick Reference to the standard classes and interfaces with their required methods is provided.

---

1. A program is to be written that simulates and keeps track of the random motion of a point whose position is represented by coordinates (x, y). The point starts at $(0, 0)$ at time = 0. It is to move randomly a large, but unknown, number of times. A record of its (x, y) positions must be kept so as to be able to re-create any part of its path starting from a given previously recorded (x, y) position. The program is to print the point's (x, y) movements, forward or backward in time, from the given (x, y) position. You may assume that no point is visited more than once. Assuming the existence of a `Point` class that holds a pair of coordinates, which of the following is the best data structure for the task?
   (A) A one-dimensional array of `Point` objects
   (B) A two-dimensional array of integers in which the array indexes represent the position visited by the point and each integer cell of the array is a counter that keeps track of the number of moves to that position
   (C) A circular doubly linked list of `Point` objects
   (D) A stack of `Point` objects
   (E) A queue of `Point` objects

GO ON TO THE NEXT PAGE

Level A Also

Questions 2–6 refer to the `TennisPlayer`, `GoodPlayer`, and `WeakPlayer` classes below. These classes are to be used in a program to simulate a game of tennis.

```
public abstract class TennisPlayer
{
    private String myName;

    //constructor
    public TennisPlayer(String name)
    { myName = name; }

    public String getName()
    { return myName; }

    public abstract boolean serve();
    public abstract boolean returnShot();
}
public class GoodPlayer extends TennisPlayer
{
    private static Random r;    //random number generator

    //constructor
    public GoodPlayer(String name)
    { implementation }

    //Postcondition: return true if serve is in (80% probability),
    //               false if serve is out (20% probability)
    public boolean serve()
    { implementation }

    //Postcondition: return true if return shot is in (70% probability),
    //               false if return shot is out (30% probability)
    public boolean returnShot()
    { implementation }
}
public class WeakPlayer extends TennisPlayer
{
    private static Random r;    //random number generator

    //constructor
    public WeakPlayer(String name)
    { implementation }

    //Postcondition: return true if serve is in (45% probability),
    //               false if serve is out (55% probability)
    public boolean serve()
    { implementation }

    //Postcondition: return true if return shot is in (30% probability),
    //               false if return shot is out (70% probability)
    public boolean returnShot()
    { implementation }
}
```

GO ON TO THE NEXT PAGE

Level A Also

2. Which of the following declarations will cause an error? You may assume all the constructors are correctly implemented.

(A) `TennisPlayer t = new TennisPlayer("Smith");`
(B) `TennisPlayer g = new GoodPlayer("Jones");`
(C) `TennisPlayer w = new WeakPlayer("Henry");`
(D) `TennisPlayer p;`
(E) `WeakPlayer q = new WeakPlayer("Grady");`

3. Which is a correct *implementation* of the constructor for the `GoodPlayer` class?

```
 I myName = name;
   r = new Random();

 II super(name);
    r = new Random();

III r = new Random();
    super(name);
```

(A) I only
(B) II only
(C) III only
(D) I and II only
(E) I, II, and III

4. Refer to the serve method in the `WeakPlayer` class:

```
//Postcondition: return true if serve is in (45% probability),
//                false if serve is out (55% probability)
public boolean serve()
{ implementation }
```

Which of the following replacements for *implementation* satisfies the postcondition of the `serve` method?

```
 I double value = r.nextDouble();
   return value >= 0 || value <= 0.45;

 II double value = r.nextDouble();
    return value < 0.45;

III int val = r.nextInt(100);
    return val < 45;
```

(A) I only
(B) II only
(C) III only
(D) II and III only
(E) I, II, and III

GO ON TO THE NEXT PAGE

Level A Also

5. A client program uses the `TennisPlayer`, `GoodPlayer`, and `WeakPlayer` classes to simulate a game of doubles (four players, two on each side of the net). Consider the following declarations:

```
TennisPlayer[] players = {new GoodPlayer("Kay"), new WeakPlayer("May"),
        new GoodPlayer("Jay"), new WeakPlayer("Fay")};

//Outputs results for one point
public static void onePoint(TennisPlayer[] players)
{ implementation }
```

Which is a *false* statement about method calls in the `onePoint` method?
   (A) The expression `players[i].serve()` has an 80% probability of being `true` if i is 0 or 2.
   (B) The expression `players[i].returnShot()` has a 30% probability of being `true` if i is 1 or 3.
   (C) The method call `players[i].getName()` is not an example of dynamic binding.
   (D) The method call `players[0].getName()` will cause an error message stating that there is no getName method in the GoodPlayer class.
   (E) The method call `players[i].serve()` will throw an `ArrayIndexOutOfBoundsException` whenever i is not in the range $0 \le i \le 3$.

6. Consider the following declaration:

```
public class Beginner extends WeakPlayer
{
    private double myCostOfLessons;

    //methods of Beginner class
        ...
}
```

Refer to the following declarations and method in a client program:

```
TennisPlayer g = new GoodPlayer("Sam");
TennisPlayer w = new WeakPlayer("Harry");
TennisPlayer b = new Beginner("Dick");

public static void giveEncouragement(WeakPlayer t)
{ implementation }
```

Which of the following method calls will cause an exception to be thrown?
   (A) `giveEncouragement((WeakPlayer) g);`
   (B) `giveEncouragement(w);`
   (C) `giveEncouragement(b);`
   (D) `giveEncouragement((WeakPlayer) b);`
   (E) `giveEncouragement((WeakPlayer) w);`

GO ON TO THE NEXT PAGE

7. Inorder and postorder traversals yield the same output for which of the following trees?

(A)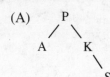

(D)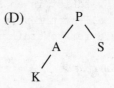

(B)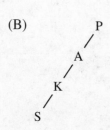

(E)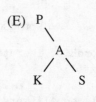

(C)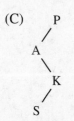

8. Worst case run time is *never* $O(n^2)$ for which of the following sorting algorithms?

    I Mergesort
    II Heapsort
    III Quicksort

(A) I only
(B) II only
(C) III only
(D) I and II only
(E) I, II, and III

Level A Also

9. Which is true of the following boolean expression, given that x is a variable of type `double`?

```
3.0 == x * (3.0/x)
```

(A) It will always evaluate to false.
(B) It may evaluate to false for some values of x.
(C) It will evaluate to false only when x is zero.
(D) It will evaluate to false only when x is very large or very close to zero.
(E) It will always evaluate to true.

GO ON TO THE NEXT PAGE

10. Refer to the `removeWord` method below:

```
//Precondition:  wordList is an ArrayList of String
//Postcondition: all occurrences of word removed from wordList
public static void removeWord(ArrayList wordList, String word)
{
    < implementation code >
}
```

Which < *implementation code* > will produce the required postcondition?

```
I  Iterator itr = wordList.iterator();
   while (itr.hasNext())
   {
       if (itr.next().equals(word))
           itr.remove();
   }
```

```
II Iterator itr = wordList.iterator();
   int i = 0;
   while (itr.hasNext())
   {
       if (itr.next().equals(word))
           wordList.remove(i);
       i++;
   }
```

```
III for (int i=0; i<wordList.size(); i++)
    {
        if (wordList.get(i).equals(word))
            wordList.remove(i);
    }
```

(A) I only
(B) II only
(C) III only
(D) I and II only
(E) I and III only

GO ON TO THE NEXT PAGE

Assume that linked lists are implemented with the `ListNode` class provided.

Refer to method `insertZero` for Questions 11 and 12.

```
//Precondition:   current refers to a node in a linear linked list.
//                current is not null
//Postcondition: the node following the node that current refers to contains 0
public static void insertZero(ListNode current)
```

Examples:

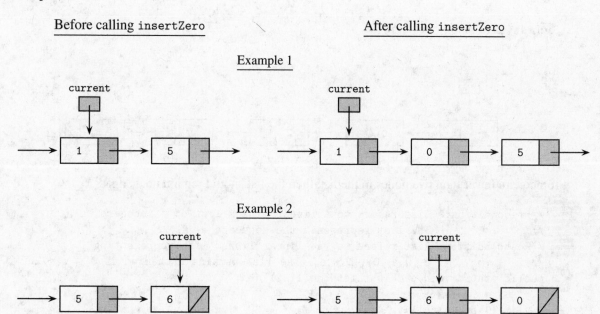

11. Which of the following could be used as the body of `insertZero` such that its postcondition is satisfied?

   I   `current.setNext(new ListNode(new Integer(0), current.getNext()));`

  II `ListNode p = new ListNode(new Integer(0), current.getNext());`
      `current = p;`

 III `ListNode p = new ListNode(null, null);`
      `p.setNext(current.getNext());`
      `p.setValue(new Integer(0));`
      `current.setNext(p);`

(A) I only
(B) II only
(C) III only
(D) I and II only
(E) I and III only

GO ON TO THE NEXT PAGE

12. A method `padList`, whose code is given below, is to insert a zero between each pair of existing nodes in its parameter, `list`, a linked list of integers. For example, if the list is initially

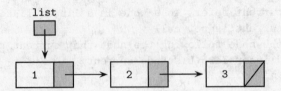

`padList(list)` should result in

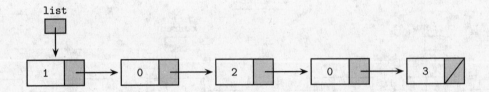

If there are fewer than two nodes in the list, then the list should remain unchanged.

```
//Precondition:  list refers to a linear linked list of n integers, n ≥ 0.
//               The list represents the sequence a₁,a₂,...,aₙ.
//Postcondition: list refers to the linear linked list representing
//               a₁,0,a₂,0,...,0,aₙ. The list remains unchanged if 0 ≤ n < 2
public static void padList(ListNode list)
{
    if (list != null)
    {
        ListNode temp = list;
        while (temp.getNext() != null)
        {
            insertZero(temp);
            temp = temp.getNext();
        }
    }
}
```

Assuming that the precondition for `padList` is satisfied, for which lists will `padList` work correctly?
(A) For all linear linked lists
(B) For no linear linked lists
(C) Only for lists that contain fewer than two nodes
(D) Only for lists that contain exactly one node
(E) Only for empty lists

13. The binary tree shown is traversed preorder. During the traversal, each element, when accessed, is pushed onto an initially empty stack s of String. What output is produced when the following code is executed?

```
while (!s.isEmpty())
    System.out.println(s.pop());
```

(A) AKCPRF
(B) CKRFPA
(C) FPRACK
(D) APFRKC
(E) FRPCKA

Questions 14 and 15 refer to the findMin method below:

```
//Precondition:  a is a nonempty list of Comparable objects
//Postcondition: returns smallest item in a
public static Comparable findMin(List a)
{
    Iterator itr = a.iterator();
    Comparable min = (Comparable) itr.next();
    while (itr.hasNext())
    {
        Comparable element = (Comparable) itr.next();
        if (min.compareTo(element) > 0)
            min = element;
    }
    return min;
}
```

14. Which is a *false* statement?
    (A) The elements of the list must be Comparable so that the compareTo method can be used.
    (B) The findMin method will work whether a is a LinkedList or ArrayList.
    (C) If the initialization of min is changed to

        Comparable min = itr.next();

        the findMin method will not work as intended.
    (D) If the list a contains duplicates, the findMin method will not work as intended.
    (E) If the statement that compares min to element is changed to

        if (min.compareTo(element) >= 0)
            min = element;

        the findMin method will still work as intended.

GO ON TO THE NEXT PAGE

15. Suppose the implementation of the findMin method is changed as follows: The statement

```
Comparable min = (Comparable) itr.next();
```

is changed to

```
Comparable min = (Comparable) a.getFirst();
```

Which of the following code segments in a client program will *fail*?

```
 I  List list = new ArrayList();
    list = readList();  //initialize list with Comparable elements
    Comparable smallest = findMin(list);
```

```
II  List list = new LinkedList();
    list = readList();  //initialize list with Comparable elements
    Comparable smallest = findMin(list);
```

```
III Comparable[] list = new Comparable[SIZE];  //SIZE is an integer constant
    list = readList();  //initialize list with Comparable elements
    Comparable smallest = findMin(list);
```

(A) I only
(B) II only
(C) III only
(D) I and III only
(E) I, II, and III

16. A large charity organization maintains a database of its donors. For each donor, the following information is stored: name, address, phone number, amount and date of most recent contribution, and total contributed so far. Two methods for organizing and modifying the data are considered:

 I A one-dimensional array of Donor objects maintained in alphabetical order by name.
 II A hash table of Donor objects implemented using an array of linked lists. The hash address for any given Donor object will be determined by a hash method that uniformly distributes donors throughout the table.

Which of the following is *false*? (Assume the most efficient algorithms possible.)
(A) Methods I and II have roughly the same memory efficiency.
(B) Insertion of a new donor is more run-time efficient using method II.
(C) Modifying an existing donor's record is more run-time efficient using method II.
(D) Printing out a mailing list in alphabetical order is more run-time efficient using method I.
(E) Printing out a list of donors in decreasing order of total amount contributed is more run-time efficient using method I.

GO ON TO THE NEXT PAGE

17. Consider a class that has this private instance variable:

    private int[][] mat;

The class has the following method, alter.

```
public void alter(int c)
{
    for (int i=0; i<mat.length; i++)
        for (int j=c+1; j<mat[0].length; j++)
            mat[i][j-1] = mat[i][j];
}
```

If mat is

    1 3 5 7
    2 4 6 8
    3 5 7 9

then alter(1) will change mat to

(A) 1 5 7 7
    2 6 8 8
    3 7 9 9

(B) 1 5 7
    2 6 8
    3 7 9

(C) 1 3 5 7
    3 5 7 9

(D) 1 3 5 7
    3 5 7 9
    3 5 7 9

(E) 1 7 7 7
    2 8 8 8
    3 9 9 9

GO ON TO THE NEXT PAGE

Level A Also

Use the program description below for Questions 18–20.

A car dealer needs a program that will maintain an inventory of cars on his lot. There are three types of cars: sedans, station wagons, and SUV's. The model, year, color, and price need to be recorded for each car, plus any additional features for the different types of cars. The program must allow the dealer to

- Add a new car to the lot.
- Remove a car from the lot.
- Correct any data that's been entered.
- Display information for any car.

18. The programmer decides to have these classes: `Car`, `Inventory`, `Sedan`, `StationWagon`, and `SUV`. Which statement is *true* about the relationships between these classes and their attributes?

    I There are no inheritance relationships between these classes.
    II The `Inventory` class *has-a* list of `Car` objects.
    III The `Sedan`, `StationWagon`, and `SUV` are independent classes.

    (A) I only
    (B) II only
    (C) III only
    (D) I and II only
    (E) II and III only

19. Suppose that the programmer decides to have a `Car` class. An `Inventory` class will maintain a list of all the cars on the lot. Here are some of the methods in the program:

    ```
    addCar          //adds a car to the lot
    removeCar       //removes a car from the lot
    displayCar      //displays all the features of a given car
    setColor        //sets the color of a car to a given color.
                    //May be used to correct data
    getPrice        //returns the price of a car
    displayAllCars  //displays features for every car on the lot
    ```

    Which of the following is the *least* suitable choice to be responsible for the given method?
    (A) `Car, setColor`
    (B) `Car, removeCar`
    (C) `Car, getPrice`
    (D) `Car, displayCar`
    (E) `Inventory, displayAllCars`

GO ON TO THE NEXT PAGE

Level A Also

20. Suppose Car is a superclass and Sedan, StationWagon, and SUV are subclasses of Car. Which of the following is the most likely method of the Car class to be overridden by at least one of the subclasses (Sedan, StationWagon, or SUV)?
    (A) setColor(newColor)   //set color of Car to newColor
    (B) getModel()   //return model of Car
    (C) displayCar()   //display all features of Car
    (D) setPrice(newPrice)   //set price of Car to newPrice
    (E) getYear()   //return year of Car

21. What is the result of running this code segment?

```
Map dwarfs = new HashMap();
dwarfs.put("Sneezy", "sick dwarf");
dwarfs.put("Happy", "merry dwarf");
dwarfs.put("Grumpy", "irritable dwarf");
String s = (String) dwarfs.get("Dopey");
```

    (A) A NoSuchElementException will be thrown.
    (B) An IllegalStateException will be thrown.
    (C) A ClassCastException will be thrown.
    (D) The code will run without error, and s will have the value "Dopey".
    (E) The code will run without error, and s will have the value null.

GO ON TO THE NEXT PAGE

Questions 22–24 are based on the following procedure, which copies items from an array A containing N distinct numbers into a binary search tree T and then prints the elements.

Procedure:

Step 1:   Initialize T to be empty.

Step 2:   Insert A[0], A[1], ..., A[N-1] into T using a standard algorithm for insertion of item A[i] into T. (Assume that the insert operation does no balancing of T.)

Step 3:   Print the elements stored in T, using an inorder traversal.

22. Which of the following best characterizes the output produced in Step 3 of the above procedure?
    (A) The items are printed in the original order in which they appear in array A.
    (B) The items are printed in sorted order, from smallest to largest.
    (C) The items are printed in sorted order, from largest to smallest.
    (D) The items are printed in the reverse of the order in which they appear in array A.
    (E) The items are printed in random order.

23. Which best describes the best case run time of the procedure?
    (A) $O(1)$
    (B) $O(N)$
    (C) $O(\log N)$
    (D) $O(N \log N)$
    (E) $O(N^2)$

24. The procedure is most likely to exhibit its best case run time when the numbers are stored in array A in which of the following ways?

    I   Ascending order
    II   Descending order
    III Random order

    (A) I only
    (B) II only
    (C) III only
    (D) I and II only
    (E) I, II, and III

GO ON TO THE NEXT PAGE

25. Assume that `ArrayList a` is initialized with `Integer` elements. Also, assume the existence of the following method:

```
//Postcondition: returns a HashSet that contains all the elements
//                of List list
public HashSet copyListToHashSet(List list)
```

Consider the following code segment:

```
Set s = copyListToHashSet(a);
System.out.println("Number of elements in ArrayList is " + a.size());
System.out.println("Number of elements in HashSet is " + s.size());
```

Suppose the output produced by this code segment is

```
Number of elements in ArrayList is 10
Number of elements in HashSet is 6
```

Which is a valid conclusion?
(A) a contains ten distinct (i.e., different) elements, and s contains six distinct elements.
(B) There is at least one element in a that occurs more than once.
(C) a contains four more distinct elements than s.
(D) There are at least four elements in a that occur more than once.
(E) There is one element in a that occurs five times.

GO ON TO THE NEXT PAGE

Level A Also

Questions 26–28 are based on the Computable interface and LargeInt class shown below.

```
public interface Computable
{
    Object add(Object obj);         //returns this object + obj
    Object subtract(Object obj);    //returns this object - obj
    Object multiply(Object obj);    //returns this object * obj
}

public class LargeInt implements Comparable, Computable
{
    //private instance variables
       ...

    public LargeInt(int n)          //converts n to LargeInt
    { implementation }

    public String toString()        //returns this LargeInt as a String
    { implementation }

    public Object add(Object obj)        //returns this LargeInt + obj
    { implementation }

    public Object subtract(Object obj)   //returns this LargeInt - obj
    { implementation }

    public Object multiply(Object obj)   //returns this LargeInt * obj
    { implementation }

    //Returns -1 if this LargeInt is less than obj, 1 if it is greater
    //than obj, and 0 if it equals obj
    public int compareTo(Object obj)
    { implementation }
}
```

26. Of the following pairs of methods, which should be coded and tested first to facilitate testing and debugging the other methods?
    (A) The constructor and add method
    (B) The constructor and compareTo method
    (C) The constructor and toString method
    (D) The toString and compareTo methods
    (E) The toString and one of the add, subtract, or multiply methods

GO ON TO THE NEXT PAGE

Level A Also

27. Consider the problem of simulating the following loop for `LargeInt` objects:

```
for (int i=1; i<n; i++)
    System.out.println(i);
```

The following code is used. You may assume that n exists and is of type `LargeInt`.

```
LargeInt i = new LargeInt(1);
LargeInt one = new LargeInt(1);
while (i.compareTo(n) < 0)
{
    System.out.println(i);
    < statement >
}
```

Which of the following should replace < *statement* > to simulate the loop correctly?
(A) `i = (LargeInt) i.add(one);`
(B) `i = (LargeInt) i.add(1);`
(C) `i = (LargeInt) One.add(i);`
(D) `i = (LargeInt) n.add(one);`
(E) `i = (LargeInt) i.add(n);`

28. Which of the following are the *least* suitable objects to implement the `Computable` interface?
(A) Telephone numbers
(B) Complex numbers
(C) Fractions
(D) Irrational numbers
(E) Matrices

29. A teacher needs to assess the reading level of a textbook. One measure used is the frequency of words that have six or more letters. A computer program scans the text and keeps track of such words and their corresponding frequencies by storing them in a `TreeMap` data structure.

   Assuming that there are *n* different words in the key set so far, which is a *true* statement about operations performed on this frequency map?
(A) Insertion of a new word into the map is $O(1)$.
(B) To check whether a given word is in the map is $O(\log n)$.
(C) To update the frequency of an existing word in the map is $O(1)$.
(D) To print a list of the `keySet` of words in alphabetical order is $O(\log n)$.
(E) To print a list of all word/frequency pairs is $O(\log n)$.

GO ON TO THE NEXT PAGE

30. A set s1 is said to be a *subset* of s2, s1 ⊆ s2, if there is no element in s1 that is not in s2. Consider the isSubset method below:

```
//Precondition:  s1 and s2 are initialized with objects of the same type
//Postcondition: returns true if s1 is a subset of s2, false otherwise
public static boolean isSubset(Set s1, Set s2)
{
    < implementation code >
}
```

Which < *implementation code* > achieves the desired postcondition? Assume the existence of the following method:

```
//Postcondition: returns a HashSet that contains all the elements of Set s
public static HashSet copySetToHashSet(Set s)
```

```
 I Set temp = copySetToHashSet(s2);
   for (Iterator itr=s1.iterator(); itr.hasNext();)
       temp.add(itr.next());
   return temp.size() == s2.size();
```

```
II for (Iterator itr=s1.iterator(); itr.hasNext();)
       if (!s2.contains(itr.next()))
           return false;
   return true;
```

```
III for (Iterator itr1=s1.iterator(); itr1.hasNext();)
    {
        Object obj1 = itr1.next();
        for (Iterator itr2=s2.iterator(); itr2.hasNext();)
            if (!obj1.equals(itr2.next()))
                return false;
    }
    return true;
```

(A) I only
(B) II only
(C) III only
(D) I and II only
(E) I, II, and III

GO ON TO THE NEXT PAGE

Refer to the following for Questions 31 and 32.

A word game uses certain five-letter words that are stored in a special dictionary file. In the game, no word may be used more than once. The game is implemented with the `WordGame` class shown:

```
public class WordGame
{
    private Map m;
    //other private instance variables
        ...
    //constructor
    public WordGame()
    {
        m = new HashMap();
        //initialization of other instance variables
            ...
    }

    /* Load hash map with all words in the dictionary and mark
     * every word as available */
    public void loadDictionary(String fileName)
    {
        < code to open inFile with given fileName >

        while (< there are words in inFile >
        {
            String word = inFile.readWord();   //read word from inFile
            < code to insert word into Map m >
        }
        //code to close inFile not shown
            ...
    }

    /* Look up word in HashMap m.
     * If present and available, mark as used and return true.
     * Otherwise return false */
    public boolean isAvailable(String word)
    {
        < implementation code >
    }

    //other methods to implement the game not shown
        ...
}
```

31. Refer to the `loadDictionary` method in the `WordGame` class. Which < *code to insert* word *into* Map m > will cause an error?
    (A) `m.put(word, new Boolean(true));` //a Boolean object wraps a boolean value
    (B) `m.put(word, "true");`
    (C) `m.put(word, true);`
    (D) `m.put(word, new Integer(0));`
    (E) `m.put(word, new Integer(1));`

GO ON TO THE NEXT PAGE

32. Suppose the HashMap m has available words marked with the Integer 1. When an available word is found in m, it is marked as used by changing its corresponding Integer value to 0. Refer to the isAvailable method of the WordGame class:

```
/* Look up word in HashMap m.
 * If present and available, mark as used and return true.
 * Otherwise return false */
public boolean isAvailable(String word)
{
    < implementation code >
}
```

Which represents correct < *implementation code* >?

```
I  if (m.containsKey(word) && ((Integer) m.get(word)).intValue() == 1)
   {
       m.put(word, new Integer(0));
       return true;
   }
   else
       return false;

II if (m.containsKey(word) && ((Integer) m.get(word)).intValue() == 1)
       return m.put(word, new Integer(0));

III if (!m.containsKey(word))
        return false;
    else
        if (((Integer) m.get(word)).intValue() == 1)
        {
            m.put(word, new Integer(0));
            return true;
        }
    }
```

(A) I only
(B) II only
(C) III only
(D) I and III only
(E) I, II, and III

GO ON TO THE NEXT PAGE

33. Consider the following code segment:

```
Queue q = new ListQueue();

< code to place Integer elements in q >

int time, val;
int limit = < some initial value >;
while (!q.isEmpty())
{
    time = 0;
    Object value = q.dequeue();
    val = ((Integer) value).intValue();
    while (val != 0 && time < limit)
    {
        val--;
        time++;
    }
    if (val > 0)
        q.enqueue(new Integer(val));
}
```

Suppose that initially the values in the queue are 1, 10, 8, 5, 12 (1 is at the front of the queue, 12 is at the back). Which of the following is the *least* value of limit that would ensure that the total number of dequeue operations is 6 or less?
(A) 3
(B) 5
(C) 6
(D) 7
(E) 10

GO ON TO THE NEXT PAGE

34. Assume that doubly linked lists are implemented with the `DoublyListNode` class below:

```
public class DoublyListNode
{
    private Object value;
    private DoublyListNode next, prev;

    public DoublyListNode(DoublyListNode initPrev, Object initValue,
                   DoublyListNode initNext)
    {
        prev = initPrev;
        value = initValue;
        next = initNext;
    }

    public DoublyListNode getPrev()
    { return prev; }

    public void setPrev(DoublyListNode theNewPrev)
    { prev = theNewPrev; }

    public Object getValue()
    { return value; }

    public void setValue(Object theNewValue)
    { value = theNewValue; }

    public DoublyListNode getNext()
    { return next; }

    public void setNext(DoublyListNode theNewNext)
    { next = theNewNext; }
}
```

For the doubly linked list shown below, which of the following code segments will remove the node containing b from the list? Following execution of the segment, `list` may refer to any element of the list. (Note that arrows pointing to the right correspond to `next` and those to the left correspond to `prev`.)

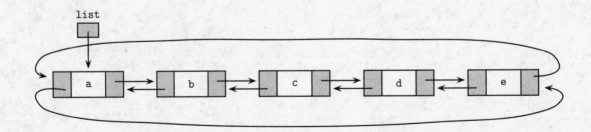

GO ON TO THE NEXT PAGE ▶

```
 I  list.setNext(list.getNext().getNext());
    list.getNext().getNext().setPrev(list));

II  list.getNext().getNext().setPrev(list));
    list.setNext(list.getNext().getNext());

III list = list.getNext().getNext();
    (list.getPrev().getPrev()).setNext(list);
    list.setPrev(list.getPrev().getPrev());
```

(A) I only
(B) II only
(C) III only
(D) I and II only
(E) II and III only

GO ON TO THE NEXT PAGE

35. Assume that binary trees are implemented with the TreeNode class provided. Refer to method mTree:

```
//Returns a reference to a newly created tree
public static TreeNode mTree(TreeNode t)
{
    if (t == null)
        return null;
    else
        return new TreeNode(t.getValue(), mTree(t.getRight()),
                mTree(t.getLeft()));
}
```

Suppose p = mTree(t) is invoked for the tree shown.

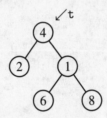

Which of the following trees will be created?

(A)
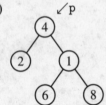

(D)
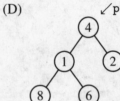

(B)
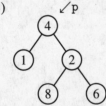

(E)
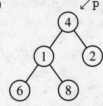

(C)
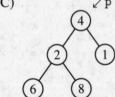

GO ON TO THE NEXT PAGE

Questions 36–40 involve reasoning about the code from the Marine Biology Simulation Case Study. A Quick Reference to the case study is provided as part of this exam.

36. The current implementation of `BoundedEnv` allows only for cells with four adjacent neighbors, the adjacent neighbors on all four sides. Suppose you need to modify the program so that cells have eight adjacent neighbors, those on the four sides plus the four neighbors on the diagonals. Which groups of methods require *no modification* in the `Fish` class when the change to eight adjacent neighbors is made?

  I   `initialize` and the three `Fish` constructors
  II `changeLocation` and `changeDirection`
  III `emptyNeighbors, breed, nextLocation` and `move`

  (A) I only
  (B) II only
  (C) III only
  (D) II and III only
  (E) I, II, and III

Level A Also

37. Assume that `env` is a valid, empty 10×10 `BoundedEnv` object. Consider the following code segment:

```
Location loc1 = new Location(10, 10);
Location loc2 = new Location(2, 3);
Location loc3 = new Location(5, 1);
Location loc4 = new Location(6, 6);
Fish f1 = new Fish(env, loc2);
Fish f2 = new Fish(env, loc3);
```

  What should be the return value of `env.numObjects()` after this code segment?
  (A) 1
  (B) 2
  (C) 4
  (D) 6
  (E) No value. The segment causes an `ArrayIndexOutOfBoundsException`.

38. Consider a large, roughly square environment whose dimensions are approximately $n \times n$. The environment is sparsely populated with fish—approximately one fish per row. What is the big-O performance of the `allObjects` method if the environment is a

  (1) `BoundedEnv` object   (2) `UnboundedEnv` object?

  (A) (1) $O(n^2)$ (2) $O(n^2)$
  (B) (1) $O(n^2)$ (2) $O(n)$
  (C) (1) $O(n)$ (2) $O(n)$
  (D) (1) $O(n)$ (2) $O(1)$
  (E) (1) $O(n)$ (2) $O(n^2)$

GO ON TO THE NEXT PAGE

39. Recall that the `BoundedEnv` is implemented with a two-dimensional array:

```
private Locatable[][] theGrid;
```

The implementation of the `allObjects` method is

```
/** Returns an array of all the environment objects
 **/
public Locatable[] allObjects()
{
    Locatable[] theObjects = new Locatable[numObjects()];
    int tempObjectCount = 0;

    // Look at all grid locations.
    for ( int r = 0; r < numRows(); r++ )
    {
        for ( int c = 0; c < numCols(); c++ )
        {
            // If there's an object at this location, put it in the array.
            Locatable obj = theGrid[r][c];
            if ( obj != null )
            {
                theObjects[tempObjectCount] = obj;
                tempObjectCount++;
            }
        }
    }
    return theObjects;
}
```

Suppose the code in the nested `for` loop is changed as follows:

```
for ( int r = 0; r < numRows(); r++ )
{
    for ( int c = 0; c < numCols(); c++ )
    {
        if ( theGrid[r][c] != null )
        {
            theObjects[tempObjectCount] = theGrid[r][c];
            tempObjectCount++;
        }
    }
}
```

What will be the effect of the change when the program is run?
(A) A `NullPointerException` will be thrown.
(B) A `ClassCastException` will be thrown.
(C) An `IllegalStateException` will be thrown.
(D) An error message to the effect that `Object is not Locatable` will be given.
(E) The change will not affect the program; it will run as intended.

GO ON TO THE NEXT PAGE

Level A Also

40. Consider a modified version of the `nextLocation` method for the `DarterFish` class that does not alter the behavior of `DarterFish` in any way. Debugging statements are omitted.

```
/** Finds this fish's next location.
 *  A darter fish darts forward two spaces if it can, otherwise it
 *  tries to move forward one space.  A darter fish can only move
 *  to empty locations, and it can only move two spaces forward if
 *  the intervening space is empty.  If the darter fish cannot move
 *  forward, nextLocation returns the fish's current
 *  location.
 *  returns the next location for this fish
 **/
protected Location nextLocation()
{
    Environment env = environment();
    Location oneInFront = env.getNeighbor(location(), direction());
    Location twoInFront = env.getNeighbor(oneInFront, direction());
    < more code >
}
```

Which replacement for *< more code >* leads to the correct return value for `nextLocation`?

```
 I if (env.isEmpty(twoInFront))
        return twoInFront;
    else if (env.isEmpty(oneInFront))
        return oneInFront;
    else
        return location();

II if (!(env.isEmpty(oneInFront) || env.isEmpty(twoInFront)))
        return location();
    else if (env.isEmpty(twoInFront))
        return twoInFront;
    else
        return oneInFront;

III if (env.isEmpty(oneInFront) && env.isEmpty(twoInFront))
        return twoInFront;
    else if (env.isEmpty(oneInFront))
        return oneInFront;
    return location();
```

(A) I only
(B) II only
(C) III only
(D) II and III only
(E) I, II, and III

END OF SECTION I

IF YOU FINISH BEFORE TIME IS CALLED, YOU MAY
CHECK YOUR WORK ON THIS SECTION.

DO NOT GO ON TO SECTION II UNTIL YOU ARE TOLD TO DO SO.

COMPUTER SCIENCE AB
SECTION II

Time—1 hour and 45 minutes
Number of questions—4
Percent of total grade—50

Directions: SHOW ALL YOUR WORK. REMEMBER THAT PROGRAM SEGMENTS ARE TO BE WRITTEN IN JAVA.

Note: Assume that the standard packages (e.g., `java.util.*`) are included in any programs that use the code segments provided in individual questions. A Quick Reference to the standard classes and interfaces with their required methods is provided.

---

1. Consider designing a simple line-oriented text editor. The text editor maintains a current line pointer and pointers to the first and last lines of the text. Each line of text is stored as a string. The text itself is stored as a linear doubly linked list of lines. The operations supported by the text editor are described in the following `TextEditor` class.

```java
public class TextEditor
{
    private DoublyListNode current;    //refers to the current line
    private DoublyListNode topPtr;     //refers to the top line
    private DoublyListNode bottomPtr;  //refers to the bottom line

    //Constructor. Lines of text read in from inFile
    //Precondition:  inFile is open for reading and contains at least
    //               one line of text
    //Postcondition: all lines of inFile inserted into TextEditor
    //               topPtr and current point to first line
    //               bottomPtr points to last line
    public TextEditor(FileReader inFile)
    { implementation }

    //Move current line pointer to next line, if line exists
    public void next()
    { implementation }

    //Move current line pointer to previous line, if line exists
    public void previous()
    { implementation }

    //Move current line pointer to first line
    public void top()
    { implementation }
```

GO ON TO THE NEXT PAGE.

```
        //Move current line pointer to last line
        public void bottom()
        { implementation }

        //Precondition:  current and bottomPtr are not null
        //Postcondition: line inserted following line pointed to by current.
        //               current remains unchanged.
        //               bottomPtr is updated to point to last line, if necessary.
        public void insert(String line)
        { implementation }

        //Print line pointed to by current line pointer to screen
        //Postcondition: current line pointer still points to that line
        public void printLine()
        { implementation }

        //Return true if current line pointer points to last line,
        //otherwise return false
        public boolean atEnd()
        { implementation }
    }
```

The doubly linked list for the text editor is implemented with the DoublyListNode class below:

```
    public class DoublyListNode
    {
        private Object value;
        private DoublyListNode next, prev;

        public DoublyListNode(DoublyListNode initPrev, Object initValue,
                        DoublyListNode initNext)
        {
            prev = initPrev;
            value = initValue;
            next = initNext;
        }

        public DoublyListNode getPrev()
        { return prev; }

        public void setPrev(DoublyListNode theNewPrev)
        { prev = theNewPrev; }

        public Object getValue()
        { return value; }

        public void setValue(Object theNewValue)
        { value = theNewValue; }

        public DoublyListNode getNext()
        { return next; }

        public void setNext(DoublyListNode theNewNext)
        { next = theNewNext; }
    }
```

GO ON TO THE NEXT PAGE.

The text editor uses the following `FileReader` class to read lines of text from an external file.

```
public class FileReader
{
    //Return next line of file
    public String getOneLine()
    { /* implementation not shown */ }

    //Return true if the last line of the file
    //has been read, otherwise return false
    public boolean endOfFile()
    { /* implementation not shown */ }

    //other methods and private instance variables not shown
        ...
}
```

(a) Write the implementation code for the `insert` method as started below. Method `insert` should insert its parameter `line` after the line pointed to by the current pointer. After insertion `current` should be unchanged, but `bottomPtr` should be adjusted to point to the last line of text if the insertion occurred at the last line.

For example, if this is the state of the `TextEditor t`

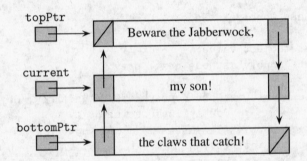

the method call

```
        t.insert("The jaws that bite,");
```

should result in

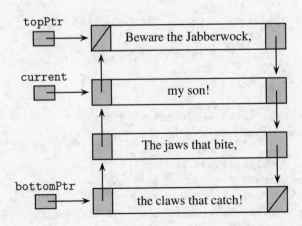

GO ON TO THE NEXT PAGE.

Complete method `insert` below:

```
//Precondition:  current and bottomPtr are not null
//Postcondition: line inserted following line pointed to by current.
//               current remains unchanged.
//               bottomPtr is updated to point to last line, if necessary.
public void insert(String line)
```

(b) Write the implementation code for the `TextEditor` constructor. The constructor reads lines from the file with name `fileName`. You may assume that the file is open for reading and contains at least one line of text. Note that the postcondition specifies that both `current` and `topPtr` should be initialized to the top line of text, while `bottomPtr` should point to the last line of text.

In writing the constructor you may wish to call the `insert` method specified in part (a), as well as the `getOneLine` and `endOfFile` methods of the `FileReader` class. You may assume that all of these methods work as specified.

Complete the constructor below:

```
//Constructor. Lines of text read in from inFile
//Precondition:  inFile is open for reading and contains at least
//               one line of text
//Postcondition: all lines of inFile inserted into TextEditor
//               topPtr and current point to first line
//               bottomPtr points to last line
public TextEditor(FileReader inFile)
```

(c) A client method `printAlternate` prints every second line of text, starting with the first line and proceeding to the end of the text. You may assume that all methods of the `TextEditor` class work as specified.

Write method `printAlternate` as started below:

```
//Precondition:  t contains at least one line of text
//Postcondition: alternate lines of text have been printed to
//               the screen, starting with the first line
public static void printAlternate(TextEditor t)
```

GO ON TO THE NEXT PAGE.

2. Assume that stacks are implemented with an `ArrayStack` class that implements the `Stack` interface provided, and that binary search trees are implemented with the `TreeNode` class provided.

This question refers to the `BinaryTree` class below:

```
public class BinaryTree
{
    private TreeNode root;

    public BinaryTree()
    { root = null; }

    public TreeNode getRoot()
    { return root; }

    public void setRoot(TreeNode theNewNode)
    { root = theNewNode; }

    public boolean isEmpty()
    { return root == null; }

    public void postorder()
    { doPostorder(root); }

    //private helper method
    //Uses an iterative method to print the elements of t, postorder
    private static void doPostorder(TreeNode t)
    { implementation }

    //other traversal methods, methods to insert and find elements
        ...
}
```

Consider the problem of writing an *iterative* algorithm for a postorder traversal of a binary tree. The iterative version of the traversal simulates recursion by maintaining a stack of tree nodes, each of which is labeled 1, 2, or 3. The stack stores nodes that have been visited, but whose recursive calls are not yet complete. The top of the stack represents the current node being visited, which can be at one of three places in the algorithm, indicated by its label:

    label = 1: about to make a recursive call to the left subtree
    label = 2: about to make a recursive call to the right subtree
    label = 3: about to process the current node

Thus each node is placed on the stack three times during the postorder traversal. The third time the node is popped, it is processed.

Here is a summary of the algorithm:

    1. Initialize the traversal by pushing the root onto the stack. Label it 1.
    2. While the stack is not empty,
        • Pop the stack.
        • If the label is 1,
            (i) Increment the label and push that node back.
            (ii) Push the root of its left subtree (if there is one) onto the stack with a label of 1.

GO ON TO THE NEXT PAGE.

- If the label is 2,
    - (i) Increment the label and push that node back.
    - (ii) Push the root of its right subtree (if there is one) onto the stack with a label of 2.
- If the label is 3,
    - (i) Process the node.

For example, here is the state of the stack for a postorder traversal of the tree shown.

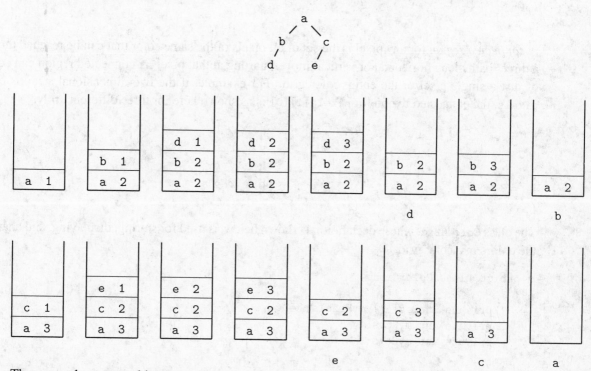

The postorder traversal is dbeca.

(a) The algorithm requires a StackNode object. Write a StackNode class in which a StackNode has a TreeNode and an integer label. When a StackNode is constructed, it must be assigned a TreeNode and a label value of 1. The StackNode should have the following operations:

- Retrieve its TreeNode.
- Retrieve the value of its label.
- Increment its label by 1.

Write the StackNode class below.

(b) Write the implementation of the doPostorder helper method. Your algorithm should be iterative and should print the elements in the tree, one per line, with a postorder traversal. You may assume that the objects in the tree have a toString method defined. You may also assume that your StackNode class works as described, irrespective of what you wrote in part (a).

Complete the doPostorder method below.

```
//private helper method
//Uses an iterative method to print the elements of t, postorder
private static void doPostorder(TreeNode t)
```

GO ON TO THE NEXT PAGE.

3. A *color grid* is defined as a two-dimensional array whose elements are character strings having values "b" (blue), "r" (red), "g" (green), or "y" (yellow). The elements are called pixels because they represent pixel locations on a computer screen. For example,

```
                                      y g r
     b b g r                          b y g
     g r g r        r r r r           g r b
                                      b b g
```

A *connected region* for any pixel is the set of all pixels of the same color that can be reached through a direct path along horizontal or vertical moves starting at that pixel. A connected region can consist of just a single pixel or the entire color grid. For example, if the two-dimensional array is called pixels, the connected region for pixels[1][0] is as shown here for three different arrays.

```
                         y g r b
     b b g r             g g y g          b b
     g r g r             b g r g          b b
```

The class ColorGrid, whose declaration is shown below, is used for storing, displaying, and changing the colors in a color grid.

```
public class ColorGrid
{
     private String[][] myPixels;
     private int myRows;
     private int myCols;

     /* constructor
      * Creates numRows X numCols ColorGrid from String s */
     public ColorGrid(String s, int numRows, int numCols)
     { implementation }

     /* Precondition:  myPixels[row][col] is oldColor, one of "r","b","g", or "y".
      *                newColor is one of "r","b","g", or "y"
      * Postcondition: if 0 ≤ row < myRows and 0 ≤ col < myCols, paints the
      *                connected region of myPixels[row][col] the newColor.
      *                Does nothing if oldColor is the same as newColor */
     public void paintRegion(int row, int col, String newColor, String oldColor)
     { implementation }

     //other methods not shown
     ...
}
```

(a) Write the implementation code for the ColorGrid constructor. The constructor should initialize the myPixels matrix of the ColorGrid as follows: The dimensions of myPixels are numRows X numCols. String s contains numRows X numCols characters, where each character is one of the colors of the grid—"r", "g", "b", or "y". The characters are contained in s row by row from top to bottom and left to right. For example, given that numRows is 3, and numCols is 4, if s is "brrygrggyyyr", myPixels should be initialized to be

GO ON TO THE NEXT PAGE.

```
b r r y
g r g g
y y y r
```

Complete the constructor below:

```
/* constructor
 * Creates numRows × numCols ColorGrid from String s */
public ColorGrid(String s, int numRows, int numCols)
```

(b) Write the implementation of the paintRegion method as started below. **Note: You must write a recursive solution.** The paintRegion paints the connected region of the given pixel, specified by row and col, a different color specified by the newColor parameter. If newColor is the same as oldColor, the color of the given pixel, paintRegion does nothing. To visualize what paintRegion does, imagine that the different colors surrounding the connected region of a given pixel form a boundary. When paint is poured onto the given pixel, the new color will fill the connected region up to (but excluding) the boundary.

For example, the effect of the method call c.paintRegion(2, 3, "b", "r") on the ColorGrid c is shown here. (The starting pixel is shown in a frame, and its connected region is shaded.)

		before						after			
r	r	b	g	y	y	r	r	b	g	y	y
b	r	b	y	r	r	b	r	b	y	b	b
g	g	r	r	r	b	g	g	b	b	b	b
y	r	r	y	r	b	y	b	b	y	b	b

Complete the method paintRegion below. **Note: Only a recursive solution will be accepted.**

```
/* Precondition:  myPixels[row][col] is oldColor, one of "r","b","g", or "y".
 *                newColor is one of "r","b","g", or "y"
 * Postcondition: if 0 ≤ row < myRows and 0 ≤ col < myCols, paints the
 *                connected region of myPixels[row][col] the newColor.
 *                Does nothing if oldColor is the same as newColor */
public void paintRegion(int row, int col, String newColor, String oldColor)
```

4. This question involves reasoning about the code from the Marine Biology Simulation Case Study. A Quick Reference to the case study is provided as part of this exam.

Consider implementing the unbounded environment with a HashMap rather than the ArrayList that is used in the UnboundedEnv class. This would be the declaration:

```
private HashMap objectMap;
```

The keys of objectMap would be only those locations in the environment that contain an object. The corresponding values would be the Locatable objects placed at those locations (i.e., the fish). No empty locations would be stored in the map.

GO ON TO THE NEXT PAGE.

(a) Write the `isEmpty` method for the `UnboundedEnv` class, using the `HashMap` implementation. In this implementation, only those locations that contain a fish are represented in the map. **The implementation of `isEmpty` that you write should not contain a call to `objectAt`.**

Complete the `isEmpty` method as started below.

```
/** Returns true if loc is empty; false otherwise
 **/
public boolean isEmpty(Location loc)
```

(b) Write the `remove` method for the `UnboundedEnv` class, using the `HashMap` implementation. The `remove` method should remove its `obj` parameter from the environment. This means that there should no longer be a mapping in the environment with this object as the value. Recall that at the time `remove` is called, `obj` stores its new location. However, it is still recorded as being at its previous location in the environment. If the object to be removed could not be found in the environment at the time of the removal, method `remove` should throw an `IllegalArgumentException` with an appropriate message.

In writing `remove` you must use an iterator that locates the object to be removed by iterating over the key set of the map.

Complete the `remove` method below.

```
/** Removes obj from the environment.
 * Precondition: obj is in this environment.
 * Throws IllegalArgumentException if the precondition is not met
 **/
public void remove(Locatable obj)
```

(c) Write the `recordMove` method that updates the environment when an object moves. If the `obj` parameter thinks that it has moved to a location that is already occupied by a different object, the `recordMove` method should throw an `IllegalArgumentException` with an appropriate message.

The `recordMove` method must update the environment: When an occupied location in the environment becomes empty, that location should no longer appear as a key in the `HashMap`. Any new location that has acquired an object should be inserted into the `HashMap`.

In writing `recordMove` you may want to use the `remove` method defined in part (b). You may assume that `remove` works as specified irrespective of what you wrote in part (b). You should also assume that all of the other methods in `UnboundedEnv` work as specified.

Complete `recordMove` below.

```
/** Updates the environment to reflect the fact that object obj has moved.
 * oldLoc is the previous location of obj.
 * Precondition:  obj.location() contains no other object
 * Postcondition: obj is at its new location, obj.location(), and
 *                either oldLoc is equal to obj.location() (there was
 *                no movement), or oldLoc is empty.
 * Throws an IllegalArgumentException if the precondition is not met
 **/
public void recordMove(Locatable obj, Location oldLoc)
```

END OF EXAMINATION

Answer Key

Section I

1. **C**		15. **E**		29. **B**	
2. **A**		16. **E**		30. **D**	
3. **B**		17. **A**		31. **C**	
4. **D**		18. **E**		32. **A**	
5. **D**		19. **B**		33. **E**	
6. **A**		20. **C**		34. **E**	
7. **B**		21. **E**		35. **D**	
8. **D**		22. **B**		36. **E**	
9. **B**		23. **D**		37. **B**	
10. **A**		24. **C**		38. **B**	
11. **E**		25. **B**		39. **E**	
12. **C**		26. **C**		40. **C**	
13. **E**		27. **A**			
14. **D**		28. **A**			

Answers Explained

Section I

1. **(C)** A circular doubly linked list works well for this program because of the ability to traverse forward and backward from any given node. Note that a stack provides easy backtracking from the current top element but does not allow for convenient access to any other specified position or for easy forward traversal. Similarly, a queue allows easy forward traversal from the front position but is awkward for backtracking and random access of elements in the "middle" of the queue. Choice A seems reasonable for both forward and backward traversal. The number of moves, however, is large and unknown, which makes a dynamic data structure preferable. Choice B doesn't satisfy the requirements of the program at all. It also has the problem of representing real-number coordinates (x, y) with the indexes of the array; the indexes must be integers.

2. **(A)** Choice A is illegal because you can't create an instance of an abstract class.

3. **(B)** Implementation I is wrong because the `GoodPlayer` subclass can't directly access the private variables of its `TennisPlayer` superclass. Implementation III doesn't work because whenever you use `super` in a constructor it must be used in the first line of the implementation.

4. **(D)** The statement `double value = r.nextDouble()` generates a random double in the range $0 \le$ `value` < 1. Since random doubles are uniformly

distributed in this interval, 45% of the time you can expect `value` to be in the range $0 \leq$ `value` < 0.45. Therefore a test for `value` in this range can be a test for whether the serve of a `WeakPlayer` went in. Since `r.nextDouble()` never returns a negative number, the test in implementation II, `value < 0.45`, is sufficient. The test in implementation I would be correct if `||` were changed to `&&` ("or" changed to "and"—both parts must be true). Implementation III also works. The call `r.nextInt(100)` returns a random integer from 0 to 99, each equally likely. Thus, 45% of the time, the integer `val` will be in the range $0 \leq$ `val` ≤ 44. Therefore a test for `val` in this range can be used to test whether the serve was in.

5. **(D)** Choice D is false because the `GoodPlayer` (and `WeakPlayer`) class inherits `getName` from `TennisPlayer`. Choices A and B illustrate polymorphism, since the appropriate `serve` and `returnShot` methods will be selected at run time. Since `players[0]` and `players[2]` represent `GoodPlayer` objects, the serve will be in 80% of the time; and since `players[1]` and `players[3]` represent `WeakPlayer` objects, the return shot will be in 30% of the time. Choice C is *not* dynamic binding: `getName` has the same implementation in all three classes, so the superclass `getName` method can be applied for each player at compile time. Remember: to be an example of dynamic binding (polymorphism), the particular method invoked must be determined at *run time*. Choice E is true—there are only four elements in the `players` array, `players[0]`, `players[1]`, `players[2]`, and `players[3]`.

6. **(A)** Choice A will cause a `ClassCastException` to be thrown—you can't cast a `GoodPlayer` to a `WeakPlayer`. Choice B is correct: `w` is an instance of a `WeakPlayer`. Choice C is fine, since a `Beginner` *is-a* `WeakPlayer`. Choices D and E are correct, but the cast is unnecessary.

7. **(B)** Since none of the nodes in choice B has a right subtree, the recursive left-root-right of the inorder traversal becomes left-root. Similarly, the left-right-root of a postorder traversal becomes left-root. In either case, the traversal yields S, K, A, then P.

8. **(D)** Worst case for quicksort is $O(n^2)$. Quicksort recursively partitions the array into two pieces such that elements in the left piece are less than or equal to a pivot element, and those in the right piece are greater than or equal to the pivot. In the worst case, the pivot element repeatedly splits the array into pieces of length 1 and $n - 1$, respectively. In this case, there will be n splits, each using an $O(n)$ partitioning algorithm. Thus, the final run time becomes $O(n^2)$. An example where this could happen is a sorted array in which one of the end elements is repeatedly chosen as the pivot. Mergesort recursively divides the array into two pieces of roughly the same size until there are n arrays of length 1. This is $O(\log n)$. Then adjacent sorted arrays are recursively merged to form a single sorted array. Thus, the algorithm is $O(n \log n)$, irrespective of the initial ordering of array elements. Heapsort creates a balanced binary tree irrespective of the ordering of the array elements, which leads to an $O(n \log n)$ algorithm in best and worst cases.

9. **(B)** Although the expression is always algebraically true for nonzero x, the expression may evaluate to false. This could occur because of round-off error in performing the division and multiplication operations. Whether the right-

hand side of the expression evaluates to exactly 3.0 depends on the value of x. Note that if x is zero, the expression will be evaluated to `false` because the right-hand side will be assigned a value of `Infinity`.

10. **(A)** Segment II fails because it calls the `ArrayList` method `remove` during iteration. During iteration with an iterator, you may not modify the list with a noniterator method. Segment I correctly invokes the *iterator* `remove` method. Segment III does not use an iterator to cycle through the list. Therefore it is OK to use the `remove` method from `ArrayList`. You must, however, be careful. When you remove the ith item from an `ArrayList`, the $(i + 1)$th item is shifted into that position. Since i is incremented after each loop iteration, consecutive duplicates will not be deleted.

11. **(E)** Segment I correctly uses the `ListNode` constructor. Segment III correctly uses the `setNext` and `setValue` methods to insert the required values in the new node and connect it to the list. Segment II uses the `ListNode` constructor correctly but has an incorrect second statement: It fails to connect the `current` node to the new node (referred to by p). Segment II would be correct if the second statement were changed to

    ```
    current.setNext(p);
    ```

12. **(C)** The problem with the code is in the last line; change it to

    ```
    temp = temp.getNext().getNext();
    ```

    and the method will work as intended for all cases. As it is, `temp` doesn't advance far enough, and you have an infinite `while` loop that produces an endless stream of zeros:

    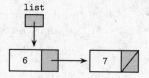

    becomes

    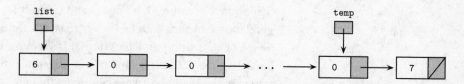

    The method works for an empty list because nothing is done. It works for a list with just one node because the `while` test fails immediately and the list remains unchanged.

13. **(E)** A preorder traversal pushes the elements onto s in the following order:
    A, K, C, P, R, F.

    The elements will be popped and printed in reverse order, namely
    F, R, P, C, K, A.

14. **(D)** Suppose the smallest value occurs more than once in the list. The variable `min` will eventually be assigned that value and then fail the comparison test for all subsequent elements, including the duplicates. The method will therefore return the correct value. Each of the other choices is true. For choice A, `compareTo` is a method of the `Comparable` interface, and only objects that implement this interface can use `compareTo`. For choice B, the iterator methods `next` and `hasNext` are applicable to all container classes. For choice C, if `min` is not cast to `Comparable`, it will be of type `Object`, which does not implement `Comparable`. The method will therefore fail when `min.compareTo` is encountered by the compiler. For choice E, replacing ">" with ">=" causes `min` to be replaced each time a duplicate value is found. This adds a slight inefficiency but doesn't cause the method to fail.

15. **(E)** In the `findMin` method `min` is initialized to the first element. The `getFirst` method is in `LinkedList` but not `ArrayList`. Therefore segment I will fail when `findMin` is invoked with an `ArrayList` parameter. It would appear that segment II will work because `getFirst` is a method of `LinkedList`. It fails because the expression `a.getFirst` causes a compile-time error: There is no `getFirst` method in `List`! In order for segment II to work, `min` would need to be initialized as follows:

```
Comparable min = (Comparable) ((LinkedList) a).getFirst();
```

Segment III will fail even with `findMin` as originally written: The parameter types are incompatible (`List` and array), and iterators are not defined for arrays.

16. **(E)** To print a list of donors in order of total contributions is equally efficient for methods I and II. Both methods require the same three steps:

   (1) Insert all `Donor` objects into a temporary array.
   (2) Sort the array with respect to total contributions.
   (3) Print the elements.

   Note that simply sorting the existing array in method I is not a good idea; the array will then need to be "sorted back" into alphabetical order. Choice A is true: All items in the database require the same amount of memory irrespective of data structure. Choices B and C are true: Insertion and searching in a good hash table are both $O(1)$, whereas in a sorted array searching for a given donor or insertion point is $O(\log n)$ (assuming that an efficient method like binary search is used). Choice D is true since method II requires sorting before printing. Method I has data items that are already sorted in alphabetical order.

17. **(A)** Method `alter` shifts all the columns, starting at column `c+1`, one column to the left. Also, it does it in a way that overwrites column `c`. Here are the replacements for the method call `alter(1)`:

```
mat[0][1] = mat[0][2]
mat[0][2] = mat[0][3]
mat[1][1] = mat[1][2]
mat[1][2] = mat[1][3]
mat[2][1] = mat[2][2]
mat[2][2] = mat[2][3]
```

18. **(E)** Statement I is false: The Sedan, StationWagon, and SUV classes should all be subclasses of Car. Each one satisfies the *is-a* Car relationship. Statement II is true: The main task of the Inventory class should be to keep an updated list of Car objects. Statement III is true: An independent class is one that does not require other classes to implement its methods.

19. **(B)** The Inventory class is responsible for maintaining the list of all cars on the lot. Therefore methods like addCar, removeCar, and displayAllCars must be the responsibility of this class. The Car class should contain the setColor, getPrice, and displayCar methods, since all these pertain to the attributes of a given Car.

20. **(C)** Each subclass may contain additional attributes for the particular type of car that are not in the Car superclass. Since displayCar displays all features of a given car, this method should be overridden to display the original plus additional features.

21. **(E)** The get method of Map returns either the value associated with the key, or null if the map contains no mapping for that key. In the given piece of code, since there is no "Dopey" key, s will be assigned the value null. Note that you need the cast to String on the right side. The get method of HashMap returns an Object, which is not type compatible with String. Without the cast a compiler error will occur.

22. **(B)** An inorder traversal of a binary search tree produces the elements in sorted increasing order. (Recall that the leftmost leaf of the binary search tree is the smallest element in the tree and that this is the first element visited.)

23. **(D)** The best case run time occurs when the binary search tree produced is balanced. This means that, for each of the N items in A, no more than $\log_2 N$ comparisons will need to be made to find its insertion point. Therefore the run time is $O(N \log N)$. Printing the elements is $O(N)$, which is less than $O(N \log N)$. Thus, the overall run time is $O(N \log N)$.

24. **(C)** Any kind of sorted array leads to worst case behavior for insertion into a binary search tree. The tree obtained is completely unbalanced, with a long chain of left links or right links. Run time of insertion becomes $O(N^2)$ (see p. 335). Choice III is thus the most likely of the three choices to lead to a balanced tree and best case behavior.

25. **(B)** As a counterexample for choices A, C, D, and E, let a be the list

    1, 1, 1, 1, 2, 2, 3, 4, 5, 6

    Then s is the set

    1, 2, 3, 4, 5, 6

    (No duplicates in a set!)

26. **(C)** Before manipulating LargeInt objects, you have to check that they've been correctly constructed, and to do that you need to output them. This means that the toString method must be defined in order to easily read the output. Therefore the constructor and toString methods should be coded before the others.

27. **(A)** You want to simulate i++ (or i=i+1). Thus eliminate choices C and D, which don't have i dot something. Eliminate choice B because a LargeInt parameter must be used. Choice E is wrong because you're not adding n to i, you're adding 1 to i.

28. **(A)** Classes that implement Computable must provide add, subtract, and multiply methods. These methods are not suitable for telephone numbers.

29. **(B)** The TreeMap class stores its elements in a balanced binary search tree. This means that TreeMap will provide $O(\log n)$ performance for insertion, retrieval, and search. Thus choices A and C are false. Choices D and E are false because printing a list of all elements involves a simple traversal: $O(n)$.

30. **(D)** In segment I temp contains all the elements of s2. Then all the elements of s1 are added to temp. If s1 is a subset of s2, all the elements of s1 will already be in temp, which means that the size of temp will remain the same as the size of s2. (If s1 is not a subset of s2, then temp.size() will end up bigger than s2.size() because there will be at least one element of s1 that was not in s2.) Segment II checks that s2 contains each element of s1. If it doesn't, the method returns false, otherwise true. Segment III iterates over both sets s1 and s2 and returns false as soon as it finds an element in s1 that is not equal to an element in s2. But for s1 to be a subset of s2, all of the elements in s2 except one will *not* be equal to a given element of s1. You would have to modify the code with a more complicated version that searches the entire set s2 for each element in s1 and returns false only if no element is equal.

31. **(C)** Both the key (first parameter) and corresponding value (second parameter) of the map must be objects. All of the choices except C satisfy this: The value in choice C is boolean, a primitive type.

32. **(A)** There are two conditions under which the isAvailable method should return false:

    - Its word parameter is not in the map.
    - The word parameter is in the map but has already been used.

    Segment I correctly takes care of both these cases. Segment II is wrong because the put method returns an object, not a boolean value. The wrong type is being returned. Segment III fails because it doesn't return false if the word is marked as used (i.e., with value 0).

33. **(E)** Note that dequeue occurs until q is empty. You want to dequeue a minimum number of times, which means that you want to avoid enqueue. This means that you want the stopping condition for the inner while loop to be value == 0, not time == limit (since value > 0 will lead to more enqueue operations). Thus limit should be made as large as possible.

34. **(E)** Segment I fails because it doesn't take into account that the next field of list was altered in the first line. Here are the faulty pointer connections (dashed lines):

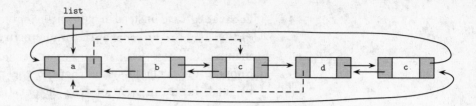

35. **(D)** The method creates a tree that is a mirror image of its parameter. Note the order of the parameters in the `TreeNode` constructor:

    ```
    (initValue, initLeft, initRight)
    ```

    In the method `mTree` the order is

    ```
    (t.getValue(), mTree(t.getRight()), mTree(t.getLeft()))
    ```

    Matching up parameters means that the right subtree of t becomes the left connection of the new tree, and the left subtree of t becomes the right connection.

36. **(E)** A `Fish` receives its initial direction from a parameter in its constructor. Whether this direction is SOUTH or SOUTHWEST does not alter the code. The `changeLocation` method is independent of which kind of neighbor `newLoc` is. The fish simply goes to the location provided by the parameter. Similarly in `changeDirection` the fish assumes the new direction provided by the `newDir` parameter. The `emptyNeighbors` method asks the environment for `neighborsOf` a given location. The immediate diagonal neighbors will therefore be provided by the environment—the `emptyNeighbors` code remains unchanged. Similarly, `breed`, `nextLocation`, and `move` get instructions from the environment on where the `Fish` must go. No changes to the code are needed. Note that the code modification that *does* need to be made to include diagonal neighbors is in the constructor of the *environment* classes. The constructor in `SquareEnvironment` that takes a boolean parameter must be called. The call `super(true)` will create an environment with eight neighbors for each cell.

37. **(B)** The new fish, `f1` and `f2`, are the only objects in the environment. Thus `env.numObjects()` should return 2. No attempt was made to add a `Fish` to the out-of-bounds location `loc1`; therefore, no error occurred.

38. **(B)** Even though `allObjects` is creating an array with approximately n objects, in the `BoundedEnv` all n^2 grid positions must be visited to retrieve these objects. This is $O(n^2)$. In the `UnboundedEnv` each object in `objectList` is visited, approximately n slots. This is $O(n)$.

39. **(E)** Since `theGrid` is declared as an array of `Locatable` objects, *and* the `Fish` objects in `theGrid` are `Locatable`, *and* `allObjects` returns an array of `Locatable` objects, there is no type discrepancy in the altered code! Here are the situations that would cause a problem:

    1. Suppose `theGrid` were declared as follows:

       ```
       private Object[][] theGrid;
       ```

       Now the compiler will complain at the attempt to assign `theGrid[r][c]` to `theObjects[tempObjectCount]` because `theObjects` is expecting a

Locatable (and instead it got an Object). You would need to cast theGrid[r][c] to Locatable, or alternatively use the original implementation!

2. Suppose the declarations of theGrid and theObjects were as in the original, but Fish were of type Object (i.e., not Locatable). If in the modified code you attempted to cast theGrid[r][c] to Locatable before inserting it in theObjects, a ClassCastException would be thrown (an attempt to cast an object to another object of which it is not an instance).

Note that choices A and C are bizarre and do not apply here: a method throws a NullPointerException if an attempt is made to invoke a method with a null reference. An IllegalStateException is thrown when a method is invoked at an illegal time (see p. 252).

40. (C) The algorithm can only return twoInFront if it's first been determined that oneInFront is also empty. Otherwise the fish gets to jump over a fish directly in front of it. This error is made in both segments I and II. In segment II, the algorithm correctly returns the current location if neither oneInFront nor twoInFront is empty. It then falls into the trap of returning twoInFront (if it's empty) without first checking that oneInFront is empty too.

Section II

1. (a)
```
public void insert(String line)
{
    DoublyListNode newLine = new DoublyListNode(current,
        line, current.getNext());
    if (current != bottomPtr)
    {
        current.getNext().setPrev(newLine);
        current.setNext(newLine);
    }
    else
    {
        current.setNext(newLine);
        bottomPtr = newLine;
    }
}
```

(b)
```
public TextEditor(FileReader inFile)
{
    String line = inFile.getOneLine();
    topPtr = new DoublyListNode(null, line, null);
    current = topPtr;
    bottomPtr = topPtr;
    while (!inFile.endOfFile())
    {
        line = inFile.getOneLine();
        insert(line);
        current = current.getNext();
    }
    current = topPtr;
}
```

(c)
```
public static void printAlternate(TextEditor t)
{
    t.top();
    t.printLine();
    while (!t.atEnd())
    {
        t.next();
        if (!t.atEnd())
        {
            t.next();
            t.printLine();
        }
    }
}
```

NOTE
- There are two cases for part (a); either current points to the last line or it doesn't. If it does, there's no prev field to be adjusted for a node that will follow the new node. The bottomPtr, however, must be adjusted.
- For part (b), the first node must be filled first because the precondition for insert requires that current and bottomPtr are not null. At the end of the algorithm, don't forget to reassign current to be at the top. You don't need to update bottomPtr—it's automatically updated by insert.

- Part (c) is tricky! You have to be sure to have the right combination of calls to next() and atEnd() so that your algorithm handles odd and even numbers of lines, as well as one and two lines.

2. (a)
```java
public class StackNode
{
    private TreeNode node;
    private int label;

    public StackNode(TreeNode n)
    {
        node = n;
        label = 1;
    }

    public TreeNode getNode()
    { return node; }

    public int getLabel()
    { return label; }

    public void incrementLabel()
    { label++; }
}
```

(b)
```java
private static void doPostorder(TreeNode t)
{
    Stack s = new ArrayStack();
    if (t != null)
    {
        s.push(new StackNode(t));
        while (!s.isEmpty())
        {
            StackNode sNode = (StackNode) s.pop();
            if (sNode.getLabel() == 1)
            {
                sNode.incrementLabel();
                s.push(sNode);
                if (sNode.getNode().getLeft() != null)
                    s.push(new StackNode(sNode.getNode().getLeft()));
            }
            else if (sNode.getLabel() == 2)
            {
                sNode.incrementLabel();
                s.push(sNode);
                if (sNode.getNode().getRight() != null)
                    s.push(new StackNode(sNode.getNode().getRight()));
            }
            else      //label == 3
                System.out.println(sNode.getNode().getValue());
        }
    }
}
```

NOTE
- In part (b), when the stack is popped, the object must be cast to StackNode before calling the methods of the StackNode class.
- Don't forget the three null tests!

3. (a)
```java
public ColorGrid(String s, int numRows, int numCols)
{
    myRows = numRows;
    myCols = numCols;
    myPixels = new String[numRows][numCols];
    int stringIndex = 0;
    for (int r=0; r<numRows; r++)
        for (int c=0; c<numCols; c++)
        {
            myPixels[r][c] = s.substring(stringIndex,
                stringIndex+1);
            stringIndex++;
        }
}
```

(b)
```java
public void paintRegion(int row, int col, String newColor,
        String oldColor)
{
    if (row >= 0 && row < myRows && col >= 0 && col < myCols)
        if (!myPixels[row][col].equals(newColor) &&
            myPixels[row][col].equals(oldColor))
        {
            myPixels[row][col] = newColor;
            paintRegion(row+1, col, newColor, oldColor);
            paintRegion(row-1, col, newColor, oldColor);
            paintRegion(row, col+1, newColor, oldColor);
            paintRegion(row, col-1, newColor, oldColor);
        }
}
```

NOTE
- In part (a) you don't need to test if stringIndex is in range: The precondition states that the number of characters in s is numRows × numCols.
- In part (b) each recursive call must test whether row and col are in the correct range for the myPixels array; otherwise, your algorithm may sail right off the edge!
- Don't forget to test if newColor is different from that of the starting pixel. Method paintRegion does nothing if the colors are the same.
- Also, don't forget to test if the current pixel is oldColor—you don't want to overwrite *all* the colors, just the connected region of oldColor!
- The color-change assignment myPixels[row][col] = newColor must precede the recursive calls to avoid infinite recursion.

4. (a)
```
public boolean isEmpty(Location loc)
{
    return !objectMap.containsKey(loc);
}
```

Alternatively,

```
public boolean isEmpty(Location loc)
{
    return objectMap.get(loc) == null;
}
```

(b)
```
public void remove(Locatable obj)
{
    // Find object to remove.
    Iterator i = objectMap.keySet().iterator();
    boolean done = false;
    Location nextLoc = null;
    while (!done && i.hasNext())
    {
        nextLoc = (Location) i.next();
        Object thisObj = objectMap.get(nextLoc);
        if (thisObj.equals(obj))
            done = true;
    }
    if (done)
        objectMap.remove(nextLoc);
    else
    // throw exception if obj was not in this environment
        throw new IllegalArgumentException("Cannot remove "
                + obj + "; not there");
}
```

Alternatively,

```
public void remove(Locatable obj)
{
    // Find object to remove.
    Iterator i = objectMap.keySet().iterator();
    boolean done = false;
    while (!done && i.hasNext())
    {
        Object thisObj = objectMap.get(i.next());
        if (thisObj.equals(obj))
        {
            i.remove();
            done = true;
        }
    }
    // throw exception if obj was not in this environment
    if (!done)
        throw new IllegalArgumentException("Cannot remove "
                + obj + "; not there");
}
```

```
(c) public void recordMove(Locatable obj, Location oldLoc)
    {
        int objectsAtOldLoc = 0;
        int objectsAtNewLoc = 0;

        // Look through the list to find how many objects are
        // at old and new locations.
        Location newLoc = obj.location();
        for (Iterator i=objectMap.keySet().iterator();
                        i.hasNext();)
        {
            Locatable thisObj =
                        (Locatable) objectMap.get(i.next());
            if (thisObj.location().equals(oldLoc))
                objectsAtOldLoc++;
            if (thisObj.location().equals(newLoc))
                objectsAtNewLoc++;
        }

        // There should be exactly one object at newLoc.
        // There should be no objects at oldLoc UNLESS
        //        oldLoc equals newLoc
        if ((objectsAtNewLoc != 1) ||
            (objectsAtOldLoc != 0 && !oldLoc.equals(newLoc)))
        {
            throw new IllegalArgumentException(
                "Precondition violation moving " + obj +
                " from " + oldLoc);
        }
        //Update the environment. Precondition is satisfied.
        remove(obj);
        objectMap.put(newLoc, obj);
    }
```

NOTE

- Suppose in part (a) you write the method body of isEmpty as

  ```
  return objectAt(loc) == null;
  ```

  The simplest implementation of the objectAt method calls isEmpty. This creates a situation of infinite mutual recursion that will crash your program! This is the reason the question specified that you not use objectAt in part (a).

- In part (b) iterate over the key set until you find the object that matches the obj parameter. You then have two choices:

  1. Save the location currently recorded for the object (its "old" location). Exit the iteration, then use the remove method of Map to remove the mapping whose key is the old location.

  2. Use the remove method of Iterator to remove the key you just found from the key set. (This is the old location.) Note that removing an element of the key set automatically removes the corresponding mapping from the map.

- Whichever solution you use for part (b), you cannot use the remove method of Map in the middle of the iteration.

- The solution to part (b) requires an iterator. A solution such as the following won't work:

```
public void remove(Locatable obj)
{
    Location loc = obj.location();
    if (objectMap.containsKey(loc))
        objectMap.remove(loc);
    else
        //throw exception ...
}
```

This is because the `obj` in the parameter already contains its *new* location, whereas the mapping is still recorded under the *old* location. The expression `objectMap.containsKey(loc)` will always be false, and the exception will always be thrown.

- In part (c) you need to iterate through all the objects counting how many are at `newLoc` and `oldLoc`. This is to make sure that the fish did not attempt an illegal move into an occupied location. When the move is found to be legitimate, don't forget to update the environment!

APPENDIX A

Glossary of Useful Computer Terms

I hate definitions.
—*Benjamin Disraeli,* Vivian Grey *(1826)*

API library: Applications Program Interface library. A library of routines for use in other programs. The library provides standard interfaces that hide the details of the implementations.

Applet: A graphical Java program that runs in a web browser or applet viewer.

Application: A stand-alone Java program stored in and executed on the user's local computer.

Bit: From "binary digit." Smallest unit of computer memory, taking on only two values, 0 or 1.

Buffer: A temporary storage location of limited size. Holds values waiting to be used.

Byte: Eight bits. Similarly, megabyte (MB, 10^6 bytes) and gigabyte (GB, 10^9 bytes).

Bytecode: Portable code, intermediate between source code and machine language. It is produced by the Java compiler and interpreted (executed) by the Java Virtual Machine.

Cache: A small amount of "fast" memory for the storage of data. Typically, the most recently accessed data from disk storage or "slow" memory is saved in the main memory cache to save time if it's retrieved again.

Compiler: A program that translates source code into object code (machine language).

CPU: The central processing unit (computer's brain). It controls the interpretation and execution of instructions. It consists of the arithmetic/logic unit, the control unit, and some memory, usually called "on-board memory" or cache memory. Physically, the CPU consists of millions of microscopic transistors on a chip.

Debugger: A program that helps find errors by tracing the values of variables in a program.

GUI: Graphical user interface.

Hardware: The physical components of computers. These are the ones you can touch, for example, the keyboard, monitor, printer, CPU chip.

Hertz (Hz):   One cycle per second. It refers to the speed of the computer's internal clock and gives a measure of the CPU speed. Similarly, megahertz (MHz, 10^6 Hz) and gigahertz (GHz, 10^9 Hz).

Hexadecimal number system: Base 16.

High-level language: A human-readable programming language that enables instructions that require many machine steps to be coded concisely, for example, Java, C++, Pascal, BASIC, FORTRAN.

HTML: Hypertext Markup Language. The instructions read by web browsers to format web pages, link to other web sites, and so on.

IDE: Integrated Development Environment. Provides tools such as an editor, compiler, and debugger that work together, usually with a graphical interface. Used for creating software in a high-level language.

Java Virtual Machine: An interpreter that reads and executes Java bytecode.

Javadoc: A program that extracts comments from Java source files and produces documentation files in HTML. These files can then be viewed with a web browser.

Interpreter: A program that reads instructions that are not in machine language and executes them one at a time.

Linker: A program that links together the different modules of a program into a single executable program after they have been compiled into object code.

Low-level language: Assembly language. This is a human-readable version of machine language, where each machine instruction is coded as one statement. It is translated into machine language by a program called an assembler. Each different kind of CPU has its own assembly language.

Mainframe computer: A large computer, typically used by large institutions, such as government agencies and big businesses.

Microcomputer: Personal computer.

Minicomputer: Small mainframe.

Modem: A device that connects a computer to a phone line or TV cable.

Network: Several computers linked together so that they can communicate with each other and share resources.

Object code: Machine language. Produced by compiling source code.

Operating system: A program that controls access to and manipulation of the various files and programs on the computer. For example, DOS, Windows, and UNIX.

Primary memory: RAM. This gets erased when you turn off your computer.

RAM: Random Access Memory. This stores the current program and the software to run it.

ROM: Read Only Memory. This is permanent and nonerasable. It contains, for example, programs that boot up the operating system and check various components of the hardware. In particular, ROM contains the BIOS (Basic Input Output System)—a program that handles low-level communication with the keyboard, disk drives, and so on.

SDK: Sun's Java Software Development Kit. A set of tools for developing Java software.

Secondary memory: Hard drive, disk, magnetic tapes, CD-ROM, and so on.

Server: The hub of a network of computers. Stores application programs, data, mail messages, and so on, and makes them available to all computers on the network.

Software: Computer programs written in some computer language and executed on the hardware after conversion to machine language. If you can install it on your hard drive, it's software (e.g., programs, spreadsheets, word processors).

Source code: A program in a high-level language like Java, C++, Pascal, or FOR-TRAN.

Swing: A Java toolkit for implementing graphical user interfaces.

Transistor: Microscopic semiconductor device that can serve as an on-off switch.

URL: Uniform Resource Locator. An address of a web page.

Workstation: Desktop computer that is faster and more powerful than a microcomputer.

Supplementary Code for Evaluating a Binary Expression Tree

The ExpressionEvaluator class on p. 346 evaluates binary expression trees. It makes use of a createTree method, whose code is given below in case you want to run the whole program. Note that you need to slot in whatever method you use to read characters from a file.

```
/* Creates binary expression tree from expression in inFile
   Precondition: inFile contains one expression, in postfix form.
   Constants (operands) are single digits.
   The characters of the expression are separated by spaces.
   For example: 9 6 + 4 2 / * represents the expression (9+6)*(4/2)
   The file should not be terminated with a carriage return!  */
public static Expression createTree()
{
    < open inFile for reading >
    char ch;
    Expression exp = null;
    Stack s = new ArrayStack();
    while (true)
    {
        ch = < the next character from inFile >
        if (< inFile is at end-of-file >)
            break;
        if (ch == ' ')
            continue;
        if (Character.isDigit(ch))    //constant (operand)
        {
            exp = new Constant(ch - '0');
            s.push(exp);
        }
        else       //binary operator
        {
            Expression right = (Expression) s.pop();
            Expression left = (Expression) s.pop();
            if (ch == '+')
                exp = new Sum(left, right);
            else if (ch == '*')
                exp = new Product(left, right);
            else if (ch == '-')
                exp = new Difference(left, right);
            else if (ch == '/')
                exp = new Quotient(left, right);
```

```
                    else
                        System.out.println("Error in input file");
                    s.push(exp);
                }
            }
        return exp;
    }
```

Index

Symbols

! operator, 7
!= operator, 5
*= operator, 7
+ operator
    concatenation, 111
++ operator, 8
+= operator, 7
-- operator, 8
-= operator, 7
. operator, 36
/ operator, 5
/= operator, 7
< operator, 5
<= operator, 5
== operator, 5
> operator, 5
>= operator, 5
% operator, 5
%= operator, 7
&& operator, 7
|| operator, 7

A

abs method, 117
abstract, 79
abstract class, 79
    when to use, 81
abstract method, 80
access specifier, 34
accessor, 36
act method, 453, 454, 456, 459, 461
actual parameter, 41
add method
    of ArrayList, 180, 372
    of BoundedEnv, 467, 470
    of Environment, 464
    of List, 371
    of ListIterator, 256
    of PriorityQueue, 306
    of Set, 377
    of UnboundedEnv, 467, 470
addFirst method, 374
addLast method, 374
algorithm, 148
    average case, 153
    best case, 153
    efficiency, 153, 177, 268
    worst case, 153
aliasing, 41
allObjects method
    of BoundedEnv, 467, 469

    of Environment, 464
    of UnboundedEnv, 467, 469
AP exam, xi, 301, 304, 307, 329, 331, 369,
        370, 380, 385, 454, 463, 474
    free-response section, xi, xii
    hints for taking, xii
    information, xi
    Level A, xi, xiii, 16, 474
    Level AB, xi, xiii, 16, 474
    mark-sense sheet, xi
    multiple-choice section, xi, xii
    quick reference, xii
    raw score, xi
    Section I, xi
    Section II, xi
AP Java subset, xi, 3, 9, 15, 16, 77, 256,
        268, 301, 304, 372, 374, 378, 380,
        382–385, 458
applet, 3
application, 3
argument, 42
arithmetic operators, 5
ArithmeticException, 16
array, 170–184
    as parameter, 171
    initialization, 170
    initializer list, 171, 182
    length, 171
    of objects, 176
    one-dimensional, 170
    two-dimensional, 181
ArrayIndexOutOfBoundsException, 16, 170,
        182
ArrayList, 179, 369, 371
    methods for case study, 473
    methods of, 179, 372
    vs. array, 179
    vs. LinkedList, 376
ArrayPriorityQueue class, 307
ArrayStack class, 301
assertion, 152
assignment operators, 7
association relationship, 150
average case, 153

B

backslash \, 9
base case, 220
behavior, 32
best case, 153
big-O notation, 154, 177, 224, 268
binary expression tree, 341–347

evaluation, 343
operand, 341
operator, 341
binary heap, 307
binary search, 421
binary search tree, 331–335
creating, 335
finding target element, 334
insertion, 332
binary tree, *see* tree
BinarySearchTree class, 331, 332
BinaryTree class, 329, 331
block, 39
boolean, 3
boolean expression, 6
compound, 7
short-circuit evaluation, 7
BoundedEnv, 466
constructor, 468
implementation, 466
breed method, 453, 456, 459, 461
bucket, 383, 423
bug, 148
built-in type, 3
bytecode, 2

C
case study, xi, 451–475
BoundedEnv class, 466
Color class, 474
darter fish, 451
DarterFish class, 458
Debug class, 472
Direction class, 472
EnvDisplay interface, 464
environment, 451
Environment interface, 462
Fish class, 453
Locatable interface, 464
Location class, 472
RandNumGenerator class, 473
Random class, 474
Simulation class, 452, 465
slow fish, 451, 452
SlowFish class, 458, 461
timestep, 451
UnboundedEnv class, 466
utility classes, 471
web site, 475
casting, 3, 5, 77, 375
chaining
in hash coding, 423
of assignment statements, 7
changeDirection method, 453, 458, 459, 461
changeLocation method, 453, 458, 459, 461
circular doubly linked list, 262
circular linked list, 259
CircularLinkedList class, 259
class, 32–48

abstract, 79
collaborator, 150
independent, 150
wrapper, 48, 114
class method, 37
class variable, 454
ClassCastException, 16, 79, 83, 115, 256
classes
ArrayList, 179, 369, 371
ArrayPriorityQueue, 307
ArrayStack, 301
BinarySearchTree, 331, 332
BinaryTree, 329, 331
BoundedEnv, 466
CircularLinkedList, 259
Color, 454, 474
DarterFish, 458
Debug, 472
Direction, 472
Double, 116
DoublyLinkedList, 263
DoublyListNode, 263
Fish, 453
HashMap, 369, 383
HashSet, 369, 378
Integer, 114
LinearLinkedList, 247
LinkedList, 369, 374
ListNode, xii, 245
ListQueue, 304
LLL_ListIterator, 256
LLLIterator, 252
Location, 472
Math, 117
Object, 108
Position, 128, 396
RandNumGenerator, 454, 473
Random, 118, 474
Simulation, 452, 465
SlowFish, 458, 461
String, 110, 114
TreeMap, 369, 384
TreeNode, xii, 329
TreeSet, 369, 378
UnboundedEnv, 466
client program, 34
col method, 472
collaborator class, 150
Collection, 369
collection, 368–387
Collections API library, 368
College Board web site, 1
Color, 454, 474
constructor, 474
color method, 453, 455, 459, 461
Comparable, 83, 112, 227, 309, 332, 375
compareTo method, 6, 83, 112, 115, 116
of Location, 472
compile-time error, 148
compiler, 2

compound assignment operator, 7
compound boolean expression, 7
concatenation operator, 111
`ConcurrentModificationException`, 370
constant, 34
constant run time, 154
constructor, 34, 73
    default, 34, 73, 74
constructors
    `Color`, 474
    `DarterFish`, 459
    `Fish`, 454
    `SlowFish`, 461
container class, 368
contains method, 377
containsKey method, 383
control structures, 10–15
    decision-making, 10–12
    iteration, 12–15

D
dangling else, 11
`DarterFish`, 458
    constructor, 459
    methods of, 459
data field, 33
`Debug` class, 472
debugging, 146, 148
default constructor, 34, 73, 74
depth of node, 329
dequeue method, 303, 304
die method, 453, 458, 459, 461
`Direction` class, 472
direction method, 453, 455, 459, 461
division
    floating-point, 5
    integer, 5
dot operator, 36
`Double`, 116
    methods of, 116
`double`, 3
double quote \", 9
doubleValue method, 116
doubly linked list, 262
`DoublyLinkedList` class, 263
`DoublyListNode` class, 263
downcasting, 77
driver method, 148
dummy parameter, 42
dynamic binding, 76
dynamic data structure, 244

E
early binding, 76
efficiency, 153, 177, 268
emptyNeighbors method, 453, 456, 459, 461
encapsulation, 33
enqueue method, 303, 304
`EnvDisplay` interface, 464
`Environment` interface, 462

    methods of, 463
environment method, 453, 455, 459, 461
equals method, 110, 115, 116, 382
    of Location, 472
equals vs. ==, 113
error, 15, 148
    compile-time, 148
    intent, 149
    logic, 149
    overflow, 3
    round-off, 6, 84
    run-time, 148
    syntax, 148
    underflow, 300, 303
escape sequence, 9
exam, *see* AP exam
exception, 15, 148
    `ArithmeticException`, 16
    `ArrayIndexOutOfBoundsException`, 16, 170, 182
    checked, 15
    `ClassCastException`, 16, 79, 83, 115, 256
    `ConcurrentModificationException`, 370
    `IllegalArgumentException`, 470, 471
    `IllegalStateException`, 16, 255, 256
    `IndexOutOfBoundsException`, 16, 180, 181, 372
    `NoSuchElementException`, 16, 250, 255, 375
    `NullPointerException`, 16, 41, 114
    `StringIndexOutOfBoundsException`, 113
    unchecked, 15
exponential run time, 154, 224
extended if statement, 12
extends, 70, 79, 82

F
final variable, 4, 34
`Fish`, 453
    constructor, 454
    methods of, 453
fixHeap method, 415
floating-point division, 5
floating-point numbers
    comparison of, 6
for loop, 12
formal parameter, 41

G
garbage collection, 247
generateChild method
    of DarterFish, 459, 460
    of Fish, 453, 456
    of SlowFish, 461, 462
generic code, 373
get method
    of ArrayList, 180

of List, 371
of Map, 383
getDirection method
  of BoundedEnv, 467
  of Environment, 463
  of SquareEnvironment, 465
  of UnboundedEnv, 467
getFirst method, 374
getInstance method, 454, 473
getLast method, 374
getLeft method, 330
getNeighbor method
  of BoundedEnv, 467
  of Environment, 463
  of SquareEnvironment, 465
  of UnboundedEnv, 467
getNext method, 246
getRight method, 330
getValue method
  of ListNode, 246
  of TreeNode, 330

H

has-a relationship, 150
hash address, 422
hash coding, 422
  bucket, 423
  chaining, 423
  hash address, 422
  hash function, 422
  key field, 422
  linear probing, 422
  rehashing, 423
  resolving collisions, 422
hash function, 422
hash table, 383, 422
  bucket, 383
  capacity, 383
  load factor, 383
hashCode method, 110, 382, 422, 472, 473
HashMap, 369, 383
  constructor, 384
HashSet, 369, 378
  constructor, 378
  vs. TreeSet, 382
hasNext method
  of Iterator, 252
  of ListIterator, 256
header, 34
header node, 262
heap, 414
heapsort, 414
height of tree, 329
helper method, 224, 340, 454, 456, 466
hints
  for taking exam, xii
  for using this book, xiii

I

id method, 453, 455, 459, 461

identifier, 3
if statement, 10
if...else statement, 10
IllegalArgumentException, 470, 471
IllegalStateException, 16, 255, 256
immutable object, 111, 116
implements, 82
implicit parameter, 39
import statement, 1
increment operator, 8
inDegrees method, 472
independent class, 150
indexOf method, 114, 466, 467
IndexOutOfBoundsException, 16, 180, 181, 372
infinite loop, 13
infinite recursion, 221
infix expression, 341
information hiding, 33
inheritance, 69–85
inheritance hierarchy, 69
inheritance relationship, 150
inherited instance variable, 72
inherited method, 72
initialization, 41, 170
initialize method, 453, 454, 459
initializer list, 171, 182
inorder traversal, 336
input/output, 9
insertion sort, 411, 414
instance method, 37
instance variable, 2, 33
  inherited, 72
  protected, 73
instanceof, 77
int, 3
Integer, 114
  methods of, 114
integer division, 5
intent error, 149
interface, 81–85
  Collection, 369
  Comparable, 83, 112, 227, 309, 332, 375
  EnvDisplay, 464
  Environment, 462
  Iterator, 252, 370, 375
  List, 369, 371
  ListIterator, 255, 370, 375
  Locatable, 464
  Map, 369, 382
  PriorityQueue, 306
  Queue, 303
  Set, 369, 377
  SortedMap, 369
  SortedSet, 369
  Stack, 300
intValue method, 115
is-a relationship, 69, 75, 150
isEmpty method

of BoundedEnv, 467, 469
of Environment, 464
of PriorityQueue, 306
of Queue, 304
of Stack, 300
of UnboundedEnv, 467, 469
isInEnv method, 453, 456, 459, 461
isOff method, 472
isOn method, 472
isValid method
    of BoundedEnv, 467, 468
    of Environment, 463
    of UnboundedEnv, 467, 468
iteration, 12–15
    for loop, 12
    while loop, 13
Iterator, 252, 370, 375
    methods of, 252
iterator, 252–259
    for circular linked list, 261
    for doubly linked list, 268
    for linear linked list, 252
    for maps, 384
iterator method, 254, 370, 384
    of List, 371
    of Set, 378

J
Java application, 3
Java introductory language features, 1–16
Java subset, *see* AP Java subset
java.lang, 1
java.util, 118, 368

K
key field, 422
keySet method, 382, 383
keyword, 2

L
late binding, 76
leaf, 328
length method, 113
level of tree, 329
level-order traversal, 366
linear linked list, *see* linked list
linear run time, 154
LinearLinkedList class, 247
link, 244
linked list, 244–268
    circular, 259
    circular doubly linked, 262
    doubly linked, 262
    ListNode class, 245
    node, 244
    vs. array, 268
LinkedList, 369, 374
    methods of, 374
linker, 2
List, 369, 371

methods of, 371
ListIterator interface, 255, 370, 375
listIterator method, 257, 370
    of List, 371
ListNode class, xii, 245
    instance variables, 245
    methods of, 245
ListQueue class, 304
LLL_ListIterator class, 256
LLLIterator class, 252
local variable, 39
Locatable, 464, 473
Location class, 472
location method, 453, 455, 459, 461
    of Locatable, 464
logarithmic run time, 154
logic error, 149
logical operators, 7
loop
    for, 12
    infinite, 13
    nested, 14
    while, 13
loop invariant, 152, 177

M
main method, 2, 37
Map, 369, 382
    methods of, 383
map, 382
    key, 382
    key set, 382
    value, 382
Marine Biology Simulation Case Study, *see*
    case study
Math class, 117
Math.PI, 117
matrix, 181
max heap, 414
merge method, 412
mergesort, 412
method, 34
    abstract, 80
    accessor, 36
    class, 37
    constructor, 34, 73
    driver, 148
    header, 34
    helper, 224, 340
    inherited, 72
    instance, 37
    mutator, 36
    overloaded, 38, 76
    overriding, 70, 73
    partial overriding, 70, 73
    public, 34
    recursive, 219, 220
    signature, 38
    static, 2, 37
    stub, 148

method overriding, 70, 73
methods
    abs, 117
    act, 453, 454, 456, 459, 461
    add, 180, 256, 306, 371, 372, 377, 464, 467, 470
    addFirst, 374
    addLast, 374
    allObjects, 464, 467, 469
    breed, 453, 456, 459, 461
    changeDirection, 453, 458, 459, 461
    changeLocation, 453, 458, 459, 461
    col, 472
    color, 453, 455, 459, 461
    compareTo, 6, 83, 112, 115, 116, 472
    contains, 377
    containsKey, 383
    dequeue, 303, 304
    die, 453, 458, 459, 461
    direction, 453, 455, 459, 461
    doubleValue, 116
    emptyNeighbors, 453, 456, 459, 461
    enqueue, 303, 304
    environment, 453, 455, 459, 461
    equals, 110, 115, 116, 382, 472
    fixHeap, 415
    generateChild, 453, 456, 459–462
    get, 180, 371, 383
    getDirection, 463, 465, 467
    getFirst, 374
    getInstance, 454, 473
    getLast, 374
    getLeft, 330
    getNeighbor, 463, 465, 467
    getNext, 246
    getRight, 330
    getValue, 246, 330
    hashCode, 110, 382, 422, 472, 473
    hasNext, 252, 256
    id, 453, 455, 459, 461
    inDegrees, 472
    indexOf, 114, 466, 467
    initialize, 453, 454, 459
    intValue, 115
    isEmpty, 300, 304, 306, 464, 467, 469
    isInEnv, 453, 456, 459, 461
    isOff, 472
    isOn, 472
    isValid, 463, 467, 468
    iterator, 254, 370, 371, 378, 384
    keySet, 382, 383
    length, 113
    listIterator, 257, 370, 371
    location, 453, 455, 459, 461, 464
    main, 2, 37
    merge, 412
    move, 453, 457, 459–461
    neighborsOf, 464, 465, 467
    next, 252, 256
    nextDouble, 119, 474

    nextInt, 118, 474
    nextLocation, 453, 457, 459–462
    numAdjacentNeighbors, 463, 465, 467
    numCellSides, 463, 465, 467
    numCols, 463, 467, 468
    numObjects, 464, 467, 468
    numRows, 463, 467, 468
    objectAt, 464, 467, 469
    partition, 413
    peekFront, 303, 304
    peekMin, 306
    peekTop, 300, 301
    pop, 300, 301
    pow, 117
    print, 472
    println, 472
    push, 300, 301
    put, 383
    randomColor, 453, 454, 459, 461, 474
    randomDirection, 463, 465, 467, 472
    recordMove, 464, 467, 471
    remove, 180, 252, 256, 372, 377, 383, 458, 464, 467, 470
    removeFirst, 375
    removeLast, 375
    removeMin, 306
    restoreState, 472
    reverse, 472
    row, 472
    set, 180, 256, 371
    setLeft, 331
    setNext, 246
    setRight, 331
    setValue, 246, 330
    showEnv, 464
    size, 180, 371, 378, 383
    sqrt, 117
    step, 452
    substring, 113
    swap, 173
    toLeft, 472
    toRight, 472
    toString, 108, 115, 116, 453, 456, 459, 461, 467, 469, 472
    turnOff, 472
    turnOn, 472
minimum heap, 307
mod, 5
move method
    of DarterFish, 459, 460
    of Fish, 453, 457
    of SlowFish, 461
mutator, 36

N
neighborsOf method
    of BoundedEnv, 467
    of Environment, 464
    of SquareEnvironment, 465
    of UnboundedEnv, 467

nested `if` statement, 11
nested loop, 14
`new`, 16, 170
newline `\n`, 9
`next` method
    of `Iterator`, 252
    of `ListIterator`, 256
`nextAvailableID`, 454
`nextDouble` method, 119, 474
`nextInt` method, 118, 474
`nextLocation` method
    of `DarterFish`, 459, 460
    of `Fish`, 453, 457
    of `SlowFish`, 461, 462
node, 244, 328
`NoSuchElementException`, 16, 250, 255, 375
`null`, 41
null reference, 41, 244
`NullPointerException`, 16, 41, 114
`numAdjacentNeighbors` method
    of `BoundedEnv`, 467
    of `Environment`, 463
    of `SquareEnvironment`, 465
    of `UnboundedEnv`, 467
`numCellSides` method
    of `BoundedEnv`, 467
    of `Environment`, 463
    of `SquareEnvironment`, 465
    of `UnboundedEnv`, 467
`numCols` method
    of `BoundedEnv`, 467, 468
    of `Environment`, 463
    of `UnboundedEnv`, 467, 468
`numObjects` method
    of `BoundedEnv`, 467, 468
    of `Environment`, 464
    of `UnboundedEnv`, 467, 468
`numRows` method
    of `BoundedEnv`, 467, 468
    of `Environment`, 463
    of `UnboundedEnv`, 467, 468

O

$O(n)$ etc., 154, 177, 224, 268
`Object`, 108
    methods of, 108
object, 32–48
    behavior, 32
    reference, 35, 40
    state, 32
    variable, 35
object-oriented program design, 149
`objectAt` method
    of `BoundedEnv`, 467, 469
    of `Environment`, 464
    of `UnboundedEnv`, 467, 469
one-dimensional array, 170
operator, 5–8
    arithmetic, 5
    assignment, 7
    concatenation, 111
    decrement, 8
    division, 5
    dot, 36
    increment, 8
    logical, 7
    mod, 5
    precedence, 5, 8
    relational, 5
overflow error, 3
overloaded method, 38, 76

P

package, 1
parameter, 34
    actual, 41
    array, 171
    dummy, 42
    formal, 41
    implicit, 39
    pass by value, 42
    passing object as, 43
    passing primitive type as, 42
    two-dimensional array, 183
parameter list, 34
partial overriding, 70, 73
`partition` method, 413
`peekFront` method, 303, 304
`peekMin` method, 306
`peekTop` method, 300, 301
PI (π), 117
pivot element, 413
pointer, 244
polymorphic method calls
    rules for, 78
polymorphism, 76–79, 470
`pop` method, 300, 301
`Position` class, 128, 396
postcondition, 152
postfix expression, 341
postorder traversal, 336
`pow` method, 117
precondition, 152
prefix expression, 341
preorder traversal, 336
primitive type, 3, 40
`print` method, 472
`println` method, 472
priority queue, 305–309
`PriorityQueue` interface, 306
`private`, 2, 34
    method, 34
    variable, 34
`probOfMoving`, 461
program analysis, 152
program correctness, 152
program design, 146–151
    object-oriented, 149
program maintenance, 149
program specification, 146, 147

protected, 73, 256
protected method, 453
public, 2, 34
    method, 34
    variable, 34
push method, 300, 301
put method
    of Map, 383

Q

quadratic run time, 154
queue, 303–305
Queue interface, 303
    methods of, 304
quick reference, xii, 454, 474, 475
quicksort, 413

R

RandNumGenerator class, 454, 473
Random class, 118, 474
random integer, 118
random number generator, 118
    seed value, 118
random real number, 119
randomColor method, 453, 454, 459, 461,
    474
randomDirection method, 472
    of BoundedEnv, 467
    of Environment, 463
    of SquareEnvironment, 465
    of UnboundedEnv, 467
recordMove method
    of BoundedEnv, 467, 471
    of Environment, 464
    of UnboundedEnv, 467, 471
recursion, 219–229
    base case, 220
    general rules, 224
    in 2-D grids, 227
    in linked structures, 341
    in trees, 337
    infinite, 221
    tail, 221
    that alters tree, 340
recursive definition, 222
recursive helper method, 224, 340
recursive method, 219, 220
    analysis of, 223
reference, 35, 40
relational operator, 5
remove method
    of ArrayList, 180, 372, 458
    of BoundedEnv, 467, 470
    of Environment, 464
    of Iterator, 252
    of ListIterator, 256
    of Map, 383
    of Set, 377
    of UnboundedEnv, 467, 470
removeFirst method, 375

removeLast method, 375
removeMin method, 306
reserved word, 2
restoreState method, 472
return type, 34
reverse method, 472
robust program, 149
root, 328
round-off error, 6, 84
rounding, 4
row method, 472
run-time error, 148

S

scope, 39
    of loop variable, 13
search
    binary, 421
    sequential, 420
Section I answer sheet, xiii
selection sort, 410
sentinel, 14
sequential search, 420
Set, 369, 377
    methods of, 377
set method
    of ArrayList, 180
    of List, 371
    of ListIterator, 256
setLeft method, 331
setNext method, 246
setRight method, 331
setValue method
    of ListNode, 246
    of TreeNode, 330
short-circuit evaluation, 7
showEnv method, 464
sibling class, 73
signature, 38
Simulation, 452, 465
    methods of, 452
size method
    of ArrayList, 180
    of List, 371
    of Map, 383
    of Set, 378
SlowFish, 458, 461
    constructor, 461
    methods of, 461
software development, 146
    waterfall model, 146
sort
    heapsort, 414
    insertion, 411, 414
    mergesort, 412
    $O(n^2)$, 410
    quicksort, 413
    recursive, 411
    selection, 410
SortedMap, 369

SortedSet, 369
sorting, 410–420
    algorithms in Java, 417
source file, 2
specification, 146, 147
sqrt method, 117
SquareEnvironment
    constructor, 465
    methods of, 465
stack, 300–303
Stack interface, 300
    methods of, 300
state, 32
static, 2, 34, 37
static binding, 76
static final variable, 34
static method, 37
static variable, 176, 454
step method, 452
stepwise refinement, 147
String, 110, 114
    comparison, 112
    concatenation operator, 111
    initialization, 111
    methods of, 113
string literal, 110
StringIndexOutOfBoundsException, 113
stub method, 148
subclass, 69
    rules for, 74
subclass object
    declaration of, 75
subpackage, 1
substring method, 113
subtree, 328
super, 73, 459
superclass, 69
swap method, 173

T
tail recursion, 221
test data, 148
testing, 146, 148
this, 39
throw, 16
toLeft method, 472
top-down design, 147
toRight method, 472
toString method, 108, 115, 116
    of BoundedEnv, 467, 469
    of Direction, 472
    of Fish, 453, 456, 459, 461
    of Location, 472
    of UnboundedEnv, 467, 469
trailer node, 262
tree, 328–347
    ancestor, 329
    balanced, 329
    binary expression tree, 341
    binary tree, 328

    child, 328
    complete binary tree, 329, 414
    depth of node, 329
    descendant, 328
    full binary tree, 329, 414
    height, 329
    inorder traversal, 336
    leaf, 328
    level, 329
    level-order traversal, 366
    node, 328
    parent, 328
    postorder traversal, 336
    preorder traversal, 336
    recursive algorithms, 337
    root, 328
    sibling, 328
    subtree, 328
    traversal, 335
tree traversal, 335
TreeMap, 369, 384
    constructor, 384
TreeNode class, xii, 329
    instance variables, 330
    methods of, 330
TreeSet, 369, 378
    constructor, 378
turnOff method, 472
turnOn method, 472
two-dimensional array, 181–184
    as parameter, 183
type, 3
    boolean, 3
    built-in, 3
    double, 3
    int, 3
    primitive, 3, 40
type compatibility, 77

U
UnboundedEnv, 466
    constructor, 468
    implementation, 466
underflow error, 300, 303
user-defined constant, 4

V
variable, 3, 34
    final, 4, 34
    instance, 2, 33
    local, 39
    public, 34
variable declaration, 3
void, 34

W
while loop, 13
worst case, 153
wrapper class, 48, 114–116